Mastering
Revit® Structure 2010

Mastering

Revit® Structure 2010

Thomas S. Weir

Jamie D. Richardson

David J. Harrington

WILEY

Wiley Publishing, Inc.

Senior Acquisitions Editor: Willem Knibbe
Development Editor: Tom Cirtin
Technical Editor: Steve Stafford
Production Editor: Dassi Zeidel
Copy Editor: Linda Recktenwald
Editorial Manager: Pete Gaughan
Production Manager: Tim Tate
Vice President and Executive Group Publisher: Richard Swadley
Vice President and Publisher: Neil Edde
Book Designers: Maureen Forys, Happenstance Type-O-Rama; Judy Fung
Proofreader: Nancy Bell
Indexer: Ted Laux
Project Coordinator, Cover: Lynsey Stanford
Cover Designer: Ryan Sneed
Cover Image: © Pete Gardner/DigitalVision/Getty Images

Library of Congress Cataloging-in-Publication Data

Weir, Thomas, 1950-
    Mastering Revit structure 2010 / Thomas Weir, Jamie Richardson, David J. Harrington. — 1st ed.
        p. cm.
      ISBN-13: 978-0-470-52141-0
      ISBN-10: 0-470-52141-4
    1. Architectural drawing — Computer-aided design. 2. Architectural design — Data processing.
3. Autodesk Revit. I. Richardson, Jamie, 1975- II. Harrington, David J., 1966- III. Title.
    NA2728.W42 2009
    720.28′40285536–dc22

                                                                            2009028750

10 9 8 7 6 5 4 3 2 1

Dear Reader,

Thank you for choosing *Mastering Revit Structure 2010*. This book is part of a family of premium-quality Sybex books, all of which are written by outstanding authors who combine practical experience with a gift for teaching.

Sybex was founded in 1976. More than 30 years later, we're still committed to producing consistently exceptional books. With each of our titles, we're working hard to set a new standard for the industry. From the paper we print on, to the authors we work with, our goal is to bring you the best books available.

I hope you see all that reflected in these pages. I'd be very interested to hear your comments and get your feedback on how we're doing. Feel free to let me know what you think about this or any other Sybex book by sending me an email at nedde@wiley.com. If you think you've found a technical error in this book, please visit http://sybex.custhelp.com. Customer feedback is critical to our efforts at Sybex.

Best regards,

Neil Edde
Vice President and Publisher
Sybex, an Imprint of Wiley

Acknowledgments

Thanks to my wonderful wife, Aida Gonzalez, for all the love and support she has given me this year while I worked all these odd hours writing this book. A wonderful photographer, she also took my photo! Thanks also to Sally, Dylan and Janice, and Josie and Steve. This is also for my grandson, Josh, so he knows that anything is possible if you are willing to work hard and really want it to happen. And as always I thank my mom, Estelle, for her constant and wise support.

I want to thank my colleagues David and Jamie for their great effort over these last six months in creating this text. There was no blueprint to follow since no other books on this subject have been published, but our combined creative forces made it happen.

I want to thank all my valued colleagues at Brandow & Johnston for supporting me through this venture. I want especially to thank Gabriel Lopez and Gautam Shenoy for their talented assistance in preparing the glossy color insert pages. I also want to thank our friend Paul Anderson for his assistance in preparation of the first chapter. And thanks to my colleague Ken Gebhart for letting me use his house model.

Thanks to Nicolas Mangon for helping create the last five amazing years, and to all the dedicated, imaginative crew at Revit Structure in Waltham. They are true revolutionaries in our field.

This whole venture also has to give a nod to the people at our publisher, Wiley, who gave us the chance and provided great professional editors who have helped us to craft a first-rate text.

— *Thomas S. Weir*

To my wife, Katie: I can't thank you enough for giving me the support I needed and for always being there to provide encouragement. A lot of things have been put on hold and my "to do list" has gotten quite large. I also want to thank my daughter, Avery, and son, Layton, for understanding why Dad was always so busy. I hope that someday this book along with my other journeys will inspire you to attempt things you didn't think were possible. Never have the "I can't do it" attitude.

Thanks to my fellow authors Tom and David for giving your time to help make this all a success. I have enjoyed working with both of you as well as strengthening our relationship in the process.

Thanks to Ericksen Roed and Associates for supporting me throughout my writing efforts and our Revit Structure user base for challenging me every day as well as maintaining great attitudes. You are the ones who help keep me motivated and encourage me to learn more.

Thanks to the Revit Structure team (the Factory). There are too many names to mention, but you have all listened to my comments and have provided support when I needed it.

Thanks to the AUGI forum community, and those who blog, for creating such a great source of information. It is great to see so many people sharing as well as expanding their knowledge.

Thanks to the entire Wiley team; you have been great to work with. I appreciated your comments and suggestions, and because of you I have become a better writer.

And finally, thanks to all of the other authors out there who are able to take the time to juggle their careers and family time as they author a book or any other form of literature. Doing this now for the second time has truly made me realize the sacrifices that are made to pull it all off.

This book has been another great experience.

— *Jamie D. Richardson*

I don't know how she did it, but my wife, Carla, surpassed my last book in the level of support and encouragement she provided this time around. She is the best wife a part-time author could possibly have! Once again, I need to thank all the kids for allowing me the time to write: Candy, Nicky, Kara, Ricky, Kaitlin, Kaylee, Krista, and Christopher. I am so happy I now have time to go into the pool! And as always I thank my dad, John, who even though he hasn't been here for over 14 years is still an inspiration for me to write about what I know.

To my fellow authors, Tom and Jamie, it once again has been a pleasant experience. To your credit it has been less challenging than before! Thanks for coming back for round two!

To my fellow coworkers at Walter P. Moore, thank you. I am the first to admit that what I know is because of the people I work with and the projects I work on. I am grateful to share the skills and knowledge I have gained while working with you all. Thanks again, Steve, you really helped me out a lot!

To Autodesk and the Revit Structure team, thank you. Your constant efforts to provide a solution to the structural field give us much to write about. It is fun modeling buildings and using your software to do it! Thank you again, Nicolas and Wai, for your support and answers.

To Willem Knibbe, our publisher, thank you for coming back for a revision to the book. Without your advocacy none of this would be possible. Special thanks to Tom Cirtin for your aid and assistance in polishing our gems!

— *David J. Harrington*

About the Authors

Thomas S. Weir

Tom is associate principal and director of BIM & CAD Operations at Brandow & Johnston, Inc., a consulting structural and civil engineering firm in Los Angeles, California. He has 30 years of structural design experience on numerous architectural-engineering building projects both large and small.

An early adopter of Revit Structure modeling software and a longtime modeling enthusiast, Tom continues to be in the vanguard of those seeking to help transform the AEC industry as it transitions into the new BIM design era. He is co-chairman and founder of the Los Angeles Revit Users Group, one of the most dynamic user groups in the United States. Tom also helped start the AUGI Revit Structural forum.

His first book is used widely for training, *Autodesk Official Training Courseware (AOTC) Revit Structure 4 Essentials*. Tom is a frequent lecturer on Revit Structure and building information modeling (BIM) and has taught classes at Autodesk University for the last several years.

Tom grew up north of Boston, Massachusetts. After high school and some college, he did a tour in the U.S. Army, leaving as a sergeant in the Military Police corps. He then studied at UMASS Amherst, where he received his BA in philosophy with minors in English and education. With few jobs available for philosophers, he went to engineering school at Northeastern University in Boston, got married, started a family, and eventually moved cross-country to California, where he began his 28-year tenure at Brandow & Johnston.

In his spare time Tom likes to camp with his family. Music and astronomy are his main hobbies. He likes to play all sorts of American roots music on his Martin D-18 guitar.

Jamie D. Richardson

Jamie is an associate and CAD/BIM manager at Ericksen Roed and Associates, a structural engineering firm based in Saint Paul, Minnesota. He has collaborated with several of the architectural firms in the Twin Cities on multiple Revit Structure projects. Jamie joined Ericksen Roed and Associates in 1996 as a structural designer and, over time, completely modernized its AutoCAD customization.

Throughout his 15 years of using Autodesk products, Jamie has been instrumental in the rollout of several versions of AutoCAD as well as the implementation of Revit Structure. His responsibilities include oversight of all Revit Structure production. Jamie has been a beta tester since RS2, an avid speaker on Revit Structure at Autodesk University, a contributor to industry publications regarding the use of Revit for BIM, as well as a contributor to the Revit Structure forums on AUGI.

His local Revit Structure involvements include being a member of the Minnesota Revit User Group (MNRUG), participating in other speaking engagements on building information modeling collaboration efforts, and mentoring students at local technical colleges.

Outside of work, Jamie enjoys spending time with his family at their cabin in northern Wisconsin. There he likes to fish, play on the water, and relax by late-night campfires.

David J. Harrington

David is a senior associate with Walter P. Moore and Associates, one of the premier consulting structural engineering firms in the United States. He has more than 22 years of structural drafting and design experience on projects ranging from the size of a convenience store up to an NFL stadium and convention center covering millions of square feet.

He has been working with Autodesk products since 1987, first starting with AutoCAD, later delving into 3D Studio, Architectural Desktop, and Tekla Xsteel (Structure). David has also been customizing the AutoCAD working environment with AutoLISP and other interfaces to aid in controlling and managing standards for Walter P. Moore. He began using Revit Structure at version 1 and conducts in-house training and customization for this application.

David has written or co-authored for many years. He created the PaperSpace newsletter produced by the North America Autodesk User Group (NAAUG), then by Autodesk User Group International (AUGI), and then began assisting in the editing arena and is the current technical editor for *AUGIWorld* magazine. Books he has worked on are *Inside AutoCAD R14*, *Inside Auto-CAD 2000*, *Inside AutoCAD 2000i*, *Inside AutoCAD 2002*, *Inside AutoCAD 2005*, and *Mastering Revit Structure 2009*.

Back in 1994, David was elected to the board of directors for NAAUG, where he served as the local user group representative. Later he was elected as the AEC industry chair, then within AUGI was elected to the position of president, where he served from 1998 to 1999. Other major contributions during these times are the AUGI Guild, an email-based support system for Autodesk users, and the formalization of the Wish List into a web-hosted system for real-time voting.

He has also been an instructor at Autodesk's annual training event, Autodesk University, teaching classes on Revit Structure adoption and other Structure-related subjects.

David has lived nearly all of his life in the Tampa area of Florida. In his spare time David enjoys wine and an occasional cigar. Hobbies are limited to relaxing and computer gaming.

Contents at a Glance

Contents

Foreword

When I was only five or six years old, I decided to become a structural engineer like my father. Every weekend, my dad would take me to visit the constructions sites he was working on. I enjoyed watching concrete being poured and rebar being bended and installed, and I was fascinated by the cranes, formwork, and cement trucks. As a teenager, I got my first computer and realized the power of programming and its ability to automate tedious work. I had a big dilemma: which career should I choose? Should I pick computer science or structural engineering? I decided to pursue both. My graduation thesis was naturally a mix of computer science and structural engineering. My passion for conceiving how I might be able to blend these two different fields of study led me to develop load distribution software for concrete structures. The software enabled engineers to presize concrete structures in a matter of hours and thus be able to evaluate the material quantities of steel and concrete. In realizing how fragmented the industry was in term of process, roles, responsibilities, and task automation, I then decided that I would spend my career trying to create tools to streamline the design-to-construction process. Over the past 20 years, I have been involved in the design of software for structural engineers, drafters, and fabricators in Europe and North America. I've worked on a wide variety of products that cover all areas of the structural industry, including structural modeling, structural analysis and design, steel and concrete detailing, and finally design of post-tensioned and precast concrete structures.

In April of 2003, one year after Autodesk acquired Revit Corporation, I was hired by the founders of Revit to extend the product beyond simply an architectural-based product to a complete structural package based on the same principles. I remember when I used Revit technology for the first time. I was amazed by its parametric approach and the great potential for the structural engineering community. I was overwhelmed. I thought to myself, how do I get started? What do I include? On the positive side, I was starting with a blank canvas. The challenge for me was that I had no paint or brushes — or even subject! Through my past experiences, I've learned that that you should never design software for yourself. I also remembered a line from a product-management course that I had taken, which was simply, "Your opinion, although interesting, is irrelevant"! Not a very comforting thought, but probably very accurate.

With that in mind, I needed to gather information and input from potential users, industry experts, and engineers. I had to find people who could help me. I found myself chasing structural folks who were interested in Revit Technology in blogs and forums when I found Tom Weir from Brandow & Johnston in Los Angeles. I sent him an email to ask for his help. His reply was a resounding, YES, YES, YES! He reminded me that he had been in the industry for over 20 years too! Tom was an early user of AutoCAD V2.6 and Softdesk Structural. He has been a model enthusiast since the beginning. Given Tom's passion and energy, I jumped on a plane to pay him a visit. We spent quite some time reviewing his process and exploring his ideas. It was the beginning of a fruitful relationship that continues to this day, and in fact, Tom has been involved in every release of Revit Structure.

A few months later, I was put in touch with Walter P. Moore and Associates (WPM). We met to discuss software and technology. At WPM, all roads eventually lead to David Harrington. When it comes to technology, David has extensive experience on model-based technology and specifically Architectural Desktop. He is also a power user of AutoCAD. David and I had some very interesting discussions on how to move from an AutoCAD environment to a Revit environment. We still share the same passions and always continue our discussions each time we meet.

In June 2005, we launched the first release of Revit Structure. Even with such a young product, we immediately experienced tremendous interest from the community. I was invited to present

BIM vision for structural engineers by Jamie Richardson from Ericksen Roed & Associates, Inc. Shortly thereafter, Jamie started working on multiple projects and rapidly became a Revit Structure expert. Jamie has made significant contributions in the development of the product.

In my opinion, these three authors are a virtual "dream team" of Revit Structure expertise and industry knowledge. They all share the energy, the passion, and even the emotion for Revit Structure. Combined with thousands of users around the world, they play a vital role for the continued success and future enhancement for Revit Structure to make it the best product for the structural engineering community.

With a tighter introduction of analysis in the BIM process, with the new simulation concepts based on analysis, with a more complete BIM including more data and details, and with more interoperability between the different disciplines (architects, MEP, fabricators, civil), we see a viral adoption of BIM within the structural community. We also know that we are just beginning a massive industry process change that will streamline the lifecycle of a project from design to construction and maintenance. Very few people have the opportunity to see their industry be transformed so dramatically. These are very exciting times and Tom, David, and Jamie are active contributors to this phenomenon.

I hope you enjoy this book. I know it will help you to become a more productive user of Revit Structure because it will open your eyes to new technologies and ideas while providing the vital tools necessary to design and build the greatest structures in the world!

Nicolas Mangon
Autodesk Building Industry Director
Autodesk, Inc.

Introduction

Thank you very much for buying this book. The three authors have been working tirelessly over many months to create something that will appeal to advanced and novice users alike. We are proud to say that this is a new edition of the first major book published on this subject.

Though the book is weighted toward the structural discipline, we think this book will also appeal to architectural and MEP designers and drafters as well, since much of the same functionality exists in all three Revit versions. We authors have all been early Revit adopters and have done scores of projects in real production over the past several years. We have taught Revit, written articles and blogs, and managed user groups, so we have a good idea of what you might want to learn. Coming from different regions of the country also helps give each of us a different perspective on the subject.

For the most part we focus on architectural engineering building projects rather than civil engineering projects. Most important, we have deliberately tried to filter the material through our experience both as project managers and as teachers. In that way we have attempted to distill the large amount of subject matter down to a manageable set of information so that you can focus on what will be most useful for you as you begin to tackle your own projects. So this book will not cover every single option of every single command and function that you find in Revit Structure, but it will try to point out the most useful items that the filter of experience has taught us you will need, and those are represented in real-world project scenarios.

For more on any of those items not covered you should refer to the documentation in the Revit Structure Help menu and tutorials. The documentation has gotten better and better in the last few years, and you need to refer to it often to keep learning in the most productive and efficient way.

If you are new to Revit Structure, a little bit of history is in order so that you are able to appreciate how far this program has progressed since it was purchased by Autodesk in 2003. At that time all of the tools you will learn about in this book were hard to use, if they existed at all. The original Revit developers focused on the architectural industry, and so the structural portions of the program were never fully developed. When Autodesk acquired the Revit product and company all that changed. Significant resources were allocated to get Revit development up to speed, and soon the Structural module was released. In a few short years Revit has become the 900-pound gorilla in the BIM world, and is the leader in this software market. With each new version of the program, and most notably when Revit Structure was developed as a separate application, it has become more complete in its capabilities. The developers at Revit Structure have constantly expanded its functionality. They definitely have been listening to the community of users and have worked very hard to provide new tools to us end users on a timely basis.

They get it! Autodesk invested heavily when BIM was in its nascent period and helped create the massive transformation that we see today in the AEC industry. Back in the 1990s when 2D computer-aided drafting started changing the industry, there were many drafters who said they did not need to learn it because hand drafting would always be available. By the late 1990s their jobs were all but gone. Today we are in a similar situation. Some say they do not need to learn about Revit Structure or BIM because there will always be 2D computer-aided drafting available. Those shortsighted people will soon suffer a fate similar to what the hand drafters suffered.

What You Will Learn

In this book you will learn the basics as well as more advanced techniques used to create a BIM model for a structural engineering project using Autodesk Revit Structure software. You will learn how to prepare construction documents after you have developed your model and how to collaborate with others by linking models or exporting to AutoCAD. You will learn how to detail and schedule the elements in your virtual building. In the last portion of the book, advanced subjects such as standards, rendering, and creating structural families will add a new dimension to your knowledge and abilities.

What You Need

Some knowledge of Revit Structure will be very helpful. Some knowledge of how buildings are designed and constructed will be helpful as well.

The *Mastering* Series

The *Mastering* series from Sybex provides outstanding instruction for readers with intermediate and advanced skills, in the form of top-notch training and development for those already working in their field and clear, serious education for those aspiring to become pros. Every *Mastering* book features:

◆ The Sybex "by professionals for professionals" commitment. *Mastering* authors are themselves practitioners, with plenty of credentials in their areas of specialty.

◆ A practical perspective for a reader who already knows the basics — someone who needs solutions, not a primer.

◆ Real-world scenarios, ranging from case studies to interviews, that show how the tool, technique, or knowledge presented is applied in actual practice.

◆ Skill-based instruction, with chapters organized around real tasks rather than abstract concepts or subjects.

◆ Self-review test "Master It" problems and questions, so you can be certain you're equipped to do the job right.

Who Should Buy This Book

All those structural, architectural, and MEP people interested in learning about Autodesk Revit Structure and building information modeling should read this book. The text is geared toward all levels, while trying especially hard to cover subjects beyond the basics that will appeal to mid-level and advanced users. Many real-world project scenarios are discussed as well as actual projects and how they were modeled.

This is a book by experienced, power Revit Structure users and not salespeople. If you are looking for a book that tells both good and bad about this subject without the sugar coating that sale types often give you, then this book is for you. We pull no punches and look under every rock in our effort to expose the underlying reality of the situation.

So if you are a Revit Structure novice, do not wait; dive in and join this exciting march into the future of building design. If you are a Revit Structure expert, you still will find many interesting concepts and procedures here that you might not have heard about before. Revit Structure rocks!

What's Inside

The chapters in this book are broken down into five parts that guide you from the moment you click on the program icon to first open the program all the way to advanced concepts such as family creation and design options. After covering the basics of the modeling environment, you move on to learn how to create a three-dimensional model. After that you learn to document and share your model with others. Finally you take an in-depth look at advanced modeling topics.

There is also a wonderful color gallery that shows off some of the many and varied design projects done by the authors. One of the most unique parts of the book is an appendix that goes into even greater detail in describing some of the gallery projects.

Here is a glance at what is in each chapter of *Mastering Revit Structure 2010*:

Part 1: Basics of the Modeling Environment

CHAPTER 1: INSIDE REVIT STRUCTURE

The basics are described in this first chapter, such as the layout of the different menus and commands. You learn about the types of elements in the modeling environment and how to create and manage project views. Another important area that is examined is how to control the graphical display of your modeled elements in a project.

CHAPTER 2: SETTING THE PROJECT ENVIRONMENT

Revit Structure, like any other program, has settings that help control the environment that you will be working in. Chapter 2 shows you how to develop different project environments through the use of templates. We discuss the various settings that are available to you as well as how the Project Browser can be organized so it can be managed. Then we discuss how content and settings can be transferred from one project to another.

CHAPTER 3: STARTING TO MODEL YOUR PROJECT

Chapter 3 explores the basics of getting a structural model started. Importing and linking CAD data and linking Revit models are explained and demonstrated. Once these files are imported/linked into your project, we will show you how you can manage and benefit from them with the use of their Visibility/Graphic Overrides and tools such as Copy/Monitor and Interference Check. After that, you will learn one of the most important tasks when starting your model, which is how to work with levels and grids before and after they are in your project.

Part 2: Developing Your Structural Model

CHAPTER 4: STRUCTURAL COLUMNS

Before we start talking about placing structural columns in Chapter 4, we talk about the basic templates used to create them as well as the various parameter settings that are available to control their behavior. We explain things you can do after they are placed that will allow the columns to adapt to other changes in the model. Modeling slanted columns is a new feature in this version, so we will discuss the tools and methods used to model them. And last we give you an in-depth explanation of everything you wanted to know about the Graphical Column Schedule for scheduling columns.

CHAPTER 5: FLOOR SLABS AND ROOF DECKS

In this chapter you learn to create many different types and shapes of slabs, floors, and roofs to add to your building model. Composite deck creation is covered as well. So-called flat roofs that really have minor sloping from ridges to drains are especially difficult to model. You will see how Revit Structure handles theses cases by using the sub-element tools.

CHAPTER 6: WALLS

Walls are system families in Revit Structure and are given plenty of attention in this chapter since they are a fundamental element of most projects. How to create walls, how to place them into your model, and how to edit them as the design process evolves are all covered.

CHAPTER 7: STRUCTURAL FRAMING

After creating the floor slabs and roof decks in Chapter 5, you now learn how to add support framing beneath them. Basic floor-framing tools are explored. Creating sloping roof framing is an especially interesting part of this chapter. You also explore framing families and their properties. We discuss how to add moment and braced frames to a project to round out this challenging subject.

CHAPTER 8: FORMING THE FOUNDATIONS

Modeling foundations can be a broad topic and cover just about everything below or at grade that supports a structure. In Chapter 8 we will explore the creation of these various foundations, which may come in many forms, with the use of the foundation tools available in Revit Structure. These tools will be discussed in great depth starting from their family type (component or system) to how they behave and how you work with them when they are in your project. You will also learn that the foundation tools available may not always be used to model certain foundation types, and we will show methods that can be used to model stepped footing conditions.

Part 3: Documenting Your Structural Model

CHAPTER 9: MODEL DOCUMENTATION

Now that you have the model up and running, you need to know how to add the notations to the various views you have created.

First you will study the datum elements and how they are added and controlled in your detail and section views. Next is a discussion of annotation elements such as text, tags, and symbols. You will examine how to add detailing elements such as detailing lines and filled regions to your views. Finally you will learn how to create a typical details library.

CHAPTER 10: MODELING REBAR

Most of the construction in the world is done in concrete, and so Revit Structure must have a very robust system to incorporate it into your virtual model and your construction documents. You will learn how to configure the rebar settings and then how to model 3D rebar. Then you will examine how 3D rebar is used and how new shapes can be made.

CHAPTER 11: SCHEDULES AND QUANTITIES

To achieve a BIM solution, you will find that your ability to extract information from your model is crucial. Here you learn to do just that by creating schedules and material takeoffs. You will also see how to export schedules to Microsoft Excel. Legends are another type of schedule that is examined.

CHAPTER 12: WORKING WITH SHEETS

In Chapter 12 we talk about creating sheets with title blocks to help organize your views and as a way to document your model. Title blocks usually include revision schedules, so we show you how to create and incorporate them into your sheets so Revit Structure can manage revisions made to the model. We also discuss creating sheet indexes and how the properties of views may change as they are placed on sheets.

Part 4: Sharing Your Structural Model

CHAPTER 13: WORKSHARING

Regardless of a project's size or the number of team members working on it, you still might want to switch from using a single-user file to a multiuser environment. In Chapter 13 we discuss when it might be right for you to enable worksharing and walk you through the steps to do so. We also talk about the typical workflow and the tools used to help you work and communicate with other team members.

CHAPTER 14: VISUALIZATION

After spending a considerable amount of time modeling your projects, you will want to gain admiration for the work. To do this you will need to render your projects! In this chapter you will learn how to evaluate what and when to model. From there you will explore the process of learning and operating the rendering engine mental ray in Revit Structure. Lastly you will uncover other options for extending your model use after you export it.

CHAPTER 15: REVIT STRUCTURE ANALYSIS

This chapter provides a close look at using the analytical model and related commands. You will learn how to configure the analytical structural settings and create loads for your project. You will examine how to place analytical load patterns onto your model. Finally you will learn how to import and export your virtual model from Revit Structure to structural analysis software.

Part 5: Advanced Topics

CHAPTER 16: PROJECT PHASES AND DESIGN OPTIONS

This chapter takes you to a new level of mastery in your ability to manipulate the model by adding phases and design options. You will examine a real-world example of a historic residence where existing and new phases had to be presented to the historical commission. Added to that were several different design possibilities. All this was done in one Revit Structure file.

CHAPTER 17: STANDARDS: INCREASING REVIT PRODUCTIVITY

You have just upgraded to Revit Structure and started to create models. But have you thought about your old AutoCAD standards? Using the information in Chapter 17, you will learn what can and cannot be done easily in Revit Structure with regard to standards. Afterward you will delve into enhancing your work through Revit Structure customization. Then you will actually implement your new model standards and apply view overrides effectively.

CHAPTER 18: FAMILY CREATION: BEYOND THE PROVIDED LIBRARIES

Family creation surely will take you much deeper into understanding the power of Revit Structure. You will learn to create a footing step family and in-place families. Groups are another powerful tool that you will find indispensable in your work. These subjects will give you a whole new perspective on modeling.

CHAPTER 19: ADVANCED STRUCTURAL FAMILIES

This chapter takes you to the next level of understanding of the family-creation process. You will study the development of several important structural families and how the families are used. Instead of building your elevator pit from scratch each time, you learn here how to develop an elevator pit family that can be inserted directly into your project.

Appendices

APPENDIX A: THE BOTTOM LINE

Every chapter ends with a collection of short exercises designed to reinforce the essential skills taught in the chapter. This appendix provides the solutions to those exercises.

APPENDIX B: THE GALLERY UP CLOSE

This appendix expands and explains the development of some of the complex projects that are presented in the color gallery section. You will see how different project types are created using Revit Structure and what difficulties were surmounted.

How to Contact the Authors

Sybex strives to keep you supplied with the latest tools and information you need for your work. Please check the website at www.sybex.com/go/masteringrevitstructure2010, where we'll post additional content and updates that supplement this book if the need arises. Alternatively, you can go to www.sybex.com, enter **Mastering Revit Structure 2010** in the Search box (or type the book's ISBN – 978-0-470-52141-0), and click Search to get to the book's update page.

Part 1

Basics of the Modeling Environment

Chapter 1

Inside Revit Structure

The Revit Structure interface is designed to be an easy-to-use, organized presentation of commands and drawing areas. The basic interface is highly configurable and can be adapted to fit most working needs that may arise as you interact with the computer in order to create a model. Multiple model views can be open at once so that you can see plan, section, elevation, and model views of an element side by side in the drawing area at one time.

This chapter will explore the interface and the arrangement of commands on the Ribbon with its tabs and panels, basic elements and their organization, as well as the types of views tools available to you in the Revit Structure workspace. The tools found here will be used to model and document your virtual structure and also help you to achieve a Building Information Modeling (BIM) solution for your project.

Underlying the graphical interface is a robust database that coordinates the graphical information through the use of a parametric change engine that controls the display of all elements in your project. In this way, a change in an element that takes place in a plan or a section view is immediately propagated to all views in the project, which in turn saves lots of time for you and allows you to focus on the design of the structure rather than the busywork of having to edit many views in order to correct one element, as occurs in most 2D drafting programs.

To succeed in this venture, you will need to add many tools to your tool chest. Imagine a construction worker who goes to work with only a hammer and a screwdriver. In all likelihood the worker will not be able to get much accomplished. So to get started, you need to add the necessary tools to your own tool chest so that you can work effectively in the virtual model-building environment.

Once you have learned the basics of the various display and modeling tools available to you in Revit Structure, you will be ready to move on to the actual modeling process in the subsequent chapters of this book.

In this chapter you will learn to:

- ◆ Use the graphical user interface

- ◆ Understand the types of elements in the modeling environment

- ◆ Create and manage project views

- ◆ Control the graphical display of elements in a project

Using the Graphical User Interface

When you double-click the Revit Structure 2010 icon on your desktop, you will first see the Recent Files window. This window shows projects and families on which you have recently been working. Click one of the existing file icons to open it, click Open to browse to a different project file, or click New to start a new project (see Figure 1.1).

FIGURE 1.1
The Recent Files window is the first window you see when you open the Revit Structure box

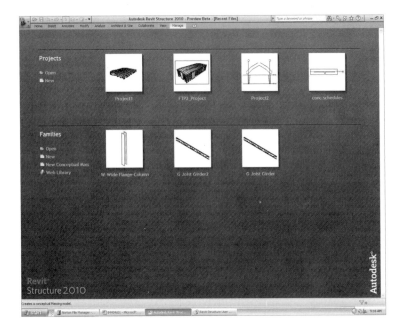

If you click New under Projects, Revit Structure puts you into the main project graphical user interface (GUI). If you click New under Families, you start the family creation process. If you click New Conceptual Mass under Families, Revit Structure puts you into the brand-new-for-this-release conceptual mass interface. We'll discuss more on each of these subjects as you proceed through the book.

The Revit Structure GUI (see Figure 1.2) is task oriented, with a compact footprint and semirigid structure. The task-oriented layout and grouping of like commands make project management and modeling within Revit Structure logical and efficient. The compact footprint of the GUI is due in large part to the lack of excessive toolbars and dialog boxes, which tend to clutter other platforms. This allows a large area in which to work and view the model. The location and size of most GUI components remain as you left them when you restart Revit Structure, making the interface somewhat friendly to user customization.

This version of Revit Structure has altered the GUI (see Figure 1.2) considerably from the previous version that contained a Menu bar, toolbars, Options bar, Type Selector, Ribbon, Project Browser, drawing area, View Control bar, and status bar. For seasoned users this will take some getting used to, but it is a significant improvement over the older interface. Revit Structure 2010 now has a Ribbon instead of the toolbars and menus that were previously used. Autodesk is now using this design for its other products as well. Going beyond similar appearances, the larger idea is that, for instance, a Trim command in one program should look and function similarly in all Autodesk programs to make it easier for users to work with multiple programs.

FIGURE 1.2
Default GUI with its intuitive display of commands

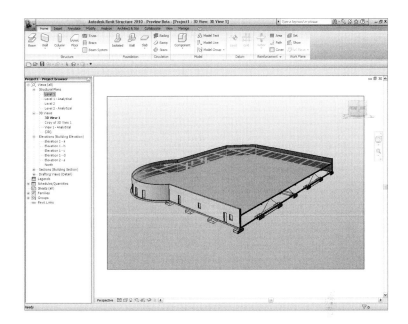

The Ribbon

The Ribbon is the central location for accessing the commands and tools that you will be using. Each tab contains multiple related panels and tools. The standard Microsoft Windows–based Ribbon (see Figure 1.3) is located near the top of the GUI and provides direct access to commands and settings available in Revit Structure. Keyboard shortcuts can also be used to display specific commands. For more information on the adoption of the Ribbon, go to the Autodesk website.

FIGURE 1.3
The Ribbon is an easy-to-use arrangement of most commands.

By clicking the small button (arrow) at the top-right end of the Ribbon you can change the way the Ribbon is displayed:

◆ Minimized to display panel titles only

◆ Minimized to display tabs

◆ Expanded to display the full Ribbon with tabs, panel titles, and command icons

Options Bar

The Options bar (see Figure 1.4) is located between the drawing area and the Ribbon and displays options specific to the active command or selected element(s). These options can be huge time-savers by negating the need to dig through a dialog box or launch another command. Even experienced users can increase productivity by keeping a watchful eye on the constantly changing Options bar and making use of the controls provided. The location of the Options bar above the display area makes it easier for the eyes to notice changes. You do not have to keep glancing up and down as much as you do in other applications with a command line at the bottom.

FIGURE 1.4
Keep an eye on the Options bar as its command options change.

Let's move on now to begin exploring some of the other important areas on the graphical user interface.

Application Menu

Click on the big purple *R* at the upper left, and you access the Application menu (see Figure 1.5). It houses frequently used commands for file management, such as exporting, publishing, and printing. On the right side you can display either a list of recently accessed files or currently open documents. At the bottom is the Options button, which when clicked opens the Options dialog box so you can configure notifications, user names, and journal file cleanup. For users familiar with earlier versions, this change is important because this information used to be found as part of Settings ➢ Options.

FIGURE 1.5
The Application menu

often be granted by simply looking to the Options bar. The following graphics illustrate the many looks of the Options bar during the execution of a single modeling command.

When you first invoke the Slab command, the default placement method is Pick Walls, and the Options bar shows various default options, as shown in the following graphic:

| Create Floor Boundary | Offset: 0' 0" | ☑ Extend into wall (to core) |

If you click the Align icon, the Options bar will change, as shown here:

| Create Floor Boundary | ☐ Multiple Alignment | Prefer: Wall faces ▼ |

When you finish the slab and select it in plan in order to modify it, the Options bar shows editing controls:

| Modify Floors | ☐ Constrain | ☑ Disjoin | ☑ Copy | ☐ Multiple |

As you can see, the Options bar had three radically different configurations, each loaded with context-specific controls that in many cases cannot be found anywhere else. In most cases, after you initiate a command you will want to look to the Options bar.

Quick Access Toolbar, InfoCenter, and Help

Adjacent to the Applications menu you will find the Quick Access toolbar, also known as the QAT (see Figure 1.6). Besides the default buttons that you find there, you can add or remove your most frequently used tools by right-clicking on a tool. You can also alter the QAT by clicking the Customize Quick Access Toolbar option at the top of the list (see Figure 1.6). The toolbar can also be repositioned below the Ribbon for easier access if so desired.

FIGURE 1.6
The Quick Access toolbar

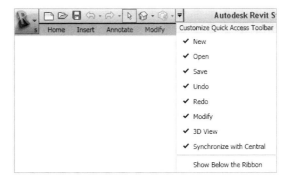

At the right side of the GUI along this bar you will find the InfoCenter and Help commands. The InfoCenter provides easy access to automatic update notifications, user groups, and other external learning resources that you may want to consult. Help offers access to help topics, tutorials, and other online resources you may need. One important item in the Help section is "Where Is My Command?" This provides you with a way to find out where the commands in Revit Structure 2009 are located in Revit Structure 2010. This will come in very handy for those users used to the old interface.

Project Browser

The Project Browser displays all of the views, families, groups, and Revit Structure links in a Windows Explorer–style format and is on the left side of the GUI (see Figure 1.7). The views in the Project Browser can be sorted, grouped, and filtered in a variety of ways depending on how you want to organize your project. The organization will be discussed more fully in the next chapter.

FIGURE 1.7
Project Browser

The Project Browser can be docked on the left (its default location), top, right, or bottom of the drawing area. You can also undock and resize it by left-click-dragging any of its borders to act as a floating dialog box. The Project Browser will remain in its location and size once you restart Revit.

Drawing Area

The drawing area (see Figure 1.8) is where all open views are displayed. Multiple views of several projects can be open at one time. Project templates and families can also be open in a single session of Revit and displayed in the drawing area. You can arrange all of these open views in the drawing area by using the window controls in typical Windows fashion. All the view controls you would expect are on the right side of the View tab on the Windows panel a tab, including: Tile, Cascade, Replicate and Switch Windows, which perform as you would expect.

FIGURE 1.8
The drawing area contains all your open views, which can be arranged in many ways.

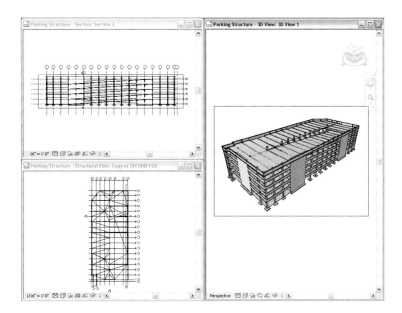

Having many views open at once, though, can lead to a slower program response. The Close Hidden Windows command is quite important in managing the performance of Revit, especially when you are working on large or complex projects. With one view maximized in the drawing area, this command will close all but the last active view of each project, project template, and family that are currently open.

If your open views are all maximized in the Revit drawing area, it is easy to quickly have numerous views of a project open at any given time without noticing it. Since Revit updates the display of all open views in real time, you can imagine how this might rapidly become a performance issue. Frequent use of this command is highly recommended, and it is a good candidate for addition to your keyboard shortcut list.

PRESENTATION GUI

While most will find the default interface more than adequate for daily use, a few simple modifications can drastically change the look of the GUI to better serve other purposes or user preferences. The following graphic shows the interface with the Ribbon minimized to show tabs only and a floating Project Browser. This clean look is great for viewing and working with the model while in meetings with the design team and/or clients.

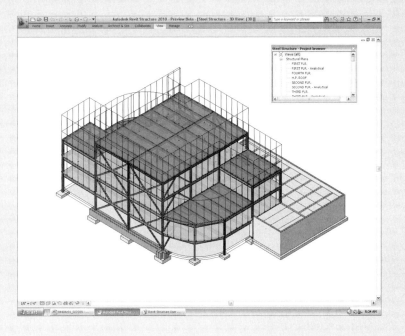

 **Real World Scenario**

NICE POSTAGE STAMP COLLECTION

I got a new PC recently and was working on a rather complex healthcare project. Impressed with the improvement in performance compared to my previous PC, I had not been paying attention to how many views I actually had open. The PC slowed considerably (a several-second pause instead of the expected near-instantaneous response) while I was attempting a rather routine procedure. It was not until I tiled my open views a few commands later that I realized what the problem was: too many open windows! They looked like a bunch of postage stamps. As I began to use the Close Hidden Windows command, as shown in the following graphic, my PC's performance returned to normal.

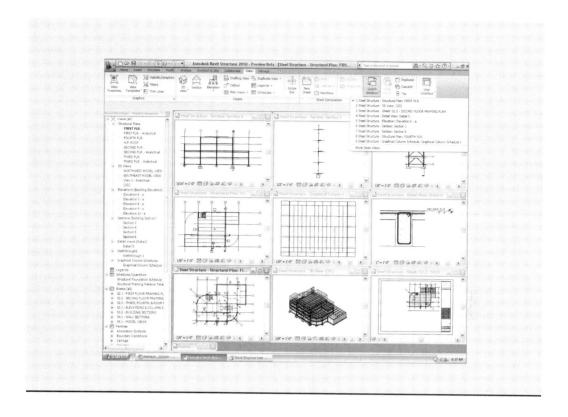

View Control Bar

The View Control bar (see Figure 1.9) is located on the bottom left of most views. The controls found on the View Control bar are for commonly used view and element display properties. They permit easy access to these features without having to open the View Properties dialog box. Each button expands when you select it and displays several context-specific settings. These are the eight buttons on the bar:

◆ Scale

◆ Detail Level

◆ Model Graphics Style

◆ Shadows

◆ Crop Entire View On or Off

◆ Crop a View Region

◆ Temporary Hide/Isolate

◆ Reveal Hidden Elements

FIGURE 1.9
The View Control bar
makes it easy to control
the view display. Detail
Level choices — Coarse,
Medium, and
Fine — are displayed
in this graphic.

Working views can change from minute to minute, for instance as you change between coarse and medium detail modes, so it is very convenient to have the View Control bar nearby for easy access to the controls.

Status Bar

The status bar is located at the very bottom of the GUI. The text on the left of the status bar will do the following:

◆ Display the name of a highlighted element

◆ Display prompts and/or additional information regarding the active command

◆ List the shortcuts that are available for a given sequence of characters, which can be navigated using the arrow keys

◆ Display the progress of a time-consuming process

At the very right of the status bar is an element selection counter, which will display the number of elements currently selected in the model. The Filter command, the small funnel icon, can also be accessed there to refine the selection set.

Keyboard Shortcuts

Keyboard shortcuts are one of the most powerful ways to increase your overall speed and productivity when using Revit Structure. Shortcuts enable you to launch commands directly from the drawing area without having to move your cursor. That significantly reduces mouse travel, saving time and your wrist. Many shortcuts are already defined, and you can create others for nearly all commands available on the Ribbon. Shortcuts are displayed when you hover over a tool and wait for the tooltip to appear. The shortcut is displayed in parentheses on the right side of the tooltip. To add a new shortcut, you open the KeyboardShortcuts.txt file in your text editor (see Figure 1.10), which is usually found in C:\Program Files\Autodesk Revit Structure 2010\Program. Editing the file is simple and straightforward.

Shortcut Menu

The Shortcut menu provides quick access to useful commands directly related to the element or object being highlighted or to view controls. As previously discussed, right-clicking on GUI objects displays a menu that controls how they are displayed:

◆ Right-clicking in the empty space of a view displays a menu (see Figure 1.11) with view navigation commands and access to the properties of the view.

◆ Right-clicking different elements and parts of elements in the model will also display various menus (see Figure 1.11) with access to element- and view-specific commands and properties.

FIGURE 1.10
The KeyboardShortcuts.txt file

```
;   ""    ribbon:"Manage-Project Location-Position-Rotate Project North"
;   ""    ribbon:"Manage-Macros-Macro Manager"
;   ""    ribbon:"Manage-Macros-Macro Security"
;
;  Add_Ins tab
;
;   ""    ribbon:"Add_Ins-External Tools-Track Changes-Highlight Changed"
;
;  ContextualTab tab
;
"PR"    ribbon:"ContextualTab-Draw-Properties"
"MV"    ribbon:"ContextualTab-Modify-Move"
"CO"    ribbon:"ContextualTab-Modify-Copy"
"RO"    ribbon:"ContextualTab-Modify-Rotate"
"MM"    ribbon:"ContextualTab-Modify-Mirror-Pick Mirror Axis"
"AR"    ribbon:"ContextualTab-Modify-Array"
"RE"    ribbon:"ContextualTab-Modify-Scale"
"PP"    ribbon:"ContextualTab-Modify-Pin"
"UP"    ribbon:"ContextualTab-Modify-Unpin"
"DE"    ribbon:"ContextualTab-Modify-Delete"
"AP"    ribbon:"ContextualTab-Edit Group-Add"
"RG"    ribbon:"ContextualTab-Edit Group-Remove"
"AD"    ribbon:"ContextualTab-Edit Group-Attach Detail"
"PG"    ribbon:"ContextualTab-Edit Group-Group Properties"
"FG"    ribbon:"ContextualTab-Edit Group-Finish"
"CG"    ribbon:"ContextualTab-Edit Group-Cancel"
```

FIGURE 1.11
View, framing element, and wall element context menus

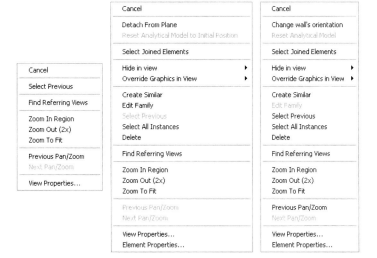

Navigation Bar

The Navigation bar appears in the upper right-hand corner of the drawing area and offers access to tools that help you navigate through views using Zoom commands, the Steering Wheel, and the Cube (see Figure 1.12).

Now that you have had a good look at the basic Revit Structure interface and command layout, let's explore the various elements that these commands create and manage in the creation of your building project.

FIGURE 1.12
The Navigation bar at
right accessing the 2D
Steering Wheel

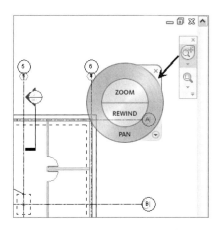

Element Types and Their Organization

One of the important things to understand about Revit Structure in its approach to modeling is that it is object (an element) oriented rather than line based as in traditional 2D drafting. Instead of drawing a series of lines on a flat sheet to represent a column, you go to a virtual library, load a column element, and then place it in your virtual working space. That column displays in every view. In addition to modeling elements, other element types are available to help you document your design, as we will discuss in this section.

Three types of elements are used to model and document a project in Revit Structure: model elements, datum elements, and view-specific elements. These elements are organized to allow you to easily control their on-screen and printed appearance and display. Let's take a look at these elements and how they function.

Model Elements

Beams, columns, walls, and other real-world building objects are represented in Revit Structure by model elements. These are the primary elements used to create the model and are typically placed as they would be constructed. This approach allows accurate quantities and views to be derived from the model.

Model elements can be altered in any view in your project in which they appear. Once they are changed, every related view is automatically updated by the underlying database. This is called *bidirectional associativity,* and it is one of the most important aspects of Revit Structure.

One of the promises of BIM (Building Information Modeling) technology like Revit Structure for project design is that much of the busywork of creating construction documents will be reduced so that you can concentrate on the design of the project rather than wrestling with the design software. The use of model elements is a good case in point.

Two distinct types of model elements exist in Revit Structure:

Host Host elements are generally system families (which will be discussed later in this chapter) that represent real-world construction elements such as walls, slabs, roofs, and stairs. These elements, as their name implies, often host other elements such as openings in a wall or reinforcement in a slab.

Component Component elements are used to represent all other real-world construction elements, including beams, trusses, columns, and reinforcing bars. These elements are typically external families that are loaded from the Revit Structure libraries into the project as needed, similar to their real-world counterparts being trucked or shipped to the site for assembly.

Most of your modeling will use these elements, so it is important for you to understand their basic properties.

Datum Elements

Grids, levels, and reference planes are datum elements. These elements provide the framework in which the building elements are placed and flexed. As you add your model elements to the project, they will become fixed to the datum elements. These basic modeling constraints then become anchors for objects so that if you need to change a bay width or the story-to-story height of a level, those elements will also move correspondingly. For example, beam elements placed in a third-floor plan view are associated with that datum. Changing the elevation of the level will take the beams along for the ride because they are defined as belonging to that level. This makes floor-to-floor clear height adjustments quick and accurate.

Datum elements also behave in a special way when it comes to the documentation of your project: they automatically appear in all relevant views. As such, datum elements are an essential part of a constraint-based modeling system and are fundamental to how you will assemble and edit the design.

View-Specific Elements

View-specific elements are used to annotate and detail specific views of the model for the creation of your construction documents:

Annotation   Annotation elements include text notes, tags, keynotes, dimensions, spot elevations, spot coordinates, and symbols. These elements play a critical role in translating the model into construction documents. Unlike simple annotations found in other platforms, the majority of the annotation elements in Revit Structure have a great deal of intelligence. Tags, for example, are annotations that display specific parameter values contained in the model elements. Change the size of a beam in the model, and all tags that you have already placed will be updated automatically. Adding text is also a view-specific element (see Figure 1.13).

FIGURE 1.13
Complete view at left, model elements in the middle, detail and datum components at the right

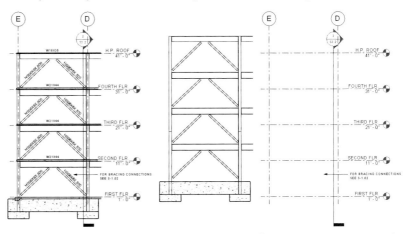

Detail   Detail elements pick up where the model elements leave off. Some items are not worth the time, effort, or performance overhead to model and can easily be handled with the addition of simple 2D line work or by adding 2D detail components, such as to a section cut through the model. These elements are used to complete in 2D the areas that are not modeled but whose display aids in showing design intent. For instance, you might add 2D earth hatching around a foundation footing.

HOW MUCH SHOULD I MODEL?

How much should you model, and how much should you just add in 2D?

You need to ask yourself this question quite often as you proceed with modeling your project. You might model the columns but not model the base plate and bolts in your project if you work for a design engineering firm. In that case, modeling a few typical cases of various connection types will be sufficient.

On the other hand, if you work for a detailing or construction management firm, you might have to model every piece in the structure. The scope and extent of your model building are relative to the documents that will be derived from it as well as the BIM solution you are trying to achieve.

The bottom line to knowing how much to model in your project is that you must maintain the essential integrity of the model by creating and maintaining the necessary elements to suit your purposes.

As the name implies, view-specific elements exist only in the view in which they are placed, with dependent views the exception to the rule. Dependent views are child views to a single parent view and share all view-specific elements with the parent and its other children. An example of a dependent view is a large framing plan that needs to be divided into several sections so it will fit onto your title sheet. If you add view-specific components to the parent view, they will also appear in the child views, which allows you to work in an overall plan view of the building without the added burden of placing annotation in each partial view.

Model elements, on the other hand, appear in every view whose extent they intersect. That saves a lot of time and coordination effort when you are making significant changes in the design. And remember: you can work on the model elements in any view in which they appear.

How Elements Are Organized

All of the elements used throughout Revit Structure are logically organized into a hierarchy of categories, families, types, and instances:

- The categories represent the different parts of the building, such as structural foundations, columns, and beams.

- Within each category are different families of objects. The structural column category, for example, has steel column families and concrete column families.

- Within each family are different types of the same object; for instance, the steel wide flange column family has many sizes, such as a W12x26 and a W24x55. These are different types of one family.

- Each type can be placed many times in your project and with various settings, which we call *instances* of a type. One instance may be a one-story column; another instance may be a four-story column.

Next we will examine these different parts of the element organization and how they work together in your virtual model as you work through the design process.

Categories

The basic set of object categories can be viewed and edited in the following way: on the Manage tab of the Ribbon, click Settings and then Object Styles from the drop-down list.

Figure 1.14 shows the Object Styles dialog box. Checking the Show Categories from All Disciplines check box will allow you to see additional categories primarily used by Revit Architecture and Revit MEP. This dialog box organizes the categories into three tabs: Model Objects, Annotation Objects, and Imported Objects. Within this dialog box you set the line weights, colors, line patterns, and materials for all elements in your project. Subcategories can also be added, deleted, or renamed as necessary.

FIGURE 1.14
The Object Styles dialog box provides display controls for element categories.

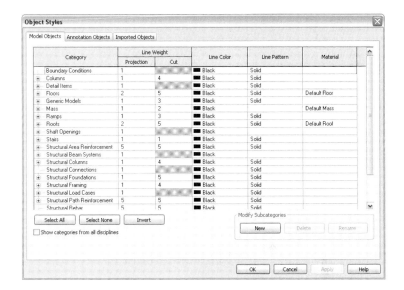

Families

The object categories are divided into families. Families can be system, in place, or component. System families are built into templates and projects, and in most cases they cannot be completely removed. Some system families are:

◆ Model elements (walls, columns)

◆ Datum elements (grids and levels)

◆ View-specific elements (text notes, tags)

System families are easily identified by checking the family name of an element in the Element Properties dialog box. The name of the family is prefaced by *System Family* (see Figure 1.15). System families are confined to a project, and the user can only create new versions from existing ones or alter the parameters for them. They can be shared with other projects, but fundamentally they exist only in a project file.

FIGURE 1.15

The name of the family is prefaced by *System Family*.

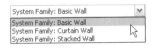

External families are loaded from the Revit Structure content libraries as well as from your own custom-created libraries. You load them in as you need them. These family files can be created from scratch using a default template shipped with the program, by using a custom template, or by copying and modifying a similar existing family.

USE THE BUILT-IN LIBRARIES TO YOUR ADVANTAGE

Copying and modifying the built-in library families are a great way to learn how families are created and to begin experimenting with your own adaptations. Learning to adapt and create families will prove to be a big benefit for you.

External families can be:

◆ Model elements such as columns and beams

◆ View-specific elements such as tags and detail components

In-place families are primarily used for custom project-specific applications. As the name suggests, these families are built in place within the project. One possible example of an in-place family is a roof truss for an old existing building structure that cannot be made from the stock library files.

Types

Families are further divided into types. A family may have one or more types. A column family (model element) type would be a W12x40 or a W18X35. A grid family (datum element) type would be a 1/4″ bubble or a 3/8″ bubble. A structural framing tag family (view-specific element) type would be Boxed or Standard.

Instances

An instance is a specific element of a given family type. For example, for a model element of the category Structural Column, whose family is a W-Wide Flange Column and whose type is a W12x40, the instance would be the specific W12x40 located at the grid intersection A-1 from Level 1 to 4′-0″ above Level 2.

Element Properties

After you place objects such as columns and beams into your building model, you can access the properties of each one by selecting it, clicking the Element Properties panel on the Ribbon (see Figure 1.16), and then clicking either Instance Properties or Type Properties, which will open one of those two Element Properties dialog boxes (see Figures 1.17 and 1.18).

The Instance properties of an element can also be accessed in other ways. With the element(s) selected:

◆ Right-click and then select Element Properties.

◆ Press Alt+Enter on your keyboard.

◆ Press the default keyboard shortcut PR.

FIGURE 1.16
Accessing the Instance and Type properties of a beam element

FIGURE 1.17
Instance Properties dialog box for a W21x44 girder

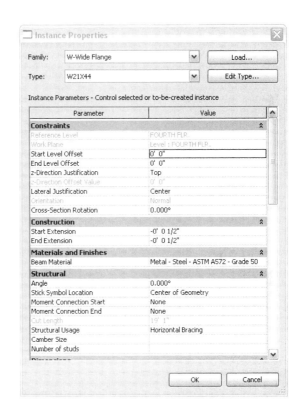

The Element Properties dialog boxes contain the parameters that define the element and are broken into two areas: instance and type parameters. You can change their values in the following ways:

◆ Changes you make to the instance parameters will affect only the element(s) that you have selected.

◆ Changes you make to the type parameters affect every instance of the element that you have in the model whether you have inserted it or selected it.

FIGURE 1.18
Type Properties dialog
box for a W21x44 girder

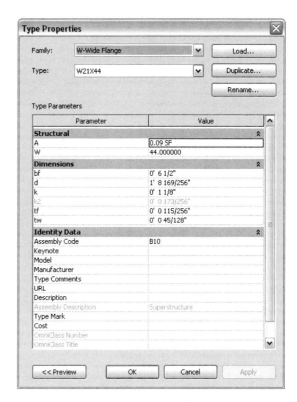

Now that you have studied the various elements that are available to you for modeling your structure, let's examine how those elements are displayed in your model. The views that you create, their interaction, and how they display the elements in the model are important considerations in the evolution of any project.

Project Views and Display

Numerous types of views are created as you work. Each view type serves a variety of purposes within your project. You access these views through the Project Browser and display them in the drawing area. In this section, we will introduce you to these various view types with a brief explanation of how they work.

◆ Plan, elevation, callout, section, and 3D views act as direct graphical "windows" to the model.

◆ View-specific elements such as notes and member tags can then be placed, and the graphical display of elements can be manipulated in these views without any effect on the actual model or other views. Modifications can be made directly to the model elements in any of these views, and those modifications will be instantaneously propagated to all other relevant views (as you will recall, this is called bidirectional associativity).

◆ Drafting views are intended to permit 2D drafting of details and as such are somewhat detached from the model itself, but they play a valuable role in the development of construction documents.

◆ Sheet views are a specialized type of view that typically contains one or more other view types and your title block. They are used for creating your finished construction documents and presentation drawings.

Now let's look at each one of these view types and see how they can be created in your project.

Plans

Probably the first view of your model you will create is a floor plan view, which for those in the structural discipline is usually cut about one foot above the floor line at each level. Structural floor plans are the default views in all preinstalled templates.

One thing to understand about plan views is their relationship to the levels you create. A floor plan view is associated with a specific level in your project. A new plan view is (at the discretion of the user) automatically added to the Project Browser every time you draw a new level in your project. Copying an existing level to create a new one will not automatically create a plan view. In these cases, you must create the view after the level is created.

To create a new plan view for a level that does not currently have one, follow these steps:

1. On the Ribbon select View ➤ Plan Views ➤ Structural Plan.

2. Select one or more levels to create plan views in the New Plan dialog box (see Figure 1.19).

FIGURE 1.19
New Plan dialog box (Since there is no dataset yours may appear different.)

Only levels that do not have floor plan views already are listed in the dialog. If you are using this method to create a duplicate plan, be sure the Do Not Duplicate Existing Views check box is not checked. Also note that you can preset the scale of the plans being created.

You can also create duplicate plan views by right-clicking a plan view name in the Project Browser and selecting Duplicate View from the shortcut menu. A fly-out menu (see Figure 1.20) will appear with three options:

◆ Duplicate

◆ Duplicate with Detailing

◆ Duplicate as a Dependent

These work like this:

◆ Duplicate will create a new plan view that is an exact copy, displaying all datum and model elements. No view-specific elements (such as text) will be copied with this option.

◆ Duplicate with Detailing works the same way except that all view-specific elements are also copied.

◆ Duplicate as a Dependent will create a child view to the selected parent view. Any number of dependent views can be created from a single parent view. This feature was added to facilitate the division of large overall plan views into smaller views for placement on sheets. All view-specific elements are shared between the parent and all child views. At any time you may change the view to an independent view.

FIGURE 1.20
You can use Duplicate View to create copies of a view.

View Range

View range is important to understand when you are dealing with plan views since it controls the basic vertical range above and below the elevation where your plan view is cut through the model. You access the View Range properties by clicking View Range in the View Properties dialog box of that particular plan view. The resulting View Range dialog box (see Figure 1.21) is used to control element visibility and display that is perpendicular to the plan view.

FIGURE 1.21
View Range dialog box

The primary range is defined by three horizontal planes: top, cut, and bottom. A fourth plane that can exist outside the primary range is the view depth. The cut plane is always defined as an offset of the view's associated level. The other three planes may be defined relative to any level in the model or set to Unlimited. The top and bottom planes of the view range define the primary vertical extents of the model that is displayed in the view:

◆ Model elements that fall within the primary range and that are not cut by the cut plane will display their projection line style as configured in Objects Styles or if altered using the Visibility Graphics dialog box.

◆ Elements that are cut by the cut plane will display their cut line style (if they have one) as configured in Object Styles or if altered using the Visibility Graphics dialog box (which will be discussed later).

◆ Elements that are outside the primary range but between the View Depth setting and the primary range will use the Line style <beyond> as configured in Object Styles or if altered using the Visibility Graphics dialog box.

A common problem with this feature results from users failing to understand that each plane cannot be assigned values that cross another. For example, the bottom of the primary range cannot cross below that View Depth setting. Imagine the planes as plates of glass that you can adjust vertically but that cannot physically pass through each other. They can share an elevation setting but not travel beyond another.

CUT LINES AND PATTERNS

Whether or not a cut line or pattern style exists for a particular category can be verified in the Object Styles or Visibility/Graphic Overrides dialog box (see Figure 1.27 later in this chapter).

Categories that have a shaded cell in the Cut-Lines column do not have a definable cut line style.

You might wonder where you would use the Beyond line style. The most obvious example is an architectural roof plan. Usually the architectural plan displays the roofs looking down from above the building on all the roof levels below. You can have a roof at the second floor and a roof at the sixth floor showing in one plan view. To do that, you extend the view depth down to the second floor so that all the roofs are within the range; you can give it a specific line style to distinguish it as being beyond the view cut plane.

MULTIPLE-VIEW CONCEPT

Although it may not seem natural at first, a good practice to adopt while working with views in Revit Structure is to create multiple copies of the same view to be used for specific purposes. When dealing with plan views, you will typically have at least three views for each level.

Using the second level of the model as an example, you can create the following views: S-FP02, S-FP02-Analytical, and S-FP02-Working. The S-FP02 view would be placed on a sheet view and would ultimately be plotted as part of the construction documents. The graphical displays of the datum and model elements in this view are always set as they are intended to plot. Only construction document view–specific elements are added to this view. The S-FP02-Analytical view is used to display an analytical view of the model elements in order to examine connection relationships and load patterns related to using analysis tools. S-FP02-Working is typically used to add/modify model elements, to coordinate with the other disciplines by linking in models and DWG backgrounds, or to adjust the display of elements to troubleshoot the model. Annotations can be placed in either of these views as reminders or notes to other team members.

Working in this manner helps safeguard the integrity of the construction documents without hindering productivity.

Callouts

Callout views are used to produce a blowup of an area for clarification and can be accessed on the Ribbon on the View tab. This usually larger-scale view is used to show a higher level of detail and additional annotation that may not be legible at the original scale.

Three distinct types of callouts are available: reference, detail, and view.

Reference callouts are ideal for tying in standard details (drafting views) or to refer to a similar existing view. Reference callouts do not create a view in the project; instead they are tied directly to the existing view they reference. You place reference views by selecting the Callout command from the View tab and selecting the Reference Other View box on the Options bar. Then, you select a view to reference from the drop-down menu on the Options bar. Finish by drawing the callout graphic in a view. While this is a logical feature to include as well as a nearly universally requested one, this feature does introduce an opportunity for error because the user can select the incorrect view to reference.

You place detail and view callouts by selecting the Callout command from View tab of the Ribbon. Then select the appropriate callout type from the Type Selector (see Figure 1.22), and finish by drawing the callout graphic in a view. Creating detail callouts will place a new view under the Detail Views (Detail) heading in the Project Browser. Detail views are typically used to embellish another detail or section at a larger scale. Detail views should be thought of as the "end of the road" in detailing, the last level of detail required. Some modeling features are restricted in detail views, so adding some elements in them may not be possible. In general, view callouts should be created until you have reached the finest scale required to communicate the intention of your design. Then use the detail callout. A view callout will place a new view under the same heading as the view it was created in. View callouts have all of the same capabilities as the view to which they refer. This makes them ideal candidates for enlarged plans.

FIGURE 1.22
Select the callout type
from the Type Selector.

Sections

Section views cut vertically through the model. These views are created for many purposes and come in three varieties: detail, wall, and building sections. They each use different annotations so that they are obviously different to the reader of your documents. The section updates automatically with any new or modified model elements falling within its scope (that is, its length, height, and depth) (see Figure 1.23). Other sections that fall within that scope are also displayed by default. That makes referencing mistakes much less likely to occur and saves you a lot of valuable time that you might otherwise spend cross-referencing details.

FIGURE 1.23
A building section
displaying depth and
other controls

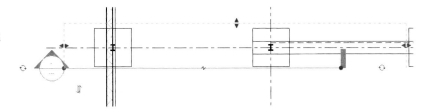

Building and wall sections are restricted to plumb or vertical representations of your building, whereas detail sections are not. This means that a detail section will permit you to provide a detail of an opening's jamb/frame condition or a sloped roof connection detail.

During the course of modeling or troubleshooting, it is often useful to cut a working section. These working views are not intended to be placed on the construction documents and are essentially disposable. To keep the Project Browser organized and the construction documents free of "view clutter," it's a good idea to create a new section view type that is easily identifiable. You need to be careful not to move sections that you have placed on sheets.

Section views that that have not been dragged onto a sheet and thus are not referenced on any sheet will not print unless you specifically enable them in the Print dialog box, so making working sections and leaving them in at print time is fine. But if you export your model to an AutoCAD DWG file, the unreferenced section callouts will be exported, so you will have to do a little cleanup of the DWG and erase them before you send it out, especially if it is an important design submission. So it is better to erase those sections before you export your sheets.

To add a section, perform these steps:

1. Click Section on the View tab of the Ribbon.

2. In the Type Selector select the section type you want: Detail, Building, or Wall.

3. Click on the location where you wish to begin the section.

4. Click where you want to finish the section.

5. The section remains selected and will display a dashed green line.

6. Click the double-triangle grips and drag the dashed green line box to adjust the depth of the section, or use the same double triangles to adjust the left and right extents of the section view.

7. Use the other controls to flip the section (double arrows), change the head and tail to the other end (circular arrows), change the location of the head or tail (blue dots), or create a gap in the section line (the jagged line symbol).

Now that you have seen how sections work in Revit Structure, let's move on to see how elevation views are created and function.

Elevations

Two types of elevations are available in Revit Structure: building and framing (see Figure 1.24).

FIGURE 1.24
Building and framing elevations

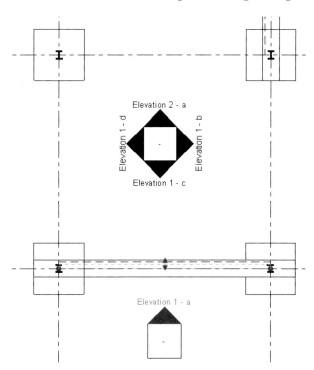

You create building elevations by selecting the Elevation command from the View tab of the Ribbon and placing the elevation tag in a plan view. Each instance of a building elevation is capable of generating four directional views.

Framing elevations are specialized elevations designed to facilitate the placement of vertical bracing and moment frames. They are anchored to a grid or reference line. You create these elevations by selecting the Framing Elevation command from the View tab of the Ribbon and hovering over a grid or named reference plane in a plan view to attach the elevation view tag. You can place the elevation view tag on either side of the grid or named reference plane; it depends on which side of the element you are on prior to placement. To release or reassign the grid anchor, highlight the elevation tag, right-click, and select Element Properties from the context menu; then change the Associated Datum parameter accordingly.

Drafting

Drafting views are 2D views that have no connection to the 3D model. To work in the drafting views, you will use the drafting tools found on the Annotate tab of the Ribbon, such as Detail Line and Filled Regions.

A good example of a drafting view is a typical detail that you wish to add or an imported scan. Detail views can be saved and inserted from detail libraries either individually or as whole sheets, as you will see later in Chapter 9.

Another useful feature (if your Revit license is on Subscription) that you can use to create a drafting view is the Freeze Drawings command from the Extensions menu. This command will take a view that contains live-model items and extract them into a 2D drafting view that is independent of the model and is just line work.

Legends

Legends are unique views that have the advantage that they are the only view types, along with schedules, that can be placed on multiple sheets. You create a legend by selecting the Legend command from the View tab of the Ribbon; then you can choose a standard legend or a keynote legend. Legend views are typically used as an explanatory list of symbols and text that are found in the project, such as framing notes that might appear on multiple sheets. Keynote legends report or summarize any keynotes that are present in the views that share the same sheet with the keynote legend. Chapter 11 will discuss alternative uses for legend views and step you through the creation of a legend.

Schedules

With the exception of the Graphical Column Schedule, schedules are typically spreadsheet-style, text-based views that report the quantities of specific elements or the values of an element's parameters. Several varieties of schedules can be created (see Figure 1.25). Graphical Column Schedules are another form of schedule that automates the process of creating and maintaining a column schedule and are covered extensively in Chapter 4.

You create a schedule by selecting Schedules from the View tab of the Ribbon and then the particular schedule type you wish to create. Creating schedules will be discussed in depth in Chapter 11.

3D

Three-dimensional (3D) views (see Figure 1.26) allow you to orbit around your model in 3D space in order to view the overall model. You can activate a section box that you use to create cutaway views in the X, Y, or Z plane through any portion of the overall model. 3D views are very important for visualization purposes, both for the client and the working engineer or draftsperson. You create a 3D view by clicking 3D Views on the View tab of the Ribbon. Using the Camera option creates a perspective 3D view. Using the Walkthrough option creates an animation sequence following a path through the model.

FIGURE 1.25
Schedule types and a
View List schedule

FIGURE 1.26
3D view with Cube,
Wheel, and Zoom navi-
gation tools

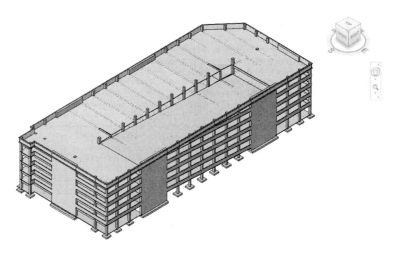

When you start your project, it is good practice to immediately create a sheet of 3D views to share with your client. Doing so quickly creates a better understanding of the structure, especially for an owner who has no experience with reading plans and sections.

Sheets

Sheet views contain your title blocks, and they are the assembly point for all the different views you create: plans, sections, elevations, and so forth. You drag the different views you have created onto the title sheet and position them as necessary. When you add a sheet view to your project, you will be prompted to select a title block to use for the new sheet. The title block is a separate file that you create and then load into your project. You will learn more about title sheet creation in Chapter 12.

Plan Regions

Plan regions are self-contained view ranges within a plan view and are used in those cases where you need the view range of a particular area on a plan to differ from the overall plan view range. Remember that the view range sets the vertical range above and below the elevation at which your plan view is cut. An example of where this might be used is an area with a stepped footing that is stepping out of the vertical range of your overall plan. If you want to control exactly which step to display on the overall plan, you would use a plan region to adjust where the stepped footing cuts off in the view.

When you start the command you are put into Sketch mode. To create a plan region, simply sketch a boundary line for the area you wish it to affect. Then adjust the View Range parameter in the View Properties dialog box to suit your needs.

Visibility/Graphic Overrides Dialog Box

The Visibility/Graphic Overrides dialog box (see Figure 1.27) provides a way to change the display of elements for a specific view.

The changes made in this dialog box have no effect on the model itself or any other views, including any dependent views and the current view. If your intention is to change the look of elements project-wide, see the appropriate dialog boxes outlined in the upcoming section, "Graphic Standard Styles and Patterns." Line style settings are located in the Visibility/Graphic Overrides dialog box. For the easiest/fastest access, learn to use the keyboard shortcut **VG**, as you will be in and out of this dialog box constantly.

FIGURE 1.27
Visibility/Graphic Over-rides dialog box

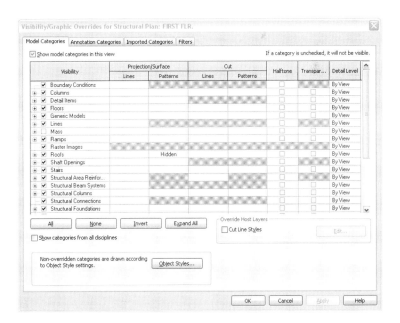

THE IMPORTANCE OF DISPLAY CONTROL

Remember that display control is half the effort that must be expended toward the goal of getting a good-looking set of construction documents from your model, like the sheet of plans in the graphic below. It is easy to get caught up with building the model and neglect setting up and creating the documents that must be derived from it. At the beginning of the project, start thinking about how you will organize your different views onto sheets and how you want each view displayed. Set up your title block and start adding sheets as soon as possible. You should be asking yourself questions such as what detail mode and view scale are appropriate, and how much of the model should a certain view expose.

Getting your modeled elements to "look right" on the final document can be a frustrating task and requires special attention to the methods that will be discussed. Keep your deadlines in mind and schedule your time accordingly so that you are not only modeling but also creating your documents in a wise manner.

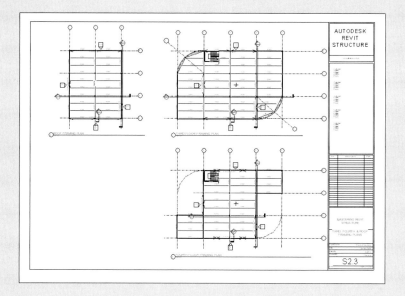

Now that you have studied the various views that are available to you for displaying your virtual structure, we'll show you how to adjust the graphical settings within those views to best display the elements in your final documents.

Graphic Standard Styles and Patterns

What if you want increase the cut line width of your structural columns and have it change in every view of the project, not just in the current view?

The graphical display of elements throughout all views of a project is efficiently managed with a handful of dialog boxes. This dynamic ability to modify project standards on the fly during production is a major benefit of the Revit Structure platform. You will now explore the different ways that you can effectively configure and control your element displays.

Object Styles

One of the most important of these dialog boxes is the Object Styles dialog box. In the Object Styles dialog box, you assign and control the following:

◆ Line weights (both projection and cut, if applicable)

◆ Line colors

◆ Line patterns

◆ Material styles

This dialog box controls the display of all categories and subcategories of elements in the project model. You organize and modify these styles using the Object Styles dialog box (see Figure 1.28), which you access on the Manage tab of the Ribbon by clicking Settings ➢ Object Styles or via the Visibility/Graphic Overrides dialog box. There you can access and edit the various display parameters, such as cut line and projection line weights.

FIGURE 1.28
Object Styles dialog box

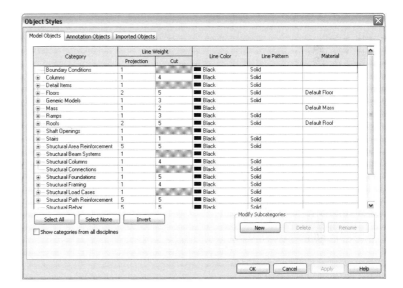

Material Styles

The Materials dialog box allows you to configure and control all the material assignments for elements in your model. For instance, what grade of steel do you want your columns to be, and in what color do you want it displayed in a 3D view?

Open the Materials dialog box (see Figure 1.29) by clicking Materials on the Manage tab of the Ribbon. This dialog box lists all of the materials currently available in the project:

◆ The Graphics tab defines the appearance of the material in all nonrendered views.

◆ The Render Appearance tab, as the name suggests, contains settings that define how the materials will appear when rendered.

◆ The Identity tab contains parameters that can be specified for each material that can be leveraged by tags and Material Takeoff schedules.

◆ The Physical tab contains structural information that can be leveraged for the structural analysis of the model.

FIGURE 1.29
Materials dialog box

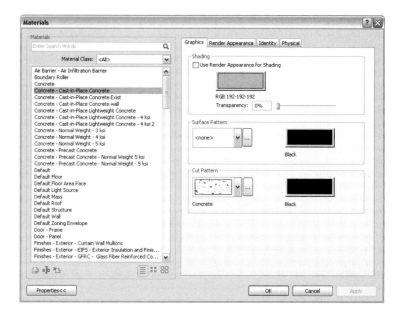

Next you will learn more about styles, in this case styles of lines.

Line Styles

Revit Structure uses many line styles to display various representations for 3D model elements, while those that users add themselves are used mostly for 2D drafting and for using the Linework tool. There are many default styles, some of which are enclosed by brackets, such as <overhead>, and some others that are not. If you find that you cannot rename or delete a line style, it is safe to assume that Revit requires it in order to function properly. Beyond that you can create your own line styles. With the Linework tool you can alter model lines so they will display in any of the line styles you have available.

Open the Line Styles dialog box (see Figure 1.30) on the Manage tab of the Ribbon by clicking Settings ➤ Line Styles. This dialog box lets you view and edit all of the line styles available in the project.

Line Weights

You define line weights using the Line Weights dialog box (see Figure 1.31). Open this dialog box on the Manage tab of the Ribbon by clicking Settings ➤ Line Weights. Line weights are divided into three categories: Model, Perspective, and Annotation. Sixteen line weights can be defined for each of these categories. The Model category can have unique weights for each of the predefined 28 imperial or 12 metric scales. Weights defined for the Perspective and Annotation categories are absolute, regardless of scale. The templates that are provided with Revit have a sample collection of typical scales and line weight assignments for each of the 16 pens. The scales that are defined in advance can be added or deleted from your templates as required.

FIGURE 1.30
Line Styles dialog box

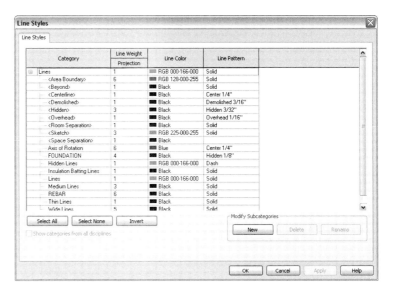

FIGURE 1.31
Line Weights dialog box

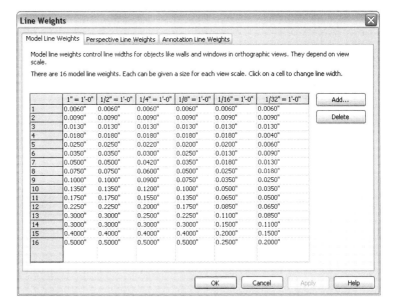

LINE WEIGHT ADJUSTMENTS

Different plotters may require adjustment of the default line weights in order to get a better print. In some cases, the thinnest pen weights will not display well on certain plotters, so you should experiment with different values to see which are best for your particular output device.

Some users find it easier to compare line weights with the technical pens used to draft on paper if the project units are assigned to millimeters. To do this, temporarily change your project's linear unit of measure to millimeter. On the Manage tab on the Ribbon choose Project Units. Click the Format button next to Length and assign it to millimeters.

Line Patterns

Line patterns are a sequence of dots, dashes, and spaces of various lengths that create distinct lines. The Line Patterns dialog box (see Figure 1.32) can be accessed on the Manage tab of the Ribbon by clicking Settings ➤ Line Patterns.

FIGURE 1.32
Line Patterns dialog box

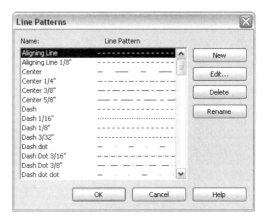

Clicking the New or Edit button in this dialog box will take you to the Line Pattern Properties dialog box (see Figure 1.33). Here you can develop new line patterns or adjust existing ones in order to perfect the different view displays. Keep in mind that the dimensions you are entering to define a pattern are the desired printed size for the pattern, and these will adjust no matter what scale of the view is used, so that the intended size will be the same across all printed views.

Fill Patterns

Fill patterns are used by filled regions for hatching. They are also used by materials for both surface and cut patterns of objects. All of the fill patterns can be viewed and edited in the Fill Patterns dialog box (see Figure 1.34). Open this dialog box on the Manage tab of the Ribbon by clicking Settings ➤ Fill Patterns. Revit Structure uses two types of fill patterns: drafting and model. Model patterns scale with the object and represent the real-world appearance of an object, such as CMU (concrete masonry units) coursing. Drafting patterns do not scale and are a symbolic representation of a material, such as the concrete pattern.

Clicking the New or Edit button in this dialog box takes you to the Modify Pattern Properties dialog box (see Figure 1.35). Here you can develop new patterns or modify existing ones.

FIGURE 1.33
Line Pattern Properties
dialog box

FIGURE 1.34
Fill Patterns dialog box

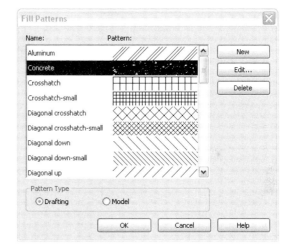

Hafltone/Underlay

New to this version of Revit Structure is an important functional improvement that provides
the ability to alter the halftone display of elements in views for underlays, such as a linked
background, as well as for views that have had the Halftone option set for categories in Visi-
bility/Graphics. The Underlay feature is part of each plan-oriented view type. Until now in many
cases the underlays were too light and could not be adjusted because the feature was not originally
intended for plotting purposes. It was intended to be used for coordination of elements from one
level to another. Due to user demand it has been expanded in this way. Open this dialog box on
the Manage tab of the Ribbon by clicking Settings ➤ Halftone/Underlay. In the dialog box (see
Figure 1.36) you can alter the Weight, Pattern, and Brightness values of the grayscale tone to fit
your needs.

FIGURE 1.35
Modify Pattern Properties dialog box

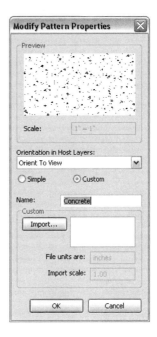

FIGURE 1.36
Use the Halftone/Underlay dialog box to control underlay tones.

This completes our first look at the Revit Structure interface and its basic set of commands. In the next chapter you will learn how to develop different project environments through the use of templates. We will discuss the various settings that are available to you as well as how the Project Browser can be organized so it can be managed. Then you will learn how content and settings can be transferred from one project to another.

The Bottom Line

Use the graphical user interface.   The Revit Structure GUI is an easy way to interact with your computer in order to efficiently create your project model and documents.

Master It   There are several ways to launch a single command in Revit Structure. List the various ways in which the Beam command can be invoked. Which method is the quickest?

Understand the types of elements in the modeling environment.   In the modeling environment, there are basic types of model and annotation elements that you use in the construction of the virtual model and construction documents that you derive from the model.

Master It   Modeled elements have a defined hierarchy that consists of categories, families, types, and instances. Select a structural column and give examples of each of these four element properties.

Create and manage project views.   Even though you are building a 3D model, most of the time you are working in views that present the model as if they are 2D views, such as plans and sections. Therefore, the view types become your working planes and must be sensibly arranged.

Master It   List all the major project view types discussed in this chapter.

Control the graphical display of elements in a project.   Creating the model is only half the story. You must also derive the 2D and 3D views you will need for your construction documents. Each of these views must be able to display the model, and those display controls are an essential subject to understand.

Master It   In your project you want to change the look of your masonry units on plans and elevations to match your company standards. Explain how to change the cut pattern for concrete masonry units to a diagonal pattern and the surface pattern to 8 × 8 block.

Chapter 2

Setting the Project Environment

To fully master Revit Structure, you need to understand the settings that are available to you and distinguish between settings that are global for the project or specific to the user's machine. Properly using these settings will easily help you achieve the look you want for your structural documentation. Most of the settings that will be discussed in this chapter will become part of your standards and should be incorporated into template files.

Getting a handle on the settings that are part of the project environment, setting them appropriately for your company's best practices, and making use of well-thought-out templates will help you start out your projects much faster. This will allow users to focus more on the project itself rather than the behind-the-scenes items that will become your standards.

To take full advantage of Revit Structure's organizational methods, you will learn how to make use of browser organization and naming conventions to aid in the modeling process and how to create a clutter-free environment. Using custom templates to start or populate your project will help you follow standards, and the documenting efforts for your model will be more efficient.

Making these settings and providing proper organizational workflows will force users to maintain standards, thus reducing errors and keeping users working efficiently.

In this chapter you will learn to:

- Develop your own custom templates

- Set project units and precision display

- Make adjustments to structural-specific settings

- Organize the Project Browser

- Transfer standards into your project

Working with Project Templates

Project templates offer the initial conditions for you when your project is started. They can also be useful to help put content into your project as you reach different stages of the modeling process. You can think of a template as a preset starting point. Templates have an `.rte` file extension rather than the `.rvt` extension that a project uses. As you create your standards and develop your working environment, be thinking about where and how that information will fit into your project template(s). Taking the time to set up your templates effectively and update them continually as the software improves or your standards change will help eliminate the redundant work of constantly making changes to your project settings. Not only that, but a properly tuned template will help maintain standards throughout your office.

It is important to know that when setting up your template(s), you definitely will not get everything you need in them the first time. Templates will more than likely change with each and every project you do. You will continue to incorporate new content as you learn the software and to reflect your workflow. Eventually you will find that the changes will be reduced, but as new versions of the software become available, you will have to adjust your templates to accommodate any new changes that you want to bring into your workflow.

What goes into a template can depend greatly on your workflow as well as your knowledge of the types of things that can be put into them — or better yet, their ingredients. Understanding these various ingredients, how they work, where they are set, and what they do can make or break a project's successful start.

The Ingredients of a Good Template

Templates can contain just about everything that a normal project would contain. They can store project information, project settings, line styles, line weights, project views that have predefined settings, and visibility/graphics settings. If you have projects that all start out with similar geometry, you could put that geometry into the template and use it to start all your projects that use that geometry. Using this approach, you won't have to model elements over and over again.

If you are transitioning from an AutoCAD environment, you probably want to take all those years that went into the look and feel of the documentation that your company has established and continue that look in Revit Structure. All this can be done, but you'll have to modify what comes out of the box. Revit Structure allows you to easily adapt your own look and feel, which will be discussed throughout this book in other chapters. However, when you do develop these standards, you need to place them in templates so they can easily be applied to projects to help keep a constant look and facilitate users following standards. Here is a list of some factors to keep in mind when developing your template files:

- The display of graphics
  - Fill patterns (hatching)
  - Materials
  - Object styles
  - Line styles
  - Line weights
  - Line patterns
  - Structural symbols
  - Halftone/Underlay settings
- The display of annotation
  - Text styles
  - Dimension styles
  - Spot elevation, coordinates, slopes

- ◆ View tags
- ◆ Annotation tags
◆ Project settings
  - ◆ Project units
  - ◆ Structural settings
  - ◆ Rebar cover settings
  - ◆ Abbreviations
  - ◆ Project parameters

This list does not contain everything, but it includes critical aspects that you will want to address prior to starting a project.

As your understanding of using Revit Structure progresses and becomes clearer, you will find yourself putting more information into your templates and even creating several different templates. You may have a template set up for projects with different structural systems. For example, a project for a precast parking garage may not use steel members of any kind, so these families would not be loaded in that template. If your company works on a lot of parking garages where the structural engineer drives the project design, your template could already contain preset views, levels, and maybe even grids, and you will just have to adjust their location.

If you have created schedules such as a Footing Schedule, Pier Schedule, Sheet Index, or schedules that allow you to do quantity take-offs, those schedules could already be created inside your templates. Users do not have to keep remaking these schedules. Not only does this approach save you time, but it also forces all schedules of different makes and types to have a consistent look.

As you become more familiar with Revit Structure and learn about the objects and the types you'll be using, you can also add the following information to your template(s):

- ◆ Wall types
- ◆ Wall footing types
- ◆ Foundation slab types
- ◆ Floor types
- ◆ Roof types
- ◆ 2D components
- ◆ Families
- ◆ Analysis loading information
- ◆ Schedules
- ◆ View templates
- ◆ Filters
- ◆ Sheet setup

NO WORKSETS ALLOWED

All commands that are used in a worksharing environment will be grayed out in a template file. Worksets cannot be included in a template.

Many of these items can be transferred from your projects into a bare template or project that you can create from the None template option when starting. Not only will this allow you to create content for your templates as you work on projects, but putting this content into an empty project first will let you clean out any non-project-specific data before placing it into your template.

Using the None Template Option

The None template option will start you out with the bare minimum of a model. It will have one structural plan view to start the modeling process, and no families will be loaded. The only families available will be system families, and they will contain only one generic type.

This template should not be used to start your projects, but it will come in handy when you want to build templates or project files to quickly add content to your project without bringing over numerous other settings. For instance, say you wanted to create a template with several wall types for concrete; you would start this process by choosing Application ➢ New ➢ Project. Figure 2.1 shows the resulting dialog box, where you will create a new project. In this case, you will create a new project template (which will use the .rte file extension) and start it by not using a template. When you specify None for a template, you will also be presented with an option to use Imperial or Metric for your units. This is also true when you're creating a project from a None template. Once your blank template is started, you can create only the wall types that you want as part of your concrete wall types. Save the template in your Imperial or Metric Template folder, and use it to transfer into your active project model when required (see the section "Transferring Project Standards" later in this chapter).

FIGURE 2.1
Starting a project template from a None template

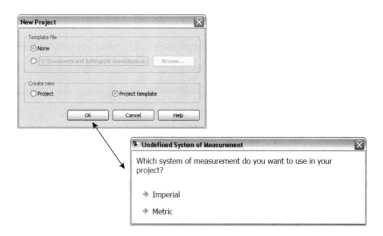

It is important to know what to put into your templates and that you will not be able to create the perfect template right out of the starting gate. Ensuring that your templates are current with your standards prior to starting each project or investing the time up front to create a template for a particular project can prevent inconsistencies as well as increase productivity downstream.

Creating a New Custom Project Template

You can create a new template in several ways:

◆ Start from Revit Structure's default template `Structural Analysis-default.rte`.

◆ Start from any other existing template.

◆ Save a current project (RVT) as a template.

If you are just starting to use Revit Structure, a good approach is to start a new template from Revit Structure's default template `Structural Analysis-default.rte`. Add, remove, or revise existing settings however you see fit for your office environment and to achieve the look and feel that you want for your documentation. Once you have completed this template, use it to start your projects. As you continue to work on and plot your projects, you will find that certain settings will need to be tweaked. Continue to make these adjustments within your active project but not on your template. At any time during the project, you can either transfer your settings from your project into your template or save your project as a template and then delete unnecessary model objects and views as required.

Your project templates should be stored on your network with all your other custom content so other users can access them. If you have a general template that will be used, you can set it as the default template to be used whenever someone starts a new project. As Figure 2.2 shows, you can do this by choosing the Application menu ➢ Options and clicking the File Locations tab. Under Default Template File, click the Browse button and select the path to your template file. When a new project is started, this is the template that it will use unless you browse to a different file.

FIGURE 2.2
Setting the default template location

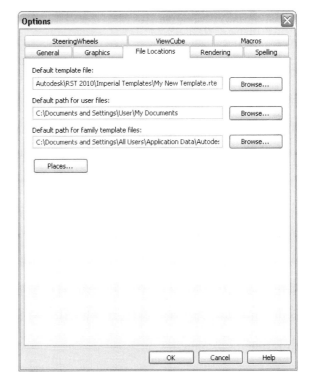

Templates should be saved to the network for all users to access and named so that users will easily know what is inside them as well as when to use them. You could consider a naming convention that reflects the structural system being used or type of content in each template if they are broken into smaller, less-populated template files. In some cases you may find that you have to have specific settings for certain clients, so you might want to include their name in the naming convention.

Starting a Project from a Template

Once you have your templates ready, you can start your new project by choosing the Application menu ➤ New ➤ Project or by going to Revit Structure's Recent File window, shown in Figure 2.3. This window is usually displayed when Revit Structure starts. If not, it can be toggled on by choosing the View tab ➤ Windows panel ➤ User Interface drop-down ➤ Recent Files. If you have already been busy at work and wish to see the Recent Files window, you'll find the check box for Recent Files is checked. You can uncheck it and check it again to open Recent Files or use Switch Windows found on the same Windows panel on the Ribbon. You will find Recent Files listed among the other open views. Choosing Recent Files simply switches the page to be active as well as display on top of other views you may have open.

FIGURE 2.3
Use the Recent Files window to start a new project or family or to open an existing project.

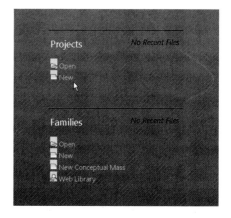

ENABLE RECENT FILES PAGE AT STARTUP

There is also a setting in the Application menu ➤ Options dialog box that controls whether the Recent Files page is displayed or not. Enabling or disabling the Enable Recent Files Page at Startup setting located at the bottom of the General tab in the Options dialog box controls this.

When you click New from the Application menu to create a project, the New Project dialog box shown in Figure 2.4 opens. Keep in mind that this dialog box appears only when starting a project through the Application menu. Using the New Project option from the Recent Files window assumes the default template will be used, and the New Project dialog box will not appear.

You will have two options to specify how you want to start out. The first one deals with the template file. You can choose not to use a template or to use one of your custom-made template files. In this example, the template that contains all the information for a high-rise post-tensioned structure will be used.

FIGURE 2.4
Starting a new project from a custom template file

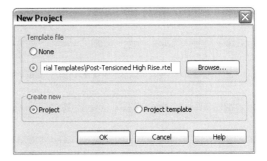

Your second option will be whether your new file will be a project or a project template. In this case, selecting Create New ➤ Project will preload your new project with all the settings stored in the template file you have chosen. Your project is under way and you are ready to start adding content. You have not named it yet, so don't forget to give your project a name and save it to your network.

Project Information

Project information is data pertaining to the project that typically does not change. You can find this category in Revit Structure by selecting the Manage tab ➤ Project Settings panel ➤ Project Information tool to open the Instance Properties dialog box shown in Figure 2.5. This information is typically shown in title blocks, and since it is specific to the project, all parameters are considered type parameters.

The initial six parameters that are available in this box are hardcoded into Revit Structure and cannot be changed. You are allowed to add parameters to this category by adding project parameters, which are parameters you can add in your project and that can be globally assigned to several categories.

To add a parameter for contractor information, follow these steps:

1. While in your project, choose the Manage tab ➤ Project Settings panel ➤ Project Parameters tool. Figure 2.6 shows the Project Parameters dialog box with some extra parameters displayed already; your project will most likely be different.

2. Click Add and fill in the information in the Parameter Properties dialog box shown in Figure 2.7. In this case, you will be adding a project parameter to the category Project Information with a name of Contractor Name. Its type will be Text and it will appear under the Other group.

Realize that just adding this new parameter as a project parameter (not a shared parameter) doesn't do much for you other than having the information shown when you display the Project Information Instance Properties dialog box. Taking advantage of this process in a slightly different way using a shared parameter gives you the ability to link the Project Information category to labels that appear in a title block.

FIGURE 2.5
The Instance Properties
dialog box for Project
Information

FIGURE 2.6
The Project Parameters
dialog box

Adding Project Information to a Title Block

If you want to see this information in a title block, you will have to add it as a shared parameter. Shared parameters are parameters that you can add to families or projects. They are stored in a separate text file where they can be accessed and shared in other families or projects. Once you select the Shared Parameter option, you will have to select a parameter from a list. If the parameter is not there, you will have to create it by clicking the Edit button (see Figure 2.8).

FIGURE 2.7
Adding a project parameter to the Project Information category

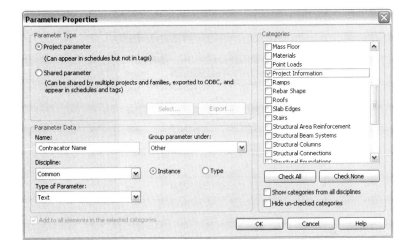

FIGURE 2.8
You can either select an existing parameter or create a new one on the fly.

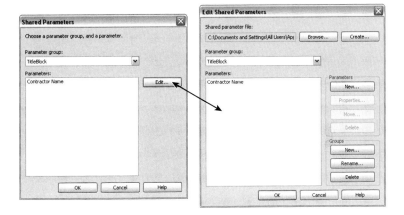

As Figure 2.9 shows, the Parameter Data options in the Parameter Properties box will be grayed out. This is because this information is stored inside the shared parameter.

HEY, WHERE DID THE CATEGORY GO?

Typically, project information acts as a type parameter. In this case, setting the Shared Parameter option to Type causes the Project Information category to disappear from the list. You only need to set it to Instance and Revit Structure will take care of the rest. This instance parameter will automatically act as a type parameter.

FIGURE 2.9
Adding a shared parameter to the Project Information category

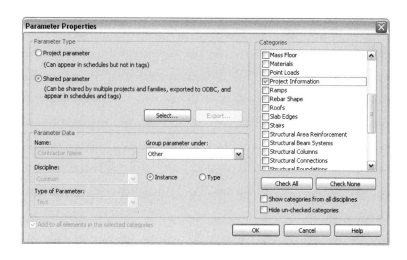

Inside the title block you will have to add the same shared parameter to a text label. Do this by placing a new label or by selecting an existing label and editing it using the Options bar. Figure 2.10 shows the Edit Label dialog box. When adding the parameter at this stage, you are only allowed to add a shared parameter. These steps are similar to those for adding a shared parameter in the project.

FIGURE 2.10
Adding a shared parameter to a label

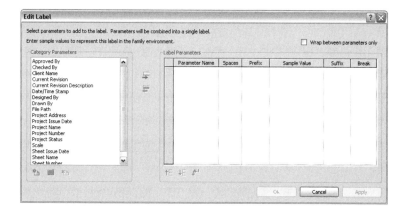

You will still need to add the shared parameter to the label by selecting the parameter in the left panel and clicking the right-arrow icon to move it over to the right panel, as shown in Figure 2.11.

When the title block is loaded into your project with that label, it will link itself to the Project Information shared parameter you created. This will allow you to change the Contractor Name information through the title block or through the Project Information dialog box. Figure 2.12 shows the information linked to the title block.

FIGURE 2.11
Putting parameters into
a label

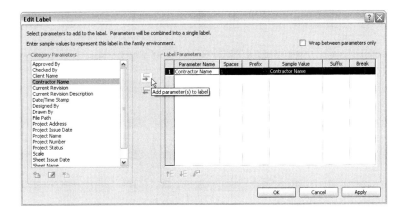

FIGURE 2.12
User-added project infor-
mation linked to a title
block

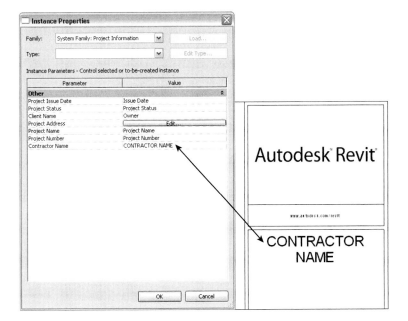

Project Location

Revit Structure acknowledges that every project needs a location with regard to where it is placed
in the coordinate system. You can find the location of this information by choosing the Manage tab
➤ Project Location panel ➤ Location tool. Figure 2.13 shows the information that can be recorded
and kept as part of your project information.

You will usually place your first object somewhere in the middle of your drawing area in that
big white space (it will be black space if your background is set to black). If you are starting your
project from an architectural model, you are probably going to link it into your project and use
the same origin point as the architect did. In Revit Structure, you not only have a location in the
left/right or up/down direction, but you have a Z direction as well. Is your first floor at elevation
0'-0″ or is it at 100'-0″? You are no longer working in 2D with sheets of paper; you are working in

an almost infinite model space, getting ready to virtually build a structure that is more than just a line on a piece of paper.

FIGURE 2.13
The Manage Place and Locations dialog box

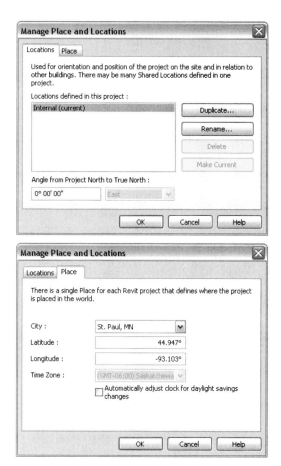

As you begin to work with several files, you will want to get familiar with their positions as well as the tools Revit Structure provides to aid in maintaining their positions. Some projects may require their positions to be revised with these tools. You should learn how each of these tools behave and what they do in the process of determining a project's position and orientation.

Project Position and Orientation

It's good practice to assume that Project North is up on your display. You start out modeling your project in the orientation that best fits on your sheet. For example, if a building is skewed, you may want to orient it so that it fits parallel or perpendicular on your sheets. In this section we'll explore tools that you can use to orient your project model as needed.

Each project you model will have its own position and orientation, which are determined by its size, shape, and geographical location. Because every project will be different, this information will not be added to your templates but is a major part of setting up your project environment. If you work for a structural firm or are part of a mechanical, engineering, and plumbing (MEP) firm, chances are that the project position and orientation will be fully denoted by the architect.

However, not every structural project is driven by an architectural concept, so you should understand what all of this means.

Since you are now working in a 3D environment, everything is tied together so you cannot just simply go to a plan view and move the entire plan over 2′ or select everything in a 3D view and move it up 1′ because the building's location needs to move. The building will move, but all the visible portions of your sections, crop regions, 2D content, and several other items will remain in their original location.

For this reason, Revit Structure provides tools that allow you to relocate, rotate, or mirror your project as needed. You access these tools by choosing the Manage tab ➢ Project Location panel ➢ Position drop-down.

The following exercises will take you through the basic steps needed to use a couple of these tools. For these exercises, you can use the RST_PROJECT_POSITION.rvt file (from the book's companion web page at www.sybex.com/go/masteringrevitstructure2010) or use one of your own projects.

EXERCISE: RELOCATE PROJECT

When you use the Relocate Project tool, Revit Structure moves the entire project relative to the shared coordinate system. It behaves much like the Move command but is more powerful. No objects need to be selected or moved, and everything maintains its position and goes along for the ride. It's kind of like a moving company placing your house on a big set of wheels and moving it across town to a new location — except with Revit Structure, you can easily toggle the location of the house from its new location back to its old location using shared coordinates.

1. With the exercise file (RST_PROJECT_POSITION.rvt) open, go to the North elevation view. Note that a project can be relocated in either a plan or elevation view. We will be relocating the project in an elevation view.

2. Choose the Manage tab ➢ Project Location panel ➢ Position drop-down ➢ Relocate Project tool.

3. Click anywhere in the drawing area, as shown in the following graphic, and move the cursor in an upward direction. While pulling in an upward direction, enter **100** (for 100′-0″) into the temporary dimension and press Enter.

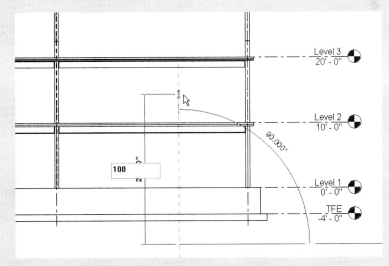

4. Step 3 just relocated your project up 100'-0". If the level's Elevation Base parameter is set to Project, it will appear that nothing has happened. This is because the Relocate Project tool has set up a shared elevation, and the level is currently not set to display the Shared Coordinate value.

5. Open the level's Type Properties dialog box. Under the Constraints group, you'll see the Elevation Base parameter. Change this value to Shared and click OK in all remaining dialog boxes.

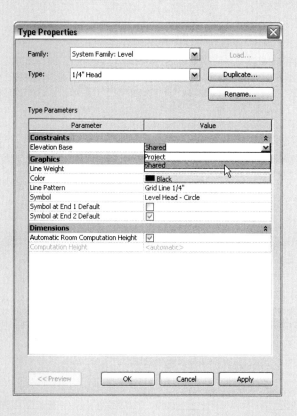

6. All elevation references should now reflect the new Shared value that you just set. The following graphic shows that the relocation of your project is complete. At first glance, it's difficult to tell what the Elevation Base parameter of a level is set to; in this example, they are set to Shared.

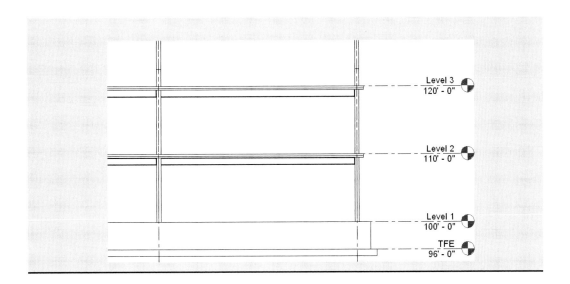

Not Everything Displays Shared in the Same Way

It is important to realize that you may need to change the Elevation Base setting to Project or Shared in other areas and that in some cases you cannot set Revit Structure to display the Shared Coordinate value.

Levels, spot elevations, and spot coordinates will allow you to toggle the display between these two coordinate systems by adjusting the Elevation Base setting.

The Graphical Column Schedule (GCS) displays the value that the level type displays. It is possible for both project and shared elevations to be displayed in the GCS at the same time. If the level's Elevation Base option is set to Project, it will display the project elevation. If the level's Elevation Base option is set to Shared, it will display the shared elevation.

The Elevation at Bottom parameter value shown in the Foundation element's Element Properties dialog box will display only the project coordinates. Take these factors into consideration when working with the project and shared coordinates.

Exercise: Rotate True North

By default, Revit Structure will set all plan views to Project North. To rotate your project to True North, you will need to be in a plan view and have the view set to display True North. Rotate True North behaves much like the Rotate command, but you'll find it is more powerful.

1. With the exercise file (RST_PROJECT_POSITION.rvt) open, go to the Level 3 plan view.

2. Open the View Properties dialog box of the view shown here, and make sure that the Orientation parameter is set to True North.

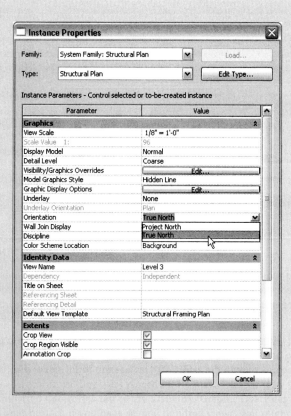

3. Select the Manage tab ➢ Project Location panel ➢ Position drop-down ➢ Rotate True North tool.

4. The default rotation symbol will display in a random location on the screen, as shown in the following graphic. You can select this symbol and move it to your chosen rotation point and rotate it as needed, or you can fill in the rotation information (45 degrees) in the Options bar at the top of the screen. Either method will produce the same results.

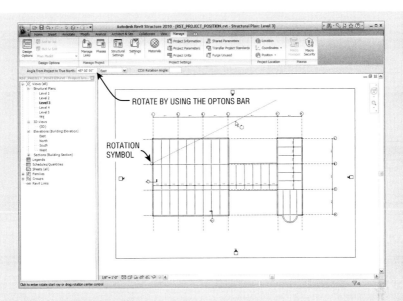

ROTATE BY USING THE OPTONS BAR

ROTATION SYMBOL

5. After completing step 4, you should see that the Level 3 view is rotated at a 45-degree angle. This is the project's True North setting. Plan views not set to the True North setting will still display at their Project North location.

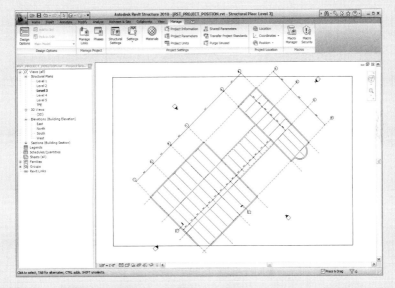

6. Observe that any annotation and detail line work has autorotated to read correctly and that the other plan views are still set to Project (which means they are not rotated 45 degrees).

Both the Relocate Project and Rotate True North tools set up shared coordinates for either the project's location or orientation. Additional settings can be set in levels or views to display these user-defined shared coordinates. Revit Structure's other tools such as Mirror Project and Rotate Project North behave much differently in that they actually affect Revit's coordinates and the position of the modeled elements.

MIRROR PROJECT

The Mirror Project tool is still fairly new to Revit Structure and hasn't changed much since its first appearance in the program, which means that it probably will not do 100 percent of everything you expect it to do. Exercise caution when using this tool; you may even want to try a few dry runs before running it on your live project. It behaves similar to the Mirror command. To mirror your project, select the Manage tab ➤ Project Location panel ➤ Position drop-down ➤ Mirror Project tool. You can mirror the project in several preset directions, as shown in the Mirror Project dialog box (Figure 2.14).

FIGURE 2.14
Mirror Project dialog box

Since this tool will mirror your project, it is going to take all annotations, section cuts, elevations, and other elements along for the ride and do its best to keep everything intact. It will not renumber grids for you so they display in the correct order or flip your section cuts on plan to maintain their original cut direction. However, it will allow you to export a list of errors that have occurred during the mirroring process so you can identify potential problem areas.

This tool is a bit different from the Relocate Project and Rotate True North tools. It does not have a setting that allows you to flip back and forth between two different mirrored views. The tool still uses the project coordinates and preserves any shared coordinates that you may have created.

OBJECTS IN MIRROR ARE CLOSER THAN THEY APPEAR

Well . . . not closer, but they might not be what you expect. The Mirror Project tool will definitely save you a lot of time when projects head down a different road than what you were originally going down. Hopefully this happens early on in the project. Either way, give this tool a try — just know that you will need to address a few things afterward. Here is a short list of the things we've come across. There may be others not mentioned, or those that have may have been fixed in an intermittent update of the software.

- Section bubbles may need to be dragged into place.
- Sections referencing other views do not get mirrored.
- The justification of text may need to be reset.
- Graphical Column Schedules do not mirror properly. They may need to be re-created.
- Elements may become unjoined.
- Dimension extension lines may need to be adjusted.
- If you mirror a project with links in it, it mirrors the instance of the link. The linked file is not actually mirrored.

Don't be discouraged by this list; just know that these are some of the things you should be looking for after the mirroring of a project. Even with this list of things that might go wrong, Mirror Project will get you much further along than if you had to use alternative methods. Keep in mind that mirroring a project in a single file as done in other software is a so-called simple task: select everything and use the mirror. In Revit, however, this command is given the job of mirroring everything in the model: all the views/sheets and related annotation. It replicates the steps that a user would have to take in every CAD file that describes a complete project, not just an individual file.

ROTATE PROJECT NORTH

The Rotate Project North tool is similar to Mirror Project in that it does not create shared coordinates: it rotates the project in its entirety based on Revit Structure's project coordinates. Revit Structure's 0,0 does not move or get relocated, but all elements such as section cuts, annotations, modeled elements, and crop boxes (basically everything) are moved. This tool was added because many users erroneously believe that to start their project they need to orient the building model with the site conditions. In fact, Revit actually suspects that you may not know what orientation the building will actually use on site yet, thus the assumption by Revit that Project North is more relevant when you start a project.

This method will do its best to realign the entire project accordingly, but, depending upon when you use this tool, you are quite likely to get a list of errors. These errors can also be exported so you can address them later more easily. Using the same file you used earlier, you begin by opening a floor plan view first and then choosing the Manage tab ➤ Project Location panel ➤ Position drop-down ➤ Rotate Project North tool. You can rotate Project North in several preset directions or select an element in the view to align the project with instead, as shown in the Rotate Project dialog box (Figure 2.15).

FIGURE 2.15
Rotate Project dialog box
with the option to show
details used

Project Units

Depending on what area of the world you are working in, you may be using either imperial or metric units. Also, depending on what types of projects you are working on, you may have set different units of precession. These units are displayed in dimensions, elevations, annotation tags, and even schedules. It is worth noting that there is an implicit understanding of "real-world" size. Changing from one unit of measure to another does not affect the size of elements, only the unit of measure displayed in dimensions and other annotation. Users of other software are probably all too familiar with the hardship of changing project units.

Revit Structure has three areas of units that are broken down into three separate sections: Common, Structural, and Electrical. You can see these sections by choosing the Manage tab ➤ Project Settings panel ➤ Project Units tool, and then clicking the Discipline drop-down list. We will discuss two of those sections next because they pertain specifically to Revit Structure. The Electrical units set is not relevant as it includes such settings as Illuminance, Luminous Flux, Luminous Intensity, Efficacy, Wattage, and Color Temperature.

Each set of units has several settings that allow you to adapt to the region and precision that you are preparing your documents for. We will not go into great depth with all of these individual levels, but we encourage you to step through each one as well as test the behavior that each setting change results in.

Common Units

The Common units include settings such as Length, Area, Volume, Angle, Slope, and Currency. Figure 2.16 shows the Project Units dialog box with Common chosen from the Discipline drop-down. This dialog box sets the units globally for the project, but you can override them when you're listing values in schedules and tags and according to dimension style types.

The Common units you see in Revit Structure are much the same as what you would see in Revit Architecture and MEP software. You will find that setting these units is similar to what you are accustomed to doing in other CAD programs. To access settings that are more specific to Revit Structure, use the Structural units, which we'll discuss next.

FIGURE 2.16
Setting your length units for the Common discipline

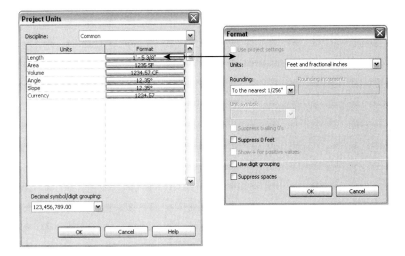

Structural Units

The Structural units include such settings as Force, Moment, Stress, Unit Weight, and Coefficient. Figure 2.17 shows the Project Units dialog box with Structural chosen from the Discipline drop-down. This dialog box sets the units globally for the project, but again, you can override them when you're listing values in schedules and tags.

FIGURE 2.17
Setting your units (Force) for the Structural discipline

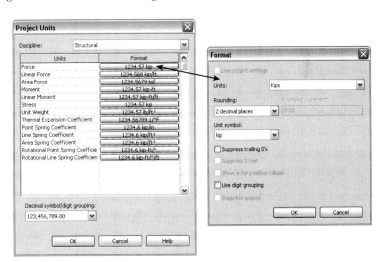

The Structural units resemble those in your analytical software. Depending on the type of work you do or where in the world your work is done, you may have separate templates that store this information to help keep your workflow efficient.

Structural Settings

The Structural Settings dialog box (Figure 2.18) contains settings for most structure-related items. These settings can be found by choosing the Manage tab ➢ Project Settings panel ➢ Structural Settings tool. You can save all information shown in this dialog box in your template files.

FIGURE 2.18
The Structural Settings dialog box

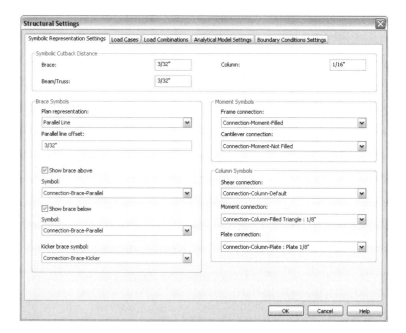

You will find that most of these settings pertain to how your documentation will look. A major aspect of showing framing for documentation involves single-line symbology as well as symbols for connection types. The next section will show how Revit Structure settings can help you adjust the symbolic representation of various structural elements for your documentation output. Following the symbolic representation settings, we will briefly discuss the settings that can be made to the analytical portions of the model.

Symbolic Representation Settings

This is the first tab in the Structural Settings dialog box. Settings on this tab control the display and representation of the different structural conditions in plans, sections, and schedules for steel shapes. These options determine how certain elements of an object display or allow you to use a symbol of your choice when certain conditions occur, such as the symbol you want to see for moment connections.

SYMBOLIC CUTBACK DISTANCE

The settings in the Symbolic Cutback Distance area shown in Figure 2.19 control the structural symbolic lines that display in a coarse detail level. Framing plans typically show a beam as offset or cut back from the column or girder it is connected to. These values govern this distance or offset from other framing members. The distance you choose is the printed dimension regardless of scale.

FIGURE 2.19
Setting the Symbolic
Cutback Distance values

Symbolic Cutback Distance			
Brace:	3/32"	Column:	1/16"
Beam/Truss:	3/32"		

These values are global (project-specific) settings that affect all beams, trusses, braces, and steel columns in your project. These are all model objects with embedded symbolic line work. The Column Cutback setting will primarily be used in a Graphical Column Schedule. Figure 2.20 shows examples of what these settings affect.

BRACE SYMBOLS

The Brace Symbols settings shown in Figure 2.21 control the symbolic display of bracing and kickers that exist throughout your project.

FIGURE 2.20
The Symbolic Cutback
Distance values can be
controlled as global set-
tings for the project.

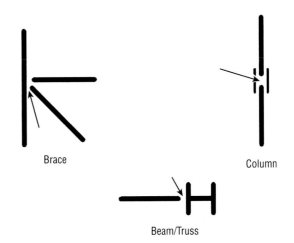

Brace

Column

Beam/Truss

FIGURE 2.21
The Brace Symbols
settings

Brace Symbols	
Plan representation:	
Parallel Line	⌄
Parallel line offset:	
3/32"	
☑ Show brace above	
Symbol:	
Connection-Brace-Parallel	⌄
☑ Show brace below	
Symbol:	
Connection-Brace-Parallel	⌄
Kicker brace symbol:	
Connection-Brace-Kicker	⌄

Revit Structure automatically places a symbol for framing members in a plan view when their Structural Usage property is set to Vertical Bracing or Kicker Bracing but only when the Structural Framing category is set to a coarse detail level.

For vertical bracing, you can choose between two different plan representation types: Parallel Line and Line with Angle. Figure 2.22 shows an example of each. The Parallel Line option has an additional offset setting so that the symbolic line can clearly be seen on your documentation. Revit Structure displays a Line with Angle symbol for the brace above and below depending on where the brace is connected.

FIGURE 2.22
Plan representation of bracing

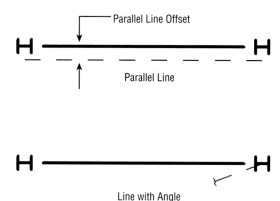

THAT IS NOT HOW WE SHOW OUR BRACING

If these two symbolic representations do not fit within your company's standard display of bracing, you can create a new symbolic bracing representation by using the Generic Annotation family. If creating a new symbol still does not give you the look you want or you dislike Revit Structure's behavior in displaying these symbolic representations, then you can deselect the Show Brace Above and Show Brace Below check boxes. This will allow you to use detail lines or other methods to achieve the look you desire.

The Kicker Brace symbol functions a bit differently than the other bracing symbols. Setting the plan representation does not have any effect on it, and you cannot toggle its above and below display. A kicker brace displays a symbol of your choice at the end of the kicker or at the kicker's uppermost connection point. Figure 2.23 shows Revit Structure's default Kicker Brace symbol: an X.

FIGURE 2.23
Plan representation of a kicker brace

Kicker Brace Symbol

EXERCISE: CREATE A NEW PLAN VIEW SYMBOL FOR A KICKER BRACE

If you choose to have a different look for the symbolic display of a kicker brace, you can do so by creating a new brace in the Plan View Symbols family.

1. Select the Application menu ➤ New ➤ Family.

2. Browse to the `Generic Annotations.rft` family template located in the `Imperial Templates - Annotations` folder.

3. Choose the Manage tab ➤ Family Properties panel ➤ Category and Parameters tool.

4. In the Family Category and Parameters dialog box shown here, select Brace in Plan View Symbols for the category type. This sets the category type of the family so it will show up as a symbolic representation to choose in the Structural Settings dialog box under Brace Symbols.

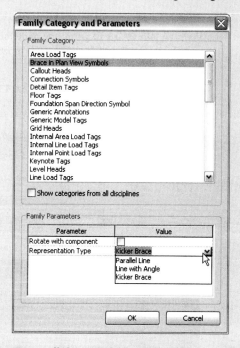

5. From the Representation Type pull-down under Family Parameters, select Kicker Brace. If this option is set to anything else, this representation type will not be available in the Kicker Brace Symbol pull-down.

6. Add line work as needed, using tools found in the Create tab on the Ribbon, for your symbolic display and delete the block of note text that was preloaded in the template.

7. Save the family and load it into your project by choosing the Insert tab ➤ Load from Library panel ➤ Load Family tool.

Note that the same steps apply for creating a new brace symbol except that in step 5 you will need to select a Representation Type setting of Parallel Line or Line with Angle.

MOMENT SYMBOLS

The settings in the Moment Symbols area shown in Figure 2.24 control the symbolic display of moment connections for framing that exist throughout your project.

FIGURE 2.24
The Moment Symbols settings

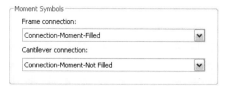

These symbols become visible only when the detail level of the Framing category is set to Coarse and the properties of the element are set such that the connections are applied. Figure 2.25 shows where these connections can be assigned for each instance of a framing member.

FIGURE 2.25
Assigning the symbolic display of a moment connection to a framing member

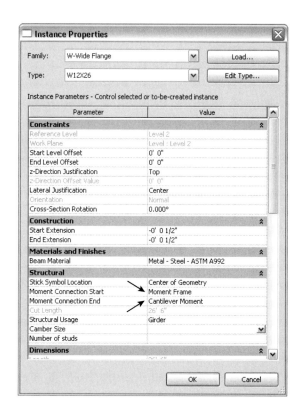

A Moment symbol falls under the category of Connection Symbol. Revit Structure has two types of framing member moment connections available: Moment Frame and Cantilever Moment. You are able to create any symbol you want for each of these two conditions. By default, Revit Structure has one set to a filled triangle and the other set to an open triangle (Figure 2.26).

FIGURE 2.26
Moment connection
symbols in plan view

COLUMN SYMBOLS

The settings in the Column Symbols area shown in Figure 2.27 control the symbolic display of connections for columns that exist throughout your project.

FIGURE 2.27
Setting the display of
Column symbols

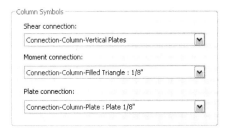

These symbols become visible only when the detail level of the Framing category is set to Coarse and the properties of the element are set such that the connections are applied. Figure 2.28 shows where these connections can be assigned for each instance of a column member.

FIGURE 2.28
Assigning the symbolic
display of a connection
to a column member

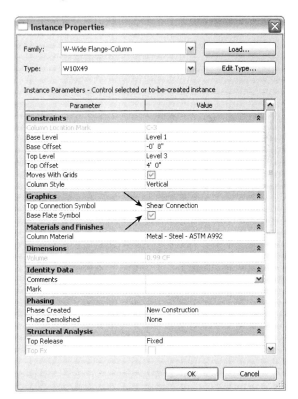

A Column symbol falls under the category of Connection Symbol. Revit Structure has three types of column member connections available: Shear Column Connection, Moment Column Connection, and Base Plate Symbol. You are able to create any symbol you want for each of these three conditions.

You can make as many different Top and Base connection types as you want, but you will only be able to display a maximum of two Top Connection symbols and a maximum of one Base Plate Connection symbol per project. Figure 2.29 shows examples of Revit Structure's default column symbols.

FIGURE 2.29
Symbolic Column symbols in Graphical Column Schedule

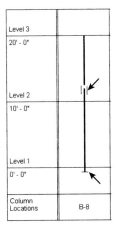

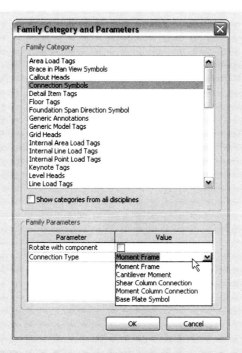

5. From the Connection Type pull-down under Family Parameters, select the type of Moment symbol you will be creating. Choosing Moment Frame or Cantilever Moment will classify the symbol as a Brace symbol. Choosing Shear Column Connection or Moment Column Connection will classify the symbol as a Column symbol, which will apply only to the top of a column. Choosing Base Plate Symbol will classify it as a Column symbol, which will apply to the base of the column.

6. Add line work as needed, using tools found in the Create tab on the Ribbon, for your symbolic display and delete the block of note text that was preloaded in the template.

7. Save the family and load it into your project by choosing the Insert tab ➢ Load from Library panel ➢ Load Family tool.

Analytical Settings

The remaining four tabs in the Structural Settings dialog box deal with the analytical portions of your project. If your project will not be taking advantage of the analytical capabilities Revit Structure offers, these settings will not matter much to you.

However, if you will be using Revit Structure for its analytical capabilities and will be placing loads inside the Revit Structure model, you will want to become familiar with these four tabs: Load

Cases, Load Combinations, Analytical Model Settings, and Boundary Conditions Settings. The settings on each tab are specific to its heading. These settings can also be accessed by selecting the Analyze tab from the Ribbon and choosing the appropriate tools from the various panels.

To learn more about these settings and how to add load cases and load combinations, go to the help sections in Revit Structure and search for "Structural Settings Dialog." The help sections serve as an excellent resource for learning about these settings so that you can incorporate them into your project templates.

Rebar Settings

Revit Structure has a separate area for adjusting settings for modeling and tagging of reinforcing bars (rebar). You'll learn more about the use of these settings and tools in Chapter 10.

Revit Structure helps automate the placement of rebar as well as how a rebar is annotated when tagged. Part of this automation is allowing the user to set rebar coverage types that can be applied to different concrete types and their conditions. This helps keep 3D rebar within the concrete element as shapes change in size and location. Once a rebar is placed, it can be tagged with predefined standard abbreviation callouts based on its placement properties.

Adjusting the Cover Distance

To set up the rebar cover distance for your project, select the Home tab ➢ Reinforcement panel drop-down ➢ Rebar Cover Settings to open the dialog box shown in Figure 2.30.

By clicking the Add button, you are able to make as many different cover types as you want, depending on the various conditions that may occur for your project. You need only specify two settings: you must enter a description and the dimension of cover from an outside edge of a concrete member to the face of a rebar element. A well-thought-out naming convention will go a long way in helping users quickly set the proper cover required throughout the project.

FIGURE 2.30
Setting up the rebar cover for your project

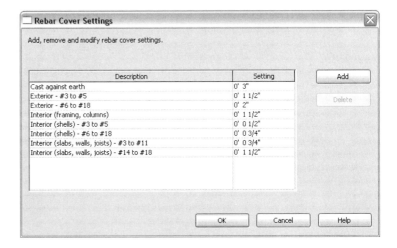

Rebar Cover Settings

Add, remove and modify rebar cover settings.

Description	Setting
Cast against earth	0' 3"
Exterior - #3 to #5	0' 1 1/2"
Exterior - #6 to #18	0' 2"
Interior (framing, columns)	0' 1 1/2"
Interior (shells) - #3 to #5	0' 0 1/2"
Interior (shells) - #6 to #18	0' 0 3/4"
Interior (slabs, walls, joists) - #3 to #11	0' 0 3/4"
Interior (slabs, walls, joists) - #14 to #18	0' 1 1/2"

Add   Delete

OK   Cancel   Help

Abbreviation for Tagging

When it comes to annotating the rebar that you have modeled, Revit Structure has a few built-in abbreviations that tags will automatically pull from depending on the properties of the rebar. To get to these settings, choose the Home tab ➤ Reinforcement panel drop-down ➤ Abbreviations. A dialog box opens whose settings reflect whether the rebar uses area or path reinforcement. Figure 2.31 shows the options for both area and path reinforcement.

You are not allowed to create new settings, but you can revise the value of the ones Revit Structure provides to match your company's standards. Making use of these settings and annotating with them helps keep your documents looking consistent no matter who is producing them.

Options

Settings in the Options dialog box are specific to the machine that Revit Structure is installed on. These settings cannot be incorporated into your template files. They deal more with how the program functions and how you interact with it than with project-specific settings. The majority of these settings are stored in the `Revit.ini` file, which is usually located in `C:\Program Files\Autodesk Revit Structure 2010\Program\`. We'll cover this file and its uses in Chapter 17.

To open the Options dialog box (Figure 2.32), select the Application Menu ➤ Options. You'll see several tabs across the top, which allow you to adjust your own working environment settings (they will not affect other users working on the project). On the General tab, you will be able to define save reminders and specify your username for workshared models, among other settings.

If you still want to work with a black background, click the Graphics tab (Figure 2.33) and select the Invert Background Color check box. Keep in mind that the visual quality while working with some elements may not be as good using a black background compared with white. Try it for yourself. If you don't like the color of objects when selected or highlighted or the object warning color when objects overlap, you can also change those settings on this tab. Allowing the user to define the color used for highlighted elements is a new addition for Revit Structure 2010.

In this release Open GL graphic support has been replaced with DirectX. This sets the stage for future graphical enhancement of Revit for the long term. Also new is Anti-Aliasing, which will generate smoother lines on screen than working without it. These two make for improved appearance of your model views on screen. These two features may require revisiting your video card settings and possibly updating drivers to make the most of them.

The File Locations tab (Figure 2.34) lets you set default locations for certain files so Revit Structure can quickly take you there when you use any Load command or start a new project. You can also click the Places button to set up your own shortcuts to folder locations; these shortcuts will appear in the Open and Load dialog boxes.

Become familiar with the settings on all the Options dialog box tabs so you can configure Revit Structure to function independently for each individual user. Also, use the Revit Structure Help documentation to further your knowledge regarding these settings.

FIGURE 2.32
User-specific settings on the General tab of the Options dialog box

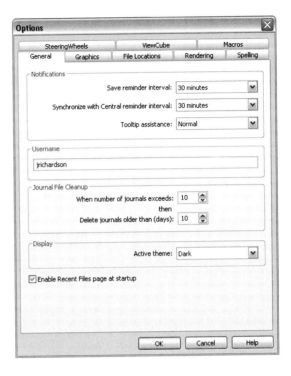

FIGURE 2.33
User-specific settings on the Graphics tab of the Options dialog box

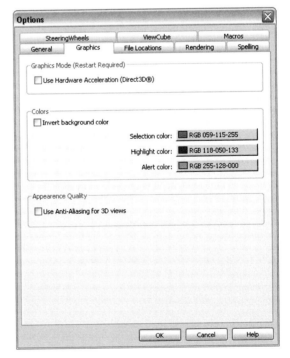

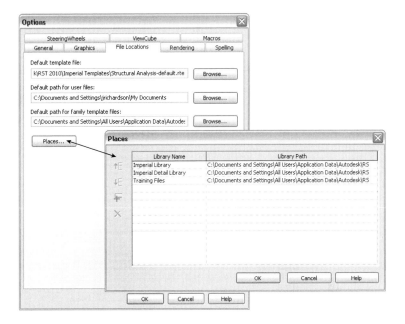

Project Browser Organization

It doesn't take long to figure out that, once you are working in Revit Structure, the Project Browser needs some type of organization or things will get very messy, very fast. The first thing you should do is devise a naming convention for your view names; second, you should sort the browser by folders and filters to help display your views in the Project Browser in a way you can quickly and easily access them.

View Naming Conventions

Firms using Revit Structure have come up with naming conventions specific to their own working methods as well as project type. A good naming convention should be developed in every Revit Structure environment, but it will have to be revisited for each project.

Revit Structure does its best to automatically name views specific to their view type. For example, a new plan is named after the level, a new detail is called Detail 1 or Detail 2 (depending on which number is next), a new section follows the same rules (except it is called Section 1), a new elevation is called Elevation 1-a or Elevation 1-b, and a drafting view is called Drafting 1 or Drafting 2. Figure 2.35 shows Revit Structure's way of helping you develop a naming convention.

This helps, but eventually the numbers can get out of sequence and make it difficult to find anything. As views are created and take on different roles, you will want assign them names that reflect those roles. Here are some examples:

Working_Detail 1   A detail used for working or looking at the model

Ref_Detail 1   A detail used to help lay out the model

Coord_Level 2   A plan used for coordinating with other disciplines

Export_Level 1   A plan used for exporting to another format

CD_Level 1   A plan used for construction documentation

ACAD_Level 2   A plan where DWG files are linked into

JDR_3D Slice - Level 2   A 3D view that belongs to a specific user

FIGURE 2.35
Revit Structure default
naming conventions

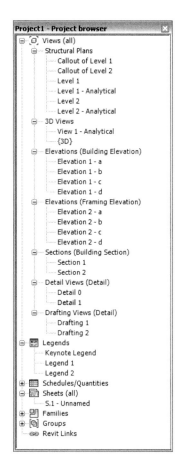

No naming convention will be handed to you on a sheet of paper that says, "This is how you name your views." It is important for you to know this and for you to make the effort up front to develop one that works best for you.

Real World Scenario

ONE APPROACH TO A NAMING CONVENTION

We have taken an approach that pretty much overrides Revit Structure's default naming convention. When a user creates a new view, the first thing he or she does is assign that view a name specific to the role it will be taking on. The use of this method along with some basic browser organization helps keep our projects neat and clean to work with.

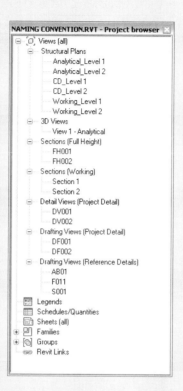

We have created various section, detail, and drafting view types to help us sort them in the browser. If it's a detail, the view is given the type Project Detail and the name DV### (for Detail View). Drafting views follow the same method, only with a DF###. The use of Revit Structure has allowed us to display more Full Height sections, so a different section type has been created for them as well (and they take on the name FH###). The Working type sections are meant to be temporary and should never be put on sheets, so they take on whichever name Revit Structure gives them.

As we get further along in our implementation, we may revise and adapt our naming convention to reflect the exciting changes Revit brings and our new working methods.

Common Methods of Organization

Revit Structure allows you to create new browser view types to sort your views for ease of working within the browser. Browser view types can be created to show you the views that have been placed on a sheet or views that have not been placed on a sheet. They can allow you to display and filter the views by discipline, detail level, or view scale or even add your own parameters to sort by. You switch to these view types when you are going to be working with only these types of views. This method filters out all those unwanted views so you do not need to weed through them. Using the Project Browser in this way will help increase your productivity as well as allow you and others to move efficiently between views.

In this section, we will take that method one step further and show you how to add your own parameter to a view and/or drawing sheet to allow you to sort your views in ways that can be more specific to your task at hand.

Just like every other object or element in Revit Structure, the Project Browser also has its own type. One way to get to the browser type list is to choose the View tab ➢ Windows panel ➢ User Interface drop-down ➢ Browser Organization. Another way, as shown in Figure 2.36, is to select the Views or the Sheets category in the Project Browser and right-click to open its properties from the shortcut menu.

FIGURE 2.36
Use the context menus for accessing the browser view types.

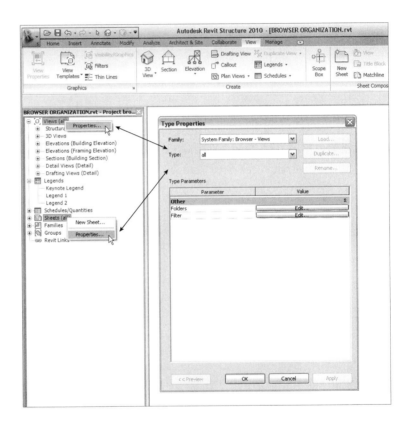

Different view types will have to be set up depending on whether you will be sorting views or sheets. These are the only types that you are allowed to sort. You cannot sort legends and schedules because they have different view properties assigned to them.

We will walk you through a couple of quick exercises designed to get you thinking about all of the possibilities you could incorporate into your working environment.

EXERCISE: CREATING A NEW BROWSER VIEW TYPE

For this project view type, we are going to create a new project parameter called View Type, which will be applied to the category View. We will then set up a new Project Browser view type to help you sort your views in the browser.

1. While in your project, choose the Manage tab ➢ Project Settings panel ➢ Project Parameters tool.

2. Click the Add button and create a new project parameter called **View Type** with the properties shown in the following graphic. Click OK to close this dialog box and then again to close the Project Parameters dialog box.

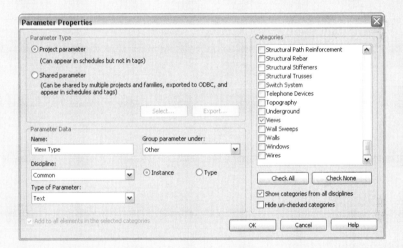

3. Choose the View tab ➢ Windows panel ➢ User Interface drop-down ➢ Browser Organization, and click the New button on the Views tab.

4. In the Browser Organization Name box, enter **View Type** and click OK. Be sure to assign a name that reflects the organization methods.

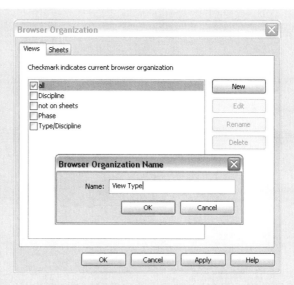

5. On the Folders tab, fill in the fields as shown in the following graphic. In the properties of a browser organization, you can set up folders to group and sort views by.

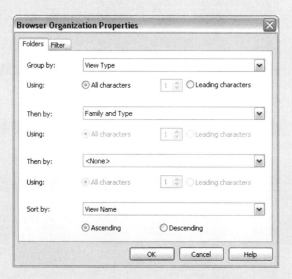

6. In this case we will not use the Filter tab, but you could apply filters to the browser view type so certain views could be hidden from view. The following dialog box shows a filter applied that would display only views that have a value of CD in the View Type parameter.

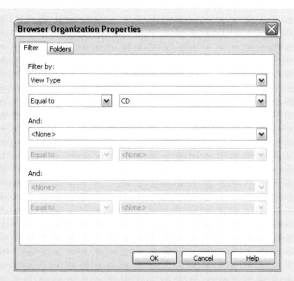

7. Choose OK until you are back to the Views tab, where you can see your new browser view type. Make it the active type by placing a checkmark in its adjacent box, and choose OK.

8. Open the properties of your views and put in a value for the View Type parameter. Watch the Project Browser reorganize into folders as you add these values. Parameters that are left without values will automatically be grouped under a "???" folder designation. The following graphic shows the browser window sorting by View Type. Keep in mind those question marks can't be replaced with something else or remain blank. Revit displays those when the criteria being used for sorting or filtering is not valid or is empty, no value supplied. There are some instances where the criteria you want to use can't apply to a view type. For example you might want to sort by the level of your project. Plan views are associated with levels, but sections and

elevations are not. They display them, but they are not associated with a single specific level; thus question marks will appear using level as a criterion for sorting or filtering.

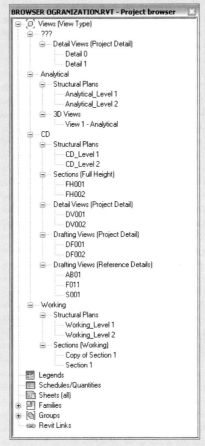

To create a browser view type for sheets, you will follow the same procedure shown here except you will apply the project parameter to the Drawing Sheets category instead of Views and use the Sheets tab in the Browser Organization dialog box.

 **Real World Scenario**

ANOTHER APPROACH TO BROWSER ORGANIZATION

This project consists of 25 stories of high-rise condos, with three levels of townhouses at the lower levels. Everything is sitting on a big podium over parking levels.

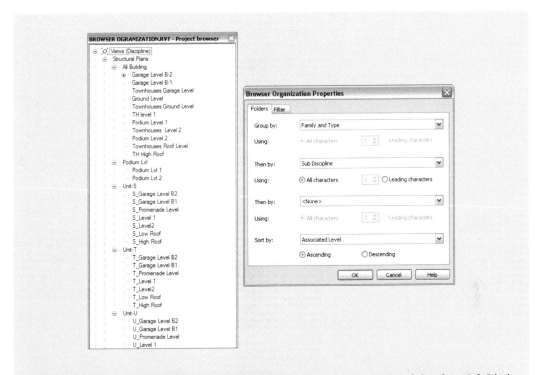

In this example we sort the browser by grouping the family and type name and then by a Sub Discipline parameter that is added as a project parameter to the views. The values of the Sub Parameter would be Podium Lvl, Unit-S, Unit-T, and so forth. In the groupings we sort by the view's associated level in ascending order. This organizes the plans from bottom to top in the browser.

Transferring Project Standards

Transferring project standards is another way of getting data from a template file or another project into your current project without having to re-create the setup. You can use the same method to transfer current standard settings that may have changed in projects with old standards to bring them up to date.

To do this, you need to have the file you will be transferring data from open at the same time as the project you will be transferring data to. Keep in mind that if both projects that are open are large in file size, you might not want to do this — you could bring your computer to a screeching halt. To get around this problem, start a new project from a None template and transfer the settings into that. Save this new file and then use it to transfer the data into your other project. The new project that was created from the None template will be much smaller in size and will allow you to clean anything out of it that you do not want transferred.

To transfer projects standards, choose the Manage tab ➤ Project Settings panel ➤ Transfer Project Standards tool while you are in the project that you want to transfer standards into. When the dialog box shown in Figure 2.37 opens, click the Copy From box and select from a list of templates or projects that are currently open. Check only the categories that you want to transfer.

In this case, we will transfer from the Concrete Wall Types template and we will transfer only wall types.

FIGURE 2.37
Transferring standards from the Concrete Wall Types template file

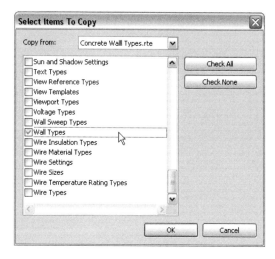

As shown in Figure 2.38, if any standards currently exist in your project, you will be given the option to add only the new ones or to overwrite the ones that are already there.

FIGURE 2.38
The Duplicate Types options when you transfer project standards

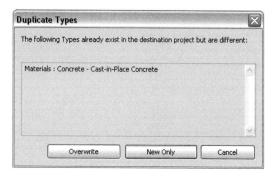

Transferring settings and already customized families from one project or template to another is a quick way to keep standards applied throughout your projects. It will also eliminate redundant creation of system family types like walls, slabs, and roofs and annotation types such as text, dimensions, and spot dimensions. Taking advantage of this feature will help you keep each project up to date with your latest project environment settings.

The Bottom Line

Develop your own custom templates. Knowing all of the items that you can store in a template file will help you avoid creating data that is the same over and over and make it easier to encourage following company standards.

Master It   What extension does a template file have? What types of things can be stored in a template file? What cannot be stored in a template?

Set project units and precision display.   Setting the units for your project and the precision of them is part of documenting your model for those who will be using it.

Master It   What are the three types of units in Revit Structure?

Make adjustments to structure-specific settings.   Revit Structure has several areas of settings that are specific to how elements display for your documentation.

Master It   Where do you go to assign the global display of symbolic representations for different types of connections? What type of family template do you use to create a new symbol type?

Organize the Project Browser.   Learning how to organize your browser depending on the workflow and requirements of the project will allow you to work more efficiently and keeps the browser free and clean of unused views.

Master It   For what two things can you create a browser view type in the Project Browser? When creating a new project parameter so that you can sort your sheets in the Project Browser, what category do you need to apply the new parameter to?

Transfer standards into your project.   Being able to use settings and content from past or other current projects allows you to avoid duplicating your efforts over and over again and ensures that standards are kept.

Master It   What command is used to bring new line weight settings into a project that is using old line weight settings?

Chapter 3

Starting to Model Your Project

Planning? Yes! Before you begin to develop your Revit Structure model, you should understand the world in which this modeling will occur. The fundamentals of Revit Structure will set the tone of your entire model and for everyone who must interact with it. A misstep here and your model, at best, will annoy others and, at worst, make completing your work in a timely fashion impossible. Imagine a contractor building a structure from the top down; it would make for a very expensive proposition.

In this chapter you will examine the basic functions and features of Revit Structure that enable you to plan your model the proper way — the first time. These initial stages of setting up your project can make or break whether or not the project will go smoothly. Nobody wants an unexpected problem midway through a project. From an improperly linked Revit/CAD file to an inaccurately placed level/grid, taking the time to sort out these issues up front will put you well on your way to mastering the process of starting to model your project.

In this chapter you will learn to:

◆ Import and link CAD data

◆ Link and work with Revit files

◆ Create levels

◆ Create grids

Importing and Linking

For decades, engineers have utilized computer-aided drafting and design programs to develop plans, sections, and details for construction drawings. They have been used to design everything from a backyard shed all the way up to the very largest buildings in the world. It is this plethora of data types that can gain new life — as a backbone for generating *Building Information Modeling* (BIM) data within Revit Structure. If you previously created AutoCAD drawings of a project that now needs a new addition, you can leverage that data by importing it. And if you have drawings from an architect who has not made the transition to Revit Architecture, you can still leverage that 2D line work to build new, smart Revit Structure objects.

With this 2D line work in your project you can use it as working overlays or you can convert the already created non-Revit line work into Revit line work. This ultimately gives you the ability to avoid redrawing information. Whether you are using the files as an import or a link, Revit Structure offers several tools that allow you to work with and manipulate them as you use the data to work inside Revit Structure. There are several software solutions on the market that other firms you collaborate with may use and exchange with you to do this. The most common one is more than likely to be AutoCAD, but the other commonly used programs being used in industry are equally recognized — or at least they can be exported to one of the data formats that Revit Structure can recognize.

Data Formats

You already know that every software program has its own specific file format. Each has its own respective "code" that enables the originating program to read and display the data contained within it. You have had to deal with these types of formats in previous programs that you have used. Revit Structure is no different. It can understand several formats, such as DWG, DXF, DGN, SAT, and SKP, that can be imported for the use of someone else's data as you work through the coordination process between other disciplines involved in a project. Once these formats have been brought into the Revit environment, you can use them to aid in your modeling efforts. The following list briefly explains the program each of these formats is associated with:

DWG This is the native format for Autodesk AutoCAD and AutoCAD LT. DWG has been the de facto standard in the building industry to date. Once the drawing has been imported or linked, you can reference objects within the single file element or even explode it into subelements.

DXF The Drawing Exchange Format was also created by Autodesk but is used more as a shared file format by software developers. Because DXF is a more widely available format, you will often find other programs, such as Computers & Structures' engineering analysis program SAP2000, that can export directly to .dxf and then into Revit Structure.

DGN The native format for Bentley Systems' MicroStation, this vector file format has been used for thousands of large commercial, infrastructure, and industrial projects.

SAT The premier format for solid modeling and machining, the ACIS specification is by Spatial. Most often used for the aerospace industry, the SAT format has been given new life by major design firms that specialize in nonlinear surface design.

SKP A new format to the world of Computer Aided Design, Google's SketchUp is a face modeler often used by architects because of its ease of use and viewing tools. It too can be imported into Revit Structure but generally only for volumetric objects contained within an in-place family.

To import or link any of these file types, choose the Link CAD tool from the Link panel or the Import CAD tool from the Import panel. These tools are positioned on the Insert tab located on the Ribbon. Depending on which one you select, the Link or Import CAD Formats dialog box opens (see Figure 3.1), where you can select a supported format and define how best to use your data file.

Importing or Linking CAD into Your Project

If you are already using Revit Structure but the architectural firm(s) or other design team members you work with are not using Revit, this does not leave you with a dilemma. You can expect that most of your projects will encounter file formats other than Revit that you will have to work with to develop your model. As we move along, we are assuming that AutoCAD is the most frequently used of those file formats; therefore we will be using the DWG file format to discuss the importing and linking of CAD files into your Revit Structure project. Make note that the same concepts apply for the various other formats that may not be used as often, but they are still able to be imported or linked into Revit Structure.

FIGURE 3.1
The Import and Link
CAD Formats dialog
boxes enable you to
import various forms
of vector data for use in
Revit Structure.

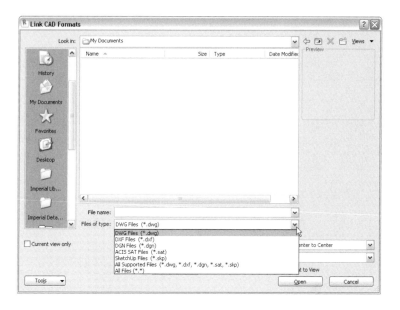

When you're importing or linking a DWG file, you must consider several factors before choosing which method to use. Be careful, as there is a difference between the two. The import embeds the file directly into your project, and the other does what it says and links the file into your project, allowing you to more easily remove it. One factor to consider is the level or work plane in which the DWG file will reside. In Revit Structure, each level constitutes a floor plan that is tied to that level and serves as a work plane. It makes sense then, if the first floor of an architectural plan is to be inserted into Revit Structure, the current floor should be Level 1. Creating levels will be discussed later in this chapter. By default, Revit Structure's template starts with Level 1 and then goes to Level 2, as illustrated in Figure 3.2. Your projects will more than likely contain more than just these two levels, so you will need to determine the correct one.

FIGURE 3.2
It is important to know
which level you are
importing or linking the
DWG into.

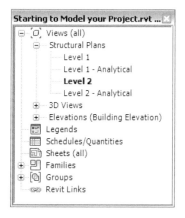

Another factor you need to consider is what the DWG will be used for. You can either import or link the DWG. When you use the import function, you are basically inserting the DWG as what is referred to in AutoCAD as a *block*. This means that when the DWG file is brought into the model, it maintains no link to the original DWG. If you link the DWG, it will maintain a live path to the original DWG, and if it is updated, you can reload it in Revit Structure. This behavior is almost the same as with the AutoCAD external reference method. This translates to one less process you need to change in order to utilize BIM.

Once you have decided how and where the DWG is going to be placed and what it is going to be used for, the rest is a straightforward process. Revit Structure separates the tools that are used to import or link a CAD file into a project. They can be found by choosing the Link CAD tool or Import CAD tool from the Insert tab, as shown in Figure 3.3. Both tools will display a similar dialog box where additional information can be set. However, the results of having the CAD file within your project will be much different depending on which tool you use.

FIGURE 3.3
Tools for importing and linking CAD files into a project

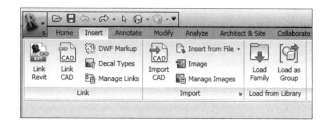

LINKING VERSUS IMPORTING CAD FILES

We would recommend that you use caution when importing CAD files into your project. At least take the time to educate yourself and others using Revit Structure about the difference between the methods of working with them. One disadvantage of importing CAD files is that users may carelessly start importing them into several views throughout a project.

They may not see that one is already in a view so they insert another one, or they just might not know what they are doing. Hey, we are all trying to master this, right? If this is the case, you just might find yourself trying to get a whole lot of unnecessary CAD files out of your project. There really isn't a good way of knowing which views they were placed in. No matter which view you are in, they will still show up in the Imported Categories tab of the Visibility/Graphic Overrides dialog box. At least you know they are in your project. If you have several hundred views, you might have to go through all of them to try to find where they were imported so you can delete them. Remember, if they are imported, they are like a block.

If you link them into your project, at least you can manage them in the Manage Links dialog box. Who cares what views they are in? If you don't need them in your project, you can remove the link. If Revit Structure cannot find the path to a linked file, it still displays the file as a block with the information from the last time it was found. Actually, this is like a block that can be more easily managed. If you are working with CAD files that are considered to be temporary or working overlays, you might want to think about linking them into your project in lieu of importing them.

In Revit Structure, all of the important choices are offered in the Import or Link CAD Formats dialog box. At the bottom of the Import or Link CAD Formats dialog box, you will see several choices, as shown in Figure 3.4.

FIGURE 3.4
As you are importing or linking a DWG, pause before clicking to make the appropriate choices.

OLD HABITS CAN BE HARD TO BREAK

Be careful not to just double-click on the file once you find it. An old habit for many is to simply browse for the file and then double-click it. In AutoCAD, the important dialog box appears after the Browse For dialog box.

Consider each of these choices carefully — they are mostly irreversible once the DWG is in the model. Whether you are importing or linking, the same options are available. The choices, as listed in order of appearance from left to right, are as follows:

Current View Only   This will limit the visibility of the DWG file specifically to this view only. Choosing this option is especially important if you are going to insert multiple floor plans on different levels. Do not check this option if you intend to use this file in conjunction with the Toposurface Site tool or if it has three-dimensional elements that you need to see in other views.

Colors   The choices for colors are:

> **Invert**   This option will take the original colors and find the opposite of each color. This feature is intended to make colors that are hard to see clearer by altering the colors; dark colors become lighter and lighter colors become darker. Aside from making the line work easier to see, you can use this option if there are two separate underlays in the same view. You will be able to differentiate between the two.

> **Preserve**   This option will keep the original colors the same.

> **Black and White**   This option will convert all the colors to black and white.

Layers   What's that? Layers? Yes! Revit Structure handles layers quite well. The choices for layers are:

> **All**   Normally you can select All here and deal with the layers from within Revit Structure. We'll explore this feature in a moment. This option will bring in all layers that are in the CAD file regardless of whether they are turned off or frozen in the file itself.

> **Visible**   This option will bring in only those layers that are turned on or are not frozen.

> **Specify**   This option presents another dialog box after opening the file, but before the file is actually placed in the view, that allows you to specify which layers to bring in. There's

no need to bring in layers if they are not needed, assuming you know which layers you really need.

Import Units   When you are importing a DWG, you are dealing with CAD. This means scale becomes a nuisance again. If you select Inches, 9 times out of 10 you will achieve the correct scale. Always measure a distance after you get into Revit Structure, just to be sure. If you are bringing in a site plan or topography, you might have to use feet. Revit looks for the assigned unit value in the DWG file to determine the correct scale. If none is assigned it may resort to "guessing." If you choose a scale incorrectly or Revit does, you can still adjust the scale in the properties of the DWG after it is imported/linked.

Positioning   Positioning basically deals with coordinates. Even in Revit Structure, there is still a need to deal with coordinates. There are several choices upon import:

Auto – Center to Center   This option will find the center of the extents of the view in Revit and center the DWG based on the center of the extents of the DWG file. If there is a rogue point in the CAD file far away from the rest of the drawing elements, the center of the extents of the file will be in a very different location than one that does not have such a rogue point.

Auto – Origin to Origin   Revit Structure finds the import's world origin and places it at the project's internal origin.

TWO-MILE LIMITATION

Revit has a limitation that the geometry in the DWG file cannot be larger than a two-mile diameter. If it is, Revit will reject the file and not import it. You can either reduce the size of the file to just the portion relevant to your work or insert it in another DWG "container" file as an attached external reference that you import instead.

Auto – By Shared Coordinates   This is available only when linking in CAD files in lieu of importing them. Shared coordinates are intended to define relationships between Revit project files and CAD files or between Revit files and other Revit files. Typically the architect will acquire the coordinate system from a civil DWG file, and the Revit Structure user will just have to import/link the architect's model using Origin to Origin. Revit Structure will place the imported instance based on coordinates that have been shared between the Revit Structure model and the import being brought in. Normally, the first imported instance will not have its coordinates shared with the Revit Structure model. If you have not shared the coordinates at this point, Revit Structure will inform you that no coordinates have been shared and that the DWG will be placed using the drawing's world coordinate system (Auto – Origin to Origin).

Manual – Origin   The inserted DWG is placed according to the DWG's 0,0 point. You then manually pick a point in the Revit Structure model to place the DWG.

Manual – Base Point   This is an optional feature in AutoCAD that allows the user to define an alternative "point" in the drawing. If one is defined, then Revit will place the DWG's base point on your cursor. This is common if the DWG file is usually used as a block in AutoCAD. You then manually pick a point in the Revit Structure model to place the DWG.

Manual – Center   The center, considering the overall extent of the inserted DWG, is based on the cursor.

MUST BE A BUG. I DON'T SEE MY DRAWING ANYWHERE.

Nope, not a bug! As you are importing or linking a DWG instance, there is a good chance that once you place the DWG, it may not be visible to you. The display of Imported Categories may be turned off in your view. If it is, go to the Visibility/Graphic Overrides dialog box and turn it back on. Another possibility is that the crop region of the view may be cropping out the placement of the AutoCAD drawing. Simply turn on the crop region and stretch it to find the import, or turn off cropping completely and show everything within that view.

Place At   If you did not select the Current View Only check box, you can select a level to place the DWG on, different from the level you may currently have open. Of course, this will become the plane that the DWG is placed on, and it will be seen in any view that crosses that plane.

Orient to View   If the orientation of your view has been rotated, Revit Structure will rotate the DWG based on the rotation of the view. When you are in elevation or section view and wish to import a CAD file for reference, you may need to use this feature. Consider that most CAD files are drawn in plan orientation in the world coordinate system of the DWG file. Consider a building section or elevation DWG file; this means that the orientation of the file would truly be a single line in an elevation view if it matched the world within Revit. If this option is checked, the world coordinate plan orientation will be aligned with the orientation of the view instead. This allows the CAD file to be viewed as if it were drawn in one of the elevation orientations in the file too. If you don't check the option, then the file will be placed in the project aligned with the world in Revit, which means that in the elevation view, the DWG file will appear as a single line on the level selected in the Place At list box/drop-down menu.

There are times where it is more appropriate to import a DWG file into your project than to link it in. One scenario when you may choose to import is when you need to add details to the project that have been drafted in another CAD package. The process is slightly different but just as simple. Most of the things that we just covered, with the exception of shared locations, apply to the process of importing CAD.

IMPORTING CAD DATA FOR PRODUCING DETAILS

More than likely, if you are going to be importing CAD files into your Revit model in lieu of linking, you are doing so because they are going to become more of a permanent fixture. Rather than making changes within the original CAD software, you will make the changes inside Revit Structure, or changes are not required at all. Most of these files will be placed in a drafting view. If you find this is not the case, you should take a closer look at your workflow and make sure that you are using the importing and linking to your advantage. A drafting view is no different than taking out a sheet of paper and drawing on it. It is a view that does not see model elements and does not have a plane. It is where you will place text, dimensions, detail components, and line work to create a 2D detail representation of your design, which is why you may be considering importing a DWG file into it.

To create a drafting view you choose the View tab ➢ Create panel ➢ Drafting View tool. Next, as shown in Figure 3.5, a dialog box will appear asking you to name the new drafting view. You are also prompted to specify a scale.

FIGURE 3.5

The New Drafting View dialog box allows you to create a blank view in which to insert your DWG.

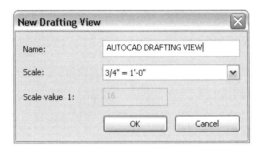

Of course, this is a DWG, so you still need to deal with the scale. Typically you should bring the imported CAD file into a Revit view (in this case a drafting view) that is set to the same scale in which the DWG was originally drawn. This will allow your annotations, if any, to be imported properly. Without matching the drafting view's scale to the imported DWG's scale, you'll get a DWG that is "blown" apart in appearance. This is because the elements in the DWG are defined according to a distinct size relative to scale — text and dimensions, for example. If the DWG does appear to be "blown" apart, you can make an attempt to change the scale of the drafting view, which will usually fix the problem when the scales match.

Once you are in the view, you can see that it is a completely blank canvas. You can always go to the Annotate tab on the Ribbon and use Detail lines to determine which is the best, purest approach. Or, as we promised, you can import a DWG here as well. If you choose the Insert tab ➢ Import panel ➢ Import CAD tool, you can browse for a DWG. The choices shown in Figure 3.6 will be the same as when you link a CAD file except that a couple of options are grayed out. The Current View Only and Place At options are not available because you are importing into a 2D view that is not looking at the model and does not have levels or planes.

FIGURE 3.6

The Import CAD dialog box for importing into a drafting view is similar to the Link CAD dialog box.

Choose the Positioning option Auto – Center to Center. The colors can be black and white because you intend to keep this information as part of your documentation. You also need to watch out for the units. Be sure to take a measurement of a known length after the import just to make sure you didn't import it at the wrong scale. Once you click OK, the DWG will be imported. If you do not see it, you can press **ZA** (zoom all) on your keyboard, and it should come into view. If your line weight settings have been configured correctly, it will come in with the correct line thicknesses, as illustrated in Figure 3.7.

There is much more that you can do with DWGs after they are brought into Revit Structure. The layers can be manipulated, deleted, or even adjusted to use a halftone. Taking the importing of your CAD files to the next level is a great way to leverage Revit Structure's capabilities of working with other CAD formats. These additional tools can also be used where you already have an extensive library of details drawn in another CAD format. It may make sense not to redraw all of them in Revit Structure but to import them instead.

FIGURE 3.7
If the imported DWG does not look the way you want, you will need to configure your import/export line weight settings.

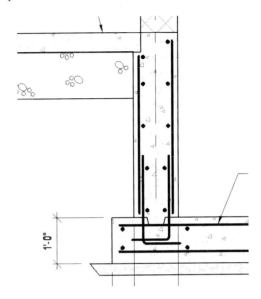

1'-0"

NATIVE REVIT CONTENT IS MORE EFFICIENT

Sometimes importing existing CAD work into your Revit views can seem to be a simple task and a natural workflow that appears to save you lots of work in the long run. In the beginning it does; however, having many imported CAD files can affect a project's performance. The more native Revit the project is, the better.

CONTROLLING THE CAD DATA'S APPEARANCE USING VISIBILITY/GRAPHIC SETTINGS

Layers are what help control the display of line work in a DWG file. Other CAD programs may use different terminology for how they refer to these functions. MicroStation calls them *levels*. Revit refers to them as *object styles* and *line styles*. Regardless of what they are referenced as, they have always been a necessary evil throughout the years. You don't think of the phrase *CAD standards* without the word *layers* jumping into your mind. Some firms have wonderful layer management; others, not so wonderful. Either way, once DWG files become referenced into one another, you still wind up with a huge convoluted list to search through. Revit Structure handles the import of layers differently. The program will actually group the layers with their corresponding imported DWG file. This is perfect! We do like layers when they can be separated so we can see what we are looking at.

There are two different ways to view and manipulate a CAD import's layers (from the Visibility/Graphic Overrides dialog box and choosing Options from the Ribbon). Say, for instance, you want an architectural underlay to be halftone. You can simply open that view, and press **VG** or **VV** on your keyboard. This will open the Visibility/Graphic Overrides dialog box for that view. If you click the Imported Categories tab, you will see the DWGs that are imported into the model, as shown in Figure 3.8.

FIGURE 3.8
Access the layers for DWG imports by using the Visibility/Graphic Overrides dialog box.

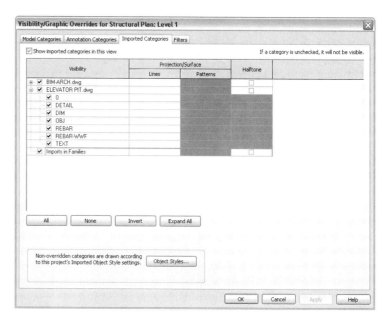

If you enable the Halftone check box, it will automatically shade the entire DWG. If you expand the tree adjacent to the DWG name, you will see all of the imported layers associated with the DWG. You can simply turn them on or off as needed for each item.

Another way to manipulate the DWG, along with its associated layers, is to select the DWG file and look at the tools available on the Ribbon. You are given some choices, as you can see in Figure 3.9. If the file is linked, some of the choices will be grayed out. If the file is imported, you can explode it into Revit Structure line elements.

FIGURE 3.9
When you select the DWG import, the Ribbon populates with applicable choices.

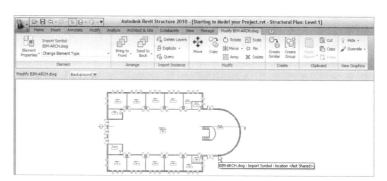

JUST BECAUSE YOU CAN DOESN'T MEAN YOU SHOULD

Exploding DWG files in the active Revit project will pollute it with line styles, text styles, and dimension styles, all named to match the layers associated with each import. It will also add filled region and fill pattern types to the project. This can make for one messy project file when users are trying to determine what line style or dimension style to use. If you really must explode a detail to change it and make it pure Revit, you should do so in a separate "quarantine" project. After the view has been cleaned up and rid of unnecessary content, you can add it into your project.

The Delete Layers option is located on the Import Instance panel of the Ribbon. Once you click this button, a list of layers will appear. You can delete any layer by simply checking it, as shown in Figure 3.10. Be careful here because this is not like AutoCAD, where you can purge only unused layers. Revit Structure will permanently delete any layer you choose, along with the elements that are on those layers. Keep in mind that it does nothing to the original DWG file. It only removes the layer and the elements assigned to the layer from the Revit database.

FIGURE 3.10
Use the Select Layers/Levels to Delete dialog box with caution. Deleting a layer also deletes elements on that layer.

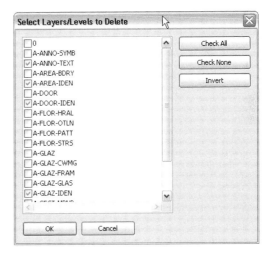

The Query option is located on the Import Instance panel of the Ribbon. Once you click this button, you can select any object in the imported DWG, and a dialog box will appear providing descriptive information. You can choose to delete the layer of the selected element or choose Hide in View (see Figure 3.11), which is really just a shortcut to turning off that layer in the Visibility/Graphic Overrides dialog box. If you use this option, you can restore it using Visibility/Graphic Overrides.

FIGURE 3.11
The Import Instance Query dialog box allows you to investigate the item and deal with it as you like.

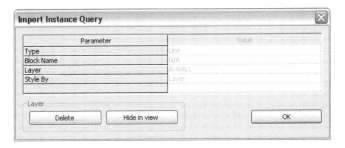

Last on the Import Instance panel is the option to explode the import instance. This option is available only for CAD files that have been imported. Choosing Explode will present two more choices, Partial Explode and Full Explode, as shown in Figure 3.12. If you perform a full explode on the item, it will "dumb" the DWG down to Revit Structure line elements, including any embedded blocks. If you perform a partial explode, it will explode the item to line elements as well, but it will not explode embedded blocks. You should try to avoid doing this in your live project file because each embedded block will result in additional tinier DWG file instances in the Revit database. These instances can be very tedious to get rid of later.

FIGURE 3.12
If the DWG is not linked, you get two additional options: Full Explode and Partial Explode.

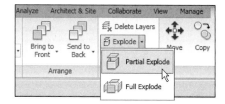

On the Arrange panel of the Ribbon are the good old-fashioned Draw Order options. They give you better control over the interference the DWG causes when laid under Revit Structure objects. You can also set the DWG as the background or foreground by selecting the pull-down located on the Options bar. Setting the import to Background allows the Revit model to hide the DWG as elements are placed. Foreground superimposes the DWG on top of the model elements. See Figure 3.13.

FIGURE 3.13
You can change the draw order of the DWG from the Arrange panel of the Ribbon.

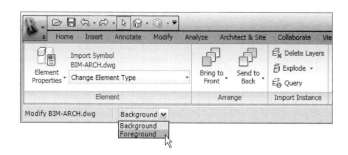

As you can see, the ability to bring in and manipulate a DWG file is something that makes Revit Structure outstanding in terms of saving time and being easy to work with. Revit Structure's ability to share coordinates for those files being linked into your project ensures accuracy of the files being placed and provides a level of comfort for team members working with them.

EXERCISE: WORKING WITH A LINKED CAD FILE

This exercise will guide you in the placement of an AutoCAD DWG reference file. The file is intended to be used as an architectural overlay for coordination as you start modeling your plan.

LINK A DWG FILE

1. At the book's companion web page (www.sybex.com/go/masteringrevitstructure2010), find the file called BIM-ARCH.DWG and save it on your local drive or a network. Or you can use your own AutoCAD file if you have one.

2. Start a new default Revit Structure model, and go to Level 1 in the Project Browser. It is good practice to create separate views for hosting imported DWG files that you will be working with. This allows you to switch between views with and without a DWG file faster than by using the Visibility/Graphics Overrides dialog box to turn on and off the CAD file. The view is usually referred to as Level 1 Import or Level 1 DWG.

3. Choose the Insert tab ➤ Link panel ➤ Link CAD tool.

4. Browse to and select the BIM-ARCH.DWG file.

5. Select the option Current View Only.

6. Assign Colors to Black and White, Layers to All, and Import Units to Inch.

7. Set the Positioning option to Auto – Origin to Origin.

8. Click Open.

This is what you need to do when you bring in a CAD file. As mentioned earlier, be deliberate with the choices made here. Most of them cannot be undone.

MANIPULATE THE DWG FILE

1. Press **VG** or **VV** on your keyboard to open the Visibility/Graphic Overrides dialog box.

2. Click the Imported Categories tab.

3. Enable the Halftone check box for the BIM-ARCH import.

4. Expand the layer list and deselect A-ANNO-SYMB.

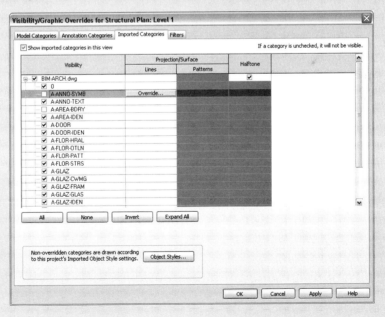

5. Click OK to close. Select the DWG.

6. On the Import Instance panel of the Ribbon, click Query.

7. Click one of the window tags.

8. Click Delete in the Import Instance Query dialog box. The Query tool stays active and expects you to pick elements, so you must remember to start another command, press the Esc key twice, or right-click Cancel twice to stop the tool.

Parameter	Value
Type	Line
Block Name	BIM-ARCH.dwg.Window Tag - Window Tag-41068-L
Layer	A-GLAZ-IDEN
Style By	Layer

Import Instance Query

Layer

[Delete] [Hide in view]   [OK]

Of course, linking CAD is one way to start a project. Hopefully this is not the only way, and most of your projects can be started by using another Revit file. Being able to start your file from the architect's model (Revit Architecture) will make your experience a whole lot different, allowing you to take full advantage of BIM!

Linking a Revit File

This is what it's all about here! When the stars are aligned, and the project team is up on Revit across the board, the building will just model itself. No? Okay, there still needs to be intervention from design professionals, but the coordination can be a real lifesaver. And it's easy for the most part. Luckily the concept is similar to linking in a CAD file except that the link is assumed. Options are not available to import another Revit file unless you link it in first and then bind it. Note that if you are sending linked models to other firms, you must include all of the models involved, similar using to the external referencing system within AutoCAD and MicroStation. Once the Revit models are linked, however, this is where the similarities end. In the linked Revit models, you will have the opportunity to physically copy objects from one linked model to the current one. Along with this copy, you can choose to monitor the movement of the elements within the Revit model each time you reload it. Almost as important, you can perform collision detection between the two models throughout the life of the project.

To begin our example, you create a blank Revit Structure model and link a partially completed Revit Architecture model. From the previous chapters you should know how to start a new project. As you move through this section of linking and working with a linked Revit file, you will be referencing a Revit Architecture file. For situations when you are working with Revit MEP or another Revit Structure file, the process involved will be the same.

Create a new Revit Structure project using the default template. To add the Revit Architecture project file, choose the Insert tab ➤ Link panel ➤ Link Revit tool. In the Import/Link RVT dialog box, you will see at the bottom that the only choice you need to make is for positioning. By now you should realize that you cannot use shared coordinates because nothing has been shared yet, so the ideal choice for this example is Auto — Origin to Origin, as illustrated in Figure 3.14. This means that the internal coordinate system will match the internal coordinate system of the Revit Architecture model. Getting everyone on the team to use this position when linking in other Revit models will ensure that all models will be placed in the same position as well as stack on top of one another. We all know that if the models/files stack, everybody is happier.

FIGURE 3.14
Choosing the Origin to Origin option when linking

Once you click Open, the architectural model will load. You may need to check the View properties before you can actually see the architectural model in its entirety. By pressing **VP** on your keyboard or by right-clicking and choosing View Properties, you can access the Instance Properties dialog box. The reason you may not be able to see much of the model is the fact that views, by default, are assigned a Discipline setting of Structural. Walls placed in Revit Architecture are normally assigned to a non-bearing usage by default, and they will not display with a Discipline setting of Structural. In order to coordinate with a Revit Architecture model, you should set the view's Discipline to Architectural or Coordination under the Graphics category, as shown in Figure 3.15.

FIGURE 3.15
Change the Discipline setting of a view to Architectural or Coordination.

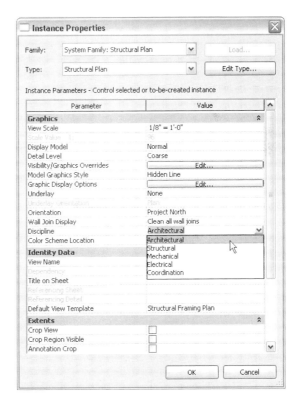

LEAVE THE VIEW'S DISCIPLINE SETTING ALONE

It is common practice to create specific views for coordination purposes and for structural documentation. This way you can easily switch between views that suit your own documentation needs and views that permit easier coordination of your models by always displaying the link. When doing this, it may be natural for you to adjust the Discipline setting in the properties of the view itself to show elements as another discipline or multiple disciplines such as Coordination. When changing this setting in the view you might find that your structural elements change how they display as well. This may or may not be what you would expect or desire. We are guessing that it is not. Better results will be found by clicking the link in the Visibility Graphic/Overrides dialog box of the view under the Revit Links tab. Setting the view to Custom allows you to modify the Discipline setting for the link only. This will result in your structural elements displaying as a structural discipline and the architectural model displaying as an architectural discipline.

This is just the start of the settings that are available for displaying data from a linked Revit file. You can reach further into the link by accessing its linked files, Phases and Design options, which affect the appearance of the linked file.

Managing the Appearance of the Linked Revit File

Some items in the architectural model you may want to see, and others you may not. If you do want to see some items, you have several choices in terms of manipulating the architectural link to suit your needs: tweaking the Visibility/Graphic Overrides settings, hiding elements in a view, using the Linework tool, and mapping phases. The first method discussed will be setting the Visibility/Graphic Overrides options. Press **VG** or **VV** on your keyboard to open the Visibility/Graphic Overrides dialog box for the current view. Click the Revit Links tab at the top. Now you can see the check box that allows you to halftone the link in its entirety, as shown in Figure 3.16.

FIGURE 3.16
The Visibility/Graphic Overrides dialog box allows you to access the display settings of the linked architectural model.

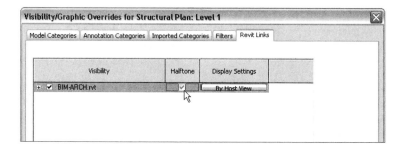

On the right side of the dialog box you will see a button under Display Settings labeled By Host View. If you click the button, the dialog box switches to the RVT Link Display Settings dialog box with tabs similar to the Visibility/Graphic Overrides dialog box for your view. You can now override the current appearance of the linked file. The Basics tab allows you to control the settings By Host View (the default), By Linked View, or Custom, as you can see in Figure 3.17. By choosing Custom, you can begin to alter the *appearance* of the architectural model as needed. This will *not* affect the actual linked file.

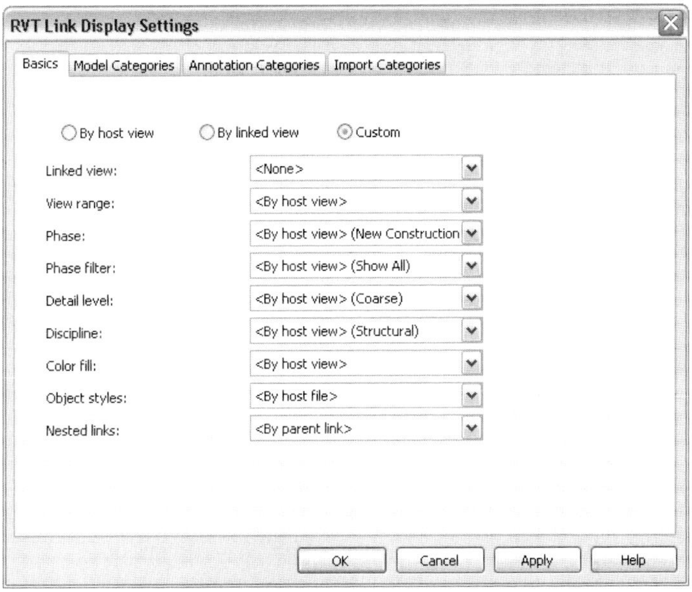

FIGURE 3.17
By changing the visibility graphics for the view, you can manipulate the graphics for the linked file any way you choose.

The other tabs — Model, Annotation, and Import Categories — break it down a little further, giving you more options. Figure 3.18 shows you the Model Categories tab, which is equivalent to the Visibility/Graphic Overrides dialog box but affects the link itself. If you choose <Custom>, you will have access to every model component category. This allows you to alter the appearance of the linked architectural model just as if it was physically constructed within the structural model.

The Annotation Categories tab allows you to change text, dimensions, and tags separately from the model categories, again just as you can in the structural model with its native elements.

The Import Categories tab lets you reach into the linked file and control the graphics of any imported or linked files that reside within the architectural model.

If design options exist in the link, you will be able to set which design option displays in that particular view. This is one spot to check if you are told that something is in the model but you cannot find it. It might just be part of a design option. Investigating this tab might help you find what you are looking for.

AM I MISSING CATEGORIES?

Revit Structure doesn't care about casework and furniture, for example, so those categories are not listed in the Visibility/Graphic Overrides dialog box. To see these you need to check the Show Categories for Other Disciplines check box at the lower-left corner of the Visibility/Graphic Overrides dialog box within the Model and Annotation tabs for the Current and the RVT Link view settings. By default this is usually unchecked, which means those categories from other disciplines are not visible in the dialog box. If you are in Revit Structure, you will be missing architectural and MEP categories. If you are in Revit Architecture, you will be missing some structural and MEP categories. Checking the box will display them, so you can stop your search and move on your way.

FIGURE 3.18
Setting the link's visibility to <Custom> allows you to change its object styles separately from the structural object styles.

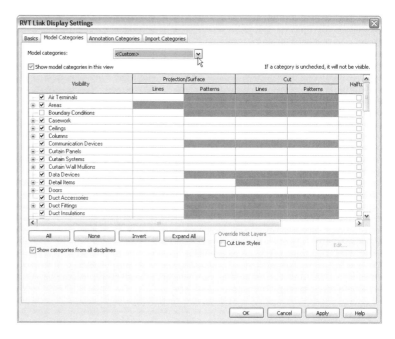

Another good way to manipulate the visibility of the Revit Structure underlay is to simply hover your mouse over a specific item in the link that you want to change graphically and press the Tab key on your keyboard. This allows you to reach through the link to select its elements individually. Doing this will highlight the item, and once the item is highlighted, you can right-click and select either Hide in View or Override Graphics in View, as shown in Figure 3.19.

This works very similarly to how you override the display of graphics for elements that are placed directly into your model. Reaching through a linked Revit model to hide individual elements in a view can come in handy when you want show only some of certain elements of the same category. You can hide the ones that you don't want. When you choose Override Graphics in View for a linked model, your option is to only do so by Category. You cannot select an element and override its appearance individually.

I WISH I COULD ADJUST THE DISPLAY OF HALFTONES AND UNDERLAYS

Well, you can. Global settings are available now in Revit Structure 2010 to control the display of halftones and underlays. These settings can be found by going to the Manage tab ➤ Project Settings panel ➤ Settings drop-down and choosing Halftone/Underlay. Keep in mind that these settings are applied to every view throughout the project that uses these settings.

You can also use the Linework tool located on the Modify tab ➤ Edit Linework panel of the Ribbon, as shown in Figure 3.20. This tool allows you to reach through the link to override individual styles of its lines. You can select the elements and apply line styles that you have created in your project. One of Revit's default styles is <Invisible Lines>, which allows you to hide things on a line-by-line basis. Keep in mind that you can also use the Tab key here to cycle through lines, and you may have to apply the Linework tool more than once if lines are on top of lines. Also, some lines cannot be overridden with this tool. It is view specific as well and can get you out of a pinch if you are displaying the link in your view for documentation purposes and need to hide or change the style of various linework.

FIGURE 3.19
By using the Tab key you can select individual items in the Revit Architecture link. You can hide them or alter their appearance in the view.

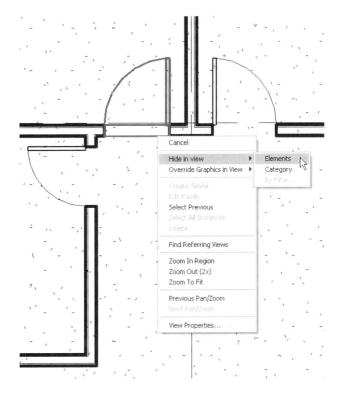

FIGURE 3.20
Use the Linework tool to make individual line style changes to the linked model.

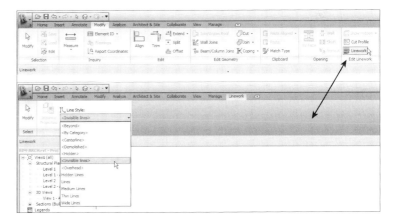

This entire link can be applied to a phase in the model. If you select the link and click the Element Properties drop-down ➢ Type Properties from the Element panel on the Ribbon, you can locate the Phase Mapping variable and click the Edit button to its right. In the dialog box shown in Figure 3.21, you can map the phases within the Revit Architecture model to the phases within the Revit Structure model. It is important that the phases of your projects match one another so that views display the correct information.

FIGURE 3.21
The Phases dialog box lets you specify which phase in the linked model is equivalent to each phase in your project.

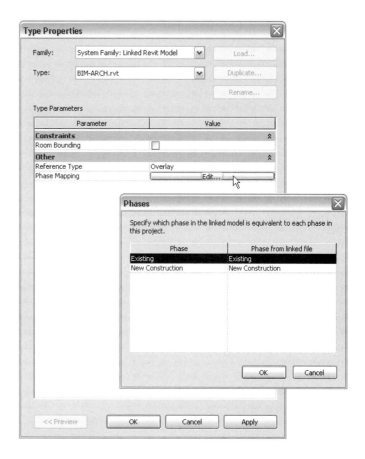

Of course, when the link is established, the architect has probably not stopped working. Revit Structure provides methods in which you can manage the linked Revit Structure models.

Managing the Revit Links

Similar to an external reference, Revit Structure keeps a live path back to the Revit linked model. This link can be managed from the Project Browser. Once you have established a link in the model, you can then right-click the Revit Links category in the Project Browser. It should be at the bottom of the browser list. The shortcut menu allows you to add a new link or access the Manage Links dialog box, which allows you to manage existing links or add new ones.

If you choose Manage Links, the Manage Links dialog box opens. The default tab is called CAD Formats. If you had a DWG or DGN linked in, you would see it listed here. If you click the Revit tab, you will see the Revit link(s) available, as shown in Figure 3.22. If you then select a Revit link, you can modify some of the options available on the row.

FIGURE 3.22

Choose the Manage tab ➤ Manage Project ➤ Manage Links tool, or right-click the Revit Links category in the Project Browser to access the Manage Links dialog box.

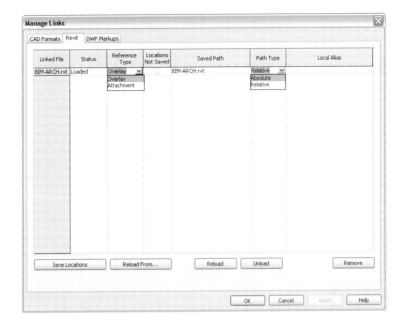

The first option lets you specify whether the link is an overlay or an attachment. Overlay and Attachment are Type parameters and can also be changed in the Element Properties ➤ Type Properties dialog box.

This option defines the relationship between a project (host) and a linked project (parent) that also contains other linked projects (children). If you choose Overlay, Revit will load the file (parent) but *not* load any nested linked models (children). If you choose Attachment, Revit will load the link (parent) and *will* load any nested linked models (children). Of course, this option can make a huge difference in the performance of the file that hosts these files!

Keep in mind that this concept of Attachment/Overlay applies equally to linked CAD files. It does not apply to imported CAD files because they are not included or listed in the Manage Links dialog box.

The next choice, Saved Path, corresponds directly to the control to the right of it, Path Type, which can be either relative or absolute. Figure 3.23 shows a relative path scheme. This means that the entire path (folder structure) up to the filename is a wildcard and irrelevant. If the two files are in the same directory, the folder names of that directory can change at any time. Revit Structure will know to look only for the RVT file with the identical name. With this method (relative), the files must be in the same directory. This is ideal for sending Revit Structure models with links to clients. All clients need to do is copy all the files in the same directory, and the links can be discovered and reestablished by Revit. If you choose an absolute path, the entire path all the way back to the drive letter is required. If any one of the folder names changes or if the file is relocated, the path is broken and Revit Structure will not be able to find the link.

With the link still selected in the Manage Links dialog box, you'll see a row of controls across the bottom, which allow you to perform tasks specific to the link (see Figure 3.23).

The first button, Save Locations, is associated with the Shared Coordinate tools. This allows the user to prompt Revit to save the new location data to the link file if the original location was altered for some reason. For the average user this tool is irrelevant to the routine managing of linked files.

FIGURE 3.23
With the link selected in the Manage Links dialog box, you can perform several functions related to how the links will be read into the model.

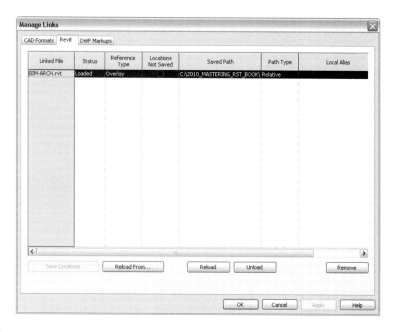

The Reload From button allows you to choose a new file or folder location for the file while retaining the original positioning data. Primarily this is used when you receive a new version of a file and wish to keep the previous version in a different archive folder. It is also a nice feature because you can keep the same link with the same coordinate location while loading different underlays for comparison. If you do load from another location for comparison purposes, be sure to load the correct model back when you have finished.

Unload permits you to temporarily remove the link from the project in all views. Reload does the opposite. Remove does what it implies: it removes the link completely from your project.

Many times when the file is getting large, simply unloading links that are not used often can greatly improve performance. If this is the case, you might want to think about putting the link on a workset and control its loading behavior through the workset. Jump ahead to Chapter 13 to learn more about worksets.

THINK BEFORE YOU REMOVE A LINK

You will want to be cautious when using the Remove option. If you are using the linked model to create your documents, have views set up with overrides to the view, have overridden its graphics in any way, or have view templates set up to control their behavior, you will lose all of these settings. Using the Unload/Reload buttons will maintain these settings. Make sure you think about what your end result will be. Think Unload/Reload for temporary changes, Remove for permanent.

A few of these choices are available without even going to the Manage Links dialog box. As you may have noticed, the Project Browser's Revit Links category will display the available links. If you expand the Revit Links category, you can right-click on the link itself and access the same tools as found in the Manage Links dialog box, as shown in Figure 3.24.

FIGURE 3.24
By right-clicking directly
on the link in the
Project Browser, you
can manage the link on
the fly.

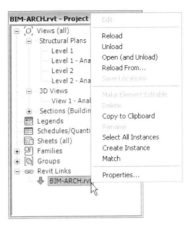

There is an additional choice available when you right-click on the link in the Project Browser, Create Instance. With Create Instance you can essentially copy the link. Revit Structure will still consider that there is only one externally linked model but provide two instances of the link in the Visibility/Graphic Overrides dialog box beneath the Parent listing. Any changes to the architectural model will be reflected in both links, or optionally you can alter the settings for each individually.

Another way to remove a link is to select it and delete it. Revit Structure will give you a warning, as shown in Figure 3.25, that says, "All instances of Linked Model 'BIM-ARCH.rvt' have been deleted, but the file itself is still loaded. Remove the Linked File using Manage Links dialog to save memory unless you are going to reuse it in this project. Removing the Link cannot be undone." If you click Remove Link, the instance is cleansed from the model.

FIGURE 3.25
Selecting a linked Revit
model and deleting it
will allow you to either
unload it or remove it
completely.

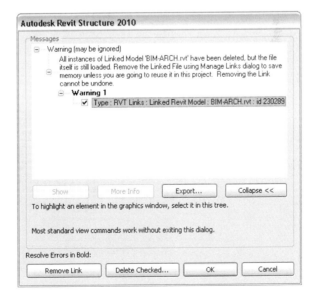

Now that the link has been established, and you know exactly how to manage it in terms of location on the network as well as the coordinate location in the model, it is time to see how to copy some of the useful items into your structural model and to let Revit monitor them for when changes occur.

Using Copy/Monitor

Next comes Revit Structure's shining moment: the ability to copy in elements from a linked architectural model and then monitor the movement of those elements is what BIM is all about. But hold on for a moment — although this is a great feature, at this point you need to remember that Revit Structure is simply a tool to aid you in your design process and workflow. If the architect changes an element you are monitoring, you will be notified, but just remember to check what those changes do to the model. As you know, in Revit Structure a change in one place will trigger changes in other places. A computer application will not replace the human eye or judgment.

Here's how it works. Once the Revit Structure link has been established, the next step in the structural design process is to basically "draw over" the top of the underlay. If that underlay has crucial structural elements you need, you can copy them. It's as simple as that. Once they are copied, they will be monitored for change. In this example, an architectural model has been linked into your Revit Structure project. The architect has defined a preliminary column grid layout in the architectural model.

There are two paths you can travel: you can place your own grids and then use Monitor to establish a relationship between your grids and theirs, or you can use Copy/Monitor to first copy their grids into your project, and Revit will automatically create the relationship between grids.

The Monitor tool assumes that you may have started your work before you received the architect's model and therefore only need to create a relationship between your existing grid layout and theirs. It also allows you to create a relationship between different types of walls; for example, a multilayered wall in the architect's model can be monitored against a shear wall in your model that's only a portion of the overall wall in the architect's model.

The Copy/Monitor tool assumes that you chose to wait until you have a copy of their model to begin your work. It also assumes that you need exact copies of their elements. We'll explore Copy/Monitor as if you did not start your model earlier, and you can see the architect's grid layout in their model.

On the Collaborate tab ➢ Coordinate panel, click the Copy/Monitor drop-down. Once you do this, you will see two choices, as shown in Figure 3.26. One is Use Current Project (which allows you to monitor similar items within your own project if desired), and the other is Select Link. Choose Select Link and pick the linked architecture model that you want to harvest the grids from.

FIGURE 3.26
Select the Copy/Monitor tool to start the process.

The Ribbon now switches to the Copy/Monitor tab. Notice there are a few tools available, as you can see in Figure 3.27. You can click the Copy tool, and Revit Structure will allow you to select the items you want to copy. These items will be monitored as part of the Copy/Monitor process. Later you can choose to stop monitoring items if necessary.

FIGURE 3.27
The Copy/Monitor tab on the Design bar has tools to aid you.

Setting the Options

The first thing that you should always do before using Copy/Monitor is review the options located on the Tools panel of the Copy/Monitor tab. The Copy/Monitor Options dialog box, shown in Figure 3.28, will show you via the display of tabs across the top what elements can be copied/monitored. These tabs are Levels, Grids, Columns, Walls, and Floors. This order implies a priority or the likelihood that you will need to use Copy/Monitor for them. You almost certainly need to coordinate the levels and grids. You may find some advantages doing the same for columns. However, floors and walls may not require Copy/Monitor as much or at all. The nature of your project and how you and the architect define your working relationship will affect how fully you use this feature.

ORDER OF OPERATION

The order of the tabs actually implies a priority or the likelihood that they will or should be used. If levels are done first, then the vertical datum is defined and additional views can be created for each floor prior to placing grids. With levels defined, column grids will inherit a more appropriate height by default than they will if you do grids first and then add the levels. Place levels into your project before grids whenever possible.

When different firms collaborate, their drafting standards can be in conflict. One firm might have a different grid symbol than you do. Since you are interested in their grids, you can define how to manage the copies that are placed into your model during the copy. Click the Grids tab, and you'll see that the Original Type column will show all of the various types for that category that are in the linked file. These are all the grid types in their project. It does not mean that they are all in use, just that each type exists in their model. The New Type column shows all of the various types that are in your structural model. You can choose Do Not Copy This Type from the pull-down that appears when you click on the value that is shown in this column, or select the grid type that you want the copy to use instead. This lets you use your standard grid type instead of theirs or agree to use their standard by copying the same type. Quite often the list of types in their project and yours will be different. You and your consultant(s) will need to decide what is necessary for the project as you are using this feature.

FIGURE 3.28
Be sure to review the
Copy/Monitor Options
dialog box before each
Copy/Monitor operation
you do.

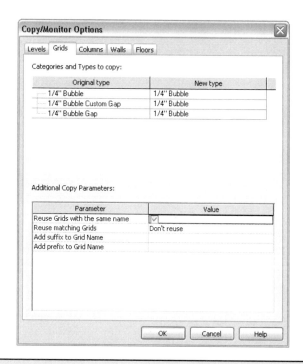

ONE CLICK, TWO CLICK, THREE CLICK

Within the Copy/Monitor options it takes three clicks to edit the values in the New Type column. The first to select the field, the second to convince Revit you want to change it, and the third to expand the drop-down list.

Take a closer look at the Additional Copy Parameters section at the bottom of each tab. These parameters offer added functionality. Your copies will behave how you want them to, and you can potentially prevent having to make additional changes afterward. Since you are interested in grids now, the settings available to you would permit you to reuse any existing grids you might have placed already according to their matching names or location. You could also include a prefix and/or suffix if necessary. Once you have reviewed these options and made any necessary changes, you are ready to use Copy to bring the grids into your model directly from the link. Click OK to close the Copy/Monitor Options dialog box.

PURGE UNUSED PLEASE

Ask your consultants to purge any unused elements from their model before sending it to you. Of course, in return, you should purge your unused elements from your model as well before sending it to your consultants. If they don't comply, you can do it yourself to the copy they send you. This way the Copy/Monitor tool will display only types that are actually in use, not all the types in the project.

Performing the Copy/Monitor

When you click the Copy tool, Revit Structure will display a few options on the Options bar. If you are going to select more than one item, it is important that you enable the Multiple check box, as shown in Figure 3.29. This tells Revit Structure to keep a running tally of the items being copied. You still need to press and hold the Ctrl key to select multiple items. If you use either the crossing or enclosing selection window, which is possible only with the Multiple option checked, make sure you use the filter (funnel icon in Figure 3.29) to select only the Grids category. Revit will allow you to select any element that the Copy/Monitor tool works with, so be certain you are selecting only the elements you really want. Once you have finished, click Finish on the Options bar. Don't click Finish from the Copy/Monitor panel on the Ribbon. Even though we told you this, you are still probably going to do it. Don't worry — we did it too, once. If you do, it will cancel all of your selections and effort so far, without warning.

FIGURE 3.29
When doing a Multiple copy, choose Finish on the Options bar or you will have to select everything again.

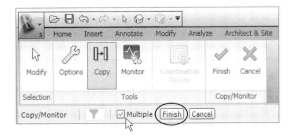

Quite often after you finish copying the items, you may see a Duplicate Types dialog box, as shown in Figure 3.30, informing you that there are some items you are copying into the Revit Structure model that match the ones in your model. Revit Structure will keep the items in your model, regarding them as more important than those from the linked model. It is safe to click OK in this dialog box.

FIGURE 3.30
The Duplicate Types dialog box that may appear after you finish copying elements with the Copy/Monitor tool

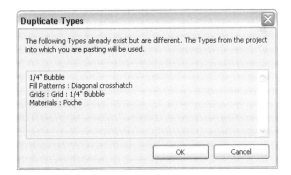

Once this process is finished, the monitor icons (symbols that look like a pulse from a heart monitor) appear, as shown in Figure 3.31. This indicates that the items have been copied and are being monitored successfully. On the Copy/Monitor tab, click Finish, and the new items are now in your model.

FIGURE 3.31
The monitor icons indi-
cate a successful mon-
itor on a given object.
Once you see this verifi-
cation, it is safe to click
Finish from the Ribbon.

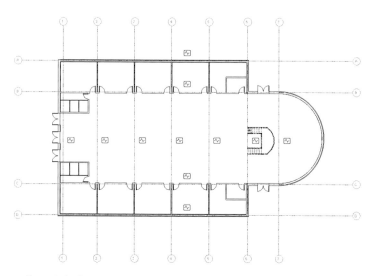

Monitoring Elements in a Link

At times, you may already have an element in your Revit Structure model that you wish to monitor against the linked model. This is done in a similar manner to the Copy/Monitor method except that you pick the element that you want to monitor and the element you want to monitor it with. Let's change our view to the south elevation. You have a Level 1 and a Level 2 in your structure model. Your Level 2 is 2'-0" lower than the architect's Level 2 in the linked model. This is fine if you want the gap to remain; for example, you may want your level to represent Top of Steel and therefore have an elevation that is 5" below the Top of Slab in the architect's model. Select your Level 2 and change its elevation value to **11'-7"**. If this was a real project, you'd probably change the level name to T.O.S. Level 2 or something similar.

The Monitor tool will allow Revit to watch for the movement of two offset elements as well. Click the same Copy/Monitor tool from the Collaborate tab on the Ribbon. You follow the same process as for the Copy/Monitor process and select the link. There's no need to review the options first because you are not copying elements too. Once you do this, the Ribbon switches to the Copy/Monitor tab again. Now, instead of clicking Copy, click the Monitor tool, as shown in Figure 3.32.

FIGURE 3.32
By clicking the Moni-
tor tool, you can keep
an eye on another ele-
ment without having to
copy it.

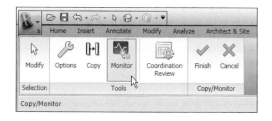

With the Monitor tool running, you must first select your level and then click the linked level you are monitoring yours against. Again, you should look for the monitor icon as an indicator that you have successfully selected the two items and have a working monitor. The Monitor tool does not allow multiple selection since it needs to define a relationship between similar elements one relationship at a time. Once you have finished with the monitoring elements, you need to remember to click Finish from the Ribbon. Now Revit is monitoring elements within the linked model, both the grids you used Copy/Monitor for and the individual level you selected.

Remember, Copy/Monitor is most useful when you don't have the elements in your project already. Monitor is handy when you've already done some work and just need to let Revit start watching them now.

 **Real World Scenario**

MAINTAINING A STEEL-TO–FINISHED FLOOR RELATIONSHIP

We find that it is much easier to maintain the Top of Steel elevation when we are using a level that is true to the Top of Steel. When doing this you will still Copy/Monitor the finished floor level that is in the architectural model, but the structural model will have an additional level for the Top of Steel. This Top of Steel level can be monitored with the finished floor level of the linked model. If the finished floor level moves, you will be notified during a Coordination Review that the relationship between the finished floor level and the Top of Steel level has changed.

If for any reason you wish to stop monitoring elements within your project, you can do so by selecting those elements that have the monitor icon and then choosing Stop Monitoring on the Monitor panel of the Ribbon.

Taking advantage of the Copy/Monitor features along with the Coordination Review, which we'll discuss next, in Revit Structure will help alleviate that feeling of having to find the proverbial "needle in the haystack."

We are confident that you'll find using Copy/Monitor for levels and grids to be very effective. However, you may find that using it for walls, floors, and columns can become a bit of a nuisance in dealing with coordination alerts that may occur early on in a project. Even if you do, using this feature for levels and grids alone will go a long way to keep you coordinated. As you begin to get comfortable with Revit Structure, you can decide for yourself how much monitoring is too much monitoring.

Coordination Alert

Now for some fun stuff. When the architect changes one of the items that Revit is monitoring for you, you will be notified as soon as you reload the link. If changes were made to the linked model when you did not have your model open, you'll get the alert when you open the file again. Be careful because you will only see a warning, as shown in Figure 3.33, and it is easy to dismiss the warning and go back to business, forgetting that the link now needs a Coordination Review.

It is always a good idea to take a second to read what these warnings are telling you. It might not be for a Coordination Review. Clicking the Expand Warning Dialog button at the right of the Warning dialog box will give you a bit more information on what has happened and what type of action you should be taking.

If you close the warning you can still open Coordination Review to check for alerts by selecting the Revit link and choosing the Modify RVT Links tab ➤ Monitor panel ➤ Coordination Review tool or by not selecting the link and then choosing the Collaborate tab ➤ Coordinate panel ➤ Coordination Review drop-down ➤ Select Link. After you select the link, the Coordination Review dialog box opens, as shown in Figure 3.34.

FIGURE 3.33
When your model is reopened, or the Revit Structure link has been reloaded, you get a coordination warning.

FIGURE 3.34
The Coordination Review dialog box allows you to modify items to match the linked items.

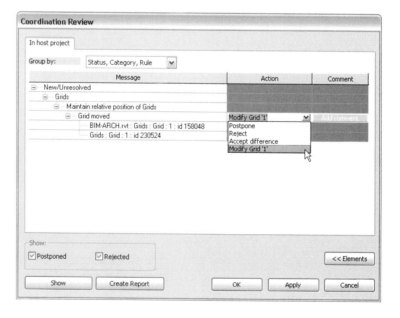

In the Coordination Review dialog box, you will see the item(s) in question. In this example, it is a grid. Once you expand the tree, you can see exactly what is different between the two models. Well, not exactly, but clicking the Show button in the bottom-left corner will when you select one of the listed items. Some of the descriptions can be vague, leaving you scratching your head trying to decide how you should respond to the Action item for the coordination alert. But this is still great, because no matter how vague the message might be, at least it is telling you something. The proverbial "haystack" has just gotten much, much smaller.

In addition, you have a decision to make and have just four options: you can choose to postpone, accept difference, reject, or modify your grid. Just make sure you think them through before taking action. In some cases it may be wise to respond to the items one at a time while reviewing and adapting to their results until the alerts are all dealt with. This will ensure that all areas of change between the models have been closely looked at and coordinated accordingly.

We've listed the essence of what each choice means here. The first three should be inspiring you to contact the architect to discuss the changes you are reviewing. While you can store these responses and the architect can review them later too, it is necessary for you to communicate with each other in order to truly coordinate your work. The software does not want you to speak to each other less; in fact, it is trying to make you do it more often!

Postpone   You are putting off making a decision. You can ignore the alert for now, and it will still remain a Coordination Review item for future review.

Accept Difference   You agree that it is okay for the two grids to be different.

Reject   You are not willing to accept the change; however, nothing will happen or change in either model. When the architect reloads your model the next time, they can review your comments and see that you have rejected the change. If you select this option, you should be prepared to contact the architect to start discussing this issue.

Modify   You will let Revit change your grid to match the grid in the linked project.

You can also create a report that will list exactly what occurred in this session by clicking the Create Report button at the bottom of the dialog box. The output of that report will be in HTML format so you can easily post it to a file-sharing site, Internet/intranet, or a local file server. Again, this is intended to encourage and facilitate communication.

Interference Check

This feature allows you to examine your model for the intersection of elements according to their categories, like Beams and Walls or Ducts and Beams. In order for an element to interfere with another, its actual volume must intersect with another element's volume. It is possible to use this feature to check for interference within your own model as well as between your model and linked models.

In our case, linking our models allows us to see where collisions are occurring. In Figure 3.35, a common collision between stairs and a beam flange has been detected. You can check an entire model for all interference, or you can be more surgical and look for specific problems. Obviously, the more elements you wish to check at one time, the longer the report will take. The most useful reports tend to focus on a few categories at a time, such as structural braces and doors/windows. These items interfere with each other all too often in our projects, and catching them sooner is always better than the alternative.

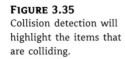

FIGURE 3.35
Collision detection will
highlight the items that
are colliding.

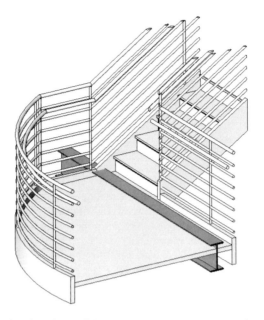

To run the Interference Check tool, select the Collaborate tab ➤ Coordinate panel ➤ Interference Check drop-down ➤ Run Interference Check tool. The resulting Interference Check dialog box contains two panels, as shown in Figure 3.36. In the left panel, the current model is selected from the menu at the top of the panel, and Structural Framing is enabled. In the right panel, the linked model is selected, and Stairs is chosen for the clash detection.

Once the suspected items are checked, click OK. Revit Structure will find all of the clashes between structural framing and stairs. In the Interference Report dialog box, you can select the items that appear in the report, as Figure 3.37 shows. The items will then be highlighted in the model. If you cannot see the items, click the Show button at the bottom of the dialog box. Revit Structure will zoom to a reasonable distance in an existing view to allow you to see the collision.

NOT ALL CONDITIONS ARE RECOGNIZED AS AN INTERFERENCE

It is important to understand that, because this feature relies on the intersection of volume, there are conditions in a model that may not be considered interference by the software but clearly are in real life. An example of this would be service clearance requirements for an air-conditioning unit suspended from a structure. If it were placed too close to an adjacent beam, it would mean that the unit could not be serviced adequately, but Revit would not detect this as a problem unless the air-conditioning unit family were made in such a way as to allow it to be detected. It is possible to develop content to do this, but most if not all the available content has not evolved to this level of detail yet. The software is trying to help us detect interference in our projects, but we still have to be vigilant.

Unlike the Coordination Report, with the Interference Check Revit Structure will not take an action to fix the solution — you have to do it manually. Once the issue is fixed, you can refresh the report, and Revit Structure will clear the field, thus giving you a clean interference report card.

FIGURE 3.36
Running Interference Check allows two models to be compared side by side.

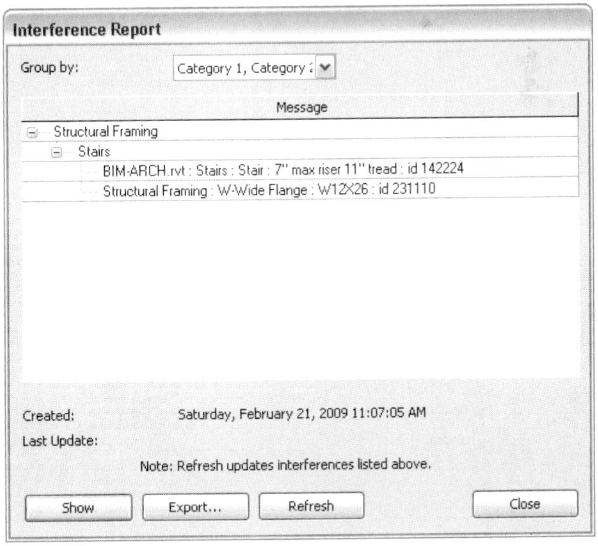

FIGURE 3.37
The Interference Report allows you to graphically review each collision.

EXERCISE: LINKING IN A REVIT MODEL

This exercise involves linking and then performing a Copy/Monitor operation to an architectural underlay. You do not need Revit Architecture or MEP to complete the exercise. At the end, to test the coordination you can close the structural model and then open the architectural model directly in Revit Structure. Make some changes to the architectural model, close it, and then open the structural model to review the report.

To start, copy the file called BIM-ARCH.rvt from the book's web page to a convenient location. (You can use your own file for this exercise as well.)

LINK IN A REVIT MODEL

1. Start a new default Revit Structure model.

2. Go to Structural plan view: Level 1.

3. Select the Insert tab ➢ Link panel ➢ Link Revit tool.

4. Browse to the BIM-ARCH.rvt file.

5. Set Positioning to Auto – Origin to Origin. This will keep both models at the same origin points.

6. Click Open.

7. Press **VV** or **VG** on your keyboard to open the Visibility/Graphic Overrides dialog box.

8. Choose the link from the Revit Links tab in the Visibility/Graphics Overrides dialog box and click the By Host View button under Display Settings. This opens the Revit Links Display Settings dialog box where you select Custom, and change the Discipline of the link to Architectural or Coordination so nonbearing/nonstructural elements such as walls will be displayed. Click OK twice to close the dialog boxes.

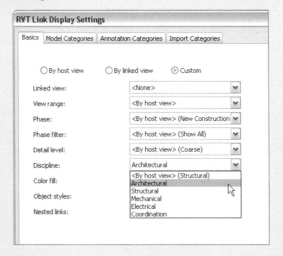

9. Open a 3D view.

10. Repeat step 8. If you don't see the doors or the curtain wall, do you remember why? Yes, the Visibility/Graphic settings for the view are set with a structural bias. You need to turn them on to see them. Remember the check box at the bottom, Show Categories from All Disciplines.

11. Go back to Structural plan view: Level 1.

See how easy it is to link Revit into Revit? The next series of steps will lead you through the Copy/Monitor functionality.

COPY/MONITOR GRIDS

1. On the Collaborate Tab of the Ribbon, click the Copy/Monitor drop-down ➤ Select Link tool. (Do this with the Structural floor plan: Level 1 open.)

2. Select the Revit link.

3. On the Copy/Monitor tab, click the Copy tool. Remember you can use the Options button to review your settings before you begin using the Copy tool.

4. On the Options bar, click the Multiple check box. This allows you to select more than one element at a time before copying it into your project.

5. While holding down the Ctrl key, select all of the structural grids one by one or do a right to left crossing window to select everything. Remember to use the Filter tool located on either the Options bar or on the Status bar in the lower-right corner of the Revit window to make sure you have only selected all the grids.

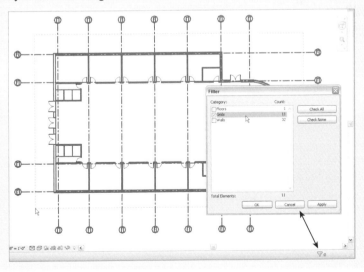

6. Once you have finished, be sure to click Finish on the Options bar, *not* on the Ribbon.

7. Click OK in the Duplicate Types warning dialog box if it appears.

8. On the Copy/Monitor panel, click Finish.

9. Select one of the grids to see if the monitor icon appears. While it is selected, remember that you can stop monitoring at any time. Just click the Stop Monitoring button on the Modify Grids contextual ribbon.

Now that you have copied and monitored the grids, it is time to monitor some levels in the structural model.

Monitor Levels

1. Go to the south elevation, and zoom in a little to bring the right side of the building into your view so it is easier to see the level annotation.

2. On the Collaborate tab of the Ribbon, click the Copy/Monitor drop-down ➤ Select Link tool.

3. On the Copy/Monitor tab, click the Monitor tool.

4. Select the Level 1 that is in the structural model (your model).

5. Select the Level 1 that is in the linked file.

6. Repeat steps 4 and 5 for Level 2. This time there is a gap between the two levels.

7. On the Copy/Monitor tab, click Finish.

8. Select either level to confirm the monitor icon is there. You'll need to zoom out a bit because the icon appears near the middle of the element.

Now that we have elements copy/monitored, let's make some changes to see how the Coordination Review works.

Coordination Review

1. Open the linked model called BIM-ARCH.rvt. You can keep your current Revit Structure session open by opening another session of Revit Structure. When you open a second session of Revit Structure, you may get a message about Visual Studio tools being disabled for this session; click OK to accept the warning. Alternatively, using the same session of Revit Structure, you can save your project and close it. Then open the BIM-ARCH.rvt file. Revit does not like linked files open in the same session.

2. In the architectural model, move Grid 1 2′ -0″ to the right.

3. Save and close the BIM-ARCH model and the extra session of Revit if applicable.

4. Now switch back to, or reopen, the session of Revit with the structural model.

5. It's time to reload the architect's model, so select the BIM-ARCH.rvt link in the Project Browser, right-click, and choose Reload.

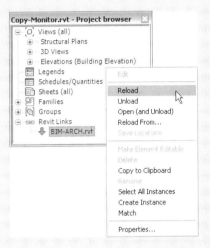

6. You will see a coordination warning. You can dismiss the warning.

7. Select the architectural link.

8. On the Modify RVT Links tab ➤ Monitor panel of the Ribbon, click the Coordination Review tool.

9. Expand the tree in the Coordination Review dialog box, and click between BIM-ARCH and Grids. If the grid in question is visible, it will be highlighted. You can click the Show button to have Revit display the grid in the current view if possible or open a view that does show the grid. When you select each item in the list, the highlighted element will change in the view as well. Note you can still use your view's navigation tools while this dialog box is open.

10. For the Action option, select Modify Grid '1'.

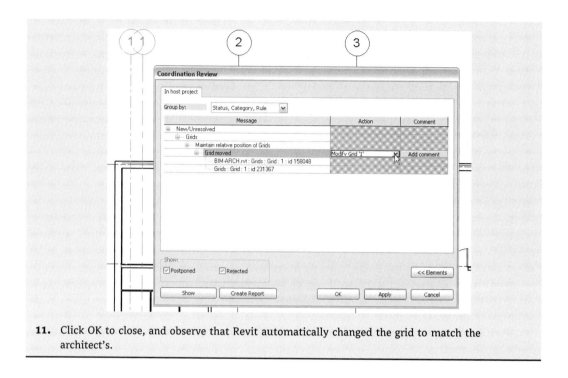

11. Click OK to close, and observe that Revit automatically changed the grid to match the architect's.

The first portion of this chapter illustrated how to import and link in CAD and Revit files. It also showed you the tools that are available to help work with these files after they are brought into your projects. We showed you how to copy/monitor elements such as grids and levels from an architectural model that was linked into your structural model. This is one way to get these elements into your project to get you off to a good start. It is also a likely approach, assuming you are working with an architect who is using Revit Architecture.

Revit Structure also has the ability to add grids and levels without the use of an architectural source. Many times you will be adding your own grids and levels. For this reason we will now focus on adding grids and levels from scratch.

Setting Your Levels

This topic is one of the most important subjects in this book. Everything in your model — walls, beams, floors, columns, foundations, and more — is associated with a level. What separates Revit Structure from a referenced file–based CAD platform is the fact that your entire model is contained within one file. All of the floors/stories of the building are defined by using levels. If you need a second-floor framing plan, you can create one in the model, but it is based on a level element. In elevations and sections you need a datum or annotation to define a building's stories and important vertical elements. These are not only for dimensional and documentation purposes but, as you've seen already, for comparison with another model you may have linked into the model.

The Level placement tool can be found by going to the Home tab ➤ Datum panel ➤ Level tool.

The Element Properties of a Level

Changes to how levels appear and display information can be made through the Element Properties dialog box. You can access these properties by selecting a level and going to Element Properties on the Ribbon or by choosing Element Properties from the Ribbon prior to placing one. In the resulting dialog box, you won't see many choices within the Instance parameters, but you can change its name and elevation here. But if you look at its Type Properties dialog box, shown in Figure 3.38, you will discover several things that you can do. Like anything else in Revit Structure, make sure you think about any changes you make. You may want to use the Duplicate button to make your own unique type. A level uses a separate annotation family (symbol) to define what you see as annotation in elevation and section views. You can customize these families if necessary, which we will discuss a little later in this section.

FIGURE 3.38
You can adjust the Elevation Base setting that a level uses through its Type Properties dialog box.

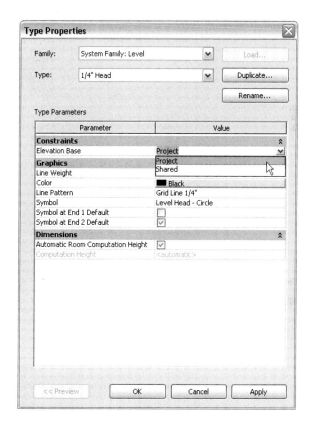

Within the Type properties of the level you can set which type of level head symbol to use. You can also set which ends of the level line the symbol will appear at by default when you create the level. You might want to set the symbol to appear at both ends since End 1 and End 2 are determined by whether you draw the level left to right or right to left. End 1 is always the first point you pick/place.

You can also set the weight, color, and pattern of the level line. In order to set the line weight of the level head symbol itself, remember that it is a separate family technically, so you will need to go to the Object styles located on the Manage tab ➤ Project Settings panel ➤ Settings drop-down ➤ Object Styles. Select the Annotation Objects tab, and you will find the Level Heads category. This setting controls the line weight of the level head symbol.

A very important thing to consider in the Type properties of a level is its Elevation Base setting, shown in Figure 3.38. This tells the level how to display your project's elevation. The two choices offered are Project and Shared. If it is set to Project, the level will display elevation information based on the project. This means that if a level is at an arbitrary 0'-0", the level will display 0'-0". If it is set to Shared, the level will display elevation information based on a shared elevation that you may have set up. This means that if a level is at 0'-0", and a shared elevation has been set that says 0'-0" equals 100'-0", the level will display 100'-0". More on setting up a shared level can be found in Chapter 2.

Real World Scenario

AUTOHIDE LEVELS IN A VIEW

In our projects we create some levels for the sole purpose of attaching elements to them so that they can be easily changed later if necessary. We typically don't want these levels to show up in some or many views. One such scenario would be the levels we create for Top of Steel. We use them to attach the steel framing to, but we do not want them to show up in our sections that we cut.

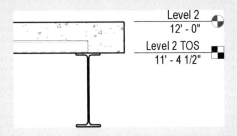

A spot dimension is used to specify the Top of Steel. We want only the finish floor-level elevations to show up so they will match what the architect is showing. Our Top of Steel levels have a level head symbol that looks like the normal level head except it is square in shape. This makes it stand out from a normal level. The new level type is named Hide in View. You can name it whatever makes most sense to you.

We then have a filter by criteria applied in our view templates to select all levels whose Type Name contains Hide in View.

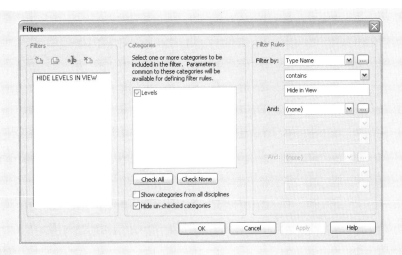

The visibility for those levels that meet the criteria for the filter's rules get toggled off.

Whenever we cut new sections, they are already toggled off by default.

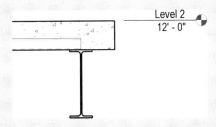

This same technique can be used for elevations, callouts, grids, and sections.

Keep in mind that the changes you make to these properties affect the Type properties of the level. Creating a level type for a specific view may not make the level appearance acceptable in another view. You may want to think about how many different level types you need and name them accordingly.

LEVEL HEAD SYMBOLS

Revit Structure has several level head symbols available for you to use. They may not be defined in the default template, but they can be found in the `Annotation` folder of the Imperial or Metric library. You also have the ability to create your own if the existing ones are not quite what you are looking for. The easiest way to accomplish this is to start from an existing family and modify accordingly. If you would like to start from scratch, you can do so by going to the Application menu and choosing New ≻ Family. In the `Imperial` or `Metric Templates` folder you will see an `Annotations` folder. This is where you will find the `Level Head.rft` template from which you can start your new family. You add linework and labels to the file — it's that simple. Once these families are loaded into your project, they will become available in the Symbol Type property of the level.

Placing Levels into Your Project

Creating a level is an easy procedure. To begin, you must be in an elevation or section view. Revit Structure's default template starts with two levels already in place. Depending on how you are starting your projects, you may use these existing levels or you may delete them and create your own.

Levels will be named sequentially as they are placed. Revit Structure does a very good job of assuming what name you want each time you place a level. If Level 4 was the last level placed, the next level placed will become Level 5. If you place a level and change it to Level A, the next level placed will become Level B. As levels are placed, Revit Structure automatically displays its elevation. It's almost as if Revit is reading your mind.

After levels are placed, the elements you add to your project will be associated automatically with them or will become associated through the settings you choose. Revit will work to maintain this association as the model progresses with change.

Levels are considered datum elements. Datum elements are special annotations because they appear in all possible views automatically. Regular annotation elements like text, dimensions, symbols, and tags appear only in the view they are placed in. This means that creating a level in one view will result in a level in all such views. Elevation and section views have a cut plane and they have a view depth; how far forward they "look" is called the far cut plane. It is possible that a level will not appear in an elevation or section view if its cut plane or far cut plane does not intersect the level.

To begin placing the first level, regardless of how it will look, select the Home tab from the Ribbon and click the Level tool on the Datum panel, as shown in Figure 3.39. Remember you need to be in an elevation view first.

FIGURE 3.39
On the Home tab of the Ribbon, you can start the Level tool.

Once you click the Level tool, the Ribbon and Options bar populate with controls. The Place Level tab that appears after you select Level is shown in Figure 3.40.

FIGURE 3.40
The various options from the Ribbon for placing a level

By default the initial choice is to draw the level by selecting two points in the active view. A second option available is to pick existing objects. In the Options bar you will see an option to automatically create a plan view after the level is placed. By default this will be always turned on.

Let's take a look at placing levels with the Pick option. You will first need to select the option from the Draw panel. Next you will need to set the distance of the floor-to-floor increment in the Offset field on the Options bar, such as 10'-0". Remember you can just enter **10 0**, entering a space between 10 and 0. As you select one of the levels, make sure before you click on the existing level that you see the alignment line above that level (so you are adding an additional level *above* the level that is there already). See Figure 3.41. The alignment line displays where the offset copy will be placed.

FIGURE 3.41
When placing levels, use the Pick option with an offset value to reference from existing levels.

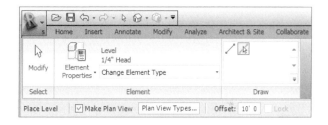

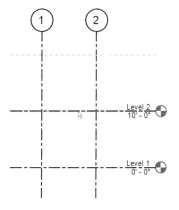

If you offset Level 2, the next level will be Level 3. You can keep offsetting levels until you have finished. You'll find that Revit created a new floor plan view of the same name for the level too. That is really all there is to adding levels into your project when using the Level tool. You place them either by sketching, by picking the first and second points, or by select existing elements and supplying an offset value. You may need to adjust their extents accordingly.

Now let's examine what is required to create floor plan views if you don't have Revit create them for you automatically. Once the floor plan views are created, you can start placing grids.

Creating Floor Plans from Levels

As you create a level by sketching or offsetting, you are also creating a plan view by default. As levels are added, you can see in the Project Browser that new plan views are being created. These new plan views are permanently associated with your new levels. However, if you create new levels using Copy, corresponding plan views are not automatically created.

You have some control of the creation of these plan views as you are adding levels to the model through the Options bar. On the Options bar, you will see a check box that controls whether or not you are creating a plan view with each level. To the right of the check box is a Plan View Types button. This allows you to specify the type of plan view you are adding to the model so you can avoid having to manually configure the plan view after it has been created, assuming you have more than one floor plan type, which the default template does not.

BLACK OR BLUE, WHAT DOES IT MEAN?

If you are looking at the levels in your project and are wondering why some are black and some are blue, we have the answer. Levels whose level head symbol is blue indicate that a plan view is associated with that level. Double-clicking on the symbol will take you to the original plan view that was created for that level. Levels whose level head symbol is black indicate that there is no plan view created for that level, commonly called a *reference level*.

If you have been creating levels with this check box turned off, or if you have used the Copy tool or Copy/Monitor tool to create levels in your model, you will have to manually create floor plans. Do so by choosing the View tab ➤ Create panel ➤ Plan Views drop-down ➤ Structural Plan tool to open the New Plan dialog box, shown in Figure 3.42. You can then choose which levels to create plan views for.

The levels that are listed initially are only those that do not have any floor plan views yet. This is fine for our circumstance, but if you wanted to create an additional floor plan for a level that already has plan views, you would need to uncheck the unassuming box at the bottom of the list called Do Not Duplicate Existing Views. This will display all the levels of the project, and you can choose any of them to create plan views.

Creating levels in your project is a rather easy task but one of the most important ones. Setting up your levels properly with a little bit of thought up front will save you lots of problems down the road. After the initial placement of your levels is complete, you can move on to getting them looking the way you want in each of your views.

Modifying Levels

Levels have controls for adjustment that are similar to grids. If you select a level, several controls appear. You can turn the level head on or off by clicking the check box adjacent to the end of the level line. If you see the alignment line and padlock icon, this means that if you drag the level head, the rest of the levels attached to that alignment line will move along with it. You may also need to make adjustments when you get into a tight situation where the level head and text have to "jog" up or down. Use the small "jog" control called Add Elbow for that. If you hover over any of the control grips long enough, a tooltip will appear to tell you a bit more about it.

FIGURE 3.42
It is easy to create new plans from levels that are in your project. Select Do Not Duplicate Existing Views to see all levels in your project.

To adjust a level, make sure you are not still in the Level Placement mode, and select a level object. A few blue grips as well as several other controls display, as you can see in Figure 3.43.

FIGURE 3.43
By selecting the level, you gain access to controls, allowing you to graphically modify each individual level.

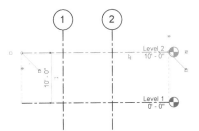

The first item is a check box that allows you to turn the level head on or off at that end. If the head is on, it will expose a jog symbol. If you click the Add Elbow icon shown in Figure 3.44, the level line will have a jog added to it, and the head will become offset. This is crucial to trying to jam several level heads into a tight spot. Keep in mind that this is considered a 2D control for the grid, which means that this display is an override that affects only this view, the one that you are applying it in.

FIGURE 3.44
Select the Add Elbow control to add a jog in the level.

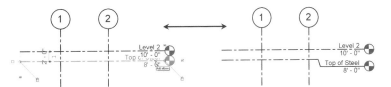

Another control you can use is the alignment line along the ends of the level lines. Attached to this alignment line is a blue drag circle, and attached to that is a blue padlock icon. Essentially these three controls tie the individual levels to the adjacent level(s). If you click and hold the blue circle and then drag the level end, all of the levels locked to it will move as well. If you first unlock this level end, it will move independently of the other level ends.

You will also see annotation indicating either 3D or 2D. If it is 3D, the level control will be an open circle. If it is a 2D grip control, it will be a filled circle. Be careful with these controls because depending on how you are changing them you may be affecting how the level displays in other views.

3D VERSUS 2D MAY BE CONFUSING

When we say "3D versus 2D," it can be a little confusing. Levels never appear in 3D views, so we don't mean *3D* in that context. *3D* means the change affects or applies to more than one view or all views, and *2D* means the change applies to this view only.

When you are moving the 3D extents of the level, you are affecting how that level displays in other views. This is a 3D control, so you will want to set these extents for your project early on and then hopefully leave them alone. If a level needs to show up in a certain portion of the building, make sure that the 3D extents cross the plane of that area. If the level is only for a low roof area on the west side of the building, make sure that the 3D extent does not run entirely through your building but through the portions of the low roof only. Paying attention to where the initial 3D extents of your levels are placed will ensure that your levels are visible throughout your project where they are required.

DON'T FORGET ABOUT FILTERS

Part of modifying datum elements such as levels and grids in a view is controlling the visibility of their line patterns and color. This can be done by creating a Define Criteria filter, which you can do by going to the View tab ➤ Graphics panel ➤ Filters tool. Filters can be created and applied to views for both levels and grids that allow you to override their graphic display. This allows you to display these elements differently than what their type or object style settings are if they meet a certain set of criteria that you set up as a rule in the filter.

If you are in a view that needs the level to be modified to show its extent for only a certain portion or something other than its 3D extent, you will need to select the 3D annotation control, which will change the level to display the filled circle and display 2D instead. You are now working with the 2D extents of the level. These extents are view specific, so like the Add Elbow control, they affect only the view you are working in.

Also, with the level selected, you see annotation turn blue. This indicates that you can modify those parameters. If you are patient and hover your cursor over these, you'll see a tooltip that says Edit Parameter as well as a rectangular box surrounding the portion you are hovering over. Take care to wait for these, and you'll be able to select and edit them with confidence even if you are zoomed out quite far. If you want the level to be at a different height, click the elevation annotation of the level and change the number; the level will move to the new height. Naturally, all other elevations or sections will reflect this change too.

If you do the same thing with the name, Revit Structure will rename the level, but you can also rename the primary plan view(s). Before Revit Structure renames the plan view, you will see a message asking if this is what you want, as shown in Figure 3.45.

FIGURE 3.45
Renaming the level also renames the primary plan view. You can rename the level by clicking on the level in an elevation view.

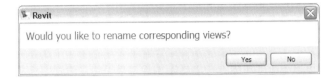

When you get messages about view and level names, be sure to read them *and* make sure you understand them. Quite often users pay little attention to them and are surprised to find a level with a name like T.O.S. Floor Plan Level 2 instead of T.O.S. Level 2. Revit tries to keep matching plan view and level names exactly the same at all times, and it will prompt you to do this every time. Once the view and level names are different, it will cease asking you about them. Sometimes the correct answer to the question asked is No.

Now that you know just about everything that there is to know about levels, you should be well on your way to getting your project started on the right foot. You should now be ready to see what it takes to put grids into your project. Fortunately, placing grids in your project and working with them to control their behavior and appearance are quite similar to how they are done with levels because they share nearly all the same features. Datum elements in Revit, levels, grids, and reference planes all share the same features.

Placing Your Grids

Just like placing levels, placing grids is one of the most important steps in starting your model. If your project is using grids, the entire model revolves around them. When you place columns, you snap to the grid intersection. If the grid intersections are not placed properly, the columns are placed improperly. When you place walls, you probably use the grids as a reference too. If a grid is not placed accurately, the wall will also be placed inaccurately. We think you get the point, and if you have worked with CAD files before, we know you have dealt with this. Revit Structure is no different. You need to spend the time up front, before you get too far into the modeling process, making sure that your grids are placed properly.

Grids have several properties that can be used to give you the look you desire. They have capabilities similar to levels that allow you to manipulate them so you can create clean and precise documentation. Learning about these properties and how to work with grids within your model will help you efficiently maintain accuracy and give you the insight required to create a clean set of documents.

The Grid placement tool can be found by going to the Home tab ➤ Datum panel ➤ Grid.

The Element Properties of a Grid

Changes to how grids appear can be made through the Element Properties dialog box. You can access these properties by selecting a grid and going to Element Properties on the Ribbon or by choosing Element Properties from the Ribbon prior to placing one. In the resulting dialog box, you won't see many choices within the Instance parameters, but the Name parameter is what you'll see at the end of your grid. If you look at its Type properties, shown in Figure 3.46, you will discover several things that you can do. Like anything else in Revit Structure, make sure you think about any changes you make. You may want to use the Duplicate button to make your own unique type. A grid uses a separate annotation family (symbol) to define what you see as annotation in plan, elevation, and section views. You can customize these families if necessary, which we will discuss a little later.

FIGURE 3.46
You can alter the appearance of a grid by editing its Type properties.

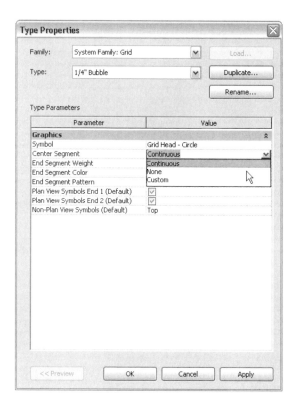

It is no coincidence that you'll see some similarity to the properties of levels. Within the Type Properties dialog box you can set the grid head symbol type that will display at the ends of the grid line. Along with setting the symbol, you can set on which ends of the grid line the symbol will appear by default when placed. You might want to set the symbol to appear at both ends since End 1 and End 2 are determined by whether you draw the grid from left to right or from right to left. End 1 will always be your first pick. There is also a setting to control how the grid bubble displays when you are looking at a section view. You can choose Top, Bottom, Both, or None for the location of the grid bubble symbol.

You can also set the line weight of the grid line. In order to set the line weight of the grid head symbol itself, you will need to go to the Object styles located on the Manage tab ➢ Project Settings panel ➢ Settings drop-down ➢ Object Styles. Within the Annotation Objects tab of the Object Styles dialog box, you will find the Grid Heads category. This setting controls the line weight of the grid head symbol.

ONE OF US DOESN'T LOOK LIKE THE OTHER

Remember that you can override the display of individual graphics in a view for levels and grids by selecting the element(s) and right-clicking to choose the Override options from the Override Graphics in View flyout.

The segment pattern and color can also be set. You can even remove the center segment if you need the grid head at each end of the building but don't want to carry the actual line all the way through the building. To modify the grid to take on these behaviors, you will need to change the Center Segment properties. Your options are Continuous, Custom, or None. Depending on which one you select, you will be given various options for determining how the segments can be set to appear. Figure 3.47 shows a graphic of the three basic center segment types. These three center segment types can be configured several ways to achieve just about any look you desire.

FIGURE 3.47
Grid 1: Continuous, Grid
2: Custom, Grid 3: None

I WISH REVIT STRUCTURE HAD A CENTERLINE

Revit Structure *can* have a centerline. All you need to do is create a grid type called Centerline. Set the Symbol parameter to None, and remove the check from the Plan View Symbols End 1 and End 2 options. Of course, you will have to uniquely name each of your centerlines because Revit Structure still thinks of a centerline as a grid, but now you have a centerline that will display in every view that the centerline intersects the plane of. Structural columns on the centerline will be placed in the Graphical Column Schedule. This may come in handy when you need to show a centerline of an element in several views or if you desire to not use the functionality that Revit Structure provides for scheduling columns offset from grid. A more in-depth explanation of this workflow can be found in the "Using a Graphical Column Schedule" section of Chapter 4.

Keep in mind that the changes you make to these properties affect the Type properties of the grid. Creating a grid type for a specific view may not make the grid's appearance acceptable in another view. You may want to think about how many different grid types you may need and name them accordingly.

GRID HEAD SYMBOLS

As it does for levels, Revit Structure has several grid head symbols available for you to use. They may not be defined in the default template, but they can be found in the Annotation folder of the Imperial or Metric library. You also have the ability to create your own if the existing ones are not quite what you are looking for. The easiest way to accomplish this is to start from an existing family and modify accordingly. If you would like to start from scratch, you can do so by going to the Application menu and choosing New ➤ Family. In the Imperial or Metric Templates folder you will see an Annotations folder. This is where you will find the Grid Head.rft template that you can start your new family from. You add line work and a label to the file; it's that simple. Once these families are loaded into your project, they will become available to be selected in the Type Properties dialog box of the grid.

Placing Grids into Your Project

Creating grids in Revit Structure is surprisingly painless to do. It basically goes like this: you use the Grid tool to draw the grid by either selecting two points or by selecting an object or reference plane. There is no wrestling match with having to specify the entire grid or working through convoluted dialog boxes that continuously pop up.

Grids will number or letter themselves sequentially as they are placed. Revit Structure does a very good job of assuming what name you want each time you place a grid. If Grid 8.5 was the last grid placed, the next grid placed will become 8.6. If you place a grid and change it to D, the next grid placed will become E. Yes, just like with levels, it is almost as if Revit is reading your mind.

After grids are placed, other elements will attach to them, maintaining a relationship as the model progresses with change. Like levels, grids are considered a datum element, so as you place them in a plan view, they have vertical and horizontal extents to them. If their 3D extents do not cross the plane of a particular level or section, then those grids will not be displayed in those views.

STOP MOVING AROUND OR WE WILL PIN YOUR POSITION

After you have levels and grids placed into your project and have taken the time to adjust their 3D extents so they look the way you want them to, you should think about pinning their position. The Pin Position tool can be applied to any element by selecting it/them and choosing the Pin tool from the Modify panel on the Ribbon or using the PP shortcut on the keyboard.

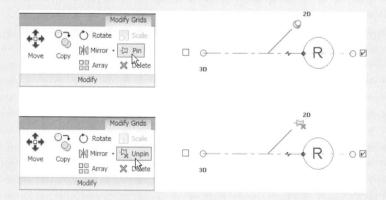

Pin Position will prevent elements from being moved. In this case it would be your levels and grids. The nice thing about levels and grids being pinned is that their 3D extents cannot be revised either.

You will be unable to select the controls to do so. However, you can still adjust their 2D extents for view-specific displays.

If changes need to be made to a particular level or grid, you will have to unpin it. To unpin the position of an element or elements, select them and choose the Unpin tool from the Modify panel on the Ribbon or use the UP shortcut on the keyboard. For quick pinning and unpinning of elements, you can simply click the Pin symbol that displays when the element is selected.

Pinning the position of your level and grids will ensure that they do not mistakenly get shifted or revised from their original intended position. As users start working with their 2D extents, they will not unknowingly be able to change the 3D extent. Another added value is that if a level or grid does mistakenly get deleted, the user doing the deleting will get a warning from Revit Structure stating that a pinned object has been deleted. Without the pin there is no warning; at least this way the user gets a chance to undo the mistake.

It is also good practice to have all of your levels created before creating the grid layout. If the grid is in place first, and a new level is added above or below existing levels, the grid won't reach those new levels unless you drag its 3D extent so it crosses the plane of the level. We will discuss how to modify the grids when this happens in your project, because we all know that levels and grids are never fully decided on before you start a project. Enough talk; let's get into the process of placing grids into a project.

PLACING LINEAR GRIDS

To begin placing the first grid regardless of how it will look, select the Home tab from the Ribbon and click the Grid tool on the Datum panel, as shown in Figure 3.48.

FIGURE 3.48
On the Home tab of the Ribbon, you can start the Grid tool.

Once you click the Grid tool, the Ribbon and Options bar populate with controls. By default the initial choice is to draw the grid by selecting two points in the active view. The Place Grid tab that appears after selecting Grid is shown in Figure 3.49.

FIGURE 3.49
The various options on the Ribbon for placing a grid

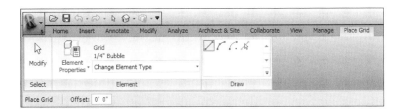

When you pick two points to create a grid, it is as easy as drawing a line. Revit Structure labels the grid, but this label may not be the one you want. If you want this label to be correct, and the subsequent labels to be sequential based on the correct label, you need to change how the grid head reads before you add the next grid. If you are careful not to start sketching another grid, you can edit the grid name by placing your cursor over the name and clicking. Notice that the value is colored blue, which means it can be edited. If you have stopped the Grid tool, you can select the grid and then click on the grid name to change it or change it with the Element Properties dialog box.

If the first grid is named grid 1, then the next grid will be grid 2. To add the second grid, restart the Grid tool. This time, you can click the Pick option from the Draw panel in conjunction with the Offset setting on the Options bar, as shown in Figure 3.50.

FIGURE 3.50
You can use the Pick option and the grid Offset option to create new grids that are offset a specified distance from existing elements.

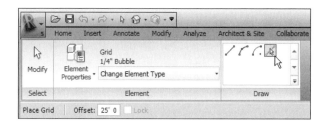

Once you select the Pick option, you can add an Offset distance. This example has a distance of 25′-0″. All you need to do is select the first grid. As you are clicking, be careful and watch for the alignment line adjacent to the either side of the grid you are picking. If it is heading in the right direction, you can click the existing grid. The new grid is created 25′-0″ away from the selected grid, and it becomes grid 2.

You can keep selecting grid after grid to create subsequent grids. A nice thing about this method of placement in Revit Structure is that the placement mode keeps running until you stop it. If you need spacing other than 25′-0″, you don't have to leave the tool to add a new increment. Simply change the spacing and offset the next grid. It could not be easier.

WHY IS THIS NUMBER ALREADY USED?

The first thing to understand is that a grid is unique — it has a unique Name parameter that it cannot share with any other grid.

The next issue is that the Grid tool remains active so you can continue to place additional grids.

Because the Grid tool remains active, the user can place a grid on top of another a bit too easily. Therefore grids that are inadvertently placed on top of another grid using the Pick option (or by copying) may mask the grid beneath them, depending on the properties of the grid head family.

Your view may appear to have only the grids you want, yet one (or more) may be lurking beneath the ones you can see. This hidden grid most likely has the name that you are being told can't be reused.

With a complicated grid layout, it can be difficult to find the offending grid so you can delete it. If you do find yourself in this situation, you can switch to a view where the majority of your grids are shown and set the view so only grids are shown. Begin by looking closely at the grid lines themselves. Occasionally the overlapping lines will alter the appearance of a grid line, making it look wrong. If that doesn't help, then select a small portion of grids at a time and examine what the status bar displays at the far right end. If it looks like you have six grids selected and the status bar says you have seven, you have just found the problem and maybe the grid in question. Hopefully there is only one.

Adding a grid in the perpendicular direction is just as easy. Click the Grid tool, and draw the grid in the other direction crossing the other grids, as shown in Figure 3.51. The clever thing here is that not only are you adding a new gridline, but you are also creating grid intersections. When the columns are placed along these lines, they will move with the grids and will display the grid location for certain types of schedules.

The first new-direction grid label should be renamed. Be sure you are not duplicating the grid name. Change the name, and start the Grid tool again. You can now work with the tools in the Place Grid tab to add several rows, as indicated in Figure 3.51.

FIGURE 3.51
Add a perpendicular set of grids with the Pick option with an Off-set setting. Be sure to label the first grid of the series.

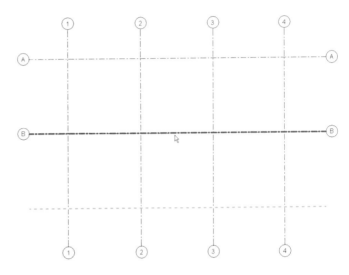

We all know that these days, most architects don't design buildings that require orthogonal grid lines. Luckily Revit Structure gives us the ability to place radial grids, so we can continue to form the skeleton structure for the building and still keep the integrity of the structural model in one piece.

WHEN DELETE IS NOT AN OPTION, HIDE IT

Sometimes you will find that you would like to remove a certain level(s) or grid(s) from a view even though its 3D extents must remain within the current view's view range. When this occurs, you can select that element(s) and right-click to choose the options from the Hide in View flyout. This does not delete the element(s) but hides it from being displayed in that particular view only. To find elements that have been hidden in a view, click the Reveal Hidden Elements button (light bulb icon) to the far right of the View Control bar.

PLACING RADIAL GRIDS

The process for creating radial grids or arc grids is basically the same as for adding a linear grid. To add an arc grid, click the Grid tool from the Home tab of the Ribbon. In the Draw panel, select the appropriate arc options. Your options are the Start-End-Radius arc or the Center-Ends arc, as shown in Figure 3.52.

FIGURE 3.52
To add a grid arc, choose
one of the arc options
from the Draw panel
when you start the Grid
tool.

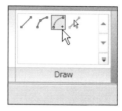

Once the option has been selected, you can draw the arc grid wherever you need it. It will behave exactly the same as a line grid, except it's an arc (see Figure 3.53). You might find the Start-End-Radius arc a bit easier to use because you don't have to know where the center of your arc is, as is required of the other option.

FIGURE 3.53
An arc grid that has
been added to the model

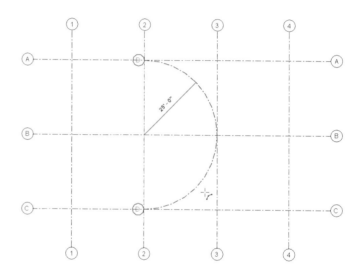

The ability to freely create a column grid "stick by stick" allows you to put a grid together in a controlled approach. Once grids are in place, you can move on to modifying them so their appearance is acceptable to your standards for documentation.

Modifying Grids

As you add the grids, you may notice that the grid head may not be on the correct side. You may even want a grid head on both sides. You may also need to make adjustments when you get into a tight situation where the grid head has to "jog" to the side.

To adjust a grid, make sure you are not still in the Grid Placement mode, and select a grid object. A few blue grips as well as several other controls display, as you can see in Figure 3.54.

The first item is a check box that allows you to turn the grid head on or off at that end. If the head is on, it will expose a jog symbol, referred to as Add Elbow. If you click this icon, as shown in Figure 3.55, the gridline will have a jog added to it, and the head will become offset. This is crucial to trying to jam several grid heads into a tight spot. Keep in mind that both of these, the On/Off check box and Add Elbow, are considered 2D controls for the grid. This means that this change alters only the view that you are applying it in.

FIGURE 3.54
By selecting the grid, you will gain access to controls allowing you to graphically modify each individual grid.

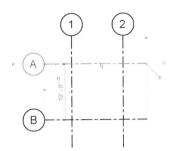

FIGURE 3.55
Select the Add Elbow control to add a jog in the grid.

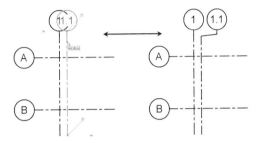

Another control you can use is the alignment line across the top of the gridline. Attached to this alignment line is a blue drag circle, and attached to that is a blue padlock icon. Essentially these three controls tie the individual grids to the adjacent grids. If you click and hold the blue circle, and then drag the grid end, all of the grids locked to it will move as well. If you first unlock this grid end, it will move independently of the other grid ends. You will also see annotation indicating either 3D or 2D. If it is 3D, the grip control will be an open circle. If it is a 2D grip control, it will be a filled circle. Be careful with these controls because changing them may affect how the grid displays in other views.

When you move the 3D extents of the grid, you affect whether that grid displays in other views. This is a 3D control, so you will want to set these extents for your project early on and then hopefully leave them alone. If a grid needs to show up in Level 5, then make sure that the 3D extents cross the plane of Level 5. If the grid is only for a canopy on the north side of the building, then make sure that the 3D extents do not run entirely through your building but run through the portions of the canopy only. Paying attention to where the initial 3D extents of your grids are placed will ensure that your grids are visible throughout your project wherever they are required.

If you are in a view that needs the grid to be modified to only show its extent for a certain portion or something other than its 3D extent, you will need to select the 3D annotation control, which will change the grid to display the filled circle. You are now working with the 2D extents of the grid. These extents are view specific, so like Add Elbow, the control affects only the view you are working in.

WATCH THAT LOCK

Yes, we know we mentioned the padlock symbol when modifying grids, but the message needs to be repeated. If you ever go to your plan views and find that someone has deleted all or several of your grids, dimensions are missing, and your Graphical Column Schedule is missing columns, take a moment (and a deep breath) to observe the situation. It might not be as bad as it looks. Somebody might have ignored the 3D lock symbol for that one grid that they were placing. Cut a few sections to see if the 3D extents of the grids have been altered. If so, you can drag them back to where they were, and your grids, dimensions, and columns should come back into place.

Let's imagine that you have spent some time on your foundation plan modifying the appearance of the grids to establish a clean and accurate view for documentation. Now you can jump up to the second floor framing plan and do it all over again. Stop! Forget we just said that — it should not be all that difficult. If you have been watching the Ribbon when selecting levels and grids, you may have noticed the Propagate Extents tool in the Datum panel. This will be your lifesaver so you don't have to do it all over again.

Working with the Extents of Datum Elements

We already talked about the importance of the 2D and 3D extents of datum elements when they are placed in a project. We also talked about how you can modify them individually for each view. Now let's talk about how you can work with these extents so they can be applied to other views. Revit Structure has several tools that allow you to do this. These tools are for continued working with the model as well as aiding and speeding up the creation of your documentation. The following sections will discuss those tools that you will want to get familiar with.

Propagating Extents

There is much to be said about the Propagate Extents tool. You should know that it is available, know how it works, and use it. This little guy (gal) allows you to select all of your grids or levels that have been modified with a jog, modified by shutting symbols on or off, or modified by dragging the 2D extents and allows you to apply (propagate) these overrides to another view or multiple views. Select the grid(s) or level(s) that have been altered in the view and choose the Propagate Extents tool from the Datum panel of the Modify Grids tab on the Ribbon. You will be presented with the dialog box shown in Figure 3.56.

Keep in mind that only those views that the selected level's or grid's 3D extents cut through will show up in this dialog box. There is no need to apply the 3D extent modifications because they are already are applied in every view — that's the purpose of 3D behavior of a datum extent. If you are performing the Propagate Extents command in a plan view, only plan views will be offered, and if you are performing it while in a section or elevation view, only those view types and only those that are parallel to the elevation or section that you applied changes to will be available in the list.

WHY DOES THE PROPAGATE EXTENTS DIALOG BOX NOT DISPLAY?

When you drag a datum extent of a level or grid outside the crop boundary of a view, you will be unable to propagate its extents to other views. The Propagate Extents tool may appear to be broken and not display a dialog box when chosen. Temporarily setting the view you are propagating from to Do Not Crop View will allow the Propagate Extents dialog box to appear, allowing you to propagate the elements. When finished, you can switch the view back to Cropping.

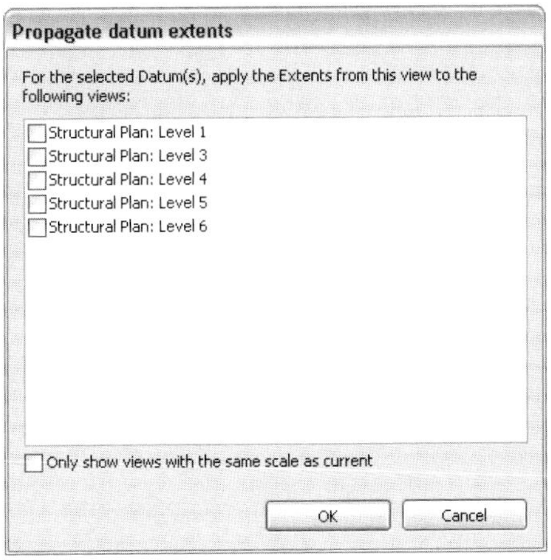

FIGURE 3.56
Propagate Datum
Extents lets you apply
modified levels or grids
to other views.

Maximizing 3D Extents

So what do you do when your grids are all in place and additional levels have been added, but the plan views for these new levels do not show your grids? First, why don't they show up? They don't because their 3D extents do not automatically adjust to cross the planes of new levels. These grids will have to have their 3D extents modified so they cross the new levels.

There are a few ways you can do this. First is to open sections or create new ones that are perpendicular to the grids. If the plane of a view is not perpendicular to a grid, you will not see it in the view. Once you see the grids, you can select them and drag their 3D extents to their new location. This can be quite easy for project with a simple grid system. For a project with a more complicated grid system using curved and radial grids, it can become time consuming and boring cutting sections so you can see the grids to readjust their extents.

For these situations you can simply select the grids from any view they are visible in and right-click to choose Maximize 3D Extents from the shortcut menu. This will adjust the 3D extents of the selected datum elements to the boundary of the model in all directions. As this may look like the best and easiest way to achieve the adjustment of your grids, you will want to use caution and know that choosing Maximize 3d Extents will adjust all of the selected elements' extents. So if the bottom extent does not need to be maximized to the bottom level but the top one does, you might want to think about the end result before using this command.

EXERCISE: WORKING WITH LEVELS AND GRIDS

This exercise will guide you through creating and placing a grid system as well as adding levels for elevations. We'll begin using a blank model and will place the grids first and add levels second, so you can see how to work with the grids when levels are placed afterward.

CREATE GRIDS

1. Open Revit Structure, and start a new default model.

2. On the Home tab of the Ribbon, click the Grid tool from the Datum panel.

3. Select a point in the Level 1 plan view window, and then click a point about 75′ below the first point.

4. If you are not still in the grid placement mode, click the Grid tool.

5. On the Draw panel, click the Pick option and type **25′ -0″** in the Offset box located on the Options bar. Offset a new grid to the right of the first grid.

6. Repeat the procedure two more times. You should be looking at grids 1 through 4.

7. Start the Grid tool again, and click the Draw option on the Draw panel. If you did not stop the Grid tool and are continuing with the same Grid tool session, be sure to reset the Offset value from 25′-0″ to 0′-0″ again. This time draw a horizontal grid across the top of the vertical grids from right to left.

8. Rename the grid head to **A**.

9. Start the Grid tool again, and click the Pick Lines option from the Draw panel. Set the Offset to **25′ -0″**. Offset grid A down three times at a 25′ -0″ increment. You should have column lines A through D.

10. While in Level 1 experiment a bit: select the grids individually and manipulate them. Add some elbows, toggle the grid head symbols on or off, and drag the 2D extents of the grid to a different location than its 3D extents. You can use the following image as an example for making the modifications. Remember that you could change the Type properties of your grids to display the "bubble" automatically at both ends instead of relying on overrides and Propagate Extents.

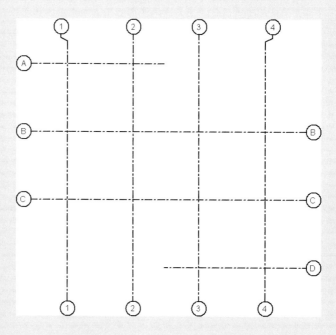

CREATE LEVELS

1. Working with the same file and grid layout, open the south elevation.

2. On the Home tab on the Ribbon, click the Level tool from the Datum panel.

3. On the Draw panel, click the Pick option, and change the offset to **10′ -0″**.

4. Offset Level 2 up. You should now have Level 3.

5. Offset Level 3 up. You should now have Level 4. Notice that the Project Browser has the new plan view for each of the new levels. If you unchecked the option Make Plan View, then these plan views will not have been created for each level. To make them, you need to use the View tab ➤ Create panel ➤ Plan Views drop-down ➤ Structural Plan tool and select the levels you added.

OBSERVE THE LEVEL AND GRIDS

1. Open the Level 4 plan view. Notice there are no grids on this plan view.

2. Go back to the south elevation view, select the 3D extents of the grids, and drag them so they cross the plane of Level 4.

3. Return to the Level 4 plan. Notice that the grids A–D are still not visible.

4. Go to the east or west elevation, select the 3D extents of those grids, and drag them so they cross the plane of Level 4.

5. Open the Level 4 plan and observe that the grids are now visible, but they do not appear the way they do in Level 1.

PROPAGATE EXTENTS

1. Go back to Level 1 plan view.

2. Select all of the grids.

3. On the Datum panel of the Ribbon, click the Propagate Extents tool.

4. In the Propagate Datum Extents dialog box, select all of the plan views and click OK.

5. Observe the other plan views. All plan views should have the same grid modifications as Level 1.

Being able to create and manipulate levels and grids is crucial to how well you work with Revit Structure. Fortunately, this process is fairly simple. Remember, though, it is through simplicity that errors can be produced as well. Take nothing for granted, and keep an eye on your model in this stage of the game. The choices you make here, right or wrong, will follow you like a shadow for the life of the model.

The Bottom Line

Import and link CAD data.   Many of your projects are likely to start with bringing in an architect's CAD data. In this chapter you learned how to bring a DWG file into your Revit Structure model and manipulate it to conform to your company's standards.

Master It   Once you add a DWG to the model, you will find that the DWG does not look the way you would like it to. Name two methods of controlling how it looks.

Link and work with Revit files.   The power of Revit Structure shines when you can get a Revit model from the architect. You can link that model and perform a Copy/Monitor operation to add superior integration unseen in CAD applications.

Master It   Although the actual import of the Revit Architecture model is quite simple, you can copy specific objects from the Revit link and keep a live connection telling you if anything changes when the model reloads. How does Copy/Monitor work?

Create levels.   One of the most compelling aspects of Revit Structure is its ability to contain the entire model in a single file. The ability to create levels and generate floor plan views that are associated with them is a huge part of this functionality.

Master It   As mentioned earlier, levels and plan views are connected. How does Revit Structure determine which level belongs to which plan view? What do you do if you need a new plan view based on an existing level?

Create grids.   Revit Structure allows you to create grids "stick by stick." This freedom is crucial to being able to easily model any building shape needed.

Master It   In this chapter you learned how to create a grid. Once the gridlines are in place, you have to make further adjustments. Explain how to do so.

Part 2

Developing Your Structural Model

Chapter 4

Structural Columns

Structural columns, which are different from architectural columns, are what help support almost every building. They are a major part of the skeleton structure that other structural elements like beams and slabs connect to. For this reason, they are probably going to be one of the first or second components that you will model in your project and will be the primary focus in this chapter.

Columns can take on many different shapes and sizes, as well as different construction materials. Depending on the type of material they consist of — wood, steel, precast, concrete — they demand different connection requirements, annotations for location, and documenting of sizes and reinforcing (if any). You should understand the various behaviors each scenario will bring.

Columns are typically defined as a vertical structural member; in today's world, they can become sloped, tapered, skewed, bent, and in some cases spiraled. Yes, you name it, and eventually a column will probably have to take on that form. Buildings are no longer square in footprint and straight-up vertical in height.

Even though columns are a major part of the building process, the basic structural column is simple to model and work with when using Revit Structure. Those that are not so basic in size and shape or vertical in height can be created and placed in a similar method but might not take on all of the functionality of a simple column.

In this chapter you will learn to:

◆ Work with the basic structural column family template

◆ Place structural columns in your project

◆ Attach structural columns to other structural components

◆ Employ the methods of placing slanted columns

◆ Document your model with the Graphical Column Schedule

Getting to Know the Column Families

Revit Structure has two column template families to help you create the behavior or intent of the columns you place in your project: column.rft and Structural Column.rft. Both templates have Upper Level and Lower Level constraints, as shown in Figure 4.1, which indicate where the top and bottom of the column should be locked and referenced to. We'll discuss the use of these levels in the section "Adding Structural Columns to Your Project." Because they are each set to a different category, they will present completely different behavior when they are loaded into your project. So when you are working with Revit Structure, make sure that you are using structural columns (Structural Columns category) and not architectural columns (Columns category). There is a dramatic difference in them, such as how they join to other elements as well as their structural properties, which will limit your capabilities if you use the wrong ones.

FIGURE 4.1
Upper Level and Lower Level constraints in a column family

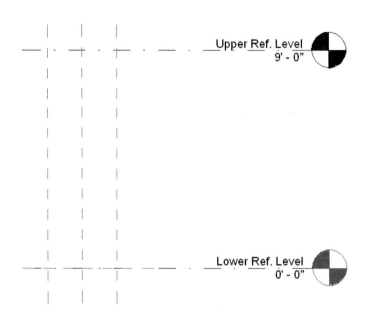

A third template is called `Generic Model.rft`. This template does not have the Upper Level parameter, which means you do not have to place it with a Top Level reference. As long as you set the category to Structural Column, it will be available to choose from within the Structural Column list and continue to behave like a column — it just will not be locked to a top level. The reference level in the family will reference a level of your choice in the project. This level can be used for uniquely shaped and placed columns that are specific to your project.

Figure 4.2 shows a unique structural column that was created with the Generic Model template. This column has two ring beams with varying heights throughout the structure. The top ring supports the roof, and the bottom ring supports the ceiling. Round skylights sit at the top of each column. This unique structural column family obviously does not work with Analysis programs, but as you can see, it proves to be valuable from a visualization standpoint as well as for documenting the model.

Getting to know the various column-related categories that are a part of Revit Structure as well as their behavior will allow you to better control how they display in the model and in your documentation. Different templates are available that have certain settings already built into them. You should also understand the various methods and reasons for loading a new column type into your project or duplicating existing types to change their properties.

FIGURE 4.2
A structural cluster column created from a Generic Model template
Courtesy of Ericksen Roed & Associates

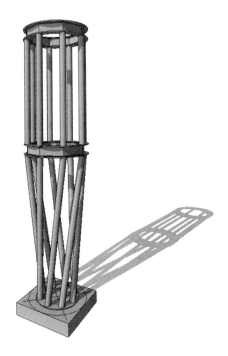

Architectural Columns

Architectural columns, which are assigned to the Columns category, are typically used by the architect to create elements such as column surrounds and structural column placeholders. This column type is useful to architects because it can automatically join with wall geometry when it comes into contact with it. This means that architects can easily convey the "column-ness" of what looks like a column without actually placing a structural column. They can focus on the space they want to allow for a structural column but not worry about the engineering-determined size until they have figured it out. Architectural columns can also be used as a design phase – related tool. In schematic design they are wonderful, but for construction documents or quantity takeoffs for walls and drywall, they don't perform as well. Architectural columns are basically intended to stand in for real columns and walls until you know what you want to use. Because of this you probably will find that you will not use these types of columns very much when working on your structure-only projects.

You can place architectural columns by selecting the Home tab ➤ Structure panel ➤ Column drop-down ➤ Architectural Column tool or dragging the column family type from the Project Browser and dropping it into your project. When you place an architectural column, the Ribbon and Options bar will display the information shown in Figure 4.3 and will make a minimum number of placement methods available, which is quite different from when you place a structural column. For instance, you can only place these columns one at a time, and by default, they will be placed unconnected going up from the level you choose to reference them to.

Architectural columns can have the same appearance as structural columns, so from the surface it can be hard to tell which category of column they are set to. Figure 4.4 shows examples of column families that have already been created and are available to use as part of the Revit Structure installation.

FIGURE 4.3
The Ribbon and Options bar when you place an architectural column

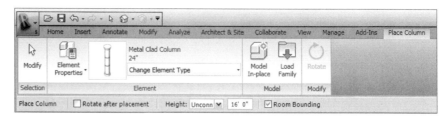

FIGURE 4.4
Architectural columns can look just like structural columns.

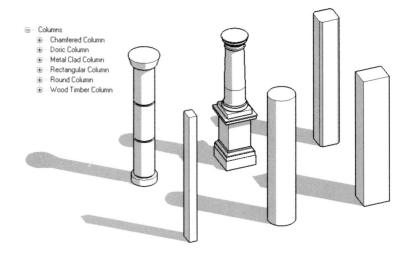

Another thing to note about architectural columns is that structural elements do not recognize them — which means that structural elements do not attach themselves to architectural columns, the columns do not have any analytical information or symbolic display, and the columns will not show up in a Graphical Column Schedule. Once you place an architectural column, you cannot easily swap it out with a structural column, so be sure to make users aware of these differences. Trying to swap out the category inside the family after it has already been placed in your project may confuse Revit Structure and create errors when you load the family back into your project.

SOMETHING JUST ISN'T RIGHT

If you are noticing strange behavior with your columns or you just can't see them in some of your views, you might want to verify whether they are architectural or structural columns. Someone may have accidentally placed an architectural column or copied it from a linked model. As you can see in the following graphic, you can easily verify which category the column is set to by hovering your mouse cursor over the column and reading the pop-up notification that displays. The first set of words indicates the category name of the object.

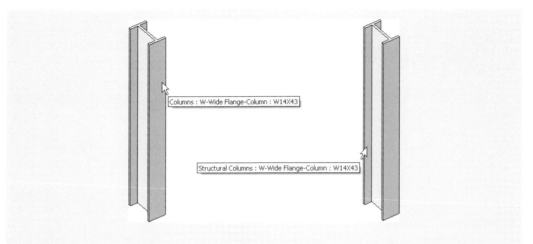

If your columns are not displaying, you might want to check the visibility settings of the view to see if the Columns category is checked to display. By default, Revit Structure will have this category set to not display in some views.

Since the architectural column is meant for nonstructural purposes, its built-in family parameters (shown in Figure 4.5) are limited and therefore much different from what you will see when you toggle to the Structural Columns category. These parameters are built into the Family template, which helps Revit Structure understand and control their behavior depending on the family category they are a part of. You can continue to add your own parameters to build additional intelligence into them.

Structural Columns

Structural columns are the columns that you should be using while modeling in your project. Therefore, the remainder of this chapter will explore the placement and behavior of structural columns. Before starting to place columns, you should have a good understanding of their properties and how they behave when placed in your project.

Structural columns are similar to architectural columns in the way that they look, but they automatically take on specific properties depending on their configuration and industry standards. They also have an analytical representation attached to them, which can be exported and used in other analysis design software.

Unlike walls, slabs, and roofs (which are *system* families), columns are considered a *component* (external) family. This means that they can be created outside your Revit Structure project as independent RFA (Revit family) files and loaded into your project. As a last resort for modeling unique items that are not repeated throughout the project, you can create structural columns as an in-place family directly inside your project. Since they are a component family, you have the freedom to create just about any shape you want. Figure 4.6 shows examples of structural column families that are part of the stock content provided with the Revit Structure installation. These families go a long way when it comes to modeling, but you will find that for some projects you will have to either modify existing ones slightly or create your own that look totally different.

FIGURE 4.5
The Family Category and Parameters dialog box for the Columns category

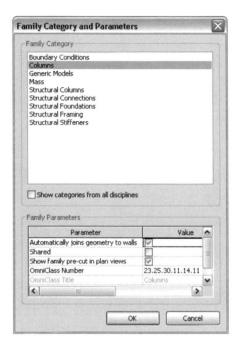

FIGURE 4.6
Revit Structure comes with a large library of structural column families.

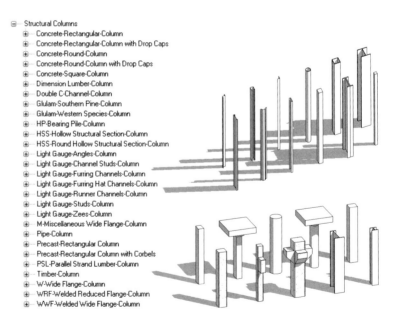

As you can see in Figure 4.7, the Structural Columns category has a few built-in parameters that allow it to behave differently depending on these parameters' settings inside the family. Setting the Structural Material Type parameter will let you add or remove additional parameters that pertain specifically to the material being used. In some cases, you might find that you need to have families containing the same geometry, but these options are set differently, so the geometry in each family displays a certain way when placed in your project.

FIGURE 4.7
The Family Category and Parameters dialog box for the Structural Columns category

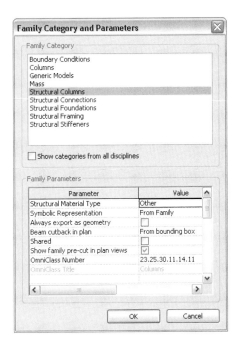

STRUCTURAL MATERIAL TYPE

When creating your own structural column, make sure that you set Structural Material Type inside the family to the proper material that it is meant to represent. You can select from five different material types: Other, Steel, Concrete, Precast Concrete, and Wood. This material property is different from the material that you assign to the family to give it surface and cut patterns and rendering appearance. This is what tells Revit Structure how the family behaves as it interacts with other structural elements and as it displays in certain views. For instance, a concrete beam that frames into a concrete column behaves differently than a steel beam that frames into a steel column or a steel beam that frames into a concrete column. Figure 4.8 shows the automatic behavior that is derived from this setting.

The Structural Material Type parameter helps determine whether the two elements should join their materials together with a construction joint or place the steel beam with a setback dimension. Each material behaves differently based on common industry conditions when it interacts with different materials. The Graphical Column Schedule also uses this setting, which allows you to schedule only columns of a certain material type. This makes this option one of the most important and the first one you should set when creating your column families.

FIGURE 4.8
The Structural Material Type setting within a structural column family helps determine how other structural elements attach to the column.

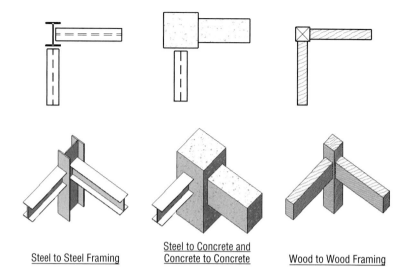

Steel to Steel Framing

Steel to Concrete and Concrete to Concrete

Wood to Wood Framing

NO, IT REALLY IS NOT THE RIGHT MATERIAL

When you are working with concrete, you might want to join two separate elements together to remove a construction joint. Let's say you need to join a concrete column to a concrete slab, and part of the column must be poured with the slab. To join these monolithically, both elements need to have the same material assigned to them. You keep checking the materials, and both the column and the slab have the same concrete material assigned to them. You have toggled among all three different Detail Level settings, and you still cannot get the construction joint to be removed. One last thing to try would be to edit the family and check the Structural Material Type setting referenced in the Family Properties panel ➤ Category and Parameters. Chances are that option is set to something other than Concrete.

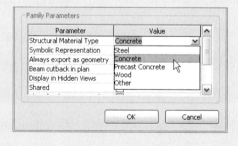

SYMBOLIC REPRESENTATION

This setting affects the family only when your views are set to a coarse detail level. If your column family is going to be a steel or wood material, you will probably want to have this option set to From Project Settings. That way, Revit Structure will automatically place symbolic lines to represent the column in a plan, section, or 3D view when set to a coarse detail level. You can control the display of this symbolic line by the subcategory Stick Symbols under the Structural Columns category. It also controls the symbols that are displayed for the Top and Bottom connection types that are set in the Structural Settings dialog box for the project and an instance parameter of a column. You can control the display of these symbols through the Connection Symbols category under the Annotation Categories tab in the Object Styles dialog box. For most companies, this will be the industry standard for showing steel or wood at reduced scales, which would also be shown in Revit Structure's coarse detail level view.

When using concrete or precast concrete, you would typically show the true double-line representation of the shape in all detail levels. For this reason, set the Symbolic Representation option for these families to By Family. This tells Revit Structure to not automatically place symbolic line work and symbols for those families.

BEAM CUTBACK IN PLAN

This is another setting that affects the family only when your views are set to a coarse detail level. Beam Cutback in Plan refers to the stick symbol symbolic line, which Revit Structure automatically generates for a beam family when its Symbolic Representation option is set to From Project Settings. If set to From Bounding Box, the symbolic line will be cut back from the bounding box of the column; if set to From Geometry, the symbolic line will be cut back from the geometry of the column. You are probably wondering, "What is a bounding box?" A *bounding box* is an invisible box that Revit Structure places to the extents of the geometry inside the family. This concept is best shown with a sloped column, as in Figure 4.9. Revit Structure uses this box to help it make decisions during its automated process. In the scenario of a beam framing into a column, the Symbolic Cutback Distance setting in the Structural Settings dialog box will start its offset dimension from the bounding box or the geometry of the column, depending on the settings in the Column family.

FIGURE 4.9
For the column on the left, Beam Cutback in Plan is set to From Bounding Box; for the column on the right, Beam Cutback in Plan is set to From Geometry.

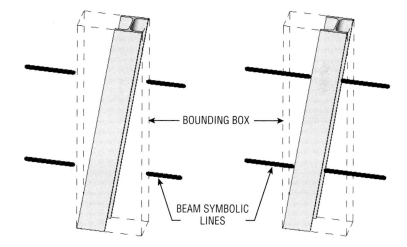

BOUNDING BOX

BEAM SYMBOLIC LINES

DISPLAY IN HIDDEN VIEWS

When Structural Material Type is set to Concrete or Precast Concrete, this parameter becomes available to help control the visibility of hidden lines that should or should not display in your concrete column families. There are three settings for this parameter: Edges Hidden by Column

Itself, Edges Hidden by Other Members, and All Edges. Figure 4.10 shows the various displays that Revit Structure will produce depending on what your family is set to.

In some cases, you may need an exact duplicate of your family with a different family name. The only difference between the two families may be the Display in Hidden Views setting. Sometimes you may have to create duplicate families with different settings so your column with special conditions displays properly once it's in your project.

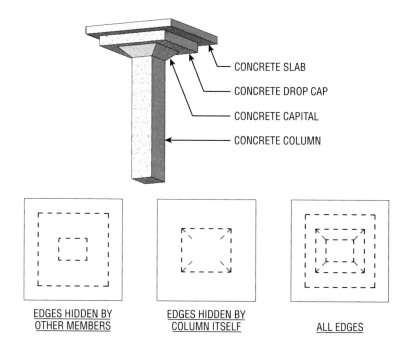

FIGURE 4.10
Setting the Display in Hidden Views option in the Structural Column family produces various plan displays.

Family Loading and Duplication

Since structural column families are component families, you will need to import them into your project in order to use them. Once the families are in your project, you will be able to duplicate them to create different sizes. Some structural column families will be created with a type catalog file that is part of the family. This type catalog file allows you to define a list of preset types that let you lock in the settings for each type and display them in a list to choose from when importing. You can find additional information on the use of type catalogs by searching the Help index in Revit Structure.

To load a structural column family or any other component family, choose the Insert tab ➢ Load from Library panel ➢ Load Family tool. You can also choose the Load Family tool on the fly from the Detail panel of the contextual tab that displays during the placement of elements such as columns and beams. Once you've selected the tool, browse to the location of your structural column family and select it to open it. You can load several families at once, similar to using Windows' standard multiple-file selection, if you hold down the Shift or Ctrl key while selecting the files. If a family is using a type catalog, Revit Structure will display a list of preset types, as shown in Figure 4.11, for you to choose from. From this list you can load all the types that you need.

FIGURE 4.11
Using a type catalog for a family to load preset types into your project

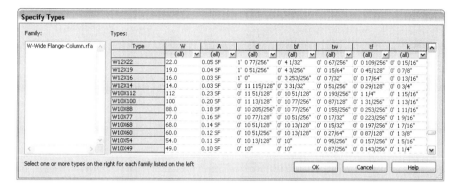

Type catalogs are typically used when the structural shape properties are pretty much static for their type. The properties of steel, light-gauge steel, and wood shapes are usually pulled right from a product catalog or are industry standards. Structural elements that are concrete or precast concrete can come in just about any shape you could imagine, so putting them in a type catalog would be exhaustive. However, if a family's types are used repeatedly throughout other projects, your exhaustive efforts will pay off.

Most families such as the wide flange member or a precast L-beam maintain their basic form; just the actual dimensions that define their size or related information change. A type catalog can make it easier for you to create a long list of sizes rather than having to create them in the Family Types dialog box each time you need a new size. It also means that you don't have to load all the types of a family when you really need to use only a couple of them. A quick look at the wide-flange family shows lots of types, but you use only a small fraction of them in a project. Certain families you create may warrant using a type catalog; you will need to decide when the right time is to use one for your families.

 Real World Scenario

REMEMBER TO CHANGE THOSE PARAMETER VALUES

When duplicating types inside your project, it is important to remember that just duplicating a structural column type with a name of W8X31 and giving it a name of W12X45 does not automatically change the parameter values that give the type its physical properties. You need to change the relevant parameter values after duplication to completely define it as a new type.

One example comes to mind: We had a user who was new to Revit Structure and was modeling a five-level composite steel structure. The template at the time had only one wide-flange column loaded in it (W8X31). As new column sizes were needed, the user continued to duplicate the W8X31. Of course, the duplicates all had names that reflected the shape of the new columns, but all 10 columns had the size properties of a W8X31. Not a good example of an accurate BIM project.

When working with families that are using type catalogs, you should load in new shapes from the catalog rather than duplicate them. You load new types in the same way you load the family for the first time. Use the Duplicate method for families that do not use type catalogs.

One method to duplicate a Structural Column, is to perform the following steps:

1. Select a column that you want to duplicate.

2. Open its Element Type Properties dialog box.

3. Click the Duplicate button in the Type Properties dialog box.

4. Give the duplicated column a new name.

5. While still in the Type Properties dialog box, make changes to all parameters that differ from the other types.

6. Click OK in all subsequent dialog boxes.

Another method to duplicate a Structural Column, is to perform the following steps. (This method allows you to create new types without touching already modeled elements.)

1. Select a column type from the Project Browser in the Structural Columns category.

2. With the column type selected, right-click and select Duplicate.

3. Give the duplicated column a new name.

4. Right-click on the new column type and select Properties.

5. While in the Type Properties dialog box, make changes to all parameters that differ from the other types.

6. Click OK in all subsequent dialog boxes.

EXERCISE: CREATING A SIMPLE STRUCTURAL COLUMN FAMILY

In this exercise, you'll use a simple structural concrete column, one that is already created for you in the Revit Structure installation. Going through the steps will help you grasp the idea and help you create structural columns of much greater complexity.

1. Choose the Application menu ➢ New ➢ Family.

2. Browse to Imperial Templates\Structural Column.rft and select it to open it.

3. From the Create tab on the Ribbon choose the Family Properties panel ➢ Category and Parameters tool.

4. Set the Structural Material Type option to Concrete. Click OK to close the dialog box.

5. While in the plan view, choose the Create tab ➢ Forms panel ➢ Solid drop-down ➢ Extrusion. Select the Rectangle line tool from the Draw/Pick gallery in the Draw panel on the Ribbon, and place the sketch lines outside the reference planes, as shown here:

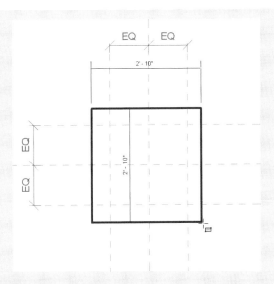

6. Use the Align command on the toolbar to align and lock the sketch lines to the reference planes, as shown here:

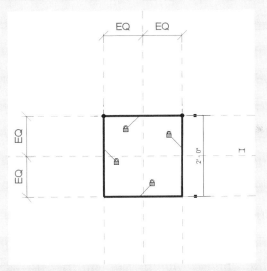

Note that placing the initial sketch lines away from the reference planes and then aligning and locking to them afterward ensures that your sketch lines are properly locked to the reference planes.

7. Click Finish Extrusion from the Extrusion panel on the Ribbon.

8. Place dimensions between the reference planes for both the width and height of the column.

9. Create a Label parameter, as shown in the following graphic, so the extrusion will flex inside your project. You can easily do this by selecting the dimension(s) and then selecting Add a Parameter from the Label box on the Options bar.

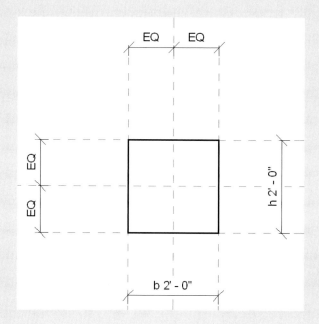

10. In the Parameter Properties dialog box, fill out the appropriate information by giving each parameter a name (here we use **b** and **h**, which is consistent with Revit Structure's references to width and height in the other structural column families) and group them under Dimensions. Make them a Type parameter and click OK.

   Note that when using this method the Type of Parameter value has already been set to Length. This is because a Length parameter is the only type that can be assigned to this type of dimension.

11. Open the Front Elevation view from the Project Browser.

12. Select the solid form, drag the top grip (triangle) up until the Upper Ref. Level is highlighted, release the mouse button, and click the padlock that appears to lock the relationship between the top of the solid and the level.

13. With the solid still selected, drag the bottom grip (triangle) up and then back down until the Lower Ref. Level is highlighted, and release the mouse button. Click the padlock that appears to lock the relationship between the bottom of the solid and the level.

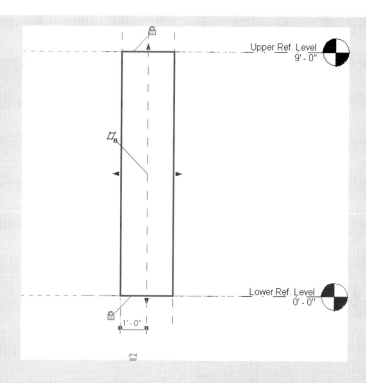

14. Select the extrusion and open its Element Properties dialog box.

15. In the Element Properties dialog box, select the little rectangular button next to the Material parameter, in the = (equals) column.

16. In the Associate Family Parameter dialog box, click Add Parameter.

17. Name the parameter **Material**, make it an Instance parameter, and group it under Material and Finishes.

18. Click OK to return to the Element Properties dialog box.

19. Notice that the little rectangular button next to the Material parameter now has an equals sign in it. Steps 15, 16, and 17 just added a parameter to your family and hardwired it to the extrusion, so when you place the parameter in your project, you are able to assign different materials to each instance of a column that you place. Click OK to close the Element Properties dialog box.

20. Perform a few safety checks by changing the Dimensions values in the Types dialog box located in the Family Properties panel of the Ribbon to make sure that your new family flexes properly. Also, choose the Lower Ref. Level and move it up or down, and do the same with the Upper Ref. Level to verify that the top and bottom of the column are constrained properly to the levels.

21. If you have not done so already, make sure to save the family in case you would like to use it later on.

Adding Structural Columns to Your Project

After learning about the various column family libraries and what makes them tick, you are ready to move on to placing columns in your project. You can use the `Structural Columns-STL.rvt` file for this section of the chapter. Before placing structural columns, you should have levels and a pretty good portion of your grids generated. The top and bottom of any columns will need to refer to levels that are already generated in the model. If you place columns on grids, you can set them to stay attached to the grids. You can do so by making sure that the Moves with Grids option on the Options bar is checked when a column is selected or that the Moves with Grids parameter is checked in the column's Instance properties. That way, when a grid moves, the column moves with it. The grids also allow modeled columns to display in a Graphical Column Schedule.

The natural tendency when starting a project is to model your columns full height from the top of the foundation to the roof. This makes perfectly good sense in a single-story structure. But you have to stop and ask yourself, "What concrete column is poured in a 100-foot lift?" or "Who erects a 100-foot-long steel column?" The preferred method is to place columns as the building will be built. Note that the Split tool doesn't work on columns, so think about how you are going to get to the finish line to achieve the "model as it's built" concept before you start.

If you are modeling a concrete post-tensioned or flat plate structure and the columns go floor-to-floor, you should model the columns floor-to-floor. A good rule is to stop the columns at the construction joint — which will most likely be the top of the slab for the bottom of the column and the bottom of the next slab above or below the beam for the top of the column. Typically, concrete structures are erected floor-by-floor, so the concrete columns would be placed level-to-level in Revit Structure just as they will be built out in the field.

If you are modeling a steel structure, the columns are more than likely going to be erected to a certain height before they will need to be spliced. This might be necessary to meet Occupational Safety & Health Administration (OSHA) requirements or because of a change in column size. A steel column usually projects above a specific level before it splices, stopping just below a level at a roof or termination of column condition. Regardless of the scenario, you should be modeling columns as they will be built.

Not only does modeling structural columns as they are constructed give you a more accurate BIM model, but when it comes to creating sections and Graphical Column Schedules and performing quantity take-offs, you will spend less time developing your sections, create a useful schedule, and have a much more accurate representation of material amounts.

The biggest part of mastering the placement of structural columns in your project is learning the ways that you can place them and knowing the best times to use those particular methods. Thinking ahead in the modeling process and attaching structural columns to other elements (so they adjust to changes in the model) will help keep element relationships consistent and their parametric behavior as you intended.

Placing Structural Columns

To begin placing your structural columns, select the Structural Column tool from the Home tab ➤ Structure panel ➤ Column drop-down, or drag the family type from the Families section of the Project Browser and drop it into your project. A third method is to select an existing column and right-click to choose Create Similar from the shortcut menu or choose it from the Create panel on the contextual tab of the Ribbon. The Options bar, as well as the contextual tab on the Ribbon, offers several methods for placing structural columns (Figure 4.12).

FIGURE 4.12
The Options bar and contextual tab give you several options for placing a structural column.

The following is an overview of what's available to you for placing structural columns into your project:

Ribbon panels

◆ Before placing a column, you can edit the Element properties of the currently selected column or duplicate it to make a new column type.

◆ From the Type Selector pull-down in the Element panel, select the type of structural column you want to place.

◆ In the Placement panel you can choose to place a vertical column or a slanted column. The Slanted Column tool is not available in a plan view.

◆ You can load a new family on the fly by choosing the Load Family tool from the Detail panel.

◆ Two additional placement options in the Multiple panel are On Grids and At Columns. These are both explained further in "Using the On Grids Option" and "Using the At Columns Option."

Options bar

◆ If you want the columns to be tagged in the current view directly after placement, select the Tag check box.

◆ Selecting the Rotate after Placement option automatically opens the Rotate command after placement, with the insertion point that is defined within the family by two reference planes serving as the center of rotation.

◆ In the Height/Depth area, you can choose to place the column with a depth (going down) or with a height (going up) with a reference to the current level you are placing it in.

◆ To the right of the Height/Depth area is the Constraint list, where you can set the constraint of the top or bottom of the column or set it to be unconnected.

◆ If you're using an unconnected height, you can give a depth or height of the column from your current level.

After you place the columns, take a look at the properties of a few of them. You will find that their Instance parameters will vary depending on the structural material type assigned to them in their family as well as how they are placed in the model. Figure 4.13 shows that a steel column will have additional Graphics parameters for the display of symbolic symbols and concrete columns will have additional Structural parameters for the concrete cover.

FIGURE 4.13
Structural col-
umn properties
vary depending
on their struc-
tural material.

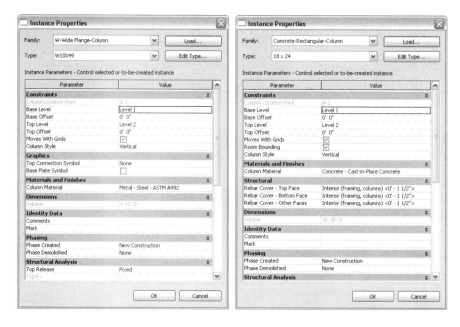

Every structural column will have a base and a top level that the bottom and the top of the column refer to. From each of those references, you can specify a top or bottom offset from the specified reference level. If you have an interior column sitting on a footing that is 8″ below the Level 1 slab on a grade, the Base Level option of the column would be set to Level 1 with a Base Offset dimension of –0′-8″. The same column that goes up and splices 4′-6″above Level 3 would have its Top Level option set to Level 3 with a Top Offset setting of 4′-6″.

You will also see a Column Style parameter. This parameter will come into play in a later section called "Adding Slanted Columns to Your Project." This parameter sets the behavior of the column in your project. Is it vertical or is it a slanted column?

When you place structural columns in Revit Structure, several tools are available that allow you to place them quickly as well as ensure that they are placed properly. Using the Single Pick option will place single columns one-by-one and also control the rotation of each specific placement. Using the On Grids or At Columns placement options allows you to place several columns at once while using other elements for their placement location.

USING THE SINGLE PICK OPTION

The Single Pick option is the initial state that Revit Structure starts in after you select one of the structural column placement tools. This allows you to place columns one at a time and easily adjust settings between each placement.

To use the Single Pick option, follow these steps:

1. Columns will be placed using the Depth option by default, so activate an upper-level plan view or change the option for Depth/Height if you prefer a lower-level plan view.

2. On the Home tab ➢ Structure panel, select the Column drop-down and choose Structural Column.

3. Select the type of column you want to place.

4. Observe the Options bar and make any necessary settings. Click the Element Properties button, and set the Top Level and Base Level values as well as any offsets that are required.

5. Start placing columns one-by-one and watch them snap to the intersection of gridlines.

6. You can rotate columns while placing them by pressing the spacebar. Each tap of the spacebar rotates the column 90 degrees. If on gridlines, the column will snap perpendicular to them and use an angle degree that's half the grid intersection angle.

7. You can tag each column as you place it by checking or unchecking the Tag check box in the Options bar.

This method is useful for placing columns that are not on grids or that require a more specific location or rotation. Even after the columns are placed, you can use the spacebar to rotate them by selecting one or more columns and pressing the spacebar.

If you use this method for grid intersection placement, take care to ensure that you are placing the column at the correct intersection point rather than at another unexpected intersection point. Keep an eye on the status bar located in the lower-left area of your Revit Structure session dialog box to verify where the column is being placed. Setting the Visibility properties of a view to show only grids and columns may help you select the correct intersection point.

USING THE ON GRIDS OPTION

The On Grids option allows you to select groups of grids for placement. Revit Structure will place a column on each intersection for all the grids that you select. This can be a quick method for getting columns into your project. Even if there is not supposed to be a column on a particular grid intersection, it can still be more efficient to place a column on it and remove it afterward.

Ask yourself which way you can do it faster. Should you place 50 columns by using the Single Pick option, or should you place 55 columns with the On Grids option and erase 5 of them afterward? Figure 4.14 shows that you can place 30 columns onto your gridlines in a matter of seconds.

For grid intersection placement, perform these steps:

1. Columns will be placed using the Depth option by default, so activate an upper-level plan view or change the option for Depth/Height if you prefer a lower-level plan view.

2. On the Home tab ➤ Structure panel, select the Column drop-down and choose Structural Column.

3. Select the type of column you want to place.

4. Observe the Options bar and make any necessary adjustments.

5. Select the On Grids Placement option from the Multiple panel.

6. While in this mode, the Options bar will refresh to display the option Tag the Column(s) after Placement. From the Ribbon, cancel out of the tool or choose Finish Selection to accept your grid selection. Note that you have to choose the option to tag before selecting grids. Otherwise, you can't check the box; it will be unavailable to select.

7. Select all grids with a right-to-left crossing window. You should see columns display at the center of all selected grid intersections.

FIGURE 4.14
Placing columns with the On Grids option will quickly and accurately place them onto gridlines.

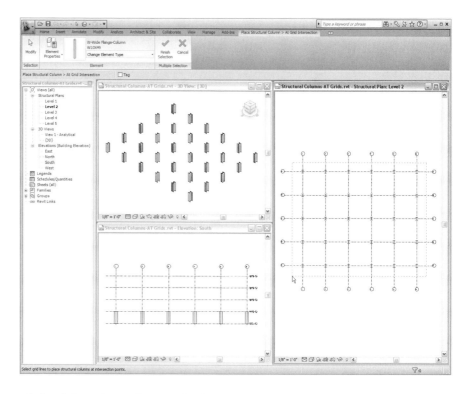

Select grids by clicking the gridlines and holding down the Ctrl key to add to your selection or by holding down the Shift key to subtract from your selection. You should see columns appear and disappear at the center of grid intersections as you add and subtract grids from your selection.

8. Once you've selected all required grids, be sure to click the Finish Selection button from the Ribbon to accept your column placement. Any other action will remove your placements.

9. You can now delete any unwanted columns that are on grid intersections and do any fine-tuning of their rotation.

Using this method will help ensure that all columns are accurately placed at the exact intersections of the grids. This will also ensure that the columns will properly be attached to the grids so that when the grids move, the columns will move with them. When columns are properly placed at grid intersections, they will continue to display in the Graphical Column Schedule (which we discuss later in this chapter).

USING THE AT COLUMNS OPTION

If you have architectural columns modeled in your project, you can use them to place your structural columns. As shown in Figure 4.15, Revit Structure will place a structural column at the center of all architectural columns that you select. If this method of placement fits in with your modeling workflow, this can be a quick method of getting columns into your project.

For At Columns placement (which requires an architectural column to place a structural column), perform the following steps:

FIGURE 4.15
When you use the At Columns option, Revit Structure will place a structural column at the center of each architectural column that you select.

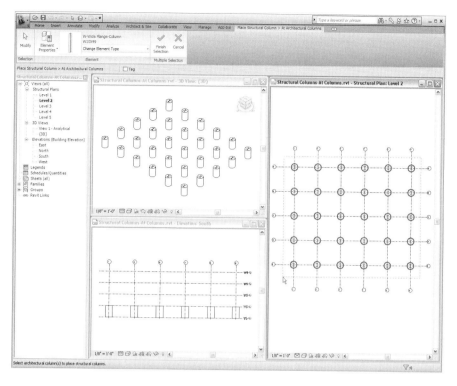

1. Columns will be placed using the Depth option by default, so activate an upper-level plan view.

2. On the Home tab ➤ Structure panel, select the Column drop-down and choose Structural Column.

3. Select the type of column you want to place.

4. Observe the Options bar and make any necessary adjustments.

5. Select the At Columns Placement option from the Multiple panel.

6. While in this mode, the Options bar will refresh to display the option Tag the Column(s) after Placement. From the Ribbon, you can cancel out of the tool or choose Finish Selection to accept your architectural column selection.

7. Select all architectural columns with a right-to-left crossing window. You should see structural columns display at the center of all selected architectural columns.

   Select architectural columns by clicking them and holding down the Ctrl key to add to your selection or by holding down the Shift key to subtract from your selection. You should see structural columns appear and disappear at the center of each architectural column as you add and subtract them from your selection.

8. Once all required architectural columns are selected, be sure to click the Finish Selection button from the Ribbon to accept your column placement. Any other action will remove your placements.

9. You can now do any fine-tuning of their rotation.

If you are using this method to place your columns and the architectural columns that you're selecting are from an outside client, make sure that architecturally the columns are accurately placed. Usually an architectural column will be in the form of a column surround, so when you place the structural column you place it within the surround. Communicating the behavior of the columns to those who created them will help achieve an accurate placement.

Some companies may use the structural linked model to display structural columns in their model, so this can be an excellent way to collaborate and keep your documents coordinated.

Copying Columns to Other Levels

Once you have columns placed in your project for one of your levels, another time-saver you can take advantage of is to copy them to other levels as needed. Each project will be a little different, so you will have to use your judgment on which tools and methods are best to use.

The basic procedure goes like this:

1. Select the column(s) that will be copied to other levels.

Switching to a 3D view to perform your selection and then using the Filter Selection tool to select only the columns can speed up the selection process. The 3D view allows you to orient to an elevation view that lets you select through the model with no clipping plane.

2. After element(s) are selected, choose Clipboard panel ➢ Copy from the contextual tab on the Ribbon, or press Ctrl+C on your keyboard.

3. If the element(s) are still selected, choose Clipboard panel ➢ Paste Aligned drop-down ➢ Select Levels from the contextual tab on the Ribbon. If the element(s) are not selected, choose the Modify tab ➢ Clipboard panel ➢ Paste Aligned drop-down ➢ Select Levels. The Paste Aligned drop-down provide several options to choose from, depending on which view you are in. The options are as follows:

Select Levels/Select Levels by Name   Choosing this option allows you to paste the element(s) you have copied by picking from a list of levels that are in your project to paste the element(s) into. Using the Ctrl and Shift keys on the keyboard while selecting the levels from the list allows you to include multiple levels in your selection.

Select Views   Choosing this option allows you to paste the element(s) you have copied by picking from a list of views. It is typically used for pasting annotation and detail items into view(s). If element(s) that will be pasted do not meet the proper criteria for any views in the project, this option will be unavailable. This is common for modeled geometry. Elements such as detail lines, annotations, dimensions, and filled regions will typically display a list of views that the element(s) can be pasted into. Using the Ctrl and Shift keys on the keyboard while selecting the views from the list allows you to choose multiple views in the list.

Current View   Choosing this option allows you to paste the element(s) you have copied into the active view. Those element(s) that are being pasted will be hosted or referenced to the level associated with your current view if they are level, hosted, or work plane based. This option may be unavailable if the proper criteria of the current view are not met for pasting the element(s), such as attempting to paste a column into a section view.

Same Place   Choosing this option allows you to paste the element(s) you have copied to the exact same place that they were copied from regardless of the view you are in. It will also display a warning that reads: "There are identical instances in the same place. This will result in double counting in schedules." This is just telling you that you now have duplicate elements on top of each other and what can happen because of it.

PASTING COLUMNS IN THE SAME PLACE

Since the Split tool does not work on columns, you can paste in the same place when you have modeled a structural column the full height of the building and need to split it into additional elements to follow the model-as-it-is-built approach. After the structural column is pasted in the same place, you can adjust the base and top constraints until there is no longer duplication of the elements.

A short example would be as follows: Column A runs from Level 1 to Level 3. Copy column A to the clipboard and use Paste Aligned ➤ Same Place; the copy now becomes a new column B directly on top of column A. Select one of the columns and adjust its top constraint to be Level 2 (after the paste the column will remain selected, making it easier to know which column you are modifying). Select the other column and adjust its base constraint to be Level 2. This allows any framing members that may be attached to the column to keep a relationship with one of the columns. Removing the column first would break that relationship.

In a floor (slab) example you could split a floor into separate floors by doing the same thing. Select one floor and modify its sketch lines. Select the other floor and modify its sketch lines. You now have two floors without having to resketch the entire floor shape.

Pick Level/Pick Level Graphics   Choosing this allows you to paste the element(s) you have copied by picking the geometry of a level. The cursor will display the usual arrow with an additional level head symbol indicating that you must select a level. If you are not in a view where levels exist, you will have to switch to one that does have them.

After you select a Paste Aligned option, the columns will be placed into your model depending on which method you select.

4. While the columns are still selected, right-click and choose Properties from the shortcut menu.

5. Make any parameter adjustments that are needed for the final location of your columns.

Using Paste Aligned ➤ Select Levels allows you to select several levels at once. If you had a 20-story concrete structure and you had the columns already placed on the first level, you could select and copy all of those columns to the clipboard. Figure 4.16 shows how you could then paste them to each of the other levels by selecting all of the remaining levels. This would place individual columns directly above the lower columns at each level. In the scenario shown, the columns that were copied were referenced from Level 1 to Level 2. Selecting Level 2 would result in placing columns over the top of the ones that you copied; selecting Level 1 would result in placing the top of the column referenced to Level 1 with the bottom projecting below. This occurs because the Paste function uses the Depth option for placing columns. There is no option to choose Height instead, so you must take care not to select the level above your work.

FIGURE 4.16
Selecting multiple lev-
els to paste columns to
other levels

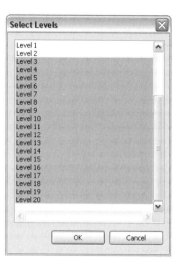

EXERCISE: PLACING STRUCTURAL COLUMNS FOR A STEEL STRUCTURE

For this exercise, you can use the `Structural Columns-STL.rvt` file. You will go through the steps of placing columns into your project first by placing the first lift . You'll then use the Copy to Clipboard method to place the upper levels. Columns will span two supported levels before requiring a splice connection.

1. Open the `Structural Columns-STL.rvt` model.

2. Open the Level 3 view (if necessary). Note that the first lift of columns will go from Level 1 to Level 3.

3. Select the Home tab on the Ribbon, and choose the Column drop-down ≻ Structural Column.

4. Select W10X49 from the Type Selector pull-down.

5. Set the column constraint option to Depth and the bottom constraint to Level 1.

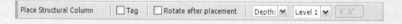

6. For the placement option, choose On Grids.

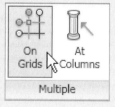

7. Select all grids from upper right to lower left. Temporary columns will display.

8. Click Finish Selection from the Ribbon to make your selection permanent.

9. Delete the columns on grids A-4, A-5, A-6, B-4, B-5, and B-6.

10. Open a 3D view, and orient the view so that you're looking south by selecting the S on the ViewCube, shown here:

Working with the controls on the ViewCube is the quickest way to maneuver the view to preset directions. However, you can also select the drop-down that appears adjacent to the ViewCube. This drop-down displays additional options for choosing the orientation of the current 3D view.

When you select columns in the following steps, it appears that you are selecting only six columns when creating a right-to-left crossing window. Since a 3D view does not have a clipping plane, you actually are selecting all columns; 24 should be listed on the status bar next to the Filter icon, bottom-right corner.

11. Select all columns that you previously placed with a right-to-left crossing window, right-click, and select Element Properties to access the columns' Instance properties.

12. Change the Top Offset value to **4′-6″** and close the Instance Properties dialog box.

13. While columns are still selected, choose Copy from the Clipboard panel on the Ribbon.

14. While columns are still selected (important because you'll have to use a different Ribbon tab if they are not still selected), choose the Paste Aligned drop-down ➤ Select Levels from the Clipboard panel on the Ribbon, and select Level 5 and Level 7 in the Select Levels dialog box.

The levels were selected for the tops of the columns because Revit Structure will place them using the Depth option when they are pasted. If columns are not still selected, you will have to choose the Paste Aligned drop-down from the Modify tab ➤ Clipboard panel.

15. Select the second lift of columns that go from Level 3 to Level 5 with a right-to-left crossing window (as shown here), right-click, and select Element Properties to access the columns' Instance properties.

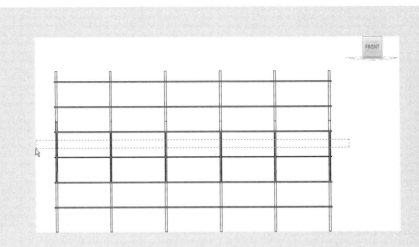

16. Change the Base Offset value to **4'-6"** and close the Instance Properties dialog box.

17. Select the third lift of columns that go from Level 5 to Level 7 with a right-to-left crossing window, right-click, and select Element Properties to access the columns' Instance properties.

18. Change the Base Offset value to **4'-6"** and the Top Offset value to **−0'-5"** (the depth of the slab), and close the Instance Properties dialog box.

19. Check that all columns are placed correctly.

Using a top offset for the column that matches the thickness of the slab will not create a relationship between the column and the slab. If the slab changes thickness, you will have to change the Top Offset value accordingly. Another option is to attach the columns to the bottom of the slab. With this method, the top of the column will automatically adjust as the slab thickness changes. To view a completed model of this exercise, see the Structural Columns-STL _Complete.rvt file.

Top and Bottom Attachment

Like walls, the top and bottom of columns can be attached to other structural elements such as floors, roofs, foundations, and structural framing members to help maintain their relationship. They can also be attached to reference planes and reference levels. The Ribbon will switch to display Attach and Detach buttons on a contextual tab, as shown in Figure 4.17, when you select a structural column. When you click the Attach button, the Options bar will display settings for the type of attachment you want to make.

FIGURE 4.17
Options bar
attachment

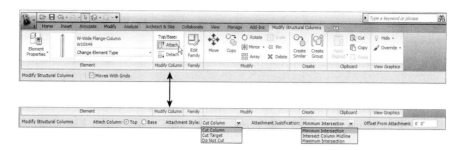

Reading from left to right, the Options bar in Figure 4.17 allows you to do the following:

◆ Select Top or Base to define which end to attach the column to.

◆ Select the attachment style type.

◆ Select the attachment justification type.

◆ Define any offset from the attachment that may be required.

To attach the top of a structural column to a slab, follow these steps:

1. Select the column(s) that will be attached.

2. In the Modify Column panel of the Ribbon, click the Attach button.

3. Select Top on the Options bar.

4. Set the style and justification methods on the Options bar.

5. Select the slab that you will be attaching to.

To attach the bottom of a structural column to the top of a beam, follow these steps:

1. Select the column(s) that will be attached.

2. In the Modify Column panel of the Ribbon, click the Attach button.

3. Select Base on the Options bar.

4. Set the style and justification methods.

5. Select the beam that you will be attaching to.

ATTACHMENT STYLE AND JUSTIFICATION

The style and justifications will react differently depending on the type of element and the material that you are attaching to. Concrete-to-concrete attachments will result in an automatic join in which neither the column nor the target will be cut. A steel column can cut to a steel beam, but a concrete column cannot. We encourage you to spend a few minutes playing around with the different style and justification types to see how they react with various material types and elements. Knowing these limits will help you put constraints in your model that will save you time further into your project. Figure 4.18 shows examples of various style and justification combinations.

FIGURE 4.18
Setting the proper attachment style and justification can eliminate tedious detail cleanup.

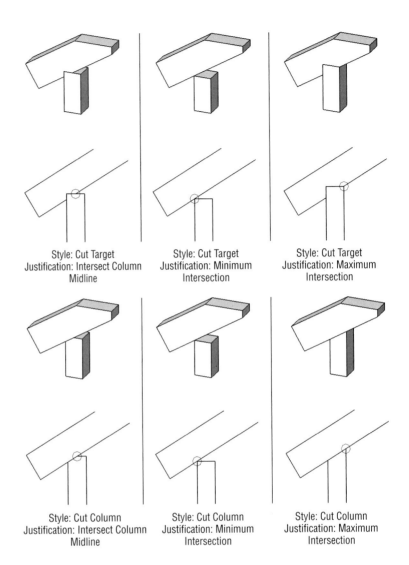

Style: Cut Target
Justification: Intersect Column Midline

Style: Cut Target
Justification: Minimum Intersection

Style: Cut Target
Justification: Maximum Intersection

Style: Cut Column
Justification: Intersect Column Midline

Style: Cut Column
Justification: Minimum Intersection

Style: Cut Column
Justification: Maximum Intersection

EXERCISE: PLACE STRUCTURAL COLUMNS FOR A CONCRETE STRUCTURE

For this exercise you can use the Structural Columns-CONC.rvt file. You will go through the steps of placing columns into your project by placing the first lift and then using the Copy to Clipboard method to place the upper levels. Individual columns will span between each supported level and will be attached to the bottom of the concrete slab.

PLACE COLUMNS USING THE ON GRIDS OPTION

1. Open the Structural Columns-CONC.rvt model.

2. Open the Level 1 view.
   Note: The first lift of columns will go from Level 1 to Level 2.

3. Select the Home tab on the Ribbon and choose the Column drop-down ≻ Structural Column.

4. Select Concrete-Square-Column: 18 x 18 from the Type Selector pull-down.

5. Set the column constraint option to Height and the top constraint to Level 2.

6. For the placement option, choose On Grids.

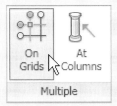

7. Select all grids, from upper right to lower left. Temporary columns will display.

   Alternatively you could create two separate crossing window selections by pressing the Alt key from the keyboard to add the second window selection to your selection. This could eliminate the steps for deleting the columns because you are selecting only those intersections that require columns. There is always more than one way to accomplish a task.

8. Click Finish Selection from the Ribbon to make your selection permanent.

9. Delete the columns on grids A-4, A-5, A-6, B-4, B-5, and B-6.

COPY AND PASTE COLUMNS TO ANOTHER LEVEL

1. Display a 3D view.

2. Select all columns with a crossing window. If more than just the columns are selected, use the Filter Selection tool on the Options bar to select only the columns.

   Using the Filter Selection tool will allow you to include only the elements in your window selection that are in the category that you choose to select in the Filter Selection dialog box.

3. Click Attach from the Modify Column panel of the Ribbon.

4. On the Options bar shown here, attach the column at the top with a style of Do Not Cut and a justification of Intersect Column Midline.

5. Select the bottom of the Level 2 slab.

6. While the columns are still selected, right-click and select Element Properties.

7. Check the parameters for Top Is Attached and Attachment Justification At Top against those shown here, and close the Element Properties dialog box.

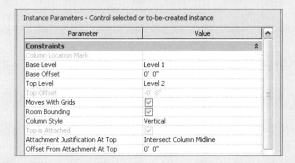

8. Select all columns, if they aren't still selected.

9. Choose Copy from the Clipboard panel on the Ribbon.

10. Choose the Paste Aligned drop-down ➢ Select Levels from the Clipboard panel on the Ribbon, and select Levels 3 through 13.

    If the floor-to-floor heights are the same as the columns you are copying from, then the columns will be placed properly. If not, the columns will be placed with incorrect top or base offset values. Revit Structure will not automatically increase or decrease the height of the column to align with the new levels the column is being associated to.

    For example, if the original columns referenced to Level 2 and Level 3 with a height between them of 10′-0″ were pasted to Level 5 and Level 6 with a height between them of 11′-6″, the pasted columns would be referenced to Level 5 and Level 6 with a Base Offset value of 1′-6″. You would see a gap between the slab and the bottom of the column. These columns would then need to have their Base Offset value reset to 0′-0″. Revit maintains the column height and a relationship with the level above and below, but to do so it must adjust the top or bottom offset parameters relative to the levels in order to maintain the same column height.

11. Verify that all columns are placed correctly.

    The columns that originally had their top attached to Level 2 maintained their top attachment to each level that they were copied to. If any of the slabs change thickness or location, the top of the column will automatically stay attached to the bottom of the slab and update the Top Offset value accordingly. To view a completed model of this exercise, open the Structural Columns-CONC_Complete.rvt file.

Revit Structure is capable of dealing with most of the requirements of how a structural column must perform. The tools provided to place structural columns into your project as well as help maintain their behavior with other elements work in sync with how you need to work with them when you are modeling. Placing a slanted column is one of those examples where Revit Structure offers tools specifically for modeling elements that are more specific to how they perform. Yes, placing a slanted column in many ways is similar to placing a vertical column; however, how it behaves and adapts to changes in the model can be quite different.

THAT ISN'T ALL YOU ARE GOOD FOR

Structural columns don't always have to be used for columns. They can also be used as piers. You would think that a pier would be part of the Foundation or Wall category since that is where a pier is usually placed. Sometimes a pier can be part of a wall, and other times it might act as a column. When piers are part of the Structural Column category, they will behave just like a column. They will show up in the Graphical Column Schedule, they will stay attached to grids, and if placed correctly, they will let isolated footings attach to them automatically. When placed in a wall, they will automatically join to the wall.

Another thing structural columns can be used for is hangers. Hangers might not be classified as a column, but they take on the same shapes and have the same characteristics as far as how you would want to place them. A hanger will still have top and bottom elevations. You can also attach the top of a hanger to the bottom of a beam; when the beam size changes depth, the hanger will adjust with it.

When using structural columns as a pier or a hanger, you might want to rename the family to something closely related to a pier or hanger and assign it to a subcategory so you can more selectively control its visibility and how you work with it inside the project.

Adding Slanted Columns to Your Project

Adding slanted columns into your project is new to this version and thus is much easier to achieve than it was in the past. Slanted columns will behave and react to other framing members the same as vertical columns do. As usual, the Help documentation that comes with Revit Structure is another resource that you should use to further your knowledge of working with slanted columns in your project.

Slanted columns use the same structural column families and tools that you use for placing a vertical column. They have the same properties along with a few added ones that are specific to their slanted nature that control how they behave when changes occur. You can create slanted columns by changing the properties of an existing vertical column or by creating a new one using the Slanted Column tool. To begin the placement of a slanted column, choose the Structural Column tool from the Home tab ➤ Structure panel ➤ Column drop-down. After the Structural Column tool is selected, you will see the Ribbon switch to a Place Structural Column contextual tab, shown in Figure 4.19 and Figure 4.20. The tools that are displayed and available to use in this contextual tab vary depending on what type of view you are currently in. Vertical columns need to be placed in a view that has its work plane set horizontal or perpendicular to the column, typically a section/elevation or 3D view. Slanted columns need to be placed in a view that has its work plane set vertical or parallel to the column. Therefore these tools are available only in the views that meet these criteria. A 3D view meets both criteria, so both tools are available.

FIGURE 4.19
The Place Structural Column contextual tab while in a plan view (Slanted Column tool is grayed out)

FIGURE 4.20
The Place Structural Column contextual tab while in a section or elevation view (Vertical Column tool is grayed out)

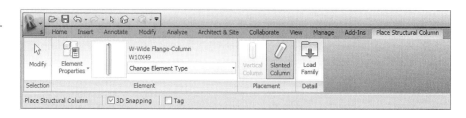

Within this contextual tab you will see the Slanted Column tool. You will also see the same Type Selector that is used for placing vertical columns as well as the Load Family tool for loading new structural column families. As we said before, slanted columns use the same families as vertical columns; it is their method of placement that is different. Depending on the view you are in while placing them, you will find different options available on the Options bar.

WHY ARE MY SLANTED COLUMNS NOT IN THE GRAPHICAL COLUMN SCHEDULE?

In the first release of Revit Structure 2010, slanted columns do not have a column location mark. Without the column location mark, slanted columns cannot be shown in the Graphical Column Schedule. This is currently a limitation, but hopefully it will be resolved in a future version. Remember, all good things have to start somewhere.

Placing Slanted Columns in a Section or Elevation View

Selecting the Slanted Column tool while in a section or elevation view requires only a few settings from the Option bar, as shown in Figure 4.20, such as choosing 3D Snapping and whether you want it to be tagged. Placing the column is a two-click process. Each of your pick points represents the top or base of the column depending on which point is higher. The endpoint at the higher elevation is the top, and the lower elevation is the base.

Prior to picking your points, you will also want to set the work plane that the column is to be placed on, or it will be assigned to an unassociated plane that will not be your expected location. If you are in a section or elevation view, you will need to tell Revit Structure which plane to place the column on. In most cases this will be a grid, so your view should be such that it is looking parallel to the grid you will be placing it on. To set the work plane choose the Home tab ➤ Work Plane panel ➤ Set tool while in the view where you will be placing the slanted column. The Work Plane dialog box appears, as shown in Figure 4.21, where you can set the work plane (via several options) for the slanted column to be placed on.

Once the work plane is set, you are ready to place the column. Figure 4.22 shows before and after placing a slanted column in a section or elevation view. This method is rather simple and similar to placing them in a 3D view.

WHAT IS THE MAGIC IN A FRAMING ELEVATION?

Before you can place a framing elevation, you must have a grid or named reference plane established for it to associate itself to. This sets the work plane for the framing elevations to the grid or reference plane you select to place it by. Creating a framing elevation for placing slanted columns can be a good way to set and maintain the proper work plane placement.

FIGURE 4.21
Setting the work plane of a view to Grid 1

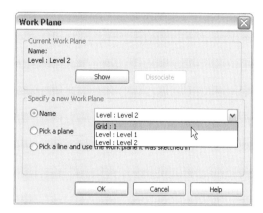

FIGURE 4.22
Before and after placing a slanted column in a section or elevation view

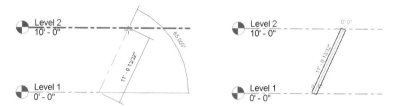

Placing Slanted Columns in a 3D View

Placing slanted columns in a 3D view is similar to the method we just discussed in the previous section for placing them in a section or elevation view. There is no need to specify a work plane because you will be making your top and base point selections by choose the 3D points of elements already placed into the model. Using a 3D view allows you to visualize how the slanted column is going to appear in your model as well as provides the ability to snap to the 3D points on other elements. In a scenario where the top and base of the slanted column may not share the same work plane, placing them in a 3D view is much easier. The process for starting the tool is the same (choose the Home tab ➤ Structure panel ➤ Column drop-down ➤ Structural Column tool, and choose the Slanted Column tool from the contextual tab). The options available in the Options bar are much different, as you can see in Figure 4.23. Here you can set the first and second click levels as well as an offset value for each level.

FIGURE 4.23
Several different options are available on the Options bar when placing slanted columns in 3D view.

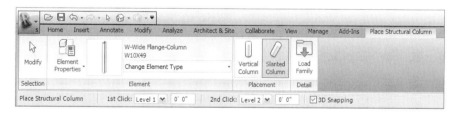

The tools for placing slanted columns into your project are easy to work with. Understanding the properties that control vertical and slanted columns will aid in your ability to work with them. The Column Style parameter, which Revit Structure uses to determine these properties, can be used to convert a vertical column into a slanted column without having to replace it.

Properties of a Slanted Column

Columns that are slanted automatically take on several additional parameters that are not available when a column is defined as vertical. These parameters vary depending on how the columns are placed and how they are positioned in the model. The major parameter that controls these properties is the Column Style parameter, shown in Figure 4.24. You have three options to choose from: Vertical, Slanted - Angle Driven, and Slanted - End Point Driven.

FIGURE 4.24

Setting the column style from the Instance Properties dialog box of a structural column

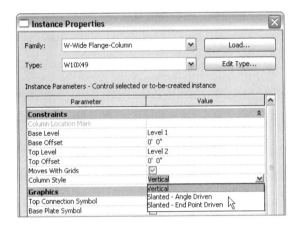

This is where you can change a vertical column to take on properties of a slanted column, which also enables type-specific modification tools. In some cases you may find that not all of the styles may be available. This is because some styles are not available when certain relationships are detected. For instance, slanted columns attached or joined at their top and base default to the Slanted - End Point Driven column style. The Slanted - Angle Driven column style is restricted to columns without joins or only a single join at their top or base. Changing the relationship so it meets these requirements allows the column style to become available for selection. You can find much more information regarding these joins and the behavior of the relationships between columns and other elements by going to the Slanted Structural Column Attachments and Joins section in Revit Structure's Help documentation.

ANGLE OR ENDPOINT DRIVEN? WHAT'S THE DIFFERENCE?

Two styles of columns are available for determining a slanted column. Their difference is in how they lock the geometry of the column's top and base endpoints, which defines the slant (slope) of the column. When the elevation of one of these points changes, how should the change affect the column's location?

SLANTED - ANGLE DRIVEN

If Column Style is set to Slanted - Angle Driven, it will maintain the angle of the column as the top or base endpoints are adjusted in elevation. The following image shows how a Slanted - Angle Driven column behaves when Level 2 is adjusted from 10'-0" to 14'-0"; the 60-degree slope is held and the base-to-top horizontal offset is revised. Given its name, you might think that you need to define the angle, but don't be fooled. Revit Structure simply focuses on maintaining the angle defined by the original position of the column when its top or base constraints are altered, whatever that angle may be.

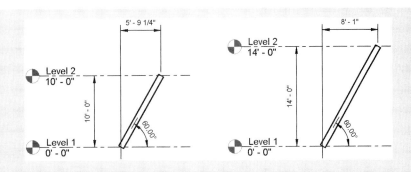

SLANTED - END POINT DRIVEN

If Column Style is set to Slanted - End Point Driven, it will maintain the horizontal offset of the base and top endpoints of the column as the top or base endpoints are adjusted in elevation. The following image shows how a Slanted - End Point Driven column behaves when Level 2 is adjusted from 10′-0″ to 14′-0″; the 60-degree slope is altered and the base-to-top horizontal offset is held.

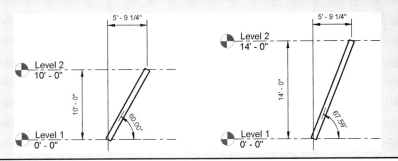

Column that are set to a slanted column style inherit additional parameters such as Move Top With Grids and Move Base With Grids, as shown in Figure 4.25. These parameters allow you to set the constraints of the top or base endpoints of the slanted columns to a grid. If the grid moves, the default is to move the top and base of the column with it.

As these columns become attached to other elements such as structural floors, roofs, foundation slabs, and reference planes or joined to other slanted columns, beams, and walls, additional parameters populate the columns' properties. Figure 4.26 shows the properties of a slanted column that is attached and joined to other framing members at its top and base endpoints.

As you can see, it is now quite easy to work with slanted columns in Revit Structure, much easier than it was in previous versions. Joins, attachment, and the behavior of the slanted columns when changes are made are not always what you would expect. This is not to be looked at as a negative but as a positive with regard to how Revit Structure now acknowledges slanted columns, which is much better than previous methods, such as using component families, in-place families, bracing, and other workarounds to create them. You also do not have the ability to take advantage of scheduling a slanted column in a Graphical Column Schedule, but you will be able to take advantage of those columns that are placed with a vertical style. Learning to use the Graphical Column Schedule to document these columns or to manipulate your model as it evolves will allow you to be more efficient as well as take advantage of Revit Structure's BIM capabilities.

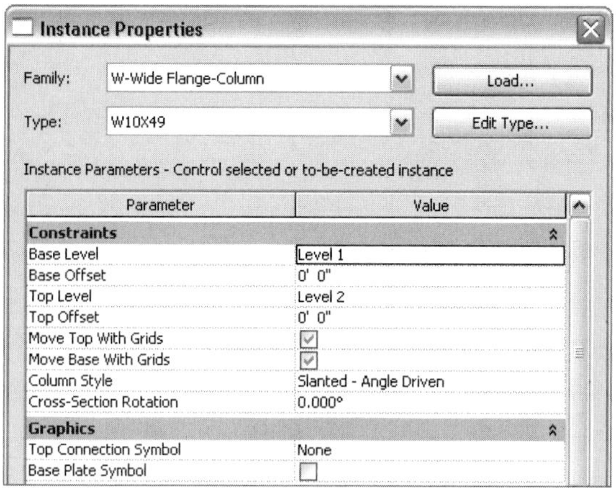

FIGURE 4.25
Setting the top and base of a slanted column's constraints to a grid in its Instance Properties dialog box

FIGURE 4.26
When slanted columns' top and base are attached to other elements, several properties become available to control their position.

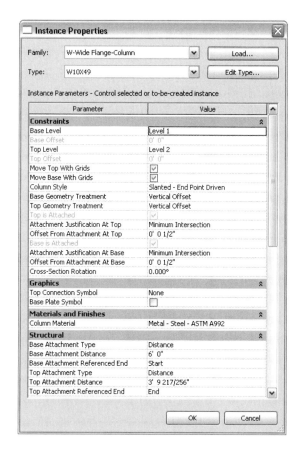

HMMM, A WALL FOR A COLUMN

If you are trying to model a concrete column that includes a taper, slope, or other odd configuration, consider using a wall. You can duplicate a wall and assign it a specific name, like Sloped Column - 24″. The wall can be modeled to the extent of the column shape, and then you can edit the profile of the wall by choosing Edit Profile from the contextual tab on the Ribbon when the wall is selected. In Edit mode, you can add, remove, or rework sketch lines to produce the shape of the column. Here is an example of a concrete sloped column with a concrete beam running over its top. The slanted column is modeled as a wall with its profile edited to create the shape of the column.

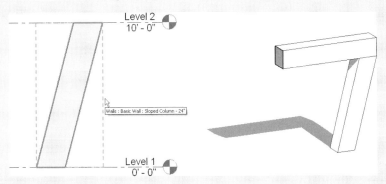

This method will give you a column with the appearance of a sloped concrete column, but it will still have the properties of a wall and schedule as a wall. You can generate other forms with this method. If you are looking only for appearance, then this might work for you.

Using a Graphical Column Schedule

As you probably already know, a Graphical Column Schedule (GCS) is extremely useful for describing the size, reinforcing, and connection information for columns on a multistory structure in an elevated graphical display rather than the standard method of using a mark number and text-only schedule. Revit Structure automatically keeps track of any structural column that is placed in your project and links it to a grid intersection. If it is not on a grid, Revit Structure will link the column to the nearest grid. Not only can the GCS shown in Figure 4.27 be used to document the information pertaining to your structural columns, but it can also be used to keep track of information while you are working and help maintain the integrity of your model.

Since GCSs are a completely different schedule (they are a hybrid of a schedule and many little section views) than Revit Structure's Standard Schedule, they get their own category in the Project Browser called Graphical Column Schedule. (We'll discuss how to create a Standard Schedule in Chapter 11.)

The basic procedure to create a GCS goes like this:

1. Select the View tab ➢ Create panel ➢ Schedules drop-down ➢ Graphical Column Schedule.

Note that if gridlines are not present in your project or the 3D extents of at least two grid intersections do not cross the plane of a structural column, you'll see the warning, "No columns are joined to grid lines, or view parameters exclude all columns." Revit Structure will create a new GCS view but will not generate a schedule displaying column information.

2. Right-click the new GCS view in the Project Browser and select Properties, or right-click anywhere in the view itself and select View Properties.

3. Make changes to the view's properties to give it the final look you want.

4. Once the GCS is placed on a sheet, change the settings to allow you to split the schedule onto multiple sheets. (You can learn more about placing GCSs on sheets in Chapter 12.)

With the GCS, you have access to only a few settings that will allow you to tweak the appearance of the schedule and control the type of columns that will show up in the schedule. There are other approaches that allow you to control the display of the graphics in the schedule, as you'll see in the next section.

Setting the Appearance

In the Instance Properties dialog box of the GCS (see Figure 4.28), you will find most of the settings for adjusting its appearance and how the information in the schedule displays. We will step through a few of the primary controls to show you how they affect the schedule's display.

The GCS has the same basic properties of any other view that Revit Structure creates, and the properties behave pretty much the same way. There are View Scale, Visibility/Graphic Overrides, Detail Level, and Discipline options. If you set Detail Level to Coarse, Revit Structure will display steel shapes as symbolic lines and include symbol representation for the top and base of column connections. You can apply view templates to the schedule, and it can have its own title separate from the title on the sheet.

COLUMN LOCATIONS PER SEGMENT

Some projects have several grid intersections with columns, which can make your schedules quite lengthy. For this reason, you can set the number of vertical rows to display in the schedule (Figure 4.29) before the schedule automatically splits into a new segment (it remains part of the same schedule). When you modify Column Locations per Segment, you are specifying the maximum number of vertical rows you want to display.

GROUP SIMILAR LOCATIONS

Select the option Group Similar Locations to combine columns that have the same (exact) information into the same vertical row (Figure 4.30). The Group Similar Locations option can also be used to change the properties of a group of structural columns all at once. This approach may be easier than selecting columns one-by-one and changing their properties.

FIGURE 4.28
Changing the properties of a Graphical Column Schedule

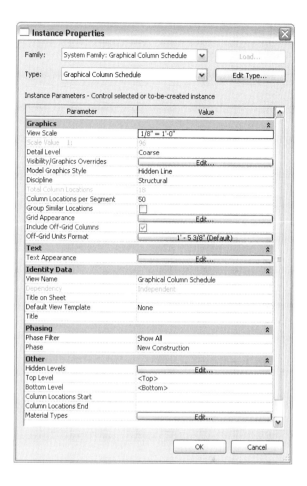

GRID APPEARANCE

The Grid Appearance tab, shown in Figure 4.31, appears when you click the Edit button for the Grid Appearance parameter in the Instance Properties dialog box for the GCS. You may have to adjust the Horizontal Widths options of the vertical rows to accommodate level names that are too long to display legibly in the schedule. Perhaps you may have to widen the vertical rows where the graphics of the structural columns display to provide adequate room for text in tags.

You may also have to adjust two of the Vertical Heights options, Above Top Level and Below Bottom Level, when structural columns exceed the GCS's upper or lower boundaries. As Figure 4.32 shows, the columns in the GCS are shown at their modeled size and length when a column is dropped well below Level 1 for a utility pipe.

The last setting in the Vertical Height options is called Between Segments. Use it to set the dimensions between columns that are broken up into multiple segments, as shown in Figure 4.29. Breaking them into multiple segments will shorten the overall width, thus allowing you to put more than one schedule on a sheet while keeping all information inside one schedule.

FIGURE 4.29
A GCS split into five segments with a vertical height between them of 1/2″

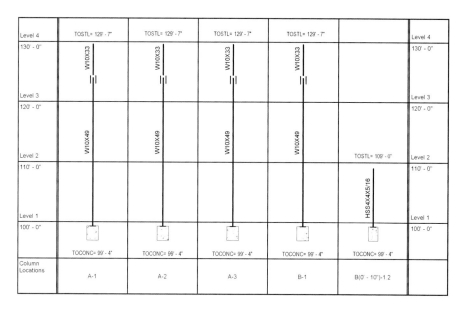

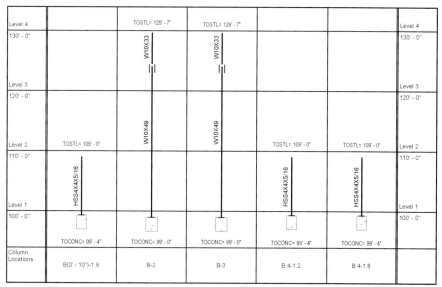

THIN LINE = GCS OUTLINE AND GRIDLINES

You can set the line weight thickness of the Graphical Column Schedule's outline and gridlines by opening the Visibility/Graphic Overrides dialog box for the view and selecting the Model Categories tab. Expand the Lines category, and for the subcategory Thin Lines, modify the Project Line value.

FIGURE 4.30
A GCS with Group Similar Locations checked can eliminate redundant cell values.

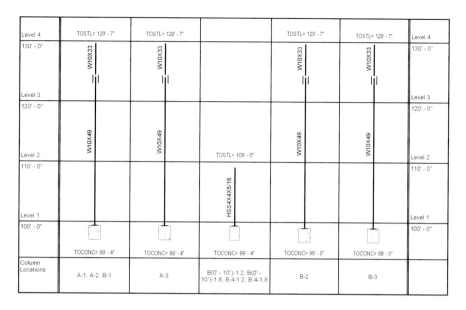

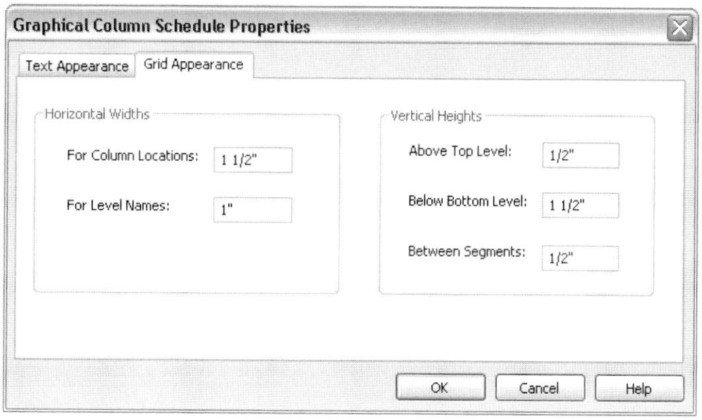

FIGURE 4.31
Setting the grid appearance of the GCS

TEXT APPEARANCE

The Text Appearance tab, shown in Figure 4.33, appears when you click the Edit button for the Text Appearance parameter in the Instance Properties dialog box for the GCS. You have seen several images in previous sections that show ways you can display the line work and column information for a GCS. Here you can also make changes to the automatic text that Revit Structure displays in the schedule.

Another way to fit level names that are too long to display legibly in the vertical level row of the GCS is to adjust the text's Width Factor value. When you are grouping similar columns, you can also do this in the Column Location field. This allows you to fit more grid intersections in the box without having to adjust the width of the grid intersection location row. You can set other text formats, such as bold, italic, and underline, to help achieve the look you want.

FIGURE 4.32
When columns exceed the segment's lower bounds of the GCS, adjust the vertical height of the Below Bottom Level value in the properties of the GCS.

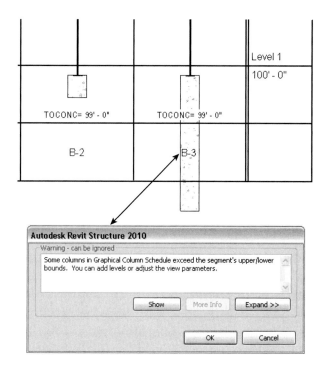

FIGURE 4.33
Setting the text appearance of the GCS

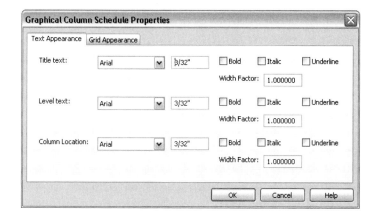

HIDDEN LEVELS

Clicking the Edit button of the Hidden Levels option in the Instance Properties dialog box of a GCS takes you to the Levels Hidden in Graphical Column Schedules dialog box, shown in Figure 4.34. Here you can turn off the display of a level by clicking its check box. All levels will appear in the schedule regardless of their 3D extents. For example, if you have created levels in your project for the sole purpose of tying together geometry or have levels for both top of slab and steel, select these levels so that Revit Structure will hide them in the GCS.

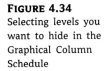

FIGURE 4.34
Selecting levels you want to hide in the Graphical Column Schedule

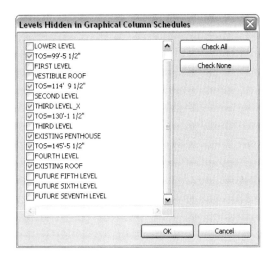

TOP AND BOTTOM LEVELS

By default, Revit Structure displays the lowest (bottom) and highest (top) levels in the GCS. You can modify the Bottom Level and Top Level settings to display only columns between a specific set of levels.

For example, suppose you have all the columns modeled on your project and you have to issue a Foundation package. You want to include structural column information for only the first lift of columns to obtain dowel reinforcing or anchor rod information. Set Bottom Level to Level 1 and Top Level to Level 2. With these settings, the GCS will show only column information for columns between Levels 1 and 2. When the next issue comes and you need to include the additional column information, you can change the Top Level setting back to the default.

Here's another example: Suppose you want to schedule only the penthouse columns on Level 10. To do so, set Bottom Level to Level 10 and Top Level to Penthouse Roof.

COLUMN LOCATIONS START AND END

The Column Locations Start and End options work in a similar way to the Top Level and Bottom Level settings, except that they use the grid intersections. You can specify a grid intersection to start from and one to end with.

For example, suppose you have three zones, Zone A, Zone B, and Zone C, and you want to separate your GCS into three different zone-specific schedules. This separation helps anyone reading the documents to easily find the grid intersection. For each GCS, set the Column Locations Start and End options to show only the extent of grid intersections for each particular zone.

Once you have the overall look of the GCS in place and you have it set up the way you want, you can move on to adding annotations to display structural column properties that you need for documentation or to put information into the model.

Annotating a GCS

The biggest display of annotations in the GCS is the tagging that pulls information from the column's properties. Any information that is part of the column's properties can be displayed with a tag that has a direct link to a particular parameter. Another form of annotation is the use of spot elevations for indicating the top or bottom of column elevations. A third form is that steel shapes display symbolic connection symbols when the view's Detail Level is set to Coarse.

These three annotation methods automatically adjust when the GCS changes form or when columns shift within it. Tags and spot dimensions maintain their relationship to the columns as other columns are added to the schedule, forcing them to shift down the line. You can add normal text as annotations, but this text will not move as the schedule changes. You will have to visually check the text for proper placement and manually move it.

TAGGING

Most of the parameters that you tag are either project or shared parameters. When creating such parameters, you must specify Instance or Type. You establish each parameter depending on the type of project and the various stages of packages you need to issue.

Figure 4.35 shows a typical steel column, which can display information such as the following:

◆ Size of the member

◆ Base plate size

◆ Anchor rod size

◆ Anchor rod embedment length

◆ Layout type

FIGURE 4.35
Placing text parameters into steel column families to create tags to display base plate information in a GCS

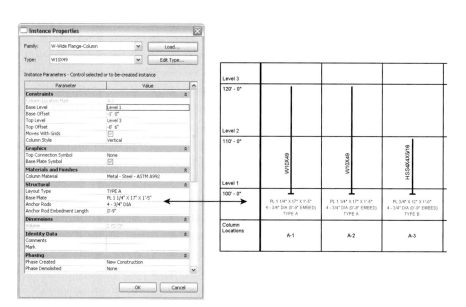

Figure 4.36 shows a typical concrete column, which can display information such as this:

◆ Size of the member

◆ Vertical reinforcing

◆ Tie reinforcing

◆ Layout type

◆ Dowel reinforcing at foundation

FIGURE 4.36
Placing text
parameters
into concrete
column fami-
lies to create
tags to dis-
play reinforcing
information in
a GCS

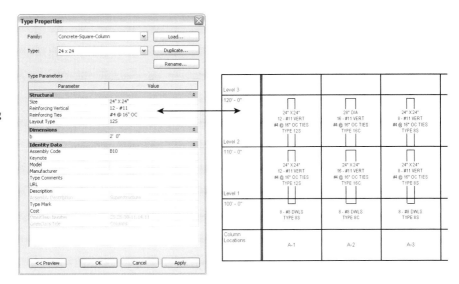

You add text parameters for this information to the structural column families. Tag families are created with labels that pull the required information from the properties of the columns to be displayed in the GCS. You can combine multiple labels inside one tag as well as add a prefix and/or suffix to the information that is being display. For example, within the properties of the column you can specify an anchor rod's information and its embedment as two separate parameters. The value for the embedment can only read 0'-9". When you create the label, you can string the two parameters together with a suffix so it all reads continuously on one line as 4 - 3/4" DIA (0'-9" EMBED). The same method can be applied for information in concrete columns such as VERTI-CAL and OC TIES. It is not necessary to call this out in the parameter value when it is already mentioned in the parameter name. Build it directly into the tag.

WIDE FLANGE COLUMNS DON'T HAVE TIE REINFORCING

When adding text parameters to columns as project parameters, you can select only the Structural Column category. This means that you may be adding concrete reinforcing parameters for concrete columns, but the parameters are also going to show up in any steel, precast, or wood columns that you have in your project. Creating shared parameters and placing this specific information directly into the family itself prevents unnecessary information from showing up in the column's properties.

SPOT ELEVATIONS

You can add spot elevations to the GCS by selecting the Annotate tab on the Ribbon and choosing Spot Elevation from the Dimension panel. As Figure 4.37 shows, not only can you use spot elevations to indicate the top and bottom elevations of columns and any other elevations that you need for documentation, but you can also use them to help control the placement of the column geometry in the model. A GCS you create simply to help control the placement of the column geometry and serve as a model consistency check can be maintained easily.

FIGURE 4.37
Using spot elevations in a GCS can help you annotate live information from the modeled geometry.

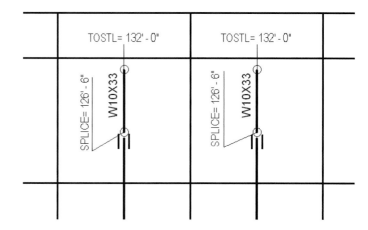

SPLICE AND BASE PLATE SYMBOLS

You know that Revit Structure displays symbolic symbols for steel shapes and their connection types in other views when they are set to a coarse detail level; the GCS does the same thing. Chapter 2 describes in great depth how Revit Structure controls these symbols for a structural column and how to create new ones as well as set their display for a project. Since structural steel is usually shown with single symbolic line work, these symbols are available only when you're working with steel shapes or families that have Structural Material set to Steel. If available for a structural column, these symbols can be found in the Graphics group of the column's properties. Making use of their display in the GCS will put the finishing touches on a well-displayed and well-documented schedule.

MODELING BASE PLATES

Revit Structure offers families for placing base plates as modeled geometry into your project. You can load these families from the Imperial Library\Structural\Connections folder. These families are face based and are part of the Structural Connection category. We attempt to take these families to the next level so we can schedule them and so they can serve as an interference check for the architect when plates and bolts tend to project outside a wall or column enclosure.

We continue to experiment with placing base plates as modeled geometry in each project, along with using text-based parameters in schedules for our documentation. Typically each new version lets us take this concept a bit further. Modeling base plates is probably not a wise approach for all your projects, so do it selectively. Keep in mind that modeling this amount of detail in a large project can decrease the performance of the model. We feel that eventually the software will catch up to this level of detail, so we are trying to dig in at whatever level we can to keep the BIM method of thinking going.

For example, we decided to develop anchor rod and a base plate families and set each as shared in the properties. We nested the new families inside the base plate connection family so that we can place them into a project as base plate connections. Since we specified these families as shared, they show up as individual families under Structural Connections in the Project Browser, as shown here. Therefore, we can easily duplicate them and create new sizes as needed.

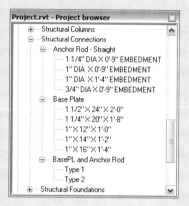

In the base plate connection family, we can select the anchor rod and base plate types (using a Family Type parameter) to create base plate connection types, which we can then schedule. These families eventually can become attached to columns when we place them into a project. Here is the overall look of the concept.

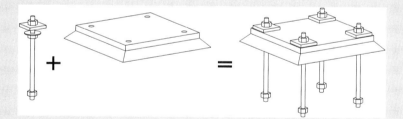

This is now a pretty advanced family and reacts well when properties of the elements change. When the anchor rod size changes, the grout changes with it, and the holes in the base plate change in size accordingly. Also, when the base plate changes size, the anchor rods and its components change with it. Visibility and subcategories are also assigned to the different components. This way, only the base plate displays at the medium detail level; everything shows up at the fine detail level. We can turn off components in the Visibility/Graphic Overrides dialog box of the view from the subcategory setup.

We continue to look at this concept, and the process still has a few kinks we need to work out. A few questions come up. For example, should this base plate, grout, and anchor rod be part of the column family, or should it be a stand-alone connection as it currently is? What happens when there are more than four anchor rods? We hope that the ability to push the limits of Revit Structure in this way will eventually become part of the GCS.

Displaying Structural Columns

As you can guess by the name Graphical Column Schedule, all columns displayed are graphically shown as their geometry. Earlier we discussed setting the appearance of the columns: We explained how you can set a steel column to display as a symbolic line, and you learned that concrete columns are usually shown as double lines. Now let's discuss what you do once the columns are actually in the schedule.

What determines that a column is put into the schedule? What do you do if columns don't show up in the schedule? What happens when you don't want certain columns to show up in the schedule? These are questions that you are going to want answers for when you're working with a GCS. Knowing these answers will help you create your schedules quickly and ensure that only the desired columns display.

STRUCTURAL COLUMNS THAT ARE OFFSET FROM THE GRID

Revit Structure gives you the ability to display only those columns that are on grids or those that are offset, and it still gives those columns a location mark based on the grid names that are intersecting them. Revit Structure creates the location marks automatically using a set of rules. In some cases, the program tries to be flexible in allowing you to choose what is displayed. After determining the best grid to reference, Revit Structure displays this value in the properties of the columns, under the Constraints group in the Column Location Mark parameter. If more than one grid can be referenced to the offset column, Revit Structure allows you to select which column location mark you want to display. Figures 4.38 and 4.39 show that the read-only behavior of this parameter changes depending on where the column is located.

FIGURE 4.38
The Column Location Mark parameter sometimes displays as a read-only value.

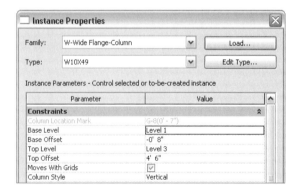

Automatically scheduling offset columns, determining their location mark, and giving the user a bit of flexibility can be complex. You may have to resort to other methods to get the GCS to perform the way you want it to.

Automatic Scheduling of Off-Grid Columns

In the properties of a GCS, you can choose Include Off-Grid Columns. With this option checked, all columns — regardless of their placement on a grid — should be placed in the GCS as long as the 3D extents of the grids cross the horizontal and vertical planes of the column(s). Revit Structure will continue to give the offset column a location mark referencing the closest grid intersection based on a set of calculations.

Figure 4.40 shows that if an offset column's bounding box (the extent of its geometry) intersects or its edges touch a grid, its location mark will reference the closest grid intersection.

FIGURE 4.39
The Column Location Mark parameter's read-only behavior is sometimes removed to allow you to select a different location mark.

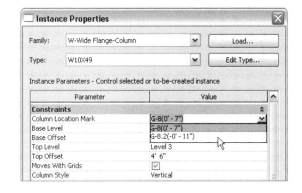

FIGURE 4.40
Offset columns with a bounding box intersecting the grid have a normal location mark.

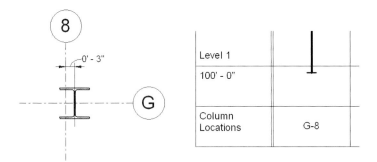

Figure 4.41 shows that if an offset column's bounding box (the extent of its geometry) does not intersect or its edges do not touch a grid, its location mark will reference the closest grid intersection, with an added annotation indicating the offset from the referenced grid.

FIGURE 4.41
Offset columns with a bounding box not intersecting the grid are noted with an added dimension in the location mark.

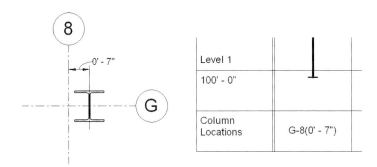

Also included in the properties of the GCS is a setting called Off-Grid Units Format. This setting, which behaves just like any other unit format override (similar to dimensions), is located just below the Include Off-Grid Columns parameter. This override allows you to have some control over the display of the offset dimension value that is placed after the grid mark in the Column Locations row.

WHAT DETERMINES THE OFFSET COLUMN LOCATION MARK?

Revit Structure calculates which grids the offset column is closest to and assigns to the column those grids for a location mark. To learn about these calculations, in Revit Structure's Help guides search for "Determining off-grid column location marks."

How the GCS displays and annotates offset columns may not be to everyone's liking. Remember that a simple rotation or size modification of an offset column can change what gets displayed for its Column Location in the GCS. An offset column is not necessarily denoted as being offset. To avoid this behavior, sometimes a quick duplication and modification to an already created structural column family will do the trick. If that doesn't quite work, you might want to try creating extra grids that will keep the column on a grid intersection. Any of these methods will work, but you will have to decide which one is best for each particular project.

Modifying the Family

In this first method we'll discuss how you make a few quick edits to an existing column family (or if you are creating your own family, keep these edits in mind). In short, you will make changes to the column family that allow Revit Structure to shift what it considers the center of the column. Make sure that you are not making changes to the normal structural column family, but that you save this family under a different name using a suffix of -Offset or something similar. One of the rules for displaying a structural column in a GCS is that it must be centered on a grid intersection (unless you have the Include Off-Grid Columns parameter checked). We'll make a few quick edits to a duplicated structural column family so it has instance parameters to adjust the location of the Center (Left/Right) and Center (Front/Back) reference planes inside the structural column family. The basic procedure looks like this:

1. Edit or open a column family that will be uniquely named for its offset behavior.

2. While in the floor plan view: Lower Ref. Level, create new reference planes parallel to both of the Center (Left/Right) and Center (Front/Back) reference planes.

   You can find these reference planes by viewing their properties and looking at the Is Reference value. These reference planes should currently be placed at the center of the column.

3. In the properties of the new reference planes, reassign the Is Reference values to the appropriate center name in the pull-down menu and select the Defines Origin check box.

   This step will automatically set the old reference planes located at the center of the column to Not a Reference and set the origin of the column to the new reference planes' intersections.

4. Place a dimension between both of the reference planes, as shown in Figure 4.42, and add an Instance parameter label to them defining the column offset.

After loading the family into the project, you can use your new family when you want to display an offset column. Just make sure that you are placing the column so the reference planes in the family that are defined as the origin are located on the grids that create the intersection. If using this method is not feasible, consider using another grid type as a centerline and using a unique grid name mark to display in the GCS.

FIGURE 4.42
Redefining the column
centerline reference
planes and origin in a
structural column family

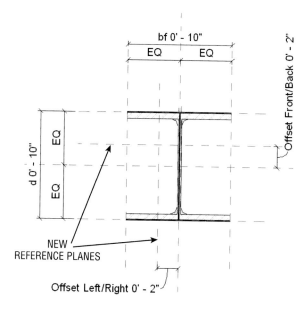

WHY THE WORKAROUND?

Revit Structure automatically schedules offset columns in the GCS. You also have the option to not
display the offset columns in the schedule. But like anything else, there will be cases where Revit
Structure's automatic methods do not perform to your standards. In such cases, you can resort to
other workarounds that go beyond the current capabilities of Revit Structure.

Using a Grid as a Centerline

In our next example, you create a new grid type by duplicating your standard one and naming
it something like Centerline. Set its Type Parameter: Symbol value to None so you will see the
gridline only when you place it in your project. Assign a color to it so it stands out from your
normal grid when viewing it on screen. Place your offset columns on this grid line. Since it is still a
grid, you will have to give it a name and set its 3D extents. If the grid you want to associate it to is
named Grid C-2 and its offset is from Grid C, then you could name the Centerline C* or something
similar. It would then show up in the GCS as C*-2, as shown in Figure 4.43.

You can add a note to the bottom of the schedule that states something like this: "Columns
shown in schedule with '*' after the grid name indicates columns that have been offset from a
grid. See plan for offset dimension." This approach allows you to see the offset centerline in all
views because it behaves as a grid; since the grid type is not assigned a symbol, the bubbles will
not display either. An offset column usually needs a centerline to denote its offset dimension,
which makes this method easy because you don't have to place a separate detail line in every view
in which you need to show the column.

FIGURE 4.43
Creating a new grid type along with a unique grid name to schedule offset columns

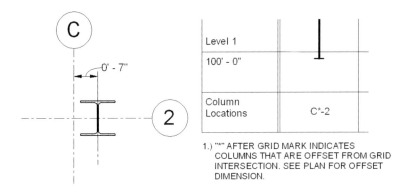

1.) "*" AFTER GRID MARK INDICATES COLUMNS THAT ARE OFFSET FROM GRID INTERSECTION. SEE PLAN FOR OFFSET DIMENSION.

WHY ARE SOME COLUMNS MISSING IN MY GCS?

There are times when a column appears to be on a grid intersection but doesn't appear in the GCS. Even if a column isn't on a grid, it should at least show up if you've selected Include Off-Grid Columns in the properties. If this is the case, you might want to check the 3D extents of the grids. In order for a column to be referenced to a grid intersection, at least two intersecting grids' 3D extents must cross the column's plane. The 3D extents might cross in the horizontal (plan) direction but might not be pulled high or low enough to intersect its plane in the vertical direction. It could also be the other way around.

Remember, grids have a 2D extent and a 3D extent. The 2D extent is specific to the view in which it is being displayed. This sometimes makes it misleading in looking like the grid is intersecting the column. Cut a couple of quick sections that look perpendicular to the grids that are intersecting to see if this is the problem. In order to see the grid you must be cutting a section that is directly perpendicular to the grid, and its 3D extents must be in your view extents. You may have to cut several sections before you can actually see the grid.

If you go through all of the motions, everything checks out, and you still can't figure out why your columns are not showing up in the GCS, you should also check the Column Style setting in the column's Instance parameters. This setting may have been switched to a slanted style, which does not allow the column to be scheduled. A column can still be modeled vertical while being set to a slanted style as well.

USING A COLUMN'S STRUCTURAL MATERIAL TYPE

Earlier we discussed setting the Structural Material property for a structural column family. Not only does this setting dictate how members frame to the column or how it displays in views, but it can be used to display or not display columns in the GCS. To use the Structural Material property to display columns in a GCS, first open the GCS's Element Properties dialog box. Under the group Other, you will find an Edit button. Click this button to open the dialog box shown in Figure 4.44. By default, Revit Structure has all five material types checked. Deselect any you don't want to include in that GCS.

This method of displaying columns can be useful when you have certain columns with material types that you don't want to appear in the GCS. Maybe you have a few wood columns scattered

FIGURE 4.44
You can remove columns from the GCS based on their structural material type.

throughout a project or a concrete structure that has a few steel columns that will be scheduled in a Basic Schedule. Deselecting those structural material types will remove them from the schedule.

If you want only a portion of those steel, wood, or concrete columns removed, you will have to apply phasing or some additional filters to remove them in a more selective way.

APPLYING PHASES

Applying phases to a GCS works the same way that it does when applying them to other views. The GCS provides a phase and a phase filter that you can apply to help drive which columns will be displayed. We'll discuss phases in much greater depth in Chapter 16. The same methods and procedures discussed in that chapter can be applied to the GCS.

You can use phases to help control the visibility of existing columns in the GCS. This is probably the easiest way to remove them from the schedule (as long as you are assigning these elements to the Existing phase by setting the Phase Created parameter to Existing). Follow these steps:

1. In the properties of the existing column, make sure the Phase Created parameter is set to Existing.

2. Right-click in the GCS's view and select View Properties, or right-click on the GCS's name in the Project Browser and select Properties.

3. Set the value of the Phase Filter option located in the Phase group to Show New. Click OK to go back to your GCS.

4. Those columns for which you set the Phase Created parameter to Existing have disappeared from the schedule.

You can use phases to display columns in the GCS depending on the project stage. You may even create schedules just to see how columns are modeled or to reveal the various stages at which they will be issued. When using phasing does not quite get you 100 percent satisfaction, you can apply filters, as you'll see next.

APPLYING FILTERS

Filters let you be a bit more selective in determining what columns show up in the GCS and — in some cases — *how* they display inside it. Filters can be a selection of elements that you save or a set of rules that you put in place to determine what is put into a selection set as your model progresses. Figure 4.45 shows a Define Criteria filter called Do Not Schedule that does the following: It finds all the project elements from the Structural Columns category, and if the value of an element's Comments parameter equals Do Not Schedule, then that element becomes part of the selection set. As this parameter value changes, columns continue to be added or removed from the selection set that the filter creates. This can be a much better method than just saving a selection set and manually having to add and remove elements as they are modeled in your project.

FIGURE 4.45
Using a Defined Criteria filter allows you to selectively display columns in a GCS.

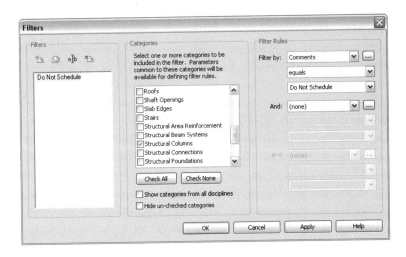

After your filter is created, you will have to apply it to the GCS view using the Visibility/Graphic Overrides dialog box.

To make a Selection Set filter, perform the following steps:

1. Select the elements that you want to be part of the set.

2. Choose the View tab ➤ Graphics panel ➤ Filters tool.

3. In the Filters dialog box click the New button to create a new filter.

4. Give the Selection Set filter a name that reflects its purpose and choose Use Current Selection. If elements are not selected, you can choose Select to be given the option to make a selection.

5. Continue to click OK to close out of all open dialog boxes to finish.

Then you have to apply this filter to a view in the Visibility/Graphic Overrides dialog box.

To create a Defined Criteria filter (which is rule-based), follow these steps:

1. Choose the View tab ➤ Graphics panel ➤ Filters tool.

2. In the Filters dialog box click the New button to create a new filter.

3. Select the Define Criteria option and assign your filter an appropriate name.

4. Apply the appropriate settings (such as the categories that the filter will apply to), and then specify any rules that will apply to the filter.

5. Continue to click OK to close out of all open dialog boxes to finish.

After you save your filter, you can add or remove elements or change the filter rules (choose the View tab ➤ Graphics panel ➤ Filters tool). Select the filter and click the Edit tab. If the filter is a Define Criteria filter, it will display the Filters dialog box, where you can change its rules. If it's a Selection set filter, you will be put into Selection Edit mode, and the Ribbon will show options for adding or removing elements from the selection.

To apply a filter to a GCS view, perform these steps:

1. While in the properties of the GCS view, click the Edit button next to the Visibility/Graphic Overrides parameter.

2. Select the Filter tab at the top of the dialog box to access the filter settings.

3. Click the Add button to add an already created filter or click Edit/New to create a new one.

4. After you add the filter on the Filter tab, you can make changes to the filter's elements.

5. Deselecting the Visibility option will remove any structural columns that are part of the filter from the GCS. You can also apply other override settings to change the look of the graphics of the scheduled columns.

Filters can be powerful tools for developing GCSs that will help you document your model. In some cases, you can use existing parameters such as the Comments field, or you may need to create your own. Filters can be used to help create separate GCSs for zones of a building.

Adding a parameter called Scheduled Zone will allow you to give each structural column a property indicating the zone the column belongs to. You can use a filter to select only those columns in a particular zone. Each time you create a GCS, those filters are applied to show only the columns for a particular zone.

NAMING YOUR FILTERS

As you continue to create filters for the GCS and other views, be sure to assign appropriate names so that anyone can quickly understand what they are being used for. A nondescriptive filter name can make it difficult to know what a filter was meant for. Naming a filter that removes hangers from a GCS "Hangers" indicates that it is a selection of hangers, when in actuality its purpose is to remove all hangers from the GCS. A name like "Hangers Omitted From GCS" is much more descriptive. Descriptive naming of filters can prevent other users from creating redundant filters as well, since they will know what existing ones are used for.

Adding a parameter called Column Usage will allow you to give each structural column a property explaining its purpose in your project. Maybe the column is being used as a pier, or a hanger, or even a smaller post, and you don't want it to show up in the GCS because it will be scheduled with a different method. You can apply such values as Pier, Hanger, or Post and use filters to prevent those columns from displaying in your GCS.

As you can see, the possibilities of using filters in the GCS are endless. They can give you the freedom you need to produce great-looking column schedules. You can take advantage of filters in any other view throughout a project using the same procedures and methods. When used properly, filters are a great way to add flexibility when producing your documentation.

The Bottom Line

Work with the basic structural column family template.   Understanding the differences between the various templates for a structural column will help you ensure that your structural columns behave properly when placed into your project.

   Master It   What setting in a structural column family gives it the characteristics that help Revit Structure determine connection and attachment properties and whether the columns display in the Graphical Column Schedule?

Place structural columns in your project.   Knowing all the methods available for placing structural columns in your project and knowing when to use each one will help you place columns quickly and accurately into your project.

   Master It   What are three options you can use to place structural columns in your project, and how can you quickly place them onto the upper levels?

Attach structural columns to other structural components.   To help maintain the top and bottom of a column's location and their relationship to other elements, they can be of different cut styles and justifications while being attached to various elements.

   Master It   What types of elements can structural columns be attached to?

Employ the methods of placing slanted columns.   Revit Structure allows you to place slanted columns into your project using similar methods used to place vertical columns. As you attach the top and base of a slanted columns to levels, you can set the slanted column's properties to determine how they behave when those levels are modified.

   Master It   What view type does not allow a slanted column to be placed, and what are the two properties that can be specified in the Column Style setting to control how slanted columns behave when their top and base locations are modified?

Document your model with the Graphical Column Schedule.   The Graphical Column Schedule can be generated automatically by Revit Structure and modified to exclude columns that you do not want displayed.

   Master It   What methods are used to remove structural columns from the Graphical Column Schedule?

Chapter 5

Floor Slabs and Roof Decks

Floors and roofs are two of the main elements for any building project, and you must contend with them when you are modeling a structure. The various floor construction types that you will encounter on a regular basis include concrete slabs-on-grade and supported decks constructed with concrete and metal, wood, or formed concrete. Along with modeling the basic slab or deck profile, you will be required to add slab edges, depressions, ramped floors, and openings to your project in order to accurately develop the design.

Although the techniques seem similar, roof modeling is quite different from floor modeling because you will be spending a lot of time and effort sloping the roof for drainage purposes. Roofs come in many forms, from a residential wooden Cape Cod–style roof to a commercial roof that warps from ridges to drains. A roof is one of the most difficult elements to model in your projects; therefore, the tools and workflow required to create and edit roofs must be up to the task. It is essential to gain a solid understanding of how to model these difficult elements to maintain the integrity of your model.

Revit Structure has many excellent tools to add to your modeling tool chest that help in the creation of these floor and roof entities. In this chapter, you will see those tools in action.

Of course, the slabs will have reinforcing bar or mesh in them, but you will learn how that works later in the book in Chapter 12.

In this chapter you will learn to:

- ◆ Create a concrete slab-on-grade with dropped slab edges
- ◆ Work with floor decks
- ◆ Work with various kinds of roof decks
- ◆ Create openings and depressions in your floors and roofs

Creating Slabs and Decks for Your Project

The first part of this chapter will deal with slabs-on-grade as well as elevated slabs and decks. An understanding of their basic properties and the tools used in their creation is an essential step to mastering Revit Structure. In this section you will have a chance to work with these elements in order to create various slab conditions. You will learn how floor types are made within the foundation slab and floor system families and how you can modify them to satisfy the many conditions that you will be required to model in the virtual environment. To that end, you will examine many forms of supported decks as well as slabs-on-grade.

Slab and Deck Properties

You can find the Slab command on the Foundation panel on the Home tab of the Ribbon; you use the Slab command to make slabs-on-grade and slab edges. When you click the Slab icon, you enable Sketch mode. Sketch mode isolates you from the rest of the model as you are working on the slab so that you can create its outline without disturbing other elements. Sketch mode is used not only for making slabs but for many other functions as well. You should have a thorough understanding of it if you want to use Revit Structure effectively. You will find the Floor command on the Structure panel of the Home tab of the Ribbon; the Floor command is used for making supported decks. For slabs supported on ground, use the Slab function on the Foundation panel.

As discussed in earlier chapters, most elements that you model have Instance and Type parameters (see Figure 5.1). The Type parameters apply to every occurrence of an element of that type in your project. In the case of slabs, an example of a Type parameter is the thickness of the slab. The Type parameters for defining the slab structure are found in the Edit Assembly dialog box and include the following:

- Function
- Material
- Thickness
- Wraps
- Variable

We will discuss those more in a bit. Instance parameters apply to a particular insertion of an object. An example of a slab Instance parameter is the height from the level to which the slab is attached. Rebar Cover is an important group of Instance parameters for slabs.

Once you're in Sketch mode you will create the slab by using the available suboptions found on the Draw panel: Boundary Line and Slope Arrow. Boundary Line (see Figure 5.2) offers the following Draw options:

Line and other sketching options   Use this option to sketch the boundary of the slab with lines or using a variety of common forms.

Pick Lines   Use this option to pick other lines or reference planes that define your slab boundary.

Pick Supports   Use this option to select beams or girders.

Pick Walls   Use this option to select walls that support the slab.

Slope Arrows   Slope arrows permit you to define the desired slope of an entire slab or a portion of slab. The head and tail define elevation change over a distance, the distance between the head and the tail. The slab will slope from tail to head, and the slope of the slab will change over the length of the slope arrow regardless of where the slab edges are. This means I could draw a 10′ long slope arrow and offset each end 10′, and the slab will "tilt" overall, but between the head and the tail it will slope exactly 10′. This is a subtle difference, but functionally this means that I can define a specific slope in a critical area without regard for what it does at the extremes of the slab and find out what that does to my assumptions about that particular area of the slab.

Using one of those methods, you draw the boundary of the slab. The slab boundary lines must be a closed sequence of lines or arcs, so you must be sure that your elements are trimmed and connected to each other. Otherwise, Revit Structure will not allow you to complete the sketch.

FIGURE 5.1

The Element Properties dialog boxes for a floor slab

FIGURE 5.2

The Draw panel on the Ribbon has the tools you need to draw your boundary.

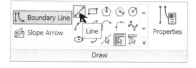

Once the boundary has been established, you will assign a slab type to the element (see Figure 5.3) by clicking Floor Properties on the Element panel of the Modify Slab tab and then choosing the desired type from the drop-down list. Some slab types are available as defaults, and some you will need to create yourself in the Type Properties dialog box. A good template will have the right collection of slab types ready and waiting for you. See Chapter 2 for an explanation of templates.

Within the foundation slab and floor families, you can create many types of floors. Let's now explore the workflow you will use to produce these elements in various forms, starting with a slab-on-grade.

Adding a Foundation Slab to Your Project

The most basic type of slab you can make is a simple slab poured against the ground, known as a slab-on-grade, or a foundation slab. You may have gotten out the hoe and wheelbarrow and mixed some concrete in your own backyard at some point to make a new slab for parking, or a basketball court, or a walkway perhaps. You began by laying out the boundary with boards

FIGURE 5.3
Default supported slab
types

or digging and letting the earth be your form, adding in some reinforcing if needed, and then pouring the concrete. You may also have had to block out certain portions to create openings or depressions. That is exactly what you have to do here: create a slab boundary and then apply a certain type of slab to it.

Let's examine the general method that you will use to create a slab-on-grade within Revit Structure:

1. Click the Slab icon and then choose Foundation Slab from the drop-down list to enter Sketch mode.

2. Once in Sketch mode, you use the various Draw tools on the Draw panel. You can choose to either draw the lines or other shapes or select an existing line that will be duplicated in the same location.

3. In the Floor Properties dialog box, choose an appropriate slab type for your project, like a 6″ concrete slab.

4. Complete the slab boundary (see Figure 5.4).

FIGURE 5.4
Sketching the
slab-on-grade boundary

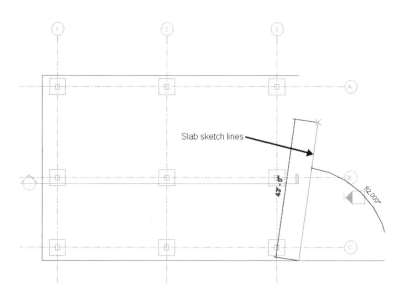

5. If necessary, use the Trim command to ensure that all lines are connected; otherwise you cannot complete the sketch.

6. Click the Finish Floor icon at the right side of the Ribbon, and the slab is complete.

The slab lines can be locked to grid lines or to the architectural stud line in order for the slab lines to adapt automatically to a change in size or location. But you need to be careful that you don't over-constrain the model because performance could suffer. Sometimes you might not want to lock your sketch lines to their boundary for this reason. It takes some time and experimentation to get a feel for those limits.

That was easy enough to do, but what if you need a 4″ thick slab for your project, and you want a 2″ layer of sand below it? In that case you will create a new slab type by duplicating the existing 6″ concrete slab and then adapting its properties. You will also add a new layer to the 4″ slab. The following section shows how the basic procedure works.

CREATING A NEW SLAB TYPE

Creating a new slab type is not very difficult at all. Follow these steps:

1. Once you enter Sketch mode, access the Floor Instance Type properties.

2. Click Edit Type and then Duplicate to create a new slab.

3. Give the slab a name, and then click on the Structure tab, which will bring up the Edit Assembly dialog box (see Figure 5.5). This allows you to alter the deck or slab structure.

FIGURE 5.5
The Edit Assembly dialog box

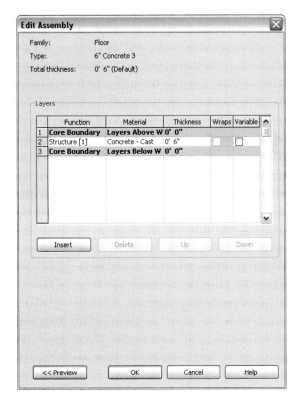

4. Now you can adjust the Material type and the Thickness value of the new slab.

5. When you click into the Material parameter, the Materials dialog box opens, and you can choose from various materials, alter the existing materials, or create new materials for that layer. Layers such as sand or metal deck can be added here (see Figure 5.6).

6. The different layers are placed inside or outside the core boundary as required.

7. The Variable field of the Edit Assembly dialog box allows your layer to vary in depth, for instance, for the purpose of drawing a sloping roof deck layer.

Now that you have seen how to add a slab and create a slab, let's look at the procedure to edit one already created and placed in your project.

FIGURE 5.6
Adding a layer of sand
to the slab structure

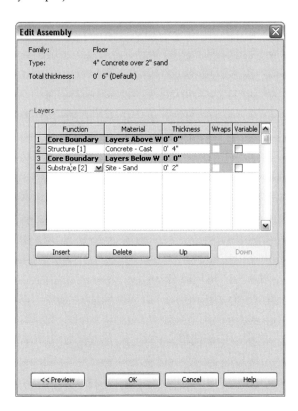

EDITING THE SLAB ELEMENT

Editing the slab once it has been created is not difficult. Just follow these steps:

1. To change the slab type, select the slab and then choose a new type in the Type Selector.

2. To edit the boundary of the slab, select the existing slab.

3. Click Edit Sketch on the Edit panel of the Modify Structural Foundations tab, which puts you back in Sketch mode.

4. Edit the slab lines as needed with the Sketch tools.

5. Click Finish Floor on the Modify Structural Foundations Floor panel.

We'll put all this together in the next exercise, where you create a new multilayered slab element for your project.

EXERCISE: CREATING A SLAB-ON-GRADE

In this exercise, you will create a basic concrete slab-on-grade with a vapor barrier below it. First, you sketch a basic rectangular shape. Then, you create a new slab type consisting of 4″ of concrete with 2″ of sand beneath it for the shape.

To sketch the basic slab shape:

1. Open a new project in Revit Structure.

2. In the Project Browser, double-click on Level 1 to open the view.

3. On the Ribbon click the Home tab.

4. Choose Slab ➤ Foundation Slab on the Foundation panel, which puts you into Sketch mode.

5. Click the Rectangle icon on the Draw panel.

6. In the drawing area draw a rectangle for the slab boundary; any size will do for this exercise.

Now let's create the new slab type:

1. On the Ribbon click the Floor Properties icon.

2. In the Type pull-down list, select 6″ Foundation Slab.

3. Click Edit Type; then in the Type Properties dialog box, choose Duplicate.

4. In the Name dialog box, type **4″ Foundation Slab over 2″ Sand**, and click OK.

5. In the Structure field click Edit.

6. In the Edit Assembly dialog box, change the Thickness to **4″**.

7. Click the Insert button to create a new layer below the concrete.

8. Click the Material field and change the material to Site-Sand. Click OK, and then click OK again to exit.

9. Click the Thickness field for the sand layer and change the value to **2″**.

10. Click OK in the remaining dialog boxes.

11. Click Finish Floor to complete your slab. Then go to a 3D view and check out your new slab.

Leave your model open for the next exercise.

Getting to Know Slab Edges

Creating the basic slab-on-grade is not too difficult. But each slab will have an edge condition that will also have to be modeled. For the basic slab-on-grade that we have been working on, there will most likely be a thickened slab 12″ to 18″ in depth around the perimeter of the slab, with a bearing surface of 8″ to 12″ (see Figure 5.7).

FIGURE 5.7
Edge of slab from the default profile family

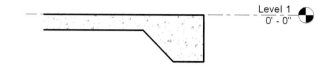

Of course, that is a simple slab edge shape in which you can add a new type to the default slab edge family. You can also start your own profile family file and create any shape you might need as long as it is a single closed boundary of lines. You can then add constraints to the basic shape to make it become a parametric family whose shape can flex to different sizes. The existing families are a good place to start by reverse engineering how they were built.

Figure 5.8 shows a more complicated slab edge profile. For this advanced case you will need to create a new profile family since the shape varies so much from the default slab edge family.

FIGURE 5.8
More complicated slab edge with curb (shaded) attached to the slab

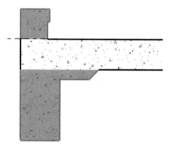

One important point to remember is that you want the slab edge material to be the same as the slab material so that when you cut a section, the final display of the slab and edge appears monolithic.

The parametric nature of Revit Structure families means you can create and manage literally thousands of modeling shapes in a well-coordinated, easy-to-understand fashion. The Slab Edge function is located on the Ribbon on the Foundation panel in the Slab drop-down list. The shape of the slab edge is controlled through the use of slab edge profile families. These families are parametrically driven, giving the profile family the ability to flex to different sizes of the same basic shape. There are limited types loaded into the default template, so you will most likely need to add new profile types, which you will learn to do later in this chapter. For now, let's explore the basic procedure for adding a slab edge type to your project.

1. On the Home tab of the Ribbon, on the Foundation panel in the Slab drop-down, click Slab Edge.

2. Then select the slab edge type you want to use from the Type Selector.

3. To add the slab edge to the slab, just begin clicking on its edges and make your way around the slab. The slab edges can be connected into chains of similar edge types if different types are required for different parts of the slab.

4. To start a new set of edges, click the Finish Current icon on the Profile panel, choose a new profile from the Type Selector, and then start picking edges again. By making groups of

slab edges, you can better control and define their behavior, especially if you have multiple types.

5. When viewed in section, the slab edges will "clean up" or appear monolithic with the foundation slab as long as the two elements have the same material, so make sure when you create the edge type that its material matches your slab material.

Now you've completed your basic slab edge. But during the period while you are designing your structure, you will undoubtedly need to revise the slab and its edges several times. You might want to eliminate one or more segments that you have added. How do you do that?

1. First, you select a slab edge segment that you want to change.

2. On the Options bar click the Add or Remove Segments button.

3. Then select the edge that defines the segment you want to remove or an edge where you want to add a slab edge.

After placement, the slab edges can be offset vertically or horizontally from the slab element. To offset the slab edge, follow these steps:

1. Select it and then click Element Properties ➤ Instance Properties on the left side of the Ribbon to access the dialog box.

2. There you can adjust the position of the slab edge by adding values for the vertical and/or horizontal Profile Offset parameter.

You can also flip the slab edge profile 180 degrees in plan view:

1. First, select the segment to flip.

2. Then click the double-arrow control that appears next to the slab edge and that will mirror the segment about the edge of slab.

The control will flip all the connected slab edges as well. If you need to flip just one of them, then you will need to define it by itself first.

In practice, you will contend with many different types of slab edges, and it can become difficult to keep them accurately modeled and displayed. This tends to be a time-consuming activity, but in order to display the model accurately, it is a necessary concern. Let's look at the profile-creation process a little closer and see how a new profile type can be made and loaded into your project.

THE POWER OF PARAMETRICS

One of the real powers of Revit lies in the parametric nature of its model and annotation families. You should learn to create parameters in your own families that allow the family elements to flex into new shapes. But if you get overly frustrated in your first attempt to do this, stick with creating the single-shape family. Later you can evolve to the higher-level creation process where your families become more parametric in nature.

Figure 5.9 shows the profile family for the edge of slab. It could be just a single four-sided shape for use as a profile. You could then create many different files, each with a similar four-sided shape but with different widths and thicknesses, such as 12 × 36, 10 × 20, or 18 × 36, all in a library of edge types. AutoCAD works that way. That approach is not parametric. Having one profile family represent similar shapes with the ability to flex the shape easily into new types is the parametric approach. Revit Structure works that way.

FIGURE 5.9
Parametric constraints
in the slab edge family
file lock the shape lines
to reference planes.

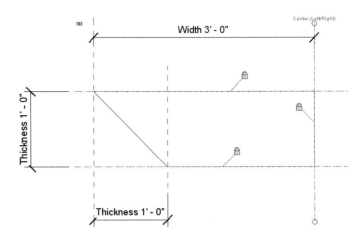

Next, let's see how to convert a simple single shape (see Figure 5.9) to a parametric one. You would do the following in the Family Editor:

1. Draw reference planes where a surface edge will be placed.

2. Draw lines along the reference planes to create the shape of the slab edge.

3. Lock the lines to the reference planes as you are drawing them. You can also lock the ends of the lines to the reference planes.

4. Create dimension strings between the reference planes.

5. Select one of the dimensions, right-click, and choose Edit Label. In the resulting pull-down box, click Add a Parameter, or choose to edit an existing one.

6. In the resulting dialog box create or edit the parameter label.

7. Finish attaching flexible parametric labels to the dimensions, which act either as Type or Instance parameters within the family.

8. Create a new type.

9. Flex the model to make sure it is working properly.

This general process gives you an insight into how to adapt and extend your modeled shapes into more generalized families.

MAKING A NEW SLAB EDGE TYPE

If you have to make a new slab edge type in your project, most likely you will also have to add a new type to the slab edge profile family because they work together. The default slab edge profile family can be found under Profiles on the Project Browser. The next exercise will show how this is accomplished.

EXERCISE: CREATING A SLAB EDGE TYPE AND ADDING IT TO YOUR SLAB

In this exercise, you will create a new slab edge type from the loaded slab edge profiles, and then you will add it to the slab that you made in the previous exercise. When you complete the exercise, make a section through the slab and check to see if the slab edge displays correctly.

First, have a slab available in an open model from the previous exercise, or create one in a new model; a basic four-sided slab is sufficient. You can now create a new slab edge type in the profile family:

1. Navigate to Project Browser ➢ Families ➢ Profiles ➢ Slab Edge-Thickened. Double-click the 24″×12″ slab edge type.

2. In the Type Properties dialog box click Duplicate.

3. Name the new profile type **30″×20″**; click OK.

4. Enter the values **30″** for the Width and **20″** for the Thickness.

5. Click OK to exit the dialog boxes.

6. Navigate to Project Browser ➢ Floors ➢ Slab Edge; then double-click on the Thickened 24″×12″ slab edge type.

7. In the Type Properties dialog box click Duplicate; then give the new type a name: **Thickened 30″×20″**.

8. In the Profile drop-down list pick the new profile type you created: Slab Edge - Thickened 30″×20″.

9. Set the Material of the slab edge to Concrete Cast-in-Place.

10. Click OK to exit the dialog box.

Now you can add the new profile to a slab edge type by doing the following:

1. On the Home tab of the Ribbon select Slab from the Foundation panel and choose Slab Edge from the drop-down list (or navigate to Project Browser ➢ Floors ➢ Slab Edge; then double-click on the Thickened 24″×12″ slab edge type).

2. On the Ribbon click Element Properties; then choose Type Properties from the drop-down list.

3. Click Duplicate and give the new slab edge a name.

4. Assign the new slab edge type the name **Thickened 30″×20″**. Then click OK.

5. In the Type Profile field, select the Slab Edge - Thickened 30″×20″ profile type that you created.

6. Click in the Type Material field to display a small button; then click it to open the Materials dialog box.

7. Select Concrete – Cast-in-Place Concrete, and click OK in each dialog box to finish your editing.

8. Click each edge of the slab successively to form a chain of edges around your slab. Click Finish Profile on the Profile panel of the Place Slab Edge Ribbon tab.

9. Click Modify on the Selection panel of the Place Slab Edge tab of the Ribbon (this completes the command).

10. On the View Control bar change the view to Hidden Line, if it isn't already, to show correctly the inside bottom edge as hidden below.

11. Select the slab edge you just created.

12. On the Options bar, click the Add or Remove Segments button.

13. Click on the right and left edges of the slab to remove those two segments.

Remember that we suggested you create a section through your slab to see if it turned out as you hoped, similar to Figure 5.7.

Now that you have learned how to use foundation slabs, let's move on to the next discussion, which is about supported slabs and decks.

Creating Floor Decks

The next important feature we will explore is working with floor decks in Revit Structure, with a focus on the nature of multilayered decks. Here are some examples of floor decks you might encounter in your projects:

◆ A steel project might have a floor deck consisting of $3\frac{1}{4}''$ lightweight concrete over a $3'' \times 18''$ gauge metal deck.

◆ A wood floor deck on the second floor of an elementary school could be $2''$ of lightweight concrete fill over a $\frac{3}{4}''$ layer of wood sheathing.

◆ A concrete flat slab over a basement could have fill topping at the street level for drainage purposes.

The process of creating different types of floor decks (see Figure 5.10) and placing them is the same as for the foundation slab, but with a few differences, most notably creating composite metal decks. The metal deck family has several default types, as shown earlier in the chapter. You learned how to add layers when you added a layer of sand below the slab-on-grade. Now let's see what we need to do to create a metal deck slab.

Making a New Composite Deck Type

The process of making steel and concrete composite decks is much the same as for the basic slab-on-grade type except the deck is multilayered. It is important to define a composite deck type in such a way that it can be cut in section and accurately show the fluted metal deck filled with concrete. This helps make your section views more complete, which means that finishing them will require much less effort. Let's see how to make the slab:

1. In the Project Browser scroll down to Families, and expand the list of families by clicking on the plus (+) sign on the left. Scroll to Floors and expand the list again and you'll see a few types.

2. From the list of Floors double-click on one that seems close to what you need. The Type Properties dialog box opens.

3. Click the Duplicate button, and then give the new deck a name.

FIGURE 5.10
Giving the new deck
type a deck profile

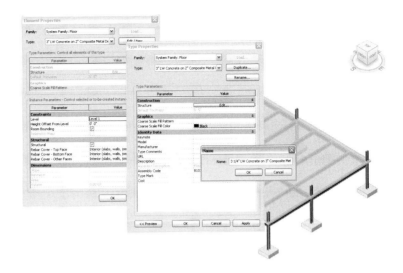

4. In the Structure parameter, click the Structure button. Depending on which floor you choose to duplicate, you may need to add a layer. Refer to Figure 5.11 to see whether you do.

5. If necessary, within the core boundary insert a layer for your concrete.

6. If necessary, insert a layer for your metal deck.

7. In the Function column for the bottom layer, click in the Function field and choose Structural Deck [1]. This is a special feature of Revit Structure to define the relationship between this layer and the layer above so the concrete can blend into this layer.

8. Choose a deck profile from the Structural Deck Properties area (see Figure 5.11) at the bottom of the dialog box. Those profiles are families and can be edited separately if desired.

9. From the Deck Usage drop-down list, choose Bound Layer Above. This choice causes Revit to include this layer as part of the layer above it; thus, the entire thickness of this slab is defined in that layer. The deck profile is bound into the layer above. The Standalone deck option treats the deck as a separate entity, making the deck thicker than required.

10. If the structural deck profile you want does not exist, you can create one by editing the deck profile family and adding new types, similar to the way you did with the slab edge profile.

 Real World Scenario

STRUCTURAL VERSUS ARCHITECTURAL FLOORS

When working on a project with an architect who was also modeling, we realized something about the different modules of Revit: there are important differences between structural and architectural floors. A Revit Structure floor and a Revit Architecture floor are of the same category element. But Revit Structure floors show analytical elements and enjoy the ability to define the function of the structural deck. They also show the span direction of the deck, which controls how the metal deck is displayed in section. In section we wanted to see the metal deck flutes automatically so we did not have to spend a lot of time adding 2D lines.

As we discovered, Revit Architecture cannot do this. It can, however, display them if the Revit Structure model is linked into the architectural model. Therefore it seemed to be a good idea to us to have the structural engineer "own" the structural deck so that this feature is available for both firms' documentation. Structure builds the deck, and the architect displays the deck in the architectural model via the link. This means the architect needs to be more forthcoming about coordinating floor penetrations, which is a good thing. Close coordination becomes essential.

FIGURE 5.11
Defining the metal deck structure in the Edit Assembly dialog box

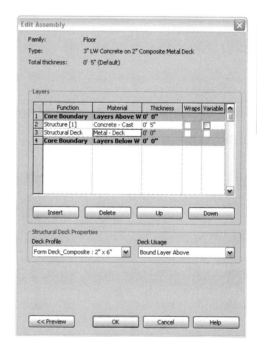

Adding a Cantilever to a Floor Deck

Edge conditions are a major consideration for floor decks. Typically the metal deck stops at the support girder, and then only concrete extends out to the inside face of the stud supported by an angle or a bent plate (see Figures 5.12 and 5.13). In order to accurately represent the edge condition in your model, the deck family has to accommodate the discontinuity of the metal deck. Fortunately this is not difficult to accomplish. Each boundary sketch line for a slab has a property for Cantilever - Concrete or Steel. To configure this you need to work in the slab's Sketch mode. While in Sketch mode select one of the boundary lines. Then on the Options bar, set the concrete or steel cantilever distance (see Figure 5.14) as required for your project. You should notice that a positive value makes the extension go to the inside of the support line, and a negative value makes the extension go to the outside of the support line.

FIGURE 5.12
The edge of the deck is parallel to the deck flutes.

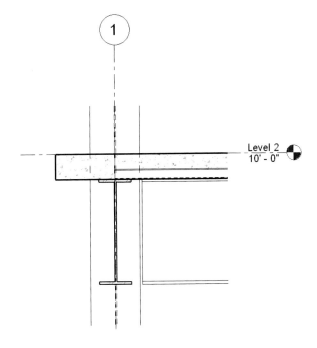

FIGURE 5.13
The edge of the deck is perpendicular to the deck flutes.

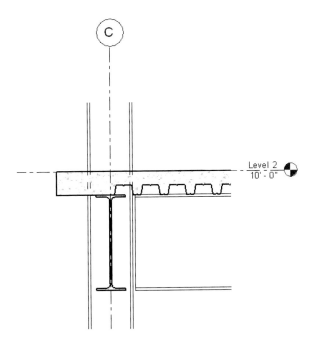

FIGURE 5.14
Adding deck cantilevers
in plan view

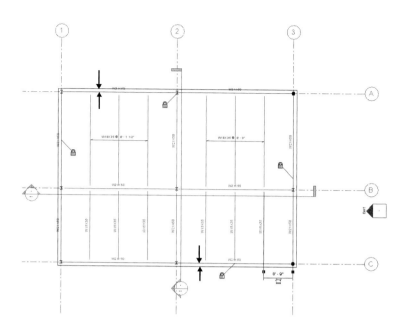

The span direction for a supported slab is another important practical element to consider. When the deck is first created, a span direction symbol is added. The half arrows shown in one direction indicate the strong direction (the span, flute direction) of the deck. You can also add the span indicator at any time by selecting the Annotate tab from the Ribbon and from the Symbol panel choosing Span Direction. If you select the span direction symbol that is already placed and rotate it, you can change the direction of the deck for a placed deck element. This will be essential in order to show the deck correctly in your section views.

OTHER EXAMPLES OF FLOOR-TYPE CONSTRUCTION

By now you might be asking, "What about different types of concrete formed structural slabs with decks, such as PT slabs, pan joist waffle slabs, and double-T slabs?" For those slabs, refer to Chapter 7 (on framing) for a full discussion. Since slab and framing are integrated, we chose that chapter to discuss the creation of those types of elements.

Creating and Placing Roof Elements

Now that you have started to get a feel for creating floors, you will find that roofs are created in much the same fashion. The big difference lies in the many varieties of wood, steel, and concrete roof shapes that you must be prepared to accommodate in your project. It could require a residential gable roof, a saltbox roof, a flat commercial-style roof deck, or perhaps even a freeform, wavelike shape.

To contend with these possibilities, you will use special tools to help create and slope your roof elements. You will then also be able to combine different roof shapes and slopes into one roof system. In Chapter 7, you will learn how to best frame your roof for these different roof conditions.

Of paramount concern in constructing your roof system is the ability to edit the roof sloping and the framing that supports it as easily as possible as the design progresses.

As you will see in Chapter 7, a sloped and warped roof will necessitate that your beam and girder system supporting the diaphragm flex automatically when you edit the diaphragm. Since each beam will most likely have a different elevation at its end, editing a complex roof shape can be time consuming. Therefore, you will need to give special consideration to your approach.

One big issue that often crops up in many projects concerns the interaction with the architectural designers as you develop the roof for your model. If the architects still use 2D techniques, they will normally not be too concerned in the design development stage about the slope of the roof. But for the person doing the modeling, that can mean trouble. Best practice is to try to work with the architect to get an idea of ridge and drain locations that you can then readily edit later in the project. To create your roof element, you will need enough information about the sloping so that you can at least get a semblance of the roof system put into place. If you simply begin by creating a flat roof, you will undoubtedly be forced later to scrap it and start over. Also, keep in mind that the integrity of the model is compromised by showing just a flat roof. Ignoring the true slope of the roof means the greater the span of the sloping structure, the worse the compromise will be and the greater the potential for conflicts.

Now let's take a close look at the techniques used to model different roof conditions. The two main areas we will focus on are the geometry of the roof diaphragm and the creation of various roof types to apply to that geometry.

Roof Deck Properties

The roof family, like every other family in Revit Structure, is populated with different types. These types are created in much the same way as floor types were created earlier in this chapter. The two basic families of roof types are basic and sloped glazing. We will concentrate on the basic type. Sloped glazing roof types are appropriate for creating a greenhouse or a skylight structure and work similar to curtain walls, except these can slope.

Let's now examine the process of creating a new roof deck. The Roof tool is on the Architect panel of the Architect & Site tab of the Ribbon. There are six related tools on its drop-down menu. We will concentrate on two: Roof by Footprint and Roof by Extrusion.

USING THE ROOF BY FOOTPRINT OPTION

Let's first see how to create a new roof deck using the Create by Footprint option. With this option you work in a plan view and draw the boundary line for the roof deck.

1. Go to your roof level view, and then on the Ribbon click the Architect & Site tab, select Roof, and then select Roof by Footprint.

2. On the Ribbon in the Element panel click Roof Properties, which displays the Instance Properties dialog box.

3. Click Edit Type, and in the resulting Type Properties dialog box, click Duplicate.

4. Give the new roof type an appropriate name.

5. In the Type Properties dialog box under Construction, click the Edit button in the Structure field.

6. In the Edit Assembly dialog box, you will create the different layers of the deck, such as a metal deck layer and a fill over that.

7. A typical roof assembly fill might be a lightweight concrete fill, wood sheathing, or solid insulation. These components of the roof assembly will be within the core layer. Create an assembly fill layer by clicking the Insert button and assigning values for Material and Thickness.

8. Use the Up and Down buttons to move the layers as needed to their correct location within the roof element.

9. Create other nonstructural layers, such as roof membranes, outside the core boundary.

ROOF CRICKETS

Adding roof crickets to your roof is difficult to accomplish, and it is usually left to the architect to model since it is not really a structural concern. You, on the other hand, will want to concentrate on the underside bearing surface of the deck in order to prepare for the addition of support framing.

---

10. Check the Variable box to the right of each layer to free up that layer so that you can vary its depth.

11. The bottom of these layers will remain constant, while the top can vary. First set the minimum thickness, and then check the Variable box to have thicker portions than the minimum setting.

12. Click OK in all remaining dialog boxes.

That is how you create a new roof deck type. Transparencies are often applied to the decking materials so that you can look through the roof deck and see the framing below. Set the Transparency value to **10%** and notice how much more of the structure you can see in your 3D views. For structural presentations it really helps. Now it is time to move on to sketching the actual deck geometry.

SKETCHING ROOF GEOMETRY FOR YOUR PROJECT

As stated earlier, sketching roof geometry is one of the most challenging things you will do when modeling with Revit Structure. Let's start by looking at some of the easier forms and work our way up to ones that are more difficult. First, let's create a simple sloped gable roof (see Figure 5.15).

The basic gable-style roof (as shown in Figure 5.15) is not difficult to model. In general, just do the following:

1. On the Ribbon, click the Architect & Site tab, choose Roof, and select Roof by Footprint.

2. You will enter Sketch mode, where you can draw the outline of the roof; the lines represent the eave or edge of the roof.

3. Click Lines on the Sketch menu.

4. On the Draw panel of the Ribbon, the basic Sketch tools are available, so you can draw or select the outline to define the footprint you want.

5. Once you create the outline, select the lines that will be at the top or base of the sloped surfaces — in this case, the line on each long side of the roof.

6. On the Options bar, check the Defines Slope box.

7. On the highlighted lines, you will see a triangle slope symbol next to the line that represents the slope value (see Figure 5.16). When you hover the mouse over the slope value, a box appears around the value. Click in the box, and you can enter a new slope value.

8. Once you have a closed boundary sketch, you can click Finish Roof on the Roof panel of the Ribbon to complete the roof.

FIGURE 5.15
A simple form of sloped roofing

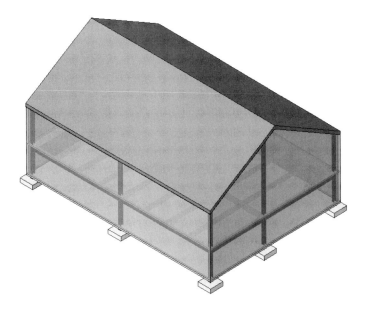

FORMATTING THE SLOPE VALUE

The format of the slope value by default is expressed in degrees, such as 30°. It can be expressed in six other ways, including a couple of different options for Rise over Run, which in many cases is how the architect will specify it. To change the display to Rise/12″ go to the Manage tab of the Ribbon, and then on the Project Settings panel click Project Units. In the Project Units dialog box click the button in the Format field for Slope. There you can select the Units format required for your project.

Figure 5.17 shows a more complicated hip roof that slopes in four directions and adds dormers on two sides.

CREATING A BASIC ROOF WITH HIPS AND DORMERS

The method to create a roof with hips and dormers in your project similar to the one shown in Figure 5.17 involves the following steps:

1. In Sketch mode, as you did on the simple roof, add lines for the four sides, set each to Define Slope, and then adjust each slope angle accordingly.

FIGURE 5.16
Sketching a basic roof
and adding slope angles
to the base lines

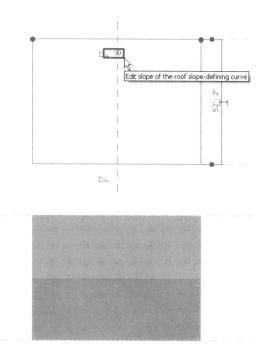

2. You need to use slope arrows to create the dormer portions. Slope arrows indicate the direction and extent of a sloping deck line, such as our dormer. There is a tail and a head; the arrow is the head.

3. The roof sketch needs individual line segments to define each portion of the gable dormer. On the top and bottom lines of the roof footprint, use the Split tool to break the existing sketch line into a total of four lines, each representing the basic roof or dormer horizontal length. The outside pair represent the slope of the main roof. For the purpose of this discussion these should be equal in length. The inner pair should also be equal and indicate the length of the gable and meet at the ridge of the dormer.

4. Click Slope Arrow on the Draw panel of the Create Roof Footprint tab. You will sketch the slope arrow from the eave to the ridge, up the dormer.

5. Sketching over the dormer lines, add the slope arrows with each arrow pointing toward the middle, the ridge of the dormer. If it helps, imagine where each segment of the roof sketch meets is a hinge that will allow the roof to slope, or change direction.

6. Select both slope arrows and then click the Properties button on the Draw panel of the Ribbon.

7. Adjust the properties to fit your dormer configuration (see Figure 5.18).

8. Repeat as necessary for the slope arrows on the other side of the roof. You can also set the slope arrow to use a Slope value like that of the roof sketch lines as opposed to entering a starting and ending elevation, as shown in Figure 5.18.

9. When you have finished, click Finish Roof on the Roof panel of the Ribbon.

Now let's look at a roof with a cutout portion, such as a mansard roof.

FIGURE 5.17
A basic roof with hips and dormers

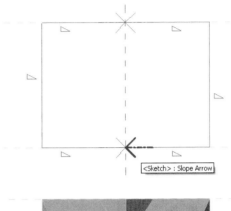

FIGURE 5.18
Slope arrow properties

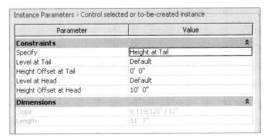

Creating a Roof with a Cutoff Portion

Another common roof shape you might encounter involves cutting out a portion of the roof to create a cutoff condition, such as for a mansard roof, or to prepare for a two-pitch roof (see Figure 5.19). The general process for this example is the same as for the roof that you just created. Once you complete the basic shape, select it, and then click the Element Properties tab next to the

Type Selector. In the Element Instance Properties dialog box, you can add a value to the Cutoff Level parameter to establish a point above the base of the roof where you would like it to be cut.

Are you getting the idea of how this works yet? Play around with these various options until you feel a little more comfortable with how this all functions. Using these various roof tools, you can create a complicated roof diaphragm configured as shown in Figure 5.20.

FIGURE 5.19
A cutoff mansard-style roof element

FIGURE 5.20
A more complicated residential roof with joined multisloped portions

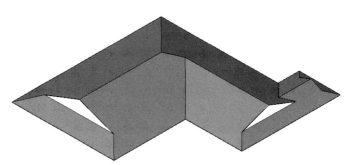

PLAY AROUND WITH THE OPTIONS

One thing that becomes clear when you start modeling with Revit Structure is that it is a satisfying way to work and is actually fun. That can be quite disconcerting to those who never equate work with having fun. "I'm working; I'm not supposed to be having fun!" some will say. But all kidding aside, working in three dimensions rather than two activates different parts of the brain and awakens a different and deeper understanding of the building that you are creating.

As you have seen by sketching the footprint and applying slope angles to the edges, you can create many distinctive roof shapes (see Figure 5.21).

Another method you can use to create a roof is to use the Roof by Extrusion tool. This option is a good one to use if you have a fairly straight multisloped roof system with areas that need to be cut out.

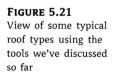

FIGURE 5.21
View of some typical roof types using the tools we've discussed so far

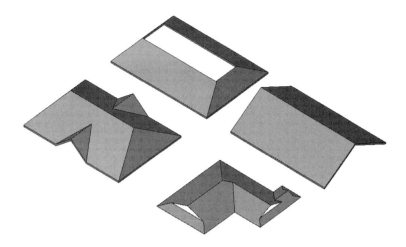

ROOF BY EXTRUSION METHOD

The Roof by Extrusion method uses a profile of the roof shape that you want to create, which is then extruded over the length of the new roof segment. Imagine drawing the roof shape in section first and then deciding how far forward and backward it should extend.

1. This tool needs a work plane. We can use a reference plane to define it. You can find it on the Work Plane panel of the Home tab. Choose the Draw Reference Plane option. In a plan view draw the reference plane (or you can use a grid line) perpendicular to the direction in which you want to extrude the roof. It is important to name the reference plane; otherwise, you won't be able to use it as the work plane for your roof sketch, and we intend to do so. You can name the reference plane in the Element Properties dialog box.

2. From the Create panel of the View tab, click the Section View tool to create one that is parallel to the reference plane or grid. It needs to "look at" and "see" the reference plane.

3. On the Ribbon click the Architect & Site tab, choose Roof, and then select Roof by Extrusion.

4. In the Work Plane dialog box that appears, choose the reference plane or grid you created as the work plane. If you didn't name the reference plane, it won't be listed.

5. The Go to View dialog box appears, suggesting that a floor plan is not the best view to use to sketch your Roof by Extrusion. The dialog box offers you some better views that are parallel to your reference plane/grid.

6. Select the new section view that you created and click Open View. In the Roof Reference Level and Offset dialog box select the level you want your roof to reference, and assign an offset if desired. This will create the relationship between your roof and this level.

7. Sketch the lines that represent the roof shape. The sketch needs to be continuous connected lines and, unlike nearly all other sketches in Revit Structure, this one does not want to be a closed boundary. The sketch you create will define the top of the roof surface.

8. Click Finish Roof. Select the finished roof, and then on the Element panel of the Home tab click the Properties box. Assign new values for Extrusion Start and Extrusion Finish. If the reference plane you created is the middle of the roof, then enter a positive value for one

side and an equal negative value for the other side to create a roof centered on your reference. Both values should be half of your desired overall roof depth or length.

EXTRUSION START AND FINISH VALUES

You do not need to be exact in establishing the Extrusion Start and Finish values, as you will soon see, though it is more accurate to do so. Each value represents a distance relative to the reference plane or grid on which you chose to draw the profile. Enter one value as a negative and one as a positive value, say −5'-0" and 5'-0".

---

9. Click OK to close the Element Properties dialog box; then open the plan view in which the roof element was drawn.

10. Select the roof you created, and using the grips that appear at either end, stretch out the roof in either direction relative to the current reference plane or grid (see Figure 5.22) to establish the full extent of the roof. If you want, you can lock the extents at either end to grids or other important elements that might flex during the design period.

FIGURE 5.22
The Roof by Extrusion method: stretching the roof extents by clicking and dragging the blue triangles

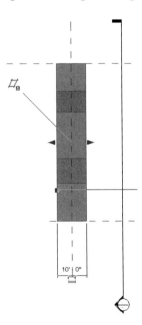

After you have finished the basic Roof by Extrusion shape, you can add openings for light shafts or other purposes such as mechanical openings, as follows.

To add an opening, you create a void that cuts out a portion of the roof you just created (see Figure 5.23). To cut an opening in the roof, follow these steps:

1. In a plan view, select the roof element.

2. On the Modify Roof panel of the Modify Roofs tab, click the Vertical Opening tool. This changes the view to Sketch mode again and displays the Create Extrusion Roof Profile contextual ribbon.

3. Sketch the shape of the opening you desire, and then click Finish Sketch. The opening is then cut out of the roof extrusion. Keep in mind that the sketch can be entirely within the roof boundary or extend beyond the boundary. Only the portion of the sketch that cuts across the roof will alter the roof. If no part of your sketch crosses the roof at all, Revit won't complain, but you won't see any change to the roof either. This sometimes happens when users attempt to add an opening in a 3D view.

FIGURE 5.23
Sketching an area to void out for a roof opening

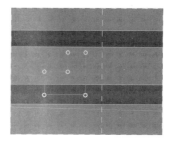

Another task you will most likely have to perform when creating the roof resembles using a cookie cutter on dough. Since the extrusion is rectangular or square, you may need to cut out a pattern from the rectangle to match your roof shape. You need to shape the edge of the rectangular extruded element to suit the shape of your structure. In this case, we are adding a void shape to cut the roof into a circular shape.

Using the same tool as before, Vertical Opening, to cut a circular shape from the rectangular roof extrusion (see Figure 5.24), sketch an inner circular boundary and then a boundary outside the overall roof extrusion. The inner circle acts as our knife edge. The outer boundary and inner boundary together define the overall vertical opening. As long as the outer boundary is larger than your roof, all of the roof outside of the circle is removed. Click Finish Roof to see the final form. Make sure that the sketch boundaries do not overlap.

Assuming that a real project may have walls under this roof and that these walls may need to extend to the underside of this roof, Revit provides an easy way to accomplish this. Select the walls and, on the Modify Wall panel of the Modify Walls tab, click Attach. Select the roof, and the walls will automatically be attached to the underside surfaces of the roof. While the Attach tool is active, the Options bar provides the opportunity to choose whether to attach the top or bottom of the walls to a roof or floor.

Keep in mind that the Vertical Opening tool defines a plumb cut through a roof. If it is necessary to define an opening that is perpendicular to the roof surface, another tool is available. You'll need to consider using the Opening by Face tool. It can be found on the Opening panel of the Modify tab. It too is defined with a Sketch mode.

FIGURE 5.24
Using the Roof by Extru-
sion method to cut a
new circular shape as
well as attach walls to
the underside of the roof

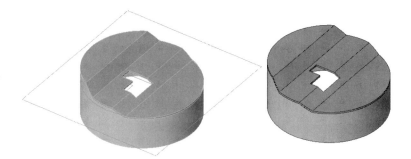

If you need to alter the openings you created in your Roof by Extrusion shape, select the roof and choose either Edit Profile (to change the extrusion profile/shape) or Vertical Opening (to return to Sketch mode for the opening(s)).

CREATING WARPED ROOF DECKS

Next we'll look at another set of roof tools to model flat roofs that slope from ridges to drains, which are found in the majority of typical commercial buildings. If you can learn to make these types of roofs, you will be able to model most of the projects that come your way.

For commercial construction, many buildings will have a "flat" roof. In reality, the roof is not flat but must slope slightly in order to drain rainwater, usually at about $\frac{1}{4}''$ per foot from ridges to drains. This can be challenging to model and edit as you are working through the design process. Not only the roof diaphragm but the support framing as well will present complications, since all framing members are at different slopes with different end elevations. Until now the roof diaphragms and support framing members we've been using have used one plane; in other words, each end of a beam has been at the same elevation. In practice, however, beams quite often have a different offset at each end to define slope. As you will see in Chapter 7, the framing members under the warped roof decks have no common plane to attach to, but they can still be created and edited in your project in an efficient way.

As you can see in Figure 5.25, the roof low point, where the water drains, will be located at –2′-0″. The roof ridges are at 0′ in relation to the roof level. Using the method of working with flat planes, you could try to model a series of triangular surfaces to make the whole roof, but modeling would be cumbersome and time consuming. Revit Structure uses a set of tools referred to as Shape Editing. These tools help you create this type of warped roof surface.

The general process looks like this:

1. Create a Roof by Footprint shape; it must not define any slope.

2. Highlight the diaphragm, and the subelements become available on the Shape Editing panel of the Modify Roofs tab on the Ribbon. The four subelements have the following properties:

   ◆ The Modify Sub Elements tool (see Figure 5.26) puts you into an editing mode where you can pick the lines and points and apply an elevation value.

   ◆ The Add Point tool lets you to add points anywhere within the roof boundary (see Figure 5.27). Once you place points, you can use the Modify Sub Elements tool to alter its elevation value relative to the level of the roof. These points can act as drain points or low points for the typical flat roof we are using as an example.

FIGURE 5.25
Roof Shape Editing tools
define the pitch of a
sloping deck to its drains
and ridges.

FIGURE 5.25
Roof Shape Editing tools
define the pitch of a
sloping deck to its drains
and ridges.

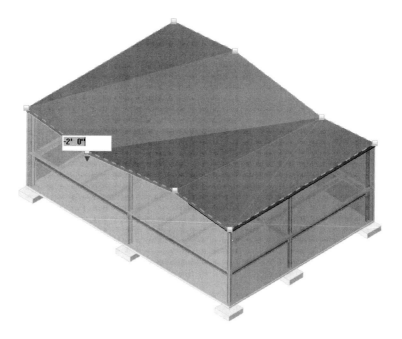

FIGURE 5.26
Select the deck and
click the Modify Sub
Elements icon.

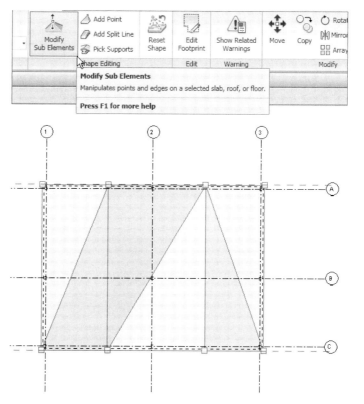

FIGURE 5.27
Adding elevation points
to the roof diaphragm

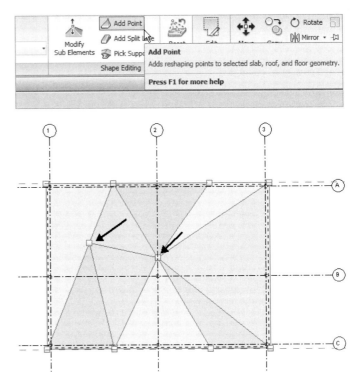

◆ The Add Split Line tool is used to add lines to the diaphragm (see Figure 5.28). Then you can add an elevation value. These lines can act as ridge lines or valley lines on your roof.

◆ The Pick Supports tool allows you to select supporting beam members that define how the roof should slope.

3. Use the Reset Shape tool to discard all of the added subelements and return the diaphragm to its original shape.

WHICH CAME FIRST, THE CHICKEN OR THE EGG?

In terms of roof creation, do you create your framing first and then apply a floor or roof to it, or do you create the roof first and then add the support framing? Truth is, there are so many conditions where either method is valid that you're wise to keep both in your tool chest.

In the case of a warped roof diaphragm though, we think the answer is definitely the latter. In Chapter 7 you will see just why that is so.

FIGURE 5.28
The Add Split Line tool
can create ridge or val-
ley lines on the roof.

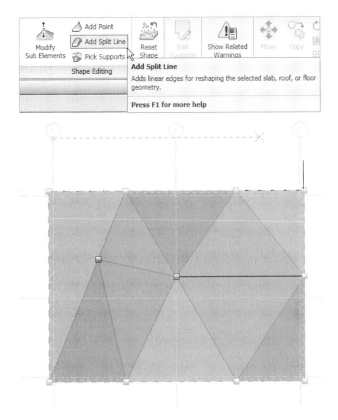

Adding and Editing Roof Subelements

Now that you have seen the editing tools at your disposal for altering roof slopes, let's step through the process. Follow these steps to use Shape Editing to create a warped roof deck:

1. Create a flat roof using Roof by Footprint. Take care not to define any sketch segments that define slope. Shape Editing is not offered as an option when a roof defines slope within its sketch.

2. Select the roof.

3. Click either Add Point or Add Split Line, and place the point or line as desired.

4. Click the Modify Sub Elements tool.

5. To edit the elevations of a point or split line, do one of the following:

   ◆ Select the point or split line, click on the Elevation value, and change it as required.

   ◆ Dynamically alter the location of the point or split line by clicking and dragging it. You can do this in a plan or 3D view.

Keep in mind that Shape Editing is designed to do one of two things: define a roof that slopes uniformly on the bottom and top surfaces (a roof with sloping structure) or define a roof that slopes only on the surface (a roof with flat structure and built-up insulation).

For roofs that use flat structure and built-up insulation, Shape Editing is limited by the ability of the roof to permit the alteration. If you recall, earlier in this chapter we described creating a roof type. Each layer in a roof has a property called Variable. When a layer is defined as Variable, the layer can be altered using Shape Editing. Layers that are above a variable layer will also be affected by Shape Editing. This means only the bottommost layer that will need Shape Editing needs to be defined as Variable.

As a practical example, consider a roof that has a 4″ layer for rigid insulation and a thinner layer above it for the membrane. If the rigid insulation layer is variable, the Shape Editing tool will alter only the top surface of the insulation and membrane layer. Creating a negative elevation offset for a point on this roof that is greater than the thickness of the rigid insulation will generate an error message. This means you can offset an elevation only by a value that's less than the overall thickness of a layer.

USING SOLID BLENDS AND SWEEPS FOR DECK CREATION

When the basic roof tools are unable to deliver what you need, there is another way to make them: Model In-Place. Making more exotic freeform types of roof shapes requires that you use solid modeling techniques. The two specific solid forms we will discuss are a sweep and a blend. You access these commands on the Home tab of the Ribbon. On the Model panel choose Model In-Place from the Component drop-down.

A solid sweep is useful for creating roof elements, such as canopies, that follow a varied path. Notice the sweep profile lines and the profile path line that they follow in Figure 5.29. You must understand these two concepts, profile and path, to create this type of modeled object.

FIGURE 5.29
Barreled roof canopy created with a solid sweep

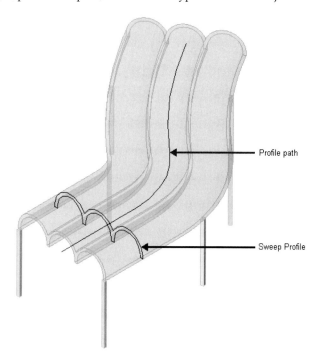

Profile path

Sweep Profile

A warped type of roof diaphragm often creates a smooth slope along its path (see Figure 5.30) from ridge to drain. In cases like that, the flat plane techniques that you learned earlier in this chapter will not work. An alternative is to use a solid sweep or a solid blend. Once you become accustomed to using the solid modeling features, you will be able to create nearly any shape imaginable (see Figure 5.31). You will undoubtedly face many challenging projects and some with exotic shapes. (We will cover these advanced solid modeling techniques in Chapter 19.)

FIGURE 5.30
Wave-style roof diaphragm created by using a solid blend

FIGURE 5.31
Freeform roof shape created using a solid blend

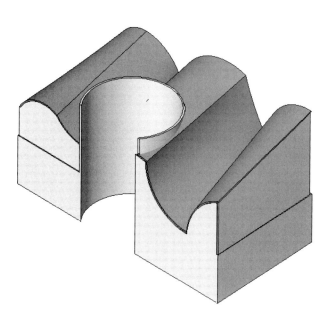

CREATING A ROOF DIAPHRAGM USING A SOLID BLEND

An interesting approach for creating a roof diaphragm is to use a blended solid form. The use of two profiles that blend together can make difficult shapes easy to create. Using a void to cut and shape the blend, you can create many complex shapes with these tools. The basic approach is as follows:

1. In a plan view, create two reference planes, one at each end of the shape you wish to create. Give them the names **1** and **2**.

2. Cut a section in front of and parallel to the first reference line; then stretch its extents past the second reference line.

3. Go to the section view you just created.

4. On the Model panel of the Home tab of the Ribbon, choose Model In-Place from the Component drop-down list.

5. Choose Roofs as the category, and name the new element.

6. On the In-Place Modeling panel click Solid and then Solid Blend from the drop-down list.

7. On the Work Plane panel of the Home tab of the Ribbon click Set, and select the first reference plane as the current plane.

8. Using the tools on the Draw panel, sketch the profile of one side of the solid (see Figure 5.32) as a closed-line sequence with the thickness of the roof.

FIGURE 5.32
Sketching the base profile at the blended solid

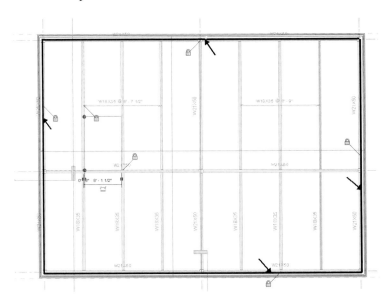

9. On the Mode panel of the Create Blend Base Boundary tab, click Edit Top.

10. On the Home tab of the Ribbon, click Set on the Work Plane panel, and then select the second reference plane to make it current.

11. Draw the second profile in the same way as you did the first except for its specific profile.

12. On the Blend panel click Finish Blend.

13. On the In-Place Editor panel click Finish Model.

That completes our look at how to create and edit roof decks. As you have seen, there are many different techniques available to you; just pick the one closest to your needs.

ATTACHING WALLS AND COLUMNS TO FLOORS AND ROOFS

An important feature of floors and roofs is that you can attach walls and columns to their underside. This is helpful in many cases, especially for roof conditions. A warped roof, for instance, with walls below would require editing the walls in elevation to match the roof warping. If the roof outline then changes during the design process, you would have to continually go back and fix the walls. That's the kind of busywork that you do not want to be spending your project fee fixing. You want to spend your fee concentrating on your design. You want your model to have the flexibility to adjust itself through its understanding of relationships between objects.

Column attachment to the floor or roof is also important. As you can imagine, with a warped or sloping roof your columns will each have a different elevation at their top. Calculating each of those values would be time consuming, and the editing process would be grueling. Another alternative to establishing the top of the column elevation is to go into a section view, measure the distance from the top of the column to the underside of deck, and adjust it in the Column Element Properties dialog box. That too is time consuming and fairly inaccurate.

The procedure to attach walls and columns to your roof (or floor) deck is straightforward:

1. In a 2D or 3D view, select a column.

2. On the Modify Column panel of the Modify Structural Columns tab of the Ribbon you will see Top/Base, where you can select Attach (or Detach if desired); take note of the Options bar to define how the attachment should be made.

3. Click on the floor or roof element to which you wish to attach the wall.

The above list describes the steps for attaching a column. The steps are the same for a wall; however, the Ribbon tab and panel names change accordingly. You won't be able to attach walls and columns at the same time because the tools will not activate if you have different categories of elements selected.

Keep in mind that walls or columns will stay attached even if the form of the roof changes, as long as the roof remains located over the wall. A warning will be displayed if the attached items can no longer be attached because of a change in the roof or floor.

FLEXING THE MODEL CAN CAUSE UNINTENDED RESULTS

Set a goal for yourself while creating your model: the elements in the model should be adequately constrained and have the ability to flex constantly. It can be intimidating when elements start moving around automatically because of the constraints to which they are attached. You have to keep an eye on those changes and anticipate them by understanding the relationship between elements in Revit Structure. Keep a check on the various views that you have placed on your sheets, and make it a habit to quickly do a survey either on screen or on the hard copy before you send out your drawings to make sure elements have not moved in unexpected ways.

OPENINGS AND DEPRESSIONS

An important consideration for any slab or deck is the ability to create openings and depressions. Slab openings are often shafts for elevators, for mechanical ductwork, for light wells, and for other things of that nature. Depressions are often necessary for setting tile in bathroom or kitchen areas. If you want to keep the model accurate, you must address these elements.

To create the openings, you can edit the deck in the following way:

1. Select the slab.

2. On the Modify Floors tab click the Edit Boundary icon on the Edit panel.

3. Using the Draw tools, sketch an enclosed polygon within the boundary of the slab where you want the opening.

4. Click Finish Floor to complete the sketch.

This is the simplest method. You can also make the opening flex with the beams that support the deck around it by locking them together. Put your plan view into Medium mode temporarily and lock the opening lines to the edges of the beam flanges (see Figure 5.33). That way, if the beam sizes change, the opening will change with them.

To add building core mechanical and elevator openings, use the Shaft Opening tool to make your openings. The advantage is that the openings are automatically created in all floors and roofs that the shaft penetrates (as determined by its parameters), and the openings are consistently in the same location floor to floor (see Figure 5.34). The Shaft Opening tool also lets you add symbolic lines so that your shaft has the graphical marking you need, such as an X to indicate a mechanical shaft opening, at each and every floor as well.

FIGURE 5.33
Locking an opening to adjacent framing while in Medium display mode

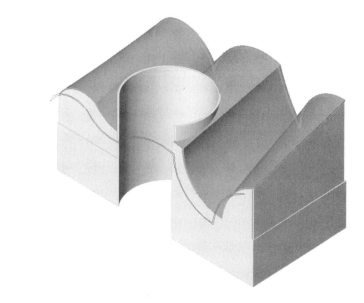

FIGURE 5.34
A 3D view of a shaft opening penetrating floors and roofs of the structure

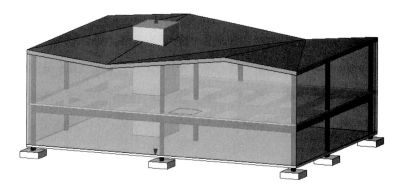

CREATE A SHAFT OPENING

Adding a shaft opening to your project is not difficult, and it works like this:

1. Go to a plan view.

2. On the Opening panel of the Modify tab of the Ribbon, click Shaft.

3. In the resulting Sketch mode, use Boundary Lines and the Draw tools to create the opening shape.

4. Click the Shaft Opening Properties icon on the Element panel to access the Element Properties dialog box.

5. Adjust the top and bottom constraints to set the vertical extents of the shaft.

6. Provide level offsets a bit below and above the roof; then exit the dialog box.

7. Using Symbolic Lines and the Draw tools, sketch the opening symbol or graphics if desired.

8. On the Shaft Opening panel click Finish Opening, and Revit Structure will create the shaft.

Another feature common to slabs that you will likely encounter is the isolated slab depression. For example, you may have thin-set tile less than an inch deep in the bathroom areas of a building (see Figure 5.35). A deeper-set tile of 3″ to 4″ is also common. How you would model these depressions depends on the type.

FIGURE 5.35
Slab depression with the void highlighted in section

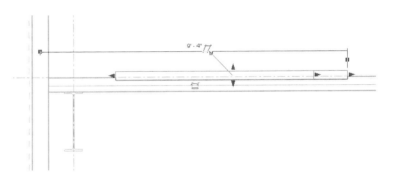

By creating and attaching a void extrusion to the slab or deck, you can hollow out the basic slab element. That will work fine for shallow depressions. Deeper depressions may require a lowering of the slab in that area. For that type of construction, you will need to create an opening in the slab, make a new slab element within that opening, and position it at the desired elevation.

CREATING SLAB DEPRESSIONS IN YOUR SLAB OR DECK

To create a depression in a slab, do the following:

1. Go to a plan view of the slab.

2. On the Model panel of the Home tab of the Ribbon, choose Model In-Place from the Component drop-down list.

3. Select Floors for the category, and name the new family something descriptive like **Depression First Floor**. You then are placed into Sketch mode.

4. On the In-Place Modeling panel click Void and then Extrusion from the drop-down list.

5. From the Draw panel use the Drawing tools to make the boundary of the depression.

6. On the Element panel click Extrusion Properties.

7. Set the Extrusion End value at **1**″ (see Figure 5.36), so that the void extrusion goes a bit above the slab.

8. Set the Extrusion Start value equal to the depth of the depression with a negative value.

9. Click Finish Model.

10. On the Modify tab on the Edit Geometry panel, click Cut Geometry from the Cut drop-down list.

11. Select the slab or deck and then select the void.

12. Click Finish Model on the In-Place Editor panel, and Revit Structure will create the depression.

A void blend can be used to create a tapering depression.

FIGURE 5.36
In the Instance Properties dialog box, you set the vertical range of the void extrusion by adding an extrusion value in each direction relative to the floor level.

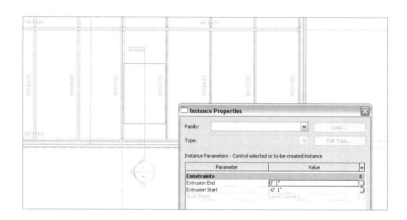

EXERCISE: CREATING A SIMPLE SLOPED ROOF WITH DORMERS

In this exercise, you will create a roof with dormers:

1. Open a new project.

2. Open Structural Plan View - Level 2.

3. Select Roof and then Roof by Footprint from the Architect panel of the Architect & Site tab.

4. Choose Boundary Line from the Draw panel.

5. Click the Rectangle tool on the Draw/Pick Gallery, and then sketch a rectangular shape to define your roof edges.

6. Click Ref Plane on the Work Plane panel of the Home tab, choose Draw Reference Plane, and draw three lines vertically inside the rectangle. Make sure they span across the top and bottom horizontal sketch lines.

7. To space them out equally, click Aligned from the Dimension panel on the Annotate tab of the Ribbon. Create a dimension string connecting all five vertical lines, the two sketch lines, and the three reference planes. Click the EQ button on the dimension string before canceling the tool, or select the dimension string to do so if you've canceled it already.

8. Erase the top and bottom lines.
   Yes, you could use the Split tool to split them instead, but the Split tool doesn't seem to detect the intersection of sketch lines and reference planes very well, so drawing four new lines is going to be more accurate.

9. Click Boundary Line on the Draw panel, and choose Line from the Draw/Pick Gallery. Sketch four equal lines across the top and bottom, using the reference planes as your guide to define each new segment.

10. Click Slope Arrow on the Draw panel, and draw a slope arrow over each of the two inner lines with the arrows facing the middle reference plane.
    The arrowhead is the head and the other end is the tail of the slope arrow. The first point of a slope arrow is always the tail. Repeat step 10 for both the top and bottom horizontal sketch lines.

11. Select all the slope arrows, and click the Properties button on the Draw panel. If isn't set already, set the Height Above level to **10′-0″**.

12. Select the six remaining lines, three each at both ends of the roof sketch. On the Options bar, check the box for Defines Slope.

13. One by one, select the other lines and click into the angle symbol. Set the slope to **30** degrees for the horizontal lines and **50** degrees for the vertical lines on the side. You can change the Slope parameter for multiple items by using the Element Properties dialog box.

14. Click Finish Sketch to finish the roof diaphragm.
    Keep in mind that the roof is an architectural element according to Revit Structure and as such may not be visible in a 3D view in the default template. Just check the view's Visibility/Graphics settings to turn on the Roof category.

The Bottom Line

Create a slab-on-grade with dropped slab edges.   Using the Slab command, you can create slabs-on-grade and apply dropped edges to them with the Slab Edge function. You can also edit the profile file for slab edges in order to create new types.

> **Master It**   You have a new project and have to add a slab-on-grade and slab edge at the bottom level. How do you do it?

Work with floor decks.   There are different methods for creating and editing roof diaphragms within Revit Structure. Composite roofs with metal deck can be created by sketching their profile in a plan view or extruding their sectional shapes.

Master It   Your project requires the metal deck to stop at the edge girder and the concrete to extend out one foot beyond to meet the inside face of the metal stud framing on the exterior. How do you accomplish this?

Work with various kinds of roof decks.   Different methods exist for creating roofs that are other than planar. Those methods include using the slab subelement tools as well as creating more exotic roof shapes with solid modeling tools.

Creating warped roof decks requires more complicated techniques because the form has no flat planes. Revit Structure has tools that help you create and edit the ridge lines and elevation points that occur in most roof elements.

Master It   Your project has a main ridge line across the middle of the roof with two drains on two edges of the roof diaphragm at points that are at one-third of the edge distance. How would you create it?

Create openings and depressions in your floors and roofs.   For nearly every project you will need to create shaft and incidental openings. The dimensions of openings such as elevator shafts that extend through several floors must be kept consistent. Revit Structure has the tools to help you accomplish that goal.

Master It   On a multistory building, you want to add shafts to the core areas for stairs and elevators. How would you do that?

Chapter 6

Walls

Walls are one of the most profound features of Revit Structure. As a wall is modeled, all aspects of that wall's functions are considered — the structural usage, the type of wall, and even architectural considerations. Also within the initial design of a wall, the cover for reinforcing is specified. Learning how to create and work with wall systems is a must, but it is easy to accomplish.

Walls, like slabs, floors, and roofs, are unique in that they are all system families. This means they are completely controlled, manipulated, and created within the current structural model. You do not import a wall type into a model. It also means that walls can change dynamically as the model changes. When a wall is "constrained" between two floors, for example, the actual dimensional difference between the floors influences the height of the wall. If a floor height changes for any reason, so does the wall height.

It is important to note right off that wall types that are to be repeated through many projects should be added to a company template. To learn more about template creation, refer to Chapter 2. If a wall object has been created in another project, the wall style can be carried into the current model by simply copying and pasting the wall into the current model from the existing one. Although this is often frowned upon in other drafting applications, Revit Structure is a database that fully allows copying and pasting without residual, unexpected side effects such as extra layers, blocks, and even shape files, which might otherwise corrupt a drawing.

The first type of wall system to be covered will be a basic wall. Don't let the name fool you — it can be anything from a plain concrete wall to a complex wall system with structural and architectural elements combined. The basic wall type, however, will certainly be the most common wall type used. Revit Structure ships with 12 predefined basic types. Some of these wall types will be fine to use as is, and some of them will be used as a starting point for a more complex wall system.

In this chapter you will learn to:

◆ Place walls in your model

◆ Create new walls

◆ Modify walls in place

Placing a Wall in Your Model

To add a new basic wall, you first need to be in either a plan view or a 3D view. You should also have all primary levels defined, but it is not imperative. After all, the power of Revit Structure lies in the fact that changes are propagated throughout the model. Also, it is recommended that you place walls in a plan view and not a 3D view. You will have much more control, and you are less likely to make mistakes. At the top of the Revit Structure 2010 graphical user interface is the Ribbon. Walls are easily created using this interface. On the Home tab ➢ Structure panel ➢ Wall drop-down ➢ Structural Wall, you will see the Structural Wall button (see Figure 6.1).

FIGURE 6.1
The Wall drop-down located on the Home tab's Structure panel

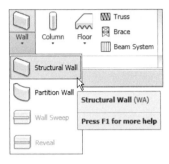

The command process in Revit Structure is quite intuitive. You select your command (in this case Structural Wall), and Revit Structure will change the active ribbon to display a contextual ribbon filled with tools that apply to that element (see Figure 6.2). When you exit the command, the contextual ribbon for that specific command will be dismissed. This greatly reduces the clutter found in most traditional CAD programs, where all the toolbar commands surround the display area.

FIGURE 6.2
The PlaceStructural Wall contextual tab

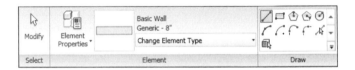

On the contextual tab, several buttons will stand out. The most important of the buttons is what is called the Type Selector (see Figure 6.3). This will display a list of the defined wall types found in this specific project. This list can simply be just a few wall types, or it can be extremely long depending on the size and stage of your project. We recommend that this list be as short as possible and that you adhere to company-wide naming conventions. There is nothing worse than having exact duplicate wall configurations with differing type names to choose from. As you start the Wall command and the Place Structural Wall tab appears, the first thing to do is select a wall type from the Type Selector.

When you select the item from the Type Selector, Revit Structure continues to provide choices from the Place Structural Wall tab and the Options bar below it. The first decision is how you will place the new wall in your model. You can either match existing geometry in the model, or you can use a Draw tool and draw the wall from scratch.

Using the Draw Method

By using a Draw tool, you are telling Revit Structure you want point-by-point placement of your wall. You will be prompted to pick a point in the view window. Click to enter the wall's start point. Because Revit Structure does not have an actual command prompt, it has a status bar to guide the user. This comes in handy for more convoluted commands. Once the first point is selected, you will see a blue alignment line. This takes the place of the traditional "ortho," or polar tracking. If you move your cursor straight in any direction, your wall will snap to a horizontal or vertical axis automatically (see Figure 6.4). You can configure additional snap settings using the Manage tab ➢ Project Settings panel ➢ Settings drop-down ➢ Snaps. Alternatively, you can press the Shift key while sketching; this will engage an automatic ortho mode, allowing easy horizontal or vertical placement.

FIGURE 6.3
The Type Selector allows you to choose the wall type you need to add to the model.

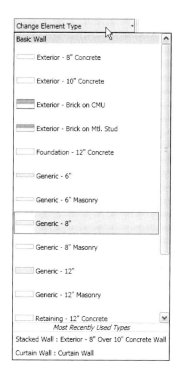

FIGURE 6.4
Alignment lines are basically the replacement for the ortho function in AutoCAD.

As you sketch the wall, a blue dimension appears. This is called a *temporary dimension*.

Instead of having to eyeball a second point, you can type in a distance value instead (see Figure 6.5), because when you see the blue dimension value Revit is "listening" for keyboard input. Since Revit Structure is, by default, using feet and fractional inches in Imperial units, you can type in the value without the foot mark. For example, if you wanted a wall that was 50′-0″ long, you could simply type in **50**. Revit Structure accepts that this value is in feet. If you wanted the wall to be 50″ long, you could enter **0 50** or **0-50**, or you could type **50″**, including the inch mark. If you wanted 50′-6-1/2″, you could enter **50 6 1/2**. Also, Revit Structure will accept equations as you draw the wall. If you wanted a 50′-0″ long wall, for example, you could type **=25*2**. Once the second point is selected, Revit Structure will place the end at the resulting distance of the equation. Another neat option is that you can use alternative units for any distance input. Even though your model may be in Imperial units, if you provide a value of **20m**, for example, Revit will provide a 20-meter distance regardless of the project unit setting.

FIGURE 6.5
You can type temporary dimensions using any valid input distance method and in any unit format.

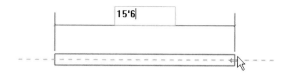

Normally, the process will be to sketch the walls, but if geometry is already placed in the model, it may be tempting to just select that geometry.

Using the Pick Lines Button

By using the Pick Lines button, you are telling Revit Structure that your method of wall placement will be to select existing geometry in the model. You typically use this approach when you are referencing an architectural model from within a structural model. In some cases, this will be a 2D architectural CAD file. We recommend that you proceed with caution while picking geometry using this method. It is possible the CAD data can contain walls that are not perfectly straight. If this is the case, and you are adding a new wall by picking the CAD geometry, Revit Structure will report the issue (see Figure 6.6).

FIGURE 6.6
The "off axis" warning informs you something is amiss.

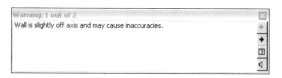

Revit Structure will generate a warning that can be bypassed. Although it is tempting to ignore, we suggest that you ensure your wall is being drawn straight and accurately. This warning can also be expanded to see exactly which wall generated the error. Revit Structure will list the error and then break the list down to the specific item(s) that are suspect. Once the items are selected, you will be able to find the "crooked" walls in the model. At that point, you can delete the offending item. Again, we recommend that you go ahead and delete the wall instead of trying to adjust it or leaving it in the model non-orthogonal. See Figure 6.7 for an illustration.

The Pick Lines method is also useful for adding walls to a sketch. Many times it is useful to use drafting lines in place of walls to establish important layout dimensional constraints. In preliminary stages of a project, it is sometimes beneficial to approach a model in this mind-set. Sketching the lines and then adding the walls afterward in many cases is much easier and actually safer (see Figure 6.8). For more information on drafting lines and sketching, see Chapter 9.

Later, once the perimeter extents have been established, you can place the walls by selecting these lines. Simply start the Structural Wall command, and then click on a line. A useful method is to use the Tab key to pick lines. While running the Wall command, you can pause your cursor over a single element. Once the item highlights, press the Tab key. All connected elements will become highlighted.

Since you are basically drawing in 2D, what about the height of the wall? Don't you need to "extrude" it? The answer is no. You can set the height based on either a level or an increment. The results would then look like Figure 6.9.

FIGURE 6.7
You can click the expanded warning button to see a full preview of the problem.

FIGURE 6.8
Drafting lines define the geometry.

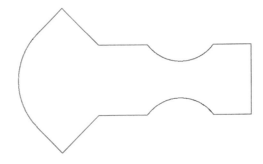

FIGURE 6.9
The 3D result of picking geometry via the Pick Lines button. Although this is a nice view, always be sure your Location Line constraint is set to the justification you need.

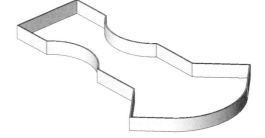

USING LINES AS A CRUTCH

You may find as you start modeling your footprint, if it is an odd shape, that the best way to be sure your geometry is where you want it is to simply start using drafting lines as a guide. Once the drafting lines are in place, you can then start selecting those lines to add your walls. In many cases this has proven to be a good fallback policy, especially in the beginning stages of your usage of Revit Structure.

Assigning Wall Constraints

As mentioned earlier, walls are special because they can be constrained to project levels. This means that the base and the top can both be "locked" to a level (see Figure 6.10). In other words, you can set a wall and forget it.

FIGURE 6.10
A wall placed and con-
strained between Level 1
and Level 2

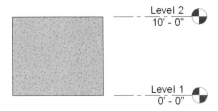

To do this, while the Wall tool is active, glance at the Options bar. It has a drop-down to handle the Height or Depth constraints (Figure 6.11). It is automatically assumed, unless specified otherwise, that you will create the wall using Depth and "build a wall" down to a level below. Once you select a depth or height, you can choose the level it will be constrained to in the adjacent drop-down list. If you choose Unconnected, you can simply provide a fixed height or depth value. We recommend that you specify a level in lieu of an unconnected height or depth when possible. Once you start sketching the wall or selecting geometry to use as a guideline, you need to consider and choose the Location Line setting, which is similar to the notion of text justification, on which the wall will be defined.

FIGURE 6.11
On the Options bar,
you will see the
Depth/Height settings.

Implementing the Location Line

Possibly the most important item on the Options bar is the location of the wall (see Figure 6.12). This determines what the points you pick/place mean. Do your points indicate the face of the structure or the face of finish? Do you care? You should, because this can ripple through a project in a negative or a positive way. When you are laying out a wall, be aware of the fact that, while the justification of a wall can always be modified, it is not always easy to do so toward the end of a project.

There are six choices for locating the justification of the wall, as explained in the following sections.

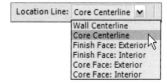

WALL CENTERLINE LOCATION LINE

The Wall Centerline option calculates the centerline of the wall based on the two outermost faces or overall thickness of the wall (see Figure 6.13). It could be made of gypsum or some lightweight finish, or it could be a structural element such as CMU or concrete. While this is fine for a single-layer-type wall such as a concrete foundation wall or concrete masonry unit (CMU) wall, it is not recommended for a compound wall such as a CMU wall with a brick veneer. Also, walls with finishes don't lend themselves well to this justification.

FIGURE 6.13
With the Wall Center-line option, the align-ment line is located on the exact middle of the overall wall width.

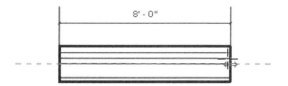

CORE CENTERLINE LOCATION LINE

The Core Centerline option allows you to justify the wall about the centerline of the structural width/thickness of the wall (see Figure 6.14). In the example used here, the compound wall is 8″ CMU with 2″ of rigid insulation, a 2″ air space, and a 4″ brick veneer. The justification of the wall is based on the center of the CMU layer because it is the core boundary. This helps in the placement of the structural face of a core layer.

FIGURE 6.14
Here, the alignment line is centered on the wall's core centerline.

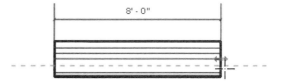

FINISH FACE: EXTERIOR LOCATION LINE

This one, we believe, is self-explanatory. The justification of the wall will be to whichever face is to the outside. If you select an existing wall, a flip control symbol will appear, and it is always located outside the exterior face of the wall. As you are placing a new wall, however, the inside and outside may not be what you expect. You have the option to press the spacebar to swap the interior and exterior faces of a wall. To do this, use the following steps:

1. Select the Structural Wall command on the Structure panel of the Home tab.

2. Select a compound wall type such as Exterior – Brick on CMU.

3. Change the Location Line value to Finish Face: Exterior.

4. Click the start point for the placement of the wall.

5. Press the spacebar.

Notice that the wall will flip about the justification axis, as illustrated in Figure 6.15.

FIGURE 6.15
This wall is justified about the finish face exterior.

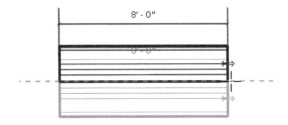

FINISH FACE: INTERIOR LOCATION LINE

This justification allows the wall to be placed using the finished face of the inside of the wall. This is normally an architectural finish and is probably the least common of the six choices, but it is still sometimes useful or necessary (see Figure 6.16) where codes require minimum clear distances between the finished walls, such as exit corridors, for example.

FIGURE 6.16
This wall is justified about the finish face interior.

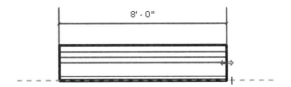

CORE FACE: EXTERIOR LOCATION LINE

This option justifies the wall to the face of the structural element of the wall. The face it chooses is the side facing the exterior. Usually this is in the middle of the wall core, as shown in Figure 6.17. This allows you to justify the wall as if there were no architectural elements, and the insulation, air space, and brick layers are ignored.

FIGURE 6.17
This wall is justified about the core face's exterior.

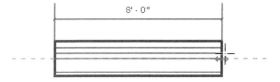

CORE FACE: INTERIOR LOCATION LINE

Like Core Face: Exterior, this option justifies the wall based on the inside face of the structural element. Any finishes on the inside of the wall will be ignored. See Figure 6.18.

FIGURE 6.18
This wall is justified about the core face's interior.

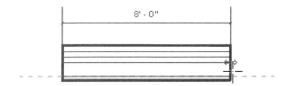

EXERCISE: JUSTIFYING WALLS

As a practice for the wall justification, perform the following steps:

1. Start a new project model and go to the Level 1 plan view.

2. Change the Detail level to Medium so that wall layers will be visible.

3. On the Structure panel of the Home tab, select the Wall button.

4. Assign the wall type Exterior – Brick on CMU on the Type Selector.

5. Change the Height to Level 2.

6. Change the justification to Finish Face: Exterior.

7. Pick a start point.

8. Toggle the Chain check box on (if needed).

9. Draw a wall 25'-0" straight to the right. If the justification location line is to the top, press the spacebar to flip it.

10. Draw another wall 25'-0" straight up. Continue to the left and down to form a box.

Although this is simply a box shape, it is important to understand how Revit Structure works and, more important, what it expects from the end user. Yes, placing walls is simple, but an eyes-open approach is needed to get the desired results. Although all of these options can be fixed later, getting the most accurate placement initially is crucial to a successful project. See the following illustration for the finished walls.

If you choose to sketch the walls, some additional tools will be available on the Options bar. These options will allow you to draw the walls in the geometry you need.

Now a final word about location line placement. Often when you copy and paste or use any other method of getting walls into your model, you might forgo worrying about the Location Line setting initially. But what if later you need to make adjustments to the wall type, such as getting rid of extra material layers you don't need structurally? If you simply adjust the Location Line setting to be a core face rather than a finish face, then when you swap to a new type the core will stay in the same position. If you need to then adjust core thickness, consider changing the location line to the core side that is in the proper location and then adjusting the type. This basic procedure will keep the primary concern of the wall, the core, in a consistent and correct location.

 **Real World Scenario**

PASTING WALLS SAVED THE DAY

We worked on a project where the client was an architect who was using Revit Architecture. We figured this should be a great treat since this project had load-bearing masonry walls all over the place. By leveraging the work the architect was doing, we could skip a lot of model work and just paste in their "stuff" into our model.

It turned out to be more of a challenge that we expected. For starters, we opened up the architect's model in the same Revit Structure session as our structural model. We then copied and pasted all the walls from their 3D view into our 3D view of the model. What did we see then? Nothing — no walls at all.

As we soon discovered, architects can't really set walls to a usage that allows Revit Structure to "see" them readily. So after a little investigation we undid the paste and then repeated it. This left the walls selected, albeit invisible in our model views. From there we went into the Element (Instance) properties for all the selected walls and changed the Structural Usage parameter to Structural Combined. Finally, we got walls we could actually see.

Next, came cleaning them up. The architect used some very nice basic walls, like those shown in the previous exercise. They had lots of layers, and these layers made up the entire wall width. But structurally, all I needed was the masonry, which was also the "core" of the wall, luckily. Well, with the walls still selected, I once again went into Element properties but this time adjusted the Location Line value to Core Face: Exterior. This relocated all the justifications to the face of the masonry part of the wall.

Then came the really cool part that really showed off Revit Structure. Using the Type Selector on the Ribbon, I selected a simple 8″ masonry wall, changing the multiple-layer walls to something with just masonry. But because I had moved the location line to the core, the walls stayed put and simply got stripped of the extra finish materials. Even doors and windows got smaller jambs, and the profile sketches were preserved.

The only other editing left to do was to extend any foundation-bearing walls down to a lower foundation level, which was quite easy. I tried to get the architect to do that for us, to lower the walls down to the footing elevation, but I guess he figured we needed something to do.

Using Sketch Tools

It does seem redundant to keep drawing walls piece by piece. After all, most drafting programs allow users to draw any shape they choose. Revit Structure is no different. With the proper height and base constraints and the proper justification, Revit Structure will allow you to "sketch" any desired shape. As a default, the Line method is selected for the placement of any new wall. To the right of the Line choice is the Rectangle method. Let's explore a couple of the other options available.

The placement of a wall using the Rectangle method involves these steps:

1. On the Structure panel of the Home tab, click the Wall button.

2. Set the Height/Depth and Location Line to the desired settings.

3. Click the Rectangle button.

4. Pick a corner point for a rectangular wall configuration.

5. Move your cursor in an angular direction.

   You will see the walls form, but they may be positioned incorrectly. Remember, before you place the second point, you can press the spacebar to flip the orientation of the wall elements about the Location Line. Unfortunately, you will have to adjust the Temporary Dimensions after you finish the rectangle because you cannot define them before or during placement.

6. Pick a final point to finish the rectangle.

The other polygon shapes we can create are inscribed polygon and circumscribed polygon.

For curves or arcs there are several other tools: Circle, Start-End-Radius Arc, Center-Ends Arc, Tangent Ends Arc, and Fillet Arc. Let's take a closer look at the placement of a wall using the Start-End-Radius Arc method, which involves these steps (see Figure 6.19). This method is easiest to use in some cases because you don't have to know where the center of the arc is located.

1. On the Structure panel of the Home tab, click the Wall button.

2. Click the Start-End-Radius Arc button.

3. Pick the start point of the arc; with the first two points you select, you are defining the chord of your arc.

4. Pick the end point of the arc.

5. Either pick a point along the arc or type in a radius distance. Remember that if the justification is incorrect, you can press the spacebar to flip the wall.

There are other wall draw options as well (see Figure 6.20).

FIGURE 6.19
An arced wall passing through three points

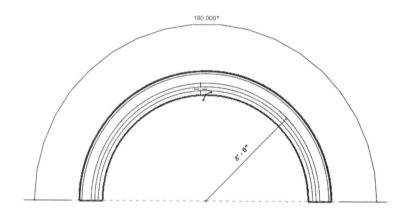

FIGURE 6.20
The available wall Draw tools

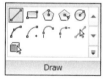

Draw

Let's try another method. Revit Structure does not have an actual Fillet command that will allow you to select the wall and add a radius at a later time. It does, however, have a Fillet Arc button built into the Draw panel during wall creation.

The creation of a filleted set of walls using the Fillet Arc option is as follows:

1. On the Structure panel, click the Wall button.

2. Create any corner condition.

3. Select the Fillet Arc button from the Draw panel.

4. Turn on the Radius check box on the Options bar, and enter a distance of **3′-0″** (see Figure 6.21). If you want, you can dynamically place the fillet arc wall segment by skipping this step, moving to step 5, and picking a point that describes where the fillet arc should go.

FIGURE 6.21
The Radius setting on
the Options bar

5. Click the two walls, and the fillet arc is added (see Figure 6.22). Note that the radius is applied to the centerline of the walls. When you sketch using the Line or Rectangle button, you also have the option to specify a radius, in the same way as in step 4 and shown in Figure 6.21, which will cause Revit to add a fillet radius at each intersection of your sketch, as you sketch.

FIGURE 6.22
The fillet arc has been
added to the walls.

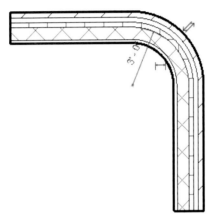

Now that we have drawn some walls in the model, it is time to see how we can further manipulate them. Simply placing a wall and then changing the visible options is literally just scratching the surface of what can be done. There is an entire dialog box filled with options and settings we can use to configure our walls. Once the wall(s) have been added to the model, we can modify the individual Element properties of each wall itself.

Accessing Element Properties

By placing a wall and then selecting Element Properties, you gain access to even more settings than were available on the Options bar. These settings are called *instance parameters*. This means that the changes will pertain only to the wall(s) selected. If you would like to change every wall instance of that wall type in the entire model, you can access the type properties by clicking the Edit Type button. This is common not only in walls but in almost all families in a Revit Structure model (see Figure 6.23).

ADJUSTING INSTANCE PARAMETERS

To gain access to the Instance parameters of a wall using the Instance Properties dialog box, follow these steps (see Figure 6.24):

1. Select a wall or many walls.

2. Click the Element Properties button on the Element panel.

3. In the resulting dialog box, you will see all of the Instance parameters.

FIGURE 6.23
In the Instance Proper-
ties dialog box, change
Instance parameters
to change individual
wall(s).

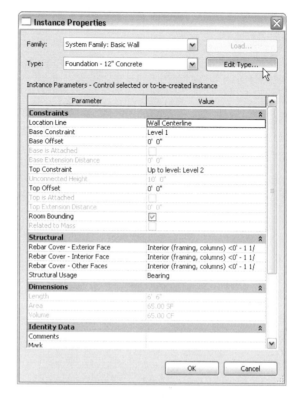

FIGURE 6.24
Instance parameters
change only the settings
of the selected wall(s).

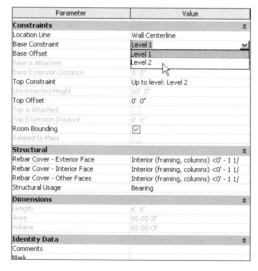

INSTANCE PARAMETER CATEGORIES

The Instance parameters for the walls are broken down into groups. One group is the Structural category. This will determine the cover of the reinforcing as it is placed into the model as well as the structural usage. This item, along with phasing and the analytical model, will be discussed in Chapter 15.

A very important parameter of each and every wall is Structural Usage. Any given wall can be set to any one of four usage parameters: Non-bearing, Bearing, Shear, Structural Combined. Each of these has intentional use conditions; for example, use Shear for walls that resist lateral forces. If you are utilizing an analysis program with the Revit Structure model, you will need to assign this property according to design intent.

In addition, if any wall usage parameter is set to Non-bearing, you will not be able to see the wall if the active view's Discipline value is set to Structural (it is assumed to be "architectural" and not as "important"). This often happens when you copy walls from an architectural model into a structural model — the walls set to Non-bearing don't show after being pasted. You then have to set the view to Coordination (or any other type), select the now-showing walls, and change those required to any bearing setting. Then those walls will be visible when the view is set back to Structural.

CHANGING TYPE PARAMETERS

Type parameters of a wall are settings that define what a wall is. These parameters, if modified, will influence every matching wall type in the model. So, if you have a CMU wall and you change the Type parameter called Material to Brick instead of Concrete Masonry Units, you have just changed *every* wall of that type to be a brick wall. So, given that, you must make changes deliberately and thoughtfully. To access these properties, first select a wall, and then click the Element Properties button on the Element panel. Next, click the Edit Type button at the top of the dialog box, as shown in Figure 6.25.

Once you click Edit Type, the Type Properties dialog box displays (see Figure 6.26).

It is important to get into the practice of creating new wall types when you are changing Type parameters and don't intend to alter the existing walls in your model. If you already have the Instance Properties dialog box open, then follow these steps to edit the Type parameters for a wall:

1. Click the Edit Type button.

2. Click Duplicate.

3. Rename the wall type to something that makes sense (see Figure 6.27).

Use the Type Properties dialog box when you plan to either change the current wall type globally or create an entirely new wall type. This sequence steps you through the process:

1. Click the Preview button at the bottom of the Type Properties dialog box. The dialog box expands to display a graphic of the wall (see Figure 6.28).

2. Beneath the preview is a View drop-down list. Select Section: Modify Type Attributes (see Figure 6.29).

FIGURE 6.25
The Edit Type button allows you to access the Type parameters.

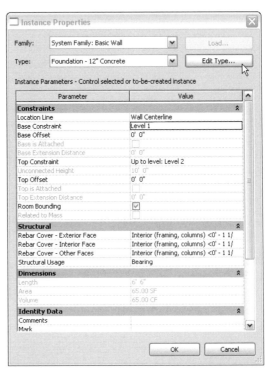

FIGURE 6.26
The Type Properties dialog box allows you to edit every wall for that type in the entire model.

FIGURE 6.27
The Name dialog box appears once you click the Duplicate button.

FIGURE 6.28
The preview allows you to see the wall.

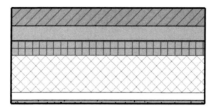

FIGURE 6.29
The Modify Type Attributes settings allow you to really see the wall components.

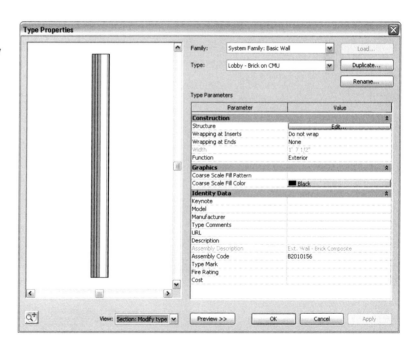

Another way of managing your wall types in Revit Structure is to use the Project Browser (see Figure 6.30). As you scroll down the list, you will come to a portion in the browser where families are listed. If you expand families by clicking the plus sign (+), you will see the Walls category. Here, the walls are broken out into the three categories: Basic Wall, Curtain Wall, and Stacked Wall. If you expand the list further, you can simply double-click on a wall type to access its Type properties. This method is slightly different than selecting a wall from the drawing area — with this method you have access only to the properties that will change all of the walls of this type in the entire model.

FIGURE 6.30
Finding a wall in the
Project Browser

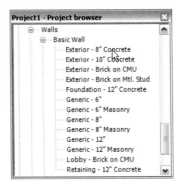

To create a new wall type from the Project Browser, perform these steps:

1. Scroll through the Project Browser until you come to the Families category.

2. Find Walls and expand it.

3. Select Basic Wall and expand the list.

4. Within the Basic Wall category, find the wall you are looking for.

5. Right-click and select Duplicate.

6. Rename the new wall type.

7. Double-click on the new wall type.

Notice you have access only to the Type properties. This is a good way to ensure you are editing only the proper wall. As mentioned earlier, there is a small sampling of walls to choose from in the out-of-the-box Revit Structure templates. You will almost certainly need to start creating your own walls at some point. Usually "some point" is the first stage of your first project.

Creating a New Compound Wall

Now that you have the basics down, it is time to create a new wall type. Depending on how you plan to use the wall type, this can be either easy or somewhat difficult. Keep in mind that the amount of effort you put into the wall at this stage of the model can have positive effects down the line when it comes time to add sections and elevations.

Let's begin with a very simple wall. Create a new model, and then in the Project Browser, scroll down to the Walls category within the Families list and then into the Basic Wall category. Right-click on Generic – 6″ and duplicate the wall type. This will create a new type of the same name with an added "2" (see Figure 6.31). Once it is created, right-click to open the context menu for the new wall type and rename it if so desired.

Use the following procedure on the new project model where we will adjust a new wall type (see Figure 6.32):

1. Double-click on the new wall type.

2. In the Type Parameters section of the Type Properties dialog box, click the Edit button in the Structure row.

3. In the Edit Assembly dialog box, make sure the Preview window is open and that the View drop-down is set to Section: Modify Type Attributes. This is important because otherwise you can't access some of the buttons we will be using (see Figure 6.33).

FIGURE 6.31

A new Generic – 6″ 2 wall

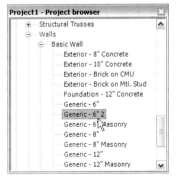

FIGURE 6.32

Edit the structure by clicking the Edit button in the Structure row.

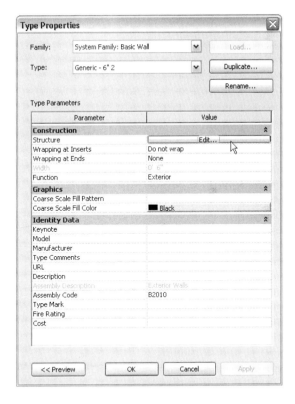

Note that before you start modifying this wall, you should plan each change carefully. Pressing the Esc key will cause you to lose all of your changes. If you make a mistake, click the Cancel button and redo the procedure. This does take practice and patience.

Revit uses wall layers to not only generate the appropriate look for a wall but also to instruct Revit on how to connect the various elements when they intersect other walls, of the same type or a different type. Core layers join to core layers, and subsequent layers join according to the hierarchy they are set to. Controls for physical materials like Substrates can supersede others such as Thermal/Air Layer.

FIGURE 6.33
The controls that describe a wall

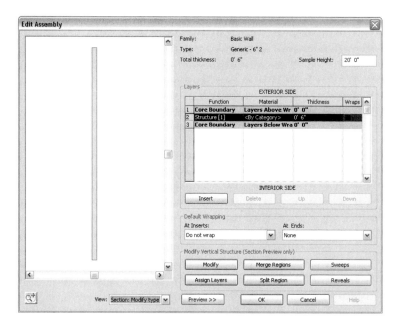

Notice a section called Layers in Figure 6.33. Two core boundaries surround a wall core. When you build a wall, anything that goes between the core boundaries is considered the *core* (typically *structure*). Above the layers you see EXTERIOR SIDE and below it you see INTERIOR SIDE. This information becomes important when it is time to set the justification (see Figure 6.34). The following procedure will step you through the process:

FIGURE 6.34
The Layers settings determine the materials and their thicknesses as they will be applied to the wall.

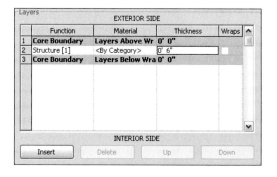

1. Click <By Category> in the Material column. A builder button will appear in the right end of the edit box (see Figure 6.35).

FIGURE 6.35
Material builder button

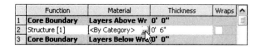

2. Click the builder button to open the Materials dialog box.

3. In the Materials section, select the material called Masonry – Concrete Masonry Units (see Figure 6.36).

FIGURE 6.36
The Materials section of
the Materials dialog box

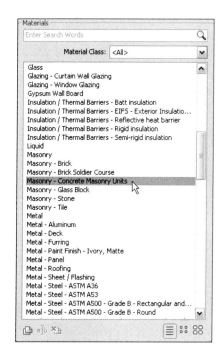

4. Click OK.

5. In the Thickness column, assign a thickness of **8″**.

6. Click on the number 1 row (next to Core Boundary).

7. Click the Insert button. This will create a new layer outside of the Core Boundary.

8. Change the new layer function from Structure to Thermal/Air Layer.

9. Click the material and then click the builder button.

10. Select Misc. Air Layers – Air Space.

11. Click OK.

12. Give it a thickness of **2″** (see Figure 6.37). The preview is starting to change. Notice the row you select in the Layers section is highlighted in the preview window. This is true only in the section view.

FIGURE 6.37
The newly added air
space layer

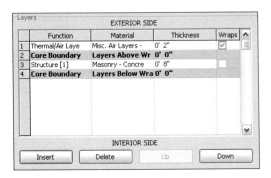

13. Select the number 1 row again, and click the Insert button.

14. Change the Function value to Finish 1.

15. Change the Material value to Masonry – Stone.

16. Click OK.

17. Change the Thickness value to **4"** (see Figure 6.38).

If you click in the preview window, notice that you can click your wheel button to pan around (see Figure 6.39). If you roll the wheel button forward or backward, you can zoom. Zoom in closer and to the bottom. You can also right-click to bring up the context menu and choose from available view options as well as click the Steering Wheel icon in the bottom-left corner to display the Steering Wheel tool.

FIGURE 6.38
Adding a masonry stone
veneer

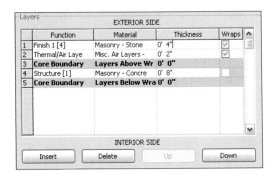

FIGURE 6.39
Zooming in the preview
window

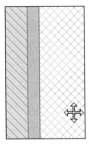

A best practice that some follow is to reserve Finish 1 for exterior placed layers and Finish 2 for interior layers. This is often used to aid in joining layers at intersections. It also can be of help when reviewing layers in a wall type. Now we are going to split and merge the bottom 3'-0'' of the wall to create a compound wall situation.

Underneath the Layers area where you were just working you will see the Modify Vertical Structure section (see Figure 6.40). This would not be available if the preview was not set to Section. Since it is set, you can chop up the wall. Before you do, though, click OK to preserve your work up to this point. This will place you back in the Type Properties dialog box. The following procedure will step you through the next process:

FIGURE 6.40
The Modify Vertical Structure section

1. Click the Edit button next to Structure to return to the Edit Assembly dialog box.

2. Click the Split Region button.

3. Your cursor turns into a knife. As you place your cursor over layers of the wall in the preview window, Revit Structure will provide a temporary dimension at your cursor. Move 3'-0'' up the wall, and split the 4'' stone material (see Figure 6.41). This may take a couple of tries to get right. Remember you can zoom in and pan. Your cursor needs to highlight the layer edge but be slightly inside the layer to cut the layer properly.

FIGURE 6.41
Split the material using the Knife tool.

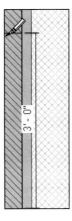

4. In the Layers section, add a new layer at row 1, specifying Function: Finish 1 and Material: Masonry – Brick (see Figure 6.42). Do not give it a thickness.

5. Using the Split Region command, split the air space at the same 3'-0'' height.

6. Click the Assign Layers button (see Figure 6.43).

7. Make sure Row 1, your brick material layer, is selected/active in the Layers section.

8. Click the lower 3'-0'' of the stone.

FIGURE 6.42
The masonry brick layer
has been assigned.

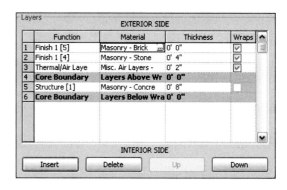

FIGURE 6.43
The Assign Layers but-
ton allows you to add
the new material to a
split section of the wall.

9. Click the Merge Regions button.

10. Hover your mouse over the line between the brick and the air space, below the 3'-0"
    cut line. You will see that an arrow forms. The direction in which the arrow points is
    the direction in which the material will merge. Merge the brick into the air space (see
    Figure 6.44).

FIGURE 6.44
Merge Regions allows
you to join two mate-
rials together.

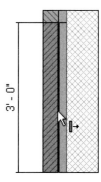

11. Click OK.

12. Click OK again.

You have a new wall type.

In some cases, the architectural finish extends above the core structure to form a small parapet.
You can do this in Revit Structure. First, place some instances of your new wall in the model. It
has been our experience that, just because something looks correct in the editor, it may not be in
the model. It is also wise to test how the wall is joining in corners (see Figure 6.45); your sketch
may look different!

FIGURE 6.45
The new wall

FIGURE 6.45
The new wall

In many cases, the architectural finish will extend above the bearing of the wall to form a small parapet for drainage blocking or to conceal structural elements. This can also be accomplished in Revit Structure with the following steps:

1. In the Project Browser, double-click on the new wall style, or open an existing compound wall.

2. Click Edit in the Structure row.

3. Zoom in to the top of the wall.

4. Under the Modify Vertical Structure (Section Preview Only) area, click the Modify button (see Figure 6.46).

FIGURE 6.46
The Modify button allows you to access the vertical structures.

5. Select the top line of the stone layer. Notice the padlock.

6. Unlock the padlock by clicking on it.
   This releases the top wall constraint so that it's independent of the wall structure (see Figure 6.47). Once the wall is placed in plan, the wall can be edited via the Element properties, in a section or in a 3D view. We recommend that you make modifications using a section view to maintain accuracy. You can edit the Element properties while looking at the wall in section to ensure the offset is as accurate as you want. If this is an extensive feature affecting many walls, it may be a good idea to set up a parapet level and extend this item to a level. You will have to use the Align and Lock feature to establish a dynamic link between the level and the top of the brick parapet. Once the wall is selected, you will see two blue arrows. One controls the finish and the other controls the structure. This indicates that the wall has been successfully released.

7. Click OK in this dialog box.

8. Click OK again.

This puts you back in the model. If you have this wall placed, cut a section through it. In the section, select the wall. See the two blue arrows? It helps to use Detail Level: Medium so you can really see the layers. They can now be independently moved, as you can see in Figures 6.48 and 6.49.

FIGURE 6.47
Unlocking the top

FIGURE 6.48
The wall section

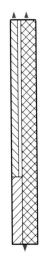

FIGURE 6.49
The parapet raised to a
parapet level added for
convenience

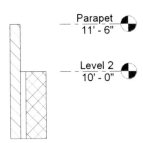

Once the wall is physically placed in the model, the battle is only half over. Revit Structure has many functions that allow you to modify the wall once it is in place.

Modifying the Wall

Once a wall is placed in a model, additional functionality is often needed. Adding an opening — penetrations, for example — and allowing the wall to attach itself to a sloping slab or a roof are a couple of tasks that often need to be done.

EDITING A WALL PROFILE

Openings are added after a wall is placed in the model. This can be done in an elevation and can be accomplished in two ways: editing the wall profile and adding a wall opening. The first method is to physically edit the wall profile. To add an opening, as well as extend the wall beyond its perimeter, perform these steps:

1. Add a wall to a new model. It can be a new wall type or a wall that has been predefined.

2. Create an elevation view looking at the wall.

3. Select the wall, and the Ribbon will display the Modify Walls tab.

4. Within the Modify Wall panel, click the Edit Profile button (see Figure 6.50).

FIGURE 6.50
Click the Edit Profile button on the Modify Wall panel.

The wall is now shaded and outlined with sketch lines. If you look at the Ribbon, you will notice that is has switched to the Modify Walls ➤ Edit Profile tab. This gives you additional functionality as you modify the sketch of the wall (see Figure 6.51).

FIGURE 6.51
The Modify Walls ➤ Edit Profile tab appears when you edit a wall.

1. Click the Rectangle button (next to Line). On the Options bar, you will notice choices similar to when you were placing the walls originally; you have controls for Offset and Radius. Draw a rectangular opening in the middle of the wall (see Figure 6.52 — your wall may look different).

2. Now, draw a step in the bottom of the wall (see Figure 6.53). You do not need to be accurate for this example, but you do need to split/trim and remove the bottom portion of the sketch so it looks like Figure 6.53.

3. Click the Finish Wall button on the Wall panel, on the far right end of the Ribbon. This will end the change and assign the new wall profile (see Figure 6.54).

FIGURE 6.52
Draw a rectangle.

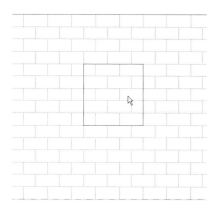

FIGURE 6.53
Step the bottom
of the wall.

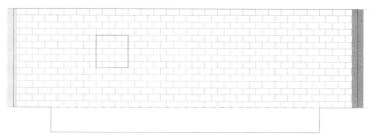

FIGURE 6.54
The new wall profile

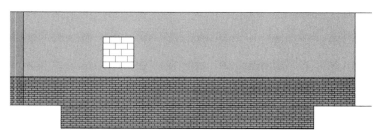

PLACING A WALL OPENING

Another technique at your disposal is the Wall Opening tool. This tool was originally designed to create openings in curved/arc walls because those walls cannot have their profile edited as we did in the previous example. These openings can be placed in an elevation view or a plan view and can only be rectangular in shape.

This tool is a bit awkward to use. For example, in an elevation view you can start sketching based on an edge or on reference planes, but setting the opposite corner accurately can be difficult. You then have to adjust the opening to achieve the size you need. In plan views you can see only the plan limits of the opening. You will have to define the opening height via the Element Properties dialog box or by switching to an elevation view. But understanding the opening parameters can aid in this work substantially. To add a wall opening in a plan view, perform these steps:

1. Starting with a plan view, add an 8″ masonry wall into a new model.

2. Click the Modify tab, and on the Opening panel click the Wall button.

3. Click your wall to select it.

4. Then click and hold the left mouse button on a wall edge.

5. Now drag your cursor along the wall. Revit Structure will provide temporary dimension strings so you can determine the width of the opening being placed (see Figure 6.55). Release the mouse button when you reach the desired width.

FIGURE 6.55
A Wall Opening creation sequence

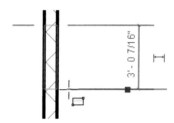

6. Click Modify or press Esc to cancel the Wall Opening tool; now select the wall opening. The Ribbon will switch to the Modify Rectangular Straight Wall Opening tab.

7. Click the Element Properties button on the Element panel. This will bring up the Instance properties for the opening (see Figure 6.56).

FIGURE 6.56
Wall Opening parameters are categorized as Constraints.

Parameter	Value
Constraints	⌄
Top Offset	-2' 0"
Base Offset	0' 0"
Unconnected Height	8' 0"
Base Constraint	Level 1
Top Constraint	Up to level: Level 2

Depending on previous actions, the values will vary and be set to unpredictable values. That is fine since we will assign proper values in a specific sequence in order to create the opening we need. For starters, we want an opening that doesn't rely on the level above it. We also need to have an opening of 8″ above the current level and 5′-4″ tall.

8. Change the Top Constraint parameter to Up to Level: Level 1. This will disconnect the opening from Level 2.

9. Change the Top Offset to **6′** and the Base Offset to **8″**. The Unconnected Height will adjust to an even 5′-4″ tall.

10. Click OK to close. Switch to an elevation view to see that the opening lines up nicely with the horizontal masonry joint lines (see Figure 6.57).

   By using the Instance parameters, you were able to adjust the wall opening without having to go to an elevation view. In your plan view, you would still adjust the opening plan extents by using the shape handles; there are no Instance parameters for opening length and placement. The Align tool can come in handy to adjust the width accurately.

It is important to understand that these opening techniques can cause a wall to lose its room-bounding behavior if the opening touches the level that an adjacent room is also on. If a wall must retain its room-bounding behavior, then openings should be created using a component family instead. Since Revit Structure does not have Room commands, it might seem an unnecessary distinction, but if you collaborate with other firms using Revit Architecture or MEP, your walls may need to be able to provide room-bounding behavior. This is the sort of thing that a collaboration meeting should include.

FIGURE 6.57
The masonry wall open-
ing can now match the
grout lines accurately.

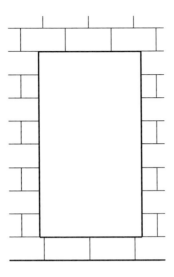

Creating a New Stacked Wall

A basic wall is restricted to maintain the same thickness overall with the exception of adding sweeps and reveals. There will be times where parts of a wall do not have a finished face that is aligned. In these situations, you can create a stacked wall instead.

A stacked wall is exactly what the name implies. It consists of two or more predefined walls that can be combined — stacked one on top of another to create a composite wall system, where the finished faces are staggered. Technically the walls are not required to have their layers align or be the same material, but in practice most walls share a common structure and the veneer varies.

In the Project Browser, in the Families category, scroll down in the list of families until you come to Walls. You will see Basic Wall, Curtain Wall, and Stacked Wall. Expand the Stacked Wall category, and you will see a single type called Exterior – 8″ Over 10″ Concrete Wall. If you double-click this wall, you will open the Type Properties dialog box. Now click the Edit button in the Structure row to open the Edit Assembly dialog box, as shown in Figure 6.58.

As you can see, the options differ from those offered in the Basic Wall Edit Assembly dialog box. With the basic wall, you are trying to define the wall laterally, layer by layer. With the stacked wall, you are defining the wall vertically, piece by piece. In other words, you build each piece in advance and then assemble them here.

In the Edit Assembly dialog box is a Types section. Here you can assign basic walls to form your stacked wall type. The default stacked wall, for example, consists of an Exterior – 10″ Concrete wall and an Exterior – 8″ Concrete wall. These are two basic walls added to the Types field. To add a new wall to the stack, click on either row 1 or row 2. Below the Types field, you will see an Insert button. Once you click the Insert button, a new wall type row will be added to the stack. You can move each wall type up or down. You can add as many walls to the stack as you need.

In the upper-right corner of the dialog box is a Sample Height field, which governs how tall the sample will be in the preview window. Usually when building a stacked wall, it is a good idea to set this to the floor-to-floor height that the wall will be constrained to. (If it is 12′-0″ from Level 1 to Level 2, set this value to **12′-0″**.) This helps to avoid unexpected results as you place the wall in the model.

Using stacked walls can save you time. They can also pose interesting problems for openings or other hosted elements like doors or windows, if these openings span more than one of the walls.

Review the help documentation for more information regarding architectural elements such as doors and windows.

FIGURE 6.58
Use the Edit Assembly dialog box to define and control all the stacked wall elements.

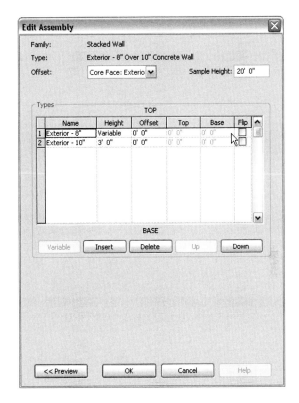

Attaching a Wall to a Roof

A common issue with walls often involves a pitched roof. You will almost certainly find yourself in a situation where you have a wall that must be extended to meet a roof.

A nice function in Revit Structure is the ability to attach the wall to a sloping or pitched floor/roof element. The following exercise explains how to attach a wall to a roof.

EXERCISE: ATTACHING A WALL TO A ROOF

To begin download walls.rvt from the book's website. It contains some walls and a roof.

1. Select the wall at the near gable end.

2. In the Modify Wall panel, you will see an Attach button under Top/Base. Click this button.

3. The Options bar changes for you to select either a top or a base. It is imperative that you notice this and select the proper option.

4. Select Top if needed.

5. Now select the roof. The wall will extend to touch the roof, as shown in the following illustration.
   The walls can be joined to any floor/roof structure. If that element then changes angle, the attached walls will change along with it.

6. Repeat the procedure on the other side.

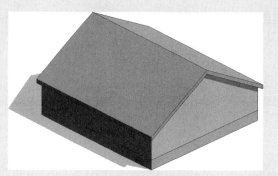

The ability to join walls in Revit Structure to a floor/roof can be quite helpful (to say the least) when you are trying to match unusual geometry. You must, however, have the element in your Revit project — you cannot attach to a linked floor/roof from another model.

The Bottom Line

Place walls in your model. When you are adding walls to your Revit Structure model, you can rely on the fact that you will get both the width and height of the wall depending on that wall's type, as well as the height constraint you have set. Once the walls are placed in the model, you can easily adjust them to change when the building changes.

Master It Walls are quite simple to place in the model, but they can also be inaccurate if they are not added to the model deliberately. What are three things to look out for when placing walls in the model?

Create new walls. There is a good amount of functionality included in the process of building a new wall type. Furthermore, walls are a system family, which can be used as a basis for any additional wall type you may wish to create.

Master It The walls in the default Revit Structure template are not going to be sufficient. Revit Structure provides the capability to modify a preconfigured wall type to suit your condition. Describe the procedures for:

- Creating a basic wall
- Creating a stacked wall

Modify walls in place.   When a wall has been placed, some additional functions are allowed in Revit Structure for modifying the wall.

> **Master It**   Walls must conform to various conditions vertically, such as odd openings and a stepped base profile. Also, if you have a pitched roof, the tops of the walls need to be extended to meet the roof. Explain how these procedures can be performed.

Chapter 7

Structural Framing

By now you are starting to get a feel for navigating the Revit Structure interface, and you are ready to delve more deeply into the techniques for modeling a structure. You have studied columns, floors, and decks, and now you will learn how to add different types of structural framing to your project.

Structural framing has many forms and materials, so you need to develop a robust set of modeling tools to create your project correctly. From the simple framing for the flat floor of an office building to a large space truss supporting an airline terminal roof, you will find many and varied conditions with which you must contend. Here you will study the methods used to frame various elevated floor and roof decks. Some of the types of roof shapes that you will learn to frame in this chapter are:

- ◆ Flat diaphragms for floors

- ◆ Sloped diaphragms for roof structures

- ◆ Warped diaphragms for roof structures

To be able to model the framing for these structures you need many tools in your tool chest. If you were out doing carpentry, having just a hammer and a saw would not get you very far. So it is with Revit Structure. This chapter will deal with floor and roof framing as well as moment and braced frames. Of course, as someone working in the structural engineering field, you will find this information of critical importance since you are responsible for putting the "bones" in the building.

Your objective in this chapter is to learn the techniques required for adding structural framing members to your working model. When you finish this chapter, you will have a good, working knowledge of how to populate your project with various steel, concrete, or wood framing members.

In this chapter you will learn to:

- ◆ Understand structural framing families and properties

- ◆ Add floor framing

- ◆ Add roof framing

- ◆ Create moment and braced frames

Structural Framing Families and Properties

Revit Structure ships with many types of framing families, each of which can be easily loaded into your project. To keep your project from getting too big and slow, you load in only those member sizes that you require for that particular project. The framing libraries encompass all those found in the AISC library, and many international libraries are included as well. You probably realize by now that Revit Structure has a truly global reach, one that works well with both metric and imperial settings. Besides the libraries that ship with Revit Structure you can create custom framing families as well either from scratch or by adapting an existing framing family to suit your needs. First, let's look at the available framing libraries, and then we'll see how to customize them.

Working with Standard Framing Libraries

Here is a partial list of the extensive framing families available in Revit Structure:

- Concrete
  - Concrete: Rectangular Beam
  - Pan Joist
  - Pan Joist with Ledges
  - Precast: Double Tee
  - Precast: Hollow Core Slab
  - Precast: I Shaped Beam
  - Precast: Inverted
  - Precast: L Shaped Beam
  - Precast: Rectangular Beam
  - Precast: Single Tee
  - Precast: Solid Flat Slab
- Light Gauge Steel
  - Light Gauge: Angles
  - Light Gauge: Furring Channels
  - Light Gauge: Furring Hat Channels
  - Light Gauge: Joists
  - Light Gauge: Runner Channels
  - Light Gauge: Zee
- Steel
  - BG Joist Girder
  - Castellated Beam

- ◆ C-Channel
- ◆ Cellular Beam
- ◆ DLH – Series Bar Joist
- ◆ Double C-Channel
- ◆ G Joist Girder
- ◆ GP – Bearing Pile
- ◆ HSS – Hollow Structural Section
- ◆ HST – Round Structural Tubing
- ◆ K-Series Bar Joist – Angle Web
- ◆ K-Series Bar Joist – Rod Web
- ◆ L-Angle
- ◆ LH-Series Bar Joist
- ◆ LL – Double Angle
- ◆ MC – Miscellaneous Wide Flange
- ◆ MT – Structural Tee
- ◆ Plate
- ◆ Round Bar
- ◆ S – American Standard
- ◆ SLH-Series Double Pitch Joist – 5 Panel
- ◆ SLH-Series Double Pitch Joist – 7 Panel
- ◆ SLH-Series Double Pitch Joist – 9 Panel
- ◆ SLH-Series Double Pitch Joist – 11 Panel
- ◆ SLH-Series Double Chord Bar Joist
- ◆ ST – Structural Tee
- ◆ VG – Joist Girder
- ◆ WRF – Welded Reduced Flange
- ◆ WT – Structural Tee
- ◆ WWF – Welded Wide Flange
- ◆ W – Wide Flange

◆ Wood

- ◆ Dimensional Lumber
- ◆ Glulam – Southern Pine

- ◆ Glulam – Western Species

- ◆ LVL – Laminated Veneer Lumber

- ◆ Open Web Joist

As you can see, there are many types and varieties of members you can use to make your virtual model.

Creating Custom Framing Libraries

But what if the framing member you require for your project does not exist in the Revit libraries? When you first start modeling, you will rely heavily on the built-in libraries. If what you want is not there, you can check for families at the websites for AUGI (Autodesk Users Group International) or Revit City, where many people have uploaded their own families for others to use. If you still cannot find what you want, you will have to build your own. After you have had a chance to try it a few times you will find that the process of adapting and creating your own families is not that hard and that it is not as intimidating as it sounds.

If a member size or shape does not exist in the Revit libraries, you have several alternatives. You can create your own structural framing member from scratch using solid modeling tools, or you can adapt an existing family to fit your needs. You adapt an existing family by editing the text database, called a Type Catalog, file that is associated with it, in order to add odd member sizes or out-of-date sizes (see Figure 7.1) that might not already be there.

The text file is located in the Framing folder along with the Revit family file (with the .rfa extension). The text file has the parameters listed on the top line that describe the basic shape of the element, such as flange width (bf) and web thickness (tw) that you will have to provide in order to make your new size work.

FIGURE 7.1
You can easily edit the Type Catalog file for wide flange beams.

To add a new size to the existing family file, first add a description of the element, such as **W12x16.5 – Obsolete**. Then fill in the values that describe its shape, as in the following parameter list for a steel beam with imperial units:

- **W**##other##

- **A**##area##inches

- **d**##length##inches

- **bf**##length##inches

- **tw**##length##inches

- **tf**##length##inches

- **k**##length##inches

Make sure each parameter is comma delimited (with no spaces), and follow this order exactly. So to add a new size to an existing library, simply add a new line anywhere in the text file and fill in the values you want for the various parameters that determine the size of the element. When you reload the family into your project, the new size you created will be available for placement into your project. This is one form of adaptation for an existing framing family.

Besides simply adding new sizes to your family, another example of family adaptation is one that not only changes the size but also changes the shape of the family. You will see an example of this kind of adaptation in Chapter 19, where you will add a wood nailer element to the top of a steel beam family for use in a project that has both wood and steel framing (which is a common occurrence for many commercial facilities).

Floor and Roof Deck Constraints

For the most part, the framing that you add to your building project, whether it is steel, concrete, or wood, will be supporting some type of elevated deck (see Figures 7.2, 7.3, and 7.4). Of course, in some projects the majority, or even all, of the framing supports piping or mechanical devices such as industrial production facilities for gas and electric plants or test frames for new aircraft.

FIGURE 7.2
Steel-framed office structure with composite metal deck and concrete floors, a sloping roof to support Spanish tile, and mechanical equipment platforms for HVAC

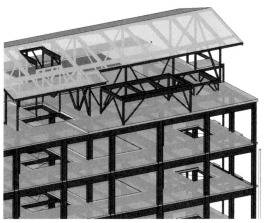

IMAGE COURTESY OF BRANDOW & JOHNSTON INC.

FIGURE 7.3
Concrete parking structure with pre-stressed, post-tensioned (PT) concrete framing supporting PT decks

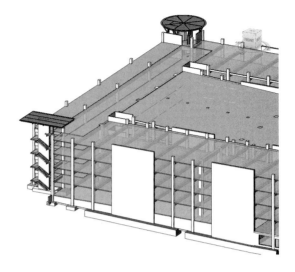

FIGURE 7.4
Multiple-housing structure framed with lumber connecting to wood bearing and shear walls

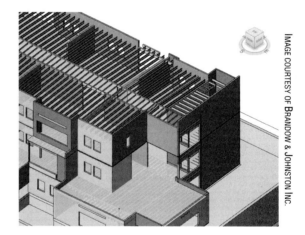

IMAGE COURTESY OF BRANDOW & JOHNSTON INC.

One important consideration when adding framing elements to your project is establishing the reference plane to which they are attached. This issue goes to the very core of Revit Structure and its constraint-based philosophy. Since you are working through an ever-changing design process, from schematics through to construction documentation, the model must always have as much flexibility as possible. You need this flexibility in your model to do such things as stretch to different-sized bay widths and adjust story-to-story heights between levels in case the design changes.

The basic vertical constraint for floor framing in your project will be the level to which the framing is attached. The basic horizontal constraints will be your grid system. Constraining your framing elements to these two datum elements will allow you to flex the model when needed as the design process continues.

The level you draw the framing on is the default for its constraint, so if the level moves, the framing will move with it. One added complication is that the framing is often below the deck, so members need to be offset downward below the deck element. You can do this by highlighting the member and changing the values for its offsets in the Instance Properties dialog box. It is easy to forget to do this, and you could end up with framing at the top of the deck unless you are paying close attention. Also, if the deck depth changes due to design updates, you have to remember to select and edit all the framing member offsets. So what is the best practice?

Many advanced users elect to use the bottom of the deck as the reference plane for attaching the framing. That way, they keep the deck constrained to the level and do not have to worry if the depth of the deck changes, because the support framing will move as well. Others create a new level or use a reference plane at the top of steel elevation so they do not have to worry about setting offsets. That seems like a better way to go. Try the different methods to determine which one works best for you.

In the next section, you will learn to create basic floor framing for an elevated deck in your virtual model. As opposed to roof framing on a sloped or warped deck, floor framing is mostly flat and fairly straightforward to model, so that is a good place for you to start in order to understand how this all works.

DEVELOPING GOOD MODELING SKILLS AND WORKFLOW

One efficient way to develop your modeling skills is to have a good understanding of the way buildings are constructed. Go out to any construction site and watch how the builders work. Study the chronological sequence of adding elements as the building is constructed. Which elements must be constructed first? Columns must be added before girders. Girders must be added before bays can be in-filled, and so on.

In the virtual building world, the workflow is not much different. For most areas of modeling, creating your virtual model similarly to how it will be sequenced in the field is a good approach.

Foundations are one virtual element that is in many cases modeled out of sequence from the actual construction process. During the design process, the foundation information usually comes after the analysis of the structure is developed because the analysis starts at the top of the structure and works down. Obviously you could not build the real building that way. So at first your foundations may be placeholders that approximate the size and material system. Or they may not be there yet. After all, the model is a virtual creation and won't fall down for lack of support.

Adding Floor Framing

As we said earlier, you will learn to create your framing in a workflow that is similar to how the members would actually be constructed in the field. Assuming that the grids and levels are established in your project and that columns and decks have been created, now you will move on to adding your floor framing. So where do you begin? The columns are there already, so the first step to framing the floor will be to connect the columns with girders as you construct your virtual model. You will find the Beam command on the Structure panel of the Home tab of the Ribbon, but first it is important to understand its available options.

How do you proceed when you want to add floor framing to your project? Depending on the way you prefer to work, you can add either the floor deck element or the framing elements first. But since the framing supports the floor deck layout, it is best practice to proceed with the deck first, though it is not absolutely necessary. That way you can easily follow the shape of the floor while you add its support framing. However, for sloping or warped roof deck framing, it is essential to create the deck first for reasons that will be explained later in the chapter.

The Beam Command and Options Settings

Let's look at the various options now on the Options bar and Ribbon to aid you in placing members into your model. When you start the Beam tool, found on the Home tab of the Ribbon, the Place Beam tab appears on the Ribbon and the Place Beam options are displayed on the Options bar:

◆ On the Element panel the Type Selector will list, in a drop-down menu, all the currently loaded beam sizes (see Figure 7.5).

FIGURE 7.5
The Type Selector lets
you choose shapes
to insert.

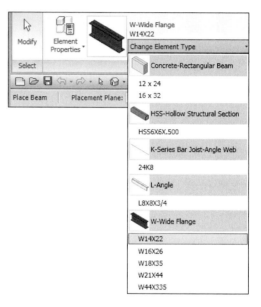

◆ Next to the Type Selector is the Element Properties icon, which you can use to set or edit the various parameters of the framing. (See the next section for a discussion of the Element properties.)

◆ On the Detail panel is the Load Family icon, which allows you to easily load new shapes from the framing libraries that you want to use in your project.

◆ To the left of that, on the Draw panel, are the tools that enable you to add the beam to the view by drawing or picking.

◆ Finally, the Multiple panel has the On Grids option, which allows you to pick grid lines and is another, faster way to place your beam members.

On the Options bar the Placement Plane drop-down menu (see Figure 7.6) allows you to choose the level (work plane) on which you want to add the beam element. Usually the value is set to the floor you are working on, but you can set it to another plane of your choosing.

FIGURE 7.6
You define the level on
which you want to add
your framing.

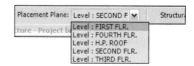

FIGURE 7.7
The Structural Usage pull-down is a convenient way to preset the beam's usage.

The next pull-down menu sets the Structural Usage field for the new beam (see Figure 7.7). As we discussed earlier, there are five categories you can use. If you leave the value on <Automatic>, Revit Structure makes its own judgment as to what structural usage the new element should be assigned. When this field is set to <Automatic>, Revit will assign elements like this: girders connect to columns, joists connect to girders, and purlins connect to joists. If you leave Structural Usage set to <Automatic>, you need to pay close attention because improperly connected beams, or ones where Revit gets confused (yes, Revit does get confused sometimes), will be assigned to the Other category. The Other line weight is usually set to a pen weight of 1 so that those members, when printed, will look very thin.

Some people like to set each Structural Usage type to a different line weight, with girders being the thickest, in order to distinguish among them. Others set all the lines the same weight regardless of Structural Usage assignments. It is one of those judgments that you need to make for yourself and your own firm.

You can configure each beam type with a different color for easy monitoring in the Object Styles dialog box (see Figure 7.8). For each of these beam categories, you can also independently define the line weight and line style properties, so you can make girders a heavier line weight than joists or alter the display in whatever way is required for your project.

FIGURE 7.8
The Object Styles dialog box lets you universally control the display of your beams and girders in their various views.

Category	Line Weight		Line Color	Line Pattern	Material
	Projection	Cut			
Structural Framing	3	4	Black	Solid	
Analytical Model	5	3	RGB 255-128-064	Solid	
Chord	6	6	Black		
Girder	6	6	Black	Solid	
Hidden Faces	1	1	Black	Hidden 3/32''	
Hidden Lines	1	1	Black	Dash	
Horizontal Bracing	4	4	Black	Dash	
Joist	5	4	Black	Solid	
Kicker Bracing	2	2	Black	Center 1/4''	
MC 1/4	3	3	Black	Solid	
MC 1/8	3	3	Black	Solid	
MC 1/16	5	5	Black	Solid	
MC Stick Symbol 1/8	6	6	Black	Solid	
MC Stick Symbol 1/16	6	6	Black	Solid	
Moment Framing	9	9	Black	Solid	
Other	7	8	Black	Solid	
Purlin	4	4	Black	Dot 1/32''	
MC Stick Symbol 1/8	6	6	Black	Solid	
MC Stick Symbol 1/16	6	6	Black	Solid	
Moment Framing	9	9	Black	Solid	
Other	7				
Purlin	4	4	Black	Dot 1/32''	
MC Stick Symbol 1/8	6	6	Black	Solid	
MC Stick Symbol 1/16	6	6	Black	Solid	
Moment Framing	9	9	Black	Solid	
Other	7	8	Black	Solid	
Purlin	4	4	Black	Dot 1/32''	
Rigid Links	5	5	RGB 000-127-000	Solid	
Stick Symbols	6	6	Black	Solid	
Vertical Bracing	6	6	Black	Solid	
Web	4	4	Black		

For a good example of how beam presentation can differ, see Figure 7.9. On a structural framing plan, the seismic system (the moment or braced frames) is usually displayed with the heaviest line weight, so it "jumps right out at you," so to speak. The plan view in the figure has the rigid frame member's Structural Usage parameter set to Other. The Other parameter is then set to a line weight of 7 in the Object Styles dialog box, for projected lines. The girders are set to line weight 6, and the joists are set to line weight 5.

FIGURE 7.9
A typical floor framing plan for a steel building with differing line weights for beam elements per usage

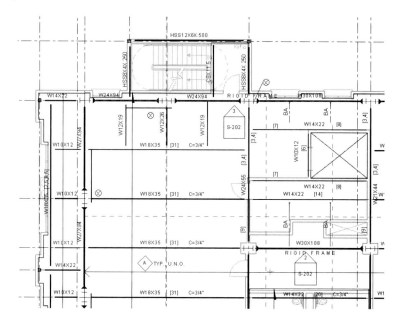

If you are using the analytical model to export to structural analysis software, you will also want to set the Structural Usage field for the floor and roof members of the frame to Horizontal Bracing in order for it to be read correctly in the analysis software.

To the right of the Structural Usage pull-down is the 3D Snapping check box. If you select this check box, the beam will snap to the elevation of the intersecting beam or girder that supports it. This is an especially important option when you're doing roof framing. When working with sloping roof members and when framing to tops of columns that are at different elevations, you have no plane on which to place the beam. So having Revit Structure automatically find the intersecting point is critical to being able to easily and efficiently place the framing member.

To the right of that check box is the Tag check box, where you can set Revit Structure to automatically add tags to the element after placement if desired. Since tagging is displayed only in the view in which it is created, you might not want to have tags in a working view, so you can uncheck this check box before placement if you wish. Of course, concrete framing will also display well when set to a hidden view, just the way you want it to, as in Figure 7.10.

Beam Element Properties

Back on the Place Beam tab of the Ribbon, next to the Type Selector, is an image of the element that Revit is ready to let you place; this could be a W-Wide Flange beam, a rectangular tube, a C- channel, and so on. To the left of the image of your selected family is the Element Properties button. When you click this button, you can set or edit the various parameters of the framing element in the resulting dialog box (see Figure 7.11). You will be constantly using this dialog box to adjust the properties of your elements. The dialog box includes the following major areas, referred to as Parameter Groups: Constraints, Construction, Materials and Finishes, Structural, Dimensions, Identity Data, Phasing, Structural Analysis, Analytical Model, and Other. Each of those categories has a set of parameters that have something in common with regard to the family. You can also open the Element Properties dialog box by selecting an existing beam, right-clicking, and selecting Element Properties at the bottom of the shortcut menu.

FIGURE 7.10
Concrete floor framing plan in a hidden mode view

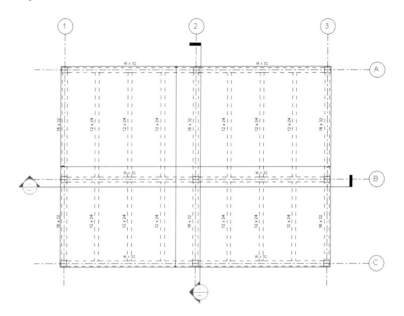

You can set some of an element's Instance parameters before placing the element, which makes multiple insertions easier and more efficient. This way you do not have to repeatedly edit the element's properties after placing it in the model. Be careful when presetting the parameters, though, and remember to change them at the appropriate time.

Adding Floor Framing to Your Virtual Model

Now that you have studied the various options for beams, their placement, and their Instance parameters, you are ready to start adding framing elements to your project. Let's begin with girder placements from column to column.

To add girders to your project one at a time, follow these steps:

1. Go to the view where you want to add the framing.

2. On the Structure tab of the Ribbon, click the Beam icon.

3. In the Type Selector, choose a size to add, or load one from the framing libraries.

4. On the Options bar, select a Structural Usage type for the beam you are adding, or leave it set to <Automatic>.

5. For floor framing make sure 3D Snapping is unchecked.

6. Check the Chain check box to easily create girders from column to column in a continuous pattern (or "chain").

7. Check the Tag check box on the Options bar to automatically add the size of the beam above the framing member once it is placed.

FIGURE 7.11

The Element Properties dialog box Instance parameters for a beam

Parameter	Value
Constraints	�
Work Plane	Level : SECOND FLR.
Reference Level	SECOND FLR.
Start Level Offset	-0' 6 1/4"
End Level Offset	-0' 6 1/4"
z-Direction Justification	Top
z-Direction Offset Value	0' 0"
Lateral Justification	Center
Cross-Section Rotation	0.000°
Construction	
Start Extension	-0' 0 1/2"
End Extension	-0' 0 1/2"
Materials and Finishes	
Beam Material	Metal - Steel - ASTM A572 - Grade 50
Structural	
Angle	0.000°
Stick Symbol Location	Center of Geometry
Moment Connection Start	None
Moment Connection End	None
Cut Length	23' 4 1/2"
Structural Usage	Joist
Camber Size	
Number of studs	
Dimensions	
Length	24' 0"
Volume	1.22 CF
Identity Data	
Comments	
Mark	
Phasing	
Phase Created	New Construction
Phase Demolished	None
Structural Analysis	
Start Release	Fixed
Start Fx	☐
Start Fy	☐
Start Fz	☐
Start Mx	☐
Start My	☐
Start Mz	☐
End Release	Fixed
End Fx	☐
End Fy	☐
End Fz	☐
End Mx	☐
End My	☐
End Mz	☐
Analyze As	Gravity
Analytical Model	
Vertical Projection	Top of beam
Auto-detect Horizontal Projection	☐
Other	
Start Extension Calculation	10' 0"
End Extension Calculation	10' 0"
RAM UniqueID	9102
RAM RevitID	
RM User Number	147
RM Unique Id	819
RS Unique Id	154155
RMBar_Labels	MEMBER_TYPE=RevitJoist

8. To place the girder, hover your cursor over a column, and then use the Tab key to cycle through the various snaps until the appropriate snapping icon appears. Use the midpoint (triangle icon) snap when possible.

9. Click to place one end of the girder onto the column.

10. In the same fashion locate the midpoint, and then click at the next column to finish placing the beam.

There are some time-saving techniques you will want to use when adding girders to your project. You can add girders by snapping from column to column individually as just described and use the Chain option for continuous placement as in step 6 above. Or you can use the On Grids tool, found on the Multiple panel, which allows you to add girders between columns automatically simply by selecting grid lines.

To place beam elements use On Grids and select the grid, following this process:

1. Perform steps 1 through 5 from the previous task in the same way.

2. Click the On Grids button on the Multiple panel.

3. Select a grid that has columns you want to frame between.

4. Revit Structure will add girders between the columns on the selected grid. The girders appear ghosted until you finish.

5. Hold down the Ctrl key to select multiple grids at one time.

6. When you have finished selecting grids, click Finish Selection on the Multiple Selection panel to complete placement.

After finishing the placement of the girders between the columns on your floor plan, you are ready to in-fill those bays with joists. After that you can add secondary framing members, such as floor openings, stair framing, and other miscellaneous framing elements, by drawing them individually. This chronology is another example of how the workflow for virtual modeling is similar to the way the building would be erected in the field.

MODELING IS HALF THE BATTLE

Creating the model is only half of the battle. The other half is to display and derive the two-dimensional plans, sections, and elevations that comprise your final construction documents set. In the current discussion on beams, this is why you must pay close attention to the Structural Usage settings, so your framing displays accordingly and has the correct assignment for analysis. Of course, you could set all of the beam line weights for the various usage settings at a single line weight and ignore the usage if you want to keep things simple. Display issues are constantly occurring, so you must understand how to use the display tools you will need in order to adjust the display accordingly. Pay close attention then to the Structural Usage categories and to the various object style assignments you are making.

In-filling Bays with the Beam System Tool

Now that the framing bays are bounded by girders, you will use the Beam System tool, found on the Structure panel of the Home tab on the Ribbon, to add the beams that will fill the framing bays (see Figure 7.12). Beam System is a powerful and versatile tool, and one that you will use on most projects. Its benefits include its ease of use and its ability to flex when or if the framing bay dimensions change.

The basic approach to using this tool consists of the following:

◆ Defining the area within which the beams will be drawn

◆ Defining the direction of the beam elements

◆ Establishing layout rules for their placement

FIGURE 7.12
Examples of in-filled framing bays using different layout rules and tag types

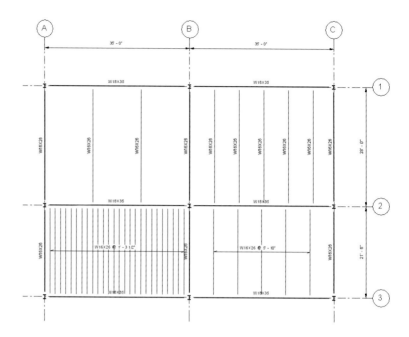

There are two approaches to defining the area and direction of the beams: the one-click method and the sketch method:

The one-click method   You simply hover your cursor over one of the girders that frame the boundary of the bay in the direction you wish the framing to be placed. You'll see a preview of the beam system in hidden line. If you don't like the orientation you see in the preview, try a girder in the other direction, and when you see the orientation you want, click to place the beam system. This method is not available in 3D views, however.

The sketch method   You sketch lines that enclose the area of the in-fill, similar to what you've done earlier with floor sketches. This method gives you greater control over the orientation and shape of the beam system and works when the one-click method fails to satisfy.

Let's take a little closer look to learn the various options available for the Beam System command.

On the Element panel of the Place Beam System tab of the Ribbon (see Figure 7.13) is the Type Selector pull-down, which allows you to select different types of beam systems that you might have created. You probably will not need to use this option because only Identity data is specified in the Type parameters. To the left of that is the Element Properties icon. On the Options bar is the Beam Type pull-down, which allows you to select the beam type for the layout. Only one beam type can be called out for any one placement of the beam system, although it is possible to override one later if necessary. The Sketch panel contains the Create Sketch tool, which we will discuss in a moment.

The Justification parameters on the Options bar (see Figure 7.14) control how the beams are spaced within the bay. The spacing can start from the beginning or end of the bay or be centered on the bay. It can take a moment to figure out which side is called Beginning and which is called End. The beam you select using the one-click method defines the Beginning side. It can be less obvious when you use the sketch method. You just need to examine the spacing and check the setting on the Options bar to get your bearings.

FIGURE 7.13
The Place Beam System tab and the Options bar for a beam system

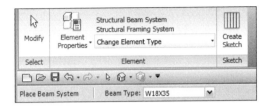

FIGURE 7.14
The Justification options

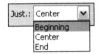

FIGURE 7.15
The four Layout options on the Options bar

Four Layout options are available when you're placing beam elements (see Figure 7.15):

◆ The Clear Spacing option sets the distance between members from the edge of the flange to the edge of the adjoining flange rather than at the centerline of the elements.

◆ The Fixed Distance and Fixed Number options do just what you'd expect from their names. Fixed Distance sets a specific distance between beam members even if the framing bay changes shape. Fixed Number sets a specific number of beams in the framing bay regardless of the spacing between members.

◆ The Maximum Spacing option in-fills the beams using the value in the box to the right of the Layout box. This is the most powerful option because it remains dynamic if the bay dimensions change. Over the course of the project, if the bay expands enough so that the members exceed the Maximum Spacing value, then new members will automatically be added into the bay. If the bay gets smaller, members will be eliminated. This helps you achieve your goal of making the model as flexible as possible during the design process.

Checking the 3D option helps you define a sloping beam system, which is needed, for example, when the member it intersects is sloping (see Figures 7.16 and 7.17 for a comparison). You will be hearing a lot about this important option later on in the chapter when we discuss roof framing.

The Tag option (see Figure 7.18), if checked, will enable two types of beam tags: System (beam system tag) or Framing (individual beam tags). The System type is best used for framing, such as for wood-framed floors with many members where spacing is very tight. If you tried to tag each one of those elements, it probably would look too crowded on your plan.

FIGURE 7.16
Without the 3D option
checked

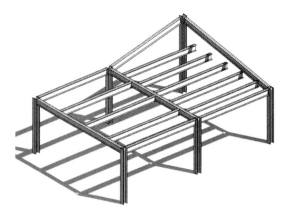

FIGURE 7.17
With the 3D option
checked

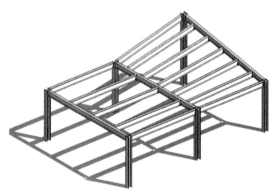

As mentioned earlier in this section, there are two methods of placement: one-click and sketch. The one-click method is easy to use (see Figure 7.19). You simply hover your cursor over an existing girder that bounds the area you are in-filling and one that is in the direction you want the framing to be added. The framing then will ghost in with blue dashed lines until you click for final placement. You will find that this method allows you to complete a whole floor of framing on your model in minutes. It is so easy that sometimes it is faster to erase the framing and redo it if design changes warrant it. Remember, though, that the one-click method is not available as an option unless you have a bay completely enclosed with beam elements.

In some cases, the one-click method does not work, and so you must use the sketch method. First, click the Create Sketch icon on the Sketch panel of the Place Beam System tab.reak The Create Beam System Boundary tab is then displayed on the Ribbon (see Figure 7.20). By using the tools in the Draw panel you can sketch the lines that define the shape you require for that bay (see Figure 7.21). Or you can use the Pick Supports option to select the supporting elements that form the boundary of the framing bay.

An important option in this menu is the Reset System function. If after placement your design criteria have changed and you must respace the elements in the bay, you will find that sometimes the display does not update correctly to the new bay shape and still displays the stick symbols as they were, without showing the new spacing or span direction. This is especially true when you're expanding a bay. The members might not display to the new extents. In that case, you need to use this option to make the display update correctly.

FIGURE 7.18
The System and Framing tag types

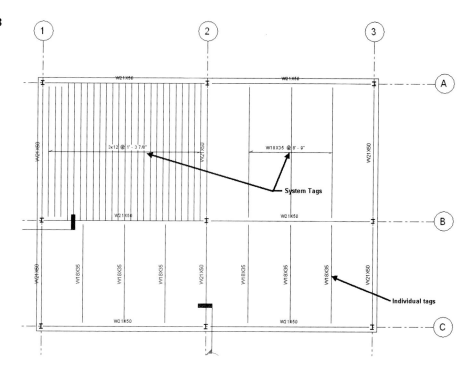

FIGURE 7.19
The beam system one-click method

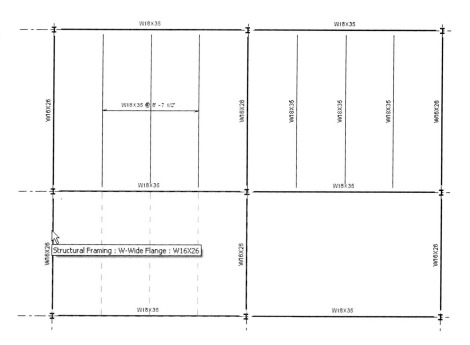

FIGURE 7.20
The Create
Beam System
Boundary tab
for sketching
the beam sys-
tem boundary

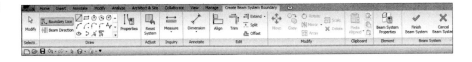

FIGURE 7.21
Sketching in
the beam sys-
tem bounded
area

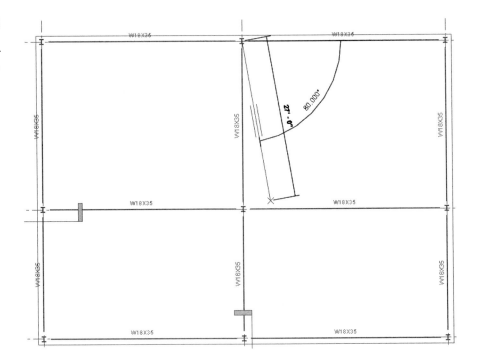

So that explains the various properties and options available for you to use in the placement of beams in your project. Next you will take a look at how to add curved beam framing to
your model.

Using Curved Beams

Almost every building project has a curved beam or two (see Figure 7.22), so it is very important
to be able to easily create them in your model. For example, you might need one in order to create
support for a barrel-style roof or for supporting an exterior curved edge of a deck. You create
curved beams by using the drawing tools on the Draw panel of the Place Beam tab. You can draw
such shapes as an arc, circle, or spline as a path for the beam shape. You can also create curved
beams by picking a curved line on your plan.

To create a curved beam on your floor plan, do the following:

1. On the Structure panel of the Home tab, click Beam.

FIGURE 7.22
Some curved beam
shapes drawn with
straight, circular, arc,
and spline options

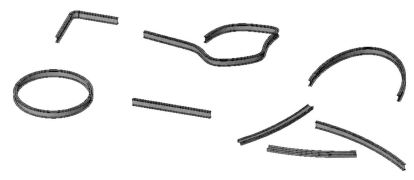

2. On the Place Beam tab, click Change Element Type, and choose the beam type from the drop-down list.

3. On the Draw panel, pick one of the drawing tools, such as Start-End-Radius Arc, Center-ends-Arc, Spline, or Tangent-End-Arc, and draw the centerline of the member on the plan. Or you can click the Pick button and select a line already present in your project, and Revit will place a curved beam to follow it.

Other Important Types of Floor Framing

You might have wondered in Chapter 5 why we didn't discuss concrete pan joist systems (waffle slabs) or precast slab systems. The reason is that these subjects are better dealt with here, since the concrete slab and concrete framing are monolithically constructed. As opposed to the approach we took for steel and concrete beams, these systems load in as units for specific layouts.

Pan joist supported slabs   A pan joist system (often called a waffle slab) can be easily constructed by using the Pan Joist concrete framing family. You create these by placing a beam system layout in each direction in the same bay (see Figure 7.23). The two beam system placements will "clean up" and display monolithically.

Precast supported slabs   Precast-Hollow-Core Slabs, Single, and Double-T system families are all available in the Revit Structure concrete framing library (see Figure 7.24). Individual panels are created to specific widths and then arrayed across the area of the floor. The framing libraries contain the basic framing shapes you will need for precast framing, with Precast Inverted-T girders, L-Shaped girders, and more.

Figure 7.25 shows some sections that have been cut from a precast structure. 2D annotation is added, as well as reinforcing. The reinforcing can be added either as a 3D component of the element or as 2D drafting detail lines.

Pre-stressed post-tensioned (PT) framed concrete structures   Concrete structures using PT (pre-stressed and post-tensioned) systems are quite common and can be readily modeled in Revit Structure (see Figure 7.26). PT beams are nonrectangular, so you can use the Pan

Joist family or adapt your own family depending on how accurate you want the beam to appear.

It is important for you to develop good judgment about the extent to which you add detail in your model families. Adding in a 1″ chamfer to the concrete beam interface with the slab might be accurate, but it might be unnecessary if you do not intend to use views in your construction documents for a lot of detailing.

In the next exercise, you will practice placing in-fill beams into a project using various methods of placement.

FIGURE 7.23
Concrete pan joist system with filled cores at the columns

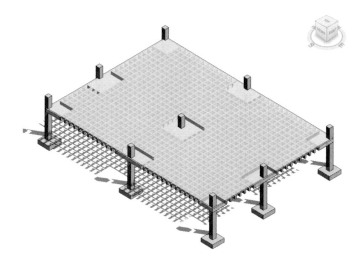

FIGURE 7.24
Many framing types are available in Revit Structure, like this precast concrete system.

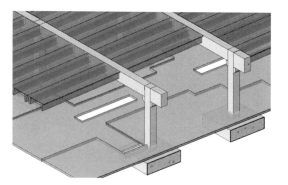

FIGURE 7.25
Sections and details for a precast concrete framing project

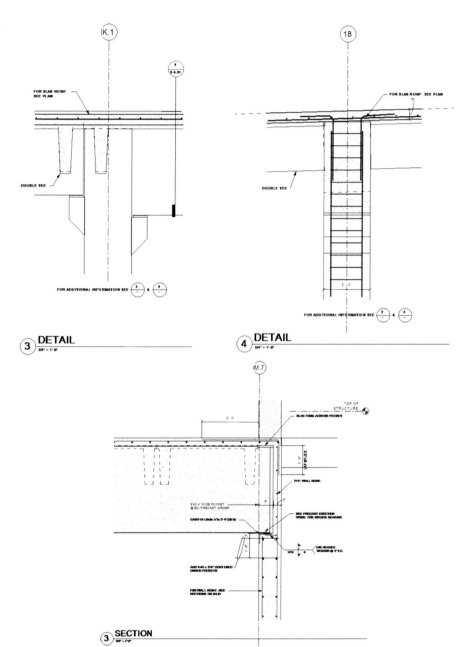

FIGURE 7.26
Elevation at ramp and
shear wall for a concrete
PT parking structure

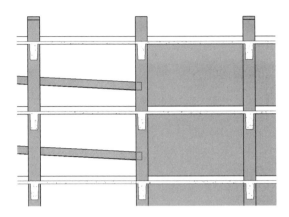

EXERCISE: ADDING GIRDERS TO A FLOOR PLAN

This exercise will have you add girders first and then in-fill beams on several bays in a simple steel structure. You'd use the same procedure for concrete or wood framing members.

First, you'll place the girders individually and then by using the On Grids method:

1. Open Dataset_0701_begin, where you should see a grid and steel columns in the view Structural Plans – Level 2.

2. On the Structure panel of the Home tab on the Ribbon, click Beam.

3. Select a W18x35 beam type in the Change Element Type drop-down list.

4. On the Options bar, select Girder in the Structural Usage field, and enable the Chain check box.

5. Hover your cursor over the column at grid A1 until a magenta (pink) triangle snap appears; then click to place one end of the girder. (If necessary, use the Tab key to cycle through snaps until you get the middle snap.)

6. Move your cursor down to hover over the column at B1 and click, and then click again at C1 to finish placing two beams across grid 1.

7. On the Multiple panel on the Place Beam tab, click the On Grids tool.

8. While holding down the Ctrl key, select grids 2 and 3. The beams should appear ghosted in.

9. Click Finish Selection on the Ribbon to complete the operation.

10. On the Multiple panel on the Place Beam tab, click the On Grids button again.

11. Holding down the Ctrl key, select grids A, B, and C; then click Finish to complete the placement. Your plan should look like the following illustration.

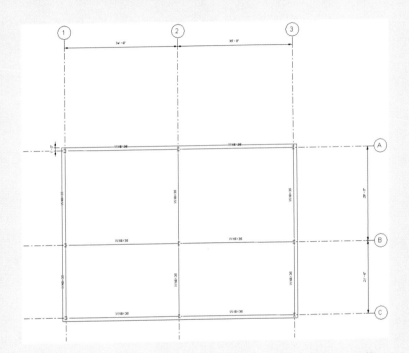

Now that the girders bounding the bays are complete, you will in-fill the four bays using the Beam System tool:

1. On the Structure panel of the Home tab on the Ribbon, click Beam System.

2. On the Options bar select W16x26 from the Beam Type drop-down list.

3. On the Options bar select Fixed Number in the Layout Rule drop-down list, and type **2** in the box next to it.

4. On the Options bar click Framing for the tag type.

5. With your mouse hover over the girder that runs from A1 to A2 (you should see two dashed blue lines parallel to the girder in the bay on the left).

6. Click the girder (A1 to A2) to finish placement in that bay.

7. Change the Beam Type to W8X10, change the Layout Rule to Maximum Spacing, and type **48″** in the box next to it.

8. On the Options bar, this time change the tag type to System.

9. With your mouse hover over the girder that runs from A2 to A3.

10. Click on that girder to create a beam system in that bay. Your plan should now look like the following illustration.

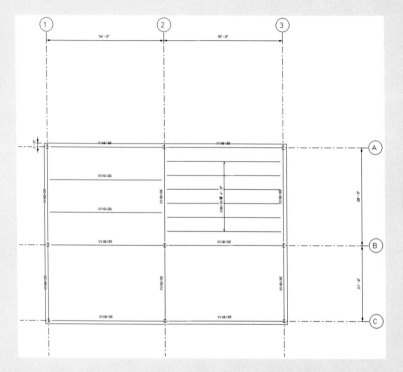

Now let's flex the bay by changing the grid spacing to see how the beam system reacts:

1. Select grid A and then click on the temporary dimension value between grid A and grid B.

2. Change it to **45′-0″**. (Click Activate Dimensions on the Options bar if no temporary dimension appears, and edit the Permanent Dimension value in the view instead.)

Notice in the following graphic that when the bay stretches, members are added to the bay with the Maximum Spacing layout rule, whereas the bay with the Fixed Number layout rule simply respaces the two members. I added a dimension so it flexes now.

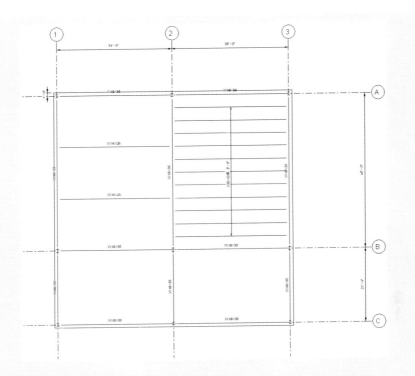

3. Click Beam System again on the Home tab of the Ribbon.

4. Click the Create Sketch icon on the Sketch panel.

5. On the Draw panel click the Rectangle icon.

6. Draw a rectangle from grid B1 to grid C2, and as before take care to snap to the midpoint of the columns; then lock each line into place by clicking on each open lock symbol.

7. On the Draw panel on the Ribbon click the Beam Direction tab and then select the girder that runs from B1 to C1.

8. On the Element panel click the Beam System Properties icon to access the dialog box.

9. Set Layout Rule to Fixed Distance, and set the value to **8'-0"** in the Fixed Distance box.

10. Set Justification to Beginning and Beam Type to W14x30.

11. Click OK to exit the dialog box, and click Finish Beam System on the Ribbon to complete the placement. Note that the Beginning side is the left side of the bay, the first 8' bay between framing.

12. In-fill the final bay with any one of the methods that you just tried.

That was not so difficult, was it? Now go to a 3D view of the model and check out the finished product.

Adding Roof Framing

Now that you have learned how basic floor framing works, the next task is roof framing. The roof framing tools in Revit Structure are quite similar to those for floor framing. You use the Beam and the Beam System commands just as you did with floor framing. The big difference is that you have to slope the framing elements to fit the roof deck slope. As you saw in Chapter 5, you can have many varieties of straight or warped sloping decks in your projects.

So let's see how to approach and master this process by starting with a simple sloped flat roof and adding steel framing to it. First you will learn how to attach framing to the underside of a roof. Then you will move on to frame more complicated roof shapes that slope from ridgelines to drain points.

CREATING THE REFERENCE LEVEL FOR A SLOPING ROOF

When you are developing your model, you create flat levels at a particular elevation for the various floors. But if you have a sloping roof, where do you create the roof level, since there isn't one constant reference elevation on the sloping surface? Best practice is to make the level at the top of the wall or (for wood) at the top plate of the wall. Your ceiling framing would be there most likely as well. Another good place to create a level is at the top of the roof, at the peak. That way, your view projects downward and you can see the whole roof. You will most likely need to adjust your view range so that the whole roof is showing. But as you expand the view range so that you can see the entire sloping roof you may start to see the ceiling framing below, which makes your display confusing. In that case, you can create a filter to hide the ceiling framing since for a roof plan you want to see only the roof framing members in the view.

Attaching Structural Framing to a Flat Sloping Plane

The first thing to do to prepare for adding the roof framing on a flat sloped roof of this type is to extend the walls and columns to the underside of the roof deck, which we discussed in Chapter 5. To attach the walls and columns, highlight them in a 3D view, click Attach on the Options bar, and then select the roof deck element where you want them attached (see Figure 7.27).

If the roof segment is a straight sloping plane, you can attach your framing to it with this technique. Using the methods you learned in Chapter 5, create a flat sloping roof deck in a new file. The general method for adding your framing is as follows:

1. Go to a section view of the roof deck.

2. On the Home tab of the Ribbon, click Set in the Work Plane panel.

3. In the Work Plane dialog box, select the Pick a Plane option, and then click OK.

4. Click the underside of the roof deck. (You may need to activate Thin Line display to make it easier for you to see the roof surface lines in section.)

5. The Go to View dialog box will appear, prompting you to choose a better view to display — that is, where you will draw the members in plan (see Figure 7.28). You must go directly to that view or the work plane will not be established.

FIGURE 7.27
Before and after views
of wall attachment
to roof deck

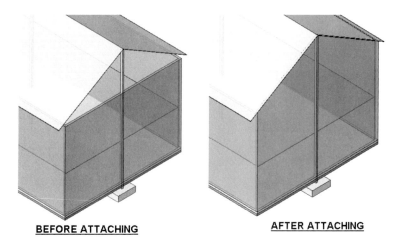

BEFORE ATTACHING   AFTER ATTACHING

FIGURE 7.28
After selecting a plane,
go directly to the view.

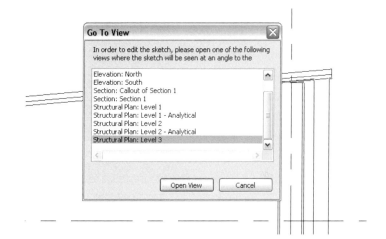

6. In plan view, you draw the members just as you did the floor members, and they will attach to the underside of the deck. The advantage of this approach is that if you need to edit the slope of the roof diaphragm during the design process, increasing or decreasing it, the attached roof framing will move with it, thus avoiding a lengthy editing process.

What about the analytical model lines? Their locations can be independently located by setting the Vertical Projection parameter of the element. See Chapter 15 for a more complete description of how the analytical lines can be adjusted.

Now you have a grasp of the basics of sloped roof framing. The material can be wood, concrete, or steel, but the modeling principles are the same. This type of modeling will work for many of the conditions that might arise. But what about those conditions where the roof varies and is not on one plane? In such cases there is no consistent flat plane where you can attach the framing. In the next section, you will learn how to work with those types of conditions.

Warped Roof Framing

It is common in building design for roofs to slope from ridges to drains in order to drain rainwater, creating a roof that warps and has no consistent flat plane (see Figure 7.29), as you saw in Chapter 5. Even if this is the case, there is a method of basic straight-line generation that will allow the warped surface to be framed using straight beam elements. In this section, you will learn how to model a roof of this type.

FIGURE 7.29
Steel midrise model with a minimally sloping roof system to accommodate drainage

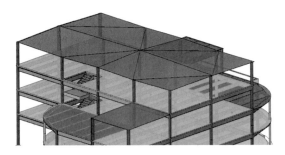

This next example will use a deck that slopes about $\frac{1}{4}''$ per foot from the ridgelines. That is not a great deal of sloping, but it is enough to drain water off and is a typical type of construction for commercial and institutional-type buildings.

In Figure 7.30, you can see that the ridgelines in this example are 8″ above the roof line datum. The drain points are –4″ below the roof line datum. (The slope values are exaggerated to make them easier to see.) The rectangular area between grids 2C and 3E has ridges on three sides; then the surface slopes down on the fourth side to the drain location. When you frame that bay, the end of each beam will have a different elevation.

Before you see how the bay is framed, you need to learn about 3D snapping. The next section will give you the essentials.

3D Snapping of Beam Elements

One of the most important concepts to discuss for sloping members is 3D snapping (no, that is not something you do to the person in the next cubicle with an elastic band). When you did the floor framing, you were able to set the members at one elevation, easily specified and controlled, with each end at the same elevation relative to the floor level or reference plane. But for a warped roof system with drains and ridges, every beam is sloping, so establishing and then editing the tops of steel can be very tedious. What tool does Revit Structure offer to help you handle this condition?

It's handled with the 3D Snapping option. When you choose the Beam or Beam System command, the 3D Snapping option will appear on the Options bar as a check box. Check it as you are creating sloping members, and they will snap to the top of column, or to the intersecting sloping girder, or to a wall. That way, you do not need to compute the elevation yourself (which would take way too much time).

Once you place the beam elements, you can also edit their Start and End elevations. When you select the member, the elevations at each end will be displayed (see Figure 7.31). Click the elevation value, and you will be able to change it. You can also modify their value(s) using the Instance Properties dialog box by setting the Start and/or End Level Offset parameters (see Figure 7.32).

These work fine when you want to edit individual conditions, but you would not want to do that for an entire roof system. 3D snapping offers a more automated approach to creating all the necessary sloping members.

FIGURE 7.30

A roof plan pattern slop-
ing from ridge to drain

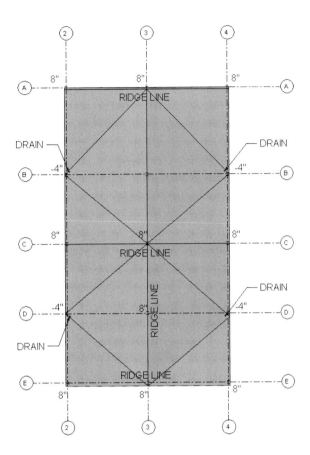

FIGURE 7.30

A roof plan pattern slop-
ing from ridge to drain

Note that 3D snapping does not work with the Grid option or with the Chain option on the Options bar.

Now that you understand how 3D snapping works, you can proceed to add the framing to your roof element. Here's how it is done. After you have placed columns and attached their tops to the underside of the roof deck, you can add the girders by snapping from column top to column top. They will be placed at the underside of the deck right where you want them without you having to compute anything. Then the framing bays are in-filled using the Beam System command, but with the 3D Snapping option checked. That way each beam will automatically snap to the elevation of the sloping girder to which it is attached, again with no need to compute any top-of-steel elevation. Furthermore, if you edit the elevation of the sloping girder, the in-fill beams will automatically flex to the new elevation.

Unfortunately, if you edit the top of the column elevation, the girder will not stay attached to the top of the column. This means that you will have to go column-by-column in a plan view and manually adjust the girders to their new position or redo the framing entirely. If only Autodesk would resolve this issue, the whole roof framing system would flex automatically when the warped diaphragm shape changes.

The next exercise will lead you step-by-step through the techniques for adding framing to a warped roof diaphragm.

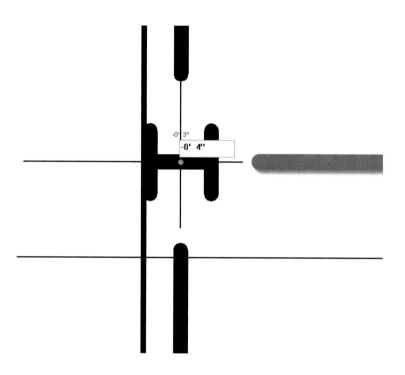

FIGURE 7.31
Adjusting the eleva-
tion at one end of the
selected girder

-0' 3"

-0' 4"

EXERCISE: ADDING ROOF FRAMING FOR A WARPED ROOF

First, we'll attach the columns and walls to the roof diaphragm:

1. Open Dataset_0702_begin.

2. Select everything, and then on the Multi-Select tab on the Ribbon, click the Filter icon on the Filter panel.

3. Leave only the Structural Column category checked, and then click OK.

4. On the Ribbon on the Modify Structural Columns tab, click the Attach icon on the Modify Columns panel, and then select the roof.

   You will get a warning that you are attaching to a nonstructural object, but that is okay. The columns will stay attached unless you detach them, even if the shape of the deck changes. Of course, now each column top is at a different elevation on the sloping surface, which is difficult to calculate manually but is exactly the way we want it. Next, let's add girders between the columns:

1. In the Project Browser, double-click the Level 3 plan view.

2. On the Ribbon on the Manage tab ➤ Project Settings panel, click Snaps from the Settings drop-down list.

3. In the Snaps dialog box, uncheck all but the Points snap, and then click OK to exit.

4. Click the Beam icon on the Home tab of the Ribbon, and then select a W16x26 size from the Type Selector.

5. On the Options bar, check the 3D Snapping check box.

6. Hover your cursor over a column top to activate the Points snap.

7. Click to place one end of the beam at the column located at 2A; then click to place the other end at column 2B.

8. Keep adding girders until all the columns are connected. The girders all slope from column top to column top. Remember that the Chain option is ignored while the 3D Snap option is active. Check your work in the 3D view.

Next, you will in-fill the bays with sloping beam systems:

1. On the Structure panel of the Home tab on the Ribbon, click the Beam System icon.

2. On the Options bar, check the 3D Snapping check box.

3. On the Options bar, set an 8′-0″ Maximum Spacing as a layout rule.

4. Change the Tag type to Framing.

5. Hover your cursor over the horizontal girder in one of the bays to set the framing direction, and then click to place the beam (the one-click method).

6. Populate the other framing bays in a similar fashion.

When you finish, your framing should look like the following illustration in a 3D view:

When you want to make larger-scale sections of sloping members, you will find that the ends of the beams needs to be cut vertically in order for them to appear correctly in your view, as the next section will demonstrate.

Shaping the Ends of the Sloping Members

Look at Figure 7.33 and notice that the ends of the sloping girders are not cut vertically as you would need for connecting the shear plate to the column. This is an important consideration for you when you are trying to detail the connection in a section.

To correct the display, you have to create a reference plane at the edge of the column flange to cut the beam vertically:

1. Highlight the girder, click on the blue triangle shape handle, and then drag the end of the girder over the column flange. (This will not affect the end node location of the girder.)

2. Draw a reference plane on the outer edge of each column.

FIGURE 7.32
You can use the Instance
Properties dialog box
to change beam Start
and End elevations.

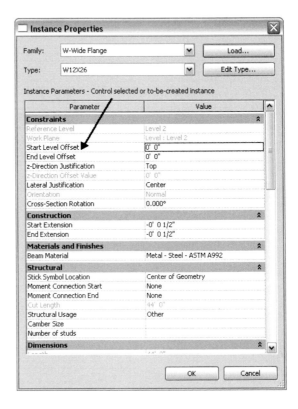

FIGURE 7.33
The girder is not cut
correctly at the column.

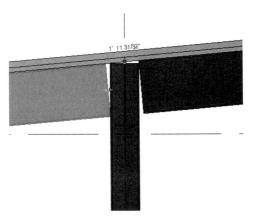

3. On the Modify tab of the Ribbon on the Edit Geometry panel, click Cut Geometry on the Cut drop-down list. Then select the girder and reference plane (see Figure 7.34). That will do it.

The final display will look like Figure 7.35. Also notice that the column and girder do not fully intersect with the roof. This is fine; it's how it would be constructed in reality. The framing members should be vertical and will have bent plates attached to the top flange to connect to the sloping surface of the roof deck.

FIGURE 7.34
Extend the beam and add a reference plane.

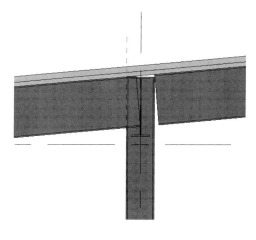

FIGURE 7.35
The final section with shaped girder ends

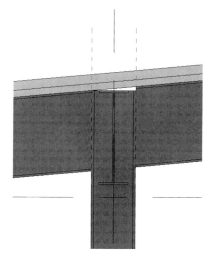

Adding Steel Braced and Moment Frames

Now that you have added your floor and roof framing, you will start work on your moment or braced frames, depending on which system your project is using. These frames will accommodate the seismic system you might be using on a steel or concrete building, depending on where your building will be located in terms of seismic zones.

Moment Frames and Cantilevered Beams

When you model moment frames, you use standard framing techniques as described earlier in this chapter, but you must adjust the display to add Moment Connection End symbols on the ends of the frame members. You might also want to display the moment frame girders with a heavier line weight, which you can do by assigning them to a particular structural category or through use of a filter.

One way to show the frame members with a heavier line weight is to assign the moment frame members to the Other category for that use, as was described earlier. Another way is to build a filter, which is used in conjunction with Visibility/Graphic overrides in views. Filters are very powerful. After you place the frame member, you should put an entry such as MF in the Comments parameter. That will identify that instance as a frame member for which you can then create a filter. In a given view, using Visibility/Graphic overrides, you can use the filter to display the member with a heavy line weight.

Though not moment frame items, cantilevered beams that are moment connected need a similar symbol, an open triangle, added to one end of the element. The symbol works just like the Moment Frame symbol. Unfortunately, it isn't obvious enough, so it can be annoying to figure out which end to select in the Element Instance Properties dialog box. The parameters Moment Connection Start and Moment Connection End are related to how you placed the member, but who remembers that when you come back to add the symbol? It is best add the symbol right after placing the member because the point you place first is the Start; otherwise, it becomes guesswork.

AN EASY WAY FOR FINDING THE START AND END OF A BEAM

One technique that can be used to graphically show where the Start and End are is to use a special tag family. The labels available to tag beams include Start Offset and End Offset, which refer to an offset relative to the work plane the beam is associated with. You can create a tag family that is set to show the Start Offset value instead of the beam type. These tags can also be assigned to use an attachment point at the Start, Middle, or End of the beam. This means that you can use a tag that will appear at the Start end of a beam.

As a working example, if you already have a beam-type tag on a beam, select it, and choose your special Start tag from the Type Selector. The new tag slides down to the Start of the beam — now you know where it is without setting the value and seeing if you guessed correctly. You can select a large number of tags, switch them, make note of their orientation, and switch them back.

To add a Moment Frame or Cantilever Moment symbol, highlight the member and click Instance Properties from the Element Properties drop-down list on the Modify Structural Framing tab of the Ribbon. In the Instance Parameter area of the resulting dialog box, set the Moment Connection Start and/or End value to Moment Frame or Cantilever Moment, which will add the corresponding symbol to the end of your beam (see Figure 7.36).

One factor you should consider when displaying the symbols is the distance of the symbol from the column in your Coarse mode plan view. If it appears too far from the column or overlaps the column, you can adjust the distance. Choose Structural Settings on the Manage tab of the Ribbon, and change the Symbolic Cutback distance for Beam/Truss to a value that displays well on your plan view. Be careful, though, because this will change the end distances for all your beams in the project throughout all views. A possible way around this would be to go into the tag family itself and adjust the symbol location.

In the Structural Settings dialog box you set the default values that control the display of Brace and Moment Frame symbols (see Figure 7.37). If the symbols do not correspond to your company standards, you can change the default version of the symbol or make your own. You assign your own symbol in the Structural Settings dialog box for the entire project.

A common display problem you will likely encounter is that the cantilever open triangle can appear too thin in plan view, and it can be quite frustrating trying to find out where to adjust its line weight. To adjust the open triangle line weight, click Settings on the Manage tab, and on the drop-down list click Object Styles ➤ Annotation Objects ➤ Connection Symbols and adjust the Projected Line Weight value. This should also be done in your company template so that you standardize the display. For more information on standards, see Chapter 17. Figure 7.38 shows how the display might look when you finish.

FIGURE 7.36
Adding the Moment Frame or Cantilever Moment symbol to an element

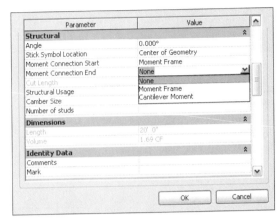

FIGURE 7.37
Moment frame and cantilevered steel framing displayed in plan view

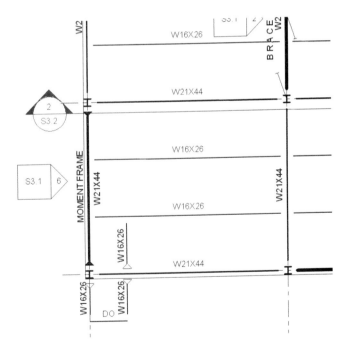

Creating Framing Elevations

Projects using steel moment and braced frames usually require the creation of frame elevations. This is an important consideration on any project, and Revit Structure has the special Framing Elevation option to make the process easier. The Framing Elevation command is found on the

View tab of the Ribbon on the Elevation drop-down list of the Create panel. It creates an elevation of the frame and is attached to a grid line. Figure 7.38 shows a typical moment frame displayed using Detail Level: Coarse, where the frame members are displayed as stick symbols. The floor and roof categories have been shut off in this view so that only the frame shows but the foundations remain. You could also display the moment frame using Detail Level: Medium, which displays the steel members showing their real shape and size and with floors and roofs turned on for a more realistic view. But Detail Level: Medium might not be the best option because you don't see the moment connection symbols since they are designed to appear only when using Detail Level: Coarse, which means the frame members are not as easily identified.

FIGURE 7.38
Moment frame elevation in coarse mode

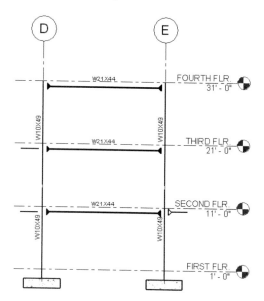

That covers the basics for creating moment frames and cantilevered framing in your virtual building. Next, you will examine the process for creating braced frames, which involves much more elaborate modeling techniques.

Real World Scenario

CONTENDING WITH MANY TYPES OF FRAMING

You may have been to some of those sales presentations where framing is quickly and easily added, every condition is covered, and everybody is really happy. Well, in real projects it just ain't so! A typical structural project will most likely have all sorts of odd framing conditions that fit no pattern and many types of different framing to place as well as many structural systems that need to be modeled. You will find that the 80-20 rule governs. Eighty percent of the framing goes in quickly and easily, but the other 20 percent is a more difficult case and creating it can cause lots of frustration. Your project fee will be spent in a corresponding fashion. As an example, let's consider a real project. For a moment turn to the Color Gallery in the middle of the book and take a look at the images of the Los Angeles Unified School District Central High School 16.

This recent project is a new high school campus in California. The campus has two large multilevel classrooms. The classroom floors are composite metal deck and concrete, with steel framing members and wide flange steel columns. The seismic system consists of steel-braced frames. The roofs slope at $\frac{1}{4}''$ per foot and are constructed of $1\frac{1}{2}''$ metal roof deck and lightweight concrete fill. Tube framing juts out from the roof to support large sloping parapets. The corridors in the floors are depressed, as is the framing.

The gymnasium structure has large steel trusses supporting the roof. The library/administration building is a two-story braced frame structure using HSS tube columns. A long canopy snakes through the campus. A subterranean parking garage is constructed with a precast concrete double-T roof that has basketball courts on top. A one-story cafeteria structure with very complicated canopies completes the campus buildings.

You will encounter numerous types of framing on your projects, and it can get quite complicated. You need lots of tools in your Revit tool chest to get it done, as well as a good deal of imagination. But once you get familiar with Revit Structure, you will find that you can accomplish most any condition you encounter.

Braced Frames

Once the floor and roof framing is completed, you are ready to add vertical braced frames (see Figure 7.39) to your model. As stated earlier in the chapter, if you are using the analytical model, you will also want to set Structural Usage for the floor members of the frame to Horizontal Bracing.

Braced frames need to be sketched in an elevation view. Usually that will be a frame elevation, as discussed earlier. The most important point to understand is that the diagonal members need to be connected to work points. A work point is usually at the center of the member that it intersects, such as a girder. As you place the diagonal member, you will see Revit trying to snap to those points. Pay close attention! Many times it will try to snap to the adjacent member, so you need to be careful. One option is to use Temporary Hide/Isolate to hide the adjacent members temporarily so it is easier to establish the correct work points.

The following exercise will lead you through the construction of a braced frame so you can see how the process works.

EXERCISE: CREATING A STEEL-BRACED FRAME

In this exercise, you will add an x-braced frame to a project.

1. Open Dataset_0703_begin. Level 1 plan view should be active.

2. Click the Framing Elevation command on the Elevation drop-down list of the Create panel on the View tab of the Ribbon. Note that on the Options bar, the check box for Attach to Grid is checked.

3. Hover your cursor slightly below grid E, and then click to select the direction of the elevation so it is facing upward on the screen.

4. Open that elevation; then on the View Control bar, change Detail Level to Medium.

5. Select the crop boundary and use its shape handles on the vertical sides to extend the boundary outside the ends of the frame on each side, making the view of the model wide enough for you to clearly see the columns.

6. On the Structure panel of the Home tab, click the Brace icon.

7. In the Type Selector, select HSSS6X6X.500 as the diagonal brace member, and be sure to uncheck 3D Snapping.

8. Hover over the base of a column, and click on the middle bottom of the column (if snaps are turned off from the previous exercise, turn them all back on).

9. Hover over the middle of the second floor beam at its center until you can snap to the work point, as shown here:

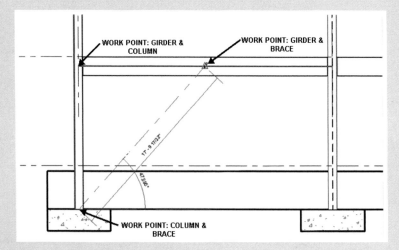

10. Repeat the sequence until the x-frame is completed.

11. Where the ends of the diagonal braces overlap the floor beams, highlight each one, and then click and drag the triangle to move the end of the brace until it clears the beam.

12. In the Project Browser activate Level 3 plan view.

13. On the Manage tab of the Ribbon click Structural Settings.

14. Change the Brace Symbol plan representation to Line with Angle, and then exit.

The brace symbols will automatically appear in plan views after you place the brace in elevation. Revit has two types of brace symbols in plan views: Line with Angle or Parallel Line. The Line with Angle option shows more information about the braced frame; in your plan views, it shows the start point of the brace and the direction it is going, up or down, as shown in the following illustration:

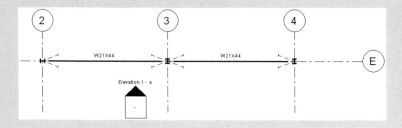

It can be important to know how the frame members are located in case there are door or window interferences on the architectural side of the design. Line with Angle, as opposed to the simple Parallel Line type, allows the architect to easily see the directions of the braces without referring to the frame elevation. You can make it even more descriptive by adapting the Line with Angle so it has a solid brace symbol, which indicates it is going up, while a dashed symbol indicates the brace is going down. Unfortunately, Revit Structure does not ship with a dashed line symbol for braces going downward. The default symbol is shown dashed in both directions. So let's see how we can create one by editing the default brace symbol. The procedure for doing that is as follows:

1. On the Application menu click Open ➤ Family ➤ Annotations ➤ Structural, and then open the Connection-Brace-Angle family.

2. On the Create tab click Line, and then add a series of short lines in a dashed pattern to replace the continuous line.

3. Erase the continuous line.

4. On the Application menu click Save As ➤ Family and save the file with the name **Connection-Brace-Angle_Down**.

5. Back in Dataset 0703_begin, on the Manage tab click Structural Settings.

6. Change the Show Brace Symbol Below setting to Connection-Brace-Angle_Down, and then click OK to finish.

7. On the Manage tab click Object Styles on the drop-down list.

8. On the Annotation Objects tab change Line Pattern for the Brace in Plan View Symbols category to Solid, and then exit.

9. Your plan views should now look like the following graphic:

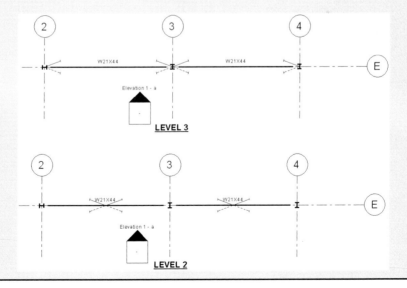

FIGURE 7.39
Steel x-braced frame elevation with no connection plates shown

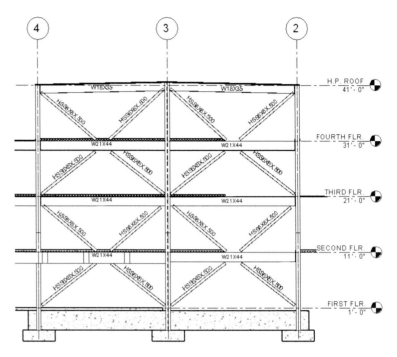

You might also wonder about the braced connection gusset plates. They are not shown unless you add them. The decision as to whether you show them in your elevation has to be a judgment call for you to make for your firm. Whereas it is best practice to show the moment frames in Coarse mode in order to see the moment connection symbols, it is best practice to show the braced frames in Medium mode. That is because braced frames are much more likely to interfere with the architecture. The frame gusset plates can sometimes get very big and might also interfere with adjacent windows or doors, so in those cases it might be a good idea to model them.

That ends our discussion about framing in Revit Structure. You have gotten a thorough overview of the capabilities and even some of the frustrations that you may encounter as you design your project. But don't be intimidated. Revit Structure is a great program and quite intuitive. If you keep adding tools to your Revit tool chest, before you know it, you will be a master.

The Bottom Line

Understand structural framing families and properties. Revit Structure modeling is a constraint-based system that allows the model to update as changes occur, keeping the overall relationships between elements the same.

Master It Describe the two primary modeling constraints for attaching beams and braces, and explain why they are important.

Add floor framing. When you add floor framing to your project, you probably start with a fuzzy idea of the size and initially use a placeholder. As the design progresses and comes into sharper detail, you will update the size and spacing in many cases. The model must have a maximum of flexibility to make the editing practical.

Master It You are in schematics and know the bay widths on your building will change considerably. You want your framing members in each bay to be about 10′ from center to center no matter how wide the bay becomes during the course of the design. What layout rule is the best to use in this case?

Add roof framing. Roof framing must support roofs that slope from ridges to drains. That means all the support beams and girders must slope as well. During the design process the roof can change in shape and slope. Be aware that costly editing can eat away your at your design fee.

Master It Calculating the end elevation for each sloping beam would be very time consuming and a nightmare to edit. What process do you use to most efficiently place the roof support system?

Create moment and braced frames. Moment and braced frames are an important element of many structural designs. Revit Structure has two methods of displaying the braces in a plan views: Parallel Line and Line with Angle. The symbols are placed automatically in plan view as you draw the braces in elevation view.

Master It Which display type is the most informative of the braced frame layouts, and how do you set it to display correctly in plan view?

Chapter 8

Forming the Foundations

The topic of modeling foundations is a broad subject that covers just about any element below or at grade that supports a structure. These elements may or may not be created with the Foundation tools, which in some cases means they are not recognized as being part of the Structural Foundations category. Elements such as walls and slabs on grade may be considered foundations, but to Revit Structure they are typically modeled using the Wall and Floor tools. Other foundation types such as grade beams are modeled as a wall or as a beam depending on your workflow and your desired results. Piers, whether they are concrete or masonry, are modeled using the Structural Column tools and families.

Some forms of foundations are created using tools that we discussed in other chapters. Even though these tools are assigned to other categories, they still serve the purpose of a foundation. To avoid redundancy this chapter focuses on the creation of foundations with the use of the Foundation tools available in Revit Structure. It also mentions how some forms of foundations may be handled without using the tools. Foundations may be the first things to be built during construction, but they tend to be modeled last. This is a direct effect of how Revit automates and keeps track of the relationships between foundations and other elements. Wall foundations need to attach to a wall, and isolated foundations below a column support attach to the column to form a relationship.

Learning the various Foundation tools and how to use them and knowing the best methods to model foundations that don't use these tools will allow you to take full advantage of what Revit Structure has to offer when working with the forms of foundations.

In this chapter you will learn to:

- ◆ Create and work with isolated foundations

- ◆ Create and work with wall foundations

- ◆ Create and work with foundation slabs

Getting to Know the Foundation Tools

Revit Structure offers tools that allow you to model footings that support columns and piers and to model footing that support walls. These tools available for modeling isolated footings (spread footings), wall footings (strip footings), and foundations slabs (pads) can be found on the Ribbon ➢ Home tab ➢ Foundation panel, as shown in Figure 8.1. The appropriate use of each tool is determined by the type of foundation you are dealing with. The name of the tool is a good clue to what it is used for.

FIGURE 8.1
Revit Structure's Foundation tools are located on the Home tab of the Ribbon.

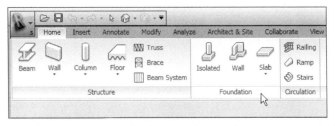

Elements placed with these tools are assigned to the Structural Foundations category in the Object styles. Revit Structure deals with these various foundation conditions as system families and component families. The use of system families like wall foundations and foundation slabs allow Revit Structure to automate more of how it interacts with other elements within the model. Using component families for unique foundation conditions gives you tremendous flexibility with regard to creating new shapes and their placement. In some situations such as complicated foundations where you may need to tie into an existing structure or conditions that may be a bit more project specific, you can use a foundation slab or, as a last resort, an in-place Structural Foundation family. The foundation families that are placed with these tools can be found in the Project Browser under the Structural Foundations category, separated into family types, as shown in Figure 8.2.

FIGURE 8.2
Foundation Slab and Wall Foundation families are system families.

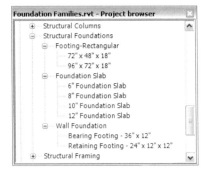

Footing-Rectangular is Revit Structure's default component family. New foundation component families that you create will be added under Structural Foundations. The Isolated Foundation tool is used to place these families into a project. Wall Foundation is a Revit Structure system family that uses the Wall Foundation tool to place it into the family. Foundation Slab is a Revit Structure system family as well. The Foundation Slab tool is used to place this family into a project. Since the wall and slab foundations are system families, you will not be able to create new families for them. However, you will be able to create new types as needed.

Using all of these tools and family types in conjunction with one another allows you to develop models like the one shown in Figure 8.3.

You use these tools similarly to how you use other tools to model elements within Revit Structure. In order to place a wall footing, you need to have a wall modeled first. Likewise, a wall must exist before you can place a wall opening. The foundation slab works the same way that a floor or roof does except its sloping capabilities are limited. An isolated footing is created the same way as any other component family, such as a structural column or a beam. The differences are that they are organized and managed under the Structural Foundation category and you use slightly different methods for placing them into a project. Once you learn how to use the tools to model elements in Revit Structure, you will find that you can model other elements in a similar manner.

FIGURE 8.3
Revit Structure's Foundation tools are used to create the various forms of foundations.

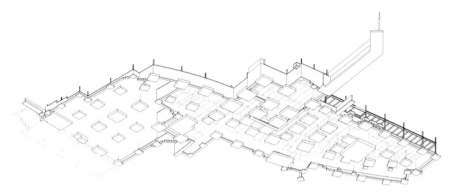

Working with an Isolated Foundation

The Isolated Foundation tool has many uses. You need to learn all the various ways it can be placed and how it behaves as it creates relationships with other elements based on its materials, location, and placement methods. It uses component families for elements that are placed, so knowing how to work with these families and how to create new ones for the many conditions you will come across, such as drilled piers, caissons, bell piers, spread footings, and pile caps, is crucial to taking full advantage of the tool. This knowledge will certainly give you an edge up on creating an accurate model, as well as make the documentation process much more efficient.

Revit Structure includes several foundation families in its library located in the Imperial Library ➢ Structural ➢ Foundations folder. Included is the `Footing-Rectangular.rfa` family, which is the most basic of the foundation component families. You may know it as a *spread footing*. Revit Structure also includes various pile and pile cap families, such as `Pile-Steel Pipe.rfa` and `Pile Cap-6 Pile.rfa`. Foundations that do not fall into these types or shapes will have to be created by making a new foundation component family.

Working with the Isolated Foundation's Component Family

Revit Structure includes a template for you to use when creating new foundation families called `Structural Foundation.rft.` You can start a new family from this template by choosing the Application menu ➢ New ➢ Family. Browse to the `Imperial Template` folder to locate this template. When using this template you will see that it already has Length and Width parameters. To see these parameters choose the Create tab ➢ Family Properties panel ➢ Types tool while in the family. This is also where you can add new parameters such as Thickness, Diameter, and Reinforcing Information to the family. You should use the default Length and Width parameters when assigning labels to your dimensions for controlling the size of the geometry in your family. With these parameters already placed into the template, analysis partners can access these fields to push and pull data between Revit Structure and their analysis program.

This template is already assigned to the Structural Foundations category. Choose the Create tab ➢ Family Properties panel ➢ Category and Parameters tool while in the family to open the dialog box shown in Figure 8.4.

You can also see in Figure 8.4 that the Structural Foundations category has a few built-in family parameters that allow the family to behave differently when it is placed into a project depending on these parameters' settings.

FIGURE 8.4
The Family Category
and Parameters dialog
box for the Structural
Foundations category

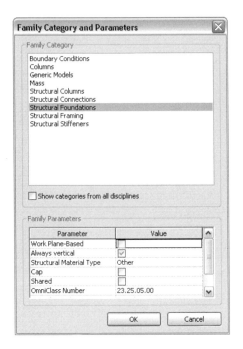

FIGURE 8.4
The Family Category
and Parameters dialog
box for the Structural
Foundations category

Work Plane-Based   Enabling the family to be work plane-based allows it to be placed with reference to a work plane (Figure 8.5) rather than a level (Figure 8.6).

FIGURE 8.5
Work Plane-Based
enabled

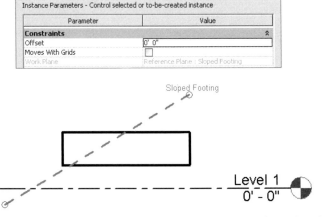

Always Vertical   Enabling the family to be always vertical keeps it vertical when placed. In the Footing-Rectangular footing family, a footing will always be placed with the top and bottom surfaces maintaining a horizontal surface regardless of whether it was placed on a level or a sloped work plane. Disabling this option, as shown in Figure 8.7, allows the footing to be rotated to the level or plane it is being referenced to.

Structural Material Type   This parameter determines some basic structural behaviors for the foundations when they are placed into a project. It does not specify the material that you

FIGURE 8.6
Work Plane-Based
disabled

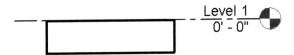

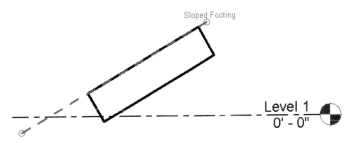

FIGURE 8.7
Work Plane-Based
enabled and Always
Vertical disabled

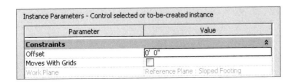

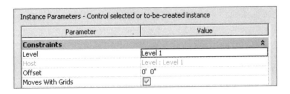

use for cut and surface patterns, physical characteristics, and rendering appearance. The main difference between the material types that are available to select is how they autojoin. In an example where a concrete beam frames between two footings, and their structural material type is set to concrete, the intersecting elements will join automatically for cleaning up. For other material types such as steel, wood, and precast concrete, the footings will not autojoin. This parameter also determines whether Revit Structure will generate reinforcement for the family. Families set to Concrete, Precast Concrete, and Other will acquire rebar cover settings in their properties, but steel and wood material types will not.

Cap   This parameter determines the value for the Elevation at Bottom parameter of an isolated footing after it is placed into a project. If Cap is enabled, the Elevation at Bottom setting will be taken from the Topmost Bottom-Facing Face. If Cap is disabled, the Elevation at Bottom setting will be taken from the Bottommost Bottom-Facing Face (Figure 8.8).

Shared   Enabling the family to be shared allows Revit Structure to take into account all the nested components when creating a schedule. It also allows the family that is set to be shared to be nested into another family while still existing as a standalone family within your project. An example would be the pile and pile cap families. The HP Shape and Steel Pipe pile families are set to be shared. They are then loaded into the family that contains the cap. These pile families can be maintained separately without opening the pile cap family.

FIGURE 8.8
The Elevation at Bottom parameter value is determined by the setting for the Cap family parameter.

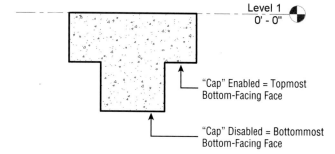

"Cap" Enabled = Topmost Bottom-Facing Face

"Cap" Disabled = Bottommost Bottom-Facing Face

 Real World Scenario

ADD FLEXIBILITY BY CREATING A SUBCATEGORY

At our firm we assign the families we create to subcategories within their main category. For example, when working with elements that are part of the Structural Foundation category, if we create a drilled pier using a structural foundation, we would assign that family to a subcategory called Drilled Pier. The same goes for a pile cap. It is assigned to a subcategory called Pile Cap. The original out-of-the-box rectangular footing is modified to be assigned to a Footing subcategory.

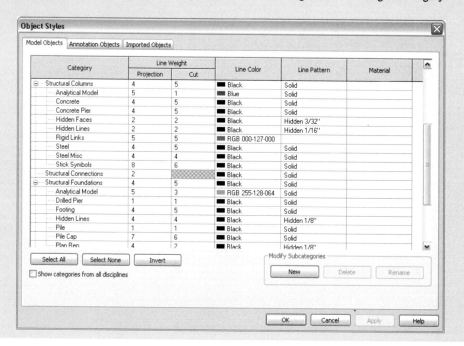

We use the same workflow with other categories such as Structural Framing and Structural Columns. This allows us to have another level of flexibility throughout our model when working with these elements. Is the element a steel, concrete, wood, precast, or light-gauge beam or column? This workflow also gives more flexibility to those who are using our model. They may want to see only certain element types in our model when they are working with it as a link inside their model. They can toggle on/off or change the display of each subcategory individually. Without doing this, one can work with these various elements only by using the main category that the element(s) are assigned to by default.

So how do you create subcategories? When in the Family Edit mode, go to the Manage tab ➢ Family Settings panel ➢ Settings drop-down ➢ Object Styles. Create a new subcategory by clicking the New button from the Modify Subcategories area in the lower right of the Object Styles dialog box. Be sure to assign the new name to the correct category in the New Subcategory dialog box.

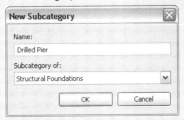

After creating the subcategory, you select all of the geometry that is in your family and open up its Instance Properties dialog box.

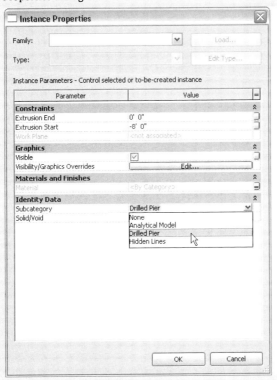

Under Identity Data you will see a parameter called Subcategory. This is where you assign the selected geometry to a subcategory. If you did everything correctly, you will be able to choose your new subcategory from the Value pull-down list.

When incorporating this workflow into your environment, consistency is incredibly important; otherwise, you could end up with several versions of subcategories that refer to the same thing but are named differently.

The Footing-Rectangular family that is provided to you in the Imperial Library includes Length, Width, and Thickness parameters in its properties. Remember what we said previously? Only the Length and Width parameters are built into the family. These parameters are system-based parameters that Revit Structure provides; basically, they are shared parameters. The Thickness parameter was added as a Family parameter that cannot appear in schedules or tags. Nor does it share the thickness parameter name of *Foundation Thickness* that the system family wall footing uses. What does all of this mean? Well, isolated footings cannot have their thickness value shown in a schedule unless you modify the family to encompass a shared parameter for their thickness. It also means that you cannot place a wall footing and an isolated footing in the same schedule and still get satisfying results. Keep this in mind as you develop your new foundation families.

Adding Isolated Foundations to Your Project

Now that you have an idea of what determines how a foundation component family behaves and that several foundation types can be placed using these types of families, you are ready to start placing them into your project. Isolated footings behave similarly to other elements in that they will move with grids if you enable them to do so. They will attach themselves to structural columns if the entire extents of the column are within the extents of the isolated foundation. For this reason, before you start placing these elements, you should already have other elements such as grids and columns placed into your model.

You can use views such as structural plan views and 3D views for placing isolated footings, but don't be alarmed when the tool is unavailable when you are in a section view. This is normal behavior because the view's work plane is not such that it allows the isolated foundation to be placed. You must be in a view whose work plane is parallel to a level, like a plan view or a 3D view, which can be set to any work plane.

Since an isolated foundation is a component family, the options for its placement will be more flexible than that of a wall or slab foundation, which are system families. You will be able to reference isolated foundations to a level or reference plane or even host them to a slab. Beyond the option to place them one by one, you can place them by selecting grids or structural columns to ensure more accurate placement.

EMPLOYING THE OPTIONS FOR PLACEMENT

To begin, select the Isolated tool from the Home tab ➤ Foundation panel, or drag the family type from the Families section of the Project Browser and drop it into the drawing area of your project. A third method is to select an existing foundation and right-click to choose Create Similar from the shortcut menu or choose it from the Create panel that displays on the contextual Ribbon tab when a foundation is selected. After the Isolated tool has been invoked, the Ribbon will switch to the Place Isolated Foundation contextual tab, as shown in Figure 8.9, as well as put you in the Single Pick placement mode for placing an isolated foundation. The contextual Ribbon tab for an isolated foundation offers several methods for placement, such as On Grids and At Columns, and the option Model In-Place.

FIGURE 8.9
The Options
bar and con-
textual tab
give you sev-
eral options
for placing an
isolated foun-
dation.

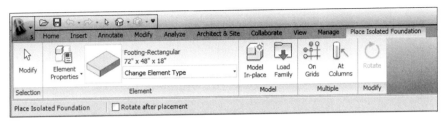

The following is an overview of what's available to you for placing isolated foundations into your project:

Ribbon panels

◆ Before placing an isolated foundation, you can select the Element properties of the currently selected isolated foundation to make changes to its properties or duplicate it to make a new type.

◆ From the Type Selector drop-down in the Element panel, select the type of isolated foundation you want to place. If the desired foundation type is not available, you will have to duplicate an existing type or load a new family that includes the foundation type you are looking for.

◆ From the Model panel you can choose Model In-Place, which allows you to create an in-place family rather than placing a component family. This is typically used for project-specific foundations that are more easily modeled in place, so you can see how they relate to elements within the model.

◆ From the Model panel you can choose the Load Family tool to load a new family on the fly. This is for those times when you don't find what you are looking for in the Type Selector; you can load a family while still in the Place Foundation mode. Once the family is loaded, you can start placing it.

◆ Two additional placement options in the Multiple panel are On Grids and At Columns. These are both explained further in "Using the On Grids Option" and Using the At Columns Option."

◆ After an isolated foundation has been placed, you can select the Rotate tool from the Modify panel. Selecting this while still in the Place Foundation mode allows you to rotate the previous footing that was placed. Once this tool is selected, additional options such as Disjoin, Copy, and an Angle designation box will appear on the Options bar.

Options bar

◆ Selecting the Rotate after Placement option automatically puts you in the Rotate command after placement, with the origin point (defined within the family by the intersection of two reference planes) serving as the center of rotation.

◆ If you are in a 3D view when you choose the Isolated tool, the Options bar will also show a Level pull-down. When placing an isolated foundation in a plan view, Revit Structure sets the level of the view as the level for its placement reference as well as its host. When in a

3D view you have to specify on what level to put the isolated foundation. This pull-down will list all of the available levels in your project and is where you specify on what level to put the isolated foundation.

You will find that isolated foundation Instance parameters will vary (similar to other elements of different categories) depending on the structural material type assigned to them in their family as well as how they are placed in the model. Figure 8.10 shows that a typical concrete isolated foundation (Footing-Rectangular family) will have additional Structural parameters for the concrete cover. The concrete cover settings are used to control the location of rebar when placing it into a foundation element. This will be discussed further in Chapter 10. Switching the structural material family parameter (while in the family edit mode) to Steel or Wood will not display this information because those materials do not require a concrete cover. It is rare that you will need to use materials for foundations that are not concrete, which means that you most likely will not have to adjust this setting. However, if you are not seeing the reinforcing information as expected, make sure that the structural material within the family is set correctly.

FIGURE 8.10
The Instance properties of a Footing-Rectangular foundation component family

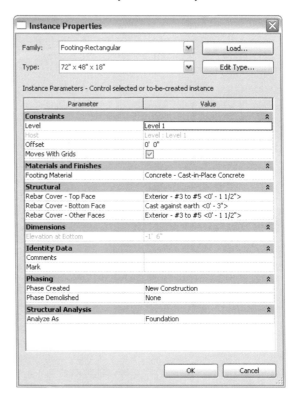

Isolated foundations will have a level, work plane, or host that they are referenced to depending on how they are placed and how you have set the Family parameters within the family. You can set an Offset value for the location of the isolated foundation from its reference location. If the level, reference plane, or slab moves, the isolated foundation will maintain its offset and move with it.

You may have a spread footing that is referenced to Level 1, with an Offset value of -0'-8″, as shown in Figure 8.11. This would place the footing 8″ below Level 1.

FIGURE 8.11
An isolated foundation
referenced to Level 1

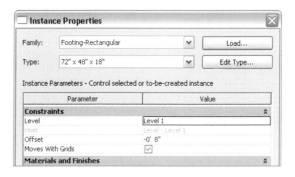

If you had a spread footing that was hosted to a 4″ Slab on Grade floor that was 1′-0″ below Level 1, and the offset value was -0′-8″, the footing would be placed 8″ below the slab, thus making it 1′-8″ below Level 1 (Figure 8.12). Note that in the example where the foundation is hosted to the slab, it can sometimes be tough to determine where the offset is from unless you cut a section and look at the geometry or look closely at the Elevation at Bottom parameter. Both the Level and Host parameters appear in the properties. If the isolated foundation is hosted to an element such as a slab, the offset is referenced from the host, not the level.

FIGURE 8.12
An isolated foundation
hosted to a 4″ Slab on
Grade floor

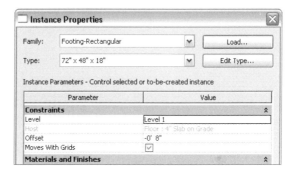

You could also place an isolated foundation with reference to a work plane that was set at a known elevation for some underground mechanical piping. Your footing family could be set so it was work plane–based so it could be placed on a named reference plane. In the example shown in Figure 8.13, the footing is placed on a reference plane named Bottom of Mech Pipe, with an Offset value of -0′-8″. As the reference plane is adjusted to match the bottom of pipe, the footing will maintain its -8″ offset.

FIGURE 8.13
An isolated foundation
referenced to a work
plane named Bottom of
Mech Pipe

Another property worth mentioning is the Moves With Grids parameter. This parameter is either enabled or disabled. If it is enabled and the isolated foundation's origin point is on a grid line, it will move with the grid if that grid is moved. Remember that the origin point is defined by the intersection of two reference planes within the family. Usually these are vertical and horizontal reference planes. If the origin point is touching only one grid instead of a grid intersection, than the isolated foundation will move only with that grid that it is touching. Paying attention to this parameter to ensure that it stays enabled will allow your footings to move with grids when changes are made.

SURE, I WOULD LOVE TO BE YOUR HOST.

When placing an isolated foundation into your project, be cautious of what the foundation takes on as its host. Once the isolated foundation has been placed, you can find this information by selecting it and going to its properties. A Host parameter will be available under the Constraints group. Typically an isolated foundation will host itself to the level that it is being placed on. For example, if you place a footing while in Level 1 view, it will host itself to Level 1. If you place a footing while in Level TFE view, it will host itself to TFE.

What happens if a slab is already placed and within your view range prior to placing the footing? In this case the footing will host itself to the slab instead of the level. Don't believe me; go ahead and try it. It is important to be aware of this behavior. If a footing is to be maintained -1'-0" below Level 1, then it should be placed so it is hosted to Level 1. If it is hosted to the slab instead, and the slab rises to be +0'-6", then the footing will move with the slab to maintain its 1'-0" offset from the slab rather than from Level 1.

In some cases where you want to have that relationship between the footing and the slab, this may be the preferred behavior. If not, you might want to place footings prior to placing slabs or temporarily turn slabs off while placing the footings. If footings are already placed and you need to change their host, all you have to do is select the footing while in a section or elevation view and choose the Pick New Host tool from the Work Plane panel in the contextual Ribbon tab.

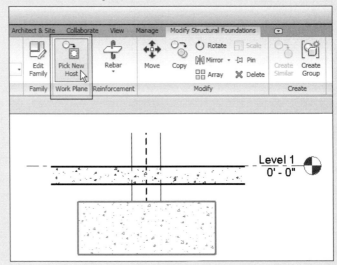

Select either a level or a slab for the new host. Hopefully, at the end of the day, you know who your host is.

When you're placing isolated foundations in Revit Structure, several tools are available that allow you to place them quickly as well as ensure that they are placed properly. Using the default Single Pick option will place single isolated foundations one by one and also allow you to control the rotation of each specific placement. Using the On Grids or At Columns placement option allows you to place several isolated foundations at once while using other elements for their placement location.

USING THE SINGLE PICK OPTION

The single-pick option is the initial state that Revit Structure puts you in after you select the Isolated Foundation tool. This allows you to place isolated foundations one at a time and adjust settings between each placement.

To use the Single Pick option, follow these steps:

1. You will typically be placing foundations in a plan view, so activate a lower-level plan view.

2. On the Home tab ➢ Foundation panel, select the Isolated tool.

3. Select the type of isolated foundation you want to place from the Type Selector.

4. Start placing isolated foundations one by one as they snap to the intersection of gridlines or the centerline of piers and columns. If you are not seeing isolated foundations appear, you may need to adjust your view range settings.

5. You can rotate isolated foundations while placing them by pressing the spacebar. Each tap of the spacebar rotates the isolated foundation 90 degrees. If the isolated foundation is at the intersection of other elements, it will snap perpendicular to them and use an angle degree that's half the intersection angle. You also have options for rotating after each placement.

This method is useful for placing isolated foundations that are not at the center of other elements or that require a more specific location or rotation. Even after isolated foundations are placed, you can rotate them by selecting one or more of them and pressing the spacebar.

WHO CONTROLS THE RELATIONSHIP?

When placing an isolated foundation that is supporting a structural column, you will get a warning telling you that an attached structural foundation will be moved to the bottom of the column.

This is normal behavior. The structural column is creating a relationship with the isolated foundation that you just placed. This relationship occurs whether you like it or not. If a structural column sees an isolated foundation touching its base, it automatically assumes that the isolated foundation wants a relationship. Once this relationship is established, the structural column will attach the isolated foundation to its base and take the isolated foundation wherever it goes. If the structural column's base changes in a vertical direction, the isolated foundation will move with it. The structural column can move in a horizontal direction, and the isolated foundation will maintain its position as long as the structural column stays within the extents of the isolated foundation. The minute that the structural column decides to leave those extents, the isolated foundation will jump back to the insertion point of the structural column.

Keep in mind that if you change the location of the footing instead of the structural column, the column will not change with it to maintain the relationship. It says, "Go ahead and move; I don't care." Their relationship will be broken. Once they come back into contact with each other, their relationship will begin again. In order to maintain the relationship, you must change the base of the structural column. This means that you should drive the location of an isolated foundation through the structural column. When you do this, the isolated foundation will stay attached and automatically move with the base of the structural column. This appears to be a relationship that is mostly controlled by the structural column.

If you use this method for intersection placement or at the origin of other elements, take care to ensure that you are correctly placing the isolated foundation at the correct point rather than at another unexpected point. Keep an eye on the status bar located in the lower-left area of your Revit Structure session dialog box to verify where the isolated foundation is being placed. Setting the Visibility properties of a view to show only grids, structural columns, and foundations may help you select the correct intersection point more easily.

USING THE ON GRIDS OPTION

The On Grids option allows you to select groups of grids for placement. Revit Structure will place an isolated foundation on all grid intersections that you select. This can be a quick method for getting isolated foundations into your project. Even if all of the isolated foundations are not supposed to be on a particular grid intersection, it can still be more efficient to place them on grids and relocate or remove those that are off grids afterward (Figure 8.14). This method of placing isolated foundations is similar to placing structural columns; it uses a tool that does the same thing.

For grid intersection placement (On Grids), perform these steps:

1. You will be placing isolated foundations (footings) in a plan view with grids, so activate a plan view that is set to the level your footings will be referenced to.

2. On the Home tab ➤ Foundation panel, select the Isolated tool. The Ribbon will switch to a contextual tab.

3. Select the type of isolated foundation you want to place from the Type Selector.

4. Select the On Grids option from the Multiple panel.

5. Select those grids that create intersections with a right-to-left crossing window. After they are selected, you should see temporary isolated foundations display at the center of all selected grid intersections.

FIGURE 8.14

Placing isolated foundations with the On Grids option will quickly and accurately place them onto gridline intersections.

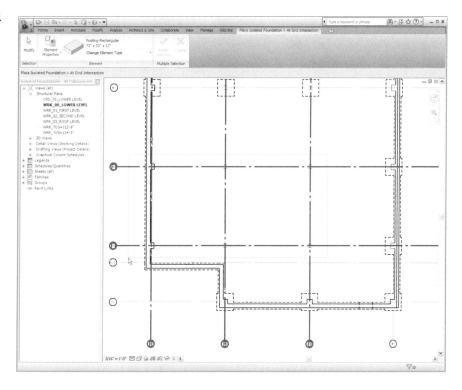

Select grids by clicking the gridlines and holding down the Ctrl key to add to your selection or holding down the Shift key to subtract from your selection. You should see isolated foundations appear and disappear at the center of grid intersections as you add and subtract grids from your selection. If you are not seeing isolated foundations appear, you may need to adjust your view range settings.

6. Once all required grids are selected, be sure to click the Finish Selection button from the Ribbon to accept your isolated foundation placement. Any other action will remove your placements.

7. You can now delete any unwanted foundations, relocate any if needed, and do any fine-tuning of their rotation.

Using this method will help ensure that all isolated foundations are accurately placed at the exact intersections of the grids. If structural columns were placed the same way, then you can feel confident that your foundations will be centered under them. This will also ensure that the isolated foundations will properly be attached to the grids so that when the grids move, the isolated foundations will move with them.

USING THE AT COLUMNS OPTION

If the Single Pick or On Grids option is not what you are looking for, than perhaps the At Columns option will do the trick. This option can work best when you are in a 3D view because you can see the location and placement of each isolated foundation as it is placed. Yes, it does say *At Columns*, but if you have piers that will need footings under them, this will work as well. Remember, a pier, even though it may be considered a foundation, is typically modeled using a structural column.

You can use structural columns and piers that are already modeled in your project to place your isolated foundations. As shown in Figure 8.15, Revit Structure will place an isolated foundation (footing) at the center (origin) of all structural columns or piers that you select. The foundation's vertical location is determined by the level that you assign it to on the Options bar. If this method of placement fits in with your modeling workflow, this can be a quick method of getting columns into your project.

FIGURE 8.15
When you use the At Columns option, Revit Structure will place an isolated foundation at the center of all structural columns that you select.

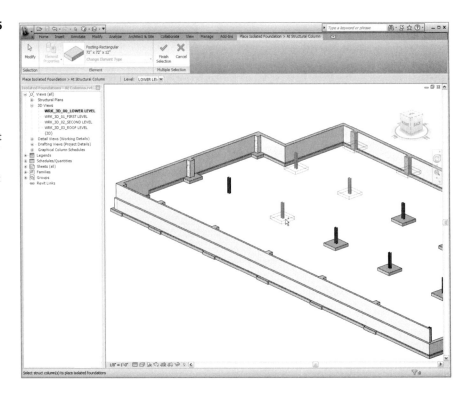

For structural column and/or pier placement (At Columns), perform the following steps:

1. Activate a 3D view that will allow you to easily select the structural columns that require isolated foundations (footings) or a plan view that is set to the level your footings will be referenced to.

2. On the Home tab ➢ Foundation panel, select the Isolated tool. The Ribbon will switch to a contextual tab.

3. Select the type of isolated foundation you want to place from the Type Selector.

4. Select the At Columns option from the Multiple panel.

5. Select groups of columns that require a footing with a right-to-left crossing window. Once they are selected, you should see isolated foundations display centered on all selected structural columns.

    Select structural columns individually by clicking a structural column and holding down the Ctrl key to add to your selection or holding down the Shift key to subtract from your selection. You should see isolated foundations appear and disappear at the center of the structural columns as you add and subtract structural columns from your selection.

    If you are in a 3D view, make sure that you specify a level for the isolated foundations to be placed on prior to placing them. This is done by using the Level pull-down on the Options bar. If this option is not set properly, you might find that your foundation will be placed in an unexpected location.

6. Once all required structural columns are selected and your isolated foundations are temporarily in place, be sure to click the Finish Selection button from the Ribbon to accept your isolated foundation placement. Any other action will remove your placements.

There should now be a relationship between the structural columns and the isolated footings. You can now do any fine-tuning of their rotation or change their elevation. Remember, if you will be changing their elevation, you should do so by changing the base elevation of the structural columns. This will change the elevation of the isolated foundations as well.

No matter what type of foundation you decide on modeling as an isolated foundation, you will use these placement methods. By using a component family, you can create all of the various shapes that are needed to model elements that are required for the Foundation category. However, the Isolated Foundation tool cannot be used for modeling all of your foundations. Revit Structure has another tool for modeling other foundations, such as those that are supporting walls like bearings and foundations. The walls that require a footing under them are modeled using Revit Structure's Wall tool, but the foundation below them is modeled using the Wall Foundation tool.

EXERCISE: PLACING ISOLATED FOUNDATIONS INTO A PROJECT

For this exercise you can use the Isolated Foundations.rvt and Isolated Foundation _Complete.rvt files (from the book's companion web page at www.sybex.com/go/ masteringrevitstructure2010). You will go through the steps of placing isolated foundations into your project.

SINGLE PICK PLACEMENT

1. Open the Isolated Foundations.rvt file.

2. Open the Level 1 Structural Plan view.

3. Choose the Home tab ➢ Foundation panel ➢ Isolated tool.

4. Initially you are in Single Pick placement mode. Set the Type Selector so you will be placing a Footing-Rectangular 72″ x 48″ x 18″.

5. Place a column footing at Grids 2-B and 2-C by hovering over the column/grid intersection. Verify in the status bar that you are snapping to the correct grid intersection. The isolated foundation will snap to various points; when it is in the correct location, pick with your mouse to place it.

   You will see a warning dialog box that says the structural foundation will be moved to the bottom of the column. This is fine because the base of the column is 8″ below Level 1 and the footing is being placed at Level 1. Revit Structural recognizes the relationship that a column and footing have and automatically attaches the footing to the base of the column.

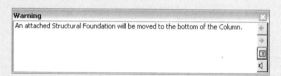

6. After these two footings are placed, select one of the footings and right-click to choose Element Properties from the shortcut menu.

7. Review the properties of the column footing. Note that Its Level is set to Level 1 and its Host is Floor: SOG 4″. It also is has an Offset of -0′-8″. Since the host is the slab, if for any reason the slab were to change elevation, the footing would maintain the 8″ offset from the slab, not the level.

8. Repeat steps 3 through 6 except place the column footing at Grid 3-B.

9. While reviewing the properties of this column footing, note that Its Level is set to Level 1 and its Host is Level: Level 1. It also is has an Offset of -0′-8″. Since the Host is set to Level 1, the column footing will maintain the 8″ offset from Level 1, not the floor.

ON-GRIDS PLACEMENT

1. Open the TFE Structural Plan view. We are using this view so our footings will reference the TFE level. Placing them in the Level 1 structural plan view would reference them to Level 1 and attach them to the base of the steel columns instead of the concrete piers.

2. Choose the Home tab ➤ Foundation panel ➤ Isolated tool.

3. Select the On Grids tool from the Multiple panel on the Place Isolated Foundation contextual tab.

4. Verify that the Type Selector is set to use Footing-Rectangular 72″ x 48″ x 18″.

5. Create a window selection by using a right-to-left crossing window to select all of the grids that are on the east wing.

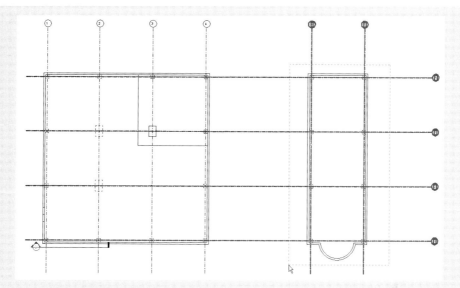

6. Once the grids are selected, you will see temporary column footings placed at any intersection that the grids create. Choose Finish Selection from the Place Isolated Foundation > At Grid Intersection contextual tab to accept their location.

Wait, did you see the warning dialog box? Selecting the Expand Warning Dialog button at the right of the warning will expand the warning to give you more information about the column footing that was moved. Checking the elements in question will highlight them in the drawing area. In this case the column footing is at grid intersection 6-C. The base of the concrete is -2′-0″ below the TFE level, so Revit Structure automatically moves it to the bottom of the concrete pier, giving it a -2′-0″ offset value from TFE level.

7. Choose Modify from the same tab or press Esc on the keyboard to close the Place Isolated Foundation contextual tab.

8. Review the properties of the column footings — the one that was moved to the bottom and one of the others.

AT-COLUMNS PLACEMENT

1. Open the 3D_Level - Slice view.

2. Choose the Home tab ➤ Foundation panel ➤ Isolated tool.

3. Select the At Columns tool from the Multiple panel on the Place Isolated Foundation contextual tab.

4. Verify that the Type Selector is set to use Footing-Rectangular 72″ x 48″ x 18″.

5. On the Options bar set the Level to TFE. This sets the level that the column footing is referenced to.

6. Rotate the 3D view to a location where you can select the concrete piers on which to place the column footings. For now just select the concrete piers individually by holding down the Ctrl key on the keyboard and selecting each one you want to add to your selection set. Remember, we talked about several other ways to select the columns; you can try these other methods as well.

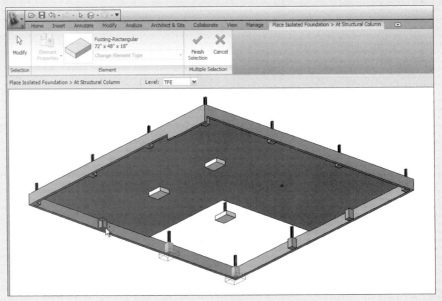

7. When your selections are complete, choose Finish Selection from the Place Isolated Foundation > At Structural Column contextual tab.

8. Choose Modify from the same tab or press Esc on the keyboard to close the Place Isolated Foundation contextual tab.

9. Review the properties of one of the column footings. You will see that it is referenced to TFE and its Host is Level: TFE. It does not have an offset because the base of the concrete pier is at the TFE level. If the base was offset from the level, you would get a warning dialog saying that your structural foundation will be moved to the bottom of the column. In this case it would be a concrete pier. The offset value would be whatever the base offset is for the concrete pier.

Continue using the methods above to finish placing the isolated foundations. Compare your work with the sample file Isolated Foundations_Complete.rvt. Naturally, every project will present different situations, and depending on what those situations are, you will use what you think is the best tool for the job.

Working with a Wall Foundation

Unlike an isolated foundation, the wall foundation (wall/strip footing) is a system family that is predefined in Revit Structure, which is much different than the isolated foundation component family. We start this section with an overview of all the properties and behaviors that can be assigned to a wall foundation as well as how you work with them as you develop your model. Before you start to place them into your project, you should have a good understanding of how they work. We will discuss the actual procedures for placing them in your project in a later section called "Adding Wall Foundations to Your Project."

In order to place a wall foundation you must have a wall in your model for the foundation to attach (hosted by) to. Without a wall you will not be able to place the wall foundation. With that said, if you delete a wall that has a wall foundation beneath it, you delete the wall foundation as well. Since the wall foundation is predefined in Revit Structure, you do not have the flexibility to create shapes that do not already exist. But then again, a wall foundation really only has one shape, a rectangle, as shown in Figure 8.16.

FIGURE 8.16
A wall foundation is a system family that requires a wall before it can be placed.

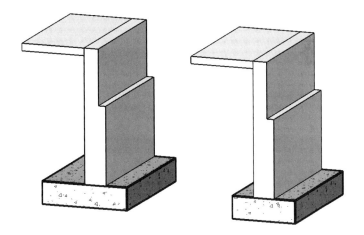

The parameters that you will need to adjust when working with a wall foundation are width, foundation thickness, location on the wall they are supporting, and length. The size of a foundation is set in its Type properties, so each different size you need, with the exception of length, will have to be a new type. Its elevation (top of footing) and length are determined by the location of the wall's base and length. Figure 8.17 shows several wall conditions that indicate how the wall foundation attaches (host) to a wall and maintains its position to the wall location.

If a wall is split to form another section of wall, then the footing will be split as well. Each segment or each individual wall requires its own wall foundation. Keep this in mind when you start changing wall footing sizes. An entire length of a wall may call for the same footing sizes, but as you continue to model your foundations, you may have had to split walls (which also splits the footings) to adjust the elevation of the wall's base for stepped foundations (footings) or to change the wall type to a different thickness. This would mean that you would have several footings to adjust for that length of the wall.

FIGURE 8.17
A wall foundation follows the same path as a wall.

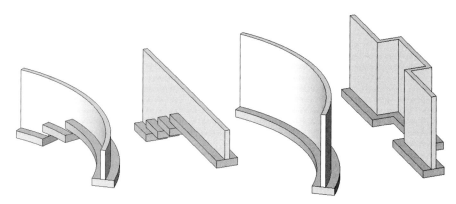

Other properties allow you to define the location of the wall footing to control whether it is centered on the wall or offset. The properties that become available for you to control this behavior depend on the Structural Usage setting that is specified in the wall foundation's Type properties: Bearing or Retaining. Depending on which one is assigned, the wall foundation will take on behavior that allows you to control the location (horizontal offset) of the wall foundation from the wall it is attaching to.

Determining the Proper Structural Usage

The default project template that Revit Structure uses includes two wall foundation types. They are Bearing Footing - 36″ x 12″ and Retaining Footing - 24″ x 12″ x 12″. The difference between the two is their Structural Usage setting. One is set to Bearing and the other is set to Retaining. The naming of these footings is such that they depict the structural usage they are set to, as well as what the values are for the properties that control their shape. Keeping the structural usage notation in the name is a good idea to help you keep track of what type the footing is, but you can choose your own naming convention for the size representation if desired. This is just Revit Structure's suggestion.

So what is the difference between a bearing and a retaining footing? The big difference is in their Type properties, which contain the parameters to control their size and location as they relate to a wall. You will want to get familiar with these properties to know how each parameter will affect the footing when it is changed.

PLACING A BEARING FOOTING

A bearing footing is defined by the Width, Foundation Thickness, and Default End Extension Length settings. Figure 8.18 shows the Type Properties dialog box of a wall footing whose Structural Usage setting is set to Bearing.

FIGURE 8.18

The Type properties of a wall footing with Structural Usage set to Bearing

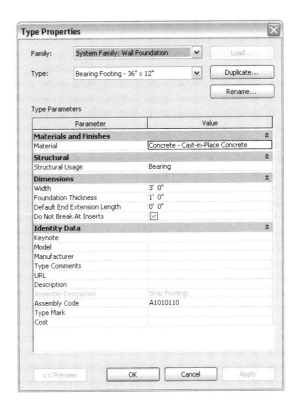

When a bearing footing is placed under a wall, it is centered by default. To offset a bearing footing, you specify an Eccentricity increment value in the Instance properties of the wall foundation (Figure 8.19).

The current version of Revit Structure does not allow you to specify an Eccentricity value that will align the edge of the bearing footing with the edge of the wall. The maximum offset value that you can achieve is determined by the thickness of the wall. So you may or may not be able to get things to go in your favor when offsetting the bearing footing. This is a known issue with the initial version of Revit Structure 2010. If you are looking to model a wall foundation that has a zero-lot line footing where this type of footing placement is desired, you will have to use the Retaining Structural Usage setting and set the Heel and Toe offset values accordingly.

PLACING A RETAINING FOOTING

Retaining Footings have additional properties that bearing footings do not have. They are defined by the Heel Length, Toe Length, Foundation Thickness, and Default End Extension Length settings. Figure 8.20 shows the Type properties of a wall footing whose Structural Usage setting is set to Retaining.

One of the most common mistakes while attempting to place a bearing footing can be unknowingly placing a retaining footing instead, or vice versa. It is easy to do because they have the same rectangular shape, but how they center themselves on the wall is much different (Figure 8.21). The two types are similar but will obviously affect the model in different ways.

FIGURE 8.19
A bearing footing with
an Eccentricity value
of 8″

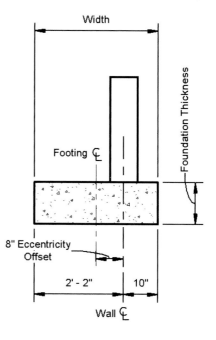

FIGURE 8.19
A bearing footing with
an Eccentricity value
of 8″

FIGURE 8.20
The type properties
of a wall footing with
Structural Usage set to
Retaining

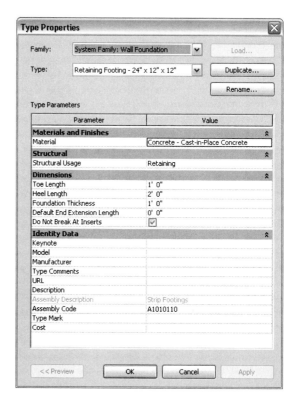

FIGURE 8.21
A retaining footing's
width takes in to
account the wall thick-
ness it is attached to.

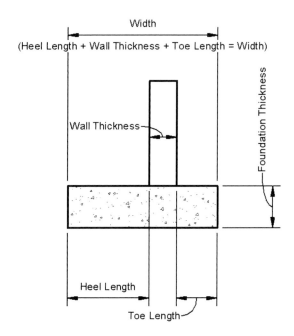

WHAT IS MY TRUE WIDTH?

The overall width of a retaining footing changes with the thickness of the wall it is attached to. This may create unexpected results.

The retaining footing allows you to set the Toe Length and Heel Length. These settings do not determine the overall width of the footing. These are only two of the three variables that determine this. The third is the thickness of the wall under which you are placing the retaining footing. Keep this in mind. You might be given an overall footing width that is required. You adjust the Toe and Heel Length settings for that footing type accordingly for its placement on the wall as well as to maintain its overall width. If that same footing type is placed under a different wall with a different wall thickness, your retaining wall footing will be a different overall thickness. You will have to make a new retaining footing type with different Toe and Heel Length settings to maintain the same overall retaining footing thickness. To see the overall retaining footing length after it has been placed, take a peek at its Instance properties.

The Structural Usage setting offers various dimensional parameters to control the location of the wall foundation with relationship to the wall's width, but what about controlling it along the wall's length? When you select a wall to place a wall foundation, the foundation will automatically adjust its length to the wall's length. If a wall is 10'-0" long, then your wall foundation will be 10'-0" long.

In a situation such as a wall thickness bumpout, termination of a wall segment, or a footing extension into an opening cutout, you may need to extend the footing past the wall end to get the proper footing extension from the end and sides of the wall. There is an additional Type parameter for the wall foundation regardless of it structural usage called Default End Extension Length that allows you to control how Revit Structure behaves for these situations. In addition, there are controls on the wall foundation that allow you to adjust their end extensions so they are not always the same length as the wall.

Adjusting the End Extension of a Wall Foundation

Earlier versions of Revit Structure made the task of extending a wall footing past the ends of a wall difficult. Your options were to just leave it the way it was and say it was a Revit thing, use an in-place family or component family that was placed at the end of the wall or footing, or use foundation slabs to model slivers of slabs to indicated the footing extension. The end extension enhancement that was added in the previous release makes this much simpler and easy to work with as well.

After selecting a wall footing, you will see blue-filled dot controls display at its ends. You can select these controls and drag the end of the footing to a new extension length as long as it extends past the end of the wall. Revit Structure does not allow you to drag the control to the inside portions of the wall. It will let you drag the control, but when you release it, it will snap back to its previous location. You can adjust wall-footing extensions from any view; a 3D view is a great view to use, and it allows you to see exactly what is happening from all angles. Figure 8.22 shows the basic steps involved when adjusting a wall foundation's end extensions.

FIGURE 8.22
After selecting a wall foundation, choose the blue-filled dot control to adjust its end extension past the end of the wall.

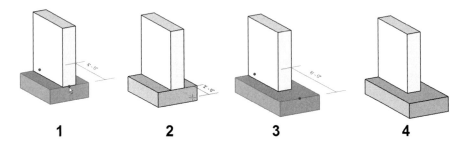

1   2   3   4

USE THOSE TEMPORARY DIMENSIONS

When selecting a wall foundation to adjust its end extension, you can use the temporary dimensions to accurately create the extension length. After selecting the blue-filled dot control and dragging it in the direction of the extension, start typing in the dimension. The temporary dimension with blue text that appears from the end of the wall to the end of the wall foundation will allow you to enter the dimension for the extension. When you've added your dimension, press Enter, and the wall foundation will adjust to that dimension length.

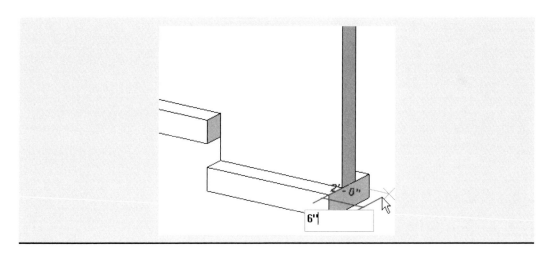

We also need to discuss the Default End Extension Length parameter located in the Type properties of a wall foundation. This parameter works in conjunction with the extension of the footing that we just talked about. It allows you to set a default dimension that the footing will use to automatically extend the footing past the ends of a wall that it is attaching to when it is placed, thus minimizing the task of having to adjust every extension manually. The default value is 0. Figure 8.23 shows this parameter set to 0'-6". After placement, each instance of the wall foundation can be modified to have a different end extension length by adjusting the end extension controls.

FIGURE 8.23
A wall footing placed with its Default End Extension Length set to 0'-6"

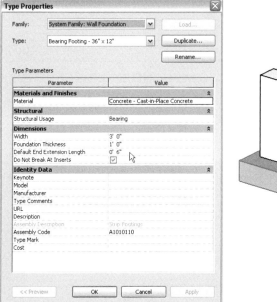

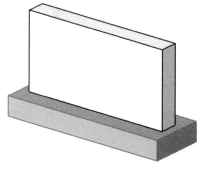

Take some time to learn how this setting behaves. If several footings have been placed and this value changes, those types will change to the new setting if they have not been previously over-ridden by dragging the blue extension control. For example, if value of the Default End Extension Length parameter for a specific wall foundation type is set to 0′-8″, and several of these types have been placed throughout your model, all of their extension lengths will be set to 0′-8″. You may have a few locations that need to be adjusted to something other than this dimension, so you do so manually by adjusting the end extension control. If somewhere down the road this value gets changed or set back to 0, all of the extensions will be reset to that new value. Those that you manually adjusted will remain the same.

YES, ONLY TWO WALL FOUNDATION EXTENSION CONTROLS PER WALL

When you edit the profile of wall to set its base location, a wall foundation that you are placing under it will split at each base offset location. However, you will only be able to adjust the extension ends of the wall foundation at the ends of the wall. Extension controls (blue dots) will not be available at the intermittent offset locations.

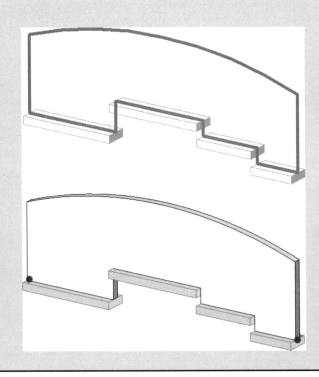

In some cases this may be thought of as good behavior, but if you place several wall foundations throughout a project, it can become difficult to keep track of which ones have been overridden as well as difficult to predict which ones are going to change. We recommend that you keep the Default End Extension Length value set to 0 and manually adjust the extensions as needed unless you have specific requirements that make sense to set the value to a known dimension. The key thing is to know what this parameter does and how it behaves so you can use it and work with it inside your project in the way that makes your modeling the most efficient.

When an opening is made in a wall such as a door, and it cuts the bottom of the wall, you might want the wall foundation to stop and slightly extend past the jambs of the opening, or you might want the wall foundation to run straight through. This is where the Do Not Break At Inserts Type parameter comes in handy. The downside of taking advantage of this setting is that it will work only if you create the opening in the wall a certain way.

Using the Do Not Break At Inserts Type Parameter

How you go about putting openings into your walls will skew your decision one way or another to use this setting. Its intended use is to break a wall footing at an opening insert if the opening cuts the bottom of the wall. The opening is the insert. This is a fairly common scenario in any type of building that you will be modeling. An interior bearing wall may extend 8″ below the slab. The bottom of the opening would extend to the top of the footing, cutting out the bottom of the wall. The slab on grade would then be thickened to tie into the footing.

Enabling this parameter, as shown in Figure 8.24, keeps the wall foundation running continuously through the opening insert.

FIGURE 8.24
The result of enabling the Do Not Break At Inserts parameter

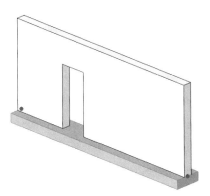
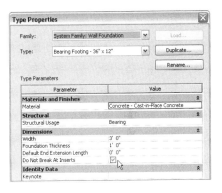

Disabling this parameter, as shown in Figure 8.25, breaks the wall foundation at the jambs of the opening, while giving you additional extension controls at the ends of each break. Even though the wall foundation appears to be broken and behaves as two separate foundations, it is still one wall foundation that is attached to the entire wall length. Deleting one side of the wall footing or the wall will delete both wall foundations.

Unfortunately, this parameter and the behavior it creates work only for openings that have been created with the window and door families (.rfa). These families can be found by going to the Imperial Library ➤ Openings folder. Once loaded into your project they behave just like other component families and can be placed into a wall by using the Home tab ➢ Model panel ➢ Component drop-down ➢ Place a Component tool.

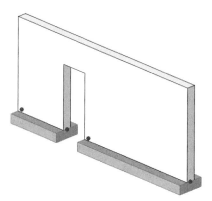

FIGURE 8.25
The result of disabling the Do Not Break At Inserts parameter

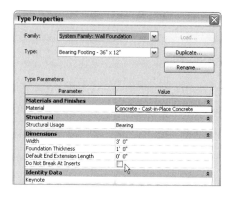

Tools that you may be using to create openings in your walls such as the Wall Opening tool or the Edit Profile tool shown in Figure 8.26 are not recognized as an opening insert; therefore, the wall foundation will not break or be continuous as you would expect in these locations.

All this talk about how to adjust the horizontal location of a wall foundation with respect to the wall, and extending its ends past the end of the wall, or that a wall foundation is attached to the bottom of the wall, but nothing has been said about creating a stepped foundation (stepped footing). What is the best way to model and show a stepped footing? There are a couple of methods that you can use to do this.

FIGURE 8.26
The Do Not Break At Inserts parameter is not recognized by the Edit Profile and Wall Opening tools.

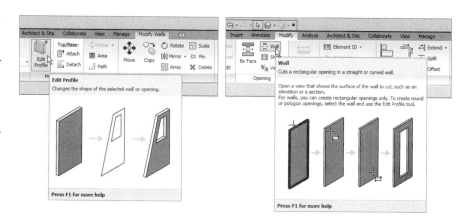

ADJUSTING A VIEW FOR HEAVY HIDDEN LINE FOOTING DISPLAY

If you desire to have all structural foundations display with a Heavy Hidden line style, then you will need to apply overrides to your view.

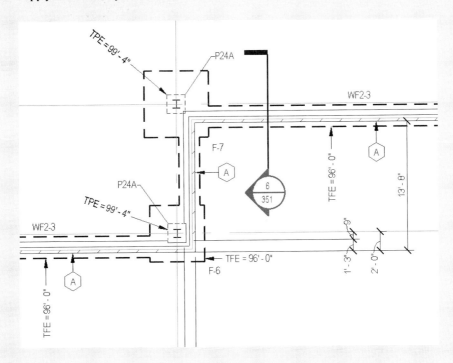

The first view adjustment you will need to make is in the View Range settings of the view. To access the View Range dialog box, choose the View Tab ➤ Graphics panel ➤ View Properties tool. Then in the Instance properties of the view, click the Edit button adjacent to the View Range parameter in the Extents group.

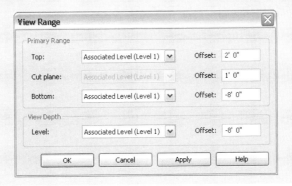

Be sure to set the Bottom Offset depth and the View Depth Level to values that are below the bottom of the lowest footing in your project. For most foundations without basements or many unexcavated areas, the Bottom and View Depth values could be set to Unlimited. Both adjustment methods allow all foundations under slabs or other elements to be displayed with the Hidden Line subcategory for structural foundations and those not under slabs or other elements to be displayed with the Projection Line settings for structural foundations. Those footings where the bottom plane of the view is cutting through or above will not be displayed on the Hidden Lines subcategory; rather they will be consider a Beyond line style, which is a solid line pattern.

The second view adjustment you will have to make is in the Visibility/Graphic Overrides dialog box of the view. To access this dialog box, choose the View tab ➢ Graphics panel ➢ Visibility/Graphics tool. Within the dialog box, scroll to the Structural Foundations category.

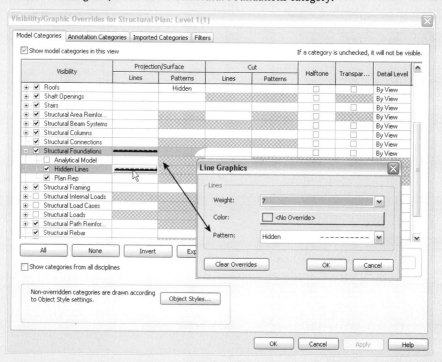

Apply Projection/Surface Lines overrides to both the Structural Foundations category and the Hidden Lines subcategory. Choose the Lines Weight and Pattern that match your standards for drawing display. If the view range of the view is set as discussed previously, those foundations that are below a slab or other elements should be assigned to the Hidden Lines subcategory, and those that are not (for instance, a perimeter wall foundation) should be assigned to the Structural Foundations category. After you apply the overrides, your foundation should appear with a Heavy Hidden line style.

If you've created additional isolated foundations and have assigned them to subcategories within the properties of the family, you will need to adjust their Projection/Surface Lines settings as well. When everything is set and you are happy with the display, create a view template that can be applied to other foundation plan views that require the same overrides.

Creating a Stepped Footing

Whether you model a wall as a curve or a straight segment can determine the method you use to create a stepped footing. In the end you will need to decide for yourself which is the best way. If it is a curved wall segment, you are stuck with one option; with a straight segment you have a couple of options. Either way, you will end up with the same results as far as how it will look in your model.

Let's start by looking at what we think is the obvious approach of creating a stepped footing, which works no matter how you model your walls. You split the wall by using Revit Structure's Split tool. This can be done before or after a wall foundation is placed. Normally when you are modeling a foundation wall for the initial stages of a project, you don't know where grade will be; therefore, you do not know where steps are required in the footing. Keeping this in mind, you model the wall at one elevation without worrying about where the steps occur. Eventually this information becomes available, and you revise the model to show steps where they are required. This is why we mention the Split tool; it's a rare occasion when you know where to step the wall when you are modeling it the first time. To access this tool choose the Modify tab ➤ Edit panel ➤ Split tool, as shown in Figure 8.27. Once the Split tool is selected, you can hover over a wall to split the wall into multiple segments. The Split tool does not always allow you to snap to the exact location where you need to split the wall, so if you are unable to split the wall at a specific location, you can adjust the ends of the split wall to a more desired location after the wall is split. To adjust these ends you can either use the Align tool or select the wall and use the solid-blue dot control at the wall ends to drag it into place.

FIGURE 8.27
Accessing the Split tool in the Edit panel of the Modify tab

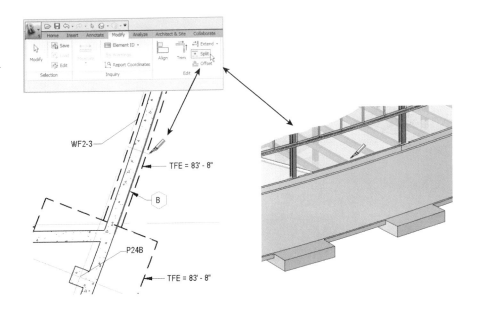

The Split tool can be used in just about any view except a schedule view; use whichever is most convenient and/or makes it easiest for you to perform the split. This method works for creating a stepped footing in both curved and straight segmented walls. Once the wall is split, you can adjust its bottom extents to the desired top of footing elevation. Sometimes splitting the walls can be a bit too time consuming and may seem like a grueling task to do. This really depends on the number of stepped footings that occur and how you have modeled your walls. Some complicated stacked walls may be difficult to split. They have more individual walls to manage, and you must be sure that they all join properly. In these cases, editing the profile of the wall may be a better road to take.

Editing the profile of the wall to create a stepped footing works well for a straight segment wall, but unfortunately it does not work on a curved wall segment. When you edit the profile of a wall, you enter into a Sketch mode where you change the extents of the wall. Revit Structure is unable to take a curved wall and flatten it out as if it were a straight wall. Because of this, Revit Structure does not know where to show the boundaries of the wall. Therefore, the Edit Profile tool for a wall will not be accessible for a wall that is modeled in this manner. Your only option is to split the wall. Remember, a wall footing hosts to the bottom extents of a wall, so if those extents change, the footing will change as well.

To start this process, cut a section/elevation that is looking perpendicular at the wall that you will be stepping; a 3D view will work as well. You decide which type of view works best. When you are in a view that allows you to look perpendicular to the wall, select the wall to edit and choose the Modify Walls contextual tab ➤ Modify Wall panel ➤ Edit Profile tool, as shown in Figure 8.28.

FIGURE 8.28
You can create stepped footings by editing the profile of a wall.

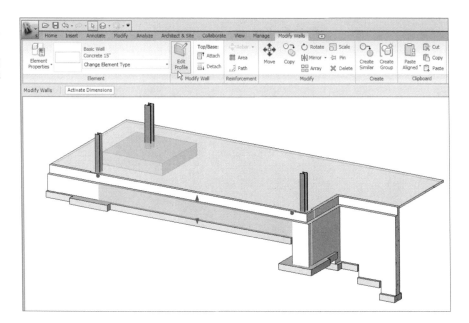

If you are modifying a wall that has not yet been modified with this tool, you will see only the Edit Profile tool while the wall is selected. You will also see only magenta sketch lines (Revit Structure's default sketch line color) at the boundaries of the wall when you are in the Sketch mode. If you select a wall that already has its profile edited, you will see an additional tool in the Modify Walls contextual tab called Reset Profile (Figure 8.29). A wall that has its profile edited will continue to show its original boundary locations with a dashed line pattern while in the Sketch mode. This allows you to see the original extents of the wall prior to it being modified. Selecting the Reset Profile tool will reset the profile back to the dashed line pattern location, removing all profile edits you have made.

FIGURE 8.29
The Edit Profile and Reset Profile tools are available in the Modify Wall contextual tab

After you select the Edit Profile tool, the Modify Walls ➤ Edit Profile contextual tab will display, as shown in Figure 8.30, where you can use tools to change the profile of the wall.

FIGURE 8.30
Revit Structure's magenta sketch lines indicate the wall's profile.

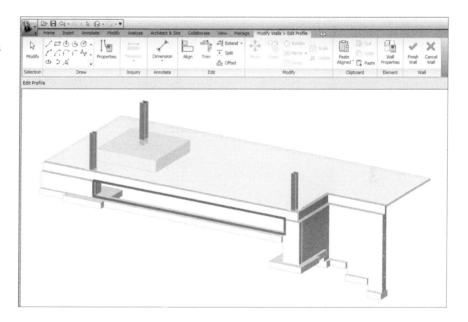

Using the tools in the contextual tab you can add additional sketch lines, split sketch lines, and trim sketch lines to form a closed-loop boundary, as shown in Figure 8.31.

FIGURE 8.31
Use the Modify Walls >
Edit Profile contextual
tab to change the profile
of a wall.

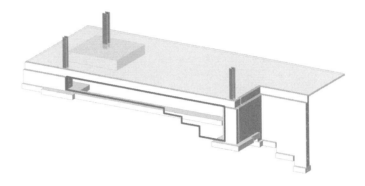

EDITING THE WALL PROFILE MIGHT PRODUCE UNEXPECTED RESULTS

You can edit the profile of a wall to create steps in your footings as well as openings and other wall shape configurations. But when you do this, the wall foundation may not always perform as expected. If the profile sketch is such that it creates two wall bases, as in the example shown below at a corner window, the wall foundation will attach to both the base of the wall and the window head.

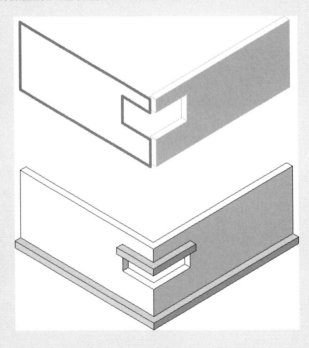

Revit Structure gets confused and thinks that both wall faces are its base. This might not be what you expected.

You must create a closed loop with no overlapping lines before the sketch will be considered valid. When you have finished completing the sketch to modify the extents or location of the base of the wall, you will need to select Finish Wall from the Wall panel on the contextual tab. Your wall and footing should now step similarly to what is shown in Figure 8.32. This example already has the wall foundations modeled, but if they were not already in the model before editing the profile, it would not be a problem. When you select the wall to place the footing, the wall footing will host to the base of each segment of the stepped profile of the wall.

FIGURE 8.32
The results from editing the profile of a wall to form a stepped footing

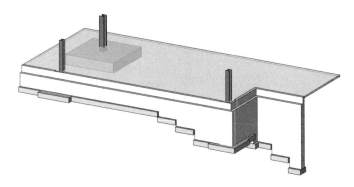

SLOPED WALL PROFILE = NO WALL FOUNDATION

Wall foundations do not attach to a wall whose base is sloped. The sloping of a base of a wall can be achieved by attaching the base to a sloped reference plane or structural slab or by editing the wall's profile. Either way you will be unable to place a wall foundation to attach to the base of the wall. In the case where you have edited the wall's profile, the wall foundation will attach only to the portions of the wall that are horizontal.

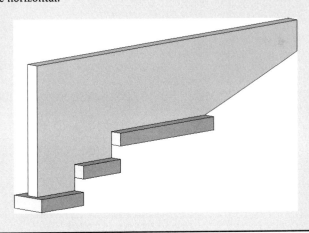

You may have noticed that these stepped footings are not shown exactly how they are going to be built. Typically the bottom of the step will be sloped, and part of the footing will be thickened where the footing overlaps the step area, as shown in Figure 8.33. You will need to decide if it makes sense to take it to the next step and model this portion of the step footing or not. It depends on the level of detail that you require in your model and how much effort you want to put into keeping the footing accurately shown in the model.

FIGURE 8.33
Use a foundation com-
ponent family to show
the finer details of a
stepped footing.

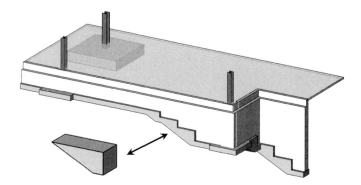

This portion of the stepped footings is created with the Isolated Foundation tool, similar to a spread or column footing. Since Revit Structure does not include a stepped footing family in its library, you will need to create or acquire one yourself. Chapter 18 includes information for creating one to help you on your way. Of course, you could do this with an in-place family by using the Form tools for creating extrusions and blends, but that eventually becomes a nightmare to manage and is not recommended. The foundation component family allows you to build much more flexibility into your project so when changes occur, your efforts of managing the model are reduced.

There is actually more to learning how to work with the properties of a wall foundation and how they function once they are in your project than there is to learning to place them. Wall foundations can be some of the easiest things to put into your project. As long as you are locating the base of your walls at the top of footing location and you have configured your family types to behave as you would expect, your wall foundations will fall into place.

Adding Wall Foundations to Your Project

Now that you hopefully fully understand how a wall foundation behaves, the properties it has, and how you work with it before and after it is placed, let's discuss how to add them into your project. It might seem odd that we talk about this last, but as we said earlier, you should really acquire a good understanding of the settings for the various elements Revit Structure deals with as well as how you can manipulate them before you randomly start modeling them. Without this understanding you risk modeling things improperly or not in the best way for modifying and working with them as your project progresses.

Wall foundation cans be placed in any view in which you are able to select a wall. You might find that it is easiest to place them in a 3D view where you crop the view with a section box to show only your foundations. Orient the view so that you can select those walls that require wall foundations, and you can see them appear as they are placed. To start, you choose the Home tab ➤ Foundation panel ➤ Wall tool, as shown in Figure 8.34. It is named the same as the Wall drop-down in the Structure panel, but it is the tool used to place wall foundations.

Once the tool has been selected, the Ribbon will switch to the Place Wall Foundation contextual tab, as shown in Figure 8.35.

If you recall what the options were for placing an isolated foundation, you will see by looking at this contextual tab that a wall foundation does not have as many. The Ribbon has the Element Properties button, a Type Selector, and on the Options bar the option to place Multiple. If Multiple is checked, you will need to choose Finish Selection from the Ribbon to accept your wall foundation placements. The options are limited because a wall foundation attaches to a wall only, so your only options are to select a wall to place it by. The placement of your wall determines the initial location of the wall foundation; without a wall you are unable to place it.

FIGURE 8.34
Choose the Wall tool from the Foundation panel to start the placement of a wall foundation.

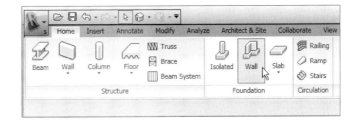

FIGURE 8.35
The Place Wall Foundation contextual tab has limited options for placing wall foundations.

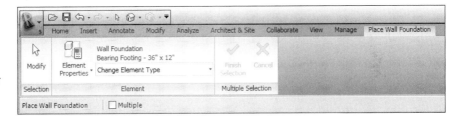

You are ready to start placing wall foundations. Start selecting walls. As you do, you should see the wall foundation appear at the base of the wall you are selecting. If you are in a view whose view settings are such that it cannot display the wall foundation, you will see a warning like the one shown in Figure 8.36. This warning is just telling you that your footing was placed, but your view settings are such that the footing cannot be displayed. Several things could make it not visible in the current view.

FIGURE 8.36
Warning stating that none of the recently created elements are visible in the current view

Here is a quick list of things you can check:

◆ The View Range settings in the View properties

◆ Whether the object's category or subcategory is turned on

◆ The Design Option settings

◆ The Phasing settings and filters

◆ Whether any filters are applied to the view

◆ The Plan Regions in the view

Once a wall footing has been placed under a wall, you will be unable to select it again. This is Revit Structure doing what it is supposed to do, which is not allowing you to place multiple wall foundations under a wall. You wouldn't pour two wall foundations out in the field on top of each other, so why would you want to model it that way?

After you finish placing your footings, you will need to select Modify from the Place Wall Foundation contextual tab or use the Esc key from your keyboard to stop the tool. Until you do this or you select another tool outside of the contextual tab, the Place Wall Foundation mode keeps running.

Checking the Multiple option from the Options bar will make the Finish Selection and Cancel tools available (Figure 8.37).

FIGURE 8.37
The Finish Selection and Cancel tools are available when the Multiple option is checked.

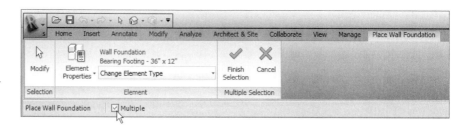

The basic steps for using the Multiple option for placing wall foundations are as follows:

1. After you choose the Wall tool from the Foundation panel, check the Multiple box on the Options bar. Note that the Finish Selection and Cancel tools in the contextual tab become activated.

2. Select the type of wall foundation you want to place from the Type Selector.

3. Select groups of walls that require a footing by using one of the following methods.

    ◆ With a right-to-left crossing window, those wall elements that are selected by the window will be part of the selection. With a left-to-right crossing window, those wall elements that are completely within the crossing window will be selected.

    ◆ Select walls individually by selecting a wall and holding down the Ctrl key to add to your selection or holding down the Shift key to subtract from your selection.

    ◆ While hovering the mouse cursor over the wall, press the Tab key from the keyboard to select a chain of walls. All walls that are chained (endpoint to endpoint) together will be highlighted. At this time you can select the wall, and all of the chain walls will be selected. This method can be used in conjunction with using the Ctrl or Shift key method from above or without the Multiple option checked.

4. When selecting walls in the Multiple selection mode, wall foundations will not display as the walls are selected. They will appear after you choose Finish Selection from the Place Wall Foundation contextual tab ➢ Multiple Selection panel. You must do this before your wall foundations placements can be committed.

With the use of the Isolated Foundation and Wall Foundation tools, you will be able to model just about all of the various foundation types that will be in your project. The content to do so might not be set up for you, but hopefully after reading the section on isolated foundations you have a better understanding of how to create that additional content as well as configure its settings. Since a wall foundation is a system family, you deal with only one shape and basically one placement method: pick a wall. Much of working with these tools is similar to how other tools work with other elements of different categories. The Foundation tool is no different. You work with this tool the same way you work with the Structural Floor tool. The main differences are that it does not have all of the sloping capabilities of a structural floor and elements it creates are not assigned to the Floor category.

EXERCISE: PLACING WALL FOUNDATIONS INTO A PROJECT

For this exercise you can use the Wall Foundations.rvt and Wall Foundation_ Complete.rvt files (from the book's companion web page at www.sybex.com/go/ masteringrevitstructure2010). You will go through the steps of adding a stepped footing with the Edit Profile method as well as the steps for placing wall foundations into your project.

STEPPING THE WALL WITH EDIT PROFILE

1. Open the Wall Foundations.rvt file.

2. Open the Section - Edit Wall Profile Section view.

3. Select the foundation wall that is running between grids 1 and 2, and choose Edit Profile from the Modify Walls ➤ Modify Wall panel.

4. The Ribbon will switch to the Modify Walls ➤ Edit Profile contextual tab, where you can use tools to change the profile of the wall. Using these tools, use the reference planes in the view as a guide and create the new profile. When you have finished, you should have a closed loop with no overlapping sketch lines.

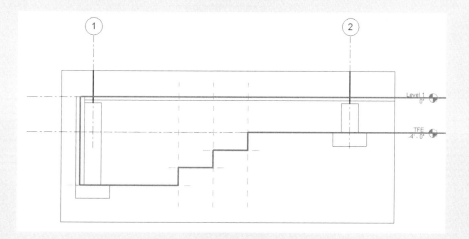

5. Choose Finish Wall from the contextual tab.

6. Switch to a 3D view and admire your new stepped wall.

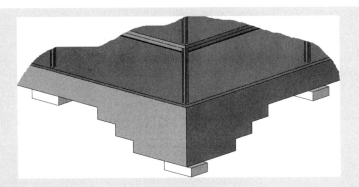

PLACING WALL FOUNDATIONS

1. Open the 3D_Level - Slice view.

2. Choose the Home tab ➢ Foundation panel ➢ Wall tool.

3. Verify that the Type Selector is set to use Bearing Footing - 36″ x 12″.

4. Move to the drawing area and start selecting foundation walls. There is no need to worry about using the Ctrl and Shift keys to create a selection because you are in a single-pick placement method and each pick of the wall will place the footing and attach it to the bottom of the wall.

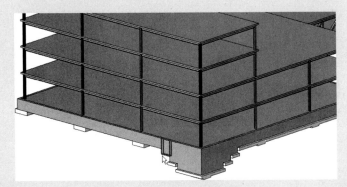

Notice that wall footings are placed at each step for those walls that have their profile edited to form steps. The other wall steps that were already created were done by using the Split tool. Each step is an individual wall, which means you have to select each one to attach a wall foundation to it.

PLACING WALL FOUNDATIONS USING MULTIPLE

1. Open the Level 1 - Structural Plan view.

2. Choose the Home tab ➢ Foundation panel ➢ Wall tool.

3. Verify that the Type Selector is set to use Bearing Footing - 36″ x 12″.

4. This time check the Multiple check box on the Options bar. Notice the Finish Selection and Cancel tools become available to use.

5. Create a window selection by making a right-to-left crossing window to select all of the foundation walls that are on the east wing. As you select walls, you will not see the wall foundations appear. Only the walls will be highlighted.

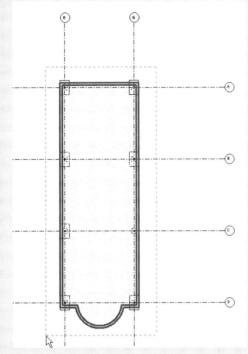

There is no need to worry about filtering elements out of your selection that are not walls because while you're in the Place Wall Foundation mode you can select only walls. You *do* have to worry about which walls you are selecting. In this exercise we have only foundation walls in the model. They are also modeled as one wall. If you had a foundation wall that was modeled with two walls on top of each other that are not a stacked wall type to form a brick ledge, you would end up with a wall foundation being placed in an unexpected location.

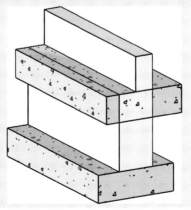

6. When your selections are complete, choose Finish Selection from the Place Wall Foundation contextual tab. Your wall foundations should appear.

7. Choose Modify from the same tab or press Esc on the keyboard to close the Place Wall Foundation contextual tab.

Continue using the methods above to finish placing the wall foundations. Compare your work with the sample file Foundations_Complete.rvt. With the quick pick/select method of placing wall foundations, you can quickly place wall foundations into your project.

Working with the Foundation Slab

There is really no need to get too in depth with the Foundation Slab tool in this chapter. It really works the same way as the Structural Floor tool, which is discussed in Chapter 5 along with using the Foundation Slab tool for a slab on grade. Like the wall foundation, the foundation slab is a system family. All of its functionality is built into the software itself, and you do not create separate families when creating foundation slabs. You only create new types within the project. One of the biggest differences between the two tools (Structural Floor and Foundation Slab) is that the elements the Foundation Slab tool creates are assigned to the Structural Foundation category, just like the isolated and wall foundations. The other difference is that it does not have the functionality with regard to sloping that the Structural Floor tool has.

We don't know about you, but because an awful lot of slabs on grades have multiple slopes to them, we believe they would be best modeled by using the Structural Floor tool, which has subelements that allow you to manipulate its points and edges. The Foundation Slab tool allows only a sloping arrow that permits you to define the desired slope of an entire slab or a portion of a slab. Only one slope arrow is permitted per slab element or slab sketch.

There are cases such as those slab on grades that don't slope where you will be able to use the Foundation Slab tool, but you will find that its biggest use will be for foundations and footing-related elements — foundations such as those that cannot be modeled successfully by using the Isolated or Wall Foundation tool. Elevator pit slabs, tower crane pads, strapped footings, irregularly shaped footings, and foundations that are required to be directly adjacent to existing construction are where the foundation slabs can be best used. Elevator pads and tower crane pads are rectangular in size like the isolated foundation component family, but controlling their size and placement in the model is easier with the sketch lines that are used in the foundation slab. It's much simpler because their size is usually determined by other elements such as walls and other foundation elements, and editing their size can be done more easily by revising the sketch in place among the related elements.

Since foundation slabs are assigned to the Structural Foundation category, they take on the same display characteristics as other foundations do in your views. In cases where the foundation slabs are being used as other footings and are square or rectangular in shape, you can use the foundation slab's Width, Length, and Default Thickness properties in a Structural Foundation Schedule. Chapter 11 will discuss more on creating schedules and quantities in Revit Structure. However, if the shape of the foundation slab is not rectangular with one length and one width, the parameter will not contain any values.

YES, ANOTHER THICKNESS PARAMETER

An isolated foundation has a parameter called **Thickness** whose value cannot be shown in a schedule. A wall foundation uses the Foundation Thickness parameter, which can be shown. A foundation slab allows only the Default Thickness parameter to be shown in a schedule. What does all of this mean? You cannot schedule the thickness of an isolated foundation, a wall foundation, and a foundation slab in the same schedule. Keep this in mind when choose your tools; you may have to create separate schedules for each foundation type: isolated, wall, and slab.

To access the Foundation Slab tool choose the Home tab ➢ Foundation panel ➢ Slab drop-down, as shown in Figure 8.38.

FIGURE 8.38
The Foundation Slab tool can be accessed in the same panel as the Isolated and Wall Foundation tools.

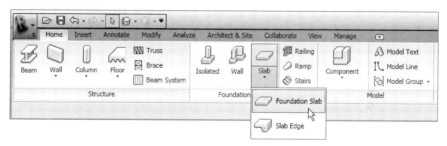

You will also see that a Slab Edge tool exists in the same location. This same tool is used to create slab edges for a structural floor. It uses the same component families and assigns the slab edge to the Floor category. Keep this in mind if you are placing a slab edge onto the edge of a foundation slab. Even though it is a slab edge from the Foundation Slab drop-down, the slab edge is assigned to the Floors category, while the foundation slab is in the Structural Foundation category. The Slab Edge tool is located with the Foundation tools rather than with the Floor tools for your convenience. If you are looking to put a slab edge onto a foundation slab, you are more than likely going to go the Foundation tools to look for it.

After you select the Foundation Slab tool, the Ribbon will switch to the Create Floor Boundary contextual tab, as shown in Figure 8.39.

FIGURE 8.39
The Create Floor Boundary contextual tab for a foundation slab is the same as it is for a structural slab.

Within the contextual tab tools are available to sketch the boundary of the foundation slab. Chapter 5 discusses how to use these additional tools to create a sketch for a slab-on-grade situation. Whether you are creating a sketch for a slab on grade or a footing-related element, the process of creating and working with the sketch and the finished element is the same.

Revit Structure's default template already has several foundation slab types created for you. They are:

- 6″ Foundation Slab

- 8″ Foundation Slab

- 10″ Foundation Slab

- 12″ Foundation Slab

You can create new types from these by going to the Type Properties dialog box and clicking the Duplicate button. Give the slab a new name and change its properties accordingly. You can view the properties of any of the foundation slab types in the Project Browser. Find the Families ➢ Structural Foundations ➢ Foundation Slab, and right-click on the slab type to choose Properties from the shortcut menu. Alternatively, you can choose Floor Properties from the Create Floor Boundary contextual tab before the foundation slab is placed into the model. Or after it is placed, you can select the element and choose Element Properties from the Modify Structural Foundations contextual tab, and you will see the foundation slab's Instance properties, as shown in Figure 8.40.

FIGURE 8.40
The Instance Properties dialog box of a foundation slab has read-only parameters in the Dimensions group.

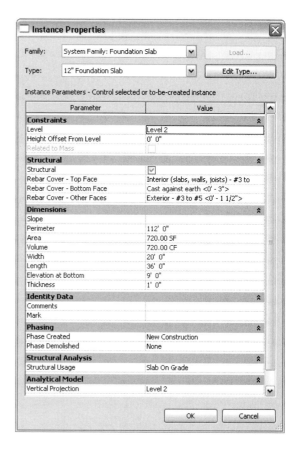

Within the Instance properties of a foundation slab you will find read only parameters under the Dimensions group such as:

♦ Slope (cannot be shown in a schedule)

♦ Perimeter

♦ Area

♦ Volume

♦ Width

♦ Length

♦ Elevation at Bottom

♦ Thickness (cannot be shown in a schedule)

♦ Default Thickness (located in the Type Parameter)

You will see that the instance properties is where the Thickness of the foundation slab is located, but it is the Default Thickness parameter located in the type properties that is shown in a schedule. Take advantage of these parameters, as most of them can be used in a Schedule/Quantities schedule to collectively view information about the foundation slabs in your project. You will also see a Structure parameter in the Type Properties of a Foundation Slab as shown in Figure 8.41.

FIGURE 8.41
Access the Edit Assembly dialog box to see the layers of a foundation slab through its Type properties.

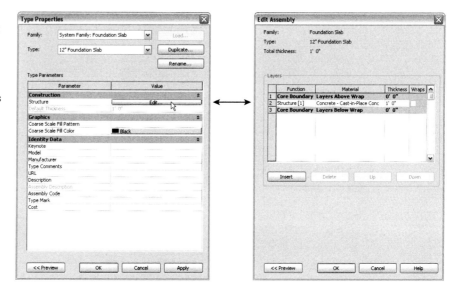

Adjacent to this parameter is an Edit button where you can edit the assembly (layers) of the foundation slab. As we said before about other characteristics of the foundation slab, it is not much different than a structural floor. Figure 8.42 shows that a foundation slab does not have a Variable setting that allows you to vary the thickness of a specified layer. This is because a foundation slab does not use subelements to slope its surface and edges.

Foundation slabs, regardless of what they are used for or how they are created, are placed no differently than structural floors. You will need to decide what tool is best in your environment for your specific situation. Each project will bring unique foundations that may not be best modeled the way you modeled them on a previous project. Knowing how these tools work will give you the knowledge to make those decisions.

FIGURE 8.42
The Edit Assembly dialog boxes for a floor and a foundation slab display different properties.

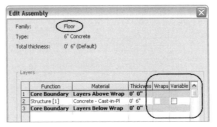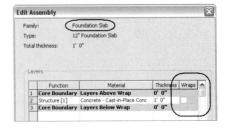

The Bottom Line

Create and work with isolated foundations. Knowing the various methods available for placing isolated foundations into your project allows you to quickly and accurately place them into your project.

> **Master It** What are some of the methods you can use to place isolated foundations into your project?

Create and work with wall foundations. Unlike an isolated foundation, a wall foundation is a system family, which has most of its behavior predefined in Revit Structure. When working with the wall foundation, the value of the Structural Usage parameter determines how it behaves in your project.

> **Master It** What values can be assigned to the Structural Usage parameter, and what are their biggest differences?

Create and work with foundation slabs. Foundation slabs are created with the same methods you use to create a structural floor. Knowing how to work with structural floors means you already know how to work with foundation slabs.

> **Master It** What are the two biggest differences between a foundation slab and a structural floor?

Part 3

Documenting Your Structural Model

Chapter 9

Model Documentation

Few structural engineering firms can afford to make a three-dimensional model for its own sake. One of the main and most important strengths of Revit Structure involves its ability to create construction documents in addition to the 3D physical and analytical models. Not all modeling software can do that. In this chapter, you will focus on those documentation features and the challenge that lies in store for you as you advance your model through the design process toward completion of your construction documents.

This chapter on documentation features in Revit Structure centers on datum, annotation, and detailing functions that are found mostly on the Home and Annotate tabs of the Ribbon. You will examine the methods necessary to annotate your view, whether it is a plan, section, elevation, or other view type, in order to complete the necessary documentation for your project. Another important topic covered in this chapter is the creation and use of a typical details library, which undoubtedly will become an essential tool for you as you generate drafting views on multiple jobs.

In this chapter you will learn to:

◆   Add datum elements to your detail and section views

◆   Add annotation elements such as text, tags, and symbols

◆   Add detailing elements such as detailing lines and filled regions

◆   Create a typical details library

Drafting Tools

Many of the features you need to finish your details that have been cut from the model, or developed as simple two-dimensional drafting views independent of the model, will be found on the Annotate tab of the Ribbon (see Figure 9.1). The tab contains several panel groups of related drafting commands:

◆   Dimension tools such as Dimension and Spot Elevation

◆   Detailing tools such as Detail Line, Filled Region, and Repeating Detail

◆   Text tools for notations

◆   Tag tools such as Tag, Tag All Not Tagged, and Keynote

◆   Symbols such as Span Direction tags, as well as symbols themselves

FIGURE 9.1
The Annotate tab on the Ribbon has most commands needed for documentation.

In this chapter you will learn how to take an undocumented view and complete it for your construction document set. It is important to remember that, like model elements, these elements are also families that can act parametrically. For example, the text family can have many types, such as a 3/32″ Arial or 1/4″ Times New Roman. Once you start developing these text types that correspond to the styles your company uses, you can add them to your project template file. Then when you begin a new project, the types will be ready to go.

Datum Elements

Datum elements aid in the precise location of elements in your model. For a structural project, it is imperative to have well-dimensioned drawings with all major elements properly located as well as an organized grid system. The next section is an overview of the various datum elements and how they aid in the documentation of your project.

Dimensions

The Dimension commands are located on the Dimension panel on the Annotate tab of the Ribbon. Clicking the panel label will display a drop-down with various dimension formatting options (see Figure 9.2). Once you choose the type of dimension you want, such as Aligned or Angular, the Place Dimensions tab is displayed. The Options bar will display other tools for you to use to aid in their placement (see Figure 9.2).

FIGURE 9.2
The Dimension panel with a drop-down list of formatting options

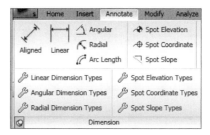

On the Place Dimensions tab on the Element panel in the Type Selector are different family types of dimension styles for you to use, or you can create your own new types corresponding to your needs. If you click the Element Properties button to the left of the Type Selector, you can then choose to open either the Instance or Type Properties dialog box. There you create or edit the graphical elements of the dimension styles, as well as the lines and tick or arrow marks. In addition to formatting, you can style the dimension text.

There are five basic forms of dimensions that you can use:

◆ Aligned

◆ Linear

◆ Angular

◆ Radial

◆ Arc Length

Figure 9.3 shows examples of these various dimension types that you can use in your project. Dimension styles can be created as baseline, linear, or ordinate styles. Notice that arrows, tick marks, and dots (as well as other symbols not shown) can be configured as dimension end point symbols depending on your preference.

FIGURE 9.3
Examples of various dimension types

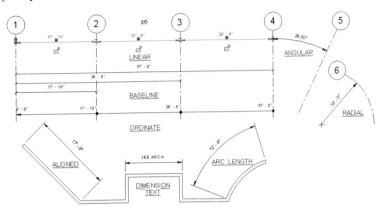

The following sections will familiarize you with the usage of dimensions, how they function, how they are placed, and how the dimension text string can be adapted to show a note instead of the dimension value.

CONSTRAINTS: LOCKS AND ANCHORS

You have been learning that Revit Structure is a constraints-based system in which relationships between elements are maintained as the model flexes to new positions during the design process. Dimensions are one of the main ways to control this movement. In Figure 9.3 the linear dimension is highlighted and two noteworthy controls are displayed. Under the linear dimension line are locks that are currently open. By clicking the locks closed, you will prevent that dimension from being changed. Above the linear dimension line, the EQ control is displayed. If you click the EQ symbol, the dimensions will be equalized and each will display an EQ value in the dimension string. This is a helpful command that allows you to easily equalize the relative locations of elements.

USING EQ AND THE PADLOCKS TOGETHER

It's important to remember that you should not use EQ and the padlocks at the same time because doing so will counter the ability of the EQ dimension string to maintain an equal spacing if the overall dimension changes. This is a common mistake that new users of Revit often make.

Dimension anchors, represented by an anchor symbol at the start of an equalized dimension string, are used in a multisegmented EQ-constrained dimension to indicate which elements remain stationary when the elements change location.

TEMPORARY, PERMANENT, AND LISTENING DIMENSIONS

As you place and locate your model elements, you will be using dimensions long before you need them for your documentation. As you place elements in your model, *temporary* dimensions begin appearing dynamically as you are working (see Figure 9.4) to help you place the element precisely. By clicking on the dimension control symbol next to the dimension, you can automatically add the dimension to your view and make it *permanent*.

FIGURE 9.4
Making temporary dimensions permanent

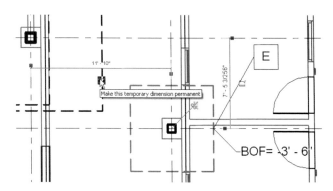

Another important concept is what is known as *listening* dimensions. As you start to add an element to your view, such as a line or an arc, after the initial click to place it, simply type in the value for the length you want in the temporary dimension that appears in order to place the second point.

DON'T FORGET YOUR DOCUMENTATION

It is easy to be caught up in building a fabulous virtual model when suddenly the boss requests a current document set of all the sheets of plans, elevations, and sections so he can show your progress to the client. You have been so absorbed in model building that you forgot to develop the views you needed for your documents. To your boss, it appears you have not done much work, even though you show him the cool 3D views of what you have been building on the computer.

The point here is that you need to start any job with this requirement in mind and document your model from the very beginning. Get the title block done and loaded into the project so sheets can be created. Begin importing your typical details into drafting views and placing them on sheets. Make a sheet of 3D views as a great source of information for the design team and client, even in schematics. As you cut working sections, keep in mind whether they might be worthy enough to be used in the documentation. If so, drag them onto a sheet.

DIMENSION PLACEMENT

Placing dimensions is as easy as clicking on successive elements in the view such as grids or beams or other elements. There are also several options for you to use for dimensioning to or from walls. When you start any but the Linear type of dimension command on the Options bar, you will find options that will allow you to dimension to wall location lines, such as the center of wall cores, or to wall faces. Just select one of these options to enable it as you begin placing the dimension strings.

When using the Align dimension type you have an added Pick option. Utilizing that option allows you to select Individual References or Entire Walls as a way to dimension your elements. If you select Entire Walls, Revit Structure enables the Options button. Clicking that will display the Auto Dimension Options dialog box, which you can configure to automatically do such things as dimension to openings in the wall. With one click, you can then create an entire string of dimensions.

After you place the dimension, you can move the whole string by selecting it and then dragging it to a new position. You can move the text string and lines together or independently by selecting and dragging them. Another important capability allows you to select intersection points of lines and grids as dimension points for anchoring the dimension string.

DIMENSION TEXT

As you are documenting your project, you will undoubtedly come upon cases where you want to show a dimension string with a text note inserted into it instead of a length or angle value. This capability comes in very handy since in many cases you want to see a note like, "SEE ARCH." To use this feature, follow these steps:

1. Select an existing text string.

2. Click on the dimension text, which then brings up the Dimension Text dialog box (see Figure 9.5).

3. Click the Replace With Text radio button.

4. Type the text string you want to use in the adjacent edit box to entirely replace the text.

FIGURE 9.5
The Dimension Text dialog box

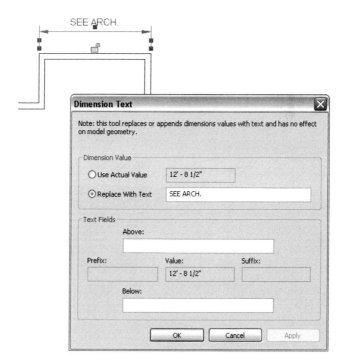

5. Or, in the Text Fields area of the dialog box, add the text string above or below the actual dimension.

6. Click OK.

In many cases you will also want the dimension to remain, but you will want to add a suffix or prefix onto the dimensions such as 5'-0" TYP. In that case enable the Use Actual Value radio button, and then type your text in the Prefix or Suffix box below.

Existing dimensions strings can be adjusted using the Witness line controls. They can be reassociated so that you can add or delete segments from an existing string. Used with dimensions to walls, they permit the user to toggle between the faces and the centerline of the wall.

You now have a basic idea of how dimensions work. The next section will introduce you to adding spot dimensions and coordinates into your project views.

Spot Dimensions and Coordinates

Spot dimensions come in two forms: spot elevations and spot coordinates. Each one can be configured in a variety of ways, using leaders with or without shoulders (horizontal lines). There are also many leader end options to choose from. If space gets tight on your plan or section, you can drag the leader to a new position (see Figure 9.6). The leader symbol will also rotate with objects.

FIGURE 9.6
The many spot elevation and coordinate family types

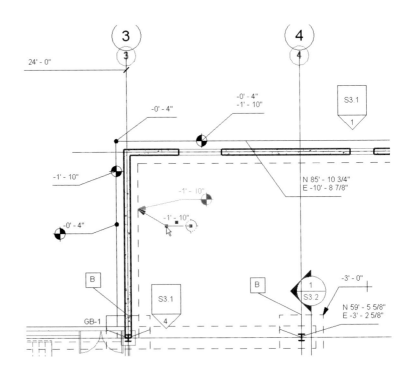

Spot coordinates can display the top elevation, the bottom elevation, or both for a particular model element and are especially helpful in documenting concrete monolithic buildings. Once you place the spot dimension, you can use it to later change the position of the object simply by changing its value (see Figure 9.7). To edit the top of a footing, follow these steps:

1. Select the element.

2. Click on the spot elevation text you want to change.

3. In the Edit Value dialog box that appears, adjust the elevation values.

4. Click OK.

FIGURE 9.7
Changing the wall footing elevation using a spot elevation

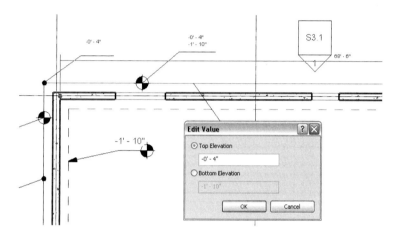

The spot coordinates cannot be edited in plan view once they are placed. The display is controlled by default through the Units Format setting, or it can be overridden (see Figure 9.8). Spot coordinates can be shown in a variety of formats, from metric to decimal to feet and inches, with various options to suit just about everyone.

Grids

Grids are an essential feature to understand. They are the basic horizontal constraint system in your model plan views. Model elements such as columns and girders can be anchored to them. When a gridline moves, those elements anchored to it also move, providing your model the ability to flex as design changes occur. Once created, they then automatically are generated in any view in which they intersect, saving you a lot of detailing time. That can be a two-edged sword, though, because managing them in the multitude of views that you use for your documents can be a frustrating task, though it is still better than in conventional CAD. Revit Structure has features to control the display in order to make managing them easier. And do not forget that the grid head can be configured as a circle, hexagon, or diamond shape, however you might prefer.

You will now examine the basic control features of grids, how to propagate grid layouts among various views, and how to use scope boxes to control their extents.

BASIC CONTROL FEATURES

Figure 9.9 shows an existing gridline and bubble with the controls displayed. A check box allows you to turn the grid bubble off or on at each end depending on how you want it shown in your view. Clicking the elbow symbol jogs the gridline so that the grid head can be dragged to a new position without moving the gridline itself, an important capability when you have numerous gridlines close together. By clicking on the grid text, you can change it on the fly. As you place the grids, Revit Structure numbers or letters them sequentially to make their annotation more automatic.

FIGURE 9.8
Overriding the default spot coordinate format

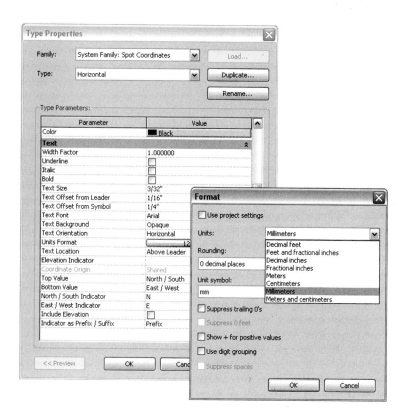

FIGURE 9.9
A basic grid element with controls displayed

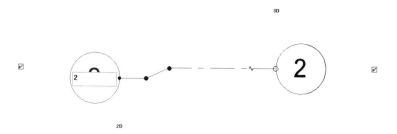

Notice in Figure 9.9 that the left grid head has a 2D control below it, while the right grid head has a 3D control above it. When you enable the 2D option, the grid length becomes specific to that view only. With the 3D bubble enabled, changing the gridline end in one view will also change it in every other view in which it intersects. As stated earlier, you can spend endless time moving grids back and forth on your views, so be aware of how this feature works. This is part of the frustration we were referring to when we said a user does not fully understand this feature and ends up spending too much time having to adjust the grid displays in other views.

Once you have placed grids on one view, say your first floor and foundation plan, and you have configured and located the grid bubbles to your liking, you will want to automatically duplicate that grid layout in other views. If you go to those other views, the grids will be there, but they may not be configured exactly like the foundation plan. To accomplish this goal, you use the Propagate Extents option, as follows:

1. Select an existing grid in a plan view, and then click the Propagate Extents button on the Options bar.

2. When the Propagate Datum Extent dialog box appears, check the views where you want to duplicate the grid display arrangement.

3. Click OK.

THE GRID DOES NOT SHOW IN ALL VIEWS! WHAT NOW?

On quite a few occasions you may find that views are missing grids and levels that should be displayed. Grids and levels must intersect or extend into a view to display automatically, but even then they may not display. What do you do? Well, don't get flustered and start faking them with 2D centerlines. What you need to do is find a view where the grid or level is showing. Highlight the gridline and right-click. Select Maximize 3D Extents from the shortcut menu to ensure that the grid or level is shown in every view in which it intersects.

SCOPE BOXES

Scope boxes are another way to control the display of grids and other datum elements in your project. Say you have a three-story steel structure sitting on a one-story concrete parking level, and suppose that the parking-level column grid layout is different from the one for the steel structure. By enclosing the concrete level in a 3D scope box, you can limit the propagation of gridlines so that in your views of the steel structure you won't have a confusing overlay of two grid systems. You use the scope box to limit their appearance in views. To add a scope box, go to a plan view and do the following:

1. On the Create panel of the View tab click the Scope Box icon.

2. On the Options bar give the scope box a name and a vertical height.

3. Then draw a rectangular region that you want to control with the scope box.

4. After placement, select the box and use the blue shape handles to further refine its exact extents.

5. To make further vertical adjustments to the scope box, go to an elevation, section, or 3D view, and adjust the box using the handles.

6. To override the scope box's visibility and its associated references in a particular view, select the box and then click the Element Properties ➢ Instance Properties icon on the Modify Scope box's tab on the Ribbon, which will display its Element properties.

7. Click Edit in the Views Visible parameter, which displays the Scope Box Views Visible dialog box (see Figure 9.10).

8. In the Override column, change the value from Visible to Invisible (or vice versa, depending on what you require).

9. Close the dialog boxes.

To enable the scope box in a view, follow these steps:

1. 1 In the plan view right-click and select View Properties.

2. In the Scope Box parameter click the drop-down menu and select from any of the existing scope boxes.

3. Exit the dialog boxes.

Note that enabling the scope box will also limit the visibility of the entire view to that area and that the view crop region will become locked to it. One of the unsung benefits of scope boxes is that they are excellent for managing the size of partial plans for multifloor buildings. Each view will show the same part of the building consistently.

FIGURE 9.10
Scope boxes control the display of datum elements in your views.

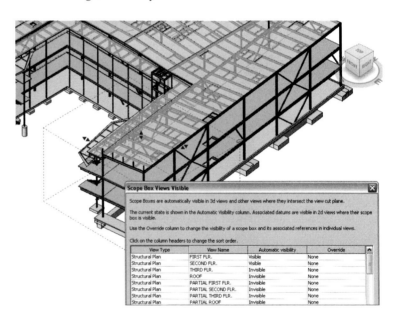

Reference Planes

Reference planes have numerous uses. They establish two-dimensional infinite work planes in the three-dimensional space of your virtual environment, to which you can then attach your model elements. If you move the reference plane, the attached objects will follow. They are also a vital part of the parametric family-creation process. For more on this subject, refer to Chapters 18 and 19.

In your model you can create reference planes and then set them as your current work plane. If you are working at an odd angle, you can work on elements on that plane while still in a straight plan view. You can then build your elements in a basic two-dimensional approach such as the way you attached roof framing to a sloping diaphragm or reference plane in Chapter 7. Even though you were drawing the members in a plan view, the objects were still drawn on the sloping reference plane. Figure 9.11 illustrates this point with a kicker brace attached to a sloping reference plane. Using the reference planes, you could add numerous braces to the model along the E grid line. Once you have created a reference plane, you should give it a name for easy use and for later identification in the project. To do that, simply select the reference plane and access its Instance Properties dialog box, where you can name it.

Figure 9.11 shows another use of reference planes that was explained in Chapter 7. In this case the reference planes are used to locate the cut of the ends of the angle kicker by using the Cut Geometry tool. This is very useful in detailing. Be careful, though, because if you delete the reference plane, the geometry reverts to its original shape.

FIGURE 9.11
Reference planes for framing and using the Cut Geometry tool

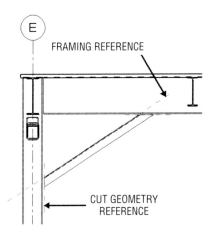

Another important use for reference planes is for the alignment of elements that are displayed in multiple views because reference planes are datum elements that can propagate across multiple views. For instance, you can create the reference plane in a plan view, and it will also be visible in your section view.

Now that you have learned about datum elements and how they are used to create your documents, let's look at annotation elements and see how you can put them to work in your project to create a good-looking, well-documented set of drawings.

Annotation Elements

Now you are going to learn how to add annotation elements to your views. Not only are you creating a three-dimensional model in order to develop your design, but at the same time you are adding documentation so that your views will be ready to be added to your sheet set. Remember that annotation elements are view specific. This section on annotation elements describes the addition of many types of tags that you will need for your documents in order to identify modeled elements such as beams and floors. You must also add text notes explaining details of the design, and as you will see, Revit Structure has it all covered. This section also explains symbols and the procedures necessary to load and add them.

Tags

Tags are element descriptors that are attached to and display parameter values for a individual modeled element (see Figure 9.12), such as a beam size or a footing mark. We cannot emphasize enough that you should always use tags, rather than writing text next to an object to describe it. By tagging elements instead, not only does the tag move with the element that needs to be relocated, but its value also updates automatically if you change the element type during the design process.

FIGURE 9.12
Typical annotated foundation plan

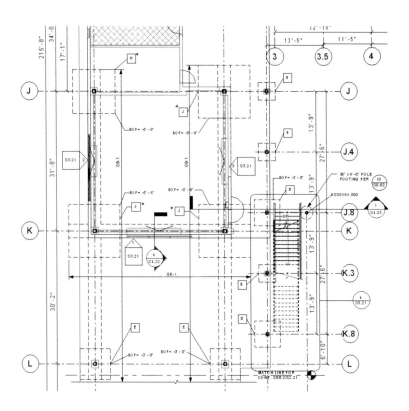

Three options exist for tagging a modeled element: By Category, Multi-Category, or Material. Of the three, By Category is the one you will most commonly use for structural projects. Tags can be found in the Annotations library installed with the software, with specific structural tags found in the Structural folder.

To add a tag to an element, do the following:

1. On the Tag panel of the Annotate tab click Tag then By Category from the pull-down list.

2. The Options bar will display the various tag placement options (see Figure 9.13).

3. Designate Horizontal or Vertical orientation of the tag.

4. Click the Tags button on the Options bar, which displays the Loaded Tags dialog box listing all the tags loaded in the current model and in all categories. You can select to make one current, or you can load others from the library directory. The tag listed next to a category is the tag that Revit will use when you select an element to tag.

5. On the Options bar, enable the automatic leader by checking the Leader check box. You can specify that the leader has its end attached or free, and you can set the leader length.

6. Hover the mouse cursor over the object you want to tag until you see the appropriate tag. Revit Structure will attempt to match the right tag with the element. In "tight quarters" you may need to use the Tab key to get at the element you want to tag.

7. Click on the screen to place the tag.

FIGURE 9.13
The Tags by Category options

As stated earlier, when you move a structural framing member in your project, any attached tag automatically moves with it to maintain its original position in relation to that element. This will allow you to place a structural beam tag at the end of a beam, which then automatically moves and repositions itself as the beam moves.

Revit Structure ships with basic tags for all structural categories. You can also edit and create your own, which inevitably you will need to do in order to adapt the default tags to ones more in conformity with your company standards and for special circumstances. For instance, the normal beam tag might read W12X26. But if you are working on an addition to an existing building, you might want to add an (E) in front of all existing framing to make it (E)W12X26. The wrong approach is to use the normal beam tag and then come back and add the (E) by using a text object in front of it. Instead, you can easily edit the tag and create a new type just for that purpose with the (E) embedded in the tag. Tags support the combination of parameters and text in one label.

Here's the general procedure for editing a structural tag:

1. Open the tag family either by browsing to the structural annotation library or by selecting a tag that exists in your project and clicking the Edit Family button on the Family panel of the Modify Structural Framing Tags tab.

2. Once you have opened the tag family for editing, highlight the text label.

3. Click Edit Label on the Label panel of the Modify Label tab.

4. In the Edit Label dialog box select new Category Parameters to add to the label (see Figure 9.14), or edit the existing Label Parameters.

5. Edit the label by changing the Sample Value field or by adding Prefix and Suffix information.

FIGURE 9.14
The Edit Label dialog box in the Wide Flange tag family

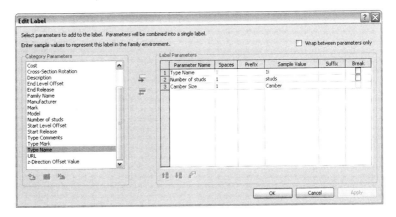

6. Enable the Wrap Between Parameters Only check box to create a multiline tag.

7. Use the Spaces field to increase or decrease the distance between the tag elements.

8. Once you've completed the label, save your work to a new tag family with an appropriate name, or if you're editing an existing tag, just save it and then load it into your project.

These are the basics of how and why you add tags to elements in your model rather than adding a text note adjacent to an element. The next section shows you how to tag a whole plan at once.

TAG ALL NOT TAGGED

Use the Tag All Not Tagged feature to automatically add tags to multiple objects that do not already have tags in any particular view. It's a very quick way to annotate your views. For instance, sometimes you might find that you need to re-create a plan in your project. At first you may think it a daunting task to reapply all the beam tags to the new plan. Maybe you think it is easier to just edit the old plan. Well, with this option, you can tag all the beams in seconds, so don't worry about the time factor.

To use this feature, follow these steps:

1. Select the elements you want to tag in a view, or do not select any if you wish all to be tagged.

2. On the Tag panel of the Annotate tab click the Tag All icon.

3. Enable one of the radio buttons to either select all objects or select the objects that you previously made to be tagged.

4. In the Category section, select the type of object tag you wish to apply (see Figure 9.15).

5. Enable the Create Leader check box, and adjust the leader length if necessary.

FIGURE 9.15
The Tag All Not Tagged
dialog box

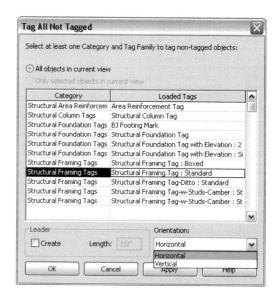

6. Choose the orientation of the tag(s).

7. Click OK to create the tags.

It's that easy, so give it a try. Even if some elements are tagged on the view, this function will find only those elements that have not been tagged and add tags to them. Revit Structure will not double-tag any element already tagged.

EXERCISE: CREATE A STRUCTURAL FRAMING TAG

In this exercise, you will make a new tag for your project to adapt the basic Beam-Stud-Camber label. Your goal is to make the beam size tag display an (E) in front of it, the stud tag to have brackets, and the camber tag to display a c= in front of it, as shown here:

(E)W12X26 [24] c=1"

1. Start a new project.

2. Level 2 should be the default plan view. If not, double-click Level 2 to make it active.

3. On the Structure panel of the Home tab click the Beam icon and then draw a beam on the plan.

4. Select the Beam tool, and then click the Element Properties icon to access the Instance Properties dialog box.

5. Type **24** for the Number of Studs value and **1″** for the Camber Size value.

6. Click OK to exit.

   Note that the stud and camber values do not display in the tag because by default the Standard Beam tag does not contain labels for them.

7. Select the tag.

8. In the Type Selector drop-down list on the Modify Structural Framing Tags tab, choose Structural Framing Tag-w-Studs-Camber: Standard to change the tag type so that the values will display in the tag.

9. With the tag still selected, click Edit Family.

10. Click Yes to open and edit the Structural Framing tag family.

11. With the tag family open, select the text and click the Edit Label button on the Label panel.

12. In the Label parameters of the Edit Label dialog box, add **(E)** as a prefix to the type name.

13. In the Number of Studs parameter, type [(left bracket) in the Prefix field and] (right bracket) in the Suffix field.

14. In the Camber field, type **c=** in the Prefix box.

15. In the Spaces field, increase the distance between elements to **3** for a better display.

16. Increase the label width to accommodate the new parameters.

17. Click OK to exit.

18. On the Application menu click Save As ➢ Family and change the tag's filename to **Structural Framing Tag-w-Studs-Camber-existing**. Place this file in your Imperial Library\Annotations\Structural folder.

19. On the Family Editor panel of the Create tab, click Load into Project.

20. Select the tag again, and use the Type Selector to specify the new tag type you just loaded.

BEAM SYSTEM TAG

The Beam System tag (see Figure 9.16) covers a whole bay of in-fill beam elements and indicates the common beam size and spacing of members in the framing bay. This tag is especially useful for wood framing where members are closely spaced; typically at 16″ center-to-center and where tagging each individual member would totally clutter the plan. Click Beam on the Symbol panel of the Annotate tab, and then hover your cursor over the beam system until it becomes highlighted. Click to place the tag in an appropriate spot in the bay. Like most things in Revit Structure, this is a tag family, so you can create other types as you need them.

FIGURE 9.16
A Beam System tag applied to wood floor framing

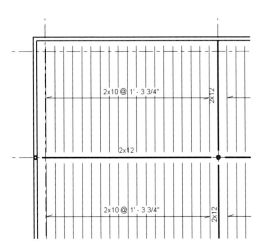

SPAN DIRECTION TAG

The Span Direction tag is applied to structural floors as they are created, or it can be added later. The filled half-arrow (see Figure 9.17) indicates the direction of the deck, while the open arrow represents the extent of the deck. The Span Direction indicator is important in steel details and sections because, once it is applied in plan, it will enable the display of the metal deck flutes correctly in section, making your sections much easier to generate.

To change the direction of the deck, highlight and rotate the tag 90 degrees. Once the tag is placed properly, you can erase it and the deck flute orientation will not change. Unfortunately, the tag works only for floor objects and not for roofs. The deck profile cannot be added to a roof type and must be drawn manually within sections using a metal deck repeating detail, which is much more time consuming to create and maintain.

FIGURE 9.17
The Span Direction tag

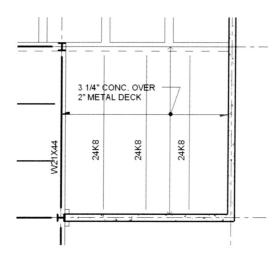

PATH AND AREA REINFORCEMENT TAGS

Path and Area Reinforcement tags (see Figure 9.18) are added to concrete plans to indicate reinforcing patterns much like the Span Direction tag does for floors. For more information, refer to Chapter 10.

FIGURE 9.18
An example of area reinforcement in plan view

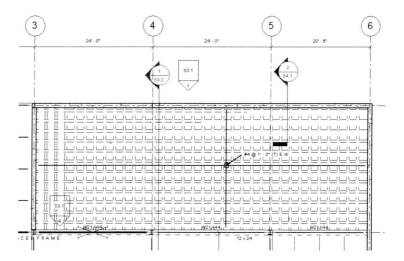

TAGGING VS. DUMB TEXT

One of the most important concepts to grasp as you learn to use Revit Structure is that your modeled elements are tagged rather than having text next to an object that has no connection to it, also known as *dumb* text. Tags are more "intelligent" than dumb text placed next to an element. When you attach a tag to an object, the tag displays a value, such as an isolated footing mark or a beam size, and connects directly to the underlying database of information. The value shown represents one of the parameters of the graphical object, such as its type mark. For example, spread footings can be organized as a schedule on a typical details sheet and will most likely be sorted by their type mark.

The same type mark value that appears in the schedule will display for the tag in the plan view as well. The underlying database controls both of them. The tags and schedules display the information stored in the elements. The schedules are reports and the tags are mini-reports. That is the parametric nature of Revit Structure, which helps it to be a powerful BIM solution: a robust, computable database that centralizes all information about the modeled elements. Changes to the basic elements represented in the database are immediately reflected in all the views that the database controls. So avoid dumb text annotation whenever possible, and really unlock the power of Revit Structure.

Beam Annotations

The Beam Annotations tool is an advanced tool for adding beam tags, spot elevations, and text notes to all or selected beams in a plan view. For instance, you can add framing tags to the middle of the beam, and you can add beam end spot elevations to the start and end of the members — all automatically. Figure 9.19 shows the Beam Annotations dialog box and its related Placement Settings dialog box. Each dialog box contains many placement options that you can set to meet various conditions.

To add a beam annotation, use the following procedure:

1. Go to a plan view where you want to annotate the beams.

2. On the Annotate tab of the Ribbon click Beam Annotations to access the dialog box.

3. In the Placement area select by enabling the check box to remove existing tags if you want to replace current ones.

4. Click the Settings button to configure the placement of the tag in relation to the text bounding box.

5. In the Annotate Location and Type area of the dialog box, select either the Level Beams in Plan or the Sloped Beams in Plan tab.

6. In either of those tabs configure the boxes in the schematic layout to show the Annotation type you want to use.

7. Finally, click OK to exit the dialog box, and the beam annotations will be added to your view.

Text

Not every element can be tagged in your project, such as lines and filled regions, so you must add text notes on various views (see Figure 9.20). As with other families, the text family is populated with many text style types formatted for your particular company needs and uses.

To place a text note in one of your views, follow these steps:

1. Click Text on the Text panel of the Annotate tab.

2. Select the text style you want to use from the Type Selector (see Figure 9.21).

3. On the Place Text tab ➤ Alignment panel, choose the text justification: Left, Centered, or Right for the text string.

FIGURE 9.19
The Beam Annotations and Placement Settings dialog boxes

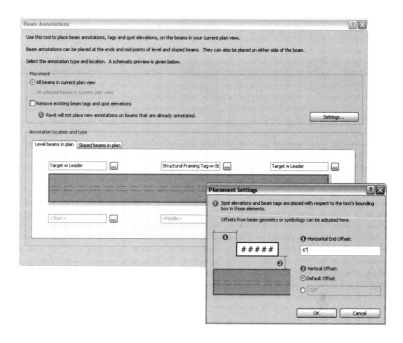

FIGURE 9.20
Adjust the text box using the controls.

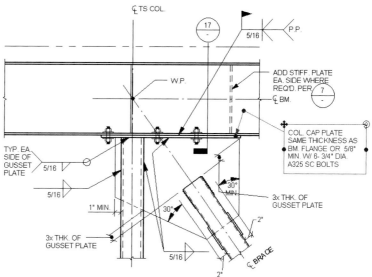

4. On the Place Text tab, select the text leader type: No Leader, One Segment, Two Segments, or Curved.

5. Choose from two placement methods:

   a. Click once to place the top-left point of the text block in your view, and then begin writing. This will make one long text box.

    b. Click the top-left corner and drag without letting up on the cursor to pick the bottom-right corner. This will result in a specific box size with text wrapping. Remember to avoid adding hard returns or the text string will not wrap correctly when the text box size is adjusted.

6. After you create the text box, the Format panel will appear, so you can make all or a portion of the text Bold, Italic, or Underlined.

7. Click outside the text box to complete the text string.

FIGURE 9.21

Accessing text types on the Place Text tab of the Ribbon

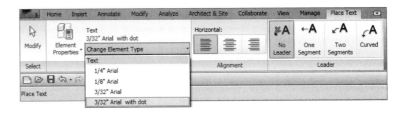

To edit the text string in one of your views, use this process:

1. Click to select the text string.

2. Pick the move grip in the upper-left corner and drag to reposition the text object.

3. Click the rotate grip in the upper-right corner and drag to rotate the text object.

4. Click and drag the grips on the sides of the text box to resize the text box.

5. Click either of the two leader line grips and drag it to reposition the leader line.

6. To edit the text itself, click into the text box and change the text as desired; then click outside the text to finish editing.

7. To add or remove leaders from the existing tag, highlight the tag that activates the Modify Text Notes tab. On the Leader tab click Remove Last to remove leaders as required.

One important consideration for your text styles is whether the background of the text box will be transparent or opaque. An opaque text box will hide what is under it. You will need to decide which way you prefer to show your notes. Covering up what is beneath can lead to problems if it covers up something important. But sometimes that might be precisely what you want. There is a Type parameter that controls this value, and you can adjust each text type as you see fit.

What about special characters in text strings, such as the centerline, plate symbol, or round symbol? They are important to structural annotation, and there is no text equivalent that can be easily used for the centerline or plate symbol. A centerline family is available, but it does not work in a text string, so you will need a workaround for that one. Many times, you will want an annotation that says something like ''Centerline W18x'' or ''Plate 3/8'' (see Figure 9.22) that includes the symbol along with some descriptive text next to it. The best thing to do is make your own annotation symbol.

To make your own text annotation symbol for the plate text symbol, do the following:

1. On the Application menu click New ➢ Annotation Symbol.

2. Select Generic Annotation as the type.

FIGURE 9.22
Simple centerline and
plate symbol with added
label

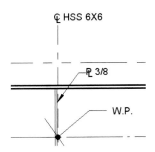

3. Create the *P* and the *L* letters with transparent text and arrange them to make the symbol.

4. Create a label next to the symbol for the text addition.

5. Make the text string left justified.

6. Save and load the family into your project, and save it to your own annotation library.

7. To use the symbol, drag it from the Annotation area under Family in the Project Browser, and click to place. You can also access the command on the Symbol panel of the Annotate tab.

For some special characters, such as the round symbol, you can use the Windows Character Map, found in the Windows Start menu, under Accessories ➢ System Tools (see Figure 9.23). As you are typing the text string, you can insert special character symbols by doing the following:

1. Open the Character Map and browse through the symbols until you find the one you want.

2. Highlight the symbol and click the Select button.

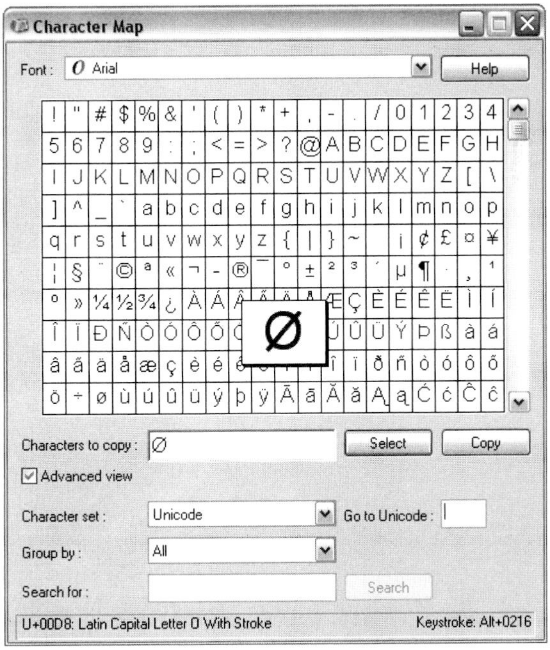

FIGURE 9.23
The Windows Character Map

3. Select other characters to copy to the string.

4. When you finish selecting, click Copy.

5. Switch back to the text string you are editing and paste in the characters (press Ctrl+V to paste).

6. Some characters have a Unicode value that can be seen at the bottom of the Character Map box, in which case you simply add that number in the text string.

   Note that the numbers have to be entered using the numeric keypad. If you just use the numbers on the regular keyboard, it will not work. For laptop users it varies from laptop to laptop, but probably you have to invoke the numeric keypad using the FN key to get it to work.

Revit Structure handles text notes efficiently and effectively, as you have just learned, but sometimes you need to add large sets of notes. The next section will show you how to approach that task.

General Notes

General notes are text but require different attention than the notes we have been discussing. General notes usually take up a large part of your first sheet in a design set of documents, and they can be heavily formatted. They can be difficult to manipulate into rows and columns and to maintain on the sheet in the way you would like them displayed. But tools are available within Revit Structure that will help to greatly reduce your effort in managing your general notes.

If you are a subscription member, you will have access to the Revit Structure Extension Text Generator, and you will undoubtedly want to start using it immediately. When you activate the command, a dialog box opens that allows you to insert and format your notes and configure how the notes will be displayed in columns and rows on the sheet (see Figure 9.24). You can open Microsoft Word documents directly from the Extension Text Generator. This is just one of a whole set of excellent extensions that Revit Structure offers. If you've struggled with AutoCAD text for many years, you'll find this function to be a breath of fresh air!

The Extension Text Generator has a text import window where you can break notes into sections on the sheet and a style area where you can create and edit the text format.

Here's the general procedure for using the text editor to import a DOC file (you must have Revit Structure Extensions 2009 loaded on your computer):

1. Click Tools ➢ External Tools ➢ Extensions for Revit. This opens the Extensions Manager dialog box.

2. Double-click Text Generator in the Miscellaneous section to start the application.

3. In the upper-right area of the Text Generator dialog box, click the Select button and browse to the file you wish to import.

4. Select and import the file.

5. Add separators where you want to break the text lines into rows or columns.

6. Click Sections.

7. Enter the number of rows or columns into which you wish to arrange the notes.

8. Adjust the row, column spacing, and order of placement for each section.

FIGURE 9.24
The Extension Text
Generator allows easy
general note formatting
into rows and columns.

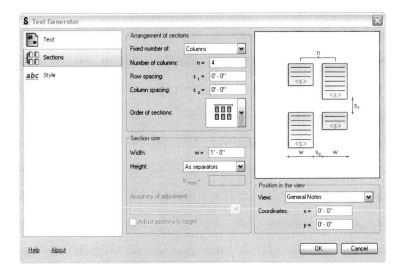

9. Adjust the section width.

10. For the height of sections, you have two options:

   a. Use the separators that you added in the text part of the dialog box.
   b. Set the value to Maximum. Then you can set a maximum height for the section.

11. Add the drafting view name for the notes and add a position (or you can just drag the note into position after import).

12. Click the Style button to access and apply text styles to the notes.

13. When you have finished, click and Revit Structure will generate the notes as a drafting view.

14. Drag the notes onto your sheet (see Figure 9.25).

You will most likely have to fine-tune the notes to fit precisely. To edit the notes, go to the drafting view and click the Extensions Modification toolbar.

Keynotes

Keynote legends report or summarize any keynotes that are present in the views that share the same sheet with the keynote legend.

Keynotes are a system of notes defined in an external text file that are applied to elements in your project and then displayed in a keynote legend or list on the side of the sheet. Keynote legends report or summarize any keynotes that are present in the views that share the same sheet with the keynote legend. This can be an effective way to annotate your details in that you can apply keynote tags to objects to display the element type, the material type, or references to a keynote in the keynote schedule. For a complete description of keynotes, refer to Chapter 11.

FIGURE 9.25
The sheet of
general notes

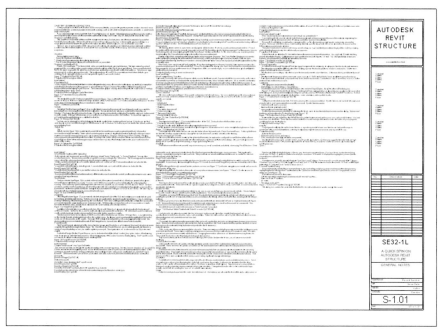

Component Symbols

Component symbols are used to provide a 2D graphic representation of an annotation or model element in your project such as a scale bar, a north arrow, or a wall type. They maintain their printed size regardless of view scale. As with other families, you can edit or make your own new symbols. It is important to build and manage a good symbol library as you transition into the Revit Structure environment. Moment frame connections (solid triangles) are an example of symbols, as are weld symbols and section marks. Figure 9.26 shows pile cap information in a legend.

Legend components are another especially useful type of symbol that you can use when you are preparing a legend (see Figure 9.27). These are not "symbols" in the same context as the Symbol tool discussed previously. They are tied to actual families in the project that will appear in the legend but not get counted in the database as a schedulable element. You can drag loaded components into your legend view. You can configure the symbols to display in any detail mode and either in plan or elevation view.

Creating a legend (see Figure 9.27) is an important task that most projects require. Model, line style, materials, annotation, and phasing symbols can all be added as well as any element that you can place in a drafting view such as lines and text. You can easily assemble a legend view by dragging the symbol and legend components into it, as well as detail and model groups. Legend views also have the unique capability that they can be dragged onto multiple sheets. No other views can do that except schedules. To create a legend for your project, do the following:

1. Click the Legend icon on the View tab of the Ribbon, and then choose Legend from the drop-down list.

2. Give the legend a name and scale.

3. On the Annotate tab, click Symbols.

4. On the Place Symbols tab, drag the symbols you want from the Type Selector into the view.

FIGURE 9.26
FIGURE 9.26

A pile cap used as a
legend component

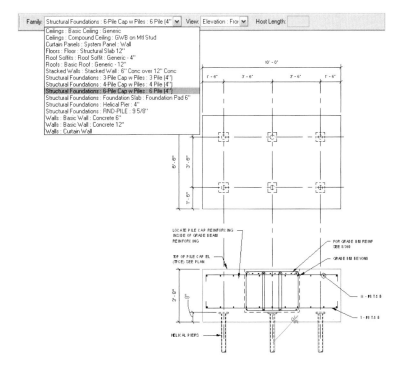

5. Click the Components icon on the Annotate tab, and then choose Legend Component from the drop-down list.

6. Select an item from the Component drop-down list.

7. On the Options bar, choose the View type and Length for the legend symbol (if applicable).

8. Place the component in the view.

9. Add any other detail or group components to the view.

10. Create descriptive text next to each item.

11. Drag the legend view onto a sheet.

WELD SYMBOLS

Weld symbols are loaded in from the structural annotation library. You access them for insertion in the Families area on the Project Browser or by choosing the Symbol command on the Annotate tab. Unfortunately, the Revit Structure weld symbol that ships with the product is a bit clumsy and awkward to use. The symbol itself is too big. And for some strange reason, there are 0″ values inserted for all the fields that must be cleared every time you use the symbol. You will probably find yourself trying to edit the family when you start working with it, or you will be looking on the Internet for better families that others might have shared. What is needed is a graphical dialog box that allows you to fully and easily configure the symbol before you place it. It is a bit astonishing that the developers have not found the time to improve such an important symbol for all who are documenting a steel structure.

FIGURE 9.27
A legend view displaying various components, groups, and symbols

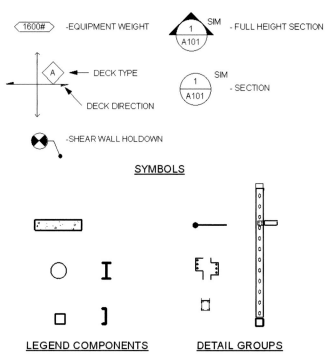

To use the default symbol, follow these steps:

1. Choose Weld System Both, Bottom, or Top from the Family Annotation area in the Project Browser (or use the Symbol command).

2. Drag and place the weld symbol into the view.

3. Highlight the weld symbol.

4. On the Modify Generic Annotations tab, click the Element Properties icon, and then choose Instance Properties on the drop-down.

5. In the Instance Parameters area, edit the Top Symbol and Bottom Symbol values as required (see Figure 9.28).

6. Add tail notes, finishes, weld sizes, the field weld symbol, the all around symbol, and others as required for your detail.

7. Use the Symbol Left check box to orient the leader line to the left or right of the symbol.

8. Click OK when you have finished.

Many of the values can also be added or edited by highlighting the weld symbol after placement and clicking into the text fields.

That concludes our section on annotation. A well-annotated set of documents is vitally important in project preparation. As you have seen, Revit Structure offers lots of help for you in this area as you are creating your documents.

Now let's move on to adding 2D detail elements to your various views. You will do this in order to show those elements you did not want or could not model.

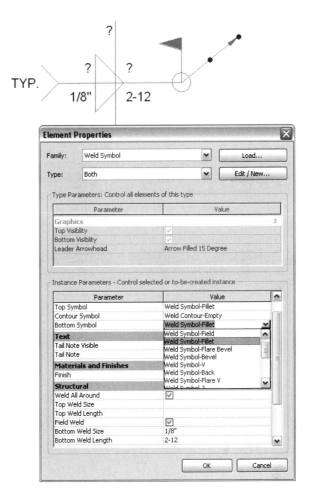

FIGURE 9.28
The Element Proper-
ties dialog box for weld
symbols

Detail Elements

Drafting views have no model elements in them. They are strictly two-dimensional views where you use traditional CAD tools to draft a detail. Section, callout, and elevation views, on the other hand, contain elements from the model as well as additional 2D detail elements. Detailing your project requires working with both element types.

If you or your company has a subscription contract with Autodesk for Revit Structure, you can download an excellent command for detailing in the Revit Structure Extensions for 2010: the Freeze Drawing extension. Any section or elevation with model elements can be turned into a drafting view. All model lines are copied and become detail lines in a new drafting view. If you are worried about shifting model elements or wish to make a typical detail, this extension will fit the bill.

Beyond using linework, you will find that Detail Component elements help you complete your sections and details. You can add those objects that you decide are not necessary to model as 2D elements to your detail views. For instance, you will model the steel column and the spread footing in your project, but you may want to show the base plate, bolts, and grout as a 2D detail group of components in an enlarged section. That is probably the case if you are working for a structural design firm where you are interested in showing only the various typical types of elements. If you are working in a structural detailing firm, on the other hand, you may choose to model all the connection elements so that they can be detailed and scheduled into piece lists.

The following sections introduce you to the various tools that you will use time and again to complete your details.

Detail Lines

Detail lines are the basic line drawing tools that you will use for 2D detailing. Use them to finish drafting views that are cut from the model and 2D drafting views as well. On the Manage tab click Settings, and then choose Line Styles from the drop-down to access the dialog box that enables you to edit existing line styles and create new line types (see Figure 9.29). These line styles are used not only for detailing lines but also for the Linework tool. With the Linework tool, you can change the line style of most model lines if they do not display as you prefer.

FIGURE 9.29
Line Styles dialog box

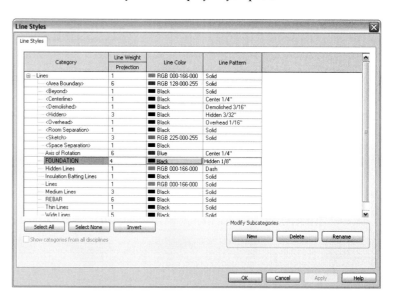

Detail lines can add important information that you might not want to model, such as piping through footings (see Figure 9.30).

Filled Regions

Filled regions are sketch based and provide hatch patterns that you use for detailing purposes (see Figure 9.31). The patterns must be sketched as a continuous boundary of lines. You then select a hatch pattern to apply to the enclosed area. The boundary element can be invisible, or each segment can be visible and use a different line style.

To add a filled region to your view do the following:

1. Click Filled Region on the Annotate tab.

2. On the Create Filled Region Boundary tab use the Draw tools to create your region boundary, and then click Finish Region.

3. On the Element panel click the Region Properties icon.

4. Select an existing region type or click Edit Type to edit or make a new type.

5. Click OK until you exit the dialog box, and then click Finish Region on the Region panel to finish.

FIGURE 9.30
Detail lines show piping run through a slab and grade beam.

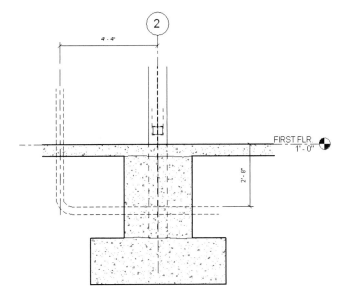

FIGURE 9.31
Earth hatching added to detail

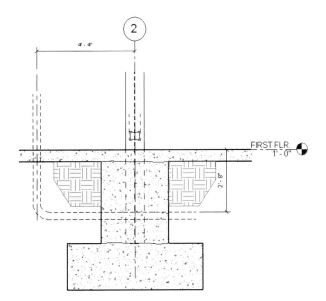

Repeating Details

Repeating details are useful in a detail view when you're adding repetitive 2D elements such as punched steel studs, 2D concrete reinforcing in section, metal deck flutes in section for a roof, or masonry block wall coursing along a line (see Figure 9.32). They are another form of component symbol. You can easily space detail components at intervals of your choosing and apply them by specifying start and end locations.

To add a repeating detail to your project do the following:

1. On the Detail panel of the Annotate tab click the Component icon, and then choose Repeating Detail from the drop-down list.

2. In the Place Repeating Detail tab select a detail component from the Type Selector.

3. To make a new Repeating Detail type, click Element Properties, and then choose Type Properties from the drop-down list.

   Note that you must load in the particular component that you will use for the new type before starting the Repeating Detail command.

4. In the Type Properties dialog box create a new type, specify the component in the Detail parameter, and then specify the Layout type as well as a Spacing value for the repeating pattern.

5. Click OK to exit, and then draw the new pattern.

FIGURE 9.32
A repeating CMU wall
detail added to a section

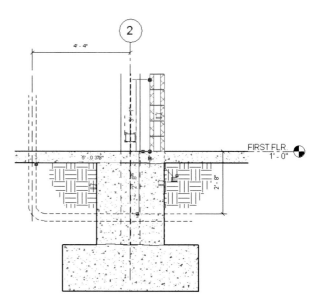

Masking Regions

Many times in your struggle to make model elements in a view display correctly, the best practice may be to cover a problem area and to finish in 2D. That is where the Masking Region function becomes useful (see Figure 9.33).

FIGURE 9.33
Masking region covering
a portion of the detail

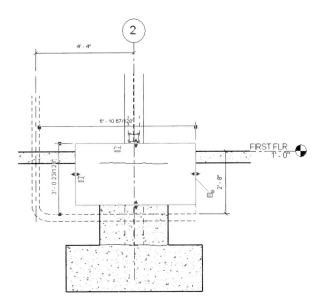

Detail Components and Groups

Detail components are 2D representations of model elements, such as wide-flange beams in section that can be used in detailing views. Detail groups are assemblies of detail components that you want to use more than once. You will be able to drag them into your views from the bottom of the Project Browser for easy insertion.

EMBEDDING DETAIL COMPONENTS IN MODELING FAMILIES

When you are cutting a section on your model, you want the section to be as complete as possible without adding lots of detached 2D lines and detail components. When the model elements move during the design process, the detail components usually do not move with them. Therefore, it can be quite time consuming to continue editing and relocating these elements as the model flexes. One way to avoid this is to build the detail components right into your model family. That way, they are automatically added and can be easily displayed in your section work, and they will move with the model element in which they are embedded.

A good example of this approach is the creation of a standard 2×6 wood-bearing wall type. In a section view you add the top and bottom wood plates as 2D components to the wall representation (see Figure 9.34). You do that by creating a profile for the flat 2×6. Within that profile, you add a 2×6 detail component. That profile is then added to the wall type.

The following general procedure will lead you through this process. First you create the required profile for the 2×6 flat stud plate:

1. Start a new project.

2. On the Application menu click New ➢ Family, and select Profile from the list of available template types. Then click Open.

3. On the Insert tab in the profile file on the Load from Library panel, click the Load Family icon.

FIGURE 9.34
Wood-bearing wall type
with embedded profiles
for plates and bolts

4. Next load in the component. In the Imperial Library section, select Detail Components and then Div 06-Wood and Plastic.

5. Select 061100 – Wood Framing, and then choose Nominal Cut Lumber – Section for the family.

6. Click Open and then specify 2×6. Click OK.

7. In the Ref. Level plan type **ZE** (keyboard shortcut for Zoom to Fit) if you do not see crossed reference planes.

8. On the Create tab on the Detail panel, click Detail Component, and place the 2×6 at the intersection of the reference planes.

9. On the Detail panel click Modify.

10. On the Detail panel click Line, and then draw and lock lines over the 2 × 6 exterior lines. (These are the actual profile lines.)

11. Select the 2 × 6 and rotate it 90°; then center the 2 × 6 on the vertical reference plane. Move the bottom line of the 2 × 6 up to the horizontal reference plane.

12. Select the detail component. Click Visibility Settings on the Visibility panel of the Modify Detail Items tab. Deselect Course and click OK.

13. The profile is now complete. On the Application menu click Save, and save the file as **Wood – 2x6 profile**.

14. On the Family Editor panel of the Create tab, click Load into Project. Then select the new project you started earlier in the exercise (open or start a new project first if necessary).

Now you add the profile with the embedded component to the wall family definition:

1. On the Structure panel of the Home tab click Wall; then choose Structural Wall from the pull-down.

2. Click the Element Properties icon, and then choose Type Properties on the Place Structural Wall tab.

3. Click Edit ➢ New; then change the wall type to Generic 6″.

4. Click the Edit button in the Structure Value field.

5. In the Edit Assembly dialog box, click the Preview button.

6. From the View list choose Section: Modify Type Attributes in order to get a sectional view of the wall.

7. Click Sweeps, and then click Add to insert a new profile.

8. In the Profile field, select the wood-2 × 6 pr profile.

9. In the Offset field, change the value to −3″. Click Apply. Notice that the profile is visible at the bottom of the wall in the section preview to the left.

10. Click OK until you exit all the dialog boxes.

Now draw a portion of the wall in plan view. Create a section view through the wall. When you open that section view, you will not see the flat stud plate at the bottom of the wall. That's because the view is using the Coarse detail level, and the Visibility option for that mode was turned off in the profile family. On the View Control bar, change the detail level of the section to Medium, and you will immediately see that the detail component appears at the bottom of the wall. For added practice go back, and using the same procedure add the two top plates to the wall definition. Notice that the From parameter offers options for Top and Base. This makes it easy to tell Revit the sweep should start at the top of the wall as a reference instead. When completed, your wall should display in section like Figure 9.35. And there you have it.

FIGURE 9.35
Adding the profiles to the wall type

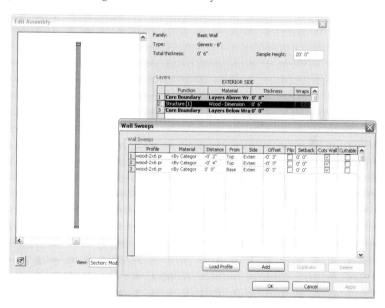

Using embedded components is the best practice for detailing. Now if the wall moves, the embedded detail components go with it. A further refinement of this procedure would be to create a profile that uses the flat 2 × 6 stud we created and also adds a bolt detail component. That profile would then be specified at the bottom of the wall to indicate the connection of the wall to the floor concrete. Chapter 19 takes this wall family even further by creating a full wood shear wall that displays well in both plan view and section view without a lot of added 2D work to complete it.

Now that you have an idea of how to use detail elements, let's explore how to create and manage typical details.

Typical Details Sheets: Creating and Managing

Typical detail preparation is a vital task in documenting any building project, and there are several ways to approach it in Revit Structure. One way is to capture sections from the model that you can then generalize to cover many typical conditions, such as typical foundation conditions (see Figure 9.36). Rather than relying on a library of sheets of foundation details, you selectively prepare what actual conditions you encounter, using the model as your guide.

Undoubtedly, you will have a standard set of details in AutoCAD or other CAD program that you will want to create eventually in Revit Structure. Most of these details have no model connection and are imported as 2D information into drafting views in your project.

To avoid becoming overwhelmed with transforming your whole workflow to modeling at once, you may want to keep your typical details in your CAD system for your first few projects. That will give you a blended construction document set of Revit Structure and CAD sheets. The CAD sheets can be managed and printed solely from the CAD program. As your staff transfers skills from CAD to BIM, you can still keep both systems going and keep everyone productive. You can also simply build the details from scratch in Revit Structure.

FIGURE 9.36
Modeled foundation section generalized as typical

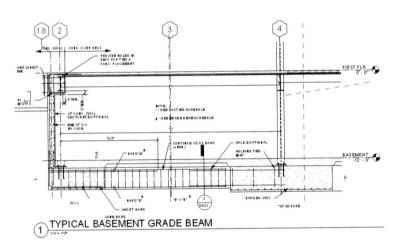

TYPICAL BASEMENT GRADE BEAM

If you decide to have a mixed set of documents, a good practice is to link the CAD detail sheets into your Revit Structure project but still do all the work in CAD. This approach allows all the printing for the project to be done in Revit Structure. That is an important consideration because it can be difficult to coordinate one project in both formats and have them look the same when it comes time to print. At the very least, you will have to maintain two title block sheets, one in Revit Structure and one in CAD.

Revit Structure has several commands that allow you to import and export drafting views and to create libraries of standard details (see Figure 9.37). They work quite well. You can import or export single drafting views or entire sheets of drafting views. Note, however, that if the sheet has any views with model elements in them, none of the views will be exported. Next you will see how to use these commands.

FIGURE 9.37
The Save Views dialog box allows you to save entire sheets of views or some of the views.

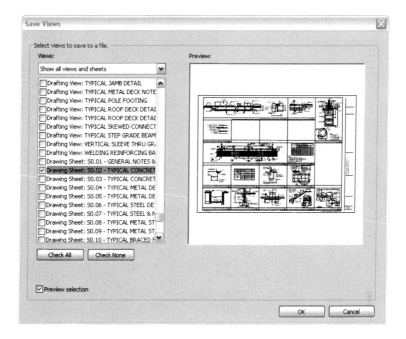

Save to Library

You can save families, groups, and views from your project (see Figure 9.38) with this command. For instance, if you want to save views to a typical details library, do the following:

1. On the Application menu click Save As ➢ Library ➢ View.

2. In the Save Views dialog box, select by checking the box next to the sheet or view names you want to export.

3. In the Save As dialog box, browse to the folder where you want to store the views.

4. Click Save.

If you choose just the sheet view, it will be created as a file with all the drafting views included.

Insert from File

Views exported from other Revit Structure files, or whole sheets of views, can be inserted with the Insert from File command. The procedure to insert drafting views is as follows:

1. On the Insert tab click Insert from File ➢ Insert Views from File (see Figure 9.39).

2. Browse to the folder and select the RVT file where the view(s) reside that you want to insert, or simply select the sheet you want to insert.

3. Click OK.

You can also insert 2D elements from a saved model view by using the Insert 2D Elements from File option. This option allows you to copy 2D detail components such as repeating details and filled regions from a view that contains model elements.

FIGURE 9.38
The Save to Library
tool is found on the
Application menu under
Save As.

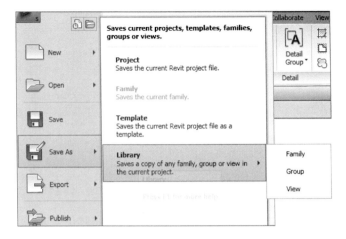

FIGURE 9.39
Insert from
File options

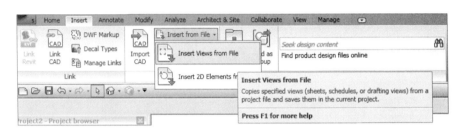

Real World Scenario

IMPORTING AND LINKING DETAILS FROM AUTOCAD

One of the biggest problems in setting up Revit Structure for first-time users is establishing proper import line-weight settings. If you use American Institute of Architects (AIA) layering standards that are found in AutoCAD, it is easier, but if they have all kinds of tweaked layers — and of course third-party SHX fonts — they are going to be shut off in terms of migration. In one such real-world case, interns in a structural engineering company were used to import AutoCAD details into Revit Structure in order to build their detail libraries. Since it can be a time-consuming and repetitive task, they used interns to keep the cost down. The template they used had to be right on, or those kids would have just been creating much more work for themselves massaging the detail once it got imported. It was important for them to have all of the filled regions already created in Revit Structure so that the AutoCAD hatch pattern was properly transferred to a Revit Structure pattern upon import and that it transferred to the predefined regions. Line types should be created in Revit Structure so the AutoCAD lines transfer directly without further editing.

If they had imported the AutoCAD layers with no mapping to a Revit Structure line style, Revit would have created a new line style with the AutoCAD layer name, which is what they did not want. AutoCAD hatch patterns and text styles will also create long unwieldy names when inserted into Revit. This can be problematic, and your details can easily be polluted with this type of junk. Some firms create AutoLISP routines or scripts to alter the detail in AutoCAD to help avoid that type of mess when the detail is then imported into Revit Structure.

You must also carefully approach importing AutoCAD hatch patterns. A detail imported from Auto-CAD will insert as a block. When you highlight the block, you have the option to explode it partially or totally. If you explode it totally, the hatch pattern will be exploded into its little line segments. This can greatly affect the performance of your file and you should avoid it. Instead, do a partial explode. In that case, the hatch patterns will not be exploded. You can then highlight them and change the pattern to a named Revit Structure pattern.

That ends our discussion on documenting your model. It is a huge subject that could fill a whole book. With this introduction of some of the most vital factors of documentation, you now should have some direction on how to prepare your projects. Remember that documentation is half the battle and must be carefully planned and executed in order to maximize the use of your model.

The Bottom Line

Add datum elements to your detail and section views.   Datum elements are necessary for your model because they are the anchors for your objects. Grids, dimensions, spot dimensions, and reference planes are basic constraints for elements within the model, and they give it the ability to flex as you are working through changes in the design of the structure.

> **Master It**   Datum elements form the basic constraints for your project. If you want to manage the columns and framing members of your project, which kind of datum is best suited for this purpose? What datum element is intended to define the vertical information like floor-to-floor height in your project?

Add annotation elements such as text, tags, and symbols.   Once the model is moving forward in development, you need to efficiently add identifying tags, beam annotations, and text to your various views in order to document your design and prepare your sheets. Tagging elements is an essential task since it taps into the properties of the object. If the object changes type, the tag automatically updates. That then allows you to use the model as a physical database for building schedules of many kinds. Text and symbols also are used to further the documentation of your model.

> **Master It**   Open Dataset_0901_Begin.rvt (from the book's companion web page at www.sybex.com/go/masteringrevitstructure2010), and then go to the second-floor plan. On the second floor, load and tag all steel members. Add a Beam System tag to at least one bay. Add a Span Direction tag to the floor. Go to the first floor and tag the columns. After placing the tags, highlight and use the grips to align them with one another for a better display. Add grid dimensions.

Add detailing elements such as detailing lines and filled regions.   Not everything should be modeled. It takes experience to find the correct level of modeling in your project. For instance, columns are modeled but base plates are not in a typical American design firm. But when taking sections and creating details, you have to add that information in 2D over the modeled objects. So you add detailing lines to show the column base plate and perhaps some earth hatching around it. These are detailing elements.

Master It   Open `Dataset_0902_Begin.rvt` and then go to the callout of Section 6. Add detail lines to show piping 4′-0″ to the left of the column going through the slab, turning 90 degrees, and going through the slab. Use a hidden line style. Add earth hatching below the slab using a filled region. Add a repeating CMU component wall to the right of the column with its outside flush with the grade beam below.

Create a typical details library.   A critical task to accomplish if you want your project to be totally documented in Revit Structure is the management of typical detail libraries. Typical details can be imported from the 2D CAD library or created from scratch in Revit Structure. You import Revit Structure details individually as drafting views, which are then added to sheets. They can also be inserted as part of a whole sheet. In similar fashion, you can export individual drafting views or sheets of drafting views to use in another job or to add to your Revit Structure library of details.

Master It   You have a new project to start and want to transfer your model and drafting views from an already completed project. How will you transfer the drafting views to the new project? What is the best way to transfer a section with model elements in it to another project as a typical drafting view?

Chapter 10

Modeling Rebar

The power of Revit Structure is no more evident in any capacity than in the procedures involved in the placement of reinforcement. To say this topic ties it all together is an understatement. In normal AutoCAD, AutoCAD Architecture, and MicroStation, reinforcement is simply a separate entity. You draft it yourself. It stands to reason that an application that allows you to place, for example, a #4 bar with a given spacing as opposed to a "donut" is a much better way to think when it comes to "drafting."

In Revit Structure, reinforcement is supplemental to the item that hosts it. With that being said, Revit Structure gives you the ability to control reinforcement long before you even place a bar (rebar) in a wall, a footing, a column, or a pier. You are provided with settings that allow you to control reinforcement cover in both the object's Element properties as well as global Revit Structure settings. Revit Structure allows you to place predefined bars via a powerful new tool called the Rebar Shape Browser, and it gives you the ability to create your own rebar and add it to the library without leaving the model to create a new family.

In this chapter you will learn to:

◆ Configure rebar settings

◆ Model a 3D rebar

◆ Add rebar shapes

Placing 3D Reinforcement

Placing a 3D rebar in Revit Structure is pretty easy. The best thing about it is that you can still basically draft reinforcement, as we explained earlier in this chapter, but now the reinforcement will allow you to specify centering and will also let you to choose from a menu of predefined shapes.

Of course, where there is 3D there are settings that we will need to look at before actually placing the bars are in the model. We need to know how thick our rebar is going to plot, and we also need to see where the rebar will appear visually unobstructed. Some of these settings are located in different areas. The following sections describe where to access these settings; we'll begin with the Object Styles dialog box.

Real World Scenario

WHAT ABOUT 2D REBAR?

There are many items in Revit Structure that should be fully modeled in 3D. There are also just as many items that, simply put, could not. Concrete reinforcement is probably the one item that falls into that gray area of "Should I model all of this in 3D, or do I draw it in?" It can be a tough decision to make in terms of what you are looking to get out of the project. On one hand, if you do model the entire project with the proper reinforcement, you can rely on the quantity takeoffs and the reinforcement scheduling to be accurate. On the other hand, if you model all of the reinforcement, it will take longer, and the model will quickly grow in size. We recommend that you look at the overall project. If it is a 650-foot-long military barracks or a football stadium, then you might want to consider placing 3D reinforcement only for the items you will be specifically cutting sections of. If it is a more manageable project in terms of size, then the advantage of fully reinforcing the model can outweigh the disadvantage of the initial time spent and the subsequent increase in the file size.

Sometimes, this decision is not easily made. There will be times where you do need to illustrate reinforcement but cannot afford either the time or the file size. Here you would simply *draft* the reinforcement. The following illustration displays a typical detail condition showing rebar both in plan and section; drafting rebar is as simple as using an appropriate detail line and whatever bar bends you need.

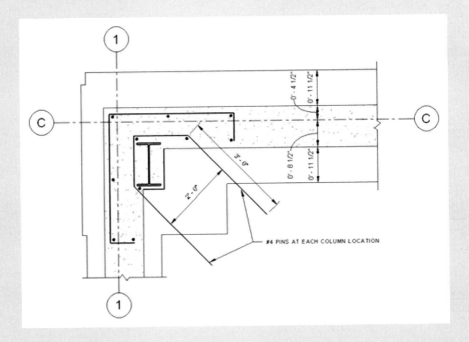

But this chapter is about real model reinforcement, not detail lines. Line styles and how they can pertain to your company standards are covered in depth in Chapter 17. If you are going to be simply drafting reinforcement as you did in AutoCAD, it makes sense to have a template set up that allows you to choose the line styles you want.

ADDING 2D REBAR DETAIL COMPONENTS

In AutoCAD it's called a *donut*. Some firms will make a block out of that donut, so if it changes, all of the bars will be updated. What are we talking about? We are referring to the perpendicular bars that need to be placed into the model. You do this by using the Detail Component tool on the Annotate tab. Once you click this button, you can then go to the Type Selector and pick the Rebar Detail family. You can then place the "sectioned" (horizontal in the case of a plan view) bars in the view, as shown in the illustration above. If you do not have the rebar family loaded in your model, click the Load Family tool. Browse to Detail Components ➢ Structural ➢ Concrete ➢ Reinf Bar Section.rfa. Once this new family is loaded, you can use the Type Selector to assign whatever bar size you need. You now have a wide choice of bars. Who says you can't draft in Revit Structure?

So, as you can see, there is a tremendous benefit to using a basic 2D drafting method of adding reinforcement with positive downstream effects. But you are here for something real, not faked, so keep reading!

Configuring Object Styles

The first item we'll examine is how the bars will appear in terms of their plotted line weight. The out-of-the-box appearance has foundation walls graphically thicker than the reinforcement, as shown in Figure 10.1. This just can't be! Although you may have the settings correct at your firm, let's get a handle on where these settings are and how you adjust them.

FIGURE 10.1
Wall line weight is thicker than rebar line weight.

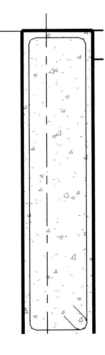

As shown in Figure 10.2, select the Manage tab ➤ Settings drop-down ➤ Object Styles. In the Object Styles dialog box are three settings you need to configure:

◆ Structural Area Reinforcement

◆ Structural Path Reinforcement

◆ Structural Rebar

FIGURE 10.2
Accessing the Object
Styles dialog box

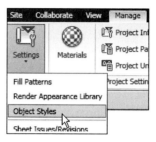

These items are set to 1 by default for both Projection and Cut. Since a line weight of 1 is ridiculously thin, we recommend that you set them to at least 4, depending on your firm's standards. See Figures 10.3 and 10.4. Refer to Chapter 17 for concepts in developing overall line weight methodologies. Gaining control of object styles in Revit Structure will greatly enhance your satisfaction with the end product.

FIGURE 10.3
The line weights are
more consistent with
how reinforcement is
typically shown.

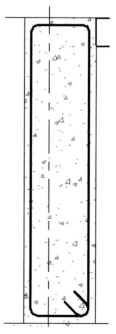

It is also worth mentioning that if you do have to change a setting in a specific project, you'll have to make the same change for the next project. So be sure to add these settings to your template file, or contact the person in charge of your company's Revit Structure standards. You know how you want the reinforcement to look as far as line weights are concerned.

FIGURE 10.4
The Model Objects tab in the Object Styles dialog box lets you controls the line weight for each object type.

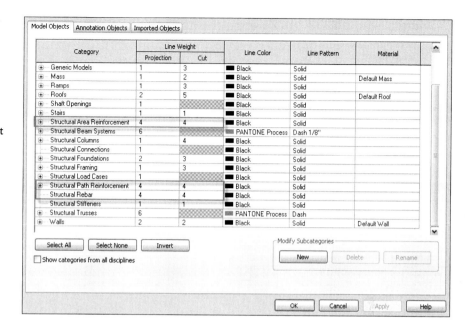

Now it is time to configure some settings that will determine the coverage that will be applied to the bars in relation to walls, slabs, and footings.

Applying Cover Settings

As mentioned in Chapter 6, each wall type has its own cover settings. You can define the minimum setback from the face, top, or bottom of a wall or foundation for which Revit Structure will allow you to automatically place reinforcement. As the rebar is graphically being placed into a wall, beam, foundation, or slab, you will see blue alignment lines. These lines, as shown in Figure 10.5, indicate the minimum allowance of cover. Once you define the reinforcement, as shown in Figure 10.6, the cover settings will serve as the guidelines for the pattern.

FIGURE 10.5
Notice the faint hidden lines, indicating the cover distance.

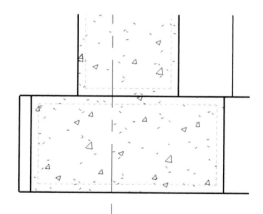

Cover settings are Instance parameters that are associated with each wall, beam, foundation, and slab. If you select any of these items, such as a concrete wall, and click the Element Properties button on the Options bar, you will see a Structural group. This group contains the cover settings for that specific item, as shown in Figure 10.6. The settings are contained in a drop-down list to the right of the parameter. There are eight choices by default. The increments of the offsets are built into these settings.

FIGURE 10.6

Instance parameters for cover settings

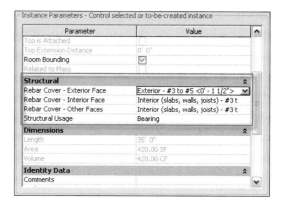

These eight choices are predefined settings built into the Revit Structure default template. You can add or subtract from these items as you see fit, as shown in Figure 10.7. To access these options, activate the Home tab ➤ Reinforcement panel drop-down list ➤ Rebar Cover Settings.

Simply click the Add button, and you are off to adding a new setting. This is one instance where the out-of-the box Revit Structure settings are sufficient — mostly. We recommend that as you are creating these new settings you keep in mind the fact that you should not overdo it. Yes, some projects will require more cover situations than others, but give careful consideration to which settings should go into the templates and which settings should be specific to a project. Once these settings are set, you are ready for the next step: adding the bars to the model.

FIGURE 10.7

The Rebar Cover Settings dialog box assigns rebar placement cover types.

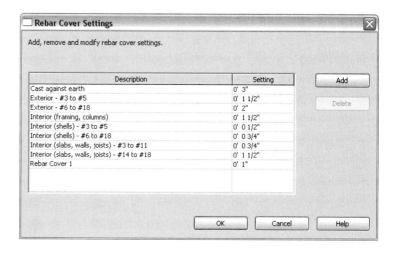

Adding Rebar Parallel to a Work Plane

As sections are cut, and the detail views start to populate the Project Browser, you may notice that when you select a beam or footing a Reinforcement panel appears on the Ribbon, as shown in Figure 10.8.

FIGURE 10.8
The Reinforcement panel of a Modify Structural Framing or Foundations ribbon

However, when you select a slab or wall element, you get a slightly different set of tools. This is because these object types are system families (built-in families), and Revit Structure perhaps has a better level of intelligent control of them. As shown in Figure 10.9, you get extra tools for the face and path of rebar you place.

FIGURE 10.9
The Reinforcement panel of a Modify Floors or Walls ribbon.

Each of these tools allows you to place reinforcement in an object, depending on the current view. For example, if you are looking at a section of a wall and you select it, the Modify Wall Framing ribbon appears. On that ribbon is the Reinforcement panel, and within that is the Rebar tool. Since you are placing stirrup cages, expand the Rebar tool and choose Place Rebar Parallel to Work Plane, as shown in Figure 10.10.

FIGURE 10.10
The Place Rebar Parallel to Work Plane option found on the Rebar tool

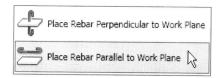

As you rest your cursor over the beam, you will see dashed blue alignment lines, as shown in Figure 10.11. This is how Revit Structure indicates the farthest location you can get to the face of an item before the rebar cover settings disallow the placement. If you exceed this distance, Revit Structure will disallow the placement. If you move up and click-right on the blue alignment line, Revit Structure will place the rebar into the model, as shown in Figure 10.12. The sides and bottom of the rebar will be set at the specified framing cover settings. The top is controlled (in this example) by the slab cover settings.

With the rebar in place, you can now select it and view the Options bar. As shown in Figure 10.13, you get placement controls you use to specify a layout. A single stirrup can be set to run the length of the beam at the spacing specified here.

After the spacing has been set, you may notice that Revit Structure will keep a running count (Quantity), as shown in Figure 10.13. Get used to having this kind of information right in view!

Adding reinforcement in Revit Structure is great. Once the rebar is placed in the model, you can then configure its visibility state by view.

FIGURE 10.11
Attempting to place rebar parallel to the work plane

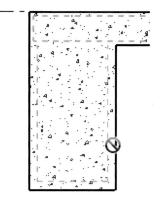

FIGURE 10.12
Valid placement of rebar parallel to the work plane

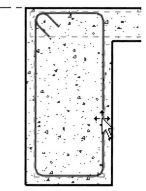

FIGURE 10.13
Options bar controls for type, layout, and spacing

CONTROLLING REBAR VISIBILITY STATES

One issue with reinforcement in Revit Structure has always been that reinforcements will show up in views where you don't want them to. Each piece of reinforcement has its own Instance parameter, which will control the appearance of reinforcement as it relates to other views. To gain access to the settings for the visibility states of a specific reinforcement item, you must select the rebar and review its properties. When the Modify Structural Rebar tab appears, click the Element Properties button. In the Instance Properties dialog box, you will see a Graphics category. In the Graphics category, you will see a View Visibility States parameter, as shown in Figure 10.14. Once you click the Edit button, you will be able to control exactly where this specific reinforcement will appear.

In the Rebar Element View Visibility States dialog box, you will see that most of the views are unchecked, as shown in Figure 10.15. The checks do not actually turn the bars off — they merely allow the bars to be obstructed by the body of the host element. When viewed unobstructed, these bars will show through the host walls, foundations, and slabs. By default, the default views that show reinforcement unobstructed are sections. Typically, plans and elevations have rebar obstructed by the host.

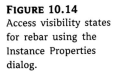

FIGURE 10.14

Access visibility states for rebar using the Instance Properties dialog.

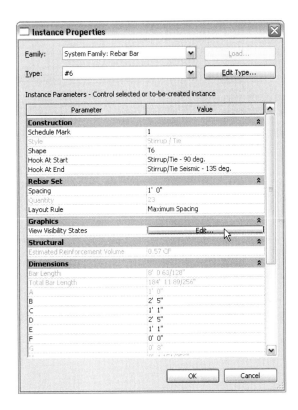

Similarly to adding bars parallel to the current work plane, you can add horizontal bars that run perpendicular to the current work plane in the same view.

Adding Rebar Perpendicular to the Work Plane

Using the same procedure as for adding parallel bars, you can place bars that are perpendicular to the work plane. In a sectional view, as illustrated earlier in Figure 10.12, these bars would be considered horizontal bars. To add these bars, simply select the beam again. You can then click the Place Rebar Perpendicular to Work Plane button. By default, these bars will come in based on a horizontal spacing. As you are placing the bar, press the spacebar to flip the orientation to a vertical plane. As you place the bar, the same cover planes will appear, limiting the bar's placement, as shown in Figure 10.16. If you were to place the bar at the top of a slab, it would not exceed the cover set for the slab top.

Once the bar is placed, you can then select it and alter the layout and the spacing. If you change the Layout to Fixed Number and change the Quantity to 3, the bars will array along that face of the beam, as shown in Figure 10.17. You can then simply mirror the bars to the opposite face of the beam once they are in place.

The same procedure can be applied to walls, footings, and slabs as well. Once you have conquered applying reinforcement to one object type, you have mastered them all!

FIGURE 10.15
Rebar Element View
Visibility States dialog
box

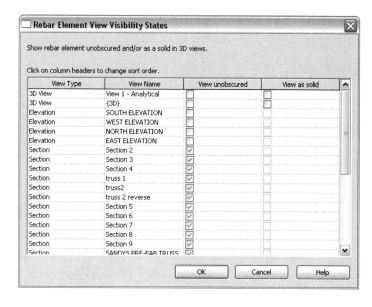

FIGURE 10.16
Adding bars perpendicu-
lar to the current work
plane

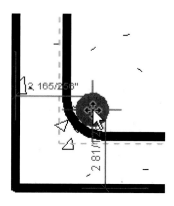

FIGURE 10.17
Horizontal bars at equal
spacing

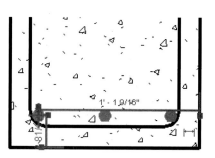

Modeling Rebar with the Rebar Shape Browser

One of the powerful features in Revit Structure is the Rebar Shape Browser. As you select an item to place reinforcement in, you then select whether you want the reinforcement perpendicular or parallel to the current work plane, as discussed earlier. Once you determine the direction of the bars, you will see a list on the Options bar. It allows you to select a rebar shape and shows the type, as shown in Figure 10.18. To the right of the list is a builder button (...). This button will turn the Rebar Shape Browser on or off.

FIGURE 10.18
The Shape list control
on the Options bar

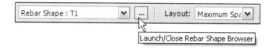

With the Rebar Shape Browser turned on, as shown in Figure 10.19, you will see that many default choices are built into the program.

FIGURE 10.19
The Shape Browser
allows you to access
any rebar shape for your
model.

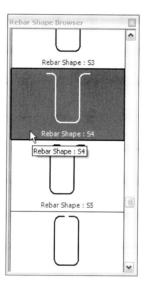

HEY! WHERE ARE MY BARS?

If you are in a model that was created in an older Revit Structure version, you may see only one shape available. If that is the case, you can activate the Insert tab and click the Load Family tool. In the default Imperial Library folder you will see a Rebar Shapes folder. Open this folder and then press Ctrl+A. This will select all of the rebar shapes. Click the Open button, and all of the selected rebar shape families will be loaded into your model.

As you find a shape and drag it into the model, you will see that the rebar cover settings are, again, dictating the height and width of the bar configuration, as shown in Figure 10.20.

FIGURE 10.20
Dragging a rebar shape
from the browser onto a
beam

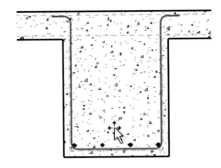

ROTATE THAT STIRRUP

As you are placing shapes with ties or other lap geometry, you can rotate the placement in a number of ways. One is the familiar method of pressing the spacebar. The other is to place your cursor over the bottom, top, or side of the item to get the rebar. The bottom of the pictured shape in the browser will be oriented and displayed according to where your cursor is positioned along the perimeter of the element. Rotating shapes will enable you to define where the lap or tie will be positioned before you place the rebar shape.

Once the bars are placed, you can select them. Notice there are quite a few grips and shape arrows. These provide you with the ability to freely change the bars to a new location if the default position is not acceptable, as shown in Figure 10.21.

FIGURE 10.21
Adjusting the
reinforcement

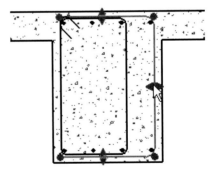

Once the bar is in place, you can change the spacing and the view settings. If you want the bars to display in 3D as a 3D solid, open the Instance Properties dialog box and change the View Visibility States settings to View Unobscured in {3D}. You can also check View as Solid. Refer again to Figure 10.15.

You place bars that are perpendicular to the current work plane in the same manner. Select the item you want reinforced, and click the Place Rebar Perpendicular to Work Plane button on the Reinforcement panel. In the Shape Browser, make sure you have the bar you want, and simply place the bars in the model just as you would if you were placing blocks. Remember to set the visibility state to show unobstructed in the 3D view if so desired; as shown in Figure 10.22, it can be very informative.

FIGURE 10.22
Showing the reinforcement in 3D but unobstructed in the view by the concrete

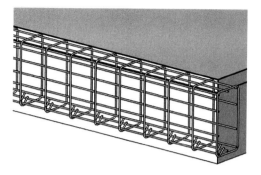

Revit Structure, as you can see, allows a tremendous amount of flexibility in terms of allowing you to model rebar as efficiently as possible, while still maintaining a true 3D modeling environment. This procedure works quite well until you come to a situation where the bars provided by Revit Structure do not provide enough choices to model a specific situation you may have. It is here that Revit Structure allows you to sketch your own rebar shape and add it to the project.

Sketching Rebar

The first time you start using the new Rebar Shape Browser, you will discover that there is no way Revit Structure could possibly include every shape possible — especially in situations where one component needs to be doweled into another. To sketch rebar in a wall, beam, slab, or foundation, simply select the component that is to receive the reinforcement. On the Reinforcement panel, select Place Rebar Parallel to Work Plane. Then on the Place Rebar tab, click the Sketch Rebar button. Revit Structure will prompt you to select the item you want to place the reinforcement in again. Once you select the object, you can then freely sketch the reinforcement. For example, you might use this method for doweling a foundation wall into a footing, as shown in Figure 10.23. You may notice that as you are drafting, if you have a 90-degree corner, Revit Structure will add the to-scale bend radius for you. Revit Structure knows you are drawing a rebar, so it stands to reason that things like this will be automatic.

 Real World Scenario

LOOK OUT FOR THE HOLE!

The ability to sketch rebar around a slab or wall opening is indispensible. Many times, modelers have faced reinforcement of massive openings created in demolition projects where the rebar needed to be carefully placed and counted around these openings. The ability to draw the bars, and space them so there was a bar counted on both sides of the wall, dramatically increased the accuracy of the quantity takeoffs and even reduced the time required to do the drafting.

One nice feature included with the rebar modeling tool is that it will automatically add the new rebar sketch to the Rebar Shape Browser for future use in this model, as shown in Figure 10.24.

The new rebar that was created has the same intelligence as the default rebar shapes. If you select the rebar you create, you will see in the Options bar that you can still specify a unique spacing layout for each instance of the reinforcement. Also, if you select the new reinforcement and click the Element Properties button, you will see that you can change the rebar size as well as the dimensions (A through R), as Figure 10.25 shows.

FIGURE 10.23
Using the rebar sketch method is simple enough even for standard conditions. For complex conditions, it is a must.

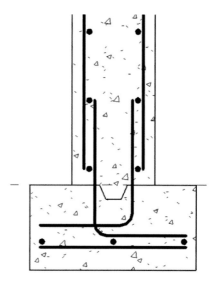

FIGURE 10.24
The newly added rebar shape

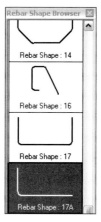

Although it seems we have explored all the methods there are for placing reinforcement into a model, there are more to go. Suppose you wanted to reinforce an entire slab in one shot. Or perhaps there are perimeter conditions you need to add to the model. Revit Structure will allow you to do these tasks with commands specific to each situation.

Reinforcing an Area

With the Area Reinforcement tool, Revit Structure will allow you to place rebar in an entire slab or wall in one action, thus eliminating the need for toiling over exact placement and configuration. However, it should be noted that area reinforcement is not visible in a 3D view.

FIGURE 10.25

The rebar's Instance Properties dialog box allows you to edit any segment dimension.

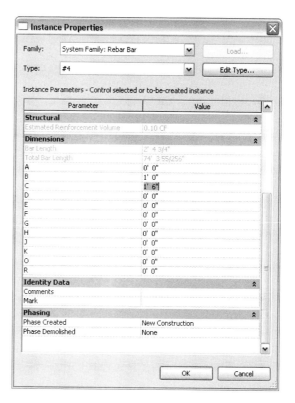

To place area reinforcement in a slab, you will need to be in the plan view where the slab is shown. Once there, you select the slab that is to be reinforced. Once you do, the Reinforcement tools appear on the Reinforcement panel. Click the Area Reinforcement button shown in Figure 10.26.

FIGURE 10.26

The Area Reinforcement button on the Reinforcement panel

This tool will put you into a Sketch mode. On the Ribbon, you can use Pick Lines tool and start selecting the edges of the slab. The first line you click will have two shorter lines on either side, similar to the sketch lines when using the Beam System tool. This indicates the slab direction. If this is incorrect, you can change the direction by clicking the Major Direction tool on the Draw panel, shown in Figure 10.27, and then pick a new starting edge line.

FIGURE 10.27

The Major Direction tool defines where the area reinforcement begins.

Another essential tool is the Area Properties button located on the Element panel of the Create Reinforcement Boundary tab. This opens a dialog box that will gain you access to the configuration and type of reinforcement that is going into your slab. A nice thing about the properties in area reinforcement is that you can specify that the reinforcement have two different layers (with separate properties for the type and spacing of the major and minor bars in each layer), as shown in Figure 10.28. Each of these layers can be turned off if one or the other is not needed (see Figure 10.29).

FIGURE 10.28

Specifying the layer configuration in the Instance properties for area reinforcement

Parameter	Value
Layers	⌃
Top Major Direction	☑
Top Major Bar Type	#6
Top Major Hook Type	None
Top Major Hook Orientation	Down
Top Major Spacing	1' 0"
Top Major Number Of Lines	5
Top Minor Direction	☑
Top Minor Bar Type	#5
Top Minor Hook Type	None
Top Minor Hook Orientation	Down
Top Minor Spacing	1' 0"
Top Minor Number Of Lines	5
Bottom Major Direction	☑
Bottom Major Bar Type	#6
Bottom Major Hook Type	None
Bottom Major Hook Orientation	Up
Bottom Major Spacing	0' 8"
Bottom Major Number Of Lines	5
Bottom Minor Direction	☑
Bottom Minor Bar Type	#5
Bottom Minor Hook Type	None
Bottom Minor Hook Orientation	Up
Bottom Minor Spacing	1' 0"
Bottom Minor Number Of Lines	5

FIGURE 10.29

Area reinforcement in the slab section shows both top and bottom bars (remember this was added in a plan view).

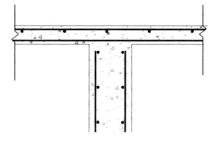

In the Instance Properties dialog box, you are also given the choice to change the additional top and bottom offsets. These will be added to the cover settings, and Revit Structure will place the reinforcement at the specified offset. For example, if the cover setting for the slab is $1\frac{1}{2}''$ down from the top face, and you specify an additional offset of 1", the rebar will be placed $2\frac{1}{2}''$ below the top face. This can be handy if there is a finish or a topping you wish to allow for.

In plan, the area reinforcement will automatically be tagged. This behavior can be changed, and a different custom tag can be specified. Select the Annotate tab on the Ribbon ➤ Tag panel drop-down ➤ Loaded Tags. In the resulting dialog box, you'll see a category for Structural Area Reinforcement, as shown in Figure 10.30. This is the tag that Revit Structure will automatically apply to the area reinforcement in plan views.

The tag will appear automatically, as shown in Figure 10.31. If you do not want to tag the item, you can delete the tag — it will not affect the actual reinforcement.

Area reinforcement is perfect for reinforcement of structural slabs, but it can be applied to walls as well. The procedure is nearly the same.

FIGURE 10.30
The Structural Area
Reinforcement category
with the automatic Area
Reinforcement Tag

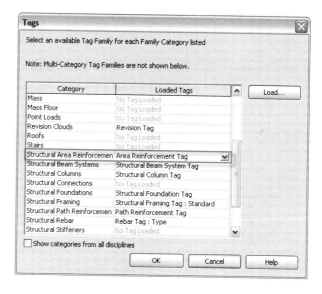

FIGURE 10.31
The automatic plan tag
that Revit Structure
inserts as you place area
reinforcement

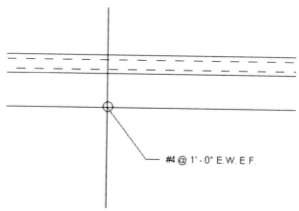

PLACING AREA REINFORCEMENT IN WALLS

Placing area reinforcement in a wall is sometimes preferred over having to place bars individually and then having to specify the spacing. Each method can have its advantages, and after you know how to do both, you can determine which process best suits your situation.

To place area reinforcement in a wall, you must first display an elevation that is looking straight at the wall that is to be reinforced.

THERE IS A DIFFERENT WAY

This chapter has enforced the procedure of selecting the item that will receive the reinforcement and then clicking the proper tool. You can, however, utilize the Home tab ➤ Reinforcement panel and choose from there as well.

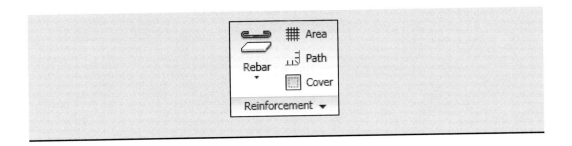

In the elevation, you can select the wall and click Area Reinforcement found on the Modify Walls tab. This will display the Create Reinforcement Boundary tab, where you can create sketch lines. At this point, you can sketch the perimeter of the reinforcement, similar to placing the reinforcement in a floor (see Figure 10.32). Make sure you do not exceed the actual boundary of the wall when doing this.

FIGURE 10.32
The area reinforcement sketch profile. The double lines on the left sketch line indicate the major direction of the bars.

Once the sketch is finished, click Finish Area. Now if you cut a section through this wall, you will see that the reinforcement is laid out as expected, as shown in Figure 10.33. If the bar layering is reversed from what was expected, you will need to use a view in which you can see the reinforcement (such as a section). Select the area reinforcement, and click Edit Boundary from the Modify Structural Area Reinforcement tab. You will then be sent back to any elevation view. In the resulting view, you can change the Major Direction setting as needed.

Now that the mass areas are reinforced, we can move on to reinforcement of specific areas, such as providing additional dowels to the perimeter for the slab by adding what Revit Structure refers to as *path reinforcement*.

Applying Path Reinforcement

There are occasions where you are going to need to reinforce the edges of a slab independent of area reinforcement. This is where the Path Reinforcement tool comes in handy. Like the other Revit Structure Reinforcement tools, you apply path reinforcement to a slab by first selecting a floor that needs the reinforcement and then clicking the Path tool (as shown in Figure 10.34), or you can click the Path tool directly from the Home tab, followed by making a floor selection.

While in Sketch mode, it is a good idea to click the Path Properties tool and then use the Instance Properties dialog box for the path reinforcement to configure the bars, as shown in Figure 10.35. Within the dialog box, you can specify in which direction the bars will hook. By default, the bars are hooking Up. If the wall was in a slab-supporting situation, you would need to change the hook direction to Down so that the bars could hook into the top of the bearing wall. Also, you can turn on alternating bars. This allows you to stagger the bars at whatever increment you have specified. The hooks are specified at each end of the bar.

FIGURE 10.33
Area wall reinforcement, as shown in section

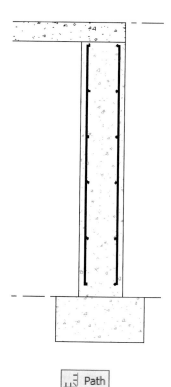

FIGURE 10.34
The Path button as shown on the Reinforcement panel

FIGURE 10.35
Parameters for edge reinforcement allow you to further control the function of the bars, such as primary spacing and the addition of alternating bars.

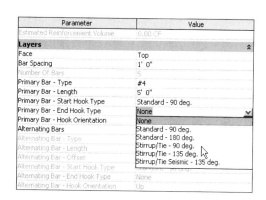

Once you have finished adjusting the properties, click OK to return to the view. From there, you can use the Draw panel to create lines along the perimeter of the reinforcement, as shown in Figure 10.36.

Once you've sketched the path, you can click Finish Path, and Revit Structure places the reinforcement into the slab. It is a good idea to cut a section through the path reinforcement and look at the spacing and the bar configuration, as shown in Figure 10.37. If it is not as expected, you can select the bars in that view, and click the Element Properties button in the Modify Structural Path

Reinforcement panel. You can then configure the properties without having to go back into Draw mode. Figure 10.37 shows the reinforcement with a 2″ offset for the alternating bars.

FIGURE 10.36
Sketching the path
reinforcement

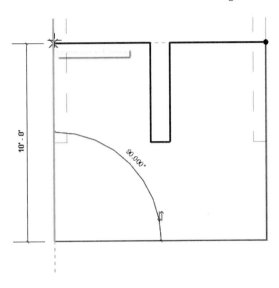

FIGURE 10.37
The slab in section view

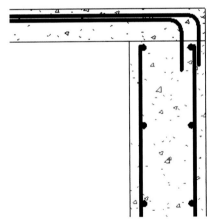

The plan view will show the depth of the bars as well as the tags and symbols. You may not want to show all of this. For example, you can select the path reinforcement outline and use the right-click context menu to select Hide in View ➤ Elements, as shown in Figure 10.38.

Another item to mention in all reinforcement is the end hook configurations, as shown in Figure 10.39. You can override the end hooks of any reinforcement by simply selecting the bars and clicking the end hook icon that appears. Many times this is an easier method than trying to specify an end hook condition in the Instance Properties dialog box. You may find it necessary to be able to graphically see in which direction the bars are going. It is also sometimes hard to determine which end of the bar you are trying to configure. This on-screen toggle makes the task much easier.

Compared to simple drafting performed in AutoCAD, adding reinforcement to a Revit Structure model is not harder but is certainly different. With the many options available to aid in the placement, this process is obviously beneficial. Also, there is a downstream benefit. As you will see in Chapter 11, reinforcement can easily be scheduled and quantified after it has been placed in the model. This is a tremendous benefit. Keep in mind, however, that if you are to provide scheduling and quantities, you must be diligent in rebar placement. You can expect Revit Structure to report back only what you put into the model.

FIGURE 10.38

Hiding the path rein-forcement in a plan view

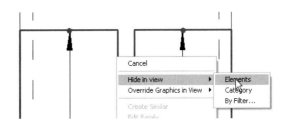

FIGURE 10.39

End hook configuration shown with the dowels extending into the top of the foundation wall

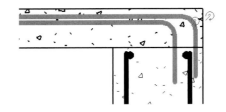

EXERCISE: USING REVIT REINFORCEMENT

In this exercise, you can either use the Revit Structure model provided at the book's companion web page at www.sybex.com/go/masteringrevitstructure2010, or you can follow along with your own model. The object of this exercise is to get you comfortable using the Revit Structure reinforcement and to make you never want to go back to drafting again. To start, follow these instructions:

1. Open the file called `reinforcement model.rvt` from the book's companion website. You may substitute your own model if you wish.

2. The first procedure is to configure the settings so the reinforcement looks correct. To do this, activate the Manage tab ➢ Settings ➢ Object Styles.

3. Starting from the top of the list, change the following line weights (the first value is Projection, and the second is Cut):

   Floors: **2,2**

   Structural Area Reinforcement: **4,4**

   Structural Foundations: **2,2**

   Structural Framing: **1,2**

   Structural Path Reinforcement: **4,4**

   Structural Rebar: **4,4**

   Walls: **2,2**

4. Click OK to close.

The next order of business is to place area reinforcement in the slab. To do this, use the 1ST FLOOR level view and select the slab. You may have to select an area around the corner of the model and click the Filter button on the Ribbon. Once you're in the Filter dialog box, select only Floors and click OK.

1. On the Reinforcement panel of the Modify Floors tab of the Ribbon, click the Area button.

2. From the Draw panel, click the Rebar Line button. (It should be on by default.)

3. Then click the Pick Lines tool from the Draw/Pick gallery.

4. Select all the outside edges of the slab. Remember that you must have a completely closed loop with no gaps or overlapping lines. If needed, use selection filters to select the floor object.

5. Click the Area Properties button.

6. Verify the Layout Rule is set to Maximum Spacing.

7. Keep the rest of the defaults the same. Remember, you can always go back and change the properties after you review a section through the model.

8. Click OK. Then click Finish Area to complete the placement.

9. Revit Structure will place the rebar into the slab. Create a new section through the slab.

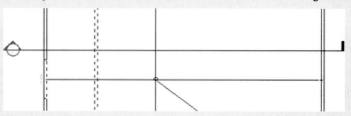

10. Create a callout of the right side of the section where the 12″ wall/beam meets the 10″ wall extending down to the footing. Make the callout's scale $\frac{1}{2}'' = 1'\text{-}0''$.

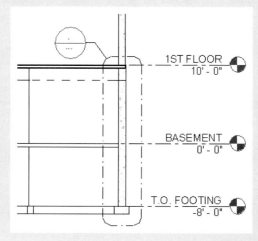

11. Open the callout view. Select the 12″ concrete bearing wall.

12. Click the Place Rebar Parallel to Work Plane button on the Ribbon.

13. In the Rebar Shape Browser, select Rebar Shape: S5. Use the spacebar to set the hooks to the top and pointing to the left. Select the rebar and grip-stretch the ends into the slab.

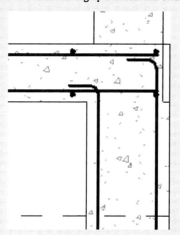

Now that the rebar is "roughed in," you can alter its behavior by accessing the instance properties.

1. Select the new rebar, and click the Element Properties button.

2. For the Rebar Set category, set the Layout Rule to Maximum Spacing, and set the Spacing to 1′-0″.

3. Click Edit Type.

4. Click Duplicate.

5. Name the rebar **#4 with 12″ hooks**.

6. Under Hook Lengths, click the Edit button.

7. Make Stirrup/Tie – 90 deg equal to 1′-0″.

8. Click OK three times to close all open dialog boxes.

9. Select the same foundation wall again.

10. Click the Place Rebar Perpendicular to Work Plane button.

11. Select Rebar Shape: 00.

12. Press the spacebar once to orient the bar vertically. This change will not be noticeable.

13. Place the bar at the top cover alignment line and to the right of the vertical bar. Click the Modify button to stop bar placement and select the new rebar itself.

14. Use the Options bar and set the Layout setting to Maximum Spacing and the Spacing to 1′-0″.

15. Mirror the bars to the left side using the centerline of the wall.

16. Pan down to the where the wall bears on the footing.

17. Select the S5 bar and grip-stretch it out of the footing.

18. Select the horizontal bars and do the same.

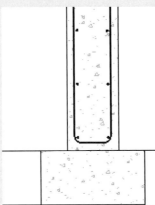

19. Select the footing, and click the Place Rebar Perpendicular to Work Plane button.

20. Select Rebar Shape: 00.

21. Place the rebar to the bottom left of the footing in the corner of the cover alignments. Cancel Placement and select the bar.

22. Change the Layout setting to Fixed Number.

23. Change the Quantity setting to **3**.

24. Select the 12″ foundation wall.

25. Click the Place Rebar Parallel to Work Plane button.

26. On the Ribbon, click the Sketch Rebar button.

27. Select the wall again.

28. Draw in a hooked dowel extending from the second bar into the footing.

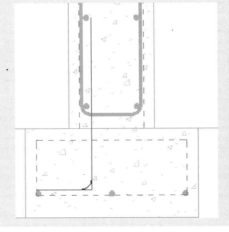

29. Click Finish Rebar. Notice that the dowel is now added to the Rebar Shape Browser.

You can now perform common drafting tasks to repeat the efforts without going through the Instance Properties dialog box.

1. Change the Spacing setting to Maximum Spacing.

2. Change the spacing to 1′-0″.

3. Mirror the dowel about the centerline of the wall.

4. Select all rebar you have put into the model.

5. Click Element Properties and then click the View Visibility States button.

6. Check View Unobscured for all 3D Views.

7. Check View as Solid.

8. Click OK to close. Click OK to close the Instance Properties dialog box.

9. Display the default 3D view.

10. Change the view Detail Level setting to Fine.

11. If needed, change the Model Graphics Style setting to Shading with Edges.

12. Click the Show Thin Lines button on the View tab.

You can now see the massive amount of steel that goes into a wall like this. All reinforcements are generated using a section view. It is good to keep in mind that this section was generated by using tools that are no more difficult to use than those you'd use in actual drafting. As a matter of fact, most of these tools are much easier to use than those you'd use in standard drafting. You do not have to add a radius to bends, and you can clearly specify hook lengths as well. As you will see in the next chapter, this reinforcement can be put into a quantity takeoff and a reinforcement schedule. As you learn to draft, you will see that this reinforcement can be tagged automatically, allowing you to maintain consistency throughout the project.

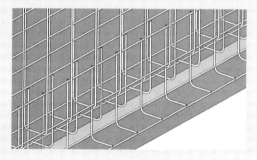

The Bottom Line

Configure rebar settings.   In Revit Structure you can place reinforcement as actual objects as opposed to simple drafting. To do this correctly, however, you need to extensively configure the rebar settings for graphics as well as performance.

Master It Walls, footings, and slabs have cover settings that allow you to place reinforcement in a more organized and accurate approach. How is this done?

Model a 3D rebar. Although Revit Structure uses a modeling approach, it is often necessary to be able to sketch reinforcement first and then add it to the 3D Shape Browser once it is completed.

Master It Placing 3D reinforcement can be done in two different ways. Describe both.

Add rebar shapes. By default in Revit Structure, you have a multitude of reinforcements to choose from. These shapes are preloaded into the template file you are using. Revit Structure allows for the importing of additional shapes.

Master It You may be working in a model that was created in an older Revit Structure version. The model will not have any rebar shapes. How do you import the shapes?

Chapter 11

Schedules and Quantities

Now that you are comfortable with modeling in a 3D environment, it is time to delve into the often talked about but never fully explained *fourth dimension*. That's right, the fourth dimension, which refers to the nongraphical side of Revit Structure. Using schedules and quantities allows us to keep track of all of the components that compose our model.

You may ask yourself, or even be asked by someone else, "Why are we using BIM over standard 2D drafting?" We were successful before — why take the risk? The answer, as it pertains to the topic of this chapter, is simple.

The effort expended to model your building begins to be rewarded by the ability to mine the vast amount of data you have created. The fact that in five minutes you can create a comprehensive steel quantity takeoff that is accurate and will adjust to changes in the model is priceless. To take this one step further, typically a firm is going to have predefined schedules and quantity takeoffs in the project before the first beam or column is placed. This means during the life of the project, this information can be viewed or printed literally at the push of a button. Not bad for having to do nothing more than place elements into a model.

In this chapter you will learn to:

- ◆ Create schedules
- ◆ Create schedule keys
- ◆ Create material takeoffs
- ◆ Export schedules to Microsoft Excel
- ◆ Create keynote legends

The Scheduling Basics

You do not need a "populated" model to create schedules. In fact, schedules can and should be provided in a template. The modeler can then focus on the modeling process while the schedules and quantity takeoffs are being populated behind the scenes.

Most every project will have different requirements for the schedule output data. In many cases, schedules are used to simply keep track of the design. This is possible because in Revit a schedule is a two-way street. Any changes to the model will immediately update the schedule. Any changes in the schedule will immediately update the model. For example, if there was a group of beam sizes you needed to change in a certain area, you could open the schedule, locate the beams, and change them right there in the schedule. This updates not only the schedule you are currently in but also the plans, elevations, and sections. This is typical Revit behavior. If you make a change in one place, other areas of the model are also influenced by the changes.

To follow along with this exercise you can open the `Scheduling Basics.rvt` file from this book's website. To create a schedule, navigate to the View tab of the Ribbon ➤ Create panel ➤ Schedules drop-down ➤ Schedule/Quantities, as illustrated in Figure 11.1.

FIGURE 11.1
The Schedule/Quantities button is on the View tab.

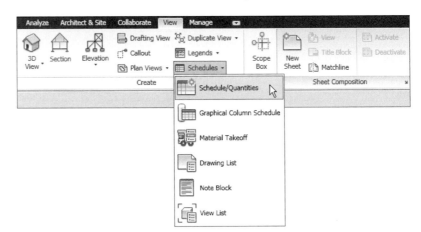

Typically the schedule of choice will be a Schedule/Quantities form of schedule. Other forms are the Graphical Column Schedule, which shows an actual view of project columns in elevation overlaid on a schedule. The Material Takeoff Schedule can quantify and total materials by volume. Finally, you can create schedules populated with a sheet list, project model symbols, and lists of the various views in the model.

Once you are presented with the New Schedule dialog, it suddenly becomes apparent there is a multitude of category choices.

ITEM COUNTS ON THE FLY!

If you choose to use a multicategory schedule, it will schedule every building component in the model. Having a multicategory schedule numerically keeping track of the model elements can be a fantastic reference as the structure is being designed. It may never be put on a sheet for issue, but it will always be there as an internal reference.

After you start the Schedule/Quantities command, you will need to make a choice in the Category area of the New Schedule dialog box, as illustrated in Figure 11.2. If, for example, you would like a schedule of all the structural framing elements in the project, you can select Structural Framing from the Category list on the left side of the dialog box. Once you choose a category, click OK.

This will bring you to the Schedule Properties dialog box, as illustrated in Figure 11.3. Once this dialog box opens, you will see a series of tabs across the top. The first tab is the Fields tab. It is the default tab when you start a new schedule for good reason. You obviously need to add some fields to tell Revit Structure which parameters to include in the schedule.

At this point, you will probably want to decide whether this schedule is going on the drawing sheets or if it will be just for internal use as the model is being created. The desired result will have an impact on what information needs to be included in the schedule and how it is arranged, among other things. Whatever its purpose, there are five basic groups of options when creating a schedule.

FIGURE 11.2
Choosing a category

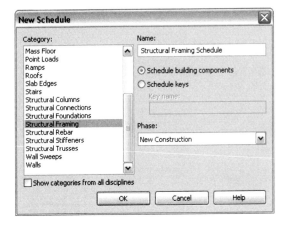

FIGURE 11.3
The Schedule Properties dialog box

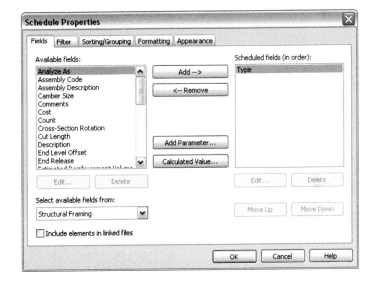

Fields This tab determines which parameters (fields) will be added to the schedule and the order in which they will appear. These form the columns of the schedule. You can also create new parameters to store information and make calculations based on other fields in the schedule.

Filter This tab determines which model elements will appear in the schedule. Filters can be used to exclude any unwanted elements or to specify which elements are desired in the schedule.

Sorting/Grouping This tab determines how the chosen fields will be arranged and grouped.

Formatting This tab determines how the data is formatted and the format of any mathematical calculations.

Appearance This tab determines how the schedule will look in terms of font types and sizes. The border and grid of the schedule are addressed here as well.

These groups are explained in detail in the following sections.

Setting Up the Fields

The Fields tab is broken into two columns. The column to the left shows all of the available fields in the chosen category. For this example the category is Structural Framing, so the available choices reflect this category. The column to the right is a list of scheduled fields. These are parameters that have been moved from the left column for inclusion in the schedule. To add a field to the schedule, simply highlight an available field in the left column and click the Add button. You can also double-click an item to move it to the opposite side.

For example, if you wanted to find all of your structural framing based on Type, Cut Length, and Count, you would add these three parameters to the Scheduled Fields column on the right of the Fields tab, as shown in Figure 11.4.

FIGURE 11.4
The scheduled fields

Once a field is added to the Scheduled Fields column, the Remove button becomes available. This can be used to remove any unwanted fields from the schedule.

When you add fields to the Schedule Fields column, the fields are displayed in the order in which they will be displayed in the completed schedule, but you do not have to worry about the order in which they are added. Below the Schedule Fields column you will see buttons that allow you to move the fields up or down to adjust their order, as illustrated in Figure 11.4.

Once the needed fields are moved to the Schedule Fields column and are in the correct order, you can click OK. This will create the new schedule view, as illustrated by the example in Figure 11.5.

To return to the Schedule Properties dialog box, first right-click anywhere in the schedule view and select View Properties, as illustrated in Figure 11.6. Alternatively, any time the schedule view is not active, you can locate and right-click on the schedule view name in the Project Browser. Select Properties from the resulting shortcut menu to bring up the Properties dialog box for the schedule.

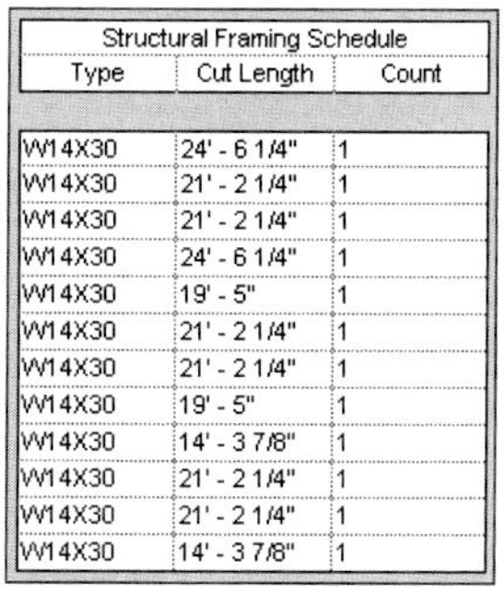

Structural Framing Schedule		
Type	Cut Length	Count
W14X30	24' - 6 1/4"	1
W14X30	21' - 2 1/4"	1
W14X30	21' - 2 1/4"	1
W14X30	24' - 6 1/4"	1
W14X30	19' - 5"	1
W14X30	21' - 2 1/4"	1
W14X30	21' - 2 1/4"	1
W14X30	19' - 5"	1
W14X30	14' - 3 7/8"	1
W14X30	21' - 2 1/4"	1
W14X30	21' - 2 1/4"	1
W14X30	14' - 3 7/8"	1

FIGURE 11.5
The schedule view

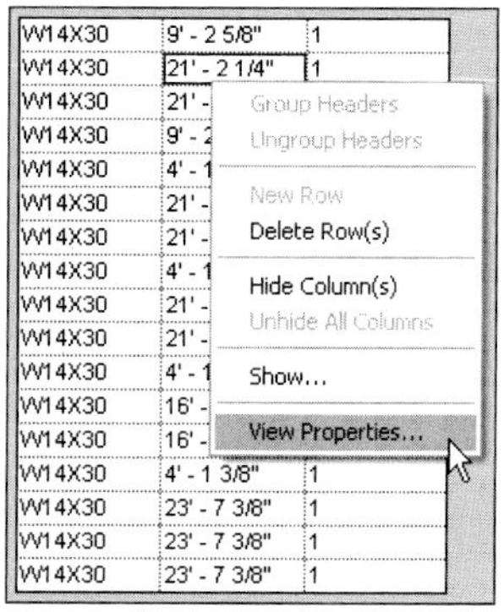

FIGURE 11.6
Right-click to return to the Properties dialog box.

If you have become accustomed to using a keyboard shortcut, for example, View Properties as VP, don't bother trying it here as it doesn't work in schedule views. Revit assumes you will be using the keyboard directly for data entry and ignores keyboard shortcuts because they are indistinguishable from normal keyboard input.

After selecting View Properties (or Properties) from the shortcut menu, you will see the Instance Properties dialog box, which will list the various tabs from the Schedule Properties dialog box under Other, as illustrated in Figure 11.7. Clicking any of the long Edit buttons in the Value column will take you to the corresponding tab in the Schedule Properties dialog box. Once there, you are free to navigate to any of the tabs.

Just because this schedule appears to simply be a list of items, it does not mean it is not live. If the field contains an editable value, you can click into the cell and edit the information. This interaction is a two-way exchange. If you change a value here, you are changing it in the model. Suggesting that you be careful here is the understatement of the century. Since all model elements associated with the schedule field will change accordingly with an edit, you should make sure any changes made in a schedule are deliberate and accurate.

Because Revit Structure acts as a database, creating a schedule filter is similar to creating a query within a specific schedule form. You can tell Revit what you want to see and how you want to see it. Revit will then display that information. Once you have included the desired fields, you can apply a filter.

FIGURE 11.7
Instance Properties dialog box

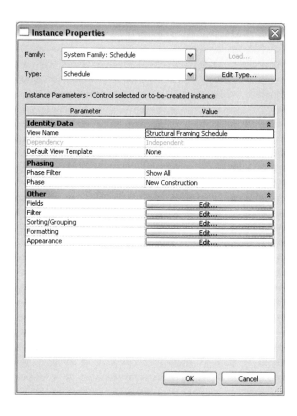

Applying a Filter

The second tab in the Schedule Properties dialog box is Filter. This is a different form of filtering than that used for Visibility/Graphic Overrides but just as powerful. The more fields you are using in the schedule, the more powerful this feature becomes. Filters are used to narrow down the elements shown on the schedule to exactly what is needed.

 **Real World Scenario**

FILTERING BEAMS BASED ON LENGTH

The Filter feature allows the design team to get specific information about the model elements in short order. For example, a schedule filter can be used to find beams that span more than a specific length. Once these beams are identified and isolated in the schedule, they can be checked by the design team and given a larger size if needed. This helps track possible problem areas and makes them reportable and printable for anyone, including project managers, to review.

Depending on the project type, it is possible that a given length of beam can actually be related to a portion of the building. Once on one of our projects, the engineer came back after much modeling and decided that the shortest beam size we were using, for filler and edge conditions, wasn't going to be deep enough for the connection requirements. So I quickly created a schedule where I could filter by beams shorter than 10 feet and see the size as well. It was a quick process from that schedule to then to edit a single schedule cell for beam size and have hundreds of beams changed.

To access the filters, click the Filter tab, as illustrated in Figure 11.8. In the Filter By: category, you can then select the field you would like to filter with. This is telling Revit that you want to see only the items that match these criteria. Any other elements in the model that don't meet the specified conditions will be excluded from this schedule. For this example, to find all beams of a certain length, you would filter by Cut Length.

To the right of the Filter By: option is a drop-down list that allows you to add a condition. To find all framing members that exceed 24'-0", you can select Is Greater Than from the drop-down list. Once this is set, you can then select or input the specific increment from the drop-down below the Filter By: category. In this case the distance would be 24' 0". These settings are illustrated in Figure 11.8.

FIGURE 11.8
The Filter feature

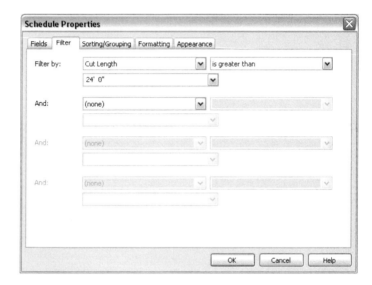

In many cases, you may wish to filter based on additional criteria. Note that each element must meet the conditions specified in the filter for it to be displayed. As more parameters are used to filter by, you increase the risk of having absolutely nothing show up in the schedule. To prevent this from happening, be sure you are targeting the exact information you would like to filter by and nothing more. If you find yourself with nothing showing in the schedule, back out of some of the specified filters until you can see data again.

Notice in Figure 11.9 that there are no framing members shorter than 24'-0". You will notice that each element is independently listed. For some scheduled items, this may be exactly what you want to see. For others, such as finding the number of beams that exceed 24'-0", you may want all identical members to be listed together. You can accomplish this within the Sorting/Grouping tab.

Activating Sorting and Grouping

The Sorting/Grouping tab of the Schedule Properties dialog box allows you to organize the schedule data. Here you can produce line item counts and totals. You can also tell Revit to combine similar instances of elements into one row and report grand totals as well as an overall count of the elements.

On the Sorting/Grouping tab, the first thing you will see is the Sort By: field followed by multiple Then By: fields. This allows you to create a sorting hierarchy. Typically, a schedule's first sorting criteria will be based on either its name or type. The second criteria can then be determined by what differentiates these similar elements. In the case of the example illustrated in Figure 11.10, the framing members are sorted first by Type, then by Cut Length.

FIGURE 11.9
24'- 0" minimum

Structural Framing Schedule		
Type	Cut Length	Count
W14X30	24' - 6 1/4"	1
W14X30	24' - 6 1/4"	1
W14X30	24' - 6 1/4"	1
W14X30	24' - 6 1/4"	1
W14X30	24' - 6 1/4"	1
W14X30	24' - 6 1/4"	1
W14X30	24' - 6 1/4"	1
W14X30	24' - 6 1/4"	1
W14X30	24' - 6 1/4"	1
W14X30	24' - 6 1/4"	1
W14X30	24' - 6 1/4"	1
W14X30	24' - 6 1/4"	1
W14X30	24' - 6 1/4"	1
W14X30	24' - 6 1/4"	1
W14X30	24' - 6 1/4"	1
W14X30	24' - 6 1/4"	1
W14X30	24' - 6 1/4"	1
W14X30	24' - 6 1/4"	1
W14X30	24' - 6 1/4"	1
W14X30	24' - 6 1/4"	1
W14X30	24' - 6 1/4"	1

FIGURE 11.10
The Sorting/Grouping tab

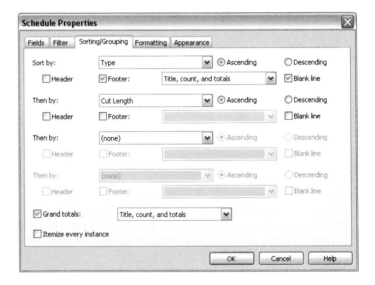

For each group, you can add a header or footer. This helps organize the display of information. A header will display the common sort criteria of the group. For example, if sorted by Type, the type name would be displayed as the header of the grouping. If you choose to provide a footer for each group, you can display the title, counts, and totals of the group or a few combinations of the three. To the right of the Header/Footer options is a Blank Line option. You can check this to insert a blank line between each entry to further break up the element listings. See Figure 11.10.

Toward the bottom of the dialog box, you will see a check box that allows you add grand totals to the end of the schedule. The grand total is calculated by counting every element eligible for the schedule regardless of its sort criteria. Just below the Grand Totals check box is the Itemize Every Instance check box. If unchecked, this option will group all identical elements in one line. See Figure 11.10.

Adding a footer will allow you to display a total count of elements that meet each sorting criteria, among other things. There will be times where you need these totals at the end of each group. In those cases, you will almost certainly require the grand totals for the project as well. See Figure 11.11 for an example of a sorted schedule with the previously implemented filter removed.

FIGURE 11.11

A sorted schedule

Structural Framing Schedule		
Type	Cut Length	Count
14K1	7' - 7 7/8"	2
14K1	8' - 11 1/8"	2
14K1	11' - 5 3/4"	2
14K1	12' - 9"	2
14K1	14' - 0 3/8"	2
14K1	16' - 7"	2
14K1	17' - 10 1/4"	2
14K1	18' - 3 1/4"	1
14K1	18' - 3 1/4"	1
14K1	19' - 1 1/2"	2
14K1	19' - 6 5/8"	1
14K1	19' - 6 5/8"	1
14K1	20' - 9 7/8"	1
14K1	20' - 9 7/8"	1
14K1	21' - 8 1/8"	2
14K1	22' - 1 1/8"	15
14K1	22' - 1 1/8"	15
14K1	22' - 11 1/2"	2
14K1	24' - 2 3/4"	2
14K1: 58		
W12X26	1' - 10 1/8"	22
W12X26	3' - 1 3/8"	22
W12X26: 44		
W14X30	4' - 1 3/8"	44
W14X30	6' - 11 1/4"	20
W14X30	8' - 2 5/8"	20
W14X30	9' - 2 5/8"	22
W14X30	10' - 9 1/4"	20
W14X30	12' - 0 1/2"	20
W14X30	13' - 3 7/8"	20
W14X30	14' - 3 7/8"	22
W14X30	15' - 10 3/8"	20
W14X30	16' - 0 1/8"	22
W14X30	17' - 1 3/4"	20
W14X30	17' - 6 3/4"	20
W14X30	18' - 5"	20
W14X30	18' - 10"	20
W14X30	19' - 5"	22
W14X30	20' - 1 3/8"	20
W14X30	20' - 11 5/8"	20
W14X30	21' - 1 3/8"	22
W14X30	21' - 2 1/4"	110
W14X30	21' - 5 1/2"	300
W14X30	22' - 3"	20
W14X30	23' - 0 1/8"	44
W14X30	23' - 1"	154
W14X30	23' - 6 1/4"	20
W14X30	23' - 7 3/8"	132
W14X30	24' - 6 1/4"	22
W14X30: 1196		
Grand total: 1298		

Improving the Formatting

On the Formatting tab, you can specify the format of each field of the schedule. This gives you additional control over how the information will be presented on the printed sheet. The left side of the tab displays the fields you have added to the schedule. The right side contains the formatting choices:

Heading   This is a text field that allows you to define the heading of the column. This allows you to name and control capitalization of the field's heading in the schedule independent of the parameter name, which is the default heading value. You can also change this by clicking in the heading cell within the schedule view.

Heading Orientation   This option sets the rotation of the heading to either horizontal or vertical. This is typically kept horizontal, but some types of schedules may require a vertical heading.

Alignment   This option horizontally justifies the heading text left, center, or right.

Field Formatting   This option pertains to parameters that are affected by Project Unit settings. Click the Field Format button with a qualified parameter highlighted to gain access to the Format dialog box, as illustrated in Figure 11.12. This is similar to the Project Units Format dialog box pertaining to length and can be used to override the project settings for each qualified field within the schedule. If you want to format a particular parameter value differently than the default, you can uncheck the Use Project Settings control at the top of the dialog box. This is useful for parameters such as beam width, where you may want to see the value in inches, as opposed to the project in general, where you want lengths to be shown in feet and inches.

FIGURE 11.12
The Format dialog box

When enabled, the Calculate Totals option of the Schedule Properties dialog box will return a total for all the elements represented by the schedule row. For example, if you had several identical beams that were represented by one row in the schedule and you wanted the Length parameter to return the total length of every instance added together, you could get that by checking the Calculate Totals check box. Compare Figure 11.13 to Figure 11.11; now that the Calculate Totals option has been enabled, as shown in Figure 11.14, the Cut Length field now returns the total length for each row. When used in conjunction with the Footer option for the Type group on the Sorting/Grouping tab, the total length of the entire group is displayed in the footer.

FIGURE 11.13

The reformatted schedule

Structural Framing Schedule		
Type	Cut Length	Count
14K1	15' - 3 5/8"	2
14K1	17' - 10 1/4"	2
14K1	22' - 11 1/2"	2
14K1	25' - 6 1/8"	2
14K1	28' - 0 3/4"	2
14K1	33' - 1 7/8"	2
14K1	35' - 8 1/2"	2
14K1	18' - 3 1/4"	1
14K1	18' - 3 1/4"	1
14K1	38' - 3 1/8"	2
14K1	19' - 6 5/8"	1
14K1	19' - 6 5/8"	1
14K1	20' - 9 7/8"	1
14K1	20' - 9 7/8"	1
14K1	43' - 4 3/8"	2
14K1	331' - 5 5/8"	15
14K1	331' - 5 3/4"	15
14K1	45' - 11"	2
14K1	48' - 5 1/2"	2
14K1: 58	1134' - 9 1/4"	
W12X26	40' - 6 1/2"	22
W12X26	68' - 7 1/8"	22
W12X26: 44	109' - 1 5/8"	
W14X30	181' - 2"	44
W14X30	138' - 10 1/8"	20
W14X30	164' - 4 1/8"	20
W14X30	202' - 9 3/4"	22
W14X30	215' - 4 3/8"	20
W14X30	240' - 10 3/8"	20
W14X30	266' - 4 1/2"	20
W14X30	315' - 0 1/2"	22
W14X30	317' - 4 5/8"	20
W14X30	352' - 3 1/4"	22
W14X30	342' - 10 3/4"	20
W14X30	351' - 2 3/4"	20
W14X30	368' - 4 3/4"	20
W14X30	376' - 8 7/8"	20
W14X30	427' - 3 1/4"	22
W14X30	402' - 2 7/8"	20
W14X30	419' - 5"	20
W14X30	464' - 6"	22
W14X30	2330' - 1"	110
W14X30	6436' - 0 3/8"	300
W14X30	444' - 11"	20
W14X30	1012' - 7 5/8"	44
W14X30	3554' - 10"	154
W14X30	470' - 5 1/8"	20
W14X30	3117' - 9 1/4"	132
W14X30	539' - 6"	22
W14X30: 119	23453' - 4 1/2"	
Grand total: 1	24697' - 3 1/2"	

If you do not want the field to be displayed at all, you can check the Hidden Field check box. This option allows the schedule to be sorted and grouped based on the information in this field even if you do not want it to be shown in the schedule view. This should be left unchecked, as illustrated in Figure 11.14, for any fields that are to be displayed in the schedule view or on the drawing sheet. The Hidden Field option can also be enabled from the schedule view. Select any cell in a column or click and drag to select multiple columns, right-click, and select Hide Column(s) from the shortcut menu. All hidden fields can be displayed similarly by right-clicking anywhere in the schedule view and selecting Unhide All Columns from the shortcut menu. Be aware, however, that just as its name implies, this command will unhide all hidden columns indiscriminately. If you do want to display just one hidden column, return to the Schedule Properties dialog box and use the Formatting tab to apply your change.

FIGURE 11.14
The Formatting tab

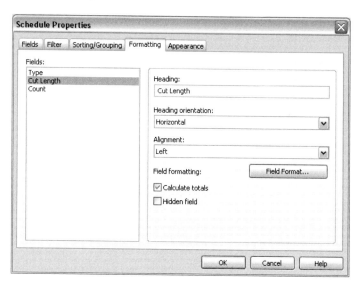

As you continue to modify items in the Schedule Properties dialog box, you will probably need to bounce back and forth between the schedule view and the various tabs quite a bit until you get the information to display the way you need it. However, you don't need to repeat this procedure every time you need a schedule. Once a suitable schedule has been created, you can add it to your project template. This particular schedule is almost ready to be placed on a drawing sheet.

You may need to create some schedules for internal use only, which are not intended to go on a drawing sheet. In that situation the next and final tab is not critical. However, if this schedule is going to be displayed on the drawings, then the Appearance tab will certainly need to be configured.

Defining the Appearance

The Appearance tab is broken into two areas:

◆ Graphics

◆ Text

The Graphics area concentrates on options for the lines that make up the grid of the schedule. The Grid Lines check box controls the display of the grid lines, as illustrated in Figure 11.15. Typically, you will want the grid lines turned on; otherwise it may be hard to tell where one cell ends and the next begins. By default, the grid lines show up very light, but you can control the line style of the grid lines with the adjacent pull-down.

To the right of the grid line and the line weight options is a check box to show the grid in headers/footers/spacers. You will typically want this checked if you are using any of these options. The grid and line weight settings can be seen only when a schedule is placed on a sheet and will not be apparent in the schedule view.

The next option, Outline, allows you to turn on a line that wraps around the entire schedule as well as assign it a different line style. If this is left unchecked, the schedule will not add the outline around the overall schedule; it will only close off the fields on the edge of the schedule. Those fields' outside lines will take on the line style assigned in the Grid Lines option above. Typically, this option is used, as illustrated in Figure 11.15, to make the outline a thicker line weight than the grid, but you can assign any line style you need. Again this option controls the display of the schedule only when it is placed on a sheet.

The Blank Row before Data option will add a blank line to serve as a separator between the schedule header and the data. This line can be added by checking the box.

FIGURE 11.15
The Graphics area of the Appearance tab

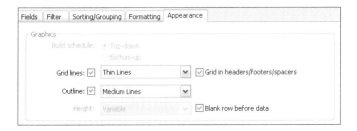

In the Text area of the Appearance tab, you can configure the appearance of the text in the schedule. The first check box is the Show Title option. This allows you to place an overall title at the top of the schedule. The Underline option to the right of the Show Title check box will allow you to override the line style of the line below the title. This option can be used, for example, to make the line under the title the same thickness as the outline, as illustrated in Figure 11.16. If the Underline option is left unchecked, the line under the title will use the grid line setting.

The next check box controls the Show Headers option. This allows you to turn the field headers on or off in the schedule. Typically, this will be left checked, as illustrated in Figure 11.16, but the option to not show headers is available if your particular schedule doesn't require field headers. This option contains Underline and line style selections just like the Show Title option.

Below the Show Headers toggle are the formatting options for Header Text and Body Text. These allow you to set the font and the font size of the headers and body text independently. You can also bold and italicize the text when needed, as illustrated in Figure 11.16.

FIGURE 11.16
Formatting the text

Now that you have explored the five tabs of the Schedule Properties dialog box, you can get some hands-on experience by creating a schedule from the beginning.

EXERCISE: CREATING A SCHEDULE FROM THE BEGINNING

The following exercise will guide you through the steps involved in creating a footing schedule. The procedure given in the example used here can then be applied to your specific needs.

To begin, open the file called `Scheduling Basics.rvt`, provided on this book's website, and follow these steps:

1. With the `Scheduling Basics.rvt` file open, activate the T.O. FOOTING plan view. If you look closely, you'll see that there are two different sizes of rectangular footings.

2. On the View tab, select Schedules ➤ Schedule/Quantities.

3. In the New Schedule dialog box, select Structural Foundations. The other options can remain at their defaults. Click OK.

4. On the Fields tab (the default tab), you can add fields to the schedule. In the Available Fields column on the left, scroll down and select Type.

5. Between the two field columns there is an Add button. Click it. The Type field moves to the Scheduled Fields column. It will now be shown in the schedule.

6. Using the same process, add the Family and Type Mark fields as well. After all fields are chosen, use the Move Up or Move Down buttons to organize them as needed.

7. Navigate to the Filter tab.

8. Filter by Type Mark.

9. In the drop-down list to the right, select Contains.

10. In the input box below the Filter By drop-down list, type the capitalized letter **F**.

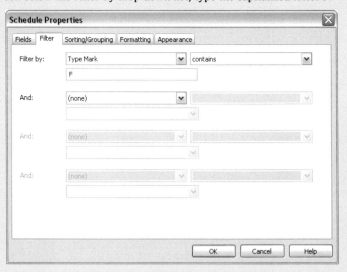

11. Navigate to the Sorting/Grouping tab.

12. Use the Sort By drop-down list and select Type.

13. Check the Footer option and choose Title, Count, and Totals. Also check the Blank Line option.

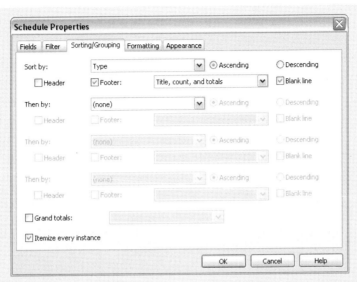

14. Click OK. The schedule is now displayed separated into two groups. Other structural foundation elements that do not have a type mark containing the letter *F* are excluded from this schedule.

Structural Foundation Schedule		
Type	Family	Type Mark
36"x36"x1	Footing-Rectangular	F33
36"x36"x1	Footing-Rectangular	F33
36"x36"x1	Footing-Rectangular	F33
36"x36"x1	Footing-Rectangular	F33
36"x36"x1	Footing-Rectangular	F33
36"x36"x1	Footing-Rectangular	F33
36"x36"x1	Footing-Rectangular	F33
36"x36"x1	Footing-Rectangular	F33
36"x36"x1	Footing-Rectangular	F33
36"x36"x1	Footing-Rectangular	F33
36"x36"x1	Footing-Rectangular	F33
36"x36"x1	Footing-Rectangular	F33
36"x36"x1	Footing-Rectangular	F33
36"x36"x1	Footing-Rectangular	F33
36"x36"x1	Footing-Rectangular	F33
36"x36"x1	Footing-Rectangular	F33
36"x36"x1	Footing-Rectangular	F33
36"x36"x1	Footing-Rectangular	F33
36"x36"x1	Footing-Rectangular	F33
36"x36"x1	Footing-Rectangular	F33
36"x36"x1	Footing-Rectangular	F33
36"x36"x1	Footing-Rectangular	F33
36"x36"x1	Footing-Rectangular	F33
36"x36"x1	Footing-Rectangular	F33
36"x36"x1	Footing-Rectangular	F33
36"x36"x1	Footing-Rectangular	F33
36"x36"x1	Footing-Rectangular	F33
36"x36"x12": 27		
42"x42"x1	Footing-Rectangular	F42
42"x42"x1	Footing-Rectangular	F42
42"x42"x1	Footing-Rectangular	F42
42"x42"x1	Footing-Rectangular	F42
42"x42"x1	Footing-Rectangular	F42
42"x42"x1	Footing-Rectangular	F42
42"x42"x1	Footing-Rectangular	F42
42"x42"x12": 7		

15. At the top of the schedule you will see the headings Type and Family. Click and hold within the Family cell, and drag your mouse to the left, selecting both cells.

16. On the Modify Schedule/Quantities tab of the Ribbon, under Headers, select Group. The headers are now grouped together with a new header of their own.

17. Name the new group header cell **Identification**.

Structural Foundation Schedule		
Identification		
Type	Family	Type Mark

Now that the schedule has been created, you should save this little gem to your standard template. This will prevent the need to re-create a frequently used schedule over and over. Refer to Chapter 2 for methods for creating templates.

Now that you have explored the basics of schedule creation, let's dig a little deeper and add some formulas to certain fields in your schedule that will provide additional functionality.

What Are Calculated Values?

When you add a calculated value, you are adding a field that contains a mathematical formula to your schedule, similar to a formula in a spreadsheet. The big difference is you are not calculating based on the contents of cells such as G2*A4. In Revit the formula is based on parameter values and would read like *Material: Volume * 2*. This would be the volume of whatever material you are scheduling multiplied by 2. A default schedule will only get you so far in terms of the information you may need reported to you, so these calculated values should be added manually as needed. If these are commonly used equations, you should definitely have these calculated values in your office template's schedule(s) so the end user does not have to create them over and over again.

Adding a Calculated Value

A good example of using a calculated value would be in a floor schedule where the designer needs a total floor volume based in cubic yards, with a given waste factor. To follow along with this example, open the `Other Schedules.rvt` file provided on this book's website.

To achieve this, create a new schedule following the steps listed below:

1. Navigate to the View tab of the Ribbon and on the Create panel, select Schedules ➤ Schedule/Quantities.

2. In the New Schedule dialog box, select Floors as the category and click OK.

3. Add the following fields:

- ◆ Level

- ◆ Area

- ◆ Volume

4. On the Fields tab of the Schedule Properties dialog box, you will see a Calculated Value button between the Available Fields and the Scheduled Fields areas, as shown in Figure 11.17. Click this button.

5. In the Calculated Value dialog box shown in Figure 11.18, fill in the name as **Cubic Yards**. Choose Common as the discipline and Volume as the type.

FIGURE 11.17
Adding a calcu-
lated value

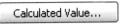
Calculated Value...

6. In the Formula field, enter **(Volume * 0.05) + Volume**. This will take the Volume field and multiply it by a factor of 0.05. This result is then added to the volume again, creating the volume plus the waste factor. See Figure 11.18. Note that references to parameters are case sensitive. Click OK.

7. With the field now created, click the Formatting tab. Select the newly created Cubic Yards field, and click the Field Format button.

FIGURE 11.18
The Calculated Value
dialog box

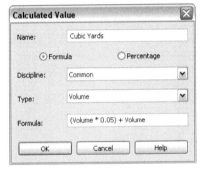

8. In the Format dialog box, uncheck Use Project Settings and set the Units to Cubic Yards, as illustrated in Figure 11.19.

9. Click OK until you are back in the schedule view. You will see the new field, as illustrated in the example shown in Figure 11.20.

FIGURE 11.19
Formatting the new Cal-
culated Value field

FIGURE 11.20
Example of a floor
schedule with a Cal-
culated Value field

Floor Schedule			
Level	Area	Volume	Cubic Yards
Level 1	6819 SF	3409.37 CF	132.59 CY
Level 2	6819 SF	3409.37 CF	132.59 CY
Level 3	6819 SF	3409.37 CF	132.59 CY
Roof	6819 SF	3409.37 CF	132.59 CY
Upper Level	711 SF	355.63 CF	13.83 CY
Upper Level	711 SF	355.63 CF	13.83 CY

As you can see, schedules can be a powerful information source regarding your model. You can use a schedule to edit, or organize, or quantify your model. The key to success is looking for opportunities during your work, as just about anything in your model can be viewed in a schedule form.

Using Schedule Keys

Creating a schedule key requires a slightly different mindset than creating a normal schedule. The purpose of a schedule key is to control multiple parameter values by creating a key designation and applying it to elements directly or within normal schedules. For this example, say you had a building with an expansion joint between the north and south halves. You may want to identify where a particular foundation exists. Let's also say a portion of this particular building was to be built over a lake, which would put the footings in this area below the water table. These are two details that may be of interest to the designer. You can follow along with this exercise by opening the Schedule Key.rvt file from this book's website.

You can create a schedule key with the same command you used to create a regular schedule. On the View tab, on the Create panel of the Ribbon, select Schedules ➤ Schedule/Quantities. For this example, select Structural Foundations in the Category column of the New Schedule dialog box. Now select the Schedule Keys radio button on the right, as illustrated in Figure 11.21. Once you click OK, you will be taken to the Schedule Properties dialog box.

FIGURE 11.21
Creating a schedule key

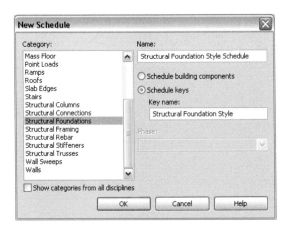

On the Fields tab, you will see only two parameters available to add to the Scheduled Fields list. Additional parameters can be added by clicking the Add Parameter button between the field columns. While you can add parameters by creating project Instance parameters manually, adding them here automatically sets the requirements for use with schedule keys.

The Key Name field will be scheduled by default. Add the Comments parameter to the Scheduled Fields list to use for the water table warning. Now you just need to add one more for the footing location. Click the Add Parameter button between the column fields. Notice the parameter defaults to a Project parameter as well as being an Instance parameter. Name this parameter **Location**, group it under Identity Data, and click OK. Move the Location parameter above the Comments parameter, as shown in Figure 11.22. Click OK.

FIGURE 11.22
Adding a new parameter

You are then presented with your new, albeit empty, schedule view. At this point, you can add new rows with the New button under Rows on the Modify Schedule/Quantities tab or by right-clicking and selecting New Row, as illustrated in Figure 11.23.

FIGURE 11.23
Adding a new row to
the key

 Real World Scenario

I once had a project where the structural concept included moment frames located in different places and in different forms. We had steel-braced frames and concrete shear walls. By using schedule keys, I was able to provide live scheduling but list only the specific data in the various schedules.

Additional parameters can be created for use with schedule keys but they must adhere to some logical restrictions. They can be created by navigating to the Manage tab and selecting Project Parameters from the Project Settings panel. If you do this you'll notice the Location parameter we just added is listed here too. Then in the Project Parameters dialog box, click the Add button. Verify that the parameter type is set to Project parameter, and in the Parameter Data area, verify that you are creating an Instance parameter. Set the other parameter data options as needed, and give the parameter a category from the list on the right side of the dialog box. This choice is derived from the element category you wish to use with the schedule key.

Create three new rows, one for each of the possible footing groups. Under Key Name, call them **Group 1**, **Group 2**, and **Group 3**. For Group 1 and Group 2, enter the Location as **North**. The Location of Group 3 will be **South**. Under Comments add **Below Water Table** to Group 2. The schedule key should now look like Figure 11.24.

FIGURE 11.24

Example schedule key

| Structural Foundation Style Schedule | | |
Key Name	Location	Comments
Group 1	North	
Group 2	North	Below Water Table
Group 3	South	

In this example, foundations are the target of this schedule key, so your next goal is to get your hands on some. Navigate to the foundation view, where you will find foundation elements that are affected by the schedule key. Select the four foundations in the upper-left corner, as illustrated in Figure 11.25, and click the upper half of the Element Properties button on the Modify Structural Foundations tab of the Ribbon.

FIGURE 11.25

Foundations set to the schedule key

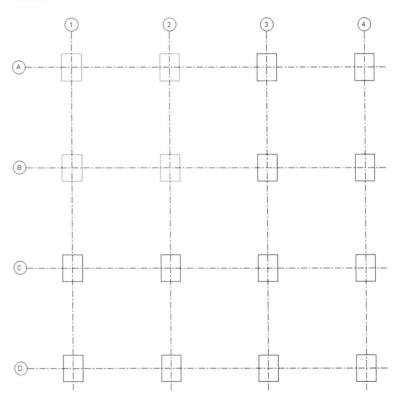

In the Instance Properties dialog box, you will see a parameter called Structural Foundation Style under the Identity Data heading. By default this will be set to (none). Notice that the Comments parameter is available for input when no Structural Foundation Style has been assigned. If you click in the Value cell of this parameter, a drop-down list will appear. In the list you will see the three groups available. Select Group 1 for this quarter of the building. The Location parameter will change to reflect the location you added to the schedule key for Group 1. The parameters affected by the schedule key will become unavailable for manual input after a key is assigned. Repeat this process for the four upper-right foundations and assign them to Group 2; see Figure 11.26. Finish by assigning the remaining eight foundations to Group 3.

FIGURE 11.26
Adding the key to elements

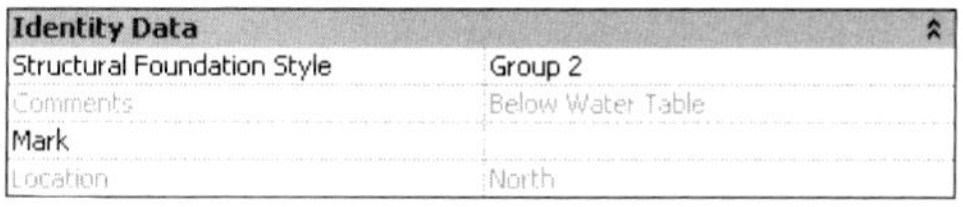

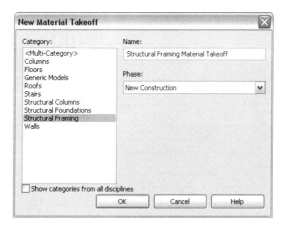

Complete this example by creating a Standard Schedule that uses these parameters. On the View tab, select Schedules ➢ Schedule/Quantities. Select Structural Foundations as the category and click OK. Notice that the parameters you created for the schedule key are now in the list of available fields. Add Type, Structural Foundation Style, Location, and Comments to the scheduled fields and click OK. To begin to see how powerful this process is, change one of the Group 1 foundations to Group 2 and notice how the controlled parameters reflect the change.

As you can see, creating a schedule in Revit is not a difficult task, and you can display quite a bit of information from the model. Next you will take it a step further and pull material quantities from the model. This might be referred to as 4D, a subject often discussed, and in this case it means an extended use of the model beyond project documentation. Material takeoffs are created using the same procedure as for schedule creation.

Material Takeoff Schedules

A nice thing about Revit Structure is that many of the procedures are similar, if not exactly the same as another. Creating a material takeoff, compared to creating a schedule, is one such example. Once you have mastered one method, the other is virtually the same.

To follow along with the description below, open the Other Schedules.rvt file found on this book's website.

A concrete structure with pan-formed joists is a good example of a material takeoff. The material of the concrete framing can be quickly quantified. Go to the View tab ➢ Create panel ➢ Schedules ➢ Material Takeoff. Within the New Material Takeoff dialog box, select Structural Framing, as shown in Figure 11.27, and click OK.

FIGURE 11.27
Creating a new material takeoff

As you are looking at the fields to add in the Material Takeoff Properties dialog box, scroll down the Available Fields column and notice the new parameter types that are prefixed with Material:

Here you can add fields such as:

◆ Reference Level

◆ Count

◆ Type

◆ Material: Name

◆ Material: Volume

See Figure 11.28 for an illustration.

FIGURE 11.28
Adding parameter fields
to the schedule

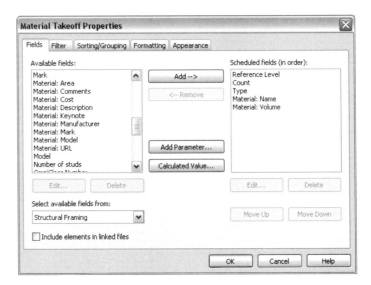

This type of schedule is oftentimes heavily dependent on how the fields are sorted. If you navigate to the Sorting/Grouping tab, you will notice you can sort the fields by many of the added parameter fields. It is also particularly important to create footers and to display the value totals in material takeoffs. At the bottom you should also uncheck Itemize Every Instance. In this example, the fields are sorted by

◆ Reference Level

◆ Type

◆ Material: Name

◆ Material: Volume

See Figure 11.29 for an illustration.

Material: Volume is an important field in this example. This field can be formatted and calculated independently of the rest of the schedule to provide a more informative material takeoff. On the Formatting tab, select the Material: Volume field, and in the Field formatting area, check the Calculate Totals option. Click the Field Format button. This button allows you to override the default unit formatting of this field. Uncheck Use Project Settings and select Cubic Yards as the units of this field, as illustrated in Figure 11.30. Click OK until you arrive at the schedule view, and you will notice the Material: Volume column displays total concrete volume for each level as well as a grand total for all the framing in the building.

FIGURE 11.29
Sorting the material takeoff

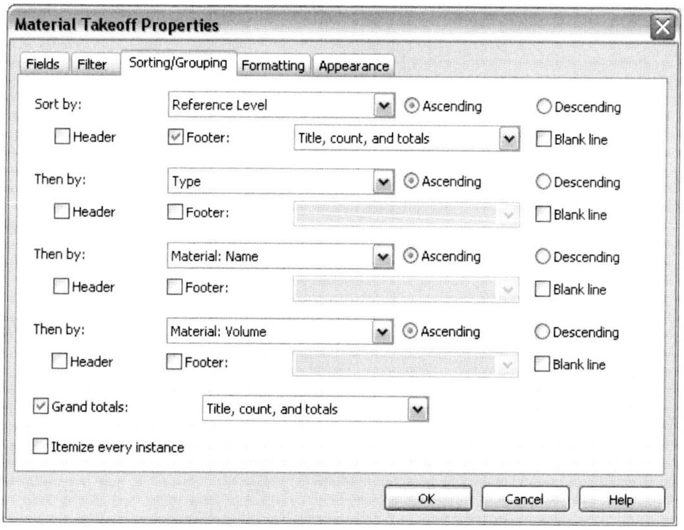

FIGURE 11.30
Field formatting

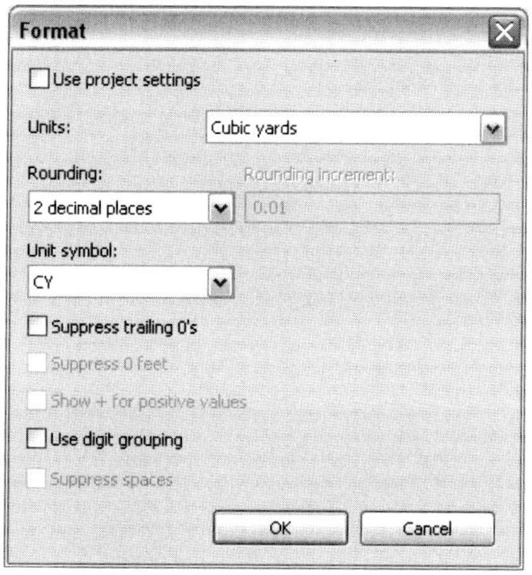

You now have a material takeoff of the volume of concrete needed to cast the framing for this structure, displayed in cubic yards. As the design of the building changes, so do the takeoff values, resulting in an accurate and current quantification of the concrete volumes throughout the life of the project.

Another good example is a floor area calculation. This takeoff can contain both area and volume information, serving as a dual-purpose schedule/takeoff. To follow along, still within the Other

`Schedules.rvt` file, go to View tab and select Schedules ➢ Material Takeoff. This time select Floors as the Category and click OK. For the fields, add

◆ Level

◆ Material: Name

◆ Material: Area

◆ Material: Volume

The Sorting/Grouping tab allows you to sort the entries according to your need. For this example, sort by Level. Grand Totals should be checked and set to display Title, Count, and Totals.

On the Formatting tab, select the Material: Area field and check the Calculate Totals option. For Material: Volume, check the Calculate Totals option, click the Field Format button to override the units to reflect Cubic Yards, and click OK until you are presented with the schedule view. The result is another accurate material takeoff that can be produced and referenced at any point in the life of the project. See Figure 11.31.

FIGURE 11.31
Another complete schedule

Floor Material Takeoff			
Level	Material: Name	Material: Area	Material: Volume
Level 1	Concrete - Cast-in-Place Concrete	6819 SF	126.27 CY
Level 2	Concrete - Cast-in-Place Concrete	6819 SF	126.27 CY
Level 3	Concrete - Cast-in-Place Concrete	6819 SF	126.27 CY
Roof	Concrete - Cast-in-Place Concrete	6819 SF	126.27 CY
Upper Level	Concrete - Cast-in-Place Concrete	1423 SF	26.34 CY
Grand total: 6		28697 SF	531.43 CY

Schedules can be used in a multitude of ways. One way is to display this information on the construction documents by adding the schedule to a drawing sheet. Another is to mine the project for material takeoff information. A third is to use the schedule to drive design changes back to the model, and we will explore this concept next.

Editing Your Schedules

As you have seen, changes to the model will be shown in your schedules automatically. Suppose you wanted the opposite to happen. It sure would be nice if you could make changes in the schedule and have them propagate back to the physical model. Well, in Revit, you can do just that. Schedules always accurately represent the model, so it makes sense that it would be impossible to change a schedule and not have that change affect the model. While it is very efficient, this two-way street burdens the modeler with the responsibility of being certain the changes made are correct. For this reason, you should be careful when editing schedules. The reality is, if you change an item in a schedule, it will change in the model.

Not every field in a schedule is editable. If the scheduled field is a calculated result (such as volume), then the field cannot be changed in the schedule. It must physically be changed in the model. If the field is a parameter that can be modified in the Element Properties dialog box (such as family type), then it can be modified in the schedule. For example, Figure 11.32 shows a Structural Column Schedule you will create in the next exercise. Notice that the Count field is a calculated value. The Count value will change only if identical instances of this element are created or deleted in the model. The Type field, however, can be modified in the schedule.

You can tell if a field is editable by clicking into the cell. If a cursor appears along with a drop-down list, as shown in Figure 11.32, the field can be changed. In an editable field you can choose one of the values in the drop-down list or type a new one. Although some parameters, such as the Type parameter here, depend on the available types of elements in the model so that a new one cannot simply be typed in, it must be created in the model to be available. The schedule and model will be updated to reflect the changes made, so be careful. Tiling the schedule view with a 3D view is a good idea in this situation so you are certain exactly what you are changing when editing model elements from a schedule view.

FIGURE 11.32
Modifying schedule
fields

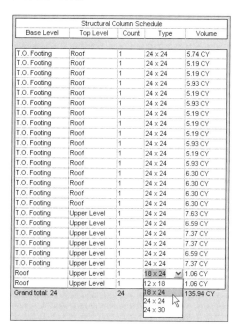

Structural Column Schedule				
Base Level	Top Level	Count	Type	Volume
T.O. Footing	Roof	1	24 x 24	5.74 CY
T.O. Footing	Roof	1	24 x 24	5.19 CY
T.O. Footing	Roof	1	24 x 24	5.19 CY
T.O. Footing	Roof	1	24 x 24	5.93 CY
T.O. Footing	Roof	1	24 x 24	5.19 CY
T.O. Footing	Roof	1	24 x 24	5.93 CY
T.O. Footing	Roof	1	24 x 24	5.19 CY
T.O. Footing	Roof	1	24 x 24	5.19 CY
T.O. Footing	Roof	1	24 x 24	5.93 CY
T.O. Footing	Roof	1	24 x 24	5.19 CY
T.O. Footing	Roof	1	24 x 24	5.93 CY
T.O. Footing	Roof	1	24 x 24	6.30 CY
T.O. Footing	Roof	1	24 x 24	6.30 CY
T.O. Footing	Roof	1	24 x 24	6.30 CY
T.O. Footing	Roof	1	24 x 24	6.30 CY
T.O. Footing	Upper Level	1	24 x 24	7.63 CY
T.O. Footing	Upper Level	1	24 x 24	6.59 CY
T.O. Footing	Upper Level	1	24 x 24	7.37 CY
T.O. Footing	Upper Level	1	24 x 24	7.37 CY
T.O. Footing	Upper Level	1	24 x 24	6.59 CY
T.O. Footing	Upper Level	1	24 x 24	7.37 CY
Roof	Upper Level	1	18 x 24 ⌄	1.06 CY
Roof	Upper Level	1	12 x 18	1.06 CY
Grand total: 24		24	18 x 24	135.94 CY
			24 x 24	
			24 x 30	

 Real World Scenario

PROCEED WITH CAUTION!

Occasionally when making a schedule view, I'll miss a step and end up with a blank cell where I expect to see values. I once made the mistake of thinking that *was expected* and changed the cell value. I then saw all my beams lose the proper stud counts — but only after plotting it out. I had missed a crucial filter and ended up with hundreds of beams listed in a single schedule row.

Being able to modify model elements using schedules is a very powerful tool, but it can also get you into trouble. Be sure when you are altering schedule field values that you are doing it deliberately and are checking the model after the changes have been made. Although Revit changes your approach to modeling, it does not negate the need for a thorough back check of the affected views and of the documents.

EXERCISE: CREATING A "WORKING" SCHEDULE

Follow these steps to create a schedule and use it to modify the model elements.

1. Open the file named `Other Schedules.rvt`.

2. On the View tab, select Schedules ➤ Schedule/Quantities.

3. Select Structural Columns as the Category and click OK.

4. Add the following fields:

    ◆ Base Level

    ◆ Top Level

    ◆ Count

    ◆ Type

    ◆ Volume

5. Navigate to the Sorting/Grouping tab.

6. Sort by Base Level and then by Top Level.

7. Navigate to the Formatting tab.

8. Highlight the Count field and check the Calculate Totals option.

9. Highlight the Volume field and check Calculate Totals.

10. With the Volume field still highlighted, click the Field Format button.

11. Uncheck Use Project Settings, set the Units to Cubic Yards, and click OK.

12. Click OK on the Schedule Properties dialog box, and the schedule will appear.

13. When editing model elements from a schedule view, it is a good idea to display both the schedule and the 3D model. With the schedule view and the {3D} view open, select Tile Windows on the View tab of the Windows panel. This allows you to more confidently modify elements from the schedule view since you can verify the affected elements and see the modification happen in real time.

14. At the bottom of the schedule, there are two 24x24 columns that run from the roof to the upper level. These columns are too big and can be sized down. Click anywhere in the row of the column; it will highlight in the 3D view. Adjust the 3D view so you can see the highlighted column. Click in the Type cell for this column and change it to **18x24**. Notice the column changes in size in both the schedule and the model.

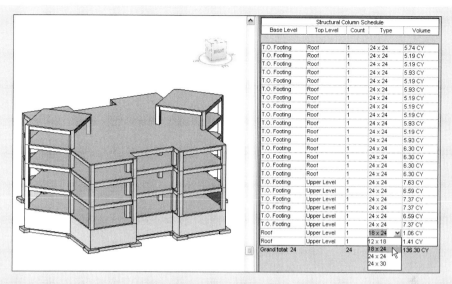

Structural Column Schedule				
Base Level	Top Level	Count	Type	Volume
T.O. Footing	Roof	1	24 x 24	5.74 CY
T.O. Footing	Roof	1	24 x 24	5.19 CY
T.O. Footing	Roof	1	24 x 24	5.19 CY
T.O. Footing	Roof	1	24 x 24	5.93 CY
T.O. Footing	Roof	1	24 x 24	5.19 CY
T.O. Footing	Roof	1	24 x 24	5.93 CY
T.O. Footing	Roof	1	24 x 24	5.19 CY
T.O. Footing	Roof	1	24 x 24	5.19 CY
T.O. Footing	Roof	1	24 x 24	5.19 CY
T.O. Footing	Roof	1	24 x 24	5.93 CY
T.O. Footing	Roof	1	24 x 24	5.19 CY
T.O. Footing	Roof	1	24 x 24	5.93 CY
T.O. Footing	Roof	1	24 x 24	6.30 CY
T.O. Footing	Roof	1	24 x 24	6.30 CY
T.O. Footing	Roof	1	24 x 24	6.30 CY
T.O. Footing	Roof	1	24 x 24	6.30 CY
T.O. Footing	Upper Level	1	24 x 24	7.63 CY
T.O. Footing	Upper Level	1	24 x 24	6.59 CY
T.O. Footing	Upper Level	1	24 x 24	7.37 CY
T.O. Footing	Upper Level	1	24 x 24	7.37 CY
T.O. Footing	Upper Level	1	24 x 24	6.59 CY
T.O. Footing	Upper Level	1	24 x 24	7.37 CY
Roof	Upper Level	1	18 x 24	1.06 CY
Roof	Upper Level	1	12 x 18	1.41 CY
Grand total: 24		24	18 x 24 / 24 x 24 / 24 x 30	136.30 CY

15. Repeat the process for the other column that runs from the roof to the upper level.

Modeling due diligence is still of paramount concern. You cannot simply model by schedule, because many of the issues like specific placement cannot be addressed in a schedule. In a pinch you can use schedules to adjust things, but always return to your plans and sections to see that orientation issues are not a problem.

Exporting Your Schedules

Although Revit Structure is a comprehensive database that is fully capable of performing most tasks, there is still — and always will be — a need to export data to other formats. You may know how to export the model to other CAD applications, but what about the data in the schedules? You will find others in the industry who don't use Revit. They could be involved in other aspects of the project that don't require Revit, or maybe they are just slower to adapt. This could even be true inside your office. An estimator or project manager probably will not be using Revit but will still need to have access to and/or manipulate data generated by the model.

In order to have something to export, you need to create a schedule or a material takeoff in Revit Structure. This example continues with the Other Schedules.rvt file. This example uses a Wall material takeoff. This material takeoff should consist of the following fields:

- Count
- Material: Name
- Length
- Material: Area
- Material: Volume

The options to choose in this example are as follows:

◆ On the Sorting/Grouping tab, sort by Material: Volume with Grand Totals checked, displaying Count and totals.

◆ Itemize every instance not checked.

◆ On the Formatting tab, override the Material: Volume field's format to Cubic Yards.

◆ Calculate totals checked for both Material: Volume and Material: Area.

See Figure 11.33.

FIGURE 11.33
Material takeoff to be exported

	Wall Material Takeoff				
Count	Material: Name	Length	Material: Area	Material: Volume	
4	Concrete - Cast-in-Place Concrete	8' - 0"	320 SF	11.85 CY	
1	Concrete - Cast-in-Place Concrete	23' - 6"	235 SF	8.70 CY	
1	Concrete - Cast-in-Place Concrete	25' - 0"	240 SF	8.89 CY	
4	Concrete - Cast-in-Place Concrete	25' - 0"	1012 SF	36.73 CY	
4	Concrete - Cast-in-Place Concrete	25' - 0"	1000 SF	37.04 CY	
3	Concrete - Cast-in-Place Concrete	25' - 0"	771 SF	28.01 CY	
1	Concrete - Cast-in-Place Concrete	25' - 0"	255 SF	9.44 CY	
18			3833 SF	140.66 CY	

Now that you have a material takeoff to export, you can get down to business. One not-so-obvious detail you need to remember when exporting takeoffs and schedules is that you need to have the schedule view you wish to export open and active. If the schedule view is not active, it will be grayed out in the list of available views to export, giving the impression it cannot be exported. As long as the view is active, the schedule will be available for export. With the Wall Material Takeoff view active, navigate to the Application menu and select Export ➤ Reports ➤ Schedule, as shown in Figure 11.34.

You should recognize the next dialog as a Save As opportunity that will allow you to name and locate the soon-to-be-scheduled export file. If applicable, you can set up a directory within the project directory where all team members have access to the files being generated from Revit. It is also a great idea to alert the team to expect this kind of information and to communicate exactly where it is to be stored. Notice that the only file type available to save as is a delimited .txt file. This file type is an application-neutral format, which is used since most database and spreadsheet programs can read these types of files. Once you verify the filename and locate the directory into which you want to save the .txt file, click Save.

The Export Schedule dialog box provides some options for how the data will be written to file. The default options should work for most situations and probably won't need to be changed unless the database software you are working with requires it or if you are an advanced user who is aware of the effects of such changes.

The defaults in the Schedule Appearance area of the dialog box will export column headers and create multiple rows as formatted in Revit, as well as include group headers, footers, and blank lines in the export. The defaults in the Output Options area will use (tab) spacing to delimit the fields. Traditionally, comma delimited is most popular, but tab delimited is a much cleaner import for software such as Excel. The text qualifier is quote marks. See these options in Figure 11.35. Click OK to write the file.

Once the .txt file has been created, it can be imported into other database software. This example will use Microsoft Excel 2007. To import the data, open Microsoft Excel and select Open using the Office button, which is similar to the Revit Application menu. For the Files of Type option, select Text Files (*.prn; *.txt; *.csv), as shown in Figure 11.36. Browse to the directory where your .txt file is stored, select the file, and click Open.

FIGURE 11.34
The Export
Schedule
command

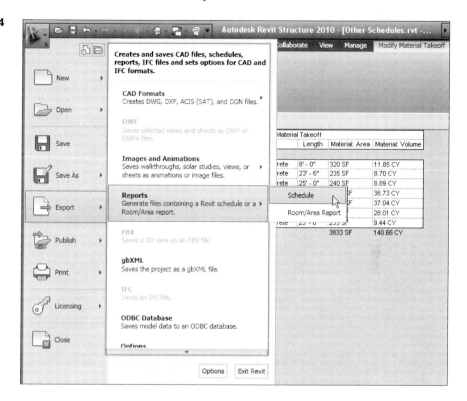

FIGURE 11.34
The Export
Schedule
command

FIGURE 11.35
The Export Schedule
options

Excel will now prompt you to make some additional choices using the Text Import Wizard, as shown in Figure 11.37. Essentially, this is a confirmation of the dialog box shown in Figure 11.35. As Excel has detected, we are using tab-delimited data. If for some reason you don't want to import the entire file from the beginning, you can set the Start Import at Row value to the desired starting row. The File Origin is 437 : OEM United States. You will also see a very basic preview of the data in the bottom window shown in Figure 11.37.

FIGURE 11.36
Opening a .txt
file in Microsoft
Excel

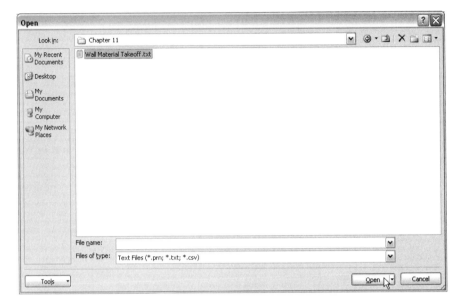

FIGURE 11.37
The Text Import Wizard
in Microsoft Excel

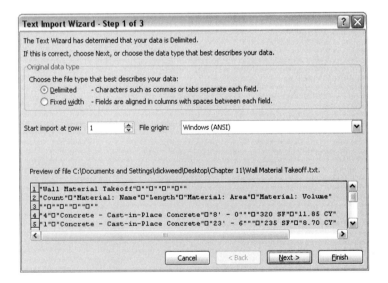

Since this is a wizard, you will see a Next button at the bottom of the dialog box. Clicking this will bring you to the next step in the process, as illustrated in Figure 11.38. Again, the defaults are simply a reflection of your initial settings in Revit. The Delimiters field is set to Tab. Here you can add additional delimiters, but the delimiter(s) should match the format of the file you are importing. If the delimiters used don't match the .txt file, the data may import unreadable or unorganized. On the flip side, if the data doesn't come in correctly, you may have to adjust these settings until the data appears the way you wish to see it. Click Next to continue.

FIGURE 11.38
Step 2 of the Text Import Wizard

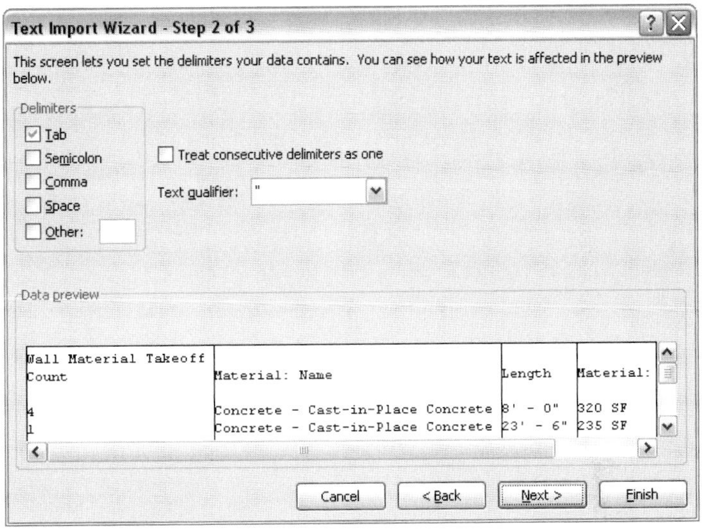

The third step in the Text Import Wizard will allow you to set the formatting of the data cells by column. Under Column Data Format, you can select the cell format for the highlighted data column below. Notice that the data columns in the Data Preview are selectable. You can format the cells of the entire column by highlighting a data column and then selecting the formatting choice in the Column Data Format area above, as illustrated in Figure 11.39. Click Finish.

FIGURE 11.39
Step 3 of the Text Import Wizard

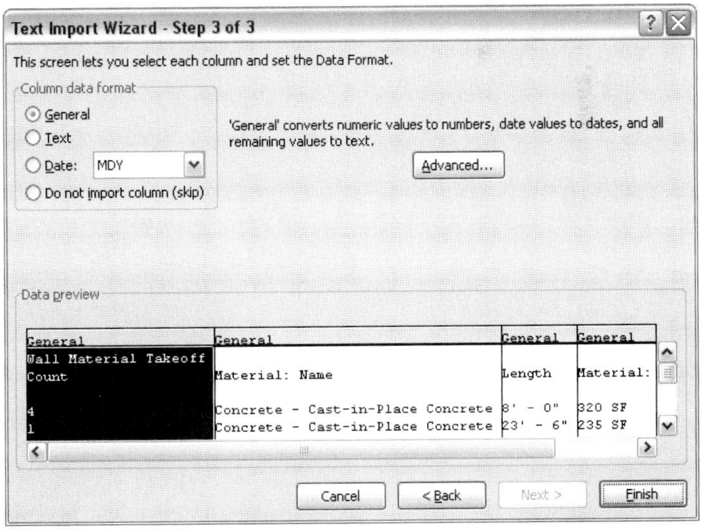

The Excel table will appear with all of the data from your Revit material takeoff. Of course some of the column widths and justifications may need to be adjusted, and perhaps the cells on the title line could be merged and the title centered, as shown in Figure 11.40. Note that the totals are not using formulas, just a strict data value extraction.

FIGURE 11.40
The schedule imported into Excel

	A	B	C	D	E
1		Wall Material Takeoff			
2	Count	Material: Name	Length	Material: Area	Material: Volume
3					
4	4	Concrete - Cast-in-Place Concrete	8' - 0"	320 SF	11.85 CY
5	1	Concrete - Cast-in-Place Concrete	23' - 6"	235 SF	8.70 CY
6	1	Concrete - Cast-in-Place Concrete	25' - 0"	240 SF	8.89 CY
7	4	Concrete - Cast-in-Place Concrete	25' - 0"	1012 SF	36.73 CY
8	4	Concrete - Cast-in-Place Concrete	25' - 0"	1000 SF	37.04 CY
9	3	Concrete - Cast-in-Place Concrete	25' - 0"	771 SF	28.01 CY
10	1	Concrete - Cast-in-Place Concrete	25' - 0"	255 SF	9.44 CY
11	18			3833 SF	140.66 CY
12					

EXERCISE: CREATING A MATERIAL TAKEOFF AND EXPORTING IT TO MICROSOFT EXCEL

The following step-by-step example will take you through creating a wall material takeoff and exporting it to Excel as explained in the previous section.

1. Open the file called `Other Schedules.rvt` from this book's website.

2. Navigate to the View tab. On the Create panel select the Schedules button and select Material Takeoff from the drop-down list.

3. Select Walls from the Category list on the left, and click OK.

4. Add the following fields:

   ◆ Count

   ◆ Material: Name

   ◆ Length

   ◆ Material: Area

   ◆ Material: Volume

5. Navigate to the Sorting/Grouping tab.

6. Sort by Material: Volume.

7. Near the bottom of the dialog box, enable the Grand Totals option and select Count and Totals from the drop-down list.

8. Uncheck Itemize Every Instance.

9. Navigate to the Formatting tab.

10. Highlight Material: Volume and click the Field Format button.

11. Uncheck the Use Project Settings option, change the Units format to Cubic Yards, and click OK.

12. With Material: Volume still highlighted, check the Calculate Totals option and click OK.

13. Navigate to the Application menu and select Export ➤ Reports ➤ Schedule.

14. Verify the name of the .txt file, browse to the directory in which you want to save the file, and click Save.

15. In the Export Schedule dialog box, use the defaults and click OK.

16. Open Microsoft Excel.

17. Open the Wall Material Takeoff.txt file. Remember to change the Files of Type drop-down in the Open dialog box.

18. In the first step of the Text Import Wizard, keep the default as Delimited and click Next.

19. In the second step of the Text Import Wizard, keep the default delimiter set to (tab) and click Next.

20. In the third and final step of the Text Import Wizard, keep the default Column Data Format set to General, and click Finish.

21. In Excel, adjust the cell widths so the data is displayed clearly, and make any other desired cell formatting changes.

22. At the bottom of the program, notice the current worksheet tab was given the same name as the Wall Material Takeoff.txt file.

23. Click the Save icon in Excel. You will get a message regarding the file format. Even though you opened the file in Excel, it is still regarded as a .txt file. When you get the message warning you of this, click No and save it to the .xls (.xls or .xlsx) format.

This procedure is useful for getting project information to the estimator or others involved in the project who do not use Revit. Some may handle their work in other software programs, and exporting the model data using this procedure will allow you to give them the information they need quickly and easily.

Employing Keynote Legends

Another option to track model elements or materials is to use keynote legends. While keynoting will allow you to change the data in many elements at once, it is a multistep process that has some special requirements. Keynoting is driven by an external .txt file that contains all the keynote entries. Each element or material's keynote parameter, located in the Element Properties dialog box, can then be given a keynote value. Note that no keynote values have been populated by default. Each element or material must then be tagged to display that entry in a keynote legend. Whew!

Thankfully, once you have set up keynotes in your template, they will be much easier to implement in future projects. To follow along with this lesson, open the Other Schedules.rvt file from this book's website.

Creating the Keynote Legend

Creating a keynote legend is very similar to creating any other schedule; we just have to start from a slightly different location. Navigate to the View tab, and from the Create panel select Legends ➤ Keynote Legend, as shown in Figure 11.41.

FIGURE 11.41
The Keynote Legend
command

This will take you to the New Keynote Legend dialog box, where you can name the view. For this example, the legend will be used with beam elements, so name the keynote legend **Beam Keynote Legend** and click OK.

You will then see the Keynote Legend Properties dialog box. This should be immediately familiar to you since it is virtually identical to the Schedule Properties dialog box you have been using throughout this chapter. On the Fields tab, there are only two available fields for keynote legends, Key Value and Keynote Text, and they are added by default, see Figure 11.42.

FIGURE 11.42
Keynote legend fields

Most of the tabs in the Keynote Legend Properties dialog box look and function exactly as within the Schedule Properties dialog box with one exception. At the bottom of the Filter tab you will find the option Filter by Sheet. If this option is left unchecked, the keynote legend will display all keynote entries for the entire project on all sheets it is placed on. When the Filter by Sheet option is checked, however, the keynote legend placed on a particular sheet will display only the entries relevant to that sheet, thus filtering the entries by sheet. This check box is typically turned on.

Once you verify the two available fields have been added and click OK, a blank keynote legend will appear. It is blank because, as mentioned before, there are multiple steps to this process. You have created the legend view; now you need to associate a keynote table file to the project.

The Keynote Table File

Before you can begin to assign keynote values to elements, you must first associate a keynote file with your project. To access the Keynoting Settings dialog box, navigate to the Annotate tab and click the Tag panel drop-down to expand it, as shown in Figure 11.43. Select Keynoting Settings from the list, and the Keynoting Settings dialog box will appear.

FIGURE 11.43
Keynoting Settings
command

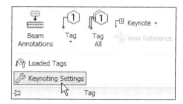

In the Keynote Table area at the top of this dialog box, you will find the path information for any associated files. There is a Browse button to use if a file has not been associated or if you need to associate a different file. Below the Browse button is a View button. This will allow you to view the keynote table in a tree format. Note that the keynote table cannot be edited from this view.

Next is the Path Type area, where you can set the resolve method for the keynote table file. Absolute specifies an exact location defined by the saved path. Relative will find the file anywhere the model file is located; thus the files can be moved and the table file will be searched for relative to the project file. At Library Locations will search for the table file wherever the libraries are defined for your particular Revit installation, whether it is a standalone installation or a network deployment.

At the bottom of the Keynoting Settings dialog box are the Numbering Method options. You can choose to number By Keynote or By Sheet when you place keynotes. The difference between these is simple but significant. When numbering by keynote, the keynote number specified in the keynotes file will be used, and it will be consistent for a given keynote across all sheets. When numbering by sheet, each keynote is assigned a number that is unique on a particular sheet; however, the same keynote could be assigned a different number on a different sheet. When you use the By Sheet numbering option, views containing keynote tags must be placed on a sheet before the keynote number will be generated. For this example, leave this set to By Keynote.

The keynote table file can be edited by opening it with a text editor or Excel, since it is created in tab-delimited format. Revit's standard keynote table file should be associated by default. If so, you can use the Browse button to determine the location of your Imperial Library. Open the default keynote table file (`RevitKeynotes_Imperial_2004.txt`) with Notepad by browsing to the Imperial Library in your library location. Note that this file is likely set with read-only protection, but you can make it editable by right-clicking on the file, selecting Properties, and unchecking the Read-Only option.

Notice that the file is not terribly easy to read in this format. For this reason, it is helpful to open this file in Excel or similar software. Open Excel and open the same file. When you're in the Open dialog box, select Text Files (.txt) using the Files of Type drop-down list, and then browse to and open the file. The Text Import Wizard will appear, just as it did when you were opening an exported schedule. Click Next twice and then click Finish to use the defaults. After you adjust the column widths a bit, the file is much easier to read than before.

There are three columns in a keynote table file. The first column represents the Keynote Value parameter. The middle column houses the Keynote Text parameter values. The last column helps define the directory tree you see when you view the file from within Revit. A blank third column means the keynote represented by the row is a top directory on the tree. If a particular keynote is located under another in the tree structure, the keynote value of the parent keynote will reside in the third column. Take a look at the default file for a minute. Notice that the rows that define the various divisions have no value for the third column. Below those, notice that the entries have values in the third column. This means these entries will be located under the various divisions in the tree within Revit.

Revit keynote table files can also be created from scratch. The format is simple: just separate each value in a row with a tab. Revit will recognize any file in this format so long as it has been associated with the project within the Keynoting Settings dialog box. For this example, verify that the default file is associated with your project. The next step involves tagging elements with the keynotes defined in the associated file.

Adding a Keynote Tag

Now that Revit has a keynote table file to draw values from, you can begin to associate those values with model elements. Navigate to the Level 2 plan view of the Other Schedules.rvt file. A keynote tag can be placed whether or not a keynote value has been assigned to a model element. If no keynote value has been assigned, the tag will prompt you for a value. Start the keynote tag command from the Annotate tab by clicking the Keynote button on the Tag panel and selecting Element from the drop-down list, as shown in Figure 11.44.

FIGURE 11.44
The Keynote Tag command

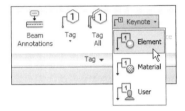

Before placing the tag, look at the Options bar. Uncheck the Leader option and change the tag orientation to Vertical. Select one of the 12x12 beams to tag, and you will be presented with the tree view of the keynote table file, as illustrated in Figure 11.45.

Here you can choose the keynote value to assign to this element. Browse the key values and expand Division 03 - Concrete ➢ 03 31 00 - Structural Concrete. Here you will find various sizes of structural concrete members. Highlight 03 31 00.C1 - 12″X12″ Cast-in-Place Beam, and click OK. The keynote tag is placed and displays the keynote value. Exit the Keynote Tag command and select the tagged beam (not the keynote tag), and look at its Element properties. Navigate to the Type properties by clicking the Edit Type button. Notice that the Keynote parameter has been populated, as illustrated in Figure 11.46.

The value can be edited after the tagging process by clicking in the Value cell of the Keynote parameter. This will display the familiar Browse button on the right side of the cell, which you can click to return to the keynote table tree. Add several keynote tags to the other beams in this plan, giving them the proper keynote value according to their size. The tag type can be changed as you would expect, by highlighting the tag and selecting a different type from the Type Selector drop-down list. Notice that when you tag a beam that is of the same type as one you have already tagged, the keynote value appears automatically.

As you have learned throughout this chapter, you can edit Element parameters by accessing the Element Properties dialog box or by editing the schedule directly, and keynoting is no different. Return to the Beam Keynote Legend schedule view. You will find a row for each type of beam for

FIGURE 11.45
Adding a
keynote tag
to an element

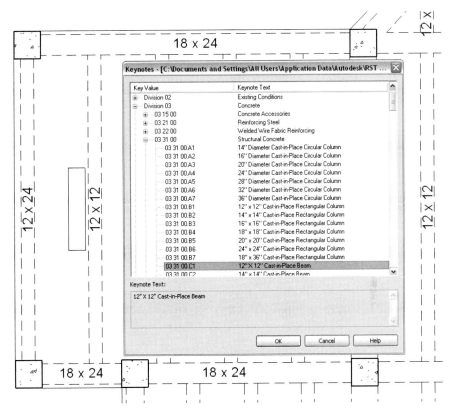

which you assigned a keynote. Click in the Key Value cell of the schedule to assess the keynote table tree and edit the value. Note that if all the tags of a particular type are deleted, the entry will no longer exist in the keynote legend.

Keynoting a material works in much the same way except instead of element types driving the value, the material of the element controls it. In order for Revit Structure to keynote a material, the element must be visible in the view, and the material may need to be displayed by adjusting the detail level in some cases.

Here are a couple of situations you may encounter:

If you are not able to keynote an element in a particular view, check the settings of the family. Nested family components must be shared in order to place or display a keynote value.

If a family is created using a keynote table file that is different from the one the project is associated with and the same value exists in each keynote table, the project's keynote file values are used. You should always try to select a value from the keynote table the project is associated with. At times this may require you to copy values from one table to another.

The last step for a keynote legend would be to put it on a sheet. Just as for other schedule views, simply make a sheet view active and then use the Project Browser to drag the sheet and place it as needed.

FIGURE 11.46
Keynote parameter in
Element properties

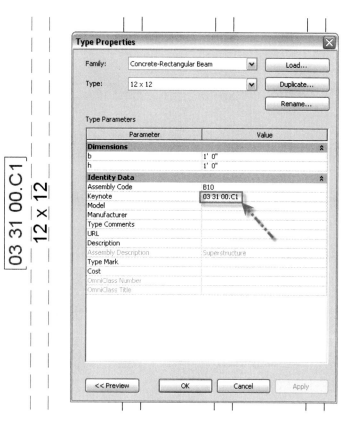

FIGURE 11.47
The keynote legend is
growing.

Beam Keynote Legend	
Key Value	Keynote Text
03 31 00.C	12" x 12" Cast-in-Place Beam
03 31 00.C	24" x 24" Cast-in-Place Beam
03 31 00.C	18" x 24" Cast-in-Place Beam

The Bottom Line

Create schedules.   Revit Structure benefits from a strong link between schedules and data. Once a schedule is created, the elements and parameter values can be manipulated either in the model or in the schedule. Each will influence the other.

Master It   The Schedule Properties dialog box can be accessed in two ways. One way is to right-click on the schedule name in the Project Browser and select Properties. What is the second way of accessing the Schedule properties?

Create schedule keys.   Schedule keys can be used to control multiple parameter values by creating a key designation and applying it to model elements.

Master It   How can you create additional parameters for use with schedule keys, and what are their restrictions?

Create material takeoffs.   Material takeoffs are known as a fourth-dimension modeling use. Using Revit Structure to track cost and material can be a big advantage in any project. Once the tools are developed and the basic takeoffs are in place, the efficiency of these features will be greater than ever.

Master It   A material takeoff is a bit different from a schedule; however, the two are similar in many ways. What is the primary difference between material takeoffs and schedules?

Export schedules to Microsoft Excel.   Keeping track of the quantities may not be in the designer's scope of work. Many times the task is assigned to an estimator who is not involved with the modeling process at all. This functionality allows the designer to output accurate model data to an estimator in a format that person can use.

Master It   Once a schedule or material takeoff is created in Revit Structure, how is it exported to Excel?

Create keynote legends.   Keynote legends are a great way to track items and materials in Revit. The keynote values and keynote text values are easily editable and create reliable keynotes for your drawings.

Master It   A keynote is tied directly into the element type being scheduled. What is the procedure for giving an element a keynote value?

Chapter 12

Working with Sheets

One aspect of using Revit Structure for BIM is creating documentation to help display the information that is part of the Revit Structure model. The method for creating these documentation pieces is pretty much the same as it is in a 2D environment. You create sheets with title blocks and then add plan views and sections or details to the sheets along with schedules and notes for plotting. In addition, you may include a sheet index and perhaps a few key plans if required. Since all this information is stored in one database, Revit Structure can help keep track of everything as the specs change during the coordination process.

You can easily keep track of these changes for others to see by using Revit Structure's built-in revision tracking. As changes are made and tagged in views, Revision Schedules placed in title blocks are automatically updated.

In this chapter you will learn to:

◆ Create a title block to display project information

◆ Create a Revision Schedule to your company standards

◆ Explore the behavior of the various view types when they are placed on a sheet

◆ Produce a drawing list/sheet index to keep track of your issued sheets

◆ Control the behavior of revisions in your project

Getting to Know Your Sheets

Sheets are a category in the Project Browser for organizing a system family called *Sheets*. Inside this system family you place other views and external component families such as title blocks. Sheets are another type of view used to display information from the model. They are somewhat like a drafting view in that they do not display information directly from the model or have a view range, but they are much more powerful in managing the information that is put inside them.

Similarly to any other views, you can place line work and annotation directly into sheets. In order to display model information, you can place other views that display the model elements inside sheets. Once other views are placed within a sheet, Revit Structure keeps track of their references and placement on the sheet as well as manages the various scales that are required to show the various levels of detail in a plan or detail view. Since sheets don't have a scale of their own and they manage the scales of those views that get placed within them, it is no longer necessary to worry about scale factors, text height, and dimension settings. As these views get moved to different locations on a sheet or onto another sheet, or when sheet numbers change, Revit Structure automatically updates the references to them throughout the model.

The basic procedure to create a new sheet in your project is as follows:

1. Right-click the Sheets category in the Project Browser and select New Sheet, or choose the View tab ➤ Sheet Composition panel ➤ New Sheet tool.

2. Within the Select a Titleblock dialog box shown in Figure 12.1, select a title block to use for the sheet. If none are available, click the Load button and browse to a title block family file to load.

3. After choosing a title block, click OK to create the new sheet.

FIGURE 12.1
Select the title block to be used when creating new sheets.

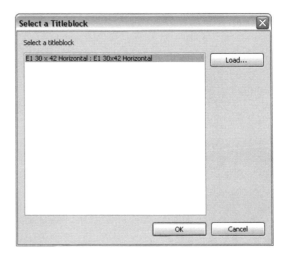

RAPID-FIRE SHEET CREATION

So you want to create multiple sheets quickly rather than creating them individually by right-clicking and selecting a title block from the shortcut menu or by choosing the New Sheet tool from the Ribbon. You can speed up this process a lot. In the Project Browser select a sheet and press Ctrl+C to copy it, or right-click the sheet and choose Copy to Clipboard. Activate the current sheet by clicking inside the view, and then press Ctrl+V to paste a copy of the sheet. A new sheet view will be created, numbered, and named, and its title block will be based on the previous sheet's number and name. You can create new sheets as fast as you can press Ctrl+V on the keyboard. As you need to change the series number of the sheet, like S100 to S200, just make an "extra" sheet view and rename/number it using the next series number, and then repeat the Copy and Paste routine.

If you have a tough time making this work, make sure that you move Revit's focus from the Project Browser back into the drawing area by clicking there before using Paste. Keep in mind that it works only on sheets that have *no* views on them yet.

When a sheet view is created, its name is automatically associated with the sheet number and sheet name, which are also properties of the view. You can change this name by changing the parameter values in the properties of the view, by right-clicking the sheet view name in the

Project Browser and selecting Rename, or by selecting the sheet and pressing the F2 key, as shown in Figure 12.2. You can also just change the sheet number and name on the title block itself; select the title block and the sheet name and number values will turn blue, which means that you can edit them.

FIGURE 12.2
Selecting a view and using the right-click shortcut menu or pressing the F2 key is a quick way to number and name sheets.

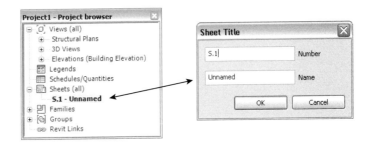

Sheets have their own category in the Project Browser, which helps keep the sheets organized and easy to work with while documenting the model. Chapter 2 discusses methods of creating browser view types to help sort views so you can easily maintain their organization. Sheets are separate from other views, but you can use these same methods for organizing your sheets. To start the creation of a new browser view type for sheets, go to the View tab ➢ Windows panel ➢ User Interface drop-down ➢ Browser Organization tool and select the Sheets tab shown in Figure 12.3. See Chapter 2 to learn how to create new types, edit them, and maneuver between them.

FIGURE 12.3
Create Project Browser view types for sheets to organize sheets in the Project Browser.

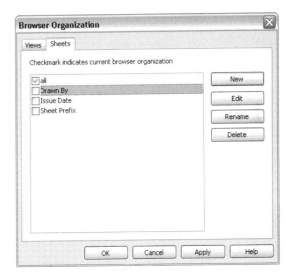

A sheet view, which is basically a drawing sheet, is where you will place your title block for displaying project-specific information with regard to location, owner, and design team as well as sheet numbering, sheet naming, and specific issue information. Like any other object or element in Revit Structure, a title block is a family. In this case it is a component family and can easily be created to match your current title block standards and/or to match another standard your client may require.

Creating a Title Block

Revit Structure has sheets and title blocks. They need each other in order to work properly, and to Revit Structure they pretty much mean the same thing. Since sheets are a system family, all information pertaining to them must be created within the project. Some information and its behavior are hardwired to the Sheets category. We will discuss some of these aspects later in this chapter. Creating the title block for a sheet allows you to display this system information on a sheet along with any other required data that pertains to the project. A title block is a component family, so you can add such information as line work, annotation, images for logos, and Revision Schedules.

The basic procedure for creating a title block is as follows:

1. Choose the Application menu ➤ New ➤ Title Block.

2. The Titleblocks folder opens, showing a list of available title block family templates. If you do not see these files, browse to the Imperial or Metric Templates - Titleblocks folder and look for them there.

3. Select a size-defined template, or select the New Size.rft file and click Open.

4. You will see the extents of a title block, with dimensions indicating its size if you choose the New Size template, as shown in Figure 12.4. You can adjust this line work to the extents of the title block. Once the extents are defined, you can delete the dimensions or turn them off to allow a clear drawing space.

FIGURE 12.4
In the New Size.rft template you can adjust the size of your title block by selecting the line work and changing the dimension values.

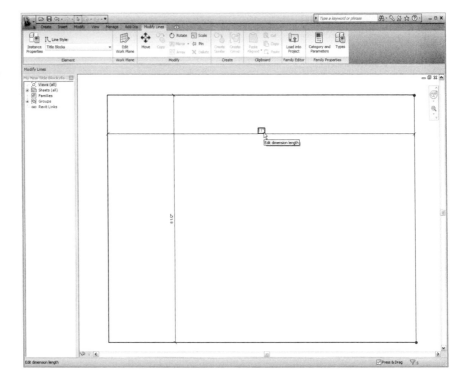

THE TITLE BLOCK TEMPLATE'S ORIGIN LOCATION

Stock templates are defined with the origin at the bottom-left corner of the rectangle; avoid changing this location unless you are prepared to do so for all your title block families so they behave consistently in projects.

---

5. Choose the Category and Parameters tool from the Create tab ➤ Family Properties panel. You will see that the new title block family is part of the Title Blocks category and that it has only one hardwired parameter within the family, Rotate with Component.

6. Right-click within the drawing area and select View Properties, and you will see that the title block family already displays project parameters and shows how it behaves in a drawing list and Revision Schedule when it is placed into a project.

7. Save your new title block family, and proceed to adding line work, annotation, logos, and any other information that may be needed.

After you define the size for your title block, you can add content to it such as line work, text, labels that hold project information, images such as company or project logos, and a Revision Schedule. This content can be imported and used from existing CAD drawings or created from scratch. A well-put-together title block will include parametric data that will allow for prompt changes.

ADDING LINE WORK TO YOUR TITLE BLOCK

Line work can be added by using the tools in the Create tab on the Ribbon within the family. You can use tools such as Lines, Masking Regions, Filled Regions, and Symbols to help place line work. Lines are defined by a subcategory of the Title Blocks category, which is located in the Annotation Objects tab of the Object Styles dialog box, as shown in Figure 12.5. You can create a new line style by choosing the Manage tab ➤ Family Settings panel ➤ Settings drop-down ➤ Object Styles.

Make sure that the Subcategory Of value is set to Title Blocks, or the new style will not be available in the Type Selector. Existing 2D CAD data can be imported into the title block family to aid you in the layout of your line work, but keep in mind you won't be able to make it parametric, if that matters to you. You can trace over the top of the imported line work, or you can explode the imported CAD data, which will convert the line work into Revit Structure lines. Creating native line work is relatively simple, so try to avoid leaving unexploded imported objects in the title block family. Convert everything to Revit Structure content so the behavior is a bit more predictable and the family remains free of unnecessary information.

WHAT IS UNNECESSARY INFORMATION?

Exploding dwg files creates "junk" in the file because it adds new object styles for each layer, new fill patterns for each hatch, and line patterns for each line type. These in turn pollute the project file too. Exploding these files is bad practice unless you are very, very careful to clean this stuff up before using the title block in a project. Though it's possible, we can't discourage this practice strongly enough.

FIGURE 12.5
Create a new line style for title blocks in the Object Styles dialog box.

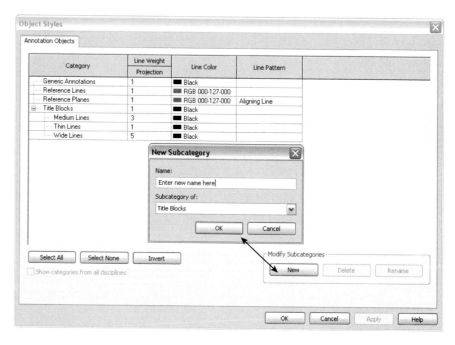

Some borders may have thicker lines to define separations within the title block or to define a boundary. In this case you can use a filled region set to a solid fill rather than using a wide line weight, as shown in Figure 12.6. Revit's lines have round ends, as if they were drawn with an ink pen. The thicker they are, the more obvious the round ends are. This technique will provide the nice "square end" look that many people prefer.

FIGURE 12.6
You can use filled regions to show extra-thick lines in a title block family.

 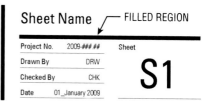

MAKING YOUR ANNOTATION INTELLIGENT

You can easily add text to your title block by using the Annotation tools located in the Create tab on the Ribbon within the family. You can create text styles and use them just as they are used in the project model environment. For each different type of text, you will need to create a new style. New text styles that are created in a title block family will not be available to the project when it is loaded in. This allows you to create the various styles that are needed only for the title block and have the comfort of knowing that they will not be cluttering up your project model. Using the Text tools to place text does not allow them to display the properties of the drawing sheet or any project information. To display this type of information you must use the Label tool. Figure 12.7 shows an example of text and labels being used together in a title block.

FIGURE 12.7
Use Text
tools where
text remains
unchanged or
changed only
once per project,
and use Label
tools where
information is
set and changed
in the project
routinely.

Sheet Name

Project No.		Sheet
Drawn By		
Checked By		
Date		

Lines & Text

+

Sheet Name

2009-###-##
DRW
CHK
01_January 2009

Labels

S1

=

Sheet Name

Project No.	2009-###-##	Sheet
Drawn By	DRW	
Checked By	CHK	
Date	01_January 2009	

Final

S1

Adding labels to your title block families allows text to automatically adapt to changes that are made to the information that they display. These labels can be used to display information such as Drawn By, Checked By, Sheet Name, Sheet Number, and other parameters. Most of these already exist as project parameters or are built into the title block family. If you need to add additional parameters, you can create them yourself. Chapter 2 discusses adding a project parameter for the contractor's name and having it display in the title block. The same procedure can be applied to other unique parameters you need to create.

To get the intended behavior when creating labels, make sure to take a moment to determine whether they should be Instance or Type parameters. For example, the Project Issue Date that is automatically created in the Project Information dialog box is a Type parameter, and the Sheet Issue Date within the title block family is an Instance parameter. All project information parameters will be Type parameters, which means you change it once and all sheets will show the same value, and the parameters that are already defined in the title block family are Instance parameters. Sheet Number is an Instance parameter because each sheet number is unique.

Another method for making your annotation, as well as other forms of line work, intelligent is to create a Yes/No parameter that allows you to turn the display of those objects on and off. The basic procedure to achieve this is as follows:

1. While in the title block family select the Types tool from the Family Properties panel located in the Manage tab.

2. Click Add from the Family Types dialog box to start the creation of a Yes/No Instance parameter.

3. Fill in the appropriate information, as shown in Figure 12.8. Name it **Not for Construction**, make it a Yes/No parameter type, group it under Graphics, and make it an Instance parameter.

4. Once the parameter is created, select the elements within the drawing area that you want to toggle on and off, and select its Instance properties through the Element Properties drop-down located in the Modify "XYZ" contextual tab ➢ Element panel. In this case we will be selecting a piece of text that reads "Not for Construction."

5. In the Instance Properties dialog box select the little rectangular button to the far right of the Visible parameter.

6. Select the Not for Construction parameter from the Associate Family Parameter dialog box, and click OK to return to the Instance Properties dialog box.

FIGURE 12.8
Add a Yes/No parameter to control the visibility of a Not for Construction note.

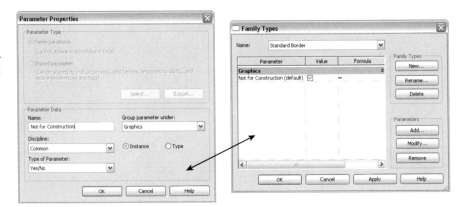

7. Observe the equal sign that now displays on the little rectangular button to the right of the parameter. This indicates that this element property is linked to the Yes/No parameter. Figure 12.9 shows the process involved to connect the text to the Yes/No parameter.

FIGURE 12.9
Create a Yes/No parameter to help control the display of elements in a title block family.

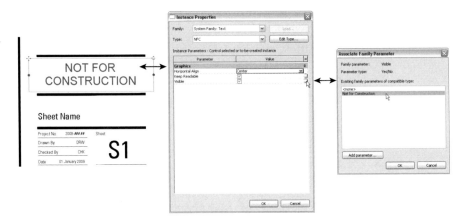

Depending on how you want the Yes/No parameter to behave, you can make it an Instance or a Type parameter. If you designate it a Type parameter, you could have two different title block types: one named For Construction and the other Not for Construction; then you can switch them as the project reaches the construction stage. If you designate it an Instance parameter, each instance of the title block family could have its own unique setting.

Another good use for a Yes/No parameter in a title block family is in creating a standard detail "grid" layout, as shown in Figure 12.10. This grid can be set to display as an Instance parameter of the title block family to be displayed and used while you are placing and arranging views on a sheet. After you have finished placing the views, you can toggle off the detail grid so it will not plot. Revit Structure will help align views to each other, but this grid can help prevent users from trying to place too many views on a sheet as well as aid in complying with sheet layout standards, like the NCS/UDS (National Cad Standard/Uniform Drawing Standard).

FIGURE 12.10
Make a grid of line work intelligent by placing it on a Yes/No Instance parameter.

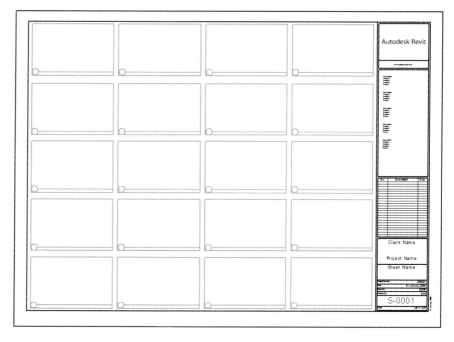

FINISHING IT OFF WITH AN IMAGE OR LOGO

Revit Structure allows you to import several different image formats into your title block families. You can see a list of these formats as well as the first step in importing an image by choosing the Insert tab ➢ Import panel ➢ Image tool. Figure 12.11 shows a logo image imported into a title block. One of the properties of an image is Lock Proportions; this ensures that the image maintains its aspect ratio when rescaling. This setting can be found in the image's properties or within the Options bar when the image is selected.

FIGURE 12.11
You can adjust the size of an image by selecting it and then dragging the grips at its corners; use Lock Proportions on the Options bar to maintain its aspect ratio.

You'll have better luck using images in Revit Structure for logos that contain fancy font display rather than using a complex filled region with line work and adjacent text, custom fonts, or imported 2D CAD graphics. If images are not created for these complex logos, you can perform screen captures with the Windows Ctrl+Alt+Print Screen keys and then paste the screen capture into editing software to crop as needed. This may not always produce a high-quality graphic, however, so you may need to use other image-capturing or printing tools.

SCREEN CAPTURE TIP

When creating a screen capture for a logo, you should try to make sure the image is "real size" first, the desired printed size. Make sure that it is not distorted to make it much bigger or much smaller. This will make the quality of the image when printed much more reliable and satisfactory.

INCORPORATING A REVISION SCHEDULE

Chapter 11 discusses in depth how to create various schedules for quantities and for displaying structural information for documentation. In this section we will discuss the things that are different in Revision Schedules from the schedules that are created within the project environment.

Revision Schedules can be created only while in a title block family. Therefore this feature will not be available in a project environment. Revision Schedules behave and are created pretty much the same way as other schedules created in the project environment. When Revision Schedules exist in a project, they populate with revision information as it is created and added to the project. Adding this revision information is discussed in the section "Keeping Track of Revisions" later on in this chapter.

The basic procedure for creating a Revision Schedule is as follows:

1. While in a title block family choose the View tab ➤ Create panel ➤ Revision Schedule tool.

2. By default, parameters that are available for schedule fields are already present, as shown in Figure 12.12. At this point you can click OK, and a schedule will be created.

3. Observe the available tabs at the top of the Revision Properties dialog box shown in Figure 12.12. These tabs all have the same look and feel that other schedules have. The only difference is that Revision Schedules do not have a Filter tab. Therefore, you will not be able to use filters when creating these types of schedules.

4. Once the schedule is created, it will appear in the Project Browser, as shown in Figure 12.13.

5. There are a couple of ways to get the Revision Schedule onto the title block sheet. One way is to select and drag the Revision Schedule in the Project Browser over to the hyphen that is located under Sheets (all). When you release the mouse button, the drawing area will switch to the view that contains the title block line work; there you can place the Revision Schedule just as you would any other schedule. Another way is to already have the title block open for editing and then drag the Revision Schedule from the Project Browser onto the sheet.

6. Adjust the appearance of your schedule in its Element Properties dialog box, and adjust its size to fit within your title block by selecting the Revision Schedule while in your title block sheet view and dragging the shape handle control as required. To access the Element properties of the Revision Schedule, you can select the schedule on the sheet, right-click it,

and choose Edit Schedule from the shortcut menu. This switches you to the schedule view where you right-click and choose View Properties from the shortcut menu. An alternative method is to select the schedule name in the Project Browser, right-click it, and choose Properties from the shortcut menu.

FIGURE 12.12
You cannot create new parameters for a Revision Schedule.

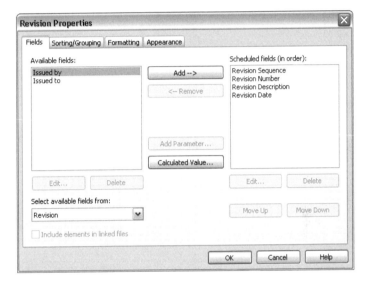

FIGURE 12.13
Revision Schedules show up in the Project Browser, where you can drag them onto the title block sheet for use in your project.

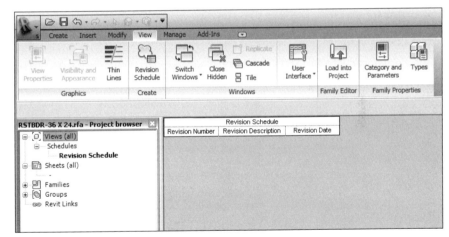

GETTING A REVISION SCHEDULE TO POPULATE

Revision schedules only list revision information when a Revision Schedule within a title block is placed into a project where cloud elements indicating a sheet issue/revision exist. Clouds have to become part of a sheet before the Revision Schedule can recognize them as a revision. To do this, you must place views containing clouds on the sheet with the Revision Schedule or place clouds directly onto the sheet.

Earlier we said that creating a Revision Schedule is pretty much the same as creating other schedules within a project. Let's discuss those aspects that are different by looking at the Appearance tab, shown in Figure 12.14. You can find this tab by going to the properties of the Revision Schedule.

FIGURE 12.14
Revision Schedules offer more functionality when it comes to their appearance.

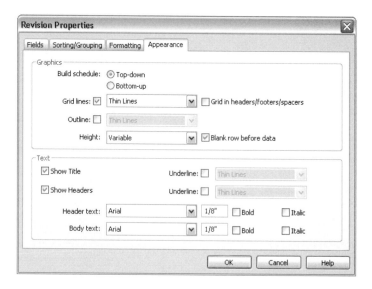

Within the Appearance tab shown in Figure 12.14 you will find fields that are available only for Revision Schedules. These appearance settings allow you to build the schedule to autopopulate from the top down or from the bottom up as well as have a variable or user-defined height. This information will display for other schedule types but will be grayed out and unavailable.

Building Your Schedules Top Down or Bottom Up

The first field that will become available is Build Schedule: Top-down or Bottom-up. This allows you to define the schedule to display schedule information from the top down, like any other schedule that is created in Revit Structure. Selecting Bottom-up allows you to create Revision Schedules that list the scheduled information starting from the bottom, as some firms prefer. Figure 12.15 shows the result of using these features.

FIGURE 12.15
Schedules can be set to be displayed Top-down or Bottom-up.

No.	Date	Revision Description
1	02/20/2009	Revision 1
2	03/13/2009	Revision 2

2	03/13/2009	Revision 2
1	02/20/2009	Revision 1
No.	Date	Revision Description

Figure 12.15 also shows the schedules with a user-defined height that allows them to show only a fixed number of rows so they can be placed in a defined area inside the title block.

Building Your Schedules with Height Adjustment

The second field that will become available is the Height field, which allows you to define the schedule height as Variable or as User Defined. Setting the Height value to a variable height allows the schedule to display as many horizontal rows as required. The height of the schedule grows as each new revision is added to a sheet. With this setting your schedule has a potential to grow to an undesirable height or length that might eventually conflict with other annotation and/or line work in your title block.

When your title block requires a limited space to be available for revision information, you should set the Height value to User Defined. This allows you to adjust the overall height of the Revision Schedule while inside the title block family. Figure 12.16 shows a selected schedule with its Height set to User Defined.

FIGURE 12.16
When Height is set to User Defined, you can adjust the fixed height by dragging the grip control.

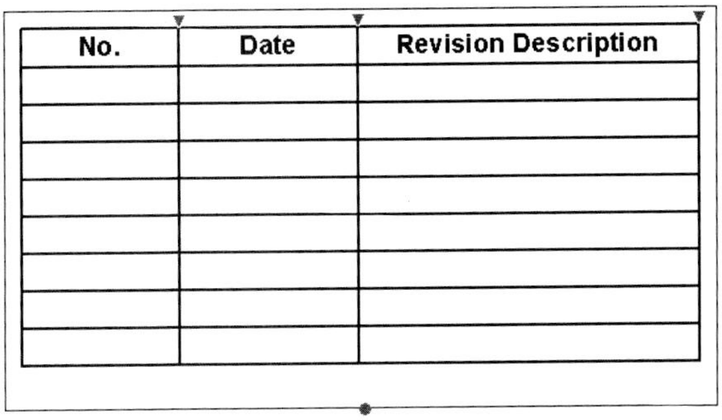

No.	Date	Revision Description

Schedules that have the Height value set to User Defined can display only a certain number of revisions, depending on the number of rows available to display the revision information. As the schedule fills up, the earlier/oldest revisions get pushed out to make room for the new ones. If a schedule is created to show only five rows of revision information and it is filled with five revisions, revision 1 will be removed from the schedule to make room for revision 6. When revision 7 is added, revision 2 is removed.

IF I COULD ONLY ROTATE MY REVISION SCHEDULE ON THE SHEET

Well, you can. While in a title block family with the Revision Schedule already placed within your title block design, select the Revision Schedule geometry and review the Options bar. You should see a drop-down list labeled Rotation On Sheet, which allows you to rotate the selected Revision Schedule 90 degrees clockwise or counterclockwise. This same feature is available for other schedules that are placed inside your project. However, like the Revision Schedules, these other schedules display the rotation option only on the Options bar; it is not part of the Element properties of the schedule.

Revision Schedules can be created to accommodate many different requirements. The best way to see all the various options is to create a new title block, add a Revision Schedule, and experiment with all of the different options. Load the title block into your project, and add revisions to the sheets to see how each change to the various settings in the Sorting/Grouping, Formatting, and Appearance tabs in the Revision Schedule properties behaves. Adding revisions to sheets will be discussed shortly.

Adding Information to Your Sheets

Sheets are one of the ways to disperse information about your project so others can access it. Typically these sheets will eventually be plotted. Beyond adding a title block to your sheets, you can add any view that was created that displays bits and pieces of the model in a schedule, section, or plan form. Placing these views onto sheets is really as simple as dragging them from the Project Browser and dropping them onto the sheet view. Once they are placed on a sheet, additional parameters become available as properties to the view. Some of these parameters are unique to the view type that is being placed, and others like the Sheet Number and Detail Number are part of almost all types of views.

Revit Structure's use of view titles helps keep your views organized onto sheets. View titles can display information about the view so those using the sheets can easily find the information they are looking for.

Sometimes thinking outside the box will allow you to take advantage of Revit Structure's views and pull information from the model. Creating a key plan from the model is an example. As the model changes, your key plan changes also. Adding more line work or text on the sheet as an overlay to the views that are placed on it allows you to provide additional information that is specific to the sheet or to combine two separate details into one. You can even overlap plan or elevation views to create nonexistent composite views.

Placing and Working with Views on Sheets

Different view types are used depending on what type of information you are showing about the model and how you want to show it. These view types are system families. Learning the parameters that appear when these views are placed onto a sheet and the different behavior each one can take on will help you produce great-looking documents that are easy to understand and work with.

There are several ways that you can add views onto a sheet. The various methods for adding any view onto a sheet are as follows:

Method 1   With the sheet view already open, drag and drop the view from the Project Browser onto the sheet.

Method 2   Drag and drop the view from the Project Browser onto the sheet name in the Project Browser. This automatically opens up the sheet view to allow you to place the view.

Method 3   Within the Project Browser, right-click the sheet onto which you will be placing a view, and select Add View. This action automatically opens to the selected sheet view and displays the Views dialog box shown in Figure 12.17. This dialog box shows a list of views that are not yet placed onto any sheet. Choosing a view and clicking the Add View to Sheet button allows you to place the selected view onto the sheet. By using this method you can avoid having to search through other views that are already placed on sheets.

Method 4   With the sheet view already open, go to the View tab on the Ribbon and select the View tool from the Sheet Composition panel. The same dialog box shown in Method 3 appears, where you can select from a list of views. The active view must be a sheet view, or the View tool will be grayed out.

As you can see, there are several methods you can use to place views onto a sheet. It is up to you to determine which one works best with your working habits. Once views are placed onto sheets, you can take advantage of those parameters that become available or those that have information available for display while they are on the sheets.

FIGURE 12.17

Selecting from a list of views that are not placed on sheets

Adding views to sheets adds another level of organization to your project. When you expand any of the sheet views in the Project Browser, every view that is placed on that particular sheet is listed, as shown in Figure 12.18. Once you expand the list, you can select any of the views and right-click it to access its properties, rename it, remove it from the sheet, or open it to edit.

You also have the ability to access the individual views that are placed on a sheet by activating a view and working through the sheet. Once you are further along in your project, this can be an efficient way to access the views that you are using for documenting the model. Figure 12.19 shows that you can right-click on any view that is on a sheet to select Activate View from the shortcut menu. This is no different from opening up the view from the Project Browser except you are seeing it displayed on your sheet with other views as well as working in the view.

FIGURE 12.18
Use the sheet views in the Project Browser to quickly access views that are placed on sheets.

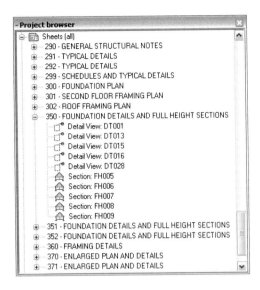

FIGURE 12.19
You can work on views through your sheets by right-clicking a view and selecting Activate View.

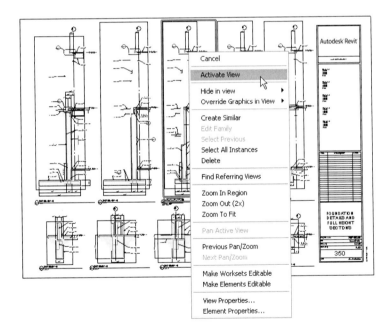

When you have finished working in the view, right-click again anywhere on the sheet and select Deactivate View from the shortcut menu. This can be an excellent method for reviewing and editing your documents while avoiding plotting the sheets or if you are picking up minor red lines that were made on a hard copy or a design review markup.

BE SURE TO DEACTIVATE YOUR VIEWS OR HALFTONE CAN HAPPEN

If you are in the process of activating and deactivating your views to work in them, Revit Structure will automatically deactivate the previous view when a new one is activated. There is no need to deactivate a view before moving onto the next one. If a new one is not activated and you forget to deactivate the current view, Revit Structure will keep it activated on that sheet. If you plot a sheet and all views on that sheet but one appears to be halftoned, then you might want to check to see that all views are deactivated.

Understanding the behavior of the various views as they are placed on sheets and learning which parameters are associated with each are definitely something that you want to master. Grasping things like the various view properties, view title manipulation, and key plan strategies will give you the edge you need to use every bit of information that is available to you to help create a good-looking set of documents that will complement your modeling efforts.

PLANS, ELEVATIONS, DETAIL, DRAFTING, AND 3D VIEWS

These view types have all the additional properties applied to them when they are placed onto a sheet. If for any reason some of them need to be rotated on a sheet, you can rotate them clockwise or counterclockwise by using the Options bar and the Rotate on Sheet drop-down list at the time of placement or after the view has been placed. The value of the Title on Sheet parameter can be filled in to override the view name that is displayed in the view title.

Other parameters that become available for these view types are as follows:

Detail Number   This contains the value that the view is given as its number on the sheet. The user can change this value, but no number can exist twice on the same sheet. When the first view is placed, Revit Structure gives it a value of 1. As additional views are placed on the sheet, Revit Structure automatically takes the next number in line or the lowest number not used.

Sheet Number   This contains the value of the sheet number that the view is placed on. This value updates as a view is moved onto a different sheet or a sheet number changes.

Sheet Name   This contains the value of the sheet name that the view is placed on. This value updates as a view is moved onto a different sheet or a sheet name changes.

Referencing Sheet   This contains the value of the sheet number that the view is referenced from. If a view is referenced from more than one sheet, then the sheet number that referenced the view first will be displayed as the value.

Referencing Detail   This contains the value of the detail number that the view is referenced from. If a view is referenced from more than one detail number, then the view that referenced the view first will be displayed as the value.

The parameters mentioned here can be used to display information in the view titles to aid in the layout and control of referencing information while you are documenting the model. Legends, schedules, and Graphical Column Schedules have behaviors that are much different from those of other views when they are placed on sheets.

LEGENDS

Legends are somewhat a combination of a detail view and a drafting view as to what is displayed inside of them, but they resemble the properties of schedules and Graphical Column Schedules when they are placed on sheets. They are like drafting views to the extent that they do not allow you to display geometric information directly from the model and they do not have a view range, but like other views they can have annotations, symbols, region fills, detail lines, and the like added to them. They are similar to detail views in that they do allow you to display model information, except that information is not graphically from the model. You can display parametric information about the various family types that exist throughout a project. A more in-depth explanation on legends and keynote legends can be found in Chapters 9 and 11.

Legends cannot be rotated when they are placed on a sheet, and they are not referenced to sheets. Since they are not referenced to sheets, they do not have the additional parameter to keep track of what sheet number they are on or what number they are assigned when placed on a sheet. They can be placed onto multiple sheets but cannot be placed multiple times on the same sheet. Revit Structure does not support multiple instances of a legend on the same sheet. You can override the display of a legend's view name in a view title by filling in the value for the Title on Sheet parameter.

SCHEDULES

Chapter 11 discusses how to create and work with schedules prior to them getting placed onto a sheet. Once a schedule is placed onto a sheet, it can be rotated clockwise or counterclockwise 90 degrees by selecting the schedule and using the Rotate on Sheet drop-down list on the Options bar. A schedule can be placed onto the same sheet multiple times; therefore it will not have a Detail Number parameter assigned to it when it is placed on a sheet, nor will it have any other parameters. Selecting the schedule while it is on a sheet and choosing Element Properties will only bring up a blank properties box.

Once a schedule is placed on a sheet, you can adjust the width of the columns by dragging the shape handle controls that display when the schedule is selected. You can do this only after the schedule is placed on a sheet. If for any reason a larger schedule needs to be split into separate chunks to fit on a sheet, you can easily do so by selecting the schedule while it is on the sheet and clicking the Split Schedule Table "break" symbol at the right of the schedule. Each click will break the schedule in equal parts. Figure 12.20 shows a single schedule that is selected and about to be split into two segments.

Figure 12.21 shows the same schedule split into two segments. Dragging the grip control (filled dot at the bottom of the first column) and moving it up or down will move rows from one segment to the other. Dragging the move control (four-way-arrow symbol) back onto the adjacent segment will join the schedules back together. Clicking the break symbol again will split the schedule into additional segments.

THIS SCHEDULE IS JUST TOO BIG FOR ONE SHEET

If a schedule is still too large for a single sheet, then you can use filters to restrict the data to a smaller subset of information. You need to create additional schedules using different filter criteria to put the remaining data on other sheets.

Graphical Column Schedules are also schedules, but they are assembled and automated much differently by Revit Structure. They are really a "hyper schedule" of little "views" of columns since they have a detail-level control for their graphical appearance, much different from a standard schedule with rows of data. They too can be split into multiple segments but take a much different approach than just clicking a break symbol.

FIGURE 12.20
Split a schedule into two by clicking the "break" symbol at the right of the schedule.

MARK	SIZE			REINFORCING	SOIL BRG PRESSURE	REMARKS
	LENGTH	WIDTH	THICKNESS			
F-5A	5'-0"	5'-0"	1'-4"	6-#5 BOT EW	6000	
F-5B	5'-0"	5'-0"	1'-0"	6-#5 BOT EW	4000	
F-6A	6'-0"	6'-0"	1'-6"	8-#6 BOT EW	6000	
F-7A	7'-0"	7'-0"	1'-8"	9-#7 BOT EW	6000	
F-7B	7'-0"	7'-0"	1'-4"	8-#7 BOT EW	4000	
F-8A	8'-0"	8'-0"	1'-10"	9-#8 BOT EW	6000	
F-8B	8'-0"	8'-0"	1'-6"	9-#7 BOT EW	4000	
F-9A	9'-0"	9'-0"	2'-2"	10-#8 BOT EW	6000	
F-9B	9'-0"	9'-0"	1'-10"	8-#8 BOT EW	4000	
F-10A	10'-0"	10'-0"	2'-6"	9-#9 BOT EW	6000	
F-12A	12'-0"	12'-0"	3'-0"	12-#9 BOT EW	6000	
F-12B	12'-0"	12'-0"	2'-4"	11-#9 BOT EW	4000	
F-13A	13'-0"	13'-0"	3'-2"	14-#9 BOT EW	6000	
F-13B	13'-0"	13'-0"	2'-6"	12-#9 BOT EW	4000	
F-14A	14'-0"	14'-0"	3'-6"	13-#10 BOT EW	6000	
F-15A	15'-0"	15'-0"	3'-10"	15-#10 BOT EW	6000	
F-20A	9'-0"	14'-7"	2'-8"	15-#8 BOT TRANS 9-#8 BOT LONG	6000	
F-21A	8'-0"	12'-0"	2'-4"	8-#9 BOT LONG 13-#7 BOT TRANS	6000	
F-22A	7'-8"	12'-0"	2'-6"	9-#9 BOT LONG 14-#7 BOT TRANS	6000	

COLUMN FOOTING SCHEDULE

Split Schedule Table

FIGURE 12.21
Split a schedule into two by clicking the break symbol at the right of the schedule.

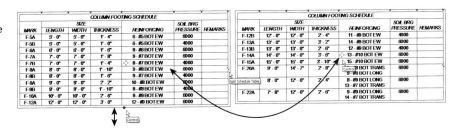

GRAPHICAL COLUMN SCHEDULES

Chapter 4 discusses in great depth how to create the Graphical Column Schedule (GCS) as well as several of its properties. The GCS has a behavior that it takes on only when it is placed onto a sheet. The only way to access this information is to select the GCS that is on the sheet and choose its Element properties. Accessing the properties by first selecting the view name in the Project Browser will not display this information. Figure 12.22 shows the additional segment information that is displayed under the Extents group of the Element properties.

The GCS does not have a Detail Number parameter when it is placed onto a sheet, so it can be placed onto different sheets multiple times but not twice onto the same sheet. Revit Structure does not support multiple instances of a GCS on the same sheet. In the properties shown in Figure 12.22, the GCS has a total of four segments. The Segments Start in Viewport and Segments in Viewport parameters are Instance parameters for each GCS that is placed on a sheet. This means each parameter can have its own value and not affect the other one but still exist as one GCS. In some cases all of the segments may not fit onto one sheet, so these values will have to be adjusted accordingly.

FIGURE 12.22
Place segments of a Graphical Column Schedule onto multiple sheets by adjusting the segment parameters in its properties.

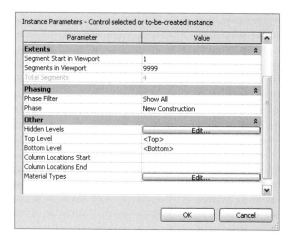

With the help of Chapter 4, create a five-segment GCS to use while reviewing the following basic procedure for distributing a GCS segments onto multiple sheets.

1. Create two sheets. The first one will contain three segments, and the second one will contain two segments of a five-segment GCS.

2. Place the five-segment GCS onto each sheet.

3. Make the first sheet view active, and review the GCS properties by selecting the GCS on the sheet and then accessing its properties from the Ribbon or by right-clicking the sheet and choosing Element Properties from the short-cut menu.

4. In the Extents group of its Instance Properties dialog box, change the value of Segments in Viewport to **3**. This will display segments 1 through 3 for this instance of the GCS. Click OK to see the results.

5. Make the second sheet view active, and review the GCS properties by selecting the GCS on the sheet and then accessing its properties from the Ribbon or by right-clicking the sheet and choosing Element Properties from the short-cut menu.

6. In the Extents group of its properties change the value of Segments Start in Viewport to **4** and the value of Segments in Viewport to **5**. This will display segments 4 through 5 for this instance of the GCS. Click OK to see the results.

Note that if you set the initial extents of the viewport values while the GCS is placed on only one sheet, Revit Structure will automatically display the remainder of the segments when the next instance of the GCS is placed on another sheet.

As you can see, these parameters allow you to adjust each instance of the GCS so you can display whatever segments you want to display as the GCS is placed on a sheet. Normally the view title displays the view name when a GCS is first placed on a sheet. This view name can be overridden by filling in a value for the Title on Sheet parameter. If a value exists for this parameter, the view name that is displayed in the view title by default is replaced with it. The GCS has a parameter to display its own title at the top of the schedule, so you may prefer that the view title be set to not display.

Working with View Titles

When views are placed on sheets, view titles are used to display information about those views. These view titles are linked directly to the view and pull information directly from the properties of the view. As properties of the view change, the information that is displayed in the view title automatically changes with it.

View titles can have different types assigned to them to allow you to display different information about a view throughout a sheet. Some views may require only a title, and some may not require anything. For each required display you create a new view title type. Three view title types exist in the `Structural Analysis-Default.rte` template that is provided by the Revit Structure installation:

◆ No Title

◆ Title Only

◆ Title w Line

These view titles are set to display the scale, the view name or title on sheet, and the detail number inside a circle. You can create additional view title types by duplicating an existing one and changing its properties as needed. If you want to display new geometry and/or parameters, then you will have to create a new view title family. For instance, some companies prefer to add the sheet number as part of their view titles.

EXERCISE: CREATING A NEW VIEW TITLE

To create a new view title you can start from an existing family that is already part of the Revit Structure installation, or you can start from scratch by using a View Title template. Revit Structure already has a family created similar to the one we are creating, except the circle element is larger. You can locate this family by browsing to the `Imperial Library - Annotations` folder.

For this exercise we will start from a View Title template so you can see the steps involved for creating one from scratch. To start we will create the look of the view title in a family and then load it into the project, where we will make it a View Title type.

CREATING A NEW VIEW TITLE FAMILY

1. Choose the Application menu ➤ New ➤ Family.

2. Browse to the `View Title.rte` family template located in the `Imperial Templates - Annotations` folder (or `Metric Templates`).

3. Choose the Category and Parameters tool from the Create tab ➤ Family Properties panel. Observe that the template already has the category set to View Titles.

4. Read the red block of note text that was preloaded in the template, and then delete it and the "dummy line" below it, as instructed.

5. Add line work and labels as shown in example graphic by using the tools in the Create tab on the Ribbon. The default Object Style for View Title in the template has a pen weight of 1. Once the family is loaded into your project, you can globally specify in the Object Styles dialog box of your project a line with that fits your standards for display. The image below has the line weight enhanced for print.

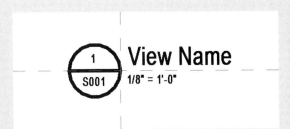

6. For the circle and line geometry, use the Line tool from the Detail panel along with various types of lines, circles, or arcs that can be found in the Draw/Pick Gallery on the Place Lines contextual tab that appears after choosing the Line tool.

7. To place the parameter information for the view data that will be part of the view title, click the Label tool located in the Create tab ➢ Annotate panel. Once you select Label, click anywhere in the drawing area to display the Edit Label dialog box, where you can choose from the available parameters.

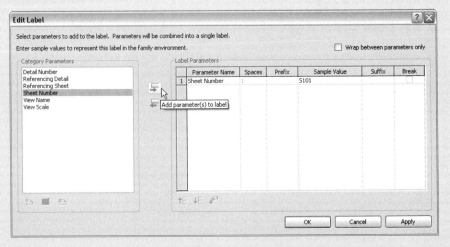

8. To add a parameter, choose it in the Category Parameters area at the left, and click the Add Parameter(s) to Label button. This is the button with the green arrow pointing to the right. Selecting this button places the parameter in the Label Parameters area to the right. Click OK to apply the parameter and close the dialog box. Tip: You can also just double-click the parameter name to shift it over as well.

9. Once the label is placed in the drawing area, drag it into its final position. Check to make sure its Justification properties are set properly, and edit its Element properties if necessary.

10. Repeat steps 7 through 9 to add the other labels to the view title.

11. Go to the Visibility/Graphic Overrides dialog box and turn off reference planes and dimensions so the thumbnail is easier to see when users load the family.

12. Save the family, naming it whatever you wish. After saving, load it into your project.

CREATING A NEW VIEW TITLE TYPE

The only way to edit or create a viewport type and assign your new view title to it is to select a view-port. If you haven't placed any views on a sheet, you'll need to do that first.

1. In your project select a view title or view that is displayed on a sheet, and click the Element Properties drop-down to access its Type properties, found on the Modify Viewports tab of the Elements panel of the Ribbon.

2. Choose Duplicate.

3. In the Name dialog box type a name and click OK.

4. Change the Title parameter value to match the view title family name that you created previously. Select the family name from the Title drop-down list, which won't be visible until you click in the field in the Value column.

5. Make adjustments, if needed, to other graphic parameters such as Line Weight, Color, Line Pattern, and the visibility of its title or extension line.

6. Click OK in the Type Properties dialog box.

7. Observe the new view title type, and check to see that its appearance is as you intended.

View titles allow you to control the display of the various components that compose them in a couple of places. To control the line weight, line color, and line pattern of the extension line, you will need to go to the Type properties of the view title, as shown in Figure 12.23.

FIGURE 12.23
Change the display of a view title extension line by going to the properties of the view type.

Type Parameters	
Parameter	Value
Graphics	⊼
Title	My New View Title : Standard
Show Title	Yes
Show Extension Line	☑
Line Weight	6
Color	■ Black
Line Pattern	Solid

To control the line weight of the annotation symbol that is created inside the family, you will need to choose the Manage tab ➤ Project Settings panel ➤ Settings drop-down ➤ Object Styles, as shown in Figure 12.24.

FIGURE 12.24
Change the appearance of view title elements by using the Object Styles dialog box.

Object Styles

Model Objects	Annotation Objects	Imported Objects		
Category	Line Weight Projection	Line Color	Line Pattern
⊞ Title Blocks	1	■ Black	Solid
View Reference	1	■ Black	
View Titles	1	■ Black	Solid
Wall Tags	1	■ Black	Solid

Within the Annotation Objects tab of the Object Styles dialog box, go to the category View Titles. Here you can change the line weight, line color, and line pattern.

CONTROLLING TEXT WRAPPING IN A VIEW TITLE

Typically Revit Structure will wrap the text in a view title based on the extent of the label length within the view title family. No matter what you set this extent to, it seems like it never wraps the text where you would like it to. A quick solution is to make the text length in the view title family long enough so the text does not autowrap. For those titles that require the text to wrap, you can force a hard return (place text on the line below) by hitting Ctrl+Enter at the keyboard while your cursor is at the point where you want the text to wrap. This should be done in the properties of the view and works only for the Title on Sheet parameter value. If you typically display the View Title parameter in your environment, you will have to utilize the Title on Sheet parameter instead. Note that if you are scheduling fields that have the text wrapped using a hard return, the values may not appear in schedules as desired.

An alternate method to the above suggestion if it does not fit into your workflow is to create different versions of the View Title families with specific-size labels for the viewport usage or text-wrapping extents. For example, a single column detail can have a label as wide as its single column or slightly less, and likewise for a two-column viewport. This way the user just chooses the correct-size viewport, and the text wraps automatically without you having to resort to a hard return.

Strategies for Creating Key Plans

In the past, in the 2D CAD environment, key plans probably consisted of line work that made up the perimeter shape of a building, some annotation for area delineation, and hatching to denote which area is shown on the sheet. There were probably other reasons for key plans even though you were not referencing zones or areas of a large-footprint building. You can still use those same strategies in Revit Structure, or you can go one step further and use modeled geometry to produce your key plans. Using modeled geometry for key plans will help keep them up to date with the current design of the building. It may even help you use key plans more often to aid in producing clearer documentation of your model.

There are several strategies for creating key plans, and they are explained in the following sections. Each strategy has pros and cons. Strategies such as the use of an annotation symbol family or images/screen captures can be embedded in title block families. Reduced structural plans and legends require them to be created directly into your project, and they are placed as views on sheets. You will need to choose which strategies will work for you as an office standard or on a project-by-project basis.

REDUCED STRUCTURAL PLANS

Using a reduced structural plan is probably the best strategy to allow the key plan to update as the model updates. The idea is that separate plan views are created at each level and then placed on sheets. The following procedure lists the necessary steps to quickly create key plans by using structural plans.

1. Create a structural plan of a level by creating a new one or duplicating an existing one. Name it accordingly.

2. Change the scale to a custom scale that allows a small key plan to be placed in a convenient and consistent location on a sheet.

3. In the Visibility/Graphic Overrides dialog box of the view, turn off the display of all model and annotation categories by selecting all and toggling their visibility off. Only a few categories will be turned back on. With everything off it is much easier to turn on the visibility of only those model categories that you want to be displayed.

4. Turn on the visibility of only those categories that you want to be displayed. Usually Walls, Floors, Roofs, and sometimes Grids will be enough categories to give you the display of the building footprint. Categories can be toggled on or off depending on how you want the key plan to display.

5. Override the line weight of the categories that are on to accommodate the reduced scale.

6. If needed, hide individual elements in the view or override their display individually.

7. Once everything is set the way you want, create a view template and name it **Key Plan**.

8. Create additional key plans for other levels, and apply the view template Key Plan to them.

9. Add additional line work, annotation, and region fills as required.

10. Drag each one to its appropriate sheet.

When using this method, you will need to create separate key plans for each zone or area of the plan you will be denoting. Structural plans can be placed on only one sheet before they have to be duplicated. The example shown in Figure 12.25 is a key plan for Zone 2 first-floor framing plan. We created this by following the procedure just outlined. Each zone is its own separate key plan with annotation, line work, and region fills specific to each view.

FIGURE 12.25
A key plan using a structural plan view to reference the Zone 2 framing plan

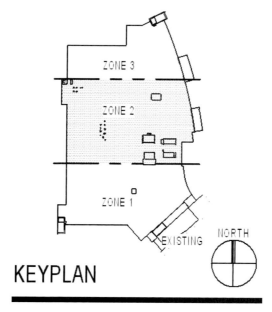

Figure 12.26 shows a similar example of a key plan displaying the parametric section cuts to reference the location of shear wall elevations that were used to document construction joints, reinforcing, and embed plate locations. Everything automatically updates in the key plan as the model changes or section references change locations.

FIGURE 12.26
A key plan using a structural plan view to reference shear wall elevations

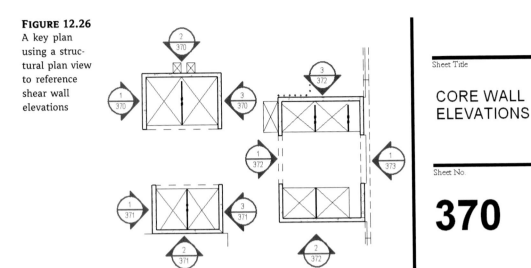

LEGENDS

Legends can also be used to create key plans. If a key plan is already created in another CAD system, the line work can be imported into the legend to be used directly or to be traced over the top of. Since legends can be placed on more than one sheet, there is potential to reduce the number of key plans you have to create. If it is not critical to follow the exact footprint, the same Zone 1, Zone 2, or Zone 3 legend could be placed on levels 1 through 10. In this scenario only three legends would have to be created. Legends can be used for building footprints just like the other methods we mention, but as you see, Figure 12.27 illustrates the use of a legend as a key to show what the information that is being displayed in a Graphical Column Schedule relates to. Using a legend as a key in this instance allows you to have one key that can be placed on multiple sheets.

FIGURE 12.27
Using a legend for a key diagram allows the same view to be placed on multiple sheets.

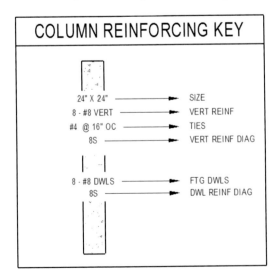

ANNOTATION SYMBOLS

Making use of annotation symbols can be a clever little way to go about creating a key plan. This allows you to create a key plan family that can be placed as a symbol onto each sheet. Line work can be added just as you would in any other example shown here. If a key plan is required to show different shades to denote zones or areas, you can add a Yes/No parameter to control the display of the hatching or filled region. An example of how to create a Yes/No parameter can be found in "Making Your Annotation Intelligent" earlier in this chapter.

The basic procedure for starting a new annotation symbol family is as follows:

1. Choose the Application menu ➢ New ➢ Annotation Symbol.

2. Browse to the Imperial Template\Annotations folder, and select the Generic Annotation.rft template.

3. A symbol used as a key plan can be categorized as Generic Annotations. You can verify this setting by choosing the Category and Parameters tool from the Create tab ➢ Family Properties panel. Highlight the Generic Annotations category, and click OK.

If the example shown in Figure 12.25 for the reduced plan method was created by using an annotation symbol, you could create the line work by placing new line work or importing existing line work. You could create a reduced plan view by using elements from the 3D model. The reduced plan view could be exported to AutoCAD to create 2D line work. This AutoCAD file could then be imported into the annotation symbol family. For the separate zones, region fills could be created and placed on Yes/No parameters. Three parameters would be created for this (Zone 1, Zone 2, and Zone 3). Each one would be set accordingly to create its own type, so depending on where the key plan was placed, it could display Key Plan Symbol Type Zone 1, Zone 2, or Zone 3.

IMAGE OR SCREEN CAPTURES

Images and screen captures can be used for key plans as well. Screen captures or images can be developed from existing key plans and placed into other views previously mentioned. Additional annotation, line work, and region fills can be used in conjunction with these images to create a look that suits your needs.

Creating a Sheet Index

Revit Structure automatically keeps track of sheets, and information such as sheet name and number can be displayed in a schedule-like format called a *drawing list*, more commonly known as a *sheet index*. As shown in Figure 12.28, creating a sheet index is similar to creating any other schedule in Revit Structure in that you can add fields, create filters, provide sorting or grouping, adjust the formatting, and set the appearance.

You can create and manipulate drawing lists using the same methods as for the schedules discussed in Chapter 11, except that when you create a drawing list you use a specific Drawing List tool that locks the category to display only information that is part of the Drawing Sheet category.

The basic procedure for creating a sheet index is as follows:

1. Choose the View tab ➢ Create panel ➢ Schedules drop-down ➢ Drawing List.

FIGURE 12.28
Creating a Drawing List is similar to creating schedules or quantities.

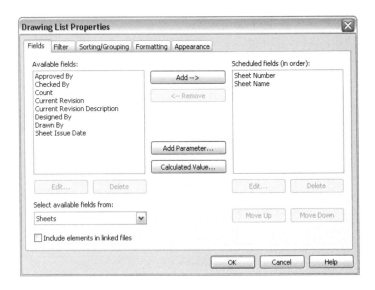

2. Within the Fields tab of the Drawing List Properties dialog box, add any of the available fields on the left-hand side of the dialog box to the scheduled fields on the right-hand side by selecting the field and clicking Add.

3. To include sheets from another Revit project file that is linked to your project, check the option Include Elements in Linked Files.

4. Reorder the scheduled fields if needed by selecting a field and clicking the Move Up or Move Down button as required.

5. Open the Filter and Sorting/Grouping tabs to create any filters and sorting or grouping rules that may be needed.

6. Open the Formatting tab to adjust the formatting of the sheet index headings and the alignment of the scheduled text.

7. Open the Appearance tab to set the appearance of the graphics and text.

8. Click OK to finish the drawing list.

Drawing lists can also be useful in helping to keep track of title block information. Viewing or populating this type of information can be easily be done through a schedule form rather than by individually viewing sheets and their properties. Information that can be added to a traditional sheet index to be used in checking for title block coordination includes the following:

◆ Checked By

◆ Designed By

- Drawn By

- Approved By

- Sheet Issued Date

- Current Revision

- Current Revision Description

SORRY, YOU CAN'T BE IN MY DRAWING LIST

Sheets can selectively be chosen to not display in a drawing list. To do this, go to the properties of the sheet that is not to be displayed, and remove the check mark from the Appears in Drawing List parameter field located in the Identity Data group. Checking the box allows that particular sheet to be displayed in a drawing list, while deselecting it prevents it from being displayed.

Sometimes you may need to create a much more advanced sheet index for larger projects or for those that have numerous issues. Keeping track of these issues can otherwise be a nightmare. Using Revit Structure to help automate some of this work will help eliminate confusion as to which sheets were issued when and for what reason. Figure 12.29 shows a more advanced drawing list that keeps track of the sheets as well as what they were issued for.

You can create a more advanced sheet index by adding additional project parameters that are linked to the Sheets category. Once these parameters are added, they will become available to be added to the scheduled fields. Within the Formatting tab, the Heading Orientation setting for the Issue field's headers is assigned to Vertical. When sheets are issued, the value of the Issue parameter in the properties of the sheet is populated with an *X* or any other character or symbol that you choose. Once the sheet index is placed on a sheet, you can adjust the columns as required.

The basic procedure for creating these additional parameters is as follows:

1. Go to the properties of the drawing list, and in the Fields tab, click Add Parameter. Adding this parameter within the properties of the schedule will automatically select the appropriate category for the parameter.

2. Select Project Parameter for Parameter Type.

3. Give it a name of **ISSUE_01_50% CD REVIEW**.

4. Select Text for the Type of Parameter.

5. Select a group to place the parameter in that makes sense to you.

6. Click OK.

7. Repeat steps 1 through 6 for as many parameters as you want to add.

8. Once the new parameters are created, they are listed under Scheduled Fields.

FIGURE 12.29
A sheet index created with additional parameters to keep track of issued sheets

STRUCTURAL SHEET INDEX							
		ISSUE					
SHEET #	SHEET TITLE	50% CD REVIEW	95% CD REVIEW	ISSUED FOR CD	ADDENDUM NO. 1	ADDENDUM NO. 3	AS-BUILTS
290	GENERAL STRUCTURAL NOTES	X	X	X			X
291	TYPICAL DETAILS	X	X	X			X
292	TYPICAL DETAILS	X	X	X			X
299	SCHEDULES AND TYPICAL DETAILS		X	X	X		X
300	FOUNDATION PLAN	X	X	X	X		X
301	SECOND FLOOR FRAMING PLAN	X	X	X			X
302	ROOF FRAMING PLAN	X	X	X	X		X
350	FOUNDATION DETAILS AND FULL HEIGHT SECTIONS		X	X	X		X
351	FOUNDATION DETAILS AND FULL HEIGHT SECTIONS		X	X	X		X
352	FOUNDATION DETAILS AND FULL HEIGHT SECTIONS		X	X			X
360	FRAMING DETAILS		X	X			X
370	ENLARGED PLAN AND DETAILS		X	X		X	X
371	ENLARGED PLAN AND DETAILS		X	X		X	X

HIDING PARAMETER INFORMATION WITHIN A SCHEDULE

Additional parameters can be added ahead of time and displayed in the schedule until used or hidden within the schedule until they are needed. To hide a parameter or column within a schedule, go to the Formatting tab within the Drawing List Properties dialog box, select the parameter to hide, and check the box named Hidden Field. You can also hide a column from within the schedule view itself. Right-click the column you don't want to show yet, and choose Hide Column(s). When you decide to show it again, you need to open the Drawing List Properties dialog box, click the Formatting tab, and uncheck Hidden Field. The Unhide All Columns option is available only from the schedule view itself.

You can create a sheet index that also keeps track of the issue date information with the addition of a drafting view or a legend. This method requires that the drafting view or legend be manually coordinated with the drawing list. Figure 12.30 shows a sheet index that has been created with this method.

The upper portion of the sheet index shown in Figure 12.30 is a drawing list, with additional parameters added to the Sheets category. Symbol characters have been added to indicate the values of these parameters depending on how the sheets are being issued. To add a symbol character you must insert the symbol via the Windows Character Map application and copy and paste it into the text field within Revit Structure.

The lower portion of the sheet index is a drafting view, with line work and text added to match the look of the sheet index. This portion has to be manually coordinated with what is shown in the sheet index above it each time you issue it. This method works well because you can display a much lengthier issue name without the sheet index getting too large, and you can also keep track of the issue dates as well as how the sheets were issued.

FIGURE 12.30
A sheet index created with additional parameters and a drafting view to help support the issue information

STRUCTURAL SHEET INDEX

SHEET #	SHEET TITLE	A	B	C	D	E	F	G	H	I	J	K	L	M	N	O
290	GENERAL STRUCTURAL NOTES	•		•	•	•	•									
291	TYPICAL DETAILS	•		•	•	•										
292	TYPICAL DETAILS	•				•	•		•							
300	FOUNDATION PLAN - ZONE 1	•		•	•	•	•	•		•		•				
300.1	FOUNDATION PLAN - ZONE 2												•		•	
301	PENTHOUSE FLOOR FRAMING PLAN - ZONE 1	•	•			•	•		•	•	▲					•
301.1	ROOF FRAMING PLAN @ INFILL - ZONE 2										▲				•	
302	PENTHOUSE ROOF FRAMING PLAN	•	•			•	•		•	•	▲					
303	PARTIAL PLAN AND DETAILS									•						
304	PENTHOUSE CONNECTOR													•		
340	FULL HEIGHT SECTIONS							•		•		•				•
360	SECTIONS AND DETAILS	•		•	•	•	•	•	•							
361	SECTIONS AND DETAILS			•	•	•	•	•		▲						•
362	SECTION AND DETAILS					•	•		•							•
363	SECTIONS AND DETAILS							•								
364	SECTIONS AND DETAILS									•		•				
365	SECTIONS AND DETAILS @ INFILL										•			•		
366	SECTIONS AND DETAILS @ INFILL												•	•		
380	COLUMN SCHEDULE AND DETAILS	•	•			•	•		•							
381	COLUMN SCHEDULE @ INFILL AND MISC DETAILS														•	

KEY FOR ISSUE

ISSUE	ISSUED FOR	ISSUE DATE
A	PRICING PACKAGE	NOVEMBER 15, 2007
B	REVISED PRICING PACKAGE	DECEMBER 03, 2007
C	BID PACKAGE #3 - FOUNDATION AND UNDERGROUND	DECEMBER 10, 2007
D	PERMIT REVIEW SET	DECEMBER 12, 2007
E	BID PACKAGE #4 - SHELL	DECEMBER 13, 2007
F	ADDENDUM #1	DECEMBER 20, 2007
G	ASI #1	JANUARY 21, 2008
H	SI #2	FEBRUARY 22, 2008
I	SI #3	MARCH 20, 2008
J	STEEL PACKAGE (INFILL)	APRIL 23, 2008
K	SI #9	APRIL 28, 2008
L	BID PACKAGE #8 (INFILL FDN)	MAY 02, 2008
M	SI #11	MAY 06, 2008
N	BID PACKAGE #9 (INFILL)	MAY 09, 2008
O	SI #15	MAY 16, 2008

• INDICATES DRAWINGS THAT ARE BEING ISSUED.

▲ INDICATES DRAWINGS THAT HAVE BEEN ISSUED ON SMALL SHEETS OR WRITE UP.

CURRENT REVISION ON A SHEET

When creating a drawing list you can also utilize such parameters as Current Revision and Current Revision Description. This is a new feature in Revit Structure 2010. Creating a Drawing List Schedule to show these parameters is a great way to display the most recent issue or revisions to a sheet. This can really come into play for projects with several sheets.

DRAWING LIST WITH CURRENT REVISION			
SHEET NUMBER	SHEET NAME	CURRENT REVISION	CURRENT REVISION DESCRIPTION
290	GENERAL STRUCTURAL NOTES	2	BID PACKAGE 1
300	FOUNDATION PLAN	3	BID PACKAGE 1, AD-1
301	SECOND FLOOR FRAMING PLAN	4	PR-1
302	ROOF FRAMING PLAN	4	PR-1
291	TYPICAL DETAILS	2	BID PACKAGE 1
292	TYPICAL DETAILS	2	BID PACKAGE 1
350	FOUNDATION DETAILS AND FULL H	2	BID PACKAGE 1
299	SCHEDULES AND TYPICAL DETAILS	3	BID PACKAGE 1, AD-1
351	FOUNDATION DETAILS AND FULL H	4	PR-1
360	FRAMING DETAILS	5	RFI-31
370	ENLARGED PLAN AND DETAILS	4	PR-1
371	ENLARGED PLAN AND DETAILS	4	PR-1
352	FOUNDATION DETAILS AND FULL H	2	BID PACKAGE 1

Learning to create a sheet index to this extent will help you to keep your sheets in sync with the revisions that you are adding to them. It may be necessary to manually keep track of these issues and revision names adjacent to a sheet index in a "Key For Issue" schedule via a Drafting View as we have shown earlier, but you will be able to use Revit Structure's revision tools to help automate the process on a sheet-by-sheet basis as well as automate the control of the information that gets displayed in a Revision Schedule.

Keeping Track of Revisions

Keeping track of revisions so others can clearly see what has changed with the model or with the documentation is another task that Revit Structure does well. Similarly to how views on sheets are repeatedly being coordinated with the sheet they are on and where they are referenced from, revisions know what sheet they are placed on, keep track of whether they are issued or not, as well as hold other valuable information about the changes being made.

When you get started your project template should already have one revision defined and waiting for the day you need it. Revit Structure uses a Sheet Issues/Revision dialog box to define all of a project's issues/revisions. In practice you'll probably find that having a single revision waiting for you in your template allows you to start off creating revision clouds to identify where your first round of changes occur. Then you can visit the Sheet Issues/Revision dialog box to deal with new changes. This section is organized that way. We'll discuss what you do with revisions and then wrap up with an in-depth explanation of all the elements that support this feature.

A typical revision consists of a cloud that displays all the information that pertains to a particular revision that is defined and stored in the Sheet Issues/Revision dialog box. We will ease into discussing this dialog box as we continue on. The cloud, which is a graphical mechanism to define where a revision affects the drawing, is placed around the area of change to indicate where the change is made. A tag that displays information from the cloud properties is placed alongside the cloud. When Revit Structure detects that a revision is on a sheet and a Revision Schedule is present in the title block, it displays and tracks the revision information for that sheet. Figure 12.31 shows revisions as they would be used on a project.

The basic procedure for placing and tagging a revision is described in the following sections.

FIGURE 12.31
Keeping track of revisions by placing a cloud and tagging it for reference

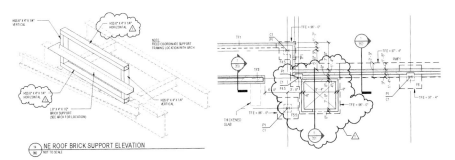

Placing a Revision Cloud

Placing clouds in Revit Structure is very similar to how you may have done it in a prior 2D/3D CAD environment. You may have used an inserted block or a tool that allowed you to sketch the extents of the cloud. Revit Structure's Revision Cloud tool allows you to sketch the boundary of the revision cloud directly in the views where the revisions occur or directly on the sheet. To place a revision cloud, follow these steps:

1. Choose the Annotate tab ➢ Detail panel ➢ Revision Cloud tool from the Ribbon. You can also right-click an existing revision cloud and choose Create Similar from the shortcut menu.

2. Placing a cloud will put you into Sketch mode, where you sketch the extents of the cloud by using the Line tool from the contextual tab that appears.

3. Clouds are sketched by consecutively clicking placement points to form a boundary. After you place your first point, each subsequent sketch point clicked creates a pair of arcs — the smaller is about a third of the size of larger arc — to represent a "sketchy" cloud shape. Pressing the spacebar while sketching an arc segment flips the orientation of the arcs. The size of the arcs increases or decreases according to the distance between the points you pick.

4. When the sketch is complete, click Finish Cloud from the Ribbon. A revision cloud does *not* have to be closed like other sketch-based elements in Revit, though most clouds, in practice, probably ought to be.

One of the best features of placing revision clouds in Revit Structure is that revision clouds are assigned to defined revisions. These clouds allow Revit Structure to keep track of those views that contain them and are on a particular sheet. Revit Structure does not know where the actual revision has occurred, but it knows that you placed a revision cloud in a view by tracking its existence. You can tag revision clouds just like other elements in Revit Structure to display their properties or denote them as a symbol that links to a Revision Schedule, where additional information can be displayed.

NO REVISION CLOUD REQUIRED

Revit Structure automatically populates a Revision Schedule with revision cloud information when it detects a revision being placed on a sheet and the presence of a revision in a view when the view is placed on the sheet. Sometimes you may want to record information about a revision within a title block that does not require a revision cloud. For example, you may want to record information about a 50 percent review set, issued for DD or issued for CD. Whatever it may be, it might not require a revision cloud.

You can create a revision on a sheet without requiring a cloud by right-clicking a sheet in the Project Browser and choosing Properties. In the properties of the sheet click the Revisions on Sheet parameter located under the Identity Data group, and click the Edit button. The following illustration shows the Revisions on Sheet dialog box, where you can choose to record a revision on a sheet without having to place a revision cloud.

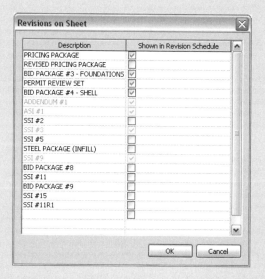

All the revisions in the project will display, and those that are already on sheets from the placement of a revision cloud will be grayed out. Checking the Shown in Revision Schedule field populates the schedule with that particular revision without having to place a revision cloud.

If multiple sheets are selected, this parameter will not be available to edit. You can select and set only one sheet at a time to display revision information.

Tagging a Revision Cloud

Before you can place a tag to reference a revision, you will need to place a revision cloud. The tag is a label that can be defined by the user to display properties about the revision cloud. To tag a revision cloud, follow these steps:

1. Choose the Annotate tab ➤ Tag drop-down ➤ By Category.

2. Use the Options bar to adjust placement properties prior to placement.

3. Select a revision cloud element to be tagged.

The Options bar shown in Figure 12.32 offers several options that you can set prior to tagging a revision cloud. The Options bar will display some settings when you select an existing tag as well.

FIGURE 12.32
Use the Options bar to toggle tag leaders on or off before and after their placement.

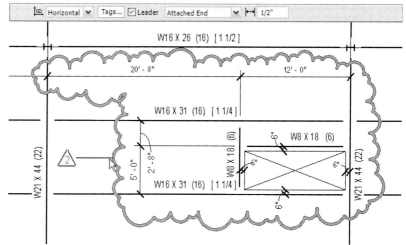

Reading from left to right, the revision-tagging Options bar in Figure 12.32 allows you to do the following:

◆ Select Horizontal or Vertical to predetermine the orientation of the tag.

◆ Click the Tags button to select which loaded tag to use. If the desired tag is not loaded, you can click Load to find it and load it now.

◆ Choose to place a tag with or without a leader.

◆ Choose to have the end of the leader attached to the cloud by setting it to Attached End or to a location of your choice by setting it to Free End.

◆ Set the initial leader length dimension from the end of the leader back to the tag. After the tag is placed, you can move it along with the leader to any location you want.

Setting the Display of Revision Clouds and Tags

You use Revit Structure's Object Styles dialog box to set the appearance of revision clouds and tags that may be used to label them. These settings can be found by choosing the Manage tab ➤ Project Settings panel ➤ Settings drop-down ➤ Object Styles. Within the Annotation Objects tab of the Object Styles dialog box, go to the category Revision Cloud Tags and Revision Clouds. Here you can change the line weight, line color, and line pattern for each. The settings in the Object Styles dialog box apply globally to the entire project, but you can apply an override for each view if necessary, giving you added flexibility in how revision cloud elements display.

You may need to assign revision clouds that are already placed throughout the model to a different revision. Revit assigns the latest revision/issue to a revision cloud when you click Finish Cloud. If a revision cloud is assigned to the wrong revision, you can change it. If revision clouds are tagged, they will automatically reflect the new revision information. You can do this by selecting the revision cloud(s) and choosing Element Properties or by going to the Options bar. Figure 12.33 shows how these methods will let you choose which revision type the cloud should be assigned to.

If you need to move several revision clouds to a different revision, you may need to individually select each revision cloud or select them all by using a window selection and filter the selection to select only the revision clouds. The Select All Instances method is not available when working with revision clouds in Revit Structure.

FIGURE 12.33
Change a revision cloud's type by going to its properties or the Options bar when it is selected.

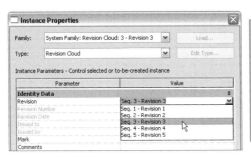
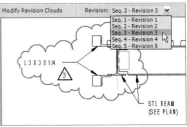

To understand the properties of revision clouds and how they are controlled, we need to introduce you to the Sheet Issues/Revisions dialog box that Revit Structure provides to let you manage them.

Understanding the Sheet Issues/Revisions Dialog Box

You access the Sheet Issues/Revisions dialog box by choosing the Manage tab ➢ Project Settings panel ➢ Settings drop-down ➢ Sheet Issues/Revisions tool. You can also get to the same location by choosing the View tab ➢ Sheet Composition panel arrow icon. Within this dialog box, shown in Figure 12.34, you can add additional revisions, merge with existing ones, as well as adjust the order in which they occur. You can mark revisions as being issued and set the display to show only the tag or both the cloud and the tag. You can also choose to display a numeric or an alphabetic value within the tag. All of this gives flexibility to you when tracking revisions. We will briefly discuss the behavior of these global settings within a project.

FIGURE 12.34
Creating new revisions, organizing their sequence, and controlling their behavior are possible with the Sheet Issues/Revisions dialog box.

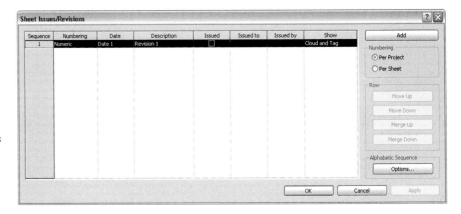

WHAT? NO TAG LOADED

Tagging a revision cloud is the same as tagging other objects in Revit Structure. The traditional symbol used for a revision is a triangular shape and that is what Revit uses, but you can revise it just as you would other tags to use another shape or to show additional information related to the revision.

Attempting to place a tag for a revision cloud without loading a matching tag will display a warning that indicates that a tag is not loaded for this type. You can load the default tag that comes with Revit Structure by browsing to the Imperial (or Metric) Library\Annotations\Revision Tag.rfa family.

When opening the Sheet Issues/Revisions dialog box for the first time, you will see that Revit Structure has already created a revision for you and it can't be removed. You can use this as a starting point. Each revision has a fixed number of parameters available.

To help you better understand the various settings in the dialog box shown in Figure 12.34, we will briefly explain what each section does. To further expand your knowledge from what is shown here, browse through the help guides that are part of Revit Structure by searching for "Revisions."

NEW PARAMETERS CANNOT BE ADDED TO REVISIONS

New parameters cannot be added, so sometimes you may have to use an unused parameter field to be able to use a revision standard that your company employs.

For example, if you were to use AD1 in your revision delta symbol to indicate Addendum 1, you could use the Issued To or Issued By parameter to hold the value of AD1. You would have to create a new revision symbol to display the value from one of those parameters. Since these parameters are global to the project, you can change the value in one place and concurrently change the display of several instances of tags.

Sequence Revit Structure gives each revision a sequence number. This parameter can be added to a Revision Schedule to help sort the order of revisions placed on a sheet. This is Revit's own unique revision ID.

Numbering The Numbering parameter is used to select the display of numeric, alphabetic, or no numbering for each revision. This value is typically displayed in a revision delta. If a numeric number method is selected, it will display numbers in sequential order, such as 1, 2, 3, 4, 5, etc., as each revision is created.

If an alphabetic numbering method is selected, it will pull its information from the alphabetic sequence list shown in Figure 12.35. This list can be found by clicking the Options button in the lower right-hand corner of the Sheet Issues/Revisions dialog box. Each revision will display the next character in line, such as *A*, *B*, *C*, *D*, *E*, etc., as each revision is created. This is intended to give you the ability to decide whether potentially ambiguous letters like *I* or *O* are allowed as revision values.

Note that the alphabetic sequence cannot contain spaces, numbers, or repeated characters. If you attempt to use this format, Revit Structure will display a warning to remind you of this.

FIGURE 12.35
Use Sequence Options
dialog box to set the
order for an alphabetic
numbering method.

Date The Date parameter is used to display the date of issue for the revision in a Revision Schedule on a title block.

Description The Description parameter is used to explain why the revision exists, and you can add it to a Revision Schedule on a title block.

Issued The Issued parameter is used to mark a revision as having been issued. This locks the revision clouds that are placed throughout the model so that they cannot be moved, deleted, or edited. If you try to move one, Revit will generate a warning dialog box that includes an option to "unissue the revision." This helps ensure that revision clouds don't get moved after they are issued. Keep in mind that the revision clouds do not automatically move when other modeled or annotation elements move, so it is possible to have the revision cloud not encompass its intended revision.

Issued revisions cannot be modified within the dialog box either except to provide Issued To or By information. You cannot place a revision cloud and assign it to an issued revision. If you need to do this, you will first need to change the revision so that it is not issued. When you place new revision clouds, they will automatically get assigned to the last unissued revision in the revision list.

Issued To The Issued To parameter can be used to display information about whom the revision is being issued to. If you don't usually show this information on documents, this field can be used as an alternative field to display information other than an Issued To value.

Issued By The Issued By parameter can be used to display information about who is issuing the revision. This field can also be used differently like Issued To if necessary.

Show The Show parameter allows you to display the tag, the cloud and tag, or neither before or after it is issued. Many firms prefer to show clouds only for the latest revisions. They leave only the tag visible for earlier revisions. Thus, these choices usually offer enough flexibility so you can display the information that you need at the time you need to display it.

MAYBE I DON'T WANT A LEADER

Sometimes you need to turn off the clouds after a revision is issued but keep the tag turned on during future revisions. This is commonly done so you can track revisions without having a cluttered mess of clouds on the sheets. If tags are placed with leaders and the Show parameter for that revision is set to show only tags, the leaders will also be visible. This can lead to an unexpected display of tags and leaders. You can turn off the leaders for tags that are related to issued revisions, but that would be some extra work. Therefore you might want to rethink using leaders for your revision tags. Many firms choose to place the tag just outside or just inside the cloud instead, without the leader, so they don't have to worry about this.

Numbering area   The Numbering area of the Sheet Issues/Revisions dialog box is where you can set the revision behavior to Per Sheet or Per Project. This affects the entire project revision scheme. This option can be set to however your company prefers to track revisions on sheets or to match how the architect is tracking them. This setting can be a big deal to the people in your firm who see the construction of the project through to completion. You can change the setting here, but it will alter how all of the revisions are identified, and you will have to verify that everything is correct.

When using the Per Project method, each revision gets assigned a numeric or alphabetic value depending on what revision it is. No matter which number of revision may be on a particular sheet, it will always display the same value. For example, if revision 3 was the fifth revision in the Sheet Issues/Revisions dialog box, it would display the value 5. Wherever that revision was detected on a sheet or set to display on a sheet through the sheet properties, it would display the value 5.

When using the Per Sheet method, each revision gets assigned a numeric or alphabetic value depending on what revision it is on that particular sheet. Each revision is given a value depending on how many revisions are on a sheet. For example, if revision 3 was the fifth revision in the Sheet Issues/Revisions dialog box and was the second revision on a sheet, it would display the value 2.

Real World Scenario

ANOTHER PERSPECTIVE OF "PER PROJECT" VERSUS "PER SHEET"

Firms that use Per Project want to define a constant reference to a revision such that it applies to the entire set of documents. This means that revision 1 is the same "thing" that was fixed or changed wherever a reader sees it. For example, revision 1 indicates that all columns have been changed to W16x31 from W10x49 in the east wing. There are sheets that have nothing to do with this portion of the project, and you will have no reference to a revision, no clouds or tags at all, but the Revision Schedule on the sheet can still indicate that there has been a revision 1. This also means that a sheet can have its first revision listed as revision 4 with no other revisions listed if these other revisions are not selected to display on the sheet too, as mentioned earlier. Consider that this sheet is usually not issued again because it is unaffected by revision 1. It would be issued when revision 4 affects it.

Other firms want to track revisions according to their impact on a specific sheet. Consider the same revision above. This firm wants the sheets that are affected by revision 1 to show revision 1. Let's imagine that several other revisions have occurred since (2–6) and they have been issued. Let's also imagine that only revision 4 affected a sheet that was issued again for revision 1. When this sheet is affected by the fourth actual revision that has been documented, the sheet will show it as just the second revision, revision 2, that applies to it, instead of showing revisions 1 and 4. This permits a reader of the documents to assess the status of a single sheet without the context of the whole set and the whole project. The reader knows that this sheet has had two revisions affect it, and based on their role in the project they may have no idea how many other revisions have occurred.

This setting is important, and the people in your firm who see a project through to completion need to be part of the decision. The "wrong" decision can be reversed, but it may involve some rework to the tagging effort completed earlier.

Row area The Row area of the Sheet Issues/Revisions dialog box is where you can rearrange the order of revisions or merge them with other ones. How often does it happen that you are working on revision 3 and you get the call, "Can we quickly issue this one detail as revision 3 and put everything else you have been working on for the past three days on revision 4?" Well, this is how you would handle it. You can add a new revision, move it up ahead of revision 3, swap the names, and can continue on your way.

Alphabetic Sequence area The Alphabetic Sequence options are used when the Numbering method is set to Alphabetic. This dialog box sets the sequence to be used for alphabetic characters as revisions are placed on sheets.

 **Real World Scenario**

EVERYBODY HAS A STANDARD

As a structural engineering firm, we work with several clients. Each one has its own standard for keeping track of revisions. Not only does each client have its own standard, but each project, depending on the construction schedule and contractor, may warrant a deviation from that standard. Revit Structure accounts for many of these standards, but in some cases we have to do a little bit of thinking outside the box in order to use Revit Structure's Revision Schedules and Tracking feature.

In one scenario we create a revision in Revit Structure for a Structure Supplemental Issue (SSI). This can be a small item or a large item. Revisions are usually issued as full-size sheets and tend to happen on a regular basis. The numbering system inside the revision tag takes the form SSI#2, depending on which SSI number it is. To get the revision tag to display this numbering method we have created a new revision tag to pull from the Issued To or Issued By parameter, which is a global parameter located in the Revision dialog box. The field that is chosen is populated with the SSI# for the revision. This parameter is also added to the Revision Schedule so that the correct numbering is displayed in the schedule on the title block.

Sometimes these SSIs may take a few days to be completed, and during this time other revisions may have to be answered in another form. For us it is usually in the form of a Request for Information (RFI). As these RFIs are answered, and if the model needs to be revised, it is denoted with a revision cloud and tag. In this case we have created a new revision tag to pull from the Instance Comment parameter of the revision cloud. The Comment parameter is populated with a value of RFI#n, depending on which RFI number it is. The revision cloud is still on an SSI revision, but the instance of the cloud would have an RFI comment. We use the revision comment tag for this.

When the SSI is officially issued, revisions not yet issued are tagged as SSI#, and those that have already been issued on smaller sheets are tagged with RFI#, or whatever method they were officially issued by. This allows a full-size sheet to display all the newly issued revised information as well as how it was issued and display the information that was previously issued but on partial sheets.

Typically Revit Structure should greatly reduce the need for RFIs because of the close collaboration we can have with other disciplines and the early detection of conflicts. However, with some projects we tend to quickly develop the model and may not always have all the discipline's correct information at the same stage of the race where we are structurally, or we may not even have a Revit Structure/BIM model available to us, just CAD documentation/files. Keeping track of these revisions in this manner allows us to stay on top of what is or has gone on with our model as we continually keep the model up to date with the construction schedule.

You will find that learning how the tools in Revit Structure work for creating sheet content and tracking revisions will help you learn some workaround solutions that can be done to achieve the behavior of several standards that may be required. You will want to take full advantage of everything pertaining to your deliverables and what sheets can do for you so you can spend your time designing and documenting the structure rather than coordinating the placement of your information, as it may change as a project evolves.

The Bottom Line

Create a title block to display project information.   The basics of creating a title block include using line work, annotations, filled regions, labels, and images. Combining these basic elements to create parametric behavior will take you way beyond 2D drafting.

>   **Master It**   What are three ways you can make your title blocks parametric to autoadapt to changes that are made within your sheets?

Create a Revision Schedule to your company standards.   Revision Schedules added to title blocks allow you to keep track of revisions on sheets. You can design these Revision Schedules to accommodate just about any company standard and title block configuration.

>   **Master It**   How do you rotate a Revision Schedule 90 degrees? How or where do you set a Revision Schedule to display its information from the bottom up?

Explore the behavior of the various view types when they are placed on a sheet.   When views are placed on sheets, new parameters become available that display information that is specific to how and where the views are placed. Each view can have a different behavior; knowing this behavior allows you to take advantage of it.

>   **Master It**   What are four parameters that become available in plan, elevation, detail, drafting, and 3D views when they are placed on a sheet? What types of views can be placed on a sheet more than once without being duplicated?

Produce a drawing list/sheet index to keep track of your issued sheets.   Revit Structure lets you easily create a drawing list/sheet index to keep track of sheets.

>   **Master It**   How can you get additional information on your drawing list to manually account for issue names and descriptions as well as to show which sheets are being or have been issued?

Control the behavior of revisions in your project.   You can control the tracking of revisions made to the model to reflect several standards that may be required as well as react to unknown project schedule changes.

>   **Master It**   How do you set a revision tag to display an alphabetic sequence "numbering" standard? How do you rearrange a revision to be put on hold so that it can be used after others instead?

Part 4

Sharing Your Structural Model

Chapter 13

Worksharing

Prior to the introduction of Revit Structure, your structural projects more than likely consisted of several files that you assembled into sheets and printed for each issue. These files were probably produced and maintained by a drafter. Another set of files was created by the engineer for the analysis portion, which eventually was put into the documentation portion of the drawings. The use of all these files kept it fairly easy to keep the work spread out so multiple users did not need to have the same file open simultaneously. Even if one person was producing all aspects of the project, at some point a second user was often brought into the project at the tail end to help.

Now Revit Structure has taken all of your individual files that you used to work on and combined them into one database that consists of a single .rvt file. This database is now where all of your plans, details, and sheets exist. This file contains all your project documentation. Chances are, more than one person will have to work in this database. This is where *worksharing* comes in.

Worksharing allows your project to be broken up into logical pieces called *worksets*, which allow multiple users to work on the same project at the same time.

In this chapter you will learn to:

- ◆ Determine when to enable worksharing
- ◆ Enable and set up the worksharing environment
- ◆ Request and grant permission of elements
- ◆ Stay in sync with other team members
- ◆ Properly maintain your project file

Understanding the Worksharing Concept

With worksharing enabled, Revit Structure allows several team members to efficiently work on a project at the same time. Revit Structure does a good job of keeping track of ownership — in other words, who has which elements borrowed or checked out. This enables you to coordinate and propagate changes between users. Worksharing involves using worksets to create a multiuser working environment.

To truly grasp the concept of worksharing, you need to understand the workflow, the various terms and concepts associated with worksharing, and when it makes sense to use worksharing and when it doesn't.

ALTERNATIVE METHOD

For very large projects, models may be broken into several smaller projects. Team members then work on individual smaller projects and link them back into another master project to produce the final documentation. Using this method might improve performance by not having everything stored inside one large working model — but at the cost of more project setup and management as well as the lack of coordination and interaction between structural elements that might otherwise be connected. This method can be used in conjunction with a multiuser worksharing environment or with just several single-user files.

Knowing the Workflow

A common scenario is where you, a single user, start a project and take it to a certain point before requiring the help of others, thus having a need to enable worksharing.

Before that time arrives you set up your project and start the modeling process. You coordinate levels and grids with the architect, and you add generic object placeholders for walls, columns, framing, and so forth to the model. You save this single-user project on your network server, as shown in Figure 13.1, so that it gets backed up, no different than how you saved your individual files in the past.

FIGURE 13.1
A single-user file saved to the network

Single-user
File
(Server)

At some point additional users are needed. You may need someone to help with the analytical model or to help out with creating details. Every company and every project will have its own scenarios. Either way, you see that it is time for multiple users, and thus it is time to enable the worksharing feature.

There are four fundamental steps to prepare any project for worksharing:

◆ Save the project in a project folder with an appropriate name

◆ Enable worksets

◆ Save the file

◆ Synchronize with Central

Once you enable this feature, Revit Structure will take all of the content that you have placed into your project and assign it to logical worksets. The first stages of this organization are all handled by Revit Structure. At this point you are no longer working on a single-user file. The only thing you need to do is save your project so it becomes a central file for other team members to use. Save the central file onto the network just as you saved your single-user file.

Once the central file is created, users will create local files, which are saved on their own workstation's hard drive, as shown in Figure 13.2. These local files maintain a bidirectional link to the central file on the network. Revit actively manages the ownership of elements in the model so that no user can edit the same element as another user at the same time. Since each user opens and works within his or her own local disk copy, multiple users can now work on the same project simultaneously.

FIGURE 13.2
This worksharing diagram shows a central file saved to the server and local files saved to each user's workstation.

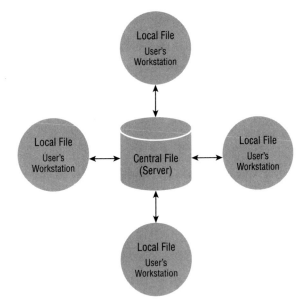

As users work they add elements and edit existing elements. As they do so they also save their changes frequently to both their own local file and to the project's central file. Revit coordinates the changes that are submitted from each user automatically. Throughout this process, users stay in sync with one another as they continue to work and make changes to the project.

This is one possible scenario, though the most common, that can exist. You will need to determine for yourself the best workflow that works for you. Regardless of your workflow, the remaining topics in this chapter will help you get the process started.

Speaking the Language

Before we get too much further, let's review some terminology. Don't worry: these terms will become second nature to you as you become more familiar with working on a project with worksharing enabled. You might even come up with your own definitions.

Worksharing   *Worksharing* is a broad term Autodesk uses to describe the tools that Revit offers to collaborate with others, such as file linking, exporting data, and using worksets. These tools permit multiple users and, if necessary, multiple firms to collaborate more effectively.

Workset   A *workset* is a grouping of elements that can be reserved for editing by a single user. These worksets usually consist of specific zones of responsibility, such as distinct wings or grouping of levels within building. Worksets can also be "checked out" (owned/borrowed) so no other user can edit them.

Element borrowing   *Element borrowing* is defined as an event that allows a person to edit an element without checking out the workset it is assigned to. When a user edits an element within the model through his or her local copy, only that element (not the workset it's on) gets checked out or borrowed from the central file by that user; that way, no one else can edit it until it is relinquished. Using a library metaphor, imagine borrowing a book (element) off a shelf (workset) in a library (central file) instead of borrowing a shelf. Borrowing a book is analogous to borrowing an element.

Checked out   While this terminology isn't actually used in Revit other than in some of its documentation, as a metaphor and again using a library as a comparison, it is useful. The term that Revit uses is "owner." This is the result of a user taking full ownership of a workset, which means no other user can edit elements that are assigned to that workset without asking that user. All elements that are part of a checked-out workset are now owned by the user who has them checked out. In contrast, a user who selects and edits an individual element or elements is a borrower, even though that person "owns" the element. Owner equals workset; borrower equals element(s).

Central file   This is the type of `.rvt` file that Revit Structure creates once you enable worksharing. It becomes the master project file and contains a building model subdivided into functional areas through worksets. This master file is saved on the network so that more than one person can have access to work on the project. Revit creates one related and important folder for this project file, a folder named the same as the project with `_backup` appended. Do not alter it or edit its contents.

Local file   Local files are the `.rvt` file(s) used to enable worksharing. A local file is a copy of the central file that resides on a user's workstation's hard drive. This file maintains a bidirectional link back to the central file, which allows all users to interact with one another. Users work on the project by working on their local file. Revit creates the same additional folder for the local file as it is did for the central file.

Editing Requests   When one user tries to edit an element that is already borrowed by another user, the user can place an Editing Request asking the current borrower/owner to relinquish it to them so they can modify the element. The current owner can grant or deny the request as long as they have not changed the element. If they have changed it, they need to Synchronize with Central (SWC) in order to save their work prior to returning the borrowed element.

Relinquish   The best way to understand this term is to look up a synonym for it. If you were to do this, you would finds phrases and words such as *give up*, *surrender*, *hand over*, and *abandon*. This is what you will do when you have finished working with borrowed elements from the project. You hand them back over, or *relinquish* them, so someone else can use them. Revit Structure has a tool called Relinquish All Mine for doing this. With a library in mind, think "return your books."

Synchronize with Central   This term will be used a lot in the worksharing environment. After you have been working on your local copy, which is linked to the central file, you will execute an SWC to update the central file with your changes so other users can see them. Said another way, it is a two-way transaction, "pulling" changes from the central file to your local file and "pushing" your changes to the central file. Veteran users will have to get used to this new phrase because it used to be called Save to Central, or STC.

Reload Latest   Just using SWC does not automatically put your changes into other users' local copies, which means they won't see your work yet. Reload Latest is a method to transfer (pull) changes that have been made in the central file into your local file. Changes that may have been made in your local file do not get transferred to the central file by this method. This is a one-way transaction, pulling changes to your local file from the central file only.

You should develop a good understanding of these terms so you are able to take advantage of the worksharing workflow that can occur using worksets. Learning to talk the talk and walk the walk early on will give you the knowledge you need to determine the best time to use worksets as well as how to properly set them up for your project.

When to Use Worksharing

You must use worksets/worksharing as soon as you want to permit more than one person to work on the project at the same time. For the most part, almost every model can benefit from having worksharing enabled. More than likely you will have at least two people working within the model at some point in time, such as the engineer and the drafter/modeler. This number may vary depending on the size of the project.

Making the decision to work in a worksharing environment and how to properly set up worksets can be determined by the project size and the potential for multiple users working in the model at the same time. Even if multiple users are not going to contribute to the project simultaneously, there are other benefits such as added visibility control and increased project performance to be gained by enabling worksharing.

WHAT'S UP WITH THIS DIALOG BOX?

By default, Revit Structure assumes that you are working in a single-user environment. If you are working in your model and another user opens that model, that user will be presented with a dialog box indicating their copy will be in read-only mode, much like any other software and files you might use. Frequently seeing this dialog box on your computer screen can become annoying, which might be a sign that you should consider using worksets/worksharing.

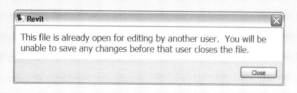

LOOKING AT PROJECT AND/OR TEAM SIZE

The project size can help determine whether worksharing should be enabled and how your worksets should be created. Prior to starting your project, discuss your options with regard to the project type and the number of potential simultaneous team members. These up-front discussions will allow you to take advantage of worksharing accordingly and allow proper setup for the following project types:

Small projects (two users) Worksharing should be enabled, but you probably don't need to create additional worksets to divide up the model. As long as you are not routinely working on the same section or same area of the project, Revit Structure's automatic element borrowing should work fine for two users working on the project. An occasional Editing Request may have to be made.

Large projects (three-plus users)   Worksharing should be enabled and most likely additional worksets ought to be created. These worksets should reflect obvious physical breakpoints of a building (for example, at expansion joints, discrete wings, and grouping of levels). If additional users are brought on only to help create sections, then automatic element borrowing should be fine.

Very large projects with multiple buildings and discrete wings   Worksharing should be enabled as well as additional worksets created. For these types of projects, you may want to consider creating and combining separate but linked structural models as well as using worksharing to help maintain more flexible and manageable files. Keep in mind that linking projects will likely hamper your ability to do analysis on the structure as a whole.

Suggested structural worksets are:

◆   By discipline (structural, architectural, MEP)

◆   By group of floors or groups of structural elements

◆   Project construction phase division

◆   Floor plan division at expansion/seismic joints

◆   By material type: steel, masonry, concrete, and so forth

These are only suggestions and certainly may not be specific in any way to how you should create worksets or set up teams. Knowing the simple logic behind determining worksets and potential roadblocks will help you put a basic standard in place. Each project has its own needs, and what worked well for one project may not be necessary for another. Try not to think of worksets as layers or a layer standard; one size does not fit all.

Not Just for Multiple Users

During the beginning stages of a project when only a single user is required on a project, it *may not* be necessary to enable worksharing. However, there are several other reasons why you should think about using worksharing regardless of the type and size of your project. In these scenarios, additional worksets more than likely would not have to be created:

◆   Saving locally to your workstation's hard drive tends to be much faster than saving across your network. Local saves can happen much more frequently.

◆   For inexperienced users, it may be necessary to allow more advanced users in the project to help perform advanced tasks or help maintain company standards within the model.

◆   It can be nice to allow inexperienced users to work only on sections and details rather than perform advanced modeling procedures. This serves as an excellent mentoring training method. However, understanding and using worksets is not a novice issue. It requires specific instruction and guidance.

There are several other reasons why you should enable worksharing regardless of being in a multiuser environment:

◆   It allows you to have another level of graphic/element visibility display for elements that are not being worked on.

◆   It allows you to load only the portions of your project that are needed for the task at hand, thus increasing computer performance.

◆ It allows you to have additional backups that are on both your local machine and your network.

If you are enabling worksharing to take advantage of the additional visibility settings and improve performance, you may need to create additional worksets. Keep in mind that if you create too many worksets for this purpose, your model can become unmanageable. Individual view overrides and the use of filters may be a better alternative.

 Real World Scenario

OH, BY THE WAY, WE HAD TO SEPARATE OUR MODEL

Our firm had a project that had already gone out a few times for issue. Over a hundred different types of views made up our construction document set. The majority of these views were from the live model. For structural, the job was almost done, and the architect had not yet completed a final issue.

The next time we received an updated model from the architect, they gave us an "Oh, by the way, we had to split the project into two files (Interiors and Shell) to increase performance." What did this mean to us? Well, whenever you link in a Revit model, it is turned on in every view by default. This meant that we had to go through every view and turn off the Visibility settings of the linked model.

Our solution was to create worksets, Arch_Shell and Arch_Interior. This allowed us to uncheck the Visible in Every View check box. It also allowed us to do selective opens of the linked models. (We will get into the Visible in Every View check box and selective opening later in this chapter.) This technique was much better than unloading the link in the file. As you start collaborating with other disciplines, you might find that this little trick with the use of worksets will work for you as well as open up many more possibilities.

Keep in mind that other disciplines that may be using your linked model will not be able to see elements from your model that are assigned to worksets with the Visible in Every View box unchecked.

Enabling Worksharing

Now that you have the concepts and terminology down, let's get into enabling worksharing. To start the process, on the Ribbon click the Collaborate tab ➢ Worksets panel ➢ Worksets tool (Figure 13.3). You can find all of the tools related to worksharing in the Collaborate tab. Notice the grayed-out commands within the Worksets and Synchronize panels. These commands are available only after worksharing is enabled.

FIGURE 13.3
Accessing the Worksets tool from the Collaborate tab ➢ Worksets panel

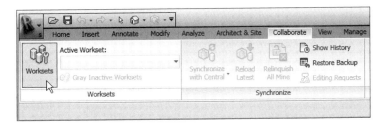

After you click the Worksets tool you will be presented with a Worksharing dialog box (Figure 13.4).

FIGURE 13.4
Revit confirms that you intend to enable work-sharing with this dialog box.

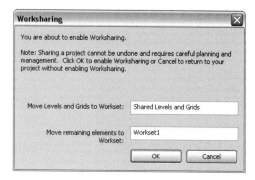

This first dialog box warns you that sharing a project cannot be undone. This sounds pretty scary at first if this is your first exposure to worksharing. But don't worry; just proceed, and we'll explain what will happen.

During the time Revit Structure takes to enable worksharing, it assigns all elements in the model to worksets. There are four kinds of worksets: User-Created, Families, Project Standards, and Views. User-Created worksets are the ones you actively manage and create with the option to create additional ones, to give you more control to manage your model. The other three workset types — Families, Project Standards, and Views — are managed by Revit Structure as you work. Let's take a closer look at each kind of workset.

User-Created Worksets

In the Worksharing dialog box (Figure 13.4) are two text fields available for editing. These are the default User-Created worksets that Revit Structure creates when worksharing is enabled. You can create additional User-Created worksets after you click OK in the Worksharing dialog box.

The Shared Levels and Grids and the Workset1 worksets are automatically defined by Revit Structure but are still called User-Created worksets. These worksets can both be renamed if you like or not used at all.

SHARED LEVELS AND GRIDS

Revit Structure will take all currently modeled levels and grids and assign them to the Shared Levels and Grids workset. Future levels and grids that you put into your project should also be assigned to this workset. This workset can be renamed to something that might make more sense to you, or it can be deleted altogether. When you delete it, it will not delete any element(s) that might be assigned to it but ask you instead what workset to reassign them to. You are also allowed to assign these elements to another User-Created workset, so if your project requires a different location, you can specify that instead. For example, you may need to separate grids into east and west wings to help control their visibility and to help define who is responsible for them.

WORKSET1

Every model element that is not a level or grid will automatically be assigned to Workset1. The elements that are assigned to this workset can be moved to another workset at a later time. You are allowed to rename this workset but do not have the option to delete it. Revit does not allow it, and the Delete button will be grayed out, making it unavailable to select. Be careful when renaming this workset because it can be confusing later when you or another user tries to delete it and can't. For this reason you may want to leave this workset alone and reassign element(s) to a workset that you create yourself. You can then leave Workset1 as an extra "catchall" for elements that may not fall into another workset.

AMAZING WHAT A NAME CAN DO

Whether you are renaming a default User-Created workset or creating a new User-Created workset, keep in mind the name you give it. Name it something more in line with your project like Main Workset, or even just Structure. Since all forms of the Revit applications (Structure, Architecture, MEP) use the same core programming, using more distinct names can help in subtle and unforeseen ways.

Explaining the Other Worksets

After you click OK in the Worksharing dialog box, Revit Structure assigns all of your modeled elements into the two User-Created worksets. It also creates a new workset for each of your project's views, families, and project standards and groups them into an additional set of default worksets, named Families, Project Standards, and Views. Like the two default User-Created worksets, these three worksets will be created automatically. Since this is hardcoded behavior in the program, you will not be able to rename them, nor will you have to do anything to them or worry about them. Revit manages them for you.

Once Revit Structure has created these worksets, you will see the Worksets dialog box shown in Figure 13.5. Note that when you first enable worksharing you are the owner of every workset — the Yes in the Editable column and your username in the Owner column indicate this. You will also notice check boxes at the bottom of the dialog box. These check boxes allow you to toggle among showing the User-Created, Views, Families, and Project Standards worksets. Your active workset is set to the default User-Created workset, Workset1.

FIGURE 13.5
The Worksets dialog box

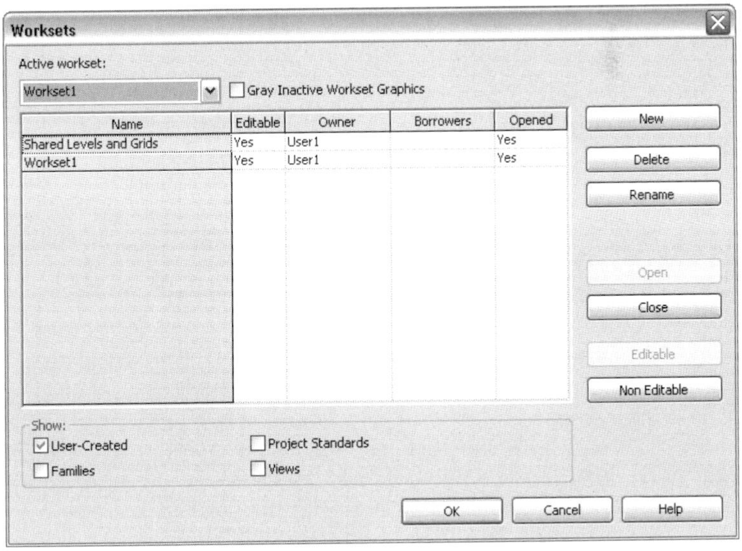

To create a new User-Created workset, click the New button in the Worksets dialog box. This opens the New Workset dialog box (Figure 13.6), where you name the workset. If you do not want to have this new workset visible in all views, deselect the Visible by Default in All Views check box.

FIGURE 13.6
Creating a new
User-Created workset

HOLD ON — YOU HAVE TO SYNCHRONIZE WITH CENTRAL FIRST

You will not be able to release your ownership of the worksets at this time. Setting the Editable column to No will prompt you to save the file first.

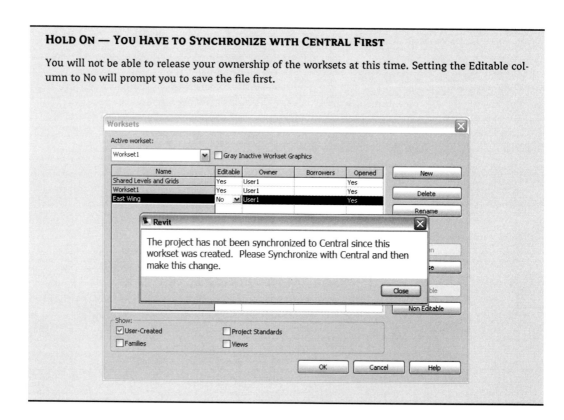

VIEWS

Revit Structure will create a workset for every view inside your project. This workset contains any view-specific elements such as annotations, as well as any view properties within the view. As you work in different views, these elements will automatically be assigned to the view's workset, regardless of which workset is current. Since Revit Structure controls all of this information, these worksets as well as the other default ones cannot be made active, nor can the elements be moved to another workset, except by removing them from one view and placing them into another, for example, by using Cut and Paste. You never have to worry about what workset text, dimensions, tags, or symbols are assigned to; Revit manages that task.

The nice thing about the view workset is that each user can have their own view of the model and control the properties. These properties will not affect other users who are in different views looking at the same portion of the model.

View worksets can be borrowed in several places. You can right-click on the view name in the Project Browser or right-click on any view-specific elements to open a dialog box that lets you select Make Workset Editable. A third method is to go directly through the Workset dialog box. And yet another less obvious but just as effective way is to change a view property. As long as no other user has already borrowed the view, you'll become the borrower of the view.

FAMILIES

Revit Structure assigns every family that is loaded into your project to its own workset, and again this is done automatically for you. The family workset governs the definition of the family or "the idea" of the family, not actual family elements themselves. You will borrow the family workset when you edit the Type properties of a family. For example, you can place structural columns all afternoon and never borrow the structural column family workset. If you change the structural column's manufacturer or Type Comments parameter, you'll borrow the structural column definition to do so. Again Revit will transparently let you borrow the structural column's workset as long as no other user has already done so.

PROJECT STANDARDS

All project settings are assigned to Project Standards worksets according to their purpose. Some of these settings include dimension styles, line styles, line weights, object styles, and text types. As Figure 13.7 shows, you can see all of them by clicking on the appropriate check box at the bottom of the Worksets dialog box. You do not need to borrow these worksets to add new information or additional settings to your project. If existing settings are modified, however, you end up borrowing them to make the changes.

FIGURE 13.7
Partial list of Project Standards worksets

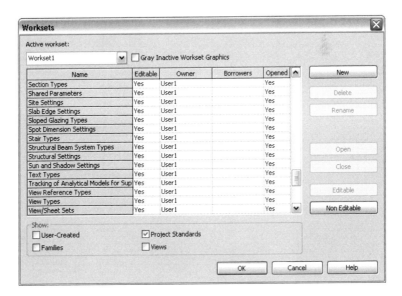

Creating the Central File

After enabling worksharing in your project, you need to save the file. This commits the changes that have been made to the database structure. Specifically, Revit has created two new data fields for each element in the project, parameters called Edited By and Workset. Once the file is saved this file becomes your central file, which will allow multiple users to then make copies of it for worksharing. When making your central file, it is a good idea to perform a Save As with a different filename instead of a Save. This will allow you to keep your original single-user file just in case you need it in the short term.

To create your central file, select the Application menu ➤ Save As ➤ Project. Before clicking the Save button, click the Options button in the lower-right corner. In the File Save Options dialog box shown in Figure 13.8, verify that Make This a Central File After Save is checked and the maximum number of backups specified is what you want. The default is 20, which might not make your IT department too happy. This number is based upon an admittedly arbitrary assumption of four users who SWC five times in a day. Twenty backups means each unique save per user would technically be preserved for restoration if necessary. Some large projects' backup folders can get quite large. You should discuss with your IT staff what your needs are and then agree on a setting.

FIGURE 13.8
File Save options

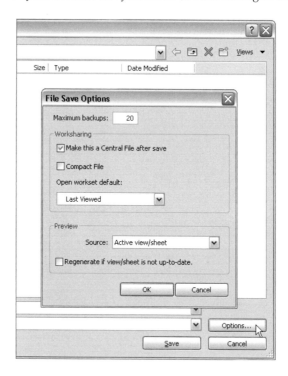

This dialog box also gives you the opportunity to set which workset becomes the default workset when the file is opened. Your options are All, Editable, Last Viewed, and Specify. You can also set which view is used to capture the preview that you see in the Recent Files window. Typically this is set to your current active view/sheet when closing, but you can set it to another view of your choice.

If during the above Save procedure you choose the Application menu ➢ Save instead of performing a Save As, the following will occur. Once you click Save, Revit will display a message (Figure 13.9) confirming that you are about to commit the changes you've made, and the file will now become a central file. This is your last chance to change your mind to wait until another time to use worksets on that file. This message occurs because you are about to override your single-user file with your new multi-user file. If this is not your expected action, be sure to choose No and perform a Save As instead.

FIGURE 13.9
Save File as Central File
message box confirming
your intention to create
the central file

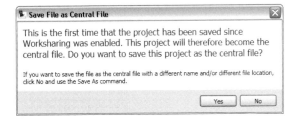

The last step is to Synchronize with Central. You need to relinquish ownership of the worksets that you still own, specifically the User-Created worksets. When you saved the file Revit relinquished the Families, Project Standards, and Views worksets for you as well as any borrowed elements. It did not do so for the User-Created worksets. On the Synchronize panel of the Collaborate tab of the Ribbon, choose Synchronize and Modify Settings from the drop-down. It is important to choose this because you don't get an opportunity to return the User-Created worksets with the other option, Synchronize Now. In the Synchronize with Central dialog box check the box for User-created Worksets and enter a comment in the Comment field. Comments are useful for troubleshooting later if necessary.

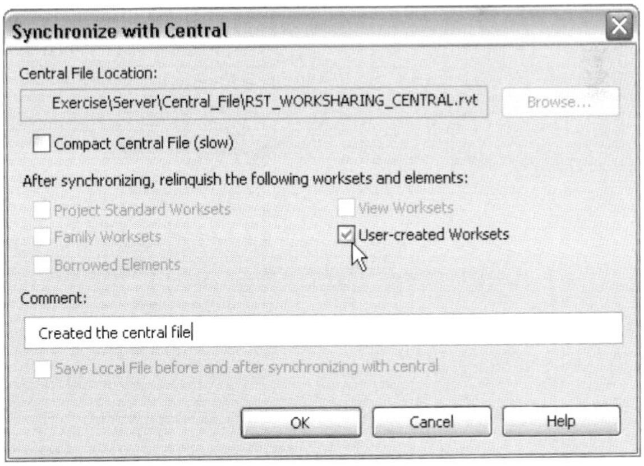

FIGURE 13.10
In the Synchronize
with Central dialog
box, check the correct
options.

Synchronize with Central

Central File Location:

Exercise\Server\Central_File\RST_WORKSHARING_CENTRAL.rvt   Browse...

☐ Compact Central File (slow)

After synchronizing, relinquish the following worksets and elements:

☐ Project Standard Worksets   ☐ View Worksets

☐ Family Worksets   ☑ User-created Worksets

☐ Borrowed Elements

Comment:

Created the central file

☐ Save Local File before and after synchronizing with central

OK   Cancel   Help

WE ALL NEED FILE-NAMING STANDARDS

You should come up with a folder and file-naming convention for your central and local files that best suits your company. The renaming is helpful to the user for visually seeing the difference between a local and a central file. It is also useful for reviewing logs and journal files. Try to avoid using special characters in your naming conventions. These characters can sometimes cause other applications to misbehave. If special characters are desired, you should check with your IT department to make sure your choice is acceptable to them.

On our server, we create a `Revit` folder inside our normal `Project` folder. This `Revit` folder holds all of our Revit-specific information for the project and keeps it apart from any AutoCAD files we may have during our transition to Revit Structure.

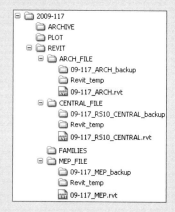

On each user's hard drive, we create a `Revit_Local` folder on the root of the C: drive. Inside this we create individual project folders, where we save our local files and any other information about the project that does not need to be backed up on the network. Once again, we put the local file in its own folder to separate it from other project file information.

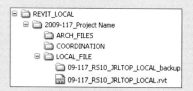

We use a file-naming convention that allows us to tie the project number to the filename as well as the version of Revit Structure that it is using. We specify whether it is a single-user, local, or central file. If it is a local file, the user will also include their initials.

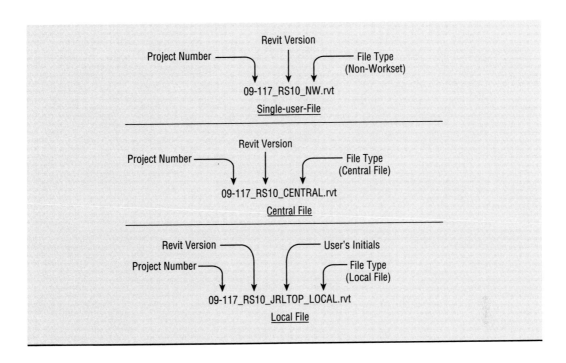

After you create the central file, you will see that a couple of folders have been automatically created where the central file is saved (see Figure 13.11). You will only see these for central and local files. One of the folders is named the same as the central file, with backup appended to it. This backup folder is where Revit Structure keeps track of all of your backups pertaining to the central file. It contains a lot of .rws and .dat files that it writes so Revit Structure can monitor permissions and ownership rights of those using local files. It also contains other various files along with a worksharing log file (.slog) that provides progress information on operations (such as Synchronize with Central) to Worksharing Monitor, a separate application created by Autodesk to enhance the workflow of teams using Revit and worksets. To preserve these backups and other critical files, users should not delete or rename these folders or files.

FIGURE 13.11
Additional folders are created in the same folder as the central file to store backup information.

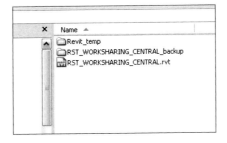

A Revit_Temp folder is also automatically created. This folder provides information for the Worksharing Monitor tool that is used to help users communicate with one another while they work together on a project. The files that are automatically created in this folder should be only a couple of kilobytes or less in size, so they will not take up much space; they are automatically deleted when users close out of the project. If this folder is deleted, Revit Structure will automatically re-create it when any user resumes work.

Creating Local Files — Getting the Team Involved

There are a few ways that you can create your local file. The method that Autodesk recommended until the release of 2010 is to open the central file and then use Save As. We don't recommend this approach for a couple good reasons.

It is slow! You open the central file (once) and then use Save As to create your local file, which is technically opening a file again (twice). Also consider that opening the central file prevents other users from accessing it, which can prevent them from saving their changes back to the central file. You may have it open for only a minute or so, but it is too easy to be interrupted or distracted by a phone call and continue working while you're still in the central file by mistake. With several team members working on a project and with this as your standard method, it is possible for more than one person to accidentally be working in the central file at the same time. Opening the central file is a bad habit, and we want you to develop good habits. Therefore, a user's normal interaction with the central file should be limited to working through the local file.

In response to user suggestions, Revit Structure 2010 has a new specific option for creating a local file. This method takes on more of an "on the fly" approach, but it leaves little flexibility as far as the name and location of the local file it creates. When you check the Create New Local check box in the Worksharing section of the Open dialog box (it is checked by default), as shown in Figure 13.12, Revit automatically creates, names, and saves the local file. The option Detach from Central appearing in the same area is also related to worksharing and will be discussed later in this chapter. The option Create New Local will be grayed out when opening project files that are not central files that need to be upgraded to 2010 format or are family files. Detach from Central will be grayed out when you open family files.

FIGURE 13.12
Using the Create New Local feature at the bottom of the Open dialog box creates a local file on the fly.

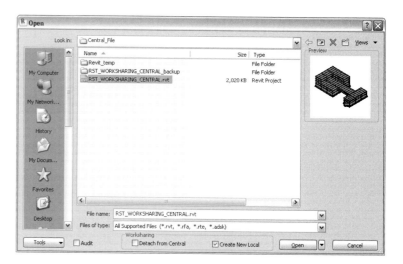

When you open a file with this feature selected, Revit Structure will automatically create the local file and name it using the exact same name as the central file but appending an underscore and the current Revit username. As an example, the central file `RST WORKSHARING-CENTRAL.rvt` is created as a local file named `RST WORKSHARING-CENTRAL_User1.rvt`.

The username is determined by the value of the Username field located in the General tab of Revit Structure's Options settings. The location of where the new local file is created is determined by the value of the Default Path for User Files field located in the File Locations tab of Revit Structure's Options settings. The Options dialog box can be found by choosing the Application menu and selecting the Options button at the bottom of the drop-down list.

If a file already exists with the same name, you will be given save preferences, as shown in Figure 13.13, to overwrite the existing file or append a timestamp to it. Appending a timestamp will prevent the file from being overwritten.

FIGURE 13.13

Revit Structure warns you with save preferences before overwriting a file when using the Create New Local option.

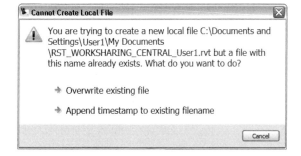

This is a good way to support a common practice of always starting the day with a new local file, but it also means that the user will be in the habit of selecting the central file daily while in Revit Structure's Open dialog box. Some might say this is dangerous and increases the chance of a user mistakenly opening a central file. To help prevent users from unintentionally opening a central file, Revit Structure determines what type of file you are opening, and if you are opening a local file, the Create New Local option will be grayed out. If you are opening a central file, however, the Create New Local feature will be checked. The user will have to purposely remove the check from the box in order to open the central file.

Though this is a great addition to Revit Structure, it does limit your choices with regard to the central file's name and location. If you desire to have file-naming conventions or folder structures as mentioned earlier, this may not be the best method for you. You may want to use a manual approach that gives you more flexibility and ensures you don't develop a habit of opening the central file at all.

We've discussed two methods so far, one we don't recommend and a second that we like but also has a limitation for file naming and location that may or may not make you consider another approach. Let's discuss another common way that users manage this process.

A third method, which many prefer, gives you lots of flexibility. You copy the central file from the network to your workstation by using Windows Explorer and then rename the copy using your company standards for name and location. When you do this, Revit Structure will regard this copy as a local file that is associated with the central file. You will see a message box when opening this file for the first time (Figure 13.14), explaining that the file has been moved or copied from its original location, and if you didn't intend this to happen, how to fix it. Otherwise it will be considered a local copy belonging to you, displaying the current Revit username.

In some cases, users may already have the central file open — for example, right after you enable worksharing and create your central file for the first time. Even though it is much more convenient to create your local file by using the Save As method at this time, you should still avoid doing so. There is no sense in creating bad user habits.

FIGURE 13.14
The Copied Central File message box, aka "the good or routine warning"

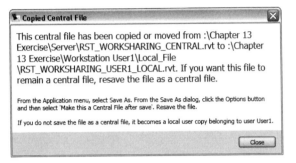

> **Copied Central File** ☒
>
> This central file has been copied or moved from :\Chapter 13 Exercise\Server\RST_WORKSHARING_CENTRAL.rvt to :\Chapter 13 Exercise\Workstation User1\Local_File \RST_WORKSHARING_USER1_LOCAL.rvt. If you want this file to remain a central file, resave the file as a central file.
>
> From the Application menu, select Save As. From the Save As dialog, click the Options button and then select 'Make this a Central File after save'. Resave the file.
>
> If you do not save the file as a central file, it becomes a local user copy belonging to user User1.
>
> [Close]

EXERCISE: CREATING A LOCAL FILE VIA A MANUAL COPY/PASTE METHOD

Let's step through the Copy/Paste method by using Windows Explorer:

1. Browse to the network where your central file is located.

2. Right-click on the central file and click Copy.

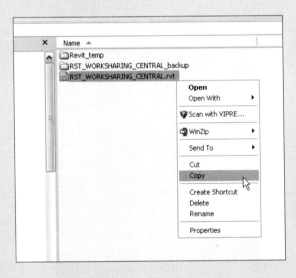

3. Browse to your workstation's hard drive (for example, `C:\Revit Local Files`) where the local file will be saved.

4. Right-click within the folder and click Paste.

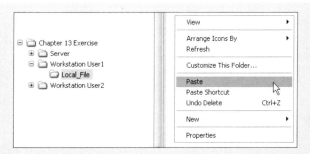

5. Select the file and press the F2 key to rename it, or right-click on the pasted file, click Rename, and rename it using your naming convention for local files.

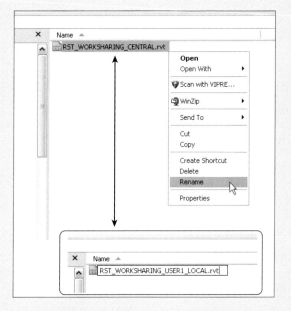

6. Launch Revit Structure and open the local file you just created to continue working on the project. You'll see the warning message we discussed earlier, shown in Figure 13.14. Just make sure your username is listed as the person whose local copy this file will belong to, and click OK.

As you can see, there are several methods that can be used to aid in the creation of a local file. Pros and cons apply to all of them. You will have your own opinions about which ones you feel are the most desirable. Decide for yourself which one will create the best workflow and decrease the potential for error in your environment. After choosing the best method and enforcing it, you will be ready to move on to staying in sync with the central file and other local files that other users may be using.

HOW CAN I SPEED UP THIS PROCESS?

Many companies have tapped into the API functionality of Revit and have created little programs that automate the creation of the local file. Others use batch/script files that copy and rename the files. This allows the user to easily click on a shortcut or use a GUI to create the local file on a daily basis. This method maintains company standards and helps eliminate errors during the Copy and Paste process. Choosing to use these tools to customize the process specifically for your workflow and your environment may be the best way to speed this up as well as maintain standards. A quick search on the Internet regarding scripts, Revit Structure, and local files should yield some examples created by users just like you. Some are even full working applications that you can put to use in your environment with little effort.

Now that you've created your local file, you are ready to work on the project with others. The next things to consider are how you work together, how you see what others are doing, and how they see what you are doing.

Staying in Sync

Revit Structure has several commands to help you stay in sync with other team members as you work together. Prior to enabling worksets, these commands are grayed out and unavailable. They can be found on the Synchronize panel of the Collaborate tab:

◆ Synchronize and Modify Settings

◆ Synchronize Now

◆ Reload Latest

These are the commands that you will use to help the local and central files stay in sync with each other. It is good practice when working with worksets to save your local file as well as Synchronize with Central often. The more consistently you do this, the less time it will take to synchronize your model with the central file, plus it will keep other users up to date with the most current information.

Synchronizing with Central

Whenever you want to share your changes with the rest of the team, you will need to do a Synchronize with Central (SWC). This can be done in a couple of ways: by choosing Synchronize and Modify Settings or by choosing Synchronize Now from the Synchronize panel on the Collaborate tab, shown in Figure 13.15. There is a difference between the two.

Clicking the Synchronize Now tool will save your most recent changes to the central file since your last save to the central file and reload any changes others have made. It is a two-way transaction, pulling changes from the central file to your local file and pushing changes you have made in your local file to the central file. You could think of it as showing others your work but not necessarily returning the "books" or "shelves" you may have borrowed. This is because it does not return any User-Created worksets that you may have borrowed. Note that it does not save your local file either.

FIGURE 13.15
The Synchronize tools behave differently depending on which one you choose.

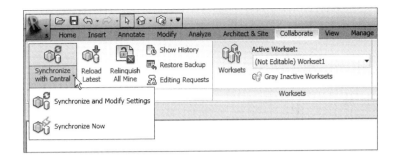

HOW DO I SAVE MY LOCAL FILE WITHOUT SYNCHRONIZING WITH CENTRAL?

The standard Save icon on the Quick Access toolbar and the Save from the Application menu only save changes to your local file. When you make changes that need to be saved to the local file and you are not ready to have them synchronized with the central file, you should choose Save from one of these two locations.

The Synchronize and Modify Settings option opens a dialog box (Figure 13.16) and provides more options for you prior to Synchronizing with Central. You can choose to relinquish worksets as well as save your local file before and after doing a Synchronize with Central. User-Created Worksets will not be checked by default. You are also given the option to enter comments about what you've done prior to synchronizing. These comments can be quite helpful later if you are looking at the backup history information. This is the most thorough way to Synchronize with Central. Using this method periodically, in particular any time you have finished working on the project such as going to lunch, attending a meeting, or leaving for the day, ensures that all borrowed elements will be returned and available for other users to use and, just as important, that your local file and the central file are in sync.

FIGURE 13.16
The Synchronize with Central dialog box with several settings for staying in sync

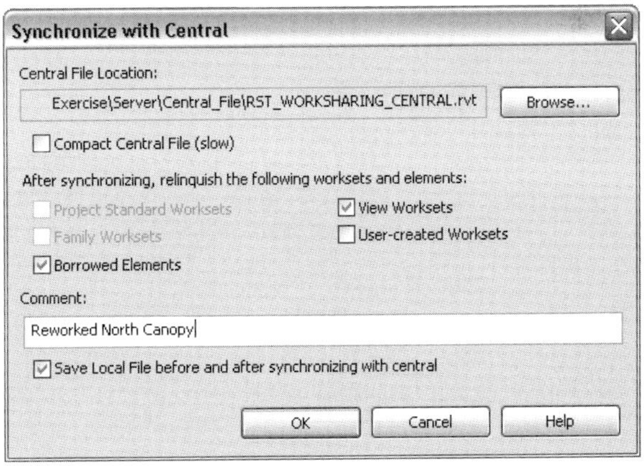

Reloading Latest

There may be times when you need to get the latest information from other team members. After they use Synchronize with Central, you can use Reload Latest from the Synchronize panel on the Collaborate tab of the Ribbon and pull any changes that have occurred since the last time you used either SWC or Reload Latest. Compared with SWC, it is a one-way transaction, pulling only changes in the central file to your local file. For this reason this command is nice to use when you want to see another user's changes but are not ready for others to see your changes. Remember to save your local file afterward. Saving accepts their changes. Until you save, you are only seeing the changes. This keeps you synchronized with the central file, except for changes that you aren't prepared to share with others yet.

Working with Worksets

While using worksets, you will be presented with several new commands and notifications that help you stay in sync and share the project with other users. The central and local files along with their backup folders bring everything together, which becomes a critical piece of the puzzle for allowing this type of environment to exist.

Making sure everyone knows the proper methods for working in this environment and when to use these methods will help keep things assigned to the proper worksets. Even then, you may still need to move elements from one workset to another. Worksets help keep all team members working in sync while keeping track of who has worked on what with ownership rights. Above and beyond the assignment of ownership to elements you will find an opportunity to improve performance by controlling the display of elements assigned to these worksets.

Moving Elements between Worksets

Once worksets are created, you will eventually have to move elements from one workset to another. This is usually done when you are moving elements from the default created Workset1 to another workset that you have created or moving added levels in grids back to the Shared Levels and Grids workset. It is also fairly common for users to place elements in the wrong workset by mistake as they are working. Elements are assigned to the active workset, which is displayed on the Worksets panel of the Collaborate tab of the Ribbon (Figure 13.17).

FIGURE 13.17
The active workset is displayed on the Work-sets panel.

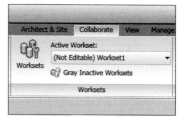

Users forget to check for the active workset because it's a bit too easy to forget and Revit doesn't make it obvious enough. The only way you can tell the active workset assignment is to display the Collaborate tab and look. It's human nature to be too busy to do that, so if you have several work-sets, you will more than likely have to perform the task of moving elements between worksets on a regular basis.

It is necessary to first borrow an element (or its assigned workset — remember the books and shelves analogy) in order to change its assigned workset; therefore it is much easier to move elements (books) between worksets (shelves) when other users do not have elements borrowed or worksets checked out. It is good practice to communicate with other team members when moving large numbers of elements from one workset to another to avoid ownership conflicts. This may mean waiting to deal with major changes when others temporarily stop working on the model or are at lunch or gone for the day. As Figure 13.18 shows, all elements will have additional Workset and Edited By parameters added to their properties under the Identity Data parameter group when worksets are enabled. The Workset parameter is what you change to reassign elements to another workset. The Edited By parameter is read-only and displays which user, if any, is currently editing the element.

FIGURE 13.18
Changing worksets in the Instance Properties dialog box

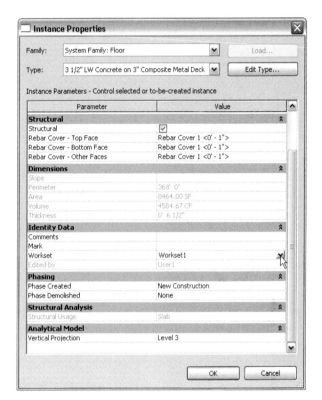

You can move elements to a different workset by selecting one or several elements at a time. Multiple selected elements that are on different worksets will not display a value for the Workset parameter because Revit Structure can display only one value at a time. In some cases where several elements of different categories are selected, the Value for the workset may not be available. Elements such as openings that become part of your selection can prevent the Workset Value from being editable. For example, a wall opening's workset is governed by the wall that it is placed in; if you change the wall workset, you'll see that the opening workset will automatically update with it. Therefore, the wall opening would prevent the workset's Value from being editable.

A quick method to resolve this is to select several elements and use the Filter option from the lower-right corner of the Status bar to select only elements of the same category or those categories that will collectively allow the workset identity to be changed. Figure 13.19 indicates that only floors will be selected. The Filter tool can also be found by choosing it from the Multi-Select contextual tab that displays on the Ribbon when multiple elements are selected.

FIGURE 13.19
Selecting elements with a filter

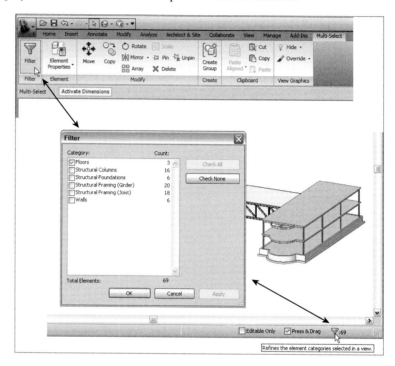

If the workset's Value is still unavailable (grayed out), you need to remember that you must borrow an element before you can assign the element to a different workset. Also remember you can only assign elements like columns and beams to User-Created worksets, and these are the only types of elements that will offer you the opportunity to reassign the workset. Other elements, such as text, dimensions, symbols, and tags, are assigned to Views worksets and will not permit you to change them. They will remain grayed out regardless.

OKAY, WHO IS PLAYING A TRICK ON ME?

Suppose you're trying to select elements, your project is using worksets, and no matter how hard you try you can't select them — you click but nothing happens. Make sure that the Editable Only check box on the status bar below the drawing area is not checked.

If this box is enabled, you will be allowed to select only elements that you own and have borrowed already. This might be why you cannot select them.

A quick way to verify which workset an element is assigned to is to hover over the element with your cursor until a tooltip appears. Not only does this box show you the element's category, family, and type name, but the first part of the description will show you the workset it is assigned to. In Figure 13.20, you can see that the element is part of the Workset1 workset. An exception to being the first information listed in the tooltip occurs when the element belongs to a design option, another potentially useful tool in Revit Structure. The design option the element is assigned to is displayed first and then the assigned workset. The bottom line is that it is easiest to hover over an element to find out the assigned workset instead of opening the Element Properties dialog box.

FIGURE 13.20
Hovering over an element to see its workset assignment

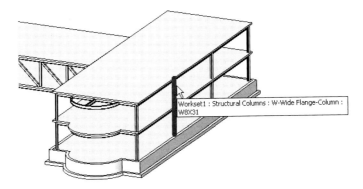

Workset1 : Structural Columns : W-Wide Flange-Column : W8X31

WHAT IS A TOOLTIP?

If you are not seeing a tooltip when hovering over elements, you may have Tooltip Assistance set to None. To verify this, go to the Application menu and choose the Options button in the lower-right corner. Within the General tab, in the Notifications section, you will be able to set Tooltip Assistance to None, Minimal, Normal, or High. This should fix the problem.

Taking Ownership

There may be a time when you will need to know whether you own a particular element. Figure 13.21 shows what you'll see if you do not own a selected element: an icon of three stacked cubes. This is the Make Element Editable icon. Selecting this symbol will make the element editable, and the symbol will disappear. Remember the "borrowing books" concept? If you select an element and you do not see the icon, you are already the owner/borrower of it and can move or modify it however you want. This icon will appear only when your project is using worksets.

The idea of borrowing elements versus borrowing worksets is how Revit Structure allows you to work simultaneously with other users. It's important to keep this in mind so that all local files can maintain communication with the central file so Revit can manage access to elements and worksets and users can make Editing Requests and respond accordingly.

FIGURE 13.21
The icon indicates that you do not own the element. Select it to borrow the element.

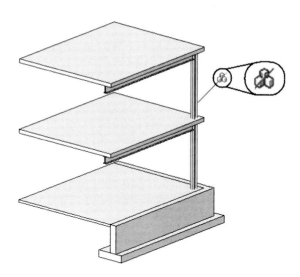

BORROWING ELEMENTS

By borrowing elements, you are taking only some of the elements that are assigned to a workset, not necessarily all of them. The notion is that you take only what you need to change right now, not what you intend to change during the course of your workday. This is a bit different mindset than users are comfortable with. With CAD they open a file and work and don't worry about anyone else needing the file until they have finished. With Revit everyone is working on the same model, and it is important to leave other things for people to work on while you do your thing "right here, right now."

Revit Structure makes the process of borrowing elements easy for you; it just gives you the element as you modify it. If someone else is already editing that element or elements, then Revit will let you know. You can also right-click an element and select Make Elements Editable from the shortcut menu or select the stacked cubes icon itself, as shown in Figure 13.22. These two methods will allow you to borrow an element even though you might not intend to modify it yet. If you recall from our earlier discussion about changing an assigned workset, you'd need to do one of these before you can assign the element to a different workset.

FIGURE 13.22
Methods of making elements editable

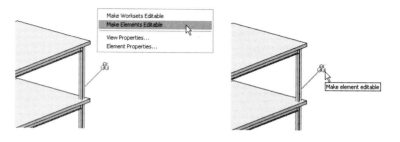

However, if a user has borrowed the East Wing workset, or just the elements you want to change, and you need to make a framing connection and rotate one of the columns that is assigned to that workset, you can make a request to borrow only that column. To make this request you just need to attempt to borrow it using one of the methods mentioned previously. When Revit detects that another user already owns the element, it will provide you with an opportunity to ask the other user for it: create an Editing Request.

Assuming the user who owns that workset hasn't changed the element in some way, that person can grant you permission, and Revit will transfer ownership to you as the new borrower. You will usually have to use the Reload Latest tool so that Revit can pass the change along to you properly. Once you have finished making your change, you can use Synchronize with Central to relinquish your changes.

If you only borrow elements but don't actually change anything, then Revit will let you use the Relinquish All Mine tool. However, if you have borrowed elements and change something as well, you'll have to use Synchronize with Central to keep your changes and relinquish the elements you've borrowed but not changed.

Borrowing Worksets

Borrowing worksets is something that ideally you shouldn't do very often, unless you need to make changes to an entire portion of the building and the elements assigned to its workset. This is a bit different from borrowing elements because you now own every element. Misuse and misunderstanding of borrowing worksets can prevent other users from being able to work efficiently. Using the book and shelf metaphor again, borrowing a workset is like borrowing the shelf instead of individual books. Borrowing elements (books) leaves more available for others, whereas borrowing a shelf restricts what others can work on.

You can borrow worksets by opening the Worksets dialog box shown in Figure 13.23. Click on the workset name at the left and then click the Editable button at the lower right, or just choose Yes from the Editable column. Yes indicates that it is editable by you, and you are also listed under the Owner column. If this is set to No, the workset is not editable by you and your name does not appear in the Owner column. If your username shows up under the Borrowers column, it means that you have elements borrowed from the workset, "books from a shelf." As a general rule your username listed under Owner column equals "bad"; your name under Borrowers column equals "good."

FIGURE 13.23
User1 is listed as the owner of a workset in the Worksets dialog box.

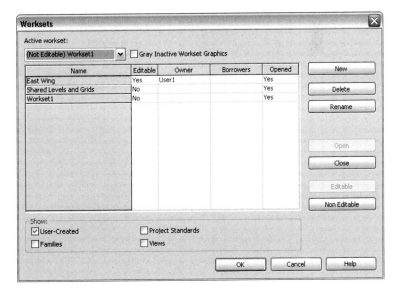

Figure 13.24 shows that you can also right-click on a selected element to select Make Worksets Editable. This means you are borrowing the workset that the selected element is assigned to and, yes, you are the owner of that workset now.

FIGURE 13.24
Borrowing a workset after selecting an element using the shortcut menu

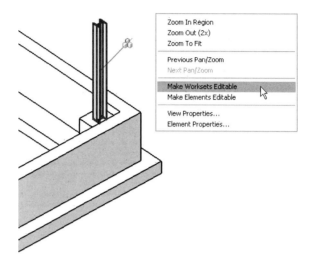

EDITING REQUESTS

If you want to edit an element that another user owns, you can create an Editing Request to borrow it. Likewise, other users can request to borrow elements that you own. If you select an element that someone else owns and try to modify it, you will be presented with the dialog box shown in Figure 13.25. Naturally this will occur only if you are working in a project that is using worksets. This dialog box indicates that another user owns the element already. You can click the Expand button to get a more in-depth list of the errors and warnings.

FIGURE 13.25
This warning dialog box tells you that another user owns the element.

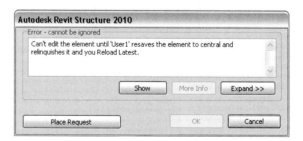

At this point, you have the option to click Cancel, in effect saying "never mind" and moving on to something else, or you can click Place Request, which will store a message for the other person to review. Clicking the Place Request button opens the dialog box shown in Figure 13.26, where you can continue checking to see if your request has been granted. Clicking the Check Now button will keep looping back to the same dialog box until the other user has taken action. If you do not want to wait, you can click Continue and then cancel out of the reminder dialog box. This will not cancel your request but will allow you to continue working on another area until your request has been granted.

FIGURE 13.26
The Check Editability Grants dialog box

Once you place the request, you have to wait until the current owner grants or denies you permission to use the workset. Other users will not automatically receive any indication that you have made a request for an element that they own. You need to contact the user by calling, emailing, tapping on the shoulder, or using Worksharing Monitor, which does improve this process. (The Worksharing Monitor tool is discussed later in this chapter.)

REVIEWING REQUESTS

Once you have the user's attention, they will need to go to their Editing Requests window by choosing the Editing Requests tool from the Collaborate tab ≻ Synchronize panel, as shown in Figure 13.27.

FIGURE 13.27
Accessing the Editing Requests tool

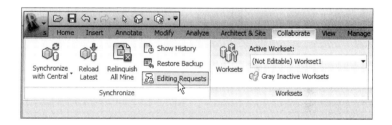

The Editing Requests dialog box will show you any requests that have been made to you as well as any pending requests that you may have. Figures 13.28 and 13.29 show two different versions of the Editing Requests dialog box. Three options are available to address the request:

Grant This option gives permission to the user making the request. You can't grant a request for an element that you have changed unless you are prepared to discard all the changes you made since your last save.

Deny/Retract This option denies permission to the user making the request or allows you to retract your request to another user.

Show This option shows you the exact element(s) that have been requested. You can examine this element in additional views by clicking Show as often as needed to see the element clearly.

FIGURE 13.28
Others' pending requests

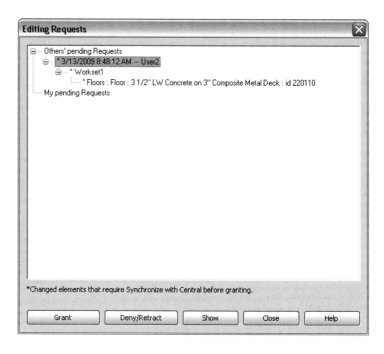

FIGURE 13.29
Your pending requests

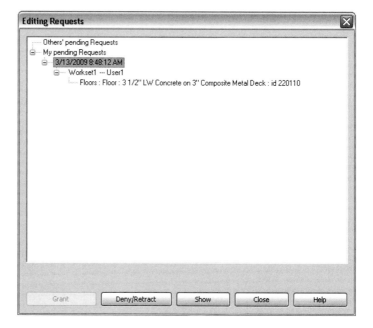

In the case where an asterisk (*) is shown, as in Figure 13.28, you will need to Synchronize with Central before granting the request. Attempting to grant a request without doing this will generate the warning box shown in Figure 13.30. This occurs because you've changed your local file and the central file does not match yours. You will need to exit the dialog box and Synchronize with Central, which will in effect grant the request automatically.

FIGURE 13.30
You'll see a warning when your local file is not in sync with the central file.

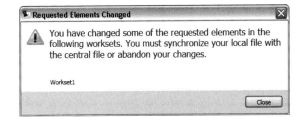

After the request has been granted, the user who is making the request will see one of the two dialog boxes shown in Figure 13.31. The ownership has been transferred over, but the local file is out of date, so a Reload Latest or a Synchronize with Central will have to be performed before editing of the element can occur.

FIGURE 13.31
Warning dialog boxes stating that your local file is out of date

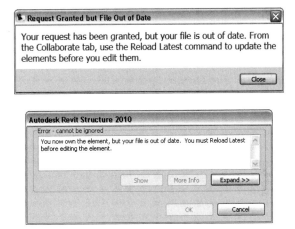

WORKING AT RISK

You may have to work on your project when the central file is not accessible for the local file to communicate with through the bidirectional link. If this is the case, you will see the warning box shown in Figure 13.32, telling you that your connection cannot be found and your changes may be lost. This means that you are working at risk. Depending on your actions, several warnings notifying you that the central file cannot be found will be displayed.

Revit Structure has no way of communicating back to the central file any ownership information that you may have created. If another user working on the project takes ownership of elements or worksets that you borrowed at risk, you will be prevented from saving to the central file, thus losing your work. Your work will be lost, although you will be able to copy and paste elements from one file to the other.

FIGURE 13.32
In situations where the central file cannot be found, you will be working at risk.

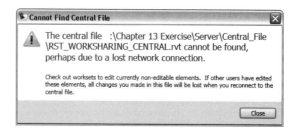

If you are working at risk and try to borrow an element, you will be given a warning stating, "Can't obtain permission to edit element: The Central File is inaccessible. You can check out worksets at risk, but consider carefully!" In order to check out worksets, you will have to do so through the Worksets dialog box. Attempting to make a workset editable through the shortcut menu will present the warning dialog box shown in Figure 13.33.

FIGURE 13.33
Worksets cannot be made editable on the fly when you are working at risk.

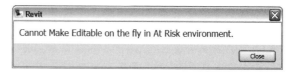

If you are working at risk and try to check out a workset through the Worksets dialog box, you will see a warning similar to the one shown in Figure 13.34, warning you yet again that you are in an at-risk workset environment.

FIGURE 13.34
Editing at-risk warning

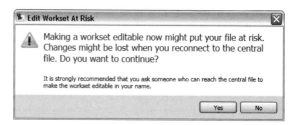

You should use caution when using this procedure. If you do decide to work at risk on your project, communicate your actions with other team members, and consider the advice within the warning dialog boxes wisely.

Improving Performance

It is pretty easy to go overboard with detail in your project. The natural tendency is to model everything down to each and every little plate and connection. When doing this, the size of your file will increase significantly and your project performance may suffer. Keep this in mind as you work.

Take advantage of the additional options that become available to you when using worksets by shutting off the display of worksets in certain views or closing them with the Selective Open options when opening your project.

USING VISIBILITY CONTROL

With worksets enabled, an additional tab called Worksets becomes available in the Visibility/Graphic Overrides dialog box. As Figure 13.35 shows, you can turn the visibility of any User-Created worksets on or off. Access this dialog box by right-clicking in the view and choosing View Properties, or by selecting the View tab ➤ Graphics panel ➤ Visibility Graphics, or using the keyboard shortcut VG or the alternate VV. On the Worksets tab, you can check the boxes to show the worksets or uncheck the boxes to hide the worksets.

FIGURE 13.35
Controlling the visibility of worksets for a particular view

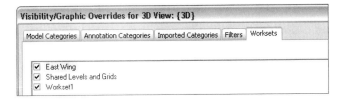

Also available is an option called Gray Inactive Workset Graphics, which can be activated from various locations: by clicking the Gray Inactive Worksets tool on the Worksets panel or by checking the check box in the Worksets dialog box (see Figure 13.36).

FIGURE 13.36
Activating the Gray Inactive Workset Graphics option

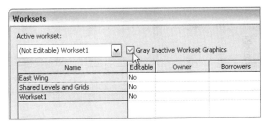

The Gray Inactive Workset Graphics command can be used to show you elements that are not in the current workset or to display the elements you might not be working with but want to see in the background as a nonemphasized element. This option can make it much easier to realize that you are assigning new elements to the wrong workset. Another nice thing about this command is that if you forget to reset it to normal and you plot, the view will still plot correctly because it affects only what you see on screen.

Using the Visibility Control allows you to easily turn off worksets that are not needed in an individual view for display or just not needed at the time when you are working in that view. Since several categories can be assigned to a workset, it is much easier to turn the workset on and off than to pick individual categories. If you turn off a workset as a temporary override, make sure that you return it to its original state because it will not reset itself.

SELECTIVE OPENING OF WORKSETS

There may be times when you do not need to see particular worksets while you are working. For instance, if you have a workset called East Wing and you are not working in that area, not opening that workset will increase your performance because those elements do not have to be displayed. When opening your local file, you can access the Open options shown in Figure 13.37 by clicking the down arrow next to the Open button.

All   Opens all the worksets in the project.

Editable   Opens all worksets checked out by you. Under normal circumstances, borrowing elements, not worksets, using this option means that nothing will be visible in the view. You will have to open the workset you want to see as a separate step using the Worksets dialog box. For this reason the last option, Specify, is a better choice.

Last Viewed   Opens the worksets that were open when the project was last closed.

Specify   Lets you decide which worksets to open by presenting you with the Opening Worksets dialog box before fully opening the project.

FIGURE 13.37
The File Open options
for workset projects

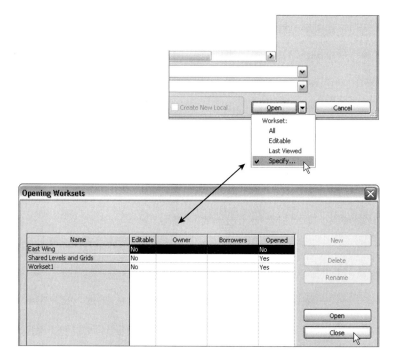

DID YOU KNOW ABOUT THE ASTERISK?

Worksets that are not opened in a project will be marked with an asterisk (*) after their names in the Worksets tab of the view's Visibility/Graphic Overrides dialog box. If a workset is set to be visible in your view and it isn't visible, check for the asterisk. If one is present, you need to open the workset using the Workset dialog box.

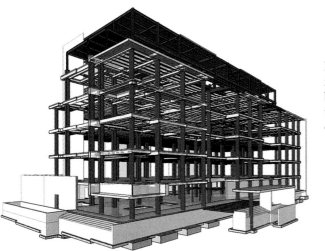

Each individual concrete framing member for this concrete pan-and-joist educational building held all of the reinforcing by use of text parameters, which were displayed and documented in a live schedule.

This concrete pan-and-joist educational building included a curved exterior with high/low slab transitions, as well as a steel-framed roof and skyway to an adjacent building.

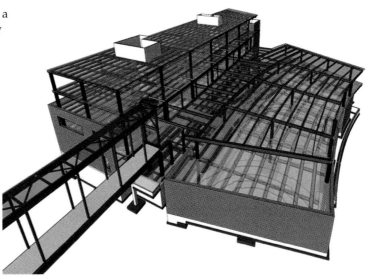

Structural: Ericksen Roed & Associates Inc.

The Thomas Aquinas College Our Lady of the Most Blessed Trinity Chapel

The chapel uses concrete, masonry, wood, and steel materials. 3D topography was a great help on this steeply graded site.

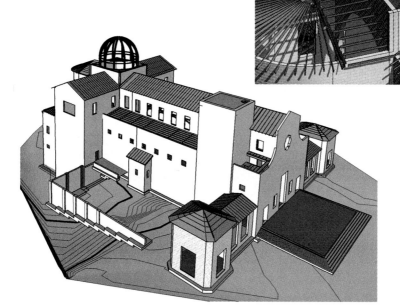

This cutaway view at the back loge area shows the interior steel-tube support framing.

Architect: Rasmussen & Associates

Structural: Brandow & Johnston Inc.

The Emory Clinic

As part of the well-known Emory University system, the Emory Clinic will provide a wide array of services including surgery and diagnostics. In addition, one wing of the building will house a very critical research component that will continue to fuel the success of the Emory system.

The structure is composed of cast-in-place concrete pan-joist floors and 3D concrete moment frames.

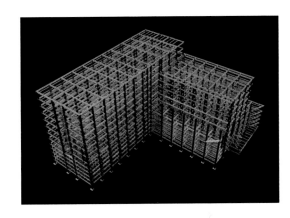

Six levels of subterranean parking anchor the structure below grade. An intricate ramping system at the main entrance provides exceptional access and wayfinding for patients.

Architect: HKS, Inc.

Structural: Walter P Moore

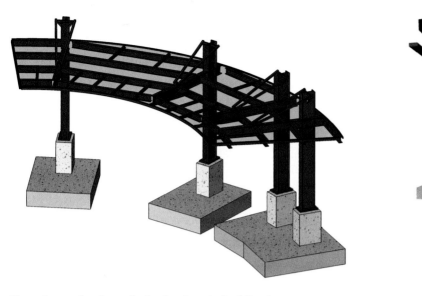

Canopies can be the main focal point of a building's exterior. Here Revit Structure is used to help disseminate the structural design of these sloped structural canopies to other team members.

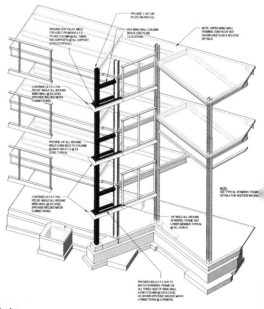

Other areas within the structure may require several sections to explain how they are being structurally supported. Here 3D views from the Revit Structure model are placed with the construction document set to facilitate the plan and section views.

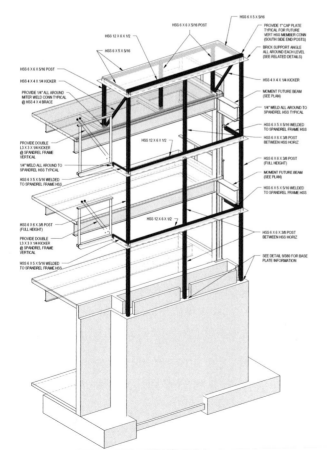

The Salvador Dali Museum

This project features an unusual facade in which the cube-like building structure is offset by an irregular structure and glass matrix, forming a cloudlike space within the building.

The building uses cast-in-place concrete primarily, including a spiral three-story stair within the lobby space.

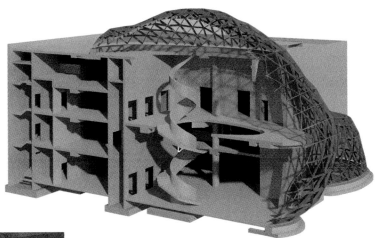

This transparent view shows the expansiveness of the entry, skin, and spiral stair.

Architect: HOK Architects

Structural: Walter P Moore

This two-story medical building uses a custom opening/lintel family. The lintel displays in section and elevation as well as in plan as a symbolic line that can be tagged and linked back to a live schedule.

This multilevel medical building has a composite steel structure. A model for a future construction phase was constructed in the analysis package and exported to a Revit Structure model, where it was linked into the project and used as part of the construction documentation.

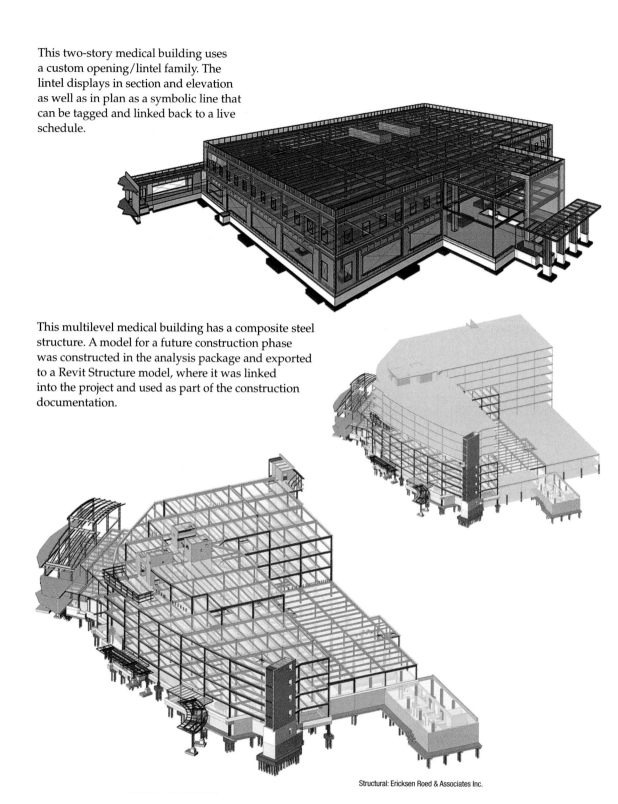

Structural: Ericksen Roed & Associates Inc.

The Rose Bowl Locker Room and Media Center Project

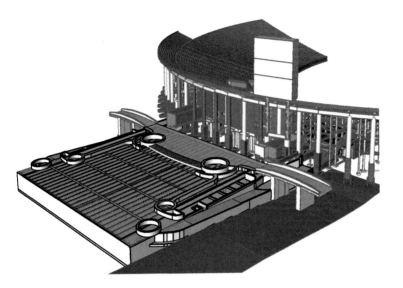

The locker rooms are located under the parking lot outside of the stadium, with connecting tunnels out onto the playing field. The media center is located beneath this end of the bowl structure.

This is an interior locker room view showing precast columns and girders. The roof is framed with concrete double-T planks.

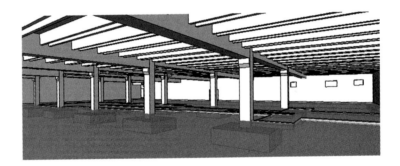

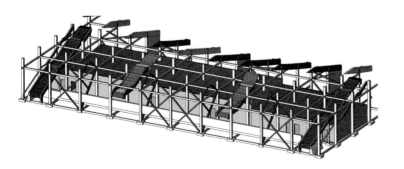

Building the media center structure around the existing concrete columns, braces, beams, and stairs was a huge effort. The Revit Structure model was invaluable for this purpose.

Architect: Margo M. Mavridis

Structural: Brandow & Johnston Inc.

The Sedgwick County Arena

The Sedgwick County Arena is a multipurpose facility capable of hosting basketball, hockey, and other entertainment events. With a seating capacity of over 14,000, the project offers great views from all seats.

The structural system is composed of cast-in-place pan-joist floors along with large-span structural steel trusses.

The seating bowl in the arena is made of precast seating units spanning between cast-in-place raker bents. Using Revit Structure not only enabled real-time coordination but also aided structural design for the floors and building skin modules.

Owner: Sedgwick County, Kansas
Arena Design Consortium consisting of:
Gossen Livingston Associates Inc.
HOK Sport + Venue + Event
McCluggage Van Sickle & Perry
WDM Architects, PA
Structural: Walter P Moore

This project consisted of outdoor lighting suspended and supported by cables below an existing structure. The cables were created with a series of sweeps inside in-place families.

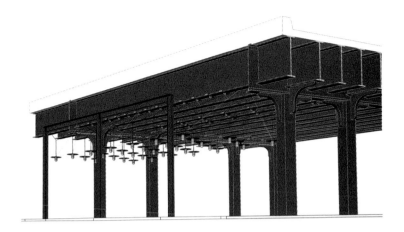

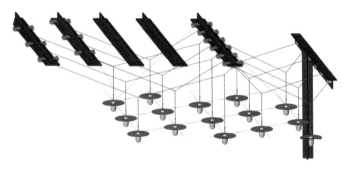

Revit Structure is used as a presentation tool to model buildings that are candidates for the ER-POST System U.S. Patent No. 7010890.

Structural: Ericksen Roed & Associates Inc.

Los Angeles Unified School District Central High School 16

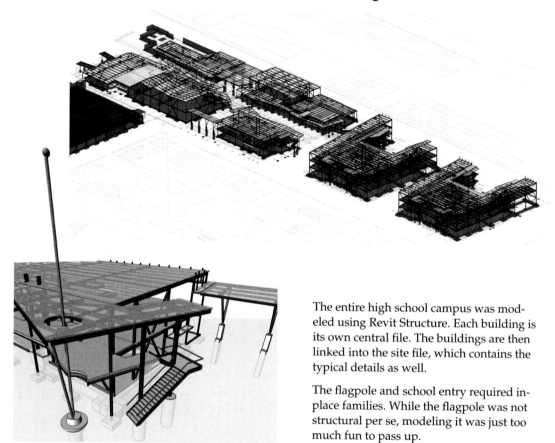

The entire high school campus was modeled using Revit Structure. Each building is its own central file. The buildings are then linked into the site file, which contains the typical details as well.

The flagpole and school entry required in-place families. While the flagpole was not structural per se, modeling it was just too much fun to pass up.

The V-shaped lunch shelter is nestled between buildings. The buildings are steel and concrete, with braced frames for seismic resistance.

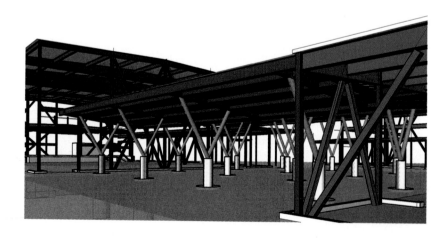

Architect: AC Martin

Structural: Brandow & Johnston Inc.

The Georgia State University Library Transformation

The key feature of the Georgia State University Library Transformation is the expansion of an existing "Link," which bridges over a downtown Atlanta street at the heart of the campus.

Portions of the two existing concrete library structures and the existing steel "Link" were modeled and coordinated with the new steel "Link" expansion.

A two-story pipe truss, column transfers, hangers, and careful sequencing were used to limit loads on existing framing and provide open spaces.

Architect: Leo A. Daly

Structural: Walter P Moore

University of South Florida - Visual and Performing Arts Teaching Facility

Three-story classroom/office/practice building with an external load-bearing tilt wall and colored precast-wall system with an internal PSI joist system.

One-story 45'- to 55'-tall concert hall building with an external load-bearing tilt-wall system with approximately 60'-long span steel bar joist with conventional steel roof decking and built-up roof system.

One-story back-of-house area with an external load-bearing tilt wall and colored precast-wall system with internal load-bearing CMU walls and a conventional built-up roof system on steel roof decking on steel bar joists.

Multiple site canopies made from a mixture of structural steel, aluminum lattice, and architectural colored precast-wall panels (aluminum and arch precast not shown in our model).

Architect: Hanbury Evans Wright Vlattas + Company

Structural: Walter P Moore

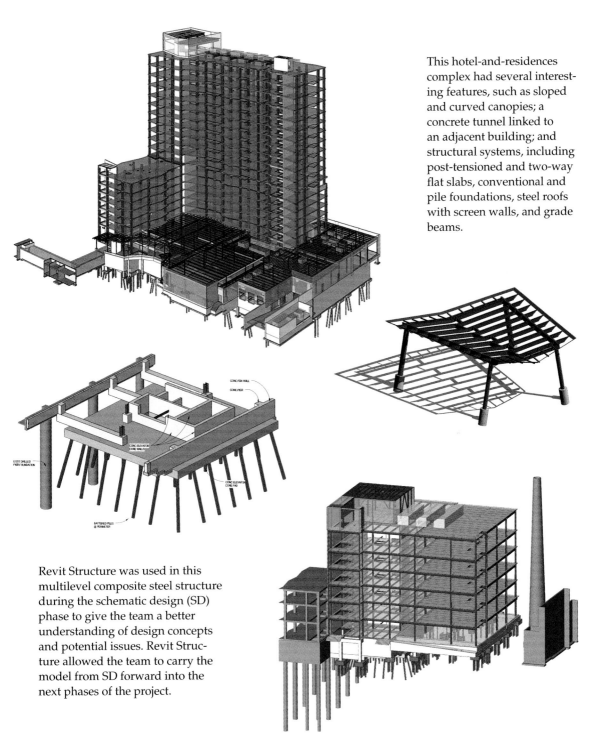

This hotel-and-residences complex had several interesting features, such as sloped and curved canopies; a concrete tunnel linked to an adjacent building; and structural systems, including post-tensioned and two-way flat slabs, conventional and pile foundations, steel roofs with screen walls, and grade beams.

Revit Structure was used in this multilevel composite steel structure during the schematic design (SD) phase to give the team a better understanding of design concepts and potential issues. Revit Structure allowed the team to carry the model from SD forward into the next phases of the project.

Structural: Ericksen Roed & Associates Inc.

The Live Show at Universal

The famous Universal Stage 1, new home of NBC's "Tonight Show," was the first TV production stage at Universal in the 1950s.

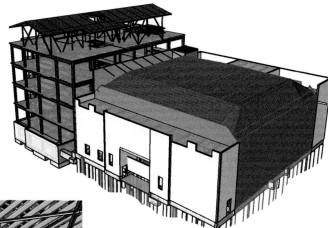

The following is a view of new interior seating platform framing in Stage 1. Diagonal double-angle steel bracing was added at the ceiling for seismic retrofit of the existing stage.

The four-story support building with a full basement is made of steel and concrete, with a steel moment frame for the seismic restraint design.

Architect: Callison Architects

Structural: Brandow & Johnston Inc.

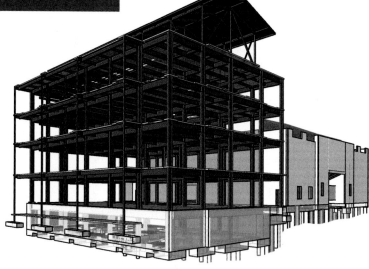

Tampa Museum of Art

Nestled along Florida's Hillsborough River, the Tampa Museum of Art is 66,000 square feet of exhibition space, a museum store, and associated administrative facilities.

The primary structural system consists of wide-flange steel beams with composite metal deck and concrete. Additional lateral bracing is done with concrete shear wall cores surrounding elevator and stair shafts.

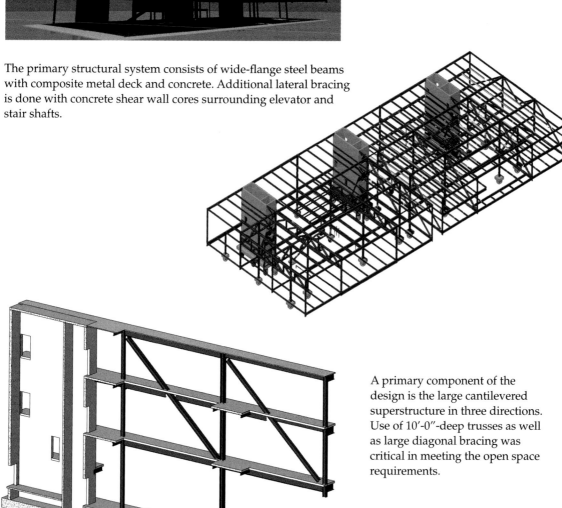

A primary component of the design is the large cantilevered superstructure in three directions. Use of 10'-0"-deep trusses as well as large diagonal bracing was critical in meeting the open space requirements.

Design Architect: Stanley Saitowitz

Executive Architect: Natoma Architects Inc.

Structural: Walter P Moore

The University Park Housing at Cal State Northridge

This project consists of two four-story wooden structures and a one-story cafeteria building. The multistory floor framing is with wood I-joists and wooden shear walls acting as the seismic restraint system.

Two exterior stairs occur on each four-story structure at the exterior, with interior steel post support.

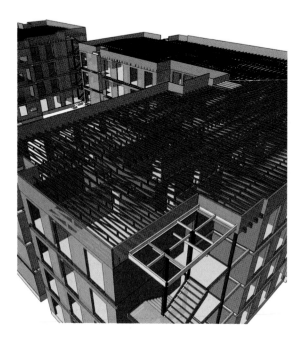

The roof structure is constructed of wooden trusses spaced at 24″ center to center.

Architect: Togawa Smith Martin Residential Inc.

Structural: Brandow & Johnston Inc.

Linking other discipline models such as architectural, mechanical, or civil into your project and having them all loaded to display at the same time can consume your computer resources. The Performance Monitor portion of the Worksharing Monitor application can help you evaluate the demand these extra linked files may put on your system's resources. We'll discuss the Worksharing Monitor in a moment.

Another benefit of making additional User-Created worksets is that you can assign each of these linked projects/files to its own workset. This will allow you to open only the ones that you need, when you need them. For example, if you will not be coordinating with mechanical for the day, you can choose to not open that workset. This is usually a much better approach than reloading and unloading the link in the Manage Links dialog box.

Using the Worksharing Monitor

The Worksharing Monitor is useful only if you are working on a project with worksets enabled. The only use for a single-user model environment is to display your current system's performance. This application is not part of Revit Structure's installation. It is a separate extension available through Autodesk and is strictly a tool that monitors temporary files that are placed in the Revit_Temp folder adjacent to your central file.

So, how can the Worksharing Monitor help you in your workflows? Well, it can answer many questions that you might have as multiple users work on your project. For instance:

◆ How long has it been since your last Synchronize with Central?

◆ Is your local file out of date?

◆ Other than yourself, who is working in the project?

◆ Is someone working in the central file?

◆ Has your request been granted yet?

◆ Who last worked on the central file?

◆ Do you need to respond to any editing requests?

Once the Worksharing Monitor is installed, you will need to launch it separately from Revit Structure. You can do this by clicking on the shortcut that the installation places on your desktop, going through the Windows Start menu, or (within Revit Structure) by choosing the Add-Ins tab from the Ribbon ➤ External Tools panel ➤ External Tools drop-down ➤ Worksharing Monitor tool.

Since this is a separate program and it has its own window, it is nice to have a dual-monitor setup. However, if you do not have dual monitors in your environment, you can configure Worksharing Monitor to display desktop alerts. These alerts will show up in the bottom-right corner of your screen with brief messages. When they appear, you can bring up the Monitor window for additional information. Keep in mind that this is only a monitoring tool, and all actions by you still need to be done from within Revit Structure.

WHEN ALL ELSE FAILS, CALL FOR HELP

Your best source of information regarding Worksharing Monitor is the help documentation in the Worksharing Monitor program. This documentation gives an in-depth look at how the tool works and looks. It also features several graphics and explanations of common day-to-day scenarios.

Using the Worksharing Monitor interface is quite simple; it allows you to set it to interact with a user's individual work methods and preferences. It displays the pertinent information needed at your fingertips while you are working.

Observing the Graphical User Interface

The Worksharing Monitor's main display shown in Figure 13.38 is organized into three sections:

Central File Access This section shows information about the project you are working on, such as the central and local filenames as well as who is working in what files. It also will tell you when other users are saving and how long before they are finished saving.

Editing Requests This section displays any Editing Requests that you may have made of other users. It displays the current status as well as who created the requests and who needs to respond.

Notifications This section displays warning information such as low memory, potential delays in saving, or users not informed of your request.

FIGURE 13.38
The main GUI screen for Worksharing Monitor

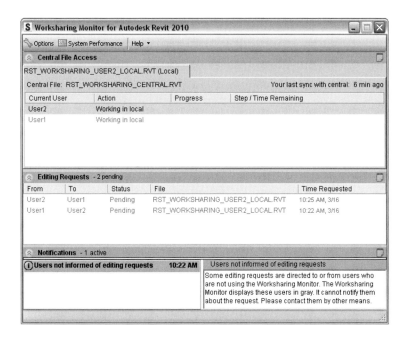

The Options button allows you to configure the notifications for behavior of each section in the main dialog box. You have control over whether you receive pop-up messages and, if so, how long they display before disappearing.

The System Performance monitor shown in Figure 13.39 is a great little tool for showing you your system's performance when you are working on your project. Since this dialog box pulls information from your system rather than from the Revit_Temp folder, this feature will work when you're working on a single-user file.

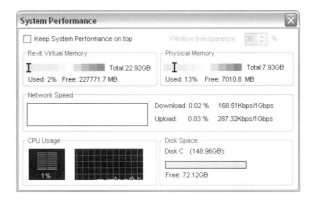

Maintaining Your Project

It is good practice to do regular maintenance on your central file. This includes keeping all users informed of how they should be working with the central and local files as well as what to do when things go wrong. Most of this maintenance should be done by a team captain or project manager so proper notification is given and tasks are performed consistently.

There are times when you will need to access the backup files for your projects. Most of the time this happens in the heat of the moment, so knowing how to do this and feeling comfortable doing it are things you will have to develop. Teaching users when to use the Detach from Central feature might help avoid trouble. Proper upgrading and routine audits will help keep your central file healthy and free of corruption.

Accessing Backup Files

Salvaging a workset project's backup file is a little different than just renaming the BAK file as you did in AutoCAD. You can use a tool that is located in the Synchronize panel of the Collaborate tab: Restore Backups.

After selecting Restore Backups, browse to the backup folder that you want to retrieve (roll back) backups from. Backups can be retrieved from either the local file backup or the central file backup. Choose whichever one is most current or contains the information that you are trying to retrieve. The number of backups you chose to keep when you created your central and local files determines how far back your backups will go.

Once you have located and opened the backup folder, you will be presented with a list of backup files similar to those shown in Figure 13.40 that are available for a Save As or Rollback operation. The number of backups is specified in the Options button when you perform a Save As. The default is 20; in Figure 13.40 it is set to 5. This is where it can become useful to add comments when you Synchronize with Central. Comments will allow you to easily determine which backup you need to get back to. If you recall, earlier we encouraged you to enter a comment when you use Synchronize with Central; you'll see comments listed in the Comment column of the Project Backup Versions dialog box (Figure 13.40). Providing comments can make it easier to determine which backup is the most appropriate one to use.

Before attempting to roll back a project, take a few minutes to think about what will be happening. Most of the time when you have to perform this action, you are caught up in the heat of the moment and not always thinking clearly. All later versions in the backup folder will be lost when you roll back a project And all team members will have to make new local files from the file that you use the Rollback feature on. For these reasons, we recommend that you use the Save As option instead of using Rollback; keep in mind that Save As creates a new local file, not a central file. It is still necessary to do a Save As ➤ Project, while checking the option to "Make this a Central File after save" in the Save As options.

FIGURE 13.40
Salvaging a backup from a workset project: choose Save As to save to a new file or choose Rollback to revert to a previous backup version.

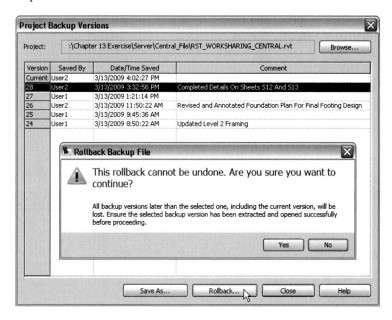

WHAT IS IT, A SINGLE-USER OR WORKSHARED FILE?

Determining what type of file your project is can be pretty simple. If your project file has additional files adjacent to it with .000*X*.rvt appended to the filenames, then it is a single-user file. These files can be renamed (remove the .000*X*) just as you would rename an AutoCAD BAK file.

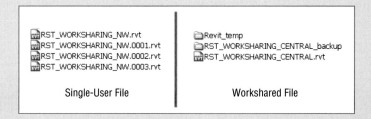

If your project file has an additional folder next to it with the same name and backup appended to it, then this is a workshared file. You need to use the Retrieve Backup tool to retrieve previous backup versions.

Detaching from Central

If for any reason you need to work inside the project and you know that you do not want to save your changes or risk borrowing elements that you do not want, you can perform a Detach from Central (DFC) prior to opening. This option is quite useful when you're performing tasks that do not need to be saved to the central file, such as:

◆   Transferring project standards

◆   Archiving a copy of the project

◆   Reviewing the project (by a manager)

◆   Exporting views for client collaboration

◆   Displaying the project in meetings

◆   Performing studies

Detach from Central is available in the Open dialog box. When you select the Detach from Central check box, you will see the notification shown in Figure 13.41 telling you that you are creating an independent file. All path and permission information is reset, and no changes can be saved back to the central file. If saved, the file will become a new central file. If this check box is selected for a single-user file, the option will be ignored and the file will open normally.

FIGURE 13.41
Detaching from Central to make an independent file

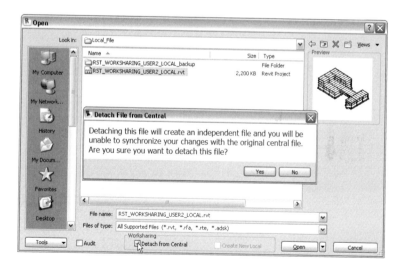

NO SAVE REQUIRED

Initially a file created from a Detach from Central isn't "anything" — it is a temporary file without a name. The application title bar displays a dash (–) for the name. The current user is the owner of all worksets. Only after the file has been saved for the first time does it become a real file. For this reason a user can use DFC and "walk away" from it without saving if desired.

Upgrading the Central File

When upgrading to a new version of Revit Structure, you should use the following procedure to upgrade the central file for each of your projects using worksets. Create a backup copy of your project in the current release before performing the upgrade. This backup file will be valuable if for any reason the new central file becomes corrupted.

To create your backup copy, make sure that all team members have saved their latest information to the central file. Using the same version of Revit that the file was created with, open the central file using the Detach from Central option. This will ensure that all user ownerships are relinquished and allow you to create a clean central file with a new name.

To retain your backup history, you will have to copy the central file and its backup folder to a new location. Be careful because Revit will regard the copy as a local file that will be looking for the original central file at its original location. If you create the new central file using the original, this can create problems later if someone tries to open the archived copy.

When upgrading the project, make sure that any Revit links in your project are upgraded first. To upgrade your file, open it in the new version of Revit Structure. You will see the message box shown in Figure 13.42, indicating that your file is being upgraded. To ensure that the backup history of the project is retained, perform a Synchronize with Central in lieu of using the Save As command from the Application menu. Remember that once your project's central file is upgraded and saved, each of your team members needs to make new local files from the upgraded central file.

FIGURE 13.42
The Project Upgrade
dialog box

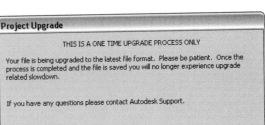

> **Project Upgrade**
>
> THIS IS A ONE TIME UPGRADE PROCESS ONLY
>
> Your file is being upgraded to the latest file format. Please be patient. Once the process is completed and the file is saved you will no longer experience upgrade related slowdown.
>
> If you have any questions please contact Autodesk Support.

TIMING IS EVERYTHING

Timing is everything when you are upgrading a project to a newer version of Revit Structure. More than likely several other Revit links also need to be upgraded. In some cases you may be waiting for the architect or mechanical teams to upgrade their files before you can open your structural model. The entire team needs to be on the same page and coordinating when it will all happen. Rather than waiting for those files and going through the agony of upgrading everybody else's model just so you can open and upgrade yours, take a different approach. If you temporarily rename the links so your structural model is unable to find them, you can easily upgrade your model. When you receive the other models that have been upgraded, rename the files back to their original name and you are back in business.

Auditing Your Project File

Part of keeping your central file healthy is occasionally performing an audit on it. This should be done at least once a month, and you definitely want to perform an audit before you upgrade to a new version. This will help fix and detect any corruption that might be inside the database. The Audit check box appears at the bottom of the Open dialog box, shown in Figure 13.43. Performing an audit on your project can increase the time it takes to open your file. Keep this in mind on some of your larger projects. Prior to performing this task, tell all users to save their local files to the central file and close out of the project. After auditing, have all users create new local files. Don't bother waiting for a status report of what the audit is doing or problems it has found and/or fixed. Don't worry; nothing is wrong. Revit does not provide any of these results for you to review.

FIGURE 13.43
Audit your project file before upgrading to a new version.

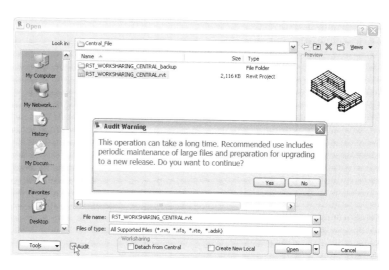

EXERCISE: WORKING IN A MULTIUSER ENVIRONMENT

For this exercise you are going to make temporary settings in your Revit Structure session(s) to simulate two users working in a worksharing environment. This will require you to open two sessions of Revit Structure on your workstation and reset the username of each session on the General tab located in the Application menu ➤ Options. *Remember these settings because you will want to set them back when you have finished with the exercise.*

Before beginning, you will need to use the RST_WORKSHARING_NW.rvt file (from the book's companion web page at www.sybex.com/go/masteringrevitstructure2010) and set up a folder structure like the one shown in the following illustration on your workstation's C: drive. This folder structure will act as both the server and user workstations. In a real-world scenario, the single-user file will be on the workstation and the central file will be on the network.

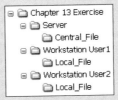

Once the folder structure is created, copy the RST_WORKSHARING_NW.rvt file into the Server folder. This will be your single-user file saved to the server.

Enable Worksharing

1. Launch two sessions of Revit Structure on your workstation.

2. In session 1, select the Application menu ➤ Options and change the username to **User1**. Repeat the same steps for session 2 but use **User2**. (From now on we will refer to User1 and User2.)

3. **User1:** Open RST_WORKSHARING_NW.rvt and take a look at the project. Notice that the tools on the Synchronize and Worksets panels in the Collaborate tab are grayed out. This indicates that worksharing is not yet enabled.

4. **User1:** Click Worksets.

5. **User1:** Acknowledge the two default User-Created worksets (Shared Levels and Grids and Workset1) and click OK.

6. **User1:** Take a look at the Worksets dialog box to see how the existing elements are organized into worksets. Toggle through the check boxes for the default worksets. Do not exit the dialog box yet.

7. **User1:** Create a new workset called **East Wing** and click OK to exit.

Create the Central File

1. **User1:** Use Save As to rename your new workset model to the server in the Central File folder as RST_WORKSHARING_CENTRAL.rvt.

2. **User1:** Choose the Synchronize and Modify Settings tool from the Collaborate tab to relinquish all worksets. Make sure all workset check boxes are checked prior to clicking OK.

3. Close out of the central file (Application menu ➤ Close).

Create the Local File

1. Using Windows Explorer, copy the central file on the server to the Local_File folder on workstation User1.

2. Rename the new local file to **RST_WORKSHARING_USER1_LOCAL.rvt**.

3. Repeat steps 1 and 2 of this section for User2's local file.

4. **User1:** Open the local file RST_WORKSHARING_USER1_LOCAL.rvt. Review the This Is Not a Central File dialog box and click OK. User1 is now working in a local file that has a bidirectional link with the central file.

5. **User2:** Repeat step 4 of this section.

REVIEW NEW ITEMS

User1/User2: Observe the additional tools and commands that are available to you:

◆ Collaborate tab ➢ Synchronize panel

◆ Collaborate tab ➢ Worksets panel

◆ Status bar

◆ Visibility/Graphic Overrides dialog box

◆ Element/View Properties

MOVE ELEMENTS BETWEEN WORKSETS

1. **User1/User2:** Choose the Synchronize and Modify Settings tool from the Collaborate panel. Click any required workset toggles to make sure you did not borrow any elements while observing the model.

2. **User1:** Borrow the Workset1 workset. You will be moving elements from this workset onto the East Wing workset. Typically you would just need to borrow the elements when moving elements from one workset to another, but since we are going to be moving several elements (an entire wing), you will borrow the workset instead.

   To borrow a workset choose the Collaborate tab ➢ Worksets panel ➢ Worksets tool. In the Worksets dialog box select the workset to borrow and click the Editable button at the right. You should see your username show up under the Owner column and a Yes appear in the Editable column. Select OK to exit the dialog box. An alternate method to do the same thing would be to select an element that is assigned to the workset you want to borrow. In your case it will be Workset1. While the element is selected, right-click to access the shortcut menu and choose Make Worksets Editable.

3. **User1:** Go to a 3D view and orient your view so you can select the East Wing objects with a left-to-right crossing window, as shown here. Once the objects are selected, use the Filter selection to select only elements of the same category, Floors.

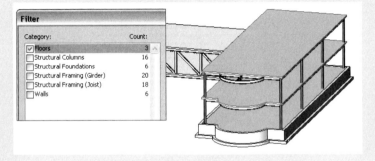

4. **User1:** Open the properties of the selected elements shown here and find the Identity Data section. Change Workset1 to **East Wing**. Click OK.

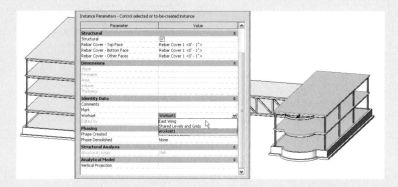

5. **User1:** Repeat steps 3 and 4 of this section for all elements until they are all on the East Wing workset.

   Tip: Turn the East Wing workset off in the Visibility/Graphic Overrides dialog box so the elements disappear when you put them in the East Wing workset. When you have finished, you can turn the workset back on to see your elements. Note that having to select elements of the same category may not always be the behavior that Revit Structure presents. Depending on the element types within your selection set, you may be able to select several elements from several categories and still have the option to switch their workset to another workset without having to repeat steps 3 and 4.

6. **User1:** With Workset1 active and the East Wing workset turned back on, gray out the inactive workset with the Gray Inactive Workset Graphics tool. You should see the East Wing grayed out, as shown here.

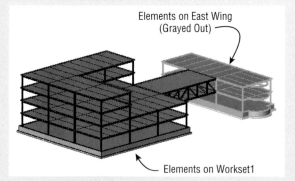

Elements on East Wing
(Grayed Out)

Elements on Workset1

7. **User1:** Choose the Synchronize and Modify Settings tool from the Collaborate panel, and click the available workset check boxes to relinquish ownership of any elements.

8. **User2:** Choose Reload Latest from the Collaborate tab to update your local file with User1's recent changes to the East Wing.

PERFORM EDITING REQUEST

1. **User1:** Switch to the Level 3 view and edit the slab edge to run to the centerline of the curved beam, as shown. When it is complete, finish the sketch.

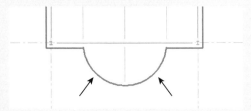

2. **User2:** Switch to the Level 3 view and attempt to edit the slab edge. Note that you do not see the new slab edge edits in the User2 local file. This is because User1 did not Synchronize with Central. Attempting to edit the slab edge at this point will prompt you to make a request because you do not own the element.

3. **User2:** Place the request and notify User1.

4. **User1:** Open the Editing Request dialog box and observe the message. In this case User1 will have to Synchronize with Central before being able to grant the request. Do the Synchronize with Central, and then grant the request.

5. **User2:** Check to see if your request has been granted. Yes, you should now own the element, but since your local file is out of date and does not reflect User2's recent slab changes, you will need to perform a Reload Latest before you can edit the elements.

This concludes the brief exercise for this chapter. Continue to work on the files on your own as if you were working in a multiuser environment. When you have finished, make sure that you set your username back to its original setting.

The Bottom Line

Determine when to enable worksharing.   Looking past day 1 of your project to help determine the proper game plan for moving forward will make things go much smoother.

> **Master It**   What can determine when you should enable worksharing?

Enable and set up the worksharing environment.   When working in Revit Structure, you'll almost always be in a multiuser environment. Knowing how to enable worksets and use the central and local files is important for communicating among team members.

> **Master It**   How do you enable worksets, and where should the central and local files be saved?

Request and grant permission of elements.   Working in a multiuser environment where you are sharing a project with ownership rights will eventually lead to team members tripping over one another. Understanding how borrowing elements works is important to work efficiently.

Master It What are the methods used so you can borrow an element(s)? What do you do if another team member has already borrowed an element(s) that you need?

Stay in sync with other team members. Creating the central file and communicating with it using a local file is how to work effectively using Revit's worksharing features.

Master It What is the most flexible method to create a local file? What commands are used to get information back and forth between the central and local files?

Properly maintain your project file. Keeping your central file as healthy as possible will decrease chances of file corruption and increase overall performance.

Master It When should you audit the central file? How should you go about upgrading your file to a new version?

Chapter 14

Visualization

You have just spent a significant amount of time learning about Revit Structure, creating models, and documenting them. But once you have your *regular* work done, you should take some time to show it off. However simple you find modeling your buildings, it may be difficult to gain a high level of familiarity with the rendering process because you may so infrequently render your projects. But keep in mind that you can gain much by exploring and implementing the rendering features contained in Revit Structure.

The rendering engine in Revit Structure enables you to create visual imagery of your models. You can then leverage these images in everyday as well as specialized uses.

In this chapter, you will learn to:

◆ Determine what and when to model

◆ Assign materials to your model

◆ Define the quality and style of your renderings

◆ Export your models for other uses

How Much Do You Need?

When you begin to plan your models, undoubtedly you make sure you are covering all the basics. You will have grids, columns, floors, beams, walls, and so forth. You will then begin your documentation process, adding details and schedules as needed. Some will be generated live by the model, whereas others will be just lines and text placed alongside your model objects. This will continue during the entire sequence of construction drawing development. Soon you will have a nice — and probably bloated — model, ripe for using beyond normal drawings.

But will you be able to use the model for these extra purposes? If you modeled every piece of steel in a composite steel structure, not only would your model be huge and probably slow, but the level of detail in it might very well be beyond extended use. If you make a highly detailed model and it takes an hour to render it once, that probably will not be suitable for your rendering needs.

In the next section we will cover developing limits on what to model, along with methods to understand and control model bloating.

Modeling beyond the Paper Documents

The normal process of modeling should be measured against several tiers. The first tier is your plan drawings. If you *see* something on plan and not in any other view, the need to model in 3D, to start with, is subjective. Sure, do it, if the object in question is easy to make and a primary component of Revit Structure. Then there are the items you see on plan and in sections or elevations. These too should probably be modeled if for no other reason than you don't want to create them twice (plan and detail). It also will help that the model is dynamic (all views will be automatically updated).

So what do you *not* model? For example, on a steel joist roof system, bracing angles are often required for the structure design. These items could be modeled and then shown on plan — but it is doubtful that you would have to model them since these small items would not normally be shown in a building section.

But let's imagine for a moment that your project has a healthy fee and you have the time to model every little thing. Not only will it be fun to create that virtual building, but you will get the added benefit of doing material takeoffs quickly. You can also use these components for the next project, where you may not have the luxury of time. You have no reason to not model every little thing. But you know there *has* to be repercussions for that!

"Speed kills" is an old adage that many relate to driving an automobile. Go too fast and you lose control. Well, excessive modeling is sort of the opposite; you will have no usability or speed and simply want to kill yourself waiting for the model to respond! Certainly this is a joke, but many times it has proven true. If you model too much, your model will become so slow that you can't work at any reasonable speed — and that is if you are lucky! Overly large models also can become unstable and crash with little warning.

Now what does this have to do with rendering? It's simple: the model you make will "make or break" your modeling efforts. If a primary goal of modeling in Revit Structure is to create a nice rendering view, you should keep that in mind while creating your model. However, if your project is small and simple, you probably cannot overmodel beyond the rendering capabilities. If your model is a convention center with tens of thousands of steel sticks, that may pose a problem.

As you have learned already, Revit Structure is a database-driven system. Every single thing in the model impacts its size. In Figure 14.1, we have a steel beam next to a concrete beam. Do you think these two are the same in the BIM world? In a way, yes, both are beams, but in every other way, no. The concrete beam has properties to help it *be* a concrete beam. Likewise, the steel beam has properties to help it *be* a steel beam. But due to the nature of this object type, there is a lot more information for a steel beam. Not only does it have connection symbols, but a steel beam has additional invisible data in this view: the stick line representation as well as the fine detail-level information, which would show the curved interior edges of the wide flange.

FIGURE 14.1
A face comparison
between a steel beam
and a concrete beam

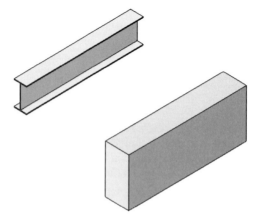

When you activate the rendering process, the surface of the shapes is what takes Revit Structure time to process. A concrete beam with six faces (four sides and two ends) will take less time to render than a wide-flange beam. A typical wide-flange beam has 12 faces, but depending on the meshing/rendering process, it can have 18 faces. To figure it out for yourself, cover your shape with "rectangles" and then count them. So it would be logical to think that a steel beam can have three times the face count of a concrete beam and then perhaps take three times as long to render. A project with 5,000 steel beams could have a face count of 90,000 — just for the beams. It is not unrealistic to have a project with over a million faces!

The key thing to keep in mind is to render what you need and not just what you have. If you can use a simplified shape, do so; it will cut down on the face count. Perform a regular basic rendering of your model, and track the model file size to compare with how long it takes to render. There is nothing worse than trying to get a high-quality render made but not have the time to create it.

Avoiding Model Creep

Model creep isn't a term to describe a mean or scary model. It simply explains a tendency to model beyond your needs, resulting in a bloated model. Imagine you have a team of people working on a project and everyone is actively contributing to the model. You should approach your virtual model just as the general contractor would. There would be regular meetings to discuss what is getting *built* today, what not to *build* at all, and what is still to be *built*. Your virtual construction should be no different, if for no other reason than to keep track of what goes into your model. You might be a frugal modeler, putting in only what needs to be put in. But your coworkers might not be so studious and go overboard. They're off modeling turndowns on slab-on-grades. They're modeling plates for steel beam-to-column connections, as shown in Figure 14.2. They're placing cold-formed steel stud members at 16″ on the center in interior walls. If these are things you need to model, then all is good. But if not, you and your team need to talk. Any valid additional items would have to be managed and/or filtered so that you can later turn them off for your renders if needed.

FIGURE 14.2
Highly detailed connections can hurt rendering times.

Real World Scenario

UNDERSTANDING CLIENT NEEDS

We were developing a rather large project in early design. The project manager asked that a detailed model be created with specifics for beam sizes and such. After a few days of model creation, the topic of renderings came up. "Can we produce some images to wow the client?" "Absolutely, no problem. Just tell me where you want to look from." "Okay, can do." Of course, more modeling went on without a word about location for point of view. A week went by and the model was ready for rendering. Seeing the deadline approaching, typical assumptions were made as to where to "see" the model and renderings began — except they took forever! The model was so dense that each rendering took 90 minutes. It turned out okay — there was enough time to run the shots. But disappointment came when the renderings were handed over and it was decided a single shot was all that was needed. We could have modeled less than 30 percent since the model was never seen by the client, internal superiors, or external customers.

The crux of creep is that you need to watch and be aware of what goes into your models so that you can better prepare for when you need to create renders. Once you know what to look for, you can begin to do some work!

Defining the Right Materials

Materials are the make-or-break component of a successful rendering. The world is your oyster, in a sense. You can make your rendering look like a cartoon, make it look realistic, or make it anywhere in between. The funny thing is that materials are often a source of so much aggravation, not because of the difficulty in using them but rather because everyone has an opinion, and just like art, beauty is in the eye of the beholder. Whereas lighting controls what you see and how flat or realistic the rendering is, materials convey object type regardless of the lighting.

As you begin to create renderings on a regular basis, you should define whatever styles you will offer to your clients, and then allow your clients to pick from your portfolio of options and the style of rendering they want you to develop. You might have a single-color material (gray) that you use for all objects. This would convey, without question, that the rendering is a computer model. This technique is best in early stages when form and volume are most important.

Another method is to have materials of a single color representing the components on the structure — for example, a white/gray for concrete objects and a deep red for steel objects, representing primer paint. You can use a photograph of a concrete wall surface with form holes as well as stains. This would be well suited for close-up images where the detail of the surface is an added bonus for faking realism.

Materials in Revit Structure can be thought of in two distinct fashions: those that are faked and those that are made of something real. In the following section, we will cover synthetic and realistic materials.

Using Synthetic Materials

The first form of material we'll refer to as *synthetic*. It does not exist in the real world and generally is just a color with various reflective properties, like paint. A synthetic material is usually the best option for large-scale renderings. One caveat: since a synthetic material itself has no patterning, you will have to rely on lighting and shadows to help define limits of objects. What you will often see is a loss of definition between a foreground object and a background object of the same color. As shown in Figure 14.3, graphically the difference between the concrete column in the foreground and the concrete wall in the background is hard to discern.

FIGURE 14.3
Can you tell the difference between the column and the wall?

So when using synthetic materials — that is, materials with no patterns — it is important to use variation in the colors to aid in the visual differences. As shown in Figure 14.4, all your concrete object types should have slightly different colors so that they contrast against one another.

FIGURE 14.4
You can use different tones to indicate object types more readily.

Creating Real-World Materials

Most people would prefer to see some sort of pattern on the rendered objects. It could be a concrete with aggregate showing, a masonry wall with grout lines, or steel with some weathering. Anything you can apply to an object that mimics its real-world properties will add a level of realism to your renderings. Take a look at Figure 14.5; this is a real photograph of a concrete surface.

FIGURE 14.5
When applied to objects, a real-world material (image) will make those objects look realistic.

EXERCISE: IT'S ALL MATERIAL

Applying materials to your various objects is fairly easy. In this exercise, you will experience first-hand the steps required. As shown here, this model has a steel material applied but lacks style. This exercise will determine what material is applied to the steel objects and then change it accordingly.

1. Access MATERIAL.RVT at the book's companion web page (www.sybex.com/go/masteringrevitstructure2010 under Resources & Downloads, Part 5 Tutorial files. This is a small model with a few beams and a column.

2. On the Ribbon choose the Manage tab, and then click the Materials button on the Project Settings panel to open the Materials dialog box.

3. Scroll down in the Materials dialog box and select Metal – Steel – ASTM A992. This is the material assigned to steel beam and column families in this model.

4. Once the material is active, select the Render Appearance tab at the top of the Materials dialog box. A quick scan of the panel will show that the style of the material is based on Aluminum Anodized Dark Bronze. This is the default in Revit Structure 2010 and probably the first thing you should change in your templates.

5. At the top of the panel, click the Replace button; then, using the Render Appearance Library, type **steel** in the Search box at the top. This will reduce the available materials to those with "steel" in their name.

6. Now locate and pick Stainless Steel Brushed, and then click OK to close. The Materials dialog box now shows Stainless Steel Brushed as the appearance. Next you need to change the shininess of the material.

7. Within the Metal Properties area is the Finish drop-down list. Change the setting from Brushed to Satin. Then click OK to close. Now this revised steel material has a more realistic render appearance, as shown here:

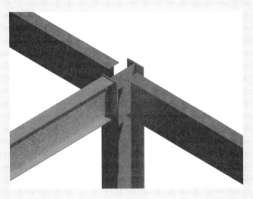

Once you have materials properly applied to your model objects, as shown in the final illustration of the preceding exercise, you will be ready at a moment's notice to create renderings. Material configuration and assignment to objects is one of the primary purposes of a template file. You can spend time doing this once and then leverage that time over and over for later projects. The key is to know how your future renderings should be set up. A great example is steel. It can come in many surface styles, from weathering steel (orange rust) to gray primer, and in many paint colors as well. A good protocol is to create a series of material recipes to recall when needed.

You may think that just duplicating Metal – Steel – ASTM A992 over and over for each style would be a good method, but there isn't a good way to change all steel objects from one steel material to another. The quick method is to change the primary material, Metal – Steel – ASTM A992, to whatever style you want for most of your objects. Then, if needed, you can create additional materials for atypical steel objects.

Once your objects are properly *materialized*, you can begin to create renderings. The following section explores the ease in which you can obtain great imagery from your Revit Structure models.

Starting a Rendering

A first step in understanding how to render is to know *what* you can render. Not every view in Revit Structure can be used for this purpose. Only isometric and camera views can be rendered. But that doesn't mean you can't render "flat" views — there are methods to follow for those as well.

To find out if you have a rendering option on a given view, look at the View Control bar for the view. Along with the scale, detail level, and other controls is a tool to open the Rendering dialog box. As shown in Figure 14.6, the icon is a teapot. This is in deference to the original teapot model used by many to develop their skills in this artistic arena.

FIGURE 14.6
Look for the teapot to know if the view can be rendered.

Before you begin to render, prepare your system for the best possible performance. The mental ray engine can use up to four computer processors for rendering computations, so whatever you can do to reduce other active applications will help. Shut down your mail client and anything else not required during the time you will be rendering.

In addition, in your model you should hide unnecessary objects in the view you will be rendering. These might be objects that are on the far side of the model but that appear in the wireframe view. If you can see objects in the wireframe view, they will be rendered and, if applicable, covered by object faces in front of them. So why bother to render them — just turn them off.

You can also gain some performance by adjusting your detail level from fine to medium or coarse. For example, steel beams have filleted corners at the web/flange interfaces. If your point of view is outside the building, this curve will be small and not visible. But the mental ray engine will see it and develop a rendered solution for it. Again, you can increase performance by reducing the detail level. Finally, you can just adjust the area to render by using a crop region or a section box or by assigning a render region. (We'll discuss render regions a little later in this chapter.)

Now that you have properly prepared your to-be-rendered view, you can click the Show Rendering Dialog button.

The Rendering dialog box might appear a bit foreign to you. It contains controls that are unlike anything else in Revit Structure. As shown in Figure 14.7, the dialog box has several panels of controls to enable you to create renderings to meet your needs.

At the very top of the dialog box is the Render button. Perhaps this should have been placed at the bottom, since you click this button only after you've made all your setting changes. Just to the right is a Region check box. Check it, and Revit Structure includes a rectangular region within your active display, with grips on all edges and corners, as shown in Figure 14.8. These grips allow you to adjust the area of the view that is to be rendered. You can alter the region even when the Render dialog box is open.

Once you have made your adjustments to the region, you return to the Rendering dialog box. If you turn off the Region check box and turn it on again, the region will reset to the view default.

Depending on your rendering needs, the quality of the output you require can vary easily using the Quality controls. The following section demonstrates the types of quality and how to achieve them.

FIGURE 14.7
The Rendering dialog box is used to make all rendered images.

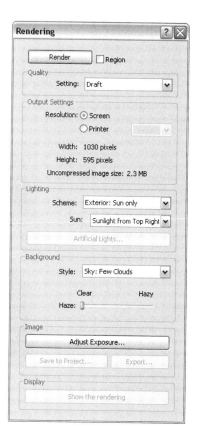

FIGURE 14.8
An example region to render

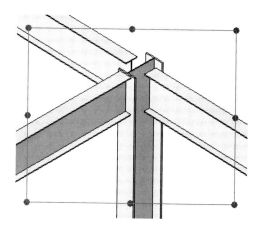

Adjusting the Quality

By default, Revit Structure provides five levels of quality: Draft, Low, Medium, High, and Best. Most users will settle for using only two or three levels, depending on the quality and time to complete they can accept. For purposes of this discussion, we ran a series of renderings on three settings. A rendering at Draft (see Figure 14.9) level took 1 minute, 3 seconds, to complete. A Medium-level (see Figure 14.10) rendering took 7 minutes, 49 seconds, to complete. Then, a rendering made at the Best level (see Figure 14.11) took over 2 hours!

FIGURE 14.9
Draft level of quality

FIGURE 14.10
Medium level of quality

In all three of these, the resolution was no different (1026 × 664) and each had a 16 million color palette. The difference was the level of quality of the computations for the rendering itself. The better the quality, the fewer mistakes, known as *artifacts*, that were left in the image. As shown in Figures 14.9, 14.10, and 14.11, each subsequent shot improved pixilation and thereby had smoother color blends. The full images are available for your review on the book's accompanying web page; look in the `Part 5 Tutorial` folder.

FIGURE 14.11
Best level of quality

In most cases you should use Draft to define your basic lighting and area of the image. That way, once you're ready, rendering at Medium will produce reasonable results for most digital uses such as a Microsoft PowerPoint slide. When you need to print an image, then (and only then) you would commit the time for a Best rendering level. Remember that the resolution isn't the issue — it is the quality of the output and how "clean" it looks.

If you review the color images, you will notice that at Draft level the grass is very spotty. But at Medium and Best you can detect little to no difference in the grass. This is because the grass is actually an image, or grass tiled onto the topography object. Also notice the jagged edges on the Draft image that don't exist on the other two.

If none of the default quality settings work for you, or you just want to delve deeper into controlling the quality, all you need to do is click the Edit option in the Setting drop-down list to open the Render Quality Settings dialog box shown in Figure 14.12.

The Render Quality Settings dialog box has several sections available for adjustment. Preset quality levels are included that provide you with a way to tell what is set for each type. For example, you can tell that at Draft level the Image Precision setting is at 1 (jagged edges), but if Medium is selected the Image Precision setting is at 4. So if you just need the speed of Draft but want fewer jagged edges, choose the Custom setting and then set Image Precision to 4. Then click OK to assign those settings and return to the Rendering dialog box.

Here are the various settings for Render Quality:

Image Precision   Adjust this value to lower the number of jagged edges in the rendered view. Values range from 1 (very jagged) to 10 (least jagged).

Maximum Number of Reflections   Increase this value if objects are not shown within reflections of a rendered view. The range is from 0 (none) to 100 (absolute most available).

Maximum Number of Refractions   Adjust this value when objects don't appear through multiple planes of glass. Values range between 0 (opaque) to 100 (transparent).

FIGURE 14.12
You can use the Render Quality Settings dialog box to create your rendering quality level.

Blurred Refractions Precision   Adjust this value when object edges or surfaces in blurred reflections are spotty. Values range from 1 (spotty) to 11 (smoothest).

Enable Soft Shadows   Choose this option to permit shadows to be soft using the Soft Shadow Precision control.

Soft Shadow Precision   If available, this option allows shadows to be set from 0 (spotty) to 10 (smoothest).

Compute Indirect and Sky Illumination   Choose this option to permit light from the sky and object-bounced light into your scene.

Indirect Illumination Smoothness   Adjust this to provide more detail on objects that are in shadow and lit by indirect lights. Values range from 1 (least detail) to 10 (most detail).

Indirect Illumination Bounces   Adjust this value to permit objects in shadow to be lit by indirect lights. It controls how many times a light ray can bounce from object to object. This can lighten objects totally in shadow so that they can be seen. Values range from 1 (single bounce for lights) to 100 (highest number of bounces), but in general more than three bounces is not perceptible.

Daylight Portals for Windows, Doors, and Curtain Walls   These controls apply only for daylight within an interior view and provide a means to get light in through the opening.

There are many components to render quality — luckily you can bypass most of them on your way to getting output. In the next section we'll examine output, settings, lighting, and backgrounds.

Changing the Output Settings

Once you have specified your quality level, you then determine the output required. The Rendering dialog box offers two options: Screen and Printer.

Screen will assign a resolution based on the visible model view. If you have a maximized viewport, the resolution will be as high as it can be. If you cascade or tile your views, the resolution will change. The resolution is directly related to the visible portion of the screen. For this reason, it can be difficult to hit specific resolution aspect ratios.

The only other option, which frankly isn't much better, is Printer. It allows you to render to a specific dpi (dots per inch). Available options include 75, 150, 300, and 600 dpi. If you need a specific resolution, you will have to render larger than you need and crop with an image-editing application such as Adobe Photoshop. Using an image-editing application to resize the image will lower the quality since the image will be pixilated.

For very high image resolutions, you will need to render in another application altogether, such as Autodesk's 3ds Max. Programs like 3ds Max permit finite control on image resolution and also have better material and lighting controls than Revit Structure.

Applying Proper Model Lighting

Lighting with Revit Structure is probably the one area where you will not need to adjust much. Structural projects are generally designed using columns rather than solid perimeter walls, so exterior lighting (the sun) typically can be used to generate the light needed for the rendering. In addition, most structural firms are quite busy with the normal building work and don't have time to delve into light placement. (An exception to this is a parking garage designer who is also responsible for garage light placement.)

As shown in Figure 14.13, Revit Structure provides a number of lighting schemes you can choose from. For a typical exterior daytime rendering, you choose Exterior: Sun Only. Selecting a Sun Only option disables the Artificial Lights control. Likewise, if you choose any of the Artificial Only options, the Sun control list will be disabled.

FIGURE 14.13
Select from various exterior or interior lighting schemes.

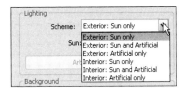

Interior schemes with sun have the added option of permitting sunlight to enter the scene via windows, doors, and curtain walls. This scheme just allows it; you would still need to use the Render Quality Settings dialog box to include the portal sunlight.

If you choose a sunlit scheme, you then have the ability to tune the sun location to whatever your needs are. As shown in Figure 14.14, you not only can point the sun at the model from a specific direction, but you can also choose to use a yearly position, such as a solstice or equinox. If none of the default Sun locations meet your needs, click the Edit/New option to display the Sun and Shadows Settings dialog box. As shown in Figure 14.15, this dialog box has Name and Settings areas. Depending on what you selected prior to clicking Edit/New, the Still, Single-Day, or Multi-Day tab will be active. If you just need a Still (single) position for the sun but want it coming from the lower left of your model, you can duplicate the Sunlight from Top Left option and modify it.

Once you've duplicated the option, rename it **Sunlight from Lower Left**; then adjust the Azimuth value to **225** (degrees) and deselect the Relative to View check box. Deselecting the Relative to View option will "pin" the location of the sun regardless of the point of view.

FIGURE 14.14
Sun-provided light can come from many directions, time of year, or relative to any point on earth.

FIGURE 14.15
Use the Sun and Shadows Settings dialog box to determine the point of origin for the sunlight.

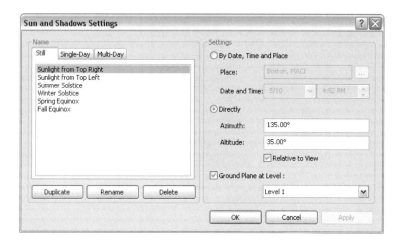

Using a Render Background

The background you choose in your Revit Structure images is an important issue: you must decide whether your goal is realism or clarity, print or digital presentation, or another personal preference. As shown in Figure 14.16, Revit Structure offers up to six styles to choose from: No Clouds, Very Few Clouds, Few Clouds, Cloudy, Very Cloudy, and Color.

The No Clouds style is simply a fading gradient from a horizon gray to a sky light blue. This is generally a great choice and allows a modest level of realism but without the distraction of visible clouds.

The other cloud styles all include increasing cloud volume overlaid on the gradient sky. The last option is Color. When you choose Color, the Haze slider control changes to a color swatch with access to a Define Color dialog box. In the Define Color dialog box you can set a simple solid color or define one using Red/Green/Blue or Pantone catalogs.

Your choice should reflect your intended use for the image. Here are some good guidelines:

Print (on paper)   Use a solid white background so that the model pops off the page. Color printers are notoriously bad when it comes to fill quality. If you must have a background image, then try to use a gradient with few clouds rather than a solid color.

Digital (on screen)   You set this depending on whether the display will be seen in a darkened room or a bright expo hall. For dark conditions, use a solid black background so that the whiteness isn't overbearing to the viewer. In well-lit rooms, choose a white background so that you have good contrast visually.

FIGURE 14.16
Revit Structure can give
you a cloudy day if you
want!

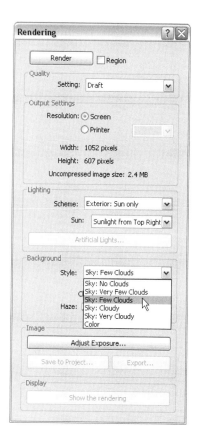

Obviously, when creating a render the end use could be just about anything. You would be wise to run renders with solid black, white, and gradients. And then for good measure, export the black background image as a PNG so that you save a version with a transparency layer. Later, using an image-editing program, you can place your building in a site photograph by using a masking and transparency layer, or you can even place it into a photograph with you in it (see Figure 14.17). The next section discusses the PNG image format.

As you can see, you can take your render to a whole other level of interest.

The last control for backgrounds is a foreground element. The Haze slider control permits you to put a level of fuzziness or fog into your render. This feature is most useful if you are designing a roadway structure, such as a large span bridge, or a major metropolitan high-rise structure.

Dealing with Images

Once you have a rendering made, you then must decide what to do with the fruit of your labor. This section exposes a few options that come into play once you have successfully rendered and are mostly satisfied with the results.

FIGURE 14.17
Get up close and personal with your models!

ADJUSTING EXPOSURE

As you begin to render models, take some time to go into the real world and look around. Develop an eye for what lighting looks like, and see how the sun and its contrast affects what you see. Contrast gives your renderings depth. Sure, you can render a model and include every little detail. But that isn't how the real world works. In the real world, some things are clearly visible, while others are hidden in darkened areas. This is where Adjust Exposure comes into play.

As shown in Figure 14.18, there is a multitude of things you can tweak to improve your renderings. In general, you will want to darken a given setting rather than lighten it.

FIGURE 14.18
Adjust the visual contrast within your images by using exposure controls.

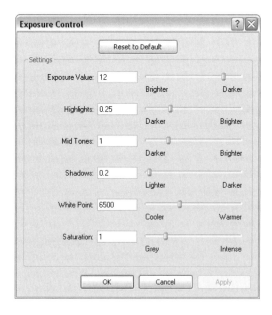

Using exposure doesn't require repeated renderings — just one. You simply open the Exposure Control dialog box before rendering, reset the default values, and then click OK to close. You then render your scene at the quality level you want. Once again, you open the Exposure Control dialog box and then modify the settings and click Apply. Your rendered image will update accordingly. Once you have the look you want, you can close the dialog box by clicking OK and then save/export as desired.

Saving to Project

If you intend to use your renderings in your project sheets, you can click the Save to Project button to place the image in a project view, and then you can drag it onto a sheet view.

This is a great feature — you can update the image simply by saving changes to the project and using the same name again. Doing so will overwrite the image, and once you return to the sheet, the revised image will be there.

Export Your Rendering

Once you have your rendering, you probably will want to save it to a file you can use later. Revit Structure provides a number of image file types for you use, but they are not all created equal. Some are best suited for viewing, others for print media, and some for use within other applications.

The choice comes when you click the Export button in the Rendering dialog box. A standard Windows file-access dialog box appears that lets you save the image. As you can see in Figure 14.19, the default filename matches the view name being exported. The Save Image dialog box also contains a Files of Type drop-down list. The following are the file format choices:

Bitmap (*.bmp)   This is an industry-standard format developed by Microsoft. The format is well known, and nearly every image-processing application can use BMPs. The format does not have a patent, which ensures its widespread use. However, the format tends to be uncompressed and therefore the images will often be very large and usable only for post-processing applications.

Figure 14.19
To save an image, use the Save Image dialog box.

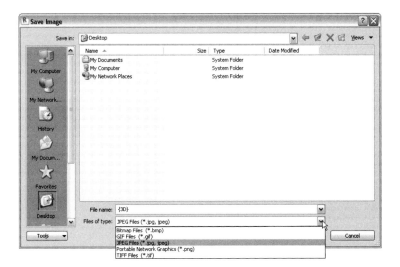

GIF (*.gif)   CompuServe developed this image standard for use within its network. Originally very popular because of their ability to contain animation, GIFs are now somewhat antiquated because of their color depth limitation of 256. GIF does still have its uses, since GIF files can contain transparent layers that can be used in post-processing to aid in masking between photographic and render image overlays.

JPEG (*.jpg, *.jpeg)   JPEG is today's standard for creation of user-ready images. The format has multiple compression levels and color depth controls, and it is generally well suited for Internet web presentation and standard-sized print uses. Due to its aliasing (pixel stepping), the JPEG is not suited for animation compiling. However, JPEG images can often be reduced in size while retaining a quality appearance.

Portable Network Graphics (*.png)   Developed as the replacement for GIF, this format offers increased color depth but no animation options. It also does not have a patent and so has been refined over the years into a great option. The color protocol is only RGB, but since it contains a transparency layer, the PNG can be used for masking easily.

TIFF (*.tif)   TIFF format is the workhorse of the professional media, including computer book publishing! The file format tends to be very large and the images can be lossless if desired. These image types are not well suited for Internet use; since they are formatted in CMYK color, they are heavily used where color-offset printing is done. A TIFF is often the best choice for post-compiling animations based on sequential images.

So, which do you use? If you are creating a single image for the Web or small 4″ × 6″ prints, use a JPEG. If you are creating an animation and intend to compile it post-render, use TIFFs for the images. If you are creating a tiny icon, use a BMP. If you desire an image you can print at 24″ × 36″, again use a TIFF for the best quality, or if size is an issue, use a JPEG. Finally, if you need to use the image layered with something else in post-render, then choose PNG.

Controlling a Rendered Display

The final option to examine in the Rendering dialog box is the simplest. The Display portion contains a single button control. Prior to rendering an image, this button is disabled. Once you have successfully rendered the view, this button reads Show the Model. And it does just that. When you click it, Revit Structure will clear the rendering from the Display area and replace it with the previous view of the model. Want to see the rendering again? Simple — click the Show the Rendering button and it comes back. We recommend that you save the model before switching back and forth between showing the model and showing the rendering.

You can close the Rendering dialog box, switch to other views, and as long as the rendered view stays open, you can recall the last rendered view any time. Once the model or view is closed, the rendered view will be discarded. Use Save to Project or Export if you will need the rendered view later.

As you now know, there is a lot of variation and control over the final product of your renderings. Next up is an exercise where you will get the chance to experience the process firsthand.

EXERCISE: RENDERING YOUR MODEL

Now that you have a complete picture of the rendering process, it is finally time to render! The model you will render is sized for speed and ease of use; yours will be much more interesting! There isn't a whole lot to successful renderings; just remember that beauty is in the eye of the beholder (see the following illustration).

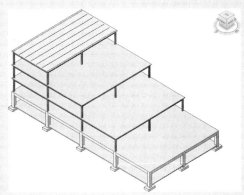

1. Open RENDER.RVT from the book's companion web page at www.sybex.com/go/masteringrevitstructure2010.

2. Using the Project Browser, open the 3D View ISOMETRIC.

3. At the bottom of the ISOMETRIC view, click the Show Rendering Dialog button (the teapot).

4. In the Rendering dialog box, change the Quality setting to Medium.

5. Click the Render button at the top to create the rendering.

Depending on the speed of your computer system, after a minute or so the ISOMETRIC view window will render. Odds are it won't look all that great. It will be washed out since no settings have been changed — yet.

1. With the Rendering dialog box still open, click Adjust Exposure.

2. Click the Reset to Default button at the top of the dialog box.

3. Change the Shadows value to **3** and then click Apply.

4. Click OK to close.

Instantly the image will darken, gain contrast in the shadows, and become more acceptable. Next we will adjust the materials.

1. Use the Manage tab on the Ribbon and click the Materials button.

2. In the Materials list panel, locate and select Concrete – Cast-in-Place Concrete.

3. Select the Render Appearance tab and then click the Replace button.

4. Using the browser window, find and select Concrete. Then click OK to apply and close.

5. Scroll the Materials list panel to find and click the Metal – Steel – ASTM 992 material. Click the Replace button.

6. In the Search box, type **Paint Dark Red Matte** and then click OK to accept and close. The preview will change to a wall corner.

7. Click OK to close the Materials dialog box.

You now have changed the material for concrete to a less-dense pattern. And now steel is a red primer color. It's time to adjust the sun and render again!

1. The Rendering dialog box should still be open; if not, click the teapot again.

2. In the Lighting area, click on the Sun list and choose Edit/New.

3. In the Sun and Shadows Settings dialog box, click Duplicate with the Sunlight from Top Right option selected.

4. Name the sun location **Sunlight from Lower Left** and click OK.

5. With Sunlight from Lower Left selected, change the Azimuth value to **225** and uncheck the Relative to View check box.

6. Click OK to apply and close.

7. In the Rendering dialog box, click the Background Style list and choose Color. You then get a color button; click it and assign a black color. Click OK to close. Consider saving your model now for real work conditions.

8. Change the Quality setting to High and then click Render. Now get some coffee or check out www.augi.com. The rendering will take a few minutes.

You have a good-looking rendering with a nice level of contrast and obvious steel elements, and it's ready for a video presentation, as shown here (the book graphic has an intentional white background).

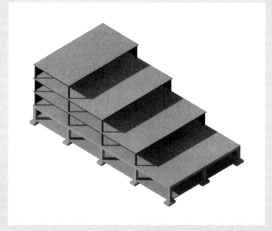

Revit Structure offers two view types to render by. One is the 3D view you just witnessed. The other is by using a camera. Next, you will use a camera and then render from the ground point of view and add some clouds.

1. Using the Project Browser, open the Level 1 plan view.

2. Using the View tab on the Ribbon, expand the 3D View button and choose Camera.

3. Note that the Options bar now contains controls for camera setting and placement. The default values are fine; start with a point on the plan view to the lower right of the building.

4. After you select a camera point, move the mouse and pick a target point in the middle of the building plan.

5. Once you set a target point, a new camera view will be generated and displayed for you, as shown here. Then you can use the grip controls to fine-tune your view. Adjust it so that the entire building, including footings, is shown within the crop box.

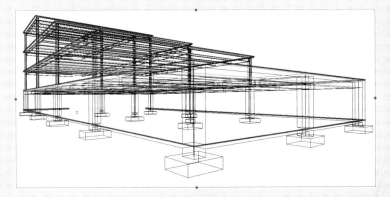

6. The Modify Camera tab becomes active, so you will need to click the View tab. Then locate and click the Visibility/Graphics button on the Graphics panel. In the Visibility/Graphic Overrides dialog box, select the Show Categories from All Disciplines check box. Then scroll down the Model Categories list for Topography and check it. Click OK to apply and close.

7. Now open the Rendering dialog box via the teapot.

8. Change the Background Style setting to Sky: Very Cloudy.

9. Open the Adjust Exposure control, reset the values, and change the Shadows value to **3**. Click OK to apply and close.

10. Change the Quality setting to High. When ready (and when you have the time) click the Render button and once again take a break while it generates. The following graphic shows the final rendering.

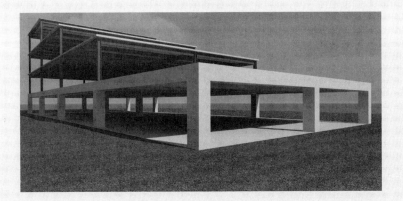

Now that you have finally rendered a view, you can sit back and enjoy the fruits of your labor, right? If you are lucky, maybe! Most likely you will have more modeling to do along with rendering new images. A great technique is to create some cameras within in your model and use them repeatedly to always have the latest version fully rendered, ready for review.

But single-frame renderings are not the only thing you can do with this technology. As the following sections show, there are some nontraditional uses for rendering your models.

Developing Sun Studies

Also included in Revit Structure is a means of creating single- and multiple-day Sun studies. In the Sun and Shadows Settings dialog box is a tab area for Single-Day and another for Multi-Day. In general, these configuration options are not a concern for the structural designer; their inclusion in the software is because Sun studies are a part of the core Revit program.

The steps to create a study are simple:

1. Activate the 3D perspective view.

2. Using the View Control bar, open the Model Graphics Style pop-up list and assign Shading or Shading with Edges.

3. Activate the View tab and within the Graphics panel, click the dialog box launch icon, the small arrow to the right of the panel name. This will open the Graphic Display Options dialog box. From this dialog box click the builder button to the right of the Sun Position drop-down list. This opens the Sun and Shadows Settings dialog box.

4. In the Sun and Shadows Settings dialog box, choose either the Single-Day or Multi-Day tab. Click the Duplicate button and name the new location the same as your model location.

5. With the new location highlighted, click the builder button for Place in the Settings area.

6. Using the Manage Place and Locations dialog box that appears, locate your city or assign specific Latitude/Longitude values. If required, turn on the Adjust Daylight Savings check box. Click OK to close.

7. Click OK to close the Sun and Shadows Settings dialog box.

8. Click OK to close the Graphic Display Options dialog box.

9. Using the View Control bar, click the Shadows On/Off control (to the right of Model Graphics Style), and turn Shadows On. Note that you can also access the Graphic Display options here with this View Control bar. After you turn on shadows, you'll find that if you click on this control again you'll be able to do a preview of your solar study. You start the preview using the tools on the Options bar.

10. To formally present your study, choose the Revit Structure Application menu (the big R icon) and choose Export ➢ Images and Animations ➢ Solar Study.

11. Using the Length/Format dialog box, adjust for desired frame length as well as image visual style and size. Click OK when ready. Keep in mind that while Rendered is an option, the final result will take as long as one rendering does multiplied by however many frames are defined.

12. Then on the Export Animated Solar Study dialog box, assign a name and location for the exported file(s). If you choose the AVI format, the Video Compression dialog box will allow you to assign compression and codec format.

That's it — you've created a Sun study. Frankly, we suspect that not many of you will use this feature of Revit Structure, but it is good to know anyway. Next we will move into how to create walkthroughs of your models.

VIDEO FILE EXPORTS

Revit Structure AVI files typically are very large. To combat this you can use either the Cinepak Codec by Radius or Microsoft Video 1 compression (see the following graphic). Most animation professionals compile videos after rendering the animation to a series of sequential images. Exporting your frames to individual TIFs or another uncompressed image file type and then compiling into an animation via something like Adobe Premier will not only give you better quality and access to many more video file types but also permit effects and other after-render changes such as resizing, watermarks, and soundtrack mixing.

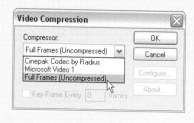

Generating a Model Walkthrough

An underused feature of Revit Structure is the Walkthrough command. Use this command to create a path that a camera will follow; the command then exports single frames or an animation of what the camera sees as it moves along the path. The technique is not hard to apply; the key is to remember that the tool is there to be used.

1. Open a plan view and then activate the View tab on the Ribbon. Locate the Create panel, and from within it expand the 3D View button and choose Walkthrough.

2. The Options bar then displays Walkthrough settings. In general, a default of 5'-6" as a head height is appropriate. You can also change the level you want to use as the basis for the walkthrough.

3. Click points on the plan; each successive point will move the camera and begin to define a spline-like pathway for the camera, as you can see in Figure 14.20. Imagine yourself the director of a movie deciding where each key frame or camera location should be for your scene. Revit will interpret what to show between each camera location along the path.

4. When you complete the path, click Finish Walkthrough on the Walkthrough tab.

5. Once the path is created, it will appear on the plan in a semi-selected state. Now click in empty space, and it will vanish from the plan view. Just as with a camera, you must select a walkthrough for it to be visible on the plan. And just like any other view, it will be stored in the Project Browser. Select any 3D view or walkthrough view in the Project Browser, and right-click to access the Show Camera option.

FIGURE 14.20
A walkthrough path-
way on the plan

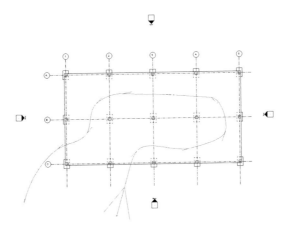

6. Using the Project Browser, find and double-click on the walkthrough view. Then click the View Properties button on the Ribbon to change the settings.

7. In the Instance Properties dialog box, change Model Graphics Style to Shading w/Edges.

8. Turn off the Far Clip Active option, thus allowing for full-depth views, as shown in Figure 14.21.

FIGURE 14.21
Adjust your walk-
through as required.

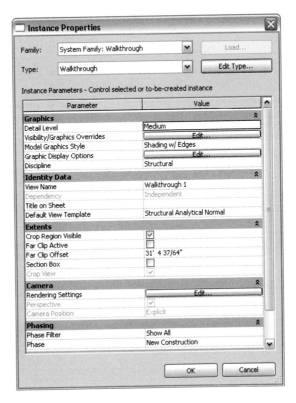

9. Scroll farther down and click the Walkthrough Frames button.

10. In the Walkthrough Frames dialog box, shown in Figure 14.22, change the Total Frames count to **200**. Click OK, and then click OK again to close the Instance Properties dialog box.

FIGURE 14.22
Scaling back the length of the walkthrough

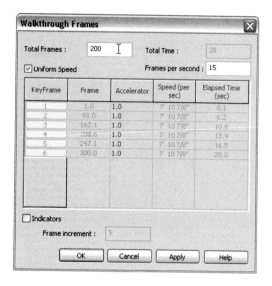

Next we'll create the walkthrough animation:

1. Using the Project Browser, locate your walkthrough and activate it. Depending on your view, you might not see anything at first.

2. Use the Revit Structure Application menu and choose Export ➢ Images and Animations ➢ Walkthrough.

3. The Length/Format dialog box will appear, which allows secondary changes to your animation timing and style. Just click OK to accept the defaults.

4. The Export Walkthrough dialog box appears, where you can specify if you want to create sequential images for later compiling or accept the default AVI format. For most walkthroughs, a Revit Structure–generated AVI will be fine.

Another method to review a walkthrough is the in-model playback feature. Once you have a walkthrough in the active view, click on the crop window, and click the Edit Walkthrough button. The Ribbon will change to the Modify Cameras tab. As shown in Figure 14.23, you now have controls for playback such as Play and Next Frame as well as Option bar adjustments for specific key frame locations.

FIGURE 14.23
The Modify Cameras tab on the Ribbon

Playback performance will be largely based on your model and the graphics style assigned, such as wireframe or shaded with edges. The purpose of a walkthrough is to study the model for coordination needs; it typically isn't for high-quality presentation, as shown in Figure 14.24.

FIGURE 14.24
A single frame of the model shows the reduced level of quality along with index text to indicate where along the walkthrough you are.

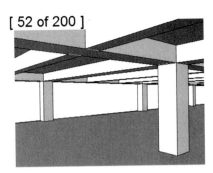

[52 of 200]

As you now know, you can put just about any view of your model out into some sort of rendered view. You can create images from basic quality level and style all the way up to high resolution and full shadows. Once you have the tools on your computer belt, you should apply them every chance you get.

For example, try taking advantage of how you break up your models. If you are doing an addition to an existing building, create another set of materials and object types for the existing structure in a flat gray, along with the new structure in a different color. Then when you render, you can present a clear difference between the old and new structures.

GO TO THE PAINT STORE FIRST

Knowing the materials that look good and meet your needs can save you lots of time. We spent tons of time assigning materials we *thought* met the client's needs. We then spent tons of time rendering stills for a 10-second animation. A single second of animation is typically 30 frames or stills. So when it took 5 minutes per rendering, it actually took 5 × 30 × 10, or 1,500 frames — which translated to 25 hours of rendering! If you don't have the proper materials, you can lose a whole day of computer time, not to mention experience a lot of frustration.

Exporting for Outside Rendering

Revit Structure comes with mental ray, which is a third-party rendering application that several Autodesk products use and is by far the best rendering solution provided within the software to date. However, as you get better at developing rendering scenes, you might want a bit more control over the finished product. Revit Structure is natively a modeler, a BIM solution, and a great documentation tool; it isn't a superior program for rendering images.

A number of awesome solutions are available for rendering images of your models, and many of those programs are created by Autodesk. Most notable is 3ds Max, a longtime program of professionals worldwide. With the introduction of the 2009 class of programs, a new version also became available: 3ds Max Design. This Revit Structure version shares the same core platform as 3ds Max. As time progresses it will be further tweaked for the Revit user and solve more and more deficiencies.

RVT Is Not Supported

The native file format for Revit Structure is not supported in any outside application. Because of this limitation, you must export the appropriate 3D model view to another file format and then use that file to import into the rendering program.

At this time the best methods for getting model data into an outside rendering application are via DWG and the newest format, FBX. Each provides the basic goal of exporting model geometry into the rendering program, but each delivers different benefits, as you'll see in a moment.

Exporting to AutoCAD DWG

The AutoCAD drawing file format DWG is probably the most-used format. It carries with it all the 3D geometry and, depending on the rendering application, can read camera and light elements. When exporting, you have a few options, such as specifying the type of objects you want in the newly created DWG file. You can access the Export CAD Formats dialog box, shown in Figure 14.25, by clicking the Application menu button and choosing Export CAD Formats ➤ DWG. Click the DWG Properties tab in the Export CAD Formats dialog box to view the options for exporting.

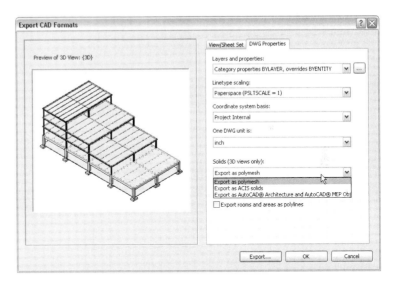

FIGURE 14.25
Limited yet functional export formats

If you choose Export as Polymesh from the Solids (3D Views Only) drop-down list, most of the model objects will be saved as blocks in the DWG. Each block (for example, W-Wide Flange-Column – W10X49_1-196959-3D View 1) is named rather intelligently, with the family name, type, unique ID, and the name of the view tacked on the end for good measure. Note that one of the odd things about this format is the block. Not all elements are bundled into blocks. Regardless, all model objects below the block level are polymesh. If you then explode the polymesh objects, you will be left with elements. This format will also provide centerline geometry for all structural objects. This can be helpful if you need to model something natively within the rendering application since you will have the wireframe to build upon. Export as Polymesh is best suited for going right into the rendering application. If you will not be editing the DWG, try Export as Polymesh first.

If you choose Export as ACIS Solids, all model objects except topography will be exported as a mix of blocks and ACIS solids. If you explode the blocks, the resulting object will be a solid. As with the polymesh option, you will also get a centerline for all structural objects. This ACIS object type is well suited for editing within AutoCAD since you can use many solid editing tools to further refine your model. If you need to work on the model prior to rendering, or if you're just going into AutoCAD, then use Export as ACIS Solids.

If you choose Export as AutoCAD Architecture and AutoCAD MEP Objects, you can further instruct Revit Structure try to make all model objects intelligent-type objects. They will contain object types that AutoCAD Architecture can understand and manipulate. Most of these objects can be exploded further. It may take a few explode executions to turn the AutoCAD Architecture objects into 3D face objects. So if the exported model is intended to be used with ADT/AutoCAD Architecture, then use Export as AutoCAD Architecture and AutoCAD MEP Objects. Also, you will need to keep an eye on any radial geometry; the function still has difficulties manipulating this data.

Why go to all this effort? Because choosing the proper method will help you when you begin your rendering work. Let's assume you will be going from Revit Structure straight into 3ds Max Design. The best choice is polymesh. It will be smallest file type and is already a mesh.

When you import your file into 3ds Max Design, you will be asked how to derive the imported model. By Layer is the best method only if you spent a lot of time organizing your model objects in the DWG file. However, if you are trying to be as time efficient as possible, then use the Entity, Blocks as Node Hierarchy method. The reason By Layer isn't a wise choice normally is that many objects within Revit Structure belong to the same class and therefore the same layer. For example, steel beams and concrete beams are both structural framing and would be on the same layer. But if you derive by entity instead, then you will end up with type name access once you're inside 3ds Max Design. The type name will be easy to locate and select, and you can then apply required materials.

Exporting to 3ds Max FBX Format

FBX is another player in the import world. This somewhat new format by Autodesk is a first stab at linking the rendering efforts in Revit Structure and AutoCAD into 3ds Max. Not only will it bring in the model objects, but it will also import cameras, lights, and materials. As you may know, you can choose one of two default rendering engines in 3ds Max. One is mental ray (the same as in Revit Structure); the other is V-Ray. You *must* set the default rendering engine in Max to mental ray, or the imported FBX file will not import correctly.

As shown in Figure 14.26, you can find this export option within the Application menu under Export ➤ FBX. You are prompted for the name and location of the newly created FBX file.

The only case where using FBX may be worth the trouble is if you are trying to match the point of view of renders done in Revit Structure. The materials, lighting, and even cameras are generally better off made in 3ds Max, so the ability to bring them in along with the model can be of little benefit.

FIGURE 14.26
Exporting as FBX

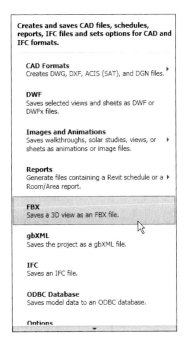

Most professional rendering work is done not in Revit Structure but in some other application. The following section discusses what is involved in rendering beyond Revit Structure.

Leveraging Outside Rendering

As mentioned earlier, rendering in Revit Structure is a great final touch for your modeling effort. You get a lot of bang for little effort. But you might want a little more from your renderings than Revit Structure can provide.

For example, you can also render clouds but are limited to the cloud generation in the software. With outside rendering engines, you gain control on material placement, tiling, transparency, and many other settings that you don't have in Revit Structure. You can also render with radiosity in Revit Structure but only with mental ray; there are many high-quality renderers out there and some are very fast. Object and subobject animation are not possible with Revit Structure; objects themselves cannot move in an animation. So if you wanted to do a construction-sequence animation, you would have to use an outside rendering solution, period.

Covering in detail the methods and applications for these is beyond the scope of this book, but here are few comparisons to consider. In Figure 14.27 is a project rendered to a high level with Revit Structure using mental ray, whereas Figure 14.28 is rendered in Autodesk 3ds Max Design.

Most would agree that there is a noticeable improvement in visual quality in Figure 14.28. For some it would be hard to quantify. But the combination of greater contrasts, smoother materials, more realistic lighting, and translucent ground surfaces provide an additional touch that may warrant investment in non–Revit Structure applications.

FIGURE 14.27
This is a reasonable-quality render made with Revit Structure.

FIGURE 14.28
The model was exported as a DWG, imported into Autodesk 3ds Max Design, and rendered with minimal material changes.

The Bottom Line

Determine what and when to model.   Once you get going in Revit Structure, the ease of creating models is both a blessing and a curse. If you model too little, you don't achieve the desired result. If you model too much, then you will have so much more than you need, your renderings will take an excessive amount of time.

Master It   Before modeling, develop a scope of what and when to model. Conduct team meetings with all project modelers so that everyone involved has rendering in mind as they do their work. Limit the complexity of your renderings by using appropriate detail levels.

Assign materials to your model.   Actually rendering in Revit Structure isn't hard — having something render worthy is the hard part. Materials make or break your renderings. You can make your model look real or *like* a real model.

Master It   As you develop your families, assign materials so that you can render on demand later. Using the Materials dialog box, create materials for steel and concrete for when they are viewed at a distance. Adjust materials for rendering even if you won't be rendering now. This will reduce the time needed to prepare for when you are asked to produce images. For real photographic needs, use materials that have few repeating patterns so that no matter the point of view, the materials you use will maintain a level of smoothness.

Define the quality and style of your renderings.   When you begin to render your model, you can be overwhelmed with all the settings at your disposal. You can define where the sun is, what time of day it is, what resolution to create, and how detailed your images should be.

Master It   Take a look around in the real world. Get a sense of what structures look like when they are under construction. Things are often dark; you don't always have to light everything up. When you create renderings, save time and create high quality only at the very end. Use the Rendering system with Autodesk mental ray to define a sun, adjust exposure, control shadows, and create renderings. Then save your rendering to any number of image types.

Export your models for other uses.   Exporting your model for outside use is a typical activity of the true professional. You don't use one kind of writing implement, so you should not use only one rendering application.

Master It   Once you have a 3D view active, you can export it to a DWG or FBX file to use in an outside application. Use the FBX format if you have Revit Structure cameras you want to export as well. Use the DWG format with polymesh for direct import into 3ds Max Design. But if you have very large models, you might want to use ACIS solids since that allows 3ds Max to control the meshing directly.

Chapter 15

Revit Structural Analysis

Revit Structure is fully capable of providing all of the information required for analysis. Revit Structure itself will not, however, perform the actual calculations. Within Revit Structure you create point loads, line loads, and area loads. These loads are defined by load cases as defined within your project. The load cases can then be grouped into load combinations for lateral and gravity cases. These loads are diagrammatically placed into the Revit Structure model in the default analytical views or new analytical views you make during the modeling process.

The analysis model coexists with the physical model but is not necessarily identical. For many reasons the analytical model can be simplified or altered by the structural engineer for analysis needs. In practice you will find that the Revit Structure analytic capabilities are most useful for preliminary analysis of your structure.

Once the loads are in place, you export the model for import into your structural analysis software. After the calculations have been performed, you then import the analysis data back into Revit Structure. Revit Structure will resize the elements in your model according to the incoming data. It is important to note that during this process there is no physical movement of the model itself. This procedure is just a flow of data. You do not have to worry about finding an insertion point or making sure the model is lined up.

In this chapter, you will learn to:

◆ Configure Revit Structure structural settings and create loads for your project

◆ Place analytical load patterns onto your model

◆ Import and export your virtual model from Revit Structure to structural analysis software

Configuring Structural Settings

To get started you will step through the process necessary to configure the structural settings for your project in the Structural Settings dialog box. You will set symbolic representations, create load patterns (see Figure 15.1), and set boundary conditions,

So let's review the structural settings (see Figure 15.2) contained within Revit Structure that pertain to the analytical model. For the procedures described in this section, please use the file `Datasest_1501.rvt` to follow along and to practice the techniques. Otherwise we would have to create all the model elements first, and this is beside the point in our current discussion. To download the files, go to the book's companion web page at `www.sybex.com/go/masteringrevitstructure2010` if you have not done so already. So go ahead and open that dataset now.

FIGURE 15.1
Various load patterns on a structure

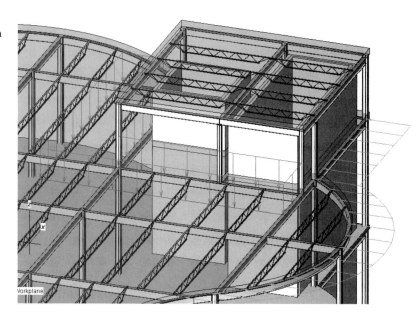

FIGURE 15.2
Structural Settings dialog box

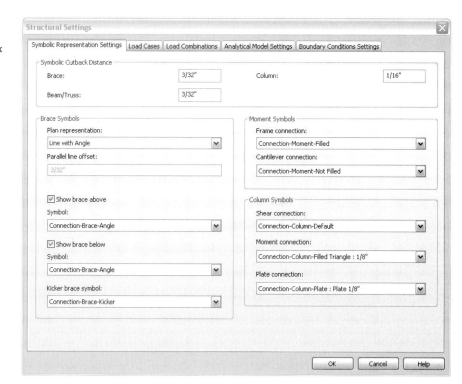

Configuring Symbolic Representation

You can access the Structural Settings dialog box on the Analyze or Manage tab on the Ribbon. On the Analyze tab click the arrow on the bottom right of the Analytical Model Tools panel to access the Structural Settings dialog box. Within the Structural Settings dialog box, there are several tabs across the top. We will cover all of these. The first tab is Symbolic Representation Settings. This tab deals mainly with the graphical model and the more common defaults.

Symbolic Cutback Distance represents the gap that Revit Structure will leave between stick symbols. This setting controls the representation of a beam in coarse detail level in order to display a gap between intersecting members, whether it is a column or another framing member (see Figure 15.3). This cutback distance is symbolic or graphic and has no bearing on the real 3D extents of a beam. For instance, in a plan view beams do not extend into columns; there is a gap between them. The same connection in a 3D view will show the beams $\frac{1}{2}''$ back from the column, more consistent with the actual construction techniques (see Figure 15.4). But most important to our discussion here is that the analytical node point at the end of members will remain attached to the intersecting beam or column.

FIGURE 15.3
Stick symbols show the cutback in coarse detail level.

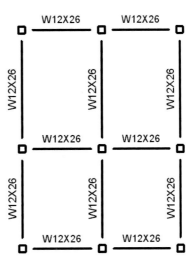

Creating Load Cases

The Load Cases tab (see Figure 15.5) allows you to view and modify existing Revit Structure load cases as well as create new ones. Before you place loads in the model, it is good practice to establish some additional load cases (if needed) here in this dialog box. To create a new load case, follow this procedure:

1. Go back to the open `Datasest_1501.rvt` file.

2. Open the Structural Settings dialog box and choose the Load Cases tab.

3. In the Load Cases tab, you will see two fields:

   ◆ The top field is Load Cases.

   ◆ The bottom field is Load Natures.

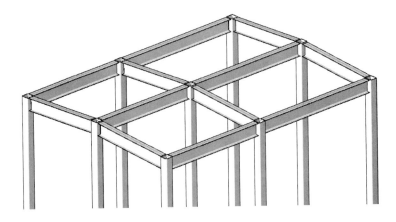

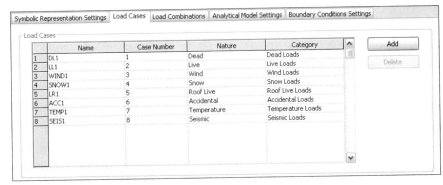

In this example you need a specific load case for an extra-large mechanical rooftop unit.

4. Click the Add button to the right of the Load Cases field.

5. Rename the new load case to **RTU-1**. Its Nature is Dead, and its Category is Dead Loads.

Now you can use this new load case as an area load and place it into the model.

Adding Load Natures

The load natures are added to a load case. The default load natures are the same as you see in most analysis applications. When you create a new load case and a new load nature in Revit Structure, they will be imported as loads into the analysis software you are using.

Normally the existing load natures (see Figure 15.6) will suit your needs for the load cases. If not, you can simply click the Add button and add a new load nature. Rename the load nature as required. It will now be available to select for your Load Cases

Combining Load Cases

In Revit Structure, you can combine load cases. This is a good thing because other analytical software programs in the past have been restricted to gravity loads only. If you wanted a 3D analysis (gravity combined with a lateral load), you had to do them separately. Revit Structure allows you to do gravity, lateral, or a combination of the two. Once you build the load combination, you can then apply it to the model. Click the Load Combinations tab. Click the Add button to the right of the Load Combination field. Rename the new load case **Wind and gravity** (see Figure 15.7).

FIGURE 15.6
You can add other load natures to these default load natures.

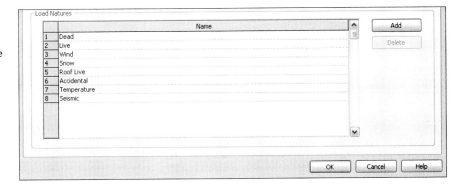

FIGURE 15.7
Creating a load combination

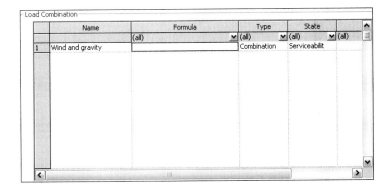

The Formula column contains a drop-down list of the load cases present in the model (see Figure 15.8). Of course, this does not help us because they are single cases.

FIGURE 15.8
The Formula drop-down menu

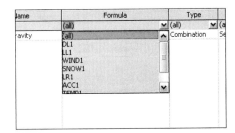

Now you will create a new formula that will combine multiple load cases.

Combining Load Cases with Edit Selected Formula

In the bottom-left corner of the Load Cases dialog box, you will see the Edit Selected Formula field (see Figure 15.9). This field will actually combine the load cases. You could consider this as a package of load cases that is inserted into a load combination. Here is a specific procedure to combine load cases:

1. Highlight the Wind and Gravity load combination you just created.

2. Click the Add button to start adding a formula.

3. Leave the Factor field set to 1.00000, and set the load to **DL1** (a dead load).

4. Click Add again, and change the factor to **0.750000**.

5. Change the Case or Combination setting to **SNOW1**.

6. Click Add again, and select WIND1 as the Case or Combination setting.

7. Set the Factor to **0.250000** (see Figure 15.10).

FIGURE 15.9
Use the Edit Selected Formula field to combine load cases.

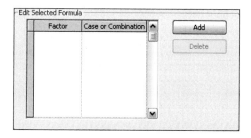

FIGURE 15.10
Adding a formula for analysis

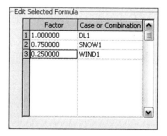

Look up at the Load Combination Wind and Gravity field. Notice that the formula is now present. This formula is an integral part of that particular load case.

Determining Load Combination Usage

This category determines what the load combination will be used for. It is not a formulaic expression; rather it is for a descriptive field. You should keep this usage naming convention consistent with your analysis software wherever possible. This will aid the interoperability as you pass loads to the analysis application and back again. As an example, in the lower-right corner of the dialog box, click the Add button in the Load Combination Usage area. Rename it **Large RTUs**. Select this load combination, and then click the Set check box. This will dedicate the usage to the current load combination (see Figure 15.11).

FIGURE 15.11
Dedicating the load
combination usage

Understanding Load Combination Types

There are two different types of load combination: Combination and Envelope. They are found on the Load Combinations tab in the Type drop-down list. Setting the load combination type to Combination provides information for a single combination. Envelope gives maximum and minimum results on a group of load combinations. Set the Load Combination type for Wind and Gravity to Combination.

Understanding Load Combination States

Revit Structure offers two different states for a load combination: Serviceability and Ultimate. They are found on the Load Combinations tab in the State drop-down list. A Serviceability state will categorize the load based on an expected force, such as wind, gravity, natural loads such as snow, and even deflection. An Ultimate state tests the load against unexpected forces and overall stability of the structure when pushed to an Ultimate state. In our example set the Load Combination state for Wind and Gravity to Serviceability. Click OK to accept the changes and exit the Structural Settings dialog box; then close your file without saving, or save it to another name.

Now that you have studied the settings for load cases and combinations, you will next learn about the analytical model settings.

Monitoring Your Model as You Work

The Analytical Model Settings tab on the Structural Settings dialog box sets the default warnings and is a means to check the structural stability of your model as you work. By default, many of the options are checked for a good reason. For example, if you place a structural column with no bearing footing or pier, a setting on this tab will alert you to the structural deficiency. As you are starting the model, it will, by the nature of the design process, be annoying. Having a warning appear every time you want to place a structural item into the model would become quite daunting and somewhat time consuming.

So in this section you will learn how to configure the automatic checks for your model and to set the correct tolerances. You will see how the analytical model is distinguished from the physical model and how analytical views are created in your project. Then you will examine particular model elements such as columns, floors, and walls to see how the analytical components for those objects work. Finally you will learn how to set up boundary conditions within your analytical model.

Setting Automatic Checks

The top of the Analytical Model Settings tab of the dialog box allows you to set the automatic checks. The following steps outline the recommended settings for automatic checks:

1. To start, open a brand new Revit Structure project.

2. Open the Structural Settings dialog box and go to the Analytical Model Settings tab (see Figure 15.12).

FIGURE 15.12
Adjusting the analytical model settings

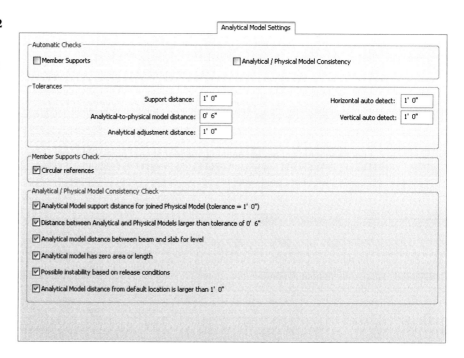

There are two items on which you can keep a running check: Member Supports and Analytical/Physical Model Consistency.

3. Check both Member Supports and Analytical/Physical Model Consistency.

4. Click OK in the Structural Settings dialog box to go back to the model.

5. You will be asked if you want to perform an analytical model check at this time. Click No. The model is still blank.

6. On the Structure panel of the Home tab of the Ribbon click the Structural Column button.

7. Go to the Level 1 plan. Place a column in the model. A warning will appear, as illustrated in Figure 15.13.

FIGURE 15.13
A warning appears
for the unsupported
column.

If you are deliberately looking for unsupported members, Revit Structure has the power and the ability to perform this function. Follow these steps:

1. Select the column.

2. On the Warning panel of the Modify Structural Column tab you will see a Show Related Warnings icon. Select it. The same warning is displayed in the Messages dialog box (see Figure 15.14).

FIGURE 15.14
Check the Messages
dialog box for unsup-
ported members.

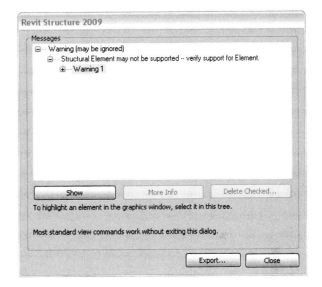

3. Click the Close button.

4. Open the Structural Settings dialog box again, and choose the Analytical Model Settings tab.

5. Check both Member Supports and Analytical/Physical Model Consistency, and then click OK to close the dialog box.

6. Click Yes to perform the analytical model check at this time.

It may appear that Revit did nothing. Select Consistency Checks on the Analyze tab, one of the main tabs on the ribbon. You will see possible model instability warnings. This is a direct result of turning on these settings. Although you cannot correct the situation here, you can select each item and click the Show button, which will give you a view of the offending member. Revit Structure will likely first tell you that there are no good views, but click Show anyway. The more you push the button, the more views of the object Revit Structure will display.

You can save the file to HTML for posting to local networks or Internet sites. Just click the Export button and save to a file.

TOLERANCES

To understand how the tolerances affect the model, you must first understand the difference between the analytical model and the physical model. We'll return to the topic of tolerances later in the chapter.

Understanding the Analytical Model

As structural elements are placed into the model, analytical representations of the elements are added as well as a component of each structural element. You may notice that next to each structural plan view in the Project Browser there is another with the word *analytical* in the name as well. These views do not actually contain additional information; they simply display different information. Illustrated in Figures 15.15 and 15.16 is the visual difference between an analytical model and a physical model.

FIGURE 15.15
The analytical model display

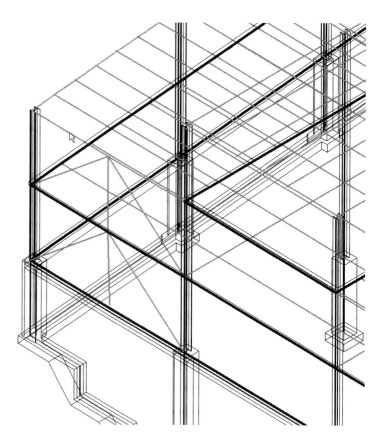

There are two sides to every model: the side you are giving to the contractor to bid and build and the side you need in order to analyze the structure. You can create both sides at the same time. Each specific structural member has its own specific analytical properties. The next sections will briefly describe these properties, beginning with structural framing.

FIGURE 15.16
The physical model display

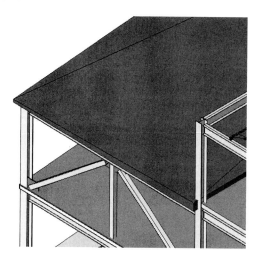

STRUCTURAL FRAMING

By default, structural framing analytical lines are displayed with an orange line (see Figure 15.17). (Since our images are not in color, note the arrows in the figure and/or draw some test members yourself.). The analytical plane always stays on the top face of the framing until the framing is attached to another framing member, usually a column. The analytical plane extends into the framing to which a beam is connected.

FIGURE 15.17
The physical and analytical beam representations

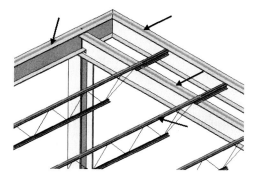

For instance, if a beam drops in elevation while attached to a column, the analytical plane will not drop with the actual beam (depending on the method used to drop the beam). It will stay at the level of the adjacent framing. A more extreme case is diagonal bracing (see Figure 15.18), where the framing is at an angle. The framing is being analyzed at a chord center line that extends into the members it is laterally supporting, extending to analytical node points.

A big concern is defining correctly where the physical model stops and the analytical line extends beyond it. This starts to influence the analytical model and can force unwanted inconsistencies.

FIGURE 15.18
Physical and analytical brace representations at different locations

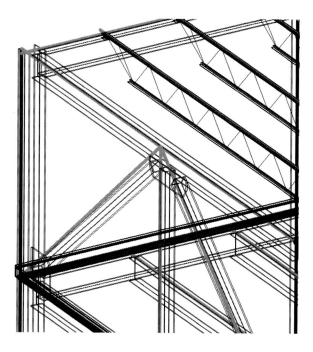

Next you will see how columns are represented in the analytical model.

COLUMNS

The analytical representation of a column in your project is normally blue and is centered on the column (see Figure 15.19). (Since our images are not in color, note the arrows and/or draw some test members yourself.). Columns and beams have some properties in common that have an influence on the plane that hosts them. The procedure to adjust the analytical column line in relation to the physical model is as follows:

1. In Datasest_1501.rvt in the Project Browser select View 1 - Analytical if it is not displayed already.

FIGURE 15.19
Physical and analytical column representations

2. Go to the Structural Settings dialog box. On the Analytical Model Settings tab enable both automatic checks and then exit.

3. Select a concrete column in the basement area.

4. On the Modify Structural Columns panel click Element Properties ➤ Instance Properties on the Element panel.

5. Scroll down to the Analytical Model settings.

6. Change the Top Vertical Projection setting from Auto-detect to Penthouse (see Figure 15.20); then click OK.

FIGURE 15.20
Changing the Top Vertical Projection setting

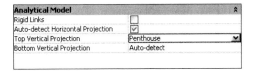

You then get a warning (see Figure 15.21) because the analytical projection will be way beyond any acceptable difference between the model and the analytical plane. Granted, some clearance is to be expected, but within reason. This is where the tolerances for the analytical settings come into play.

FIGURE 15.21
The distance between analytical and physical models must stay within a defined tolerance.

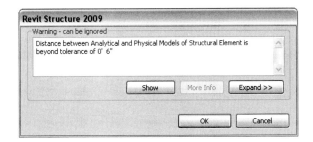

Next you will examine how wall and footing analytical properties are managed.

WALLS AND FOOTINGS

Walls have analytical properties similar to framing (see Figure 15.22). The analytical model can be dependent upon its host geometry, or it can be configured to extend to other members regardless of its host's offset from level. The analytical plane for walls and footings is typically represented in green. (Since our images are not in color, note the arrows in the figure and/or draw some test members yourself.). To see the analytical properties of a wall, follow these steps:

1. Find an open area in the Level 1 plan view of the `Datasest_1501.rvt` model.

2. On Structure panel of the Home tab of the Ribbon click Wall ➤ Structural Wall.

3. On the Options bar set the constraints to Depth and T.O. Footing, respectively.

4. Draw a structural wall. Make its type Foundation - 12″ Concrete.

5. Start the Structural Wall command again. Make its type Generic 8″ Masonry.

6. Set the constraints to Height and to Level 2.

7. Set the justification for the wall to Finish Face: Exterior.

FIGURE 15.22
Wall, column, and framing analytical properties have similarities.

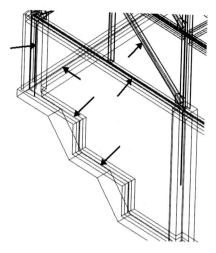

8. Draw the new wall on top of the 12″ foundation wall with the inside face flush (see Figure 15.23).

FIGURE 15.23
Coordinating analytical lines in stacked walls

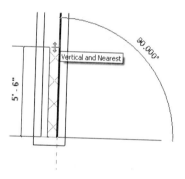

9. Once the wall is drawn, go to the 3D view View 1 - Analytical. Notice that the analytical plane of the masonry wall above is aligned with the analytical plane of the concrete wall below (see Figure 15.24).

10. Select the 8″ masonry wall; then click the Instance Properties icon on the Element Properties pull-down.

11. Find the Analytical Model parameters, and browse through the choices. Change the Horizontal Projection value to Exterior Face. Notice that the analytical line changes location but the physical wall does not. Best practice is to keep these settings on Auto-detect (see Figure 15.25) and enabled.

12. Change the value for the Horizontal Projection back to Auto-detect.

The next structural category whose analytical properties we will examine is floors.

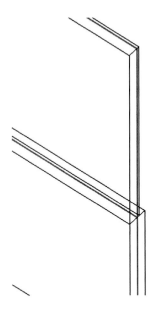

FIGURE 15.24
Aligning the analytical wall lines for stacked walls of different thickness

FIGURE 15.25
Setting the Analytical Model parameters to Auto-detect is the best practice.

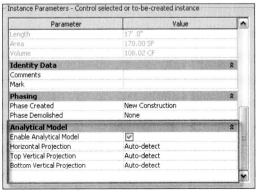

FLOORS

The same analytical functionality that occurs in beams and walls occurs in floors as well. If a floor is placed in the model, the default analytical positioning will occur at the top outside edge of the extents (see Figure 15.26). The analytical line is typically represented by a brown line.

If the same floor is placed so that it bears on walls below, the analytical plane will adjust to align with the analytical plane settings in the bearing wall. The floor analytical plane will also adjust so that it is positioned at the bottom.

The following example illustrates this analytical plane positioning for a wall and floor:

1. Find an open area in the Datasest_1501.rvt model on the Level 2 view.

2. Place four Structural 10″ concrete walls in a closed rectangular shape from Level 2 to Level 1.

FIGURE 15.26
Physical and analytical
floor representations

3. On Structure panel of the Home tab click Floor ➤ Structural Floor.

4. Using the Pick Walls option on the Draw panel, pick the four walls.

5. On the Element panel access the Floor Properties dialog box and select a 6″ concrete slab.

6. On the Options bar uncheck the option Extend into Wall (to Core).

7. Click Finish Floor on the Floor panel.

8. Answer No to the wall-join question.

Now go back to the analytical model view and examine the slab and wall analytical lines. The floor horizontal analytical plane is automatically set at the bottom of the floor and intersects the wall vertical analytical lines. Figure 15.27 demonstrates the floor and wall interaction.

FIGURE 15.27
Intersection of wall and
floor analytical lines

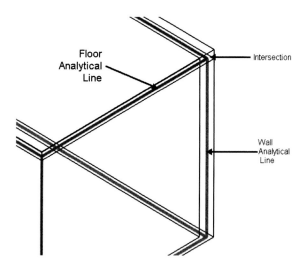

Creating an Analytical View

Any view can be turned into an analytical view. It is just a matter of setting the display correctly by turning off the physical model, which is easily accomplished by using a view template. The following is an example of how the procedure works:

1. In `Datasest_1501.rvt` right-click the Penthouse structural plan view in the Project Browser.

2. Select Duplicate ➤ Duplicate with Detailing.

3. Rename the new view to **Penthouse - Analytical**.

4. In the Project Browser highlight and right-click the new Penthouse - Analytical view.

5. Select Apply View Template.

6. In the Names field of the Apply View Template dialog box, select Structural Analytical Stick (see Figure 15.28).

7. In the View Properties field, note that all the boxes in the Include column are checked.

KNOW THE ANALYTICAL AND PHYSICAL MODELS

Now you know that there are two interrelated parts of the model you are keeping track of as you build your virtual model. The settings that control the behavior and the relationship between the physical model and the analytical model should now be more understandable and relevant. It is important to note that as you model a structure, it is good practice to study how your model is coming together analytically as well as physically. The time and discipline it takes to set up a model for analysis will be rewarded when you actually send the model to your analysis software package.

---

8. Click OK at the bottom of the dialog box, and your view should look like that illustrated in Figure 15.29.

In the next section on analytical model properties, we are finally going to get back to the tolerances functionality that we referred to in the beginning of the chapter.

Configuring Tolerances

Now that you better understand the differences between the analytical model and the physical model, you can begin to learn how tolerances are configured. The following steps give a short summary of each parameter that you will need to consider when you configure your analytical model.

1. On the Project Settings panel of the Manage tab, click Structural Settings.

2. Choose the Analytical Model Settings tab.

Under the Tolerances category, there are a few choices listed (see Figure 15.30):

Support Distance   This determines how far a cantilever will extend before Revit Structure generates warnings. This is normally set differently depending on the nature of the specific project.

FIGURE 15.28
To display the analytical model, use the existing view template.

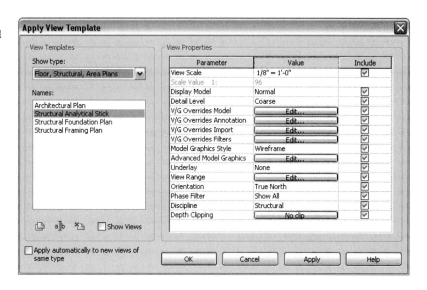

FIGURE 15.29
The analytical view display

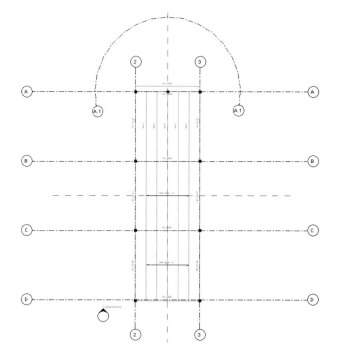

Analytical-to-Physical Model Distance   This determines how far past the actual member the analytical line can extend.

Analytical Adjustment Distance   This determines how far an autodetect analytical plane is allowed to move.

FIGURE 15.30
The Tolerances
settings

Tolerances			
Support distance:	1' 0"	Horizontal auto detect:	1' 0"
Analytical-to-physical model distance:	0' 6"	Vertical auto detect:	1' 0"
Analytical adjustment distance:	1' 0"		

Horizontal and Vertical Auto Detect   When a floor bears on walls, the analytical plane will drop to the bottom of the floor to be in alignment with the top of the wall. If this plane drops (or rises) at an increment greater than 1'-0", you will need to change the settings to something other than Auto Detect in the object's Element properties.

CHECKS

The remainder of the Analytical Model Settings tab deals with checks that can be enabled so that you will receive timely warnings of possible defects to the analytical model.

Member Support Checks   A circular reference will occur when a system of beams frames back to the origin (see Figure 15.31), transferring the load back to the same system rather than transferring the load to a separate bearing member. With this check on, Revit Structure will warn you that you have a circular reference.

FIGURE 15.31
A circular reference
caused by insuffi-
cient bearing of the
beam elements

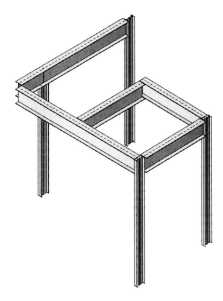

Analytical/Physical Model Consistency Check   These settings (see Figure 15.32) are used in conjunction with the automatic checks at the top of the dialog box. When you want to run checks against constructability and structural integrity, these settings will generate a line in the Review Warnings dialog box as you prepare to send your model for analysis.

BOUNDARY CONDITIONS

These settings are applicable when defining a condition where other forces are assumed to be in some support of a structural element. A good example of a typical boundary condition is the support of earth underneath a footing or a slab-on-grade. As we place a boundary condition into the model, the appearance in the model will be derived from these settings.

FIGURE 15.32
Set the Consistency Check parameters that will control the warnings reported.

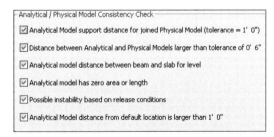

Revit Structure will add a family symbol as the boundary condition is placed in the model. To view the Boundary Condition settings (see Figure 15.33), do the following:

1. On the Project Settings panel of the Manage tab, click Structural Settings.

2. Choose the Boundary Condition Settings tab. There are four definable boundary conditions: Fixed, Pinned, Roller, and User Defined.

3. Set the Area and Line Symbol Spacing value.

4. Exit the dialog box.

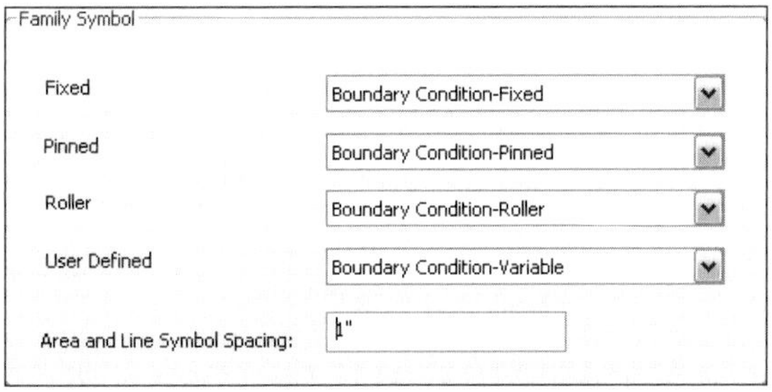

FIGURE 15.33
Setting the analytical boundary conditions

The following exercise will show how to add a boundary condition to your project. The items you are going to select are the orange analytical lines, which indicate the footings. You are specifying a boundary condition based on the footing bearing on earth. Although we do not have topography, this exercise will send the data to your analysis application indicating that there is a natural bearing surface not actually defined in the model.

EXERCISE: ADDING A BOUNDARY CONDITION

In this exercise you will add an analytical boundary condition to your project.

1. Open the Datasest_1501.rvt project file if it is not open already.

2. Right-click the T.O. Footing plan view in the Project Browser, and select Duplicate with Detailing.

3. Rename the new plan to **T.O. Footing - Analytical**.

4. Right-click the T.O. Footing - Analytical plan view, and select Apply View Template.

5. Select Structural Analytical Stick, and click OK.

6. On the Analyze tab click Boundary Conditions.

7. On the Boundary Conditions panel click the Line icon.

8. Select the orange analytical lines in the center of the footings all the way around the building, as shown in the following illustration.

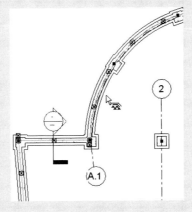

9. Once the entire perimeter is selected, click the Point button. On the Boundary Conditions panel, and make sure the State setting is set to Fixed.

10. Select the blue dots on the spread footings that the piers bear on in the middle of the building, as shown in the following illustrations.

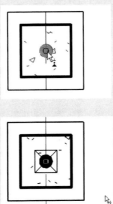

11. Switch to the View 1 - Analytical 3D view to verify, as shown in this graphic.

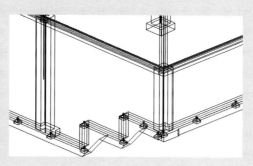

12. Save the model if you want to.

Now it is time to pull all this information together with an exercise on structural settings.

EXERCISE: STRUCTURAL SETTINGS

This exercise is intended to provide you with a comfort level in the configuring of structural settings within your project. In the next section you will learn how to actually place the loads into the model.

TASK 1: CONFIGURING STRUCTURAL SETTINGS

1. Open Datasest_1502.rvt.

2. Find the T.O. Footing Structural Floor plan in the Project Browser.

3. Right-click and select Duplicate View ➢ Duplicate with Detailing.

4. Right-click the newly created view and select Rename. Call the view **T.O. Footing - Analytical**. Click OK.

5. Right-click the new view and select Apply Template.

6. In the Names category, select Structural Analytical Stick, and click OK.

7. On the Project Settings panel of the Manage tab, click Structural Settings.

8. Choose the Load Combinations tab.

9. In the Load Combination category click the Add button.

10. Rename the load condition to **Dead+Wind+Snow**, as shown here.

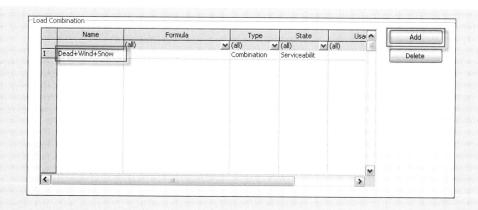

11. In the Load Combination Usage category, click the Add button.

12. Name it **Combined Dead and Snow+Wind**.

13. Click the Set check box.

14. Click OK in the Structural Settings dialog box.

Placing Loads

There are three different kinds of load placements: line, point, and area. The loads can be placed independently or you can choose a host. That is, the three load-placement types can be applied by clicking on the screen to place them or by selecting an object to host them.

An area load is a good example to show how to choose a host. If you have a snow load case, it would be a good idea to place it into the model as an area load hosted by the roof or floor element.

To add a load to a model, follow this procedure:

1. Open the file `Dataset_1501.rvt`.

2. Make sure you are in 3D views, and choose View 1 - Analytical.

3. Click Loads on the Analyze tab.

The first thing to observe is the new Workplane icon that is placed within the view window (see Figure 15.34). This is your guide as you set the properties of the direction to which the load is reacting. This icon indicates the work plane, and it is directly related to the load you are about to place.

1. Select the Hosted Area Load icon on the Loads panel.

2. Click the Element Properties icon ➤ Instance Properties. You will see the following properties:

   ◆ **Load Case** can be applied to the load you are physically adding to the model.

FIGURE 15.34
Directional guide as
you place your load

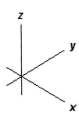

Workplane

- **Orient To** specifies if you are in an orientation to the work plane (see the Workplane icon at the bottom left of your drawing area).

- **Fx, Fy, Fz** indicates the direction the load is coming from (see Figure 15.35) and is called The Project Coordinate system. Again, you can tell by looking at the new icon in the view window which item needs to contain a value.

FIGURE 15.35
Directional load
indications

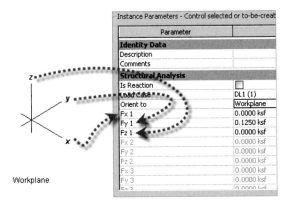

We want to place an area load with a load case of DL1(1) on the right side of the foundation. Looking at the x, y, z icon, we know that Fz1 seems like it should be blank; however, once we place the load, the work plane will orient to reflect the angled wall.

1. For Fz1, type **-.1000** (notice, this is a negative value) and then click OK.

2. In the View 1 - Analytical view, select the basement foundation wall to the right of the model. Once it is created, select the new load, and notice that the Host work plane is now oriented to reflect a z value at the skewed angle of the wall, as illustrated in Figures 15.36 and 15.37.

Leave the model open for the next section, where you will add a line load to your project.

Adding a Line Load with Host

Adding a line load with a host is a little less confusing than adding an area load. Since a line load has no z direction whatsoever, the initial host work plane will point the force based on 0, 90, 180, and 270 degrees. For an example of how to place a line load with a host, we will be using the roof plan. The load will be placed laterally along the west side of the roofline.

FIGURE 15.36
Note the orientation of the work plane

Host work plane

FIGURE 15.37
Note the orientation of the work plane in relation to the loads and model

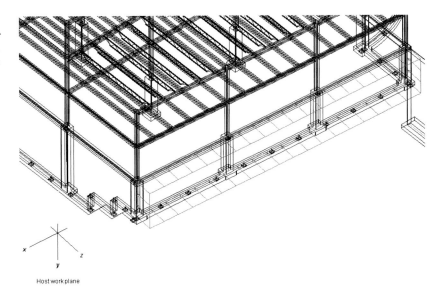

1. In the Project Browser, right-click the Roof plan view, and select Duplicate View ➢ Duplicate with Detailing.

2. Rename the new copy **Roof - Analytical**.

3. Right-click Roof - Analytical, and select Apply View Template.

4. Choose Structural Analytical Stick from the Names category; then click OK.

5. If you have previously placed a boundary condition on the footing, it may be visible. If it is, leave it on.

6. Click Loads on the Analyze tab.

7. Select the Hosted line Load icon on the Loads panel.

8. Click the Element Properties icon ➢ Instance Properties.

9. Change Fx 1 to **1.0000**, and Fy 1 and Fz 1 should be 0.0000 (see Figure 15.38). Click OK to exit the dialog box.

10. Click the orange analytical planes along column line 1 (see Figure 15.39).

FIGURE 15.38
Setting analytical
instance parameters

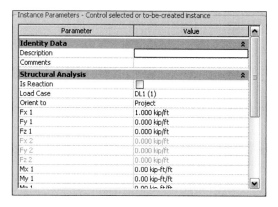

FIGURE 15.39
Selecting the ana-
lytical lines

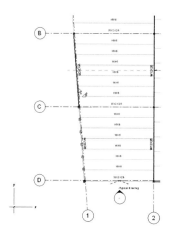

11. Once the west column line is done, right-click and choose Cancel to end the command.

The next section will add an area load to your project.

Adding an Area Load (By Sketch)

An area load by sketch allows the designer to draw an area where a concentrated load will occur. A good example would be a drifting snow load. Normally in this situation, it is a good idea to create a new load case as well.

1. On the Manage tab click Structural Settings ➤ Load Cases.

2. Click the Add button, and rename the new load case **DRIFT** (see Figure 15.40).

3. Set the parameters as follows: the Nature is Snow, and the Category is Snow Loads. Click OK to exit the dialog box.

4. Go to the Roof - Analytical plan if needed.

FIGURE 15.40
Adding an area load case

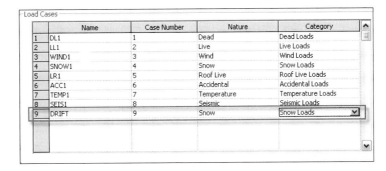

5. Click Loads on the Analyze tab.

6. Select the Area Load icon on the Loads panel, as shown in Figure 15.41.

FIGURE 15.41
Click the Area
Load button on
the Loads panel.

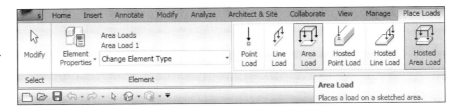

Notice that for this command, you are working in sketch mode.

7. Click Area Load Properties.

8. Change the Load Case setting to DRIFT (9).

9. Change the Fz 1 value to **-.1000 ksf** (negative). All other F values are 0.0000 (see Figure 15.42). Click OK to exit the dialog box.

10. Draw an area about 8′-0″ wide that abuts the framing leading up to the penthouse.

FIGURE 15.42
Setting the F val-
ues for analysis

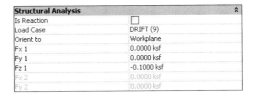

11. Mirror the area to the opposite side of the penthouse (see Figures 15.43 and 15.44), and then click Finish Sketch.

12. Save the model if desired.

FIGURE 15.43
Placing the area load in
sketch mode

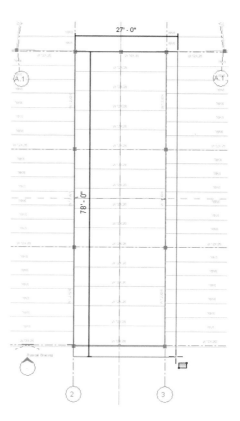

FIGURE 15.44
Loads adjacent to the
penthouse in 3D view

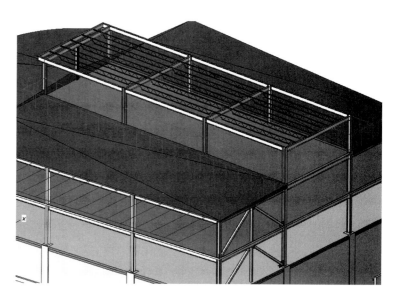

EXERCISE: PLACING LOADS

In this exercise you have three tasks to accomplish: you will create load cases, create an analytical plan, and place loads onto the roof of the project.

TASK 1: CREATE A LOAD CASE

1. Open the file called Dataset_1502.rvt.
2. On the Manage tab click Structural Settings ➤ Load Cases.
3. Click the Add button, and call the new load case **DRIFT**.
4. Set Nature to Snow and Category to Snow Loads; then click OK to exit.

TASK 2: CREATE AN ANALYTICAL ROOF PLAN

1. In the Project Browser, right-click 14 ROOF.
2. Choose Duplicate View ➤ Duplicate with Detailing.
3. Rename it **14 ROOF - analytical**.
4. Right-click 14 ROOF - analytical, and select Apply View Template.
5. Choose Structural Analytical Stick. Click OK to exit.

TASK 3: PLACE LOADS

1. Open the 14 Roof - analytical plan if needed.
2. On the Analyze tab click Loads.
3. Select the Area Load icon on the Loads panel.
4. Draw a drift region around the two higher penthouse areas, about 8'-0" away from the penthouse. You can also click the Pick Lines button to aid in the drawing of the loads.
5. Click the Load Properties button.
6. Under Structural Analysis, change the load case to DRIFT (9).
7. Change Fz 1 to **-0.1000**.
8. Click OK, and then click Finish Sketch. Go back to View 1 - Analytical; it should now look like the following graphic.

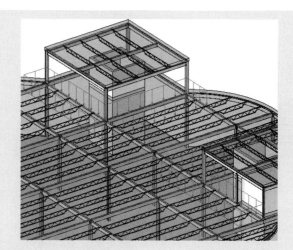

9. On the Analyze tab click the Loads icon again.

10. This time you are going to place a line load by host on the south edge of the building. Click the Line Load with Host icon.

11. Click the Element Properties icon ➢ Instance Properties.

12. Set the Load case to WIND1 (3) if needed.

13. Set the Fy 1 value to **0.500 kip/ft**; then click OK.

14. Using the 14 Roof - analytical plan view, click the analytical beam lines on the south edge of the building, as in the following graphic.

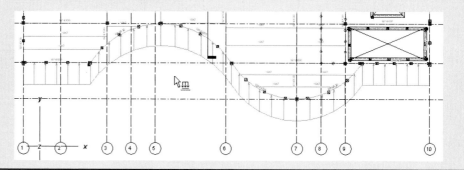

Exporting for Structural Analysis

With the loads in place, the Revit Structure model is now ready to be exported. You have done everything you can to add information that will allow your analysis application to take the model the rest of the way.

Out-of-the-box Revit Structure 2010 does not come with a link to any analysis software packages. It is up to the analysis vendor to provide links and enablers for its applications to establish the relationship between Revit Structure and its products. All of the major vendors do have this link available, fortunately. The first thing you need to do is either contact your analysis software provider, or simply go to its website and do a search for "Revit Structure." Some sites are easier than others to use to find the various components, but once you do find them, they are usually free of charge.

After downloading the integration link software from your analysis vendor, you will need to install it, as shown in Figure 15.45. The procedure to export your model to the software is as follows:

1. Make sure the applications have been loaded, and then open Revit Structure.

2. Go to the Add-ins tab ➤ *Name of analysis program*.

3. The application's dialog box then will be displayed (see Figure 15.46). You will be given some choices as to the following:

FIGURE 15.45
The Bentley Ram link

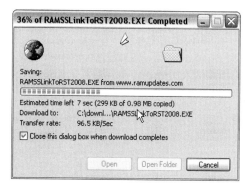

FIGURE 15.46
Export options in the RISA analytical package

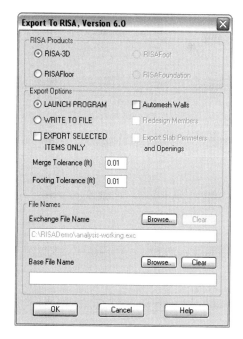

◆ The extent of elements that you are exporting

◆ Specific application questions you will need to answer for that particular analysis package

4. Depending on the application, Revit Structure will either export a file in that program's native format or create a `.bim` file. Some applications will read this format, while others will not.

Real World Scenario

THE VIABILITY OF ANALYTICAL MODEL INTEGRATION

This part of Revit Structure is constantly evolving as the AEC industry and BIM technologies mature and use ever-more-powerful computing tools. It's an incredibly complex notion to combine and coordinate analytical and physical models all in one file. At this moment the promise of integrating Revit Structure with analysis links has not proven itself totally in practice. Numerous difficulties may occur that will deter you from using it as intended.

But the situation seems to be changing even as this book is being published. With its recent purchase of Robobat, Autodesk has incorporated its own analysis software into its software suite. Already with the Revit Structure Extensions, analytical capabilities are being nicely integrated into Revit Structure. We are bound to see dramatic changes in the near future as the software makers contend with the ever-expanding reality of BIM design.

Autodesk also has just recently entered into an agreement with Bentley to coordinate their efforts more and to better integrate products such as RAM Concept with Revit Structure. The importance of this agreement cannot be understated, since for several years there has been fierce competition between these two AEC software giants for control of the BIM market. It got so bad that you could not even find the integration link or any mention of Revit on the Bentley website. It was hidden away and took much scrounging around to find it. Whether or not this agreement will succeed could well foretell the success of a more open source approach to BIM software development. This is not a truly open source agreement, but since these two companies control an overwhelming market share, in practical terms it could have a great influence on that happening.

At this time it must be said that analysis integration is very challenging to undertake in your project, which is more the reason why collaboration between Revit Structure and its analysis partners needs to be strengthened. The idea that you can import and export the model through the analysis package multiple times through the entire design period is for the most part still theory. Very few structural design firms have been able to accomplish that goal. The reasons are many and varied and quite dependent on which analysis package you are using. Each has its own problems.

Your best bet to get started in using this functionality is to use it for preliminary analysis of your structure. Work on one import or export of data as a starting point, and try to make that work in a project. Start your model in the analysis package and import it into Revit Structure or vice versa. That in itself will save valuable time and should not be ignored.

But keep a close eye on upcoming events since this story is changing almost daily. At some point the theoretical vision of integrating analytical and physical model activity will be achieved and will create a very dynamic flow of structural design data. Hopefully that goal will be achieved sooner rather than later, since the efficiencies to be gained are quite substantial.

Transferring Data

The good thing about this method of importing and exporting is that regardless of the analysis application to which Revit Structure is linked, it is merely an exchange of data, not a physical model. This is important because there is no worry about insertion points or items that did not get selected.

To import a model back into Revit, or to import a model that may have started in an analysis application, you follow the same procedure as you did to export the model.

1. Go to the Add-Ins tab on the Ribbon.

2. The application will prompt you to make some choices based on geometry that is not loaded into the Revit Structure model at the time of import (see Figure 15.47).

3. At this point, you can click the Browse button and find the model that you wish to import into Revit Structure.

FIGURE 15.47
Updating the model from the RISA analysis application

This has been a brief glimpse at this complex and often difficult subject, showing how the analytical model can be exported and imported into Revit Structure.

The Bottom Line

Configure Revit Structure structural settings and create loads for your project. The Structural Settings dialog box contains the tabs that will allow you to configure loads for your project. Load Cases, Load Natures, Load Combinations, and their usage form the basis for preparing your analytical model for export to analysis software.

Master It

1. True or False: Revit Structure has the ability to perform structural analysis.

2. True or False: Revit Structure cannot combine load cases.

3. True or False: A circular reference will occur when a system of beams frames back to the origin.

4. True or False: A good example of a typical boundary condition is the support of earth underneath a footing or a slab on grade.

5. Where are the settings located that allow you to turn on automatic checks for Member Supports and Analytical/Physical Model Consistency?

Place analytical load patterns onto your model. Loads are placed in the model in anticipation of using them for preliminary analysis. Several placement methods are possible within Revit Structure. Each of these methods can be applied in two ways.

Master It

1. Name the three different kinds of load placements.

2. The analytical properties of an element can depend on one of two things. What are they?

3. True or False: The Project Coordinate system directional guide is an icon that indicates the work plane for the load you are about to place.

4. What two ways can load placements be applied?

5. True or False: Adding a line load with host is a little less confusing than adding an area load since a line load has no z direction whatsoever.

Import and export your virtual model from Revit Structure to structural analysis software. Once the loading is created and placed, the model is ready to be exported to an analysis application. Once the analysis is complete, it can then be imported back in to Revit Structure and will automatically update the model.

Master It

1. True or False: The integration links come prepackaged with Revit Structure.

2. When the application's dialog box is displayed, you will be given some choices. To what do they refer?

3. What type of file will Revit Structure export to the analysis application?

4. True or False: Importing and exporting to the analysis application exchanges the physical model back and forth between Revit Structure and the analysis application.

Part 5

Advanced Topics

Chapter 16

Project Phases and Design Options

To appreciate the power of Revit Structure in working through the design process of a typical building project, you must improve your skills in the basics to the point where you start to feel comfortable using project phases and design options. As you will see in this chapter, you can manipulate the project data to describe multiple building scenarios for your design — and all in one Revit Structure file. Many people tend to shy away from using project phases and design options at first. But once you learn how they work and the logic behind their use, you will find yourself employing them more and more. Using these features is an efficient way to develop your model.

In this chapter you will examine the basic commands and rules for phases and design options, and you will learn how they can be applied to your projects. We'll introduce several real-world situations to illustrate their application.

In this chapter you will learn to:

◆ Create project phases to manage element assignments

◆ Display project phases in your project views

◆ Understand the relationship among phases, views, and elements.

◆ Create design options to manage element assignments

◆ Display design options in your project views

Working with Project Phases

Working with project phases is a task that many projects will require. Revit Structure has a good system for you to create and manage them. What kind of phases? A phase could involve the objects in your model that belong to an existing building to which you are adding a new addition. Or it could involve the items that are being demolished. Each can be identified as a phase. You can create your own phases or use the default ones.

You assign elements in your model to an appropriate phase. You then create views that display the phases accordingly. It sounds simple enough, but you must pay close attention to your Element and View properties when you are working with phases.

Probably the most common application of phasing will be in cases where an existing building is related to your new design. You have two basic options for setting up this type of project environment: either create the existing model and new model together in one file, or create the existing model in a separate file and link it to your new model. Depending on the particulars of the project, you could decide to go either way, and both are appropriate.

Figure 16.1 shows a view of the Williams-Drummond House historical remodel project where only the existing structure is displayed. In this project, historical preservation was an important factor for the owners. The design ideas for the residence received close scrutiny from the local building department and historical committee of the city. Figure 16.2 shows the same house design in its final completed stage after the remodel.

As you will see later in this chapter, various design options were created to show several completed remodeling ideas. These were then documented and presented in the early part of the project to the building department and historical committee for review. The phasing for new and existing elements was done within the various design options presented. We will return to this example later.

FIGURE 16.1
The existing historic residence

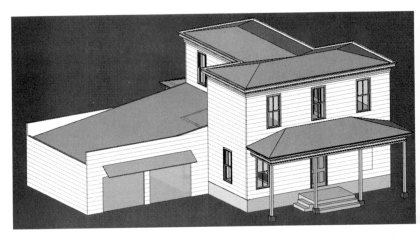

FIGURE 16.2
A new construction option for the residence

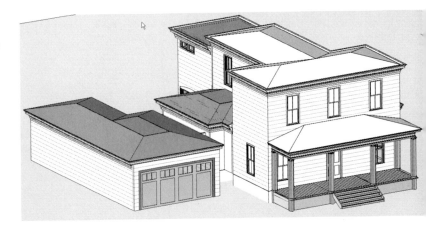

Understanding the Properties of Phases

Project phasing basically means that structural elements within the scope of your design are categorized and ordered in such a way that identifies their chronological building order or some other organizational task. Revit Structure allows you to organize and manage the many types of design and construction tasks that you may encounter. As the BIM approach matures and becomes normal practice, you will no doubt be faced with this task more and more.

CREATING PHASES IN YOUR PROJECTS

When working on a project, you will need to consider how to *phase,* or make into discrete portions, the segments of the design or construction process you are documenting. Revit Structure helps you by assigning the elements you introduce in your model to specific phases. The remodel of an existing building will have two basic phases — existing construction and new construction. Revit requires only two phases to properly document the new, existing, temporary, and demolished states of the building process. The new construction can be broken down again into subphases.

For example, remodel work in an existing hospital may require moving staff and machinery out of the way and then back again during the course of a project. All that would have to be phased correctly to allow for the continuation of normal operations in the overall hospital. So in your model you develop views that show the various conditions, and you assign to elements in the model an identification relevant to the phases you create.

CREATING PROJECT PHASES

The Phasing dialog box is accessed by selecting Phases on the Manage Project panel of the Manage tab of the Ribbon. There are three areas in the dialog box that are used to create and configure your project phases and that you need to study and understand to get started. Those are accessed with the tabs Project Phases, Phase Filters, and Graphic Overrides.

There are two default project phases, Existing and New Construction (see Figure 16.3), although you can add as many as you like. To add a new phase to your project simply click the Before or After button in the Insert area. You cannot reorder phases. You can eliminate a phase by using Combine With. You cannot simply choose to move one phase into a different place in the sequence; you have to reassign elements to the correct phase. This restriction makes true construction sequencing difficult to accomplish with the Phasing tool.

EMPLOYING PHASE FILTERS

Each phase that you use has associated filters that control how elements are displayed in any particular view where that phase filter is applied (see Figure 16.4). Each view in your project has parameters that let you set a phase and apply a phase filter for that view. Setting these options in the View Display dialog box controls what is shown in that view. Each element also has phasing controls. When these options are set in conjunction with the view controls, it creates what is referred to as the *phase status* for the element.

For instance, if the phase is set to New Construction in your view, what might you want to display? You probably just want the new work shown. By setting Phase Filters to Show New, you create a phase status for elements so that

- ◆ The model elements defined as New Construction will be displayed By Category.

- ◆ Existing, Demolished, and Temporary items will not be displayed.

You apply phases and phase filters in each view by setting parameters in the View Properties dialog box. More on this subject of assigning phases to elements will be presented in greater depth in the section "Assigning Elements to Phases."

FIGURE 16.3
The Phasing
dialog box
showing the
two default
phases

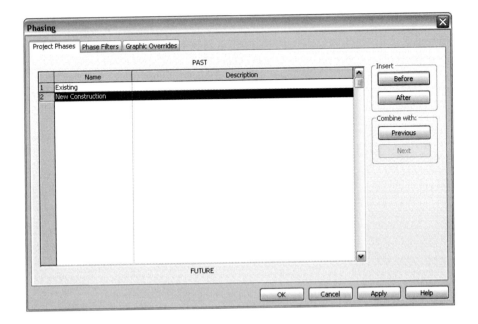

FIGURE 16.4
Examining
phase filters
in the Phasing
dialog box

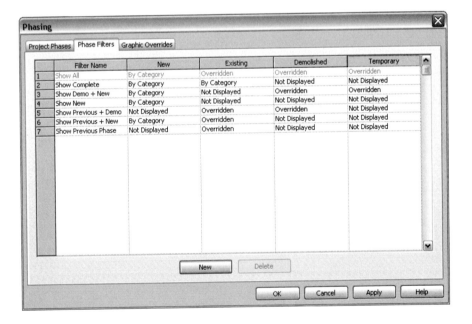

There are six default phase filters that you can use immediately, and others can be created as needed. The default configuration of any phase filter can also be changed to suit your needs.

Suppose you have a phase set as New Construction, with only the Existing phase preceding it. The following list explains each filter associated with this phase:

Show All   This filter displays all elements, including existing, demolished, and temporary elements. It cannot be changed or deleted.

Show Demo + New   This filter displays demolished elements and all of the new elements that you add to your model.

Show New   This filter displays only the new elements that you have added to your model.

Show Previous + Demo   This filter displays all elements from phases before the current, demolished, and temporary elements.

Show Previous + New   This filter displays all elements from the previous phase that were not demolished, as well as all added new elements.

Show Previous Phase   This filter shows all elements from the previous phase.

Note that if you are in the first phase there is no previous phase, so if you enable the Show Previous Phase filter, nothing will be displayed.

The phase filter categories include the following:

Not Displayed   The elements will not be displayed in that phase.

By Category   An element will be displayed as it is defined in the Visibility/Graphic override dialog box of each view.

Overridden   The graphic display is overridden for those elements in each view.

You will most likely display new elements by category. At the same time, you may want existing elements to appear shaded or with a particular line style so they are easily discernible in comparison to the new work. Demolished items as well may be best displayed in a common way, such as the default, which is visually shown as red and a hidden line pattern. The next section will show you how to use the graphic overrides and configure them to your needs.

To create a new phase filter, click New in the Phase Filters tab and then provide an appropriate name for that filter. Any number of phase filters can be created and configured in your project.

MODIFYING GRAPHIC ELEMENTS

You can modify the appearance of elements in each phase filter to something other than By Category by using graphic overrides. Figure 16.5 shows the Graphic Overrides tab, which controls assignments of the various line styles, patterns, and materials within your project views. The overrides work like this:

◆   Line styles and patterns can be altered for all for elements that are in projection or that are surfaces in projection.

◆   Line styles and patterns can be altered for all for elements that are cut by the view plane.

◆   The Halftone check box will tone the elements.

◆   The Material display of different phase statuses can be configured and applied universally.

All of these phases, filters, and overrides seem a bit daunting at first, but do not be scared off from learning to use them since they will help coordinate your project efforts tremendously. Start with a simple case and get that to work. Later you can move to more complex uses.

FIGURE 16.5
The Graphic Overrides tab in the Phasing dialog box, used for modifying graphic elements

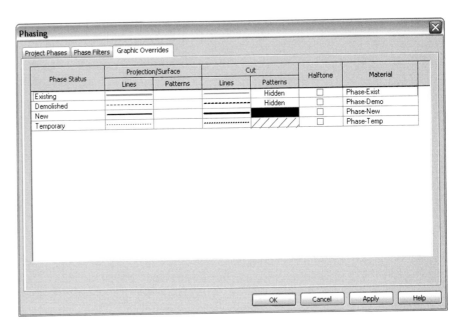

Now that you have created the phase and configured the filters to your liking, you can move on to assigning the elements in your model to a phase. This assignment will be an Instance parameter setting for each element.

Assigning Elements to Phases

You must understand how an element *is*. What do we mean by that? An existing element, for instance, is new in one view but existing in another. Its reality is dependent on what phase it was created in and what phase view it is being viewed from.

In the default setup, you configure the Phase Created and Phase Demolished settings for an element to create a phase status for that element. The phase status can be one of the following:

Existing   This refers to an existing element in the project. This is an element that was created in a previous phase than the phase of the view being used.

New   This refers to a new element in the project.

Demolished   This refers to an existing element in one phase that is demolished in a subsequent phase of the project.

Temporary   This refers to an element that is created and demolished in the same phase of the project.

In your project you will assign each element to a phase. Each element has two phase parameters: Phase Created and Phase Demolished. The default value for Phase Created is New Construction, and the default for Phase Demolished is None. It makes sense that a new element is not demolished (see Figure 16.6). An element assumes the phase of the view it is created in, so the default value depends on the view, not just the default setting.

FIGURE 16.6
Phase parameters for a new element

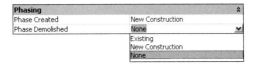

DEMOLISHING AN ELEMENT

For an existing element, set the Phase Demolished parameter to the phase in which you want it to be demolished (see Figure 16.7).

FIGURE 16.7
Setting the phase parameters for a demolished element

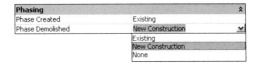

The Demolish tool is found on the Phasing panel of the Modify tab (appropriately marked with a hammer icon) and is used to mark elements as demolished in the current phase.

CREATING TEMPORARY ELEMENTS

Temporary elements are those that are created and demolished all in the same phase, such as temporary shoring (see Figure 16.8). For a temporary element, simply set the Phase Created and Phase Demolished parameters to the same phase.

FIGURE 16.8
Temporary shoring (shaded and hidden line) supporting new concrete

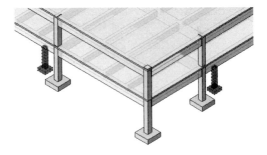

Our discussion so far has centered on elements that are all in one file. But many times you must create and maintain phasing for linked models. Let's take a look at how that works.

Linking Revit Structure Models and Phasing

Another important consideration to how you approach your project phasing is whether you are linking other Revit Structure files into your project. For instance, how would you approach a project with an existing building that is being remodeled? There are two obvious approaches:

◆ Create one Revit Structure file that incorporates the existing structure and the new remodel work that has to be done.

◆ Create a Revit Structure file for the existing structure and link that file into a file that contains only the new work.

Depending on the project, a case can be made for going either way. You may find that linking in the existing building will give you greater flexibility. One important reason for this approach is that computer performance could be improved by being able to unload the file when you do not need it displayed in your views. It might also be easier with multiple people working on the project if there are several files on which they can work. One potential challenge, though, is that controlling the phasing through the link can be a little difficult.

With a linked model, you control the phase and phase filters in the RVT Link Display Settings dialog box, as shown in Figure 16.9, which you access through the Visibility/Graphic Overrides dialog box. You can set the phase settings for a particular view from the host view file or the linked view file, or you can employ a custom approach that uses settings from each file. Be careful though, because things can get somewhat confusing when you start altering the settings. When you get the settings the way you want them, create a view template that you can apply in similar circumstances.

FIGURE 16.9

Control the phase of the linked file using the RVT Link Display Settings dialog box.

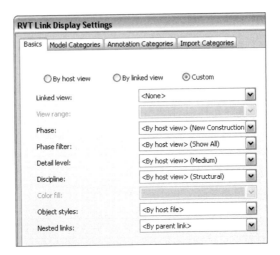

Next you will see how phases can be used to your great advantage to display a complex situation within a project. Then you will do an exercise to demonstrate how all this goes together.

Displaying Phases in Views

First you learned how basic phases are created. Then you learned how to assign to your modeled elements the phase in which they occur. Now let's look at how a view is configured to display elements in a particular phase. We'll consider two examples that illustrate both ways of working.

🌐 Real World Scenario

USING PHASING IN A DIFFICULT DESIGN SITUATION

The project examined in this scenario was a remodel of a large existing industrial building. The project model had two files, with the existing structure linked into the new structure. A large amount of demolition had to be documented. With one corner of the existing structure in particular, understanding in two dimensions what needed to be demolished in relation to the new work was quite difficult. By using three-dimensional cutaway views that showed the phasing of that area, we, the project team, ensured that the challenge of the remodel came more clearly into perspective.

First we created a view that showed the existing and demolished model elements, as shown in the following illustration. The demolished elements appear in red and as hidden lines. The existing elements that remain are shown gray and toned.

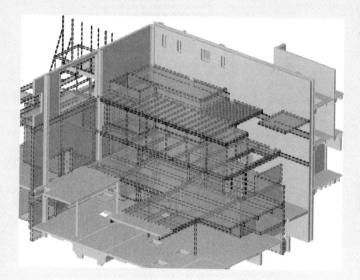

We then created a second view from the same orientation and adjusted the phasing for that view to show all elements regardless of status. So in this case the view displayed new, existing, demolished, and temporary elements, as shown in the following graphic. The Phase option was set to New Construction and the Phase Filter set to Show All. This view really helped since there were numerous stacked tube columns and lots of cantilevered framing. Using this view we could easily identify and set for demolition those elements that interfered with the new construction.

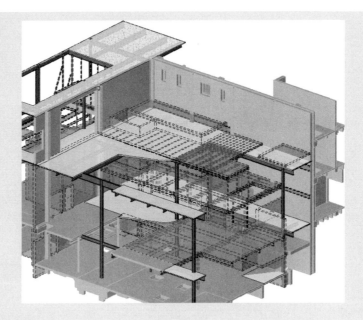

The last view we created displayed the final completed structure after the remodeling was finished. We set the Phase to New Construction and the Phase Filter to Show Complete, as shown here. You can't see the demolished elements. The existing model is shown in gray and the new elements are shown By Category.

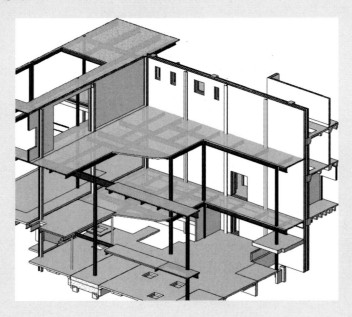

The three views just described are going to be added to the construction document set to help illustrate this hard-to-understand area of the structure and its transformation to the new design specifications. You should incorporate views like these into your documents as a matter of good BIM practice.

EXERCISE: WORKING WITH PHASES IN A PROJECT

In this exercise, you will remodel a concrete structure. One bay is being removed and replaced with steel members. You are required to create an existing view, a demolition view, and a view of the completed remodel. Your office did the original project and you have the design model of the structure that you can reuse. Your first step is to change all the current elements in the model to the Existing phase since this will be an existing building now. The second task is to identify the items to be demolished. Then, the new work can be added. Finally, you will create views that display all three phases: Existing, Demo, and New.

First let's change the properties of elements in the existing model:

1. Open the model of the concrete structure, Dataset_CH1601_begin.rvt (from the book's companion web page at www.sybex.com/go/masteringrevitstructure20010).

2. Click the Default 3D View button (the house icon on the Quick Access toolbar) to access the full model view. Use the Zoom Extents tool if necessary.

3. Select the two floor decks, and then click the Element Properties button on the Element panel of the Modify Floors tab to access the Element Properties dialog box.

4. Scroll down and change the Phase parameter for the objects to Existing. Click OK to apply and exit. Deselect the floors.

   Notice that the slabs are no longer transparent because they have assumed the Phase - Exist material display. You will change that next.

5. On the Manage tab click the Manage Project panel ➤ Phases, and then choose the Graphic Overrides tab in the Phasing dialog box.

6. Click twice in the Material field of the Existing category, which displays the Materials dialog box for Phase - Exist.

7. On the Graphics tab in the Shading section, change the Transparency value for the Phase - Exist material to 10%. Click OK twice to save and exit the dialog boxes.

8. Select any column, and then right-click to bring up the context menu. Then click Select All Instances.

9. With all members highlighted, click the Modify Structural Columns tab ➤ Element Properties to access the Instance Properties dialog box.

10. Scroll down, and change the Phase option for the selected columns to Existing. Click OK to apply and exit.

11. Select one spread footing, and then repeat steps 8 and 9 to add them to the existing phase.

It would be nice if you could select all the elements at once and change their Phase setting to Existing, but that is not possible. The easiest way to get things assigned to the correct phase is to model them in a view assigned to that phase to begin with so that no reassignment is required later. If you have not done that, you need to isolate the different model object categories and then change their phase category. Other than using the Select All Instances method, the easiest way is to filter your selection set. In the case of structural framing you cannot select the Beam System and the Structural Framing (joists) and then change the phases. The phasing is controlled by the Beam System. The Filter procedure works like this:

1. Select the entire model with a crossing window. On the Multi-Select tab click the Filter icon.

2. Click Check None and then check only Beam Systems .

3. Click OK to close; then only the Beam System elements are selected.

4. With all members highlighted, click the Element Properties icon ➤ Modify Structural Beam Systems ➤ Instance Properties.

5. Scroll down, and change the Phase option to Existing. Click OK to apply and exit.

Repeat the previous steps for the Structural Framing elements. Now all of the elements have been changed to the Existing phase, and you are ready to demolish objects. (You can verify if you have successfully changed all elements by changing the Phase Filter to Show New to see if elements are still displayed.) You will demolish all the elements in the lower-right bay, from grid 2B to grid 3C, except you will leave the girders that run along grid 2 and along grid B:

1. In the Project Browser, double-click Level 2.

2. Click the Demolish icon on the Phasing panel of the Modify tab.

3. Hover your mouse over the bottom-right bay until you highlight the beam system (use the Tab key if necessary). Click to demolish its members.

4. Next, demolish the edge structural framing in the bay on lines C and 3.

5. Go to Level 3 and repeat the demolition process.

6. Finally, go to Level 1 and demolish the column and spread footing at grid 3C.

Click the Default 3D View on the Quick Access toolbar, and note that those elements are now shown in red and with hidden lines. The last item to demolish is part of the existing floor on Levels 2 and 3. This process is a bit different because rather than a whole object being demolished, only part of this one will be removed. How are you going to deal with that? Well, you will create a solid void that cuts out the area. Of course, you do not want the void to appear in the existing view of the structure, but by phasing your views correctly, you will be able to display all the conditions correctly.

1. Go to the Level 2 plan view. On the Home tab ➤ Model tab ➤ Component, choose Model In-Place from the drop-down list.

2. Select Floors for the Family Category and click OK.

3. Name the element **Level 2 floor demo** and then click OK.

4. On the Model In-Place tab click Void ➤ Extrusion.

5. On the Create Void Extrusion tab click the Rectangle icon on the Draw panel, and then draw a rectangle from the edges of the existing girders to the edges of the slab portion to be removed.

6. On the Create Void Extrusion tab click Extrusion Properties on the Element panel and set the Extrusion End to **−6″**.

7. Click Finish Extrusion.

8. Click the Modify tab. On the Edit Geometry panel click the Cut icon ➢ Cut Geometry.

9. Select the floor and then the void that will cut it to complete the operation.

10. Finally, click Finish Model on the In-Place Editor panel.

11. Perform the same process for the Level 3 floor slab to void out a portion of that slab. If the extents of the voided-out portions in both floors are the same, you could also extend the void vertically above Level 3 and have it cut that deck as well.

At this point, your 3D view of the model should look something like this:

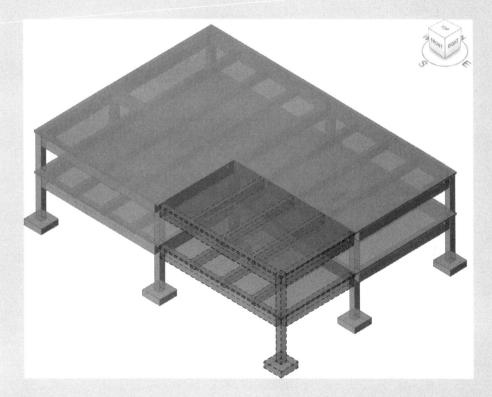

Now you will add the new construction to the project. First, go to Level 2. Right-click and select View Properties from the context menu. Scroll down and notice the phase settings:

◆ Show All for Phase Filter

◆ New Construction for Phase

Remember that for the Show All phase the phase filters are displaying new, existing, demolished, and temporary construction in the view. That works fine as a Demolition view but not as a New Construction view. In the New Construction view we do not want to see any demolished items or the existing items that we want to remove. Also, if you want the existing construction to display as grayed out, you need to override the Phase filter in the following way:

1. On the Manage tab click the Phases icon on the Manage Project panel.

2. Click the Phase Filters tab.

3. On the Show Complete line, change the Existing option from By Category to Overridden.

4. Click the Graphic Overrides tab, and notice that the cut and projected line styles are set to display a gray tone.

5. Click OK to exit the dialog box.

Now all the existing objects in the view will be displayed in gray tone, helping you to distinguish them from the new work.

So now let's duplicate the view we have been working on and then set the phase parameters to show the completed construction:

1. In the Project Browser, highlight the Level 2 plan. Right-click and select Rename from the context menu. Rename the view **Level 2 Demo**. Click No when prompted to rename the level and views.

2. Right-click in the drawing area and click View Properties. Change the Phase Filter parameter to Show Previous + Demo; then click OK to exit. The phase should be set to New Construction.

3. In the Project Browser, select the Level 2 Demo plan, right-click, and choose Duplicate View ➢ Duplicate with Detailing. Rename the new view **Level 2 Existing**.

4. Go to the Level 2 Existing view, right-click in the drawing area, and click View Properties. Change the Phase option to Existing and change the Phase Filter option to Show Previous + New; then exit.

5. In the Project Browser, highlight the Level 2 Demo plan view, right-click, and choose Duplicate View ➢ Duplicate with Detailing. Rename the view **Level 2 New**.

6. In the Project Browser, highlight the {3D} view. Rename it to **3D Demo**.

7. As you did for the floor views, create two other 3D views, one for the existing and one for the new phase, and set their phases accordingly. Name them **3D New** and **3D Existing**.

Check out the following graphic of the 3D views you just created. Is that cool or what? Of course, you can create multiple views for your other floors as well, but we will no go that far in this exercise. But you are not finished yet!

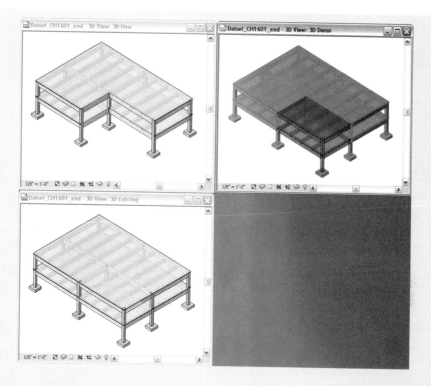

Now you will add the new construction elements to the model:

1. Go to the Level 2 New plan view.

2. On the Home tab click Column ➤ Structural Column.

3. Add a W10×49 wide flange column to grid 3C from the second to the first level.

4. Click the Home tab ➤ Beam, and in the Type Selector select W21×50.

5. Place a girder between grids 2C and 3C and one between grids 3B and 3C. Change the girder's Start and End Level Offset value to −5″ below the floor level.

6. On the Home tab, click Beam System and select W18×35 from the Options bar as the Beam Type. Set the Beam System offset to −5″.

7. In-fill the bay with beams by selecting the grid 3 girder.

8. On the Home tab, click Floor ➤ Structural Floor. Add a 3″ LW Concrete on 2″ Composite Metal Deck type floor into the new area.

9. On the Home tab, click the Isolated icon on the Foundation panel, and add a 5′-square footing for the new steel column at grid 3C. It will be placed at the bottom of the column and will not be visible in this view.

And there you have it! Pull up your various plan and 3D views, and play around with the phasing and phase filters to see how the options display your elements. Your final completed remodel in your 3D New view should resemble the following graphic.

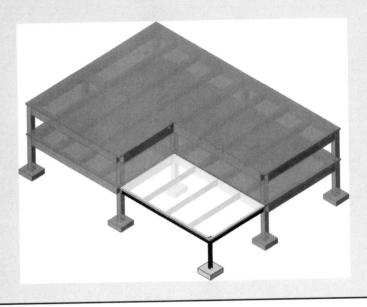

That ends our discussion on project phases, which as you have seen are very powerful as well as a bit confusing at first to understand. Next we will examine design options and how they are used in your project.

Working with Design Options

Design options are at the core of the design process. Professional architects and engineers bring life to an idea that slowly resolves itself into precise details and specifications that can actually be built. During that process, at every stage, various options are considered, analyzed, and then accepted or rejected based on their merits. You might be exploring two different concepts for a canopy on a part of a building you are designing, for example, or different mechanical support layouts on a roof. Juggling multiple options and producing the graphics necessary to display each one can be a time-consuming and confusing process. Using the design options in Revit Structure can greatly ease the difficulty of managing all those design ideas. Using design options in your projects can save you considerable time and effort because you can display multiple design ideas without having to duplicate files. You can then keep them organized in one file, where each option can be displayed in a particular view.

So let's dig into the particulars and see how this process works. First you will see how to create the basic design options in your project.

How Design Options Work

Design options are created as sets of modeled elements. A building project can have multiple option sets. Figures 16.10 and 16.11 show one set containing two options for new tunnel walls at a sports stadium project. One option within the set is for a concrete tunnel wall, and the other is for a CMU tunnel wall. The new tunnel is meant to connect the locker rooms to the main playing field. More options could be added as well for the tunnel — for instance, another option for a wider tunnel. The option set was created because the contractor wanted to compare prices and materials required for the different possibilities.

FIGURE 16.10
The Concrete Tunnel wall option

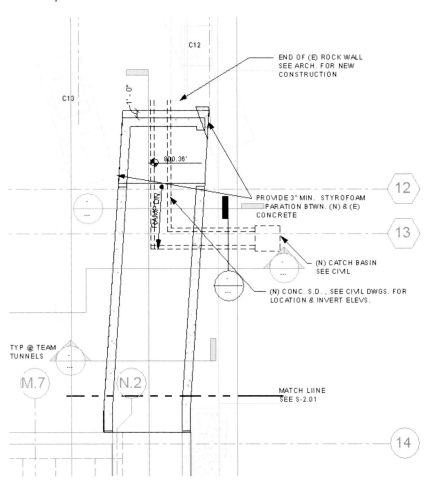

No matter how many options are added to an option set, only one can be displayed in a view at any one time. That one is called the primary option. The others are referred to as secondary options. Each view is then set to display one of the options in an option set. So create multiple views of an area, and in each view make one option primary for that view. This works well in the schematic and design development phase of a project as you organize your ideas and fit them to the whole design. Then as you start finalizing your design in the construction document phase, you can eliminate the views of those options that you do not want to use.

FIGURE 16.11
The CMU Tunnel wall
option

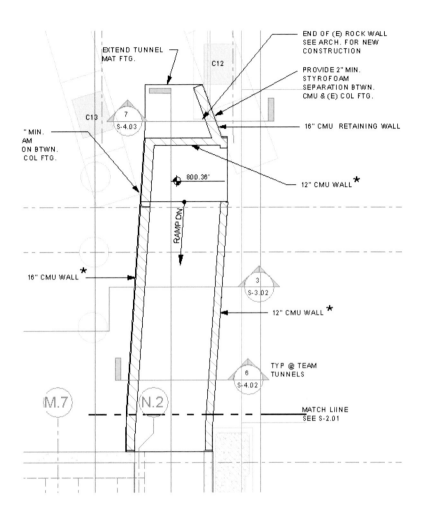

Creating Design Option Sets

You can access these commands on the Design Options panel of the Manage tab. The panel has three functions. The Design Options icon on the left accesses the Design Options dialog box. Add to Set permits us to assign selected elements from the main model to a design option; Pick to Edit activates an existing option in a view by selecting an element in the desired option set. Figure 16.12 shows the Design Options panel. Elements that are in design options are not editable until the option is enabled unless you uncheck the Exclude Options feature on the status bar. You can select an option set from the dialog box, or you can make one active from the drop-down list on the Design Options panel.

The Design Options dialog box lists each design option set. For each option set, the primary view will show by default unless overridden to display a specific alternate option. As you can see in Figure 16.13, the sports stadium project has two other design option sets as well. One option set is for Foundations and one option set is for Entry Stairs. The Foundations option set has an option for Spread Footings and one for Piles. The Entry Stairs option set has options for Concrete and

Steel stair types. By default, the main model will display the primary option of the set. To change the option in a set to primary, select the option and click the Make Primary button under Option.

FIGURE 16.12

The Design Options panel on the Manage tab

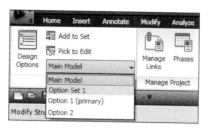

FIGURE 16.13

Design option sets for our stadium project

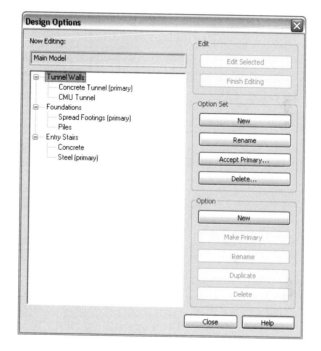

But what if you want to completely hide an option in a view? Maybe you have an alternative design that you don't want to show your client yet. In this case, create an option in your set that has no elements and make it the primary option. When you are ready to show the new option to the client, you can then make primary that particular option you have been working on.

To create a design option set, follow these steps:

1. Click the Design Options icon on the Design Options panel of the Manage tab to display the Design Options dialog box.

2. Under Option Set, click New to create the new design option set and one design option for the set.

3. Highlight the new option set, and then click Rename.

4. Rename the option set.

5. Highlight the option and rename it.

6. Under Option, click New and create other options in that set as needed.

7. Create other design option sets and options in the same way as needed.

Okay, that was not so bad, was it? Now that you have created and configured your design option set, let's add elements to it.

Adding and Editing Design Option Elements

Now that you have created your design options, how do you populate them with modeled elements? First you must enable the design option set and select the particular option within that set on which you want to work. Use the Design Options tool on the Design Options panel of the Manage tab to activate it, or you can select a design option from the pull-down list in the Design Options panel.

When working in a design option, you are isolated from the main model, which becomes grayed out and whose elements are not selectable.

All the elements that you create while in Editing mode are automatically designated as belonging to that design option. In some cases, you may want to add elements from the main model to your design option. Since the main model is not selectable while you are in Editing mode, you need to add main model elements to your option before entering the option-editing mode.

You do that by selecting the element and clicking Add to Option on the Design Options panel. Click the button and then select the main model element you want to transfer to a design option. The Add to Design Option Set dialog box appears, where you can assign the element. The element is then deleted from the main model and will display only when the option is enabled.

The following elements are not supported in design options:

Levels If you are working in a design option, you can create a level but it will nevertheless be assigned as an element to the main model. It will appear grayed out in the option.

Views Views cannot be created in design options, but rather an option is assigned to a view in the main model.

Annotations and details These elements are view specific. You are able to write text notes while editing an option, but you cannot turn them on and off if you switch between options. They remain visible in the view in either case.

Some elements depend on other elements, such as a doorway in a wall. The door element is hosted by the wall and cannot exist without it. The door cannot independently be assigned to a design option without the wall that hosts it. Elements of this sort include the following:

◆ Inserts that cut their hosts (doors, windows, equipment)

◆ Host sweeps and their hosts (slab edge profiles)

◆ Curtain panels

◆ Window mullions

◆ Grids

◆ Topographical surfaces and building pads

◆ Attachments like walls attached to roofs or floors

Also keep in mind that elements that are added to a group must be in the same design option as the group.

You have added elements to your design option. Next you must configure your views to display the options that you have created.

Displaying Design Options in Your Views

So far you have learned how to create design option sets and how to add elements to the options in those sets. The next piece in the puzzle is to configure your views to display the options that you created. These are often called *dedicated* views since they are developed to display only one design option. Figure 16.14 shows the Project Browser for the Williams-Drummond House historical remodel project. Study how the various views are set up. There are three basic view types that were created in the project: one for the existing structure, one for the option with bay windows, and one for the option without bay windows. Each view is configured to show a particular phase and design option. Then the various views are dragged onto the appropriate sheets.

The primary view is displayed automatically in your view. To choose another option to display in a particular view, if one exists, go to the Design Options tab in the Visibility/Graphic Overrides dialog box and select the Option parameter (see Figure 16.15). Elements in that option will then become visible in your view.

Another tool to be aware of is the Visible In Option parameter that you will find in the View Properties dialog box. This parameter permits you to control whether certain view annotations in the option appear in other views. For instance, if you have an elevation of an exterior stairway that shows an alternative design option solution, then you probably do not want that annotation to show up in the main model view.

You can develop a fairly complicated set of views when you also include phasing of the project along with design options, such as that in the residential project. The elements in the various design options you create can be phased to show construction sequencing. For instance, the existing structure of the historical residence in Figure 16.16 shows a 3D view of the back kitchen area and porch side of the house.

◆ Phase is set to Existing.

◆ Phase Filter is set to Show Complete.

◆ The design option is not relevant since only the existing elements are being displayed.

Figure 16.17 is a view that shows the existing elements that remain after demolition. Along with that, the new construction is displayed with the bay window.

◆ Phase is set to New Construction.

◆ Phase Filter is set to Show Complete.

◆ Design Option is set to Wall with Bay Window.

Figure 16.18 is a view that shows the existing elements that remain after demolition as well. Along with that, the new construction is displayed without the bay window.

◆ Phase is set to New Construction.

◆ Phase Filter is set to Show Complete.

◆ Design Option is set to Wall Without Bay Window.

FIGURE 16.14

The mix of views representing various phases and design options

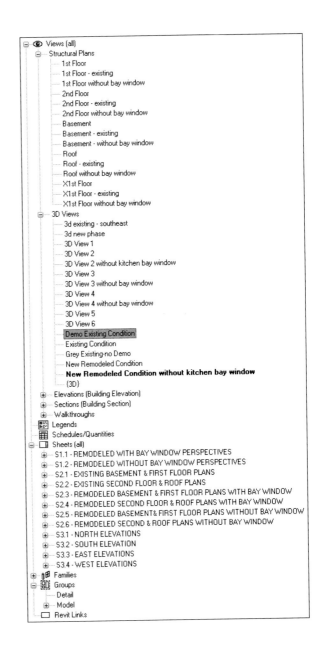

As with phasing, the creation of design options can be confusing at first, so try something simple to build up your knowledge of the subject. In the long run, you will be glad you did. Figures 16.19 and 16.20 illustrate an easy example of design options. When designing the stairway leading to the locker rooms from the upper level, we debated whether to use steel or concrete. So we created an option set for the stairways with two options. We modeled the two stairways, one in steel and one in concrete, and assigned them to their respective options. We then developed cutaway views and configured them to display one of the options. In the end, we went with the steel option and deleted the other option. It was quite easy to do.

FIGURE 16.15
Adding a design option to a view

Parameter	Value
Underlay	None
Underlay Orientation	Plan
Orientation	Project North
Wall Join Display	Clean all wall joins
Discipline	Structural
Color Scheme Location	Background
Visible In Option	Option Set 1 : Wall with Bay Window (primary) ⌄
Identity Data	⌃
View Name	1st Floor
Dependency	Independent
Title on Sheet	REMODELED FIRST FLOOR WITH BQAY WINDO
Sheet Number	S2.3
Sheet Name	REMODELED BASEMENT & FIRST FLOOR PLANS WIT
Referencing Sheet	
Referencing Detail	
Default View Template	Structural Framing Plan

FIGURE 16.16
The existing Williams-Drummond House

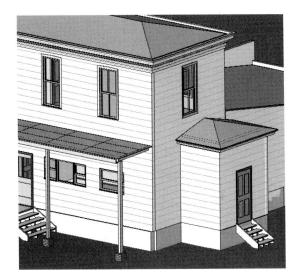

What would have been an alternative way to deal with this situation? Well, we could have created two sets of stairways and then saved each one of them as a group. Then we could have erased one and replaced it with the other as needed. But that approach is rather clumsy and time consuming for you to manage. Why not let design options manage it for you?

Design Option Considerations

By now you should have a good grasp of the basic process for creating and using design options. Let's explore other considerations that you should take into account as you are using them in your projects:

Deleting design options   You delete a design option in the Design Options dialog box. You cannot delete the primary option but only secondary options, or if there is only one option, you can delete the entire option set. Deleting will remove all elements from the model that are designated as part of that design option set.

FIGURE 16.17
The remodeled Williams-Drummond House, with Design Option set to Wall with Bay Window

FIGURE 16.18
The remodeled Williams-Drummond House, with Design Option set to Wall Without Bay Window

Duplicating design options   You cannot duplicate a design option set, but you can duplicate the options themselves. Simply highlight the option and click the Duplicate tab; then rename the new option.

Adding design options to the main model   When you finalize your design, you may decide to incorporate your design options into the main model. You do this using the Design Options dialog box by clicking the Accept Primary button. All options will be deleted as well as all views that contain secondary options.

FIGURE 16.19
Cutaway view of steel stair option at the sports stadium

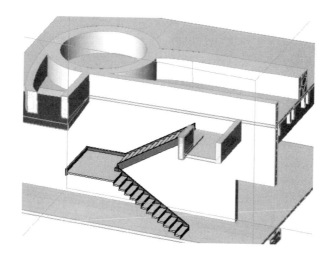

FIGURE 16.20
Cutaway view of concrete stair option at the sports stadium

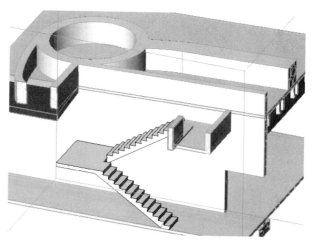

Designs options and wall joins   Element joining can be a bit tricky to do between main model elements and elements within option sets. For instance, wall cleanup at intersections will not occur if one element is in the main model and one in a secondary option. Wall attachment to a roof or floor also will not work. In such cases, you are better off adding the main model element to your design option.

Dimensioning elements in design options   You can dimension between elements in the main model and the primary design option. But secondary options work only one way: the secondary option can add a dimension to the main model. The main model, on the other hand, cannot add a dimension reference to the secondary option.

Scheduling design options   The options that you create can each be scheduled separately for comparison.

So those are a few items that you need to consider as you deploy design options into a project. The next exercise will give you some practice in using design options.

EXERCISE: WORKING WITH DESIGN OPTIONS FOR A BUILDING PROJECT

In this example you will further develop the project that you were working on earlier in this chapter. One bay was removed from an existing concrete building, and you added a one-story steel structure in its place. You also created views of the various building phases. Now your client has decided that he wants to compare the price of steel and concrete options. In this exercise you will create design option sets to document the steel and concrete alternative design schemes for the project.

First, let's create the design option set:

1. Open Datset_CH1602_begin.rvt.

2. On the Manage tab click the Design Options icon.

3. Under Option Set, click New.

4. Highlight Option Set 1, and then click Rename.

5. Name the option **One Story Addition**.

6. Under Option, click New.

7. Highlight the Option 1 (primary) option, and then click Rename.

8. Rename the primary option to **Steel Framing**.

9. Highlight the secondary option, and then click Rename.

10. Rename Option 2 to **Concrete Framing**, and then click Close to exit the dialog box.

Next, you will assign the steel elements already present to the primary option:

1. In the Project Browser, double-click on the 3D New view.

2. In that view, select the two new steel-edge girders, the new floor deck, the new steel column and footing, and the new beams and beam system. (A crossing window will get most, if not all, of it for you.)

3. On the Design Options panel of the Manage tab, click the Add to Set icon, which will display the Add to Design Option Set dialog box.

4. Make sure both the Steel and Concrete options are checked, and then click OK.

The highlighted elements are assigned from the main model to each option in the set. The items are then deleted from the main model. If you try to highlight the elements now, you'll find you cannot select them until you enable one of the options.

Next, you will change the steel elements in the Concrete option to concrete:

1. On the Design Options panel click the Pick to Edit icon, and select One Story Addition: Concrete Framing from the drop-down list to enable that option.

2. While still in the 3D New view, highlight the column at grid 3C and change it to a Concrete - Rectangular - Column: 18″ SQ.

3. Highlight the two steel girders and change them to a Concrete - Rectangular Beam: 16 × 32.

4. Highlight the beam system (you may need to use the Tab key while hovering over a beam), and change the member sizes to Concrete - Rectangular Beam: 16 × 32.

Now you will add more views to display the two options:

1. .Type **VG** to access the Visibility/Graphic Overrides dialog box

2. In the Design Options tab, select One Story Addition: Steel Framing (Primary); then click OK to exit.

3. In the Project Browser, highlight the 3D New view, right-click, and select Rename from the context menu.

4. Rename the view to **3D New - Steel Option**; then click OK to exit.

5. Right-click again and select Duplicate View ➢ Duplicate.

6. Select that new view, right-click, and select Rename from the context menu.

7. Rename the view to **3D New - Concrete Option**; then click OK to exit.

8. Type **VG** to access the Visibility/Graphic Overrides dialog box.

9. In the Design Options tab, select One Story Addition: Concrete Framing; then click OK to exit.

There you have it: two options, one concrete and one steel, displayed in different views that should look like the following:

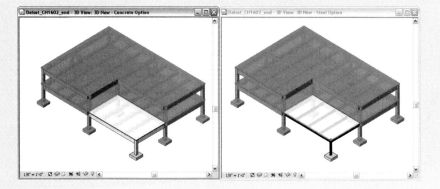

The Bottom Line

Create project phases to manage element assignments.   Creating and managing phases in a project is an important task that will help establish the sequence of construction of your structure. Phases apply existing and new statuses on elements so you can manage them. A good example of using phases is in distinguishing existing elements from new when you add a wing onto a hospital complex.

Master It What steps do you take in developing phases for your building document set?

Display project phases in your project views. Views in Revit Structure are configured to display your various phases. Using the Phase and Phase Filter parameters, you set each view to display new, demo, or existing objects or any number of construction sequence views.

Master It The current view's phase is set to New Construction, with only the Existing phase preceding it. Name the default phase filter that will show elements as they are described below:

1. All elements from the phase before New Construction

2. Demolished elements and all of the new elements that you add to your model

3. Only the new elements that you have added to your model

4. All elements, including existing, demolished, and temporary elements

5. All elements from the previous phase that were not demolished, as well as all added new elements

Understand the relationship among phases, views, and elements. It is critical to understand how these three relate to one another when using phasing. An element can display as existing in one view, demolished in another, and new in yet another. This is all governed with just four parameters, two for views and two for elements. Revit interprets the values stored in these parameters to determine how to display them in your views.

Master It Match the following phase settings for elements with their corresponding phase status, assuming that they are visible in a view assigned to Phase: New.

1. Phase Created: Existing - Phase Demolished: None

2. Phase Created: Existing - Phase Demolished: New

3. Phase Created: New - Phase Demolished: None

4. Phase Created: New - Phase Demolished: New

Create design options to manage element assignments. In a design situation, you have to create sets of design options in order to evaluate various issues and problem areas. All of these options are created and managed in one Revit Structure file. They are then displayed in various views that you create.

Master It Answer the following questions:

1. How many options from an option set can be shown in one view?

2. What elements are not supported in design options?

3. What is a dedicated view?

4. How does the use of design options in your project save you time and resources?

Display design options in your project views.   Once design options are created in your project, you assign them to different views. Those views are then added to a sheet for comparison. In that way, you are able to evaluate and select primary options and discard ones you do not want as the design process progresses.

> **Master It**   Some modeled elements in your project depend on other elements and so cannot be independently assigned to a design option. Name three of those types of elements.

Chapter 17

Standards: Increasing Revit Productivity

In this chapter, you will discover how simple it is to get your company's "look and feel" back into your documentation. With Revit Structure you can develop templates that ensure automatic compliance with standards, while also helping you and your team focus on modeling rather than trying to develop clear and readable drawings.

In this chapter you will learn to:

◆ Ascertain what can and cannot be done easily

◆ Enhance your model through customization

◆ Implement model standards and view overrides

Get to Work?

No doubt, the first thing you did when you installed Revit Structure was start up the software and begin making a basic model. But how did you prepare for that? Did you take a training class? Did you research graphic standard needs? Did you take your AutoCAD Standards Manual and begin mimicking that in Revit Structure? No? Exactly! Well, we have all been there. Take this new product and get it done now. So you model away for a while and then print out drawings. Then your managers take a peek and think "Yuck" when they see how poor your drawings look.

This isn't totally your fault. Most people get so excited about this new application, BIM, and 3D that they forget about the basics. Most structural engineering firms consult for someone else, and there is an expectation of quality in the final product. But unless you carve out development time, the end product will be short in quality. Sure, the information will be there and you will have BIM and a nicely coordinated set of documents. But do these drawings convey importance? Can you tell the difference between a concrete beam and a masonry wall?

As you begin to delve into the following sections, you will expose where most of our standards come from and how to develop a plan for standards. Then you will touch on typical standard containers like fonts. You'll round off this section by examining line styles and patterns.

Knowing Your Limitations

When talking with other Revit Structure users, we've found that the subject of standards often crops up. Nearly everyone has some prior history with AutoCAD. If that is your history as well, then you are probably familiar with .LIN, .PAT, .CTB, and .STB files. These Autodesk files have set the stage for standards worldwide for over 25 years. People bought AutoCAD and went right to work using the standards the software offered right out of the box.

Why did the standard from Autodesk become the *standard* for users? Simple! Because it was hard to create standards yourself and even harder to manage them. If you had the skill to develop your own custom files, you then owned the responsibility to manage them; in the AutoCAD world, those file types contain the standard. See the following list for an explanation of AutoCAD standard "containers":

ACAD.LIN   In this file you define line patterns (dot, space, dash, and letters) then load them into a given DWG file to be assigned to objects and/or layers.

ACAD.PAT   This file is where hatch patterns (a regular sequence of pen strokes) are defined and then read when used within a given .DWG.

ACAD.CTB   You define color to pen weight here. The file is used only at print or plot time.

ACAD.STB   This file is where you define pen weight names; your .DWG then references these names via layer or object overrides.

Seems like a good way to do it? It is, as long as your standards are what Autodesk suggested. But what if you don't like their standards?

◆   If you create new line types or hatch patterns, you then have to provide the .LIN/.PAT file to everyone who will need to use it for new .DWG files. You can put your custom line patterns in the ACAD.LIN or ACAD.PAT or a new .LIN/.PAT file. You have to be sure to tell people where the .LIN/.PAT file is stored and to archive it with the drawings.

◆   If you customize a .CTB/.STB file, you also need to store that file on the network so that the team has access to it when they plot. Be sure to back up your files — if you lose them, you will not be able to plot properly. And make them read-only so that changes won't happen behind your back.

The joy of Revit Structure is that all four of these standard containers are now in your model directly. Don't like a line type? Change it or make a new one and apply it. Want a heavy pen? Assign it where you want. Need a tighter pattern? Make it on the fly and use it right then. Not customizing Revit Structure is almost a crime — it is that easy. So don't just copy your AutoCAD standards; improve them and make them even better! And again, the great thing about Revit Structure is that your customization is contained in the model, so that anywhere your model goes, your standards go along for the ride.

Now that you understand where historically standards have been managed and customized, it is time to learn how to begin to customize standards in Revit Structure.

Planning Your Standards

It is wise to have a plan of attack before you begin. When it comes to standards, you need to know where you want to go and then build the road to get there. In Revit Structure the first step is to determine the line weights you will use for your model. In the following sections you will assign these weights accordingly.

DEFINING LINE WEIGHTS

Revit Structure has 16 "pen slots" you can define and use. In early versions of AutoCAD, you had 16 pen options, so to some, this will be familiar. As shown in Figure 17.1, the pens are simply numbered 1 through 16. The Model Line Weights tab lets you assign weights for model objects in orthogonal views such as plans and elevations.

FIGURE 17.1
The Model Line Weights
tab of the Line Weights
dialog box

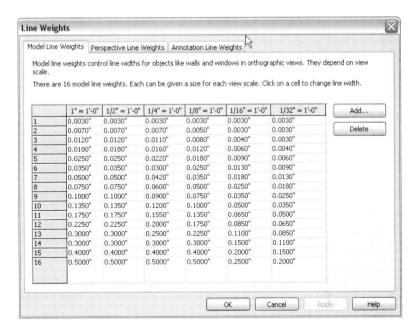

Now as you look at this dialog box, it may seem a little expansive with all the various scales. Don't let this deter you — all the various scales are not important, and you really don't need them. The scales listed provide a means of controlling differing scales. But if your standards are like most, you will apply the same pen sizes to every scale option. An exception, however, can be made for certain types of plan work. Imagine you have a $\frac{1}{8}'' = 1'\text{-}0''$ steel framing plan with a fairly heavy pen for the steel beams. Using a line weight scale control for $\frac{1}{8}'' = 1'\text{-}0''$, you can make the heavy pen number thinner, perhaps 50 percent thinner, thus enabling your $\frac{1}{16}''$ plan to truly look half-size.

The default setup provided in Revit Structure has a series of sizes ranging from 0.003″ to 0.5″. It is uncommon, to say the least, to see a $\frac{1}{2}''$ wide line; that would use up a lot of ink or toner. This should be your first clue that perhaps Autodesk isn't the proper source of your standards. So what should you use? What you want, of course, but here are some baseline schemes.

If you have had manual drafting training, you will recall technical pens. Those ink-filled devices for drawing crisp, black lines on vellum or Mylar did very well back then, and their sizes can still be used today. A popular brand manufactured by Koh-I-Noor offered pens ranging from 0.13mm to 2mm wide. The goal of any line weight change is to offer a visual clue that something is to be seen more important or less important than something else. By proper assignment you can visually *layer* objects in your drawings, drawing attention to important elements and fading elements that are needed visually but don't have to stand out.

In the construction industry, the most basic drawing is a $\frac{1}{8}''$ scale plan, so we can use that as a starting point in our setup. As an added control, you assign a size 0.025mm to pen 1. With Revit Structure, everything has a pen assignment. And with most model object defaults, Projection is set to pen 1 and Cut is often set to pen 2. By assigning pen 1 the value 0.025mm, the absolute thinnest line a modern printer/plotter can produce with Revit Structure will be used. You will then make things thicker as required for your documentation. As shown in Table 17.1, there are many very real pens you can use within Revit Structure. Note that 0.45mm is a valid size but is not manufactured by Koh-I-Noor; however, it is available from other manufacturers.

TABLE 17.1:　　Pen Weights

PEN SLOT	SIZE
1	0.025mm
2	0.13mm
3	0.18mm
4	0.25mm
5	0.30mm
6	0.35mm
7	0.45mm
8	0.50mm
9	0.60mm
10	0.70mm
11	0.80mm
12	1.00mm
13	1.20mm
14	1.40mm
15	2.00mm
16	0.025mm

I use millimeter (mm) values here (rather than inches) because I am a purist. Back in the day, technical pens used mm values, and to maintain precision, I do so as well. But it doesn't matter that much whether you assign 0.13mm, 0.051″, or 0.05″ — only someone with a super laser printer and a microscope could tell the difference. It should be noted that once set, this value will be pretty static and should not change often. So why not be precise?

As for pen 16, it isn't needed for most work, but you could think of it as your "super-thin pen" just in case it prints. You can use that pen slot as a flag of sorts for tracking changes you will make later.

EXERCISE: DEFINING LINE WEIGHTS

This exercise examines the process for filling out the Line Weights dialog box and making adjustments to various scales. Start with a new project based on the default Imperial template:

1. Under the Manage tab, choose the Settings drop-down and click the Line Weights command.

2. Select the first column on the Model Line Weights tab and then click the Delete button.

3. Repeat for all scale columns except $\frac{1}{8}'' = 1'\text{-}0''$.

4. Fill in all sizes, as shown in Table 17.1.

5. Click the Add button and create a new scale for $\frac{1}{16}''$. Notice how the scale adopts the sizes from the only existing column.

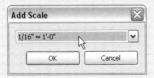

6. Adjust each pen width for the $\frac{1}{32}'' = 1'\text{-}0''$ scale to be a half value. Just take the normal size and divide it in half for every pen slot for $\frac{1}{32}''$ scale.

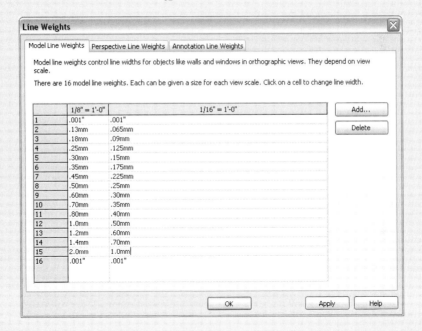

7. Click OK to close the Line Weights dialog box.

WHICH PENS ARE USED FOR UNDEFINED SCALES?

If the drawing scale you're using does not have a corresponding scale in the Pen Weights dialog box, Revit Structure will use the closest, or if evenly split between two, the larger scale. For example, if pen 1 for $\frac{1}{8}''$ is 0.25mm and pen 1 for $\frac{1}{32}''$ is 0.13mm, if a $\frac{1}{16}''$ scale plan is developed, it will use the sizes from the $\frac{1}{8}''$ scale.

Using this knowledge, you can avoid having to assign pen weights for all scales simply so that they follow your standards. If you want all drawings to use the same pen sets, create one scale, and every view at every scale will use it.

As shown earlier in the Line Weights dialog box, you have defined two scales for your model objects. Objects shown in $\frac{1}{8}''$ or smaller will use the $\frac{1}{8}'' = 1'\text{-}0''$ pens, and those objects shown at $\frac{1}{16}''$ or larger will use the $\frac{1}{16}'' = 1'\text{-}0''$ pens. With this technique, you can have consistent quality while also getting control of conditions with small scale factors.

Defining Line Patterns

Often referred to as a line type, Revit Structure *line patterns* are a defined series of dots, spaces, and lines that can convey a purpose. Whereas line weight in an object will indicate importance, a line pattern will help paper-document readers know what they are looking at. A good example of this is a concrete beam below a slab. The lines for beams below slabs are typically drawn in a hidden line type indicating that the beam is, in fact, below.

Users of AutoCAD will access and develop new line types via a `.LIN` file. This then will be read into an active `.DWG` to permit use of the line type. If you need to modify an actively used line type in AutoCAD, you first have to change the `.LIN` code (A, .75, -.125, .125, -.125, for example) in the `.LIN` file, save, and then reload the file. If you create a custom pattern and then lose the `.LIN` file, you are out of luck. There is no way to re-create the `.LIN` from the definition stored in a `.DWG`. It is precisely this tedious work that has forced the architecture, engineering, and construction (AEC) industry to adopt the standard put forth by Autodesk.

Where Did Revit Structure Come From?

Autodesk did not invent Revit. In fact, other than purchasing the company and then spinning off Revit Structure and setting release cycles, Autodesk has done well to stay out of the way and let the people who created it keep the program moving in a positive direction.

But it is this "separation" that causes some discontinuity. In nearly all cases, you will be using Auto-CAD alongside or to support Revit Structure. For example, in Revit Structure the default pattern for gridlines is Grid Line $\frac{1}{4}''$. AutoCAD, on the other hand, doesn't have gridlines. Rather, it has line types that look like a gridline (or something else defined by you) but interestingly enough, CENTER, CEN-TER2, and CENTER2X (in AutoCAD) do not have the same settings as Grid Line $\frac{1}{4}''$ (in Revit). This is what nearly everyone using AutoCAD has been using for over 20 years. What will you do?

Revit Structure users have the option to use the standard provided in the software or develop what they want much easier than in AutoCAD. It is impossible to match AutoCAD immediately when you open Revit Structure; you must customize your template to get an identical line style appearance. But I think you should do what you like and what you think looks good rather than simply adopting a graphic standard that goes back 25 years.

To develop standards, look back at old hand-drawn plans, sections, and elevations to see what the *hand* would typically do. You will notice that hand-drawn lines tended to be more continuous and unbroken than what typical CAD systems display. Knowing why is subjective, of course, but if you think about it, that was probably done for two reasons. First, it took more effort to lift and drop the pencil/pen when creating long lines. But also the drafter often kept the line breaks away from important intersections. For example, the gridline pattern would be continuous at column locations. The dashes would be placed between grid intersections instead. With Revit Structure a 30′-0″ bay will have eight line breaks, using Grid Line $\frac{1}{4}$″, at $\frac{1}{8}$″ scale. Back on the board (hand drafting), this same distance would instead have no more than three breaks, besides being drawn with a very thin pen.

PROTECTING CUSTOM STANDARDS

You might think about redefining patterns or other default settings in Revit Structure. We recommend that you stay away from this practice. It is easy to create new definitions and just as easy to overwrite them. You could spend time redefining Grid Line $\frac{1}{4}$″, and then later you load in standards from a client or default template file. All your settings can be reset with no way to re-create them easily.

We recommend that you develop a naming protocol to provide a level of safety for your custom styles, patterns, families, and so forth. For example, you could use a # sign as a prefix in front of anything new you create. Not only is it unique (it's not used by Revit Structure), but also it will be shown first due to alphabetic listings. Use this or another character or company initials, but you certainly should not just redefine any out-of-the-box standards.

So the first step to improve your Revit Structure standards is to define a new, longer pattern for gridlines to use and then apply it.

EXERCISE: CREATING A NEW LINE PATTERN

This exercise shows the steps to create a new line pattern and then assign it to Grid Line objects. Start with a new model based on the default Imperial template:

1. Click the Manage tab on the Ribbon. Then on the Project Settings panel expand the Settings button and choose Line Patterns. This will display the Line Patterns dialog box, as shown here:

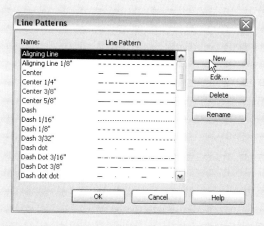

2. Click New to display the Line Pattern Properties dialog box.

3. Type **#Grid Line** as the name, and then use the values shown in the following graphic for the various fields. Click OK to close the dialog box.

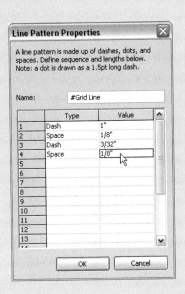

4. Click OK to close the Line Patterns dialog box.

5. If not displayed already, switch to any $\frac{1}{8}''$ scale plan view.

6. Using the Home tab, click the Grid button in the Datum panel, and create a vertical grid in the center of the drawing area.

7. Select that grid and then copy it to the right $15'-0''$.

8. With the new grid selected expand the Element Properties button, and click the Type Properties button on the list. This will display the Type Properties dialog box.

9. Click the Duplicate button. Name the new grid type **#Grid Bubble** and click OK.

10. Once you're back in the Type Properties dialog box, select the End Segment Pattern parameter box, scroll to the top of the list, and choose #Grid Line. The new #Grid Bubble type is now assigned to use the new #Grid Line pattern.

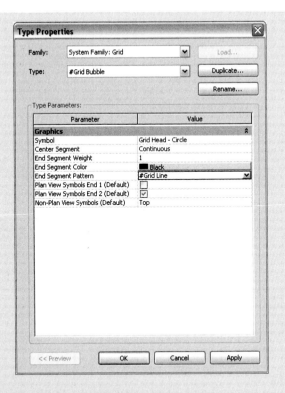

11. Click OK to close the Type Properties dialog box.

The following illustration is a comparison of the out-of-the-box grid and a new custom grid type; grid 2 now has a much-less-busy line pattern. It is less likely to be misinterpreted as something else, and some find that it's more pleasing to the eye. Also, when placed closely to a hidden line, the grid pattern will not "compete for attention" with the hidden line. Again, this can aid recognition and interpretation.

If you can keep in mind how your models (drawings) look and work to keep them clear, you will make your future drawing reader much happier. It takes a conscientious effort to keep those readers in mind. Remember they don't have a computer display that they can zoom in with to see something more clearly. Developing your standards is a twofold process — creating the style and then applying it.

CONTROLLING OBJECT LINE PATTERNS

Revit Structure elements, like columns and beams, are managed in much different ways than grid-type objects. Access to the multitudes of model objects is done via the Visibility/Graphic Overrides and Object Styles dialog boxes. If you want to set how the entire model is displayed, you use object styles. If you want to change only a single view, you use visibility/graphic overrides. In general, try to get the model itself looking right for the majority of views and then, if needed, tweak specific views.

Our first step is to learn what we have to start with. We will create a new model and then make some basic objects: a set of intersecting grids, a concrete slab with supporting beams, and a column below and one being cut by the view range. As shown in Figure 17.2, this doesn't exactly pop visually.

FIGURE 17.2
The basic objects for concrete models and their default line weights and patterns

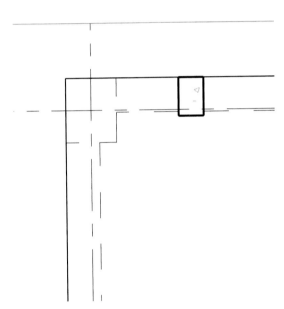

Next, we will adjust your pen weights as described earlier in this chapter. The linework will begin to change thickness — but may not be for the better. That's because we have yet to tell the objects what weights to use!

Then we can create new line patterns for gridlines and hidden line patterns for beams and columns below the slab. Finally, we fire up the Object Styles dialog box and begin to adjust the line weight and line pattern assignments. Once complete, the grids, columns, and beams all should look different and ideally better.

TRACKING YOUR CHANGES

If you recall from earlier in this chapter, pen 16 will plot super thin, and since no default Revit Structure setting uses pen 16, you can easily see what has not yet changed as you work to adjust your standard requirements.

EXERCISE: ASSIGNING NEW LINE WEIGHTS AND PATTERNS

This exercise walks you through the steps to assign line weights and line patterns. Use the book's companion web page at www.sybex.com/go/masteringrevitstructure2010, look in the Part 5 zip for Chapter 17 files, and open Line Weights.RVT. This model has the proper line weights defined as well, containing several line patterns for concrete objects.

1. Activate the Manage tab on the Ribbon, and within the Project Settings panel, expand the Settings drop-down and click the Objects Styles command to display the Object Styles dialog box.

2. On the Model Objects tab, expand by clicking the [+] icons in front of all Revit Structure categories. You will need to use the scroll bar to see and expand all categories.

3. Click the Select All button. Then use any Projection column slot and change the value to **16**. Repeat for the Cut column, and change all Cut values to **16**.

4. Click OK to close the Object Styles dialog box. This will collapse all the categories. Then reopen the Object Styles dialog box.

5. Select the Floors Projection cell and change it to pen **6** (0.35mm).

6. Select the Floors Cut cell and change it to pen **8** (0.50mm).

7. Select the Structural Columns Projection cell, change it to pen **6** (0.35mm), and change the Cut cell to pen **8** (0.50mm).

8. Now expand the Structural Columns category. Change the Hidden Lines Projection cell to pen **6** (0.35mm). Change the Hidden Lines Line Pattern from Hidden $\frac{3}{32}''$ to **#CIP Column Below**.

9. Scroll down to the Structural Framing category and change the Projection cell to pen **6** and Cut to pen **8**. Expand the category and change the Hidden Lines Projection cell to pen **6** (0.35mm). Finally, change the Hidden Lines Line Pattern cell from Dash to **#CIP Framing Below**.

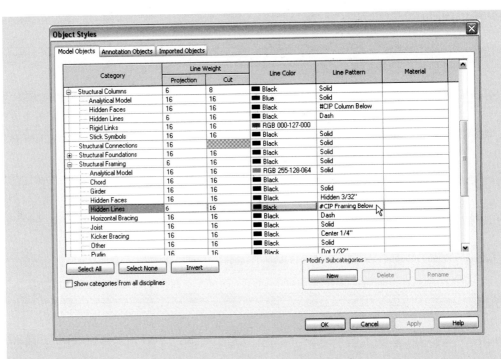

10. Click OK to close the Object Styles dialog box. Your model should now match the following illustration.

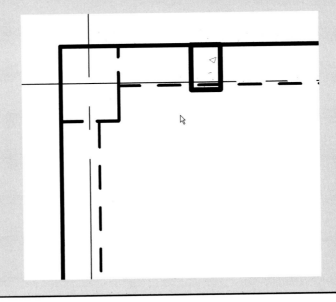

You've made only the beginning steps to control your standards as you see fit. Every cell with pen 16 is a potential location to customize weight. Every Line Pattern cell that isn't set to Solid is a candidate for customization. But take note that sometimes for any given view, an object's hidden lines may be managed via the Hidden Faces category rather than the Hidden Lines category.

It will take some work to fully customize your modeling styles. The key to success is to tackle your model objects one at a time. Some users have gone so far as to set all pen slots to 16 and change all colors to something bold and easy to see, like hot pink. Then they proceed to reset hot pink to black, item by item, from within a model that has all model objects in it. Eventually when they don't see any hot pink model objects, they know they have addressed all projection/cut issues for the objects they placed while they were incorporating their line weight and line pattern standards.

Most of the work in Revit Structure is line work of some sort. Strokes of the pen can convey a great deal of information. But undoubtedly great line work will not do for all. Eventually you will need to provide something that can be read.

Developing Annotation Standards

Another class of objects in Revit Structure is *annotation objects*. These are elements that present themselves in only one form for any view; they don't have a cut style and they tend to scale with the active view scale. Tags, level heads, and sections are all annotation objects.

Getting your annotation standards in place isn't as difficult as developing standards for model objects, so temporarily changing the line weight for all projects will reap little reward for the effort. Also, most annotation objects categories are just text, and all text in Revit Structure uses Windows True Type fonts (TTF). A TTF contains the full letter stroke in it, so line weight will have little impact. Therefore, making them any weight from pen 1 to pen 16 will be impossible to notice onscreen.

However, there are things worth customizing. For example, callouts have a boundary box that usually should be a medium line weight as well as unique line pattern. Also, you may prefer that grid heads have a heavier weight for the circle, and there are other examples.

EXERCISE: ASSIGNING ANNOTATION PEN WEIGHTS AND PATTERNS

This exercise quickly runs through the steps to control pen weights and line patterns for annotation objects. Open Chapter 17's Annotation.RVT file (from the book's companion web page). This model picks up where the previous exercise ended, but a callout has been placed around the column.

1. Activate the Manage tab, and click Settings ➢ Line Patterns to display the Line Patterns dialog box.

2. Click the New button and name the new pattern **#Callout**.

3. Create a Dash type at $\frac{1}{2}''$ value and then a Space type at $\frac{3}{8}''$ value. Click OK to close the Line Pattern Properties dialog box.

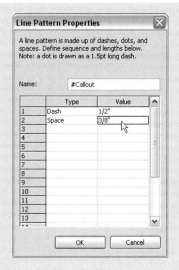

4. Click OK to close the Line Patterns dialog box.

5. Choose Settings ➢ Object Styles to display the Object Styles dialog box.

6. Select the Annotation Objects tab.

7. Expand the Callout Boundary category. Change the Projection line weight to pen **5**. Change the Callout Boundary Line Pattern from Dash Dot $\frac{3}{16}''$ to **#Callout**.

8. Change the Callout Leader Line to pen **5** and also change the Callout Heads category to pen **5**.

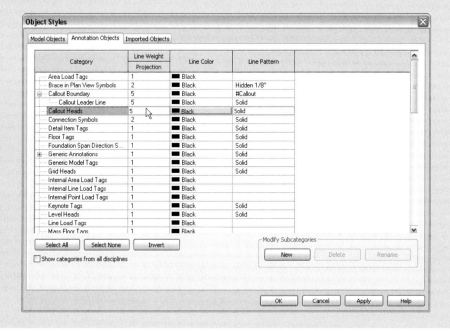

9. Now change the Grid Heads Projection to pen **5**.

10. Scroll down to Section Line and Section Marks and make both slots pen **5**. Click OK to close the Object Styles dialog box. As shown here, the section and callout symbols are now heavier and stand out clearly.

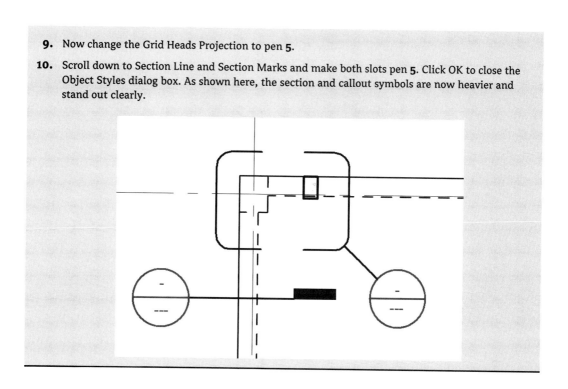

Obviously this should not be the end to changes to your standards, but you should have a better idea of the connection between the various controls at your disposal. First you define line weights, then define line patterns, and then assign the pair to your object styles so that you get the desired results. This combined pair, known as a *line style*, is covered in the following section.

Applying Line Styles

Once you have developed your line weights and patterns, you will probably want to use them for non-objects as well, such as drafting lines and detail components. This is done in Revit Structure through the creation and application of line styles. A line style is essentially a set of style controls saved into a single style that can then be applied to numerous objects later.

After you have defined your line styles, you will be able to use them not only to draw basic line geometry but also to override an object's native appearance as the need arises. Creating line styles is fairly simple; a line style consists of a weight, a pattern, and a color. Refer to Figure 17.3 for the styles provided with the `Structural Analysis-default.RTE` file.

Now just as before, you would be wise to keep your standards away from default styles so that they can be protected from being overwritten, but also so that you can keep track of how your standards are organized. For example, there is a default line style named Medium Lines, and it has pen 3 as a weight. However, there is also a generic annotation style named Medium Lines, and it has pen 4 as a weight. These are not the same thing, so this not a problem — technically. But the possibility for confusion is high — unless your customized style is unique and you follow that naming convention across the board. A good policy is to leave everything in place and simply add your customization to a new template and then build on this as needed. If desired, you can purge extraneous styles as permitted by the program.

FIGURE 17.3
Revit Structure default template line styles

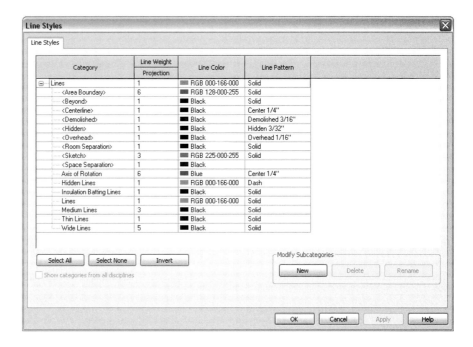

EXERCISE: CREATING MODEL OBJECT–DERIVED LINE STYLES

This exercise will step through making line styles based on model object standards. Open the Chapter 17 Line Styles.RVT file (from the book's companion web page). This model picks up where the previous exercise ended. Our goal is to create a few styles for conditions when the model must be "faked."

1. From the Manage tab, choose Settings ➤ Line Styles to display the Line Styles dialog box.

2. At the lower right, click the New button.

3. In the New Subcategory dialog box, type **#CIP Column Below** and click OK.

4. Locate the new #CIP Column Below line style and change the Projection slot line weight to pen **6**. This is the same size used in the earlier exercises for the concrete column line weight in hidden line projections.

5. Change the Line Pattern setting to #CIP Column Below and click OK to close the dialog box.

Category	Line Weight Projection	Line Color	Line Pattern	
⊟ Lines	1	RGB 000-166-000	Solid	
#CIP Column Below	6	Black	#CIP Column Below ☑	
<Area Boundary>	6	RGB 128-000-255	Solid	
<Beyond>	1	Black	#Callout	
<Centerline>	1	Black	#CIP Column Below	
<Demolished>	1	Black	#CIP Framing Below	
<Hidden>	1	Black	#Grid Line	
<Overhead>	1	Black	Aligning Line	
<Room Separation>	1	Black	Aligning Line 1/8"	
<Sketch>	3	RGB 225-000-255	Solid	
<Space Separation>	1	Black		
Axis of Rotation	6	Blue	Center 1/4"	
Hidden Lines	1	RGB 000-166-000	Dash	
Insulation Batting Lines	1	Black	Solid	
Lines	1	RGB 000-166-000	Solid	
Medium Lines	3	Black	Solid	
Thin Lines	1	Black	Solid	
Wide Lines	5	Black	Solid	

Now that you have a style, you can apply it in two primary ways. One is to draw "dumb" lines when and where required. Perhaps you just had a bunch of changes come in, and there isn't enough time to fully model them.

1. On the Annotate tab of the Ribbon, click the Detail Line button on the Detail panel.

2. Using the Type Selector on the Element panel, select #CIP Column Below. Choose the Rectangle button from the Draw panel.

3. Move into the drawing area, to the lower right of the real column below the slab. Create a 24″ x 30″ box shape to match the size of the real concrete column.

Understand that this is poor modeling practice. However, it very well may save the day, and you will go back later and model properly, right? The tool is there for a reason: to aid you in your work. With this tool, you can mimic your concrete columns below slabs. Creating other line styles that match your object style standards will also permit 2D DWG conversion into the Revit Structure "look and feel." Perhaps you are renovating an old AutoCAD-based project; with this procedure, you can import the drawing data and then reassign line work to your current documentation standards for a seamless 2D/3D presentation.

Finally, perhaps you have modeled in 3D but for whatever reason the object style being presented isn't accurate. You can use your line styles to "paint" model objects. Imagine for a moment that the vertical concrete beam on the Level 2 plan view at the last minute was changed to a concrete wall below a slab:

1. Using the Modify tab, click the Linework button on the Edit Linework panel.

2. Change the Type Selector to #CIP Column Below, and then select the right edge of the vertical concrete beam.

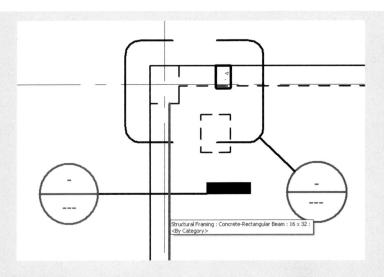

Structural Framing : Concrete-Rectangular Beam : 16 x 32 : <By Category>

Notice that the line pattern changed to match the columns below. This beam now has the appearance of a column as demanded by a project change but without the hassle of remodeling just before the deadline. Again, this is *not* the best thing to do as a normal practice but it can be handy. If you end up needing to reset an object, use the Linework <By Category> style. This will clear any *painting* you may have done. Taking the time to develop line styles that match your modeling line work will not only provide you with a means to clean up problems but also provide a means to draw in 2D just as you model in 3D.

Not everything in proper documentation is line work. Another valuable technique is to use hatching, otherwise known as fill patterns and filled regions.

Employing Patterns and Filled Regions to Indicate Material

Known in the AutoCAD world as *hatch*, filled regions in Revit Structure enable you to provide tone to your drawings. This tone conveys that a simple box is made of steel, concrete, precast, masonry, or some other material. AutoCAD has had a healthy selection of hatch patterns for years, and Revit Structure can leverage them — and more. Not only can you bring in your favorite AutoCAD hatch patterns, but you can also set up patterns for your model that can be used over and over again without keeping track of scale and rotation. In AutoCAD you must determine the scale of the pattern, its rotation, and its layer every time you place a hatch pattern on your drawings. In Revit Structure, those questions are answered when the fill pattern is defined; you decide the scale, rotation, line weight, opaqueness, and color (if needed).

An added perk with Revit Structure filled regions is the inclusion of the boundary in the filled region itself, along with a line style control for the boundary line work. And since filled regions have a type property, also known as a style, if for some reason you want to globally change a given filled region pattern, you can do so and the entire model file will update with the changes.

You can place filled regions in any model view except 3D, and you can place them into legends. A great use is for plan notes and legends on sheets. You also have patterns that are also printed 1:1, known as drafting fill patterns. You also have model fill patterns, which are used to represent real model objects such as tile and masonry stacking.

To define a new pattern or adjust an existing pattern, activate the Manage tab and choose Settings ➢ Fill Patterns. This displays the Fill Patterns dialog box, shown in Figure 17.4.

FIGURE 17.4
Use the Fill Patterns dialog box to define your project hatch styles.

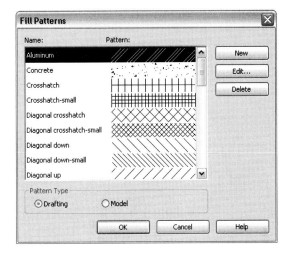

Let's say, for example, you want a honeycomb-style hatch you used before in AutoCAD. That doesn't exist natively in Revit Structure, but you still have your ACAD.PAT file available. Open the Fill Patterns dialog box and click the New button. This will display the New Pattern dialog box. Here you can create a basic line-based pattern or, as in this case, read an existing .PAT file for a pattern. At this point, click the Custom radio button. The dialog box changes to a custom import format, allowing you to browse to a .PAT file (see Figure 17.5).

FIGURE 17.5
Browsing to a .PAT file

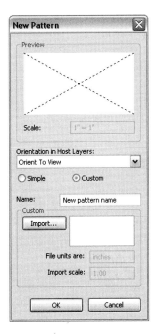

Now, click the Import button to open the Import Fill Pattern dialog box, where you can hunt down your AutoCAD-installed ACAD.PAT file. Normally this is stored in the AutoCAD\support directory — find yours by typing (findfile "acad.pat") at the AutoCAD command line and pressing Enter.

If AutoCAD can locate the file, it will return the directory location. Once you have found your .PAT file, Revit Structure will list all included patterns in the Custom list panel. Next, assign the name **Styrofoam** and then decide if you want the same 1:1 scale as in AutoCAD. In this case, the hatch scale in AutoCAD is set to one-half the old AutoCAD scale value. Revit Structure doesn't have a DIMSCALE or a scaling problem, so here you can use 0.5 to make the pattern half the size as the 1:1 scale in AutoCAD. Finally, if this pattern was going to be used for something like a wall, then you would adjust the Orientation in Host Layers setting to Align with Element. In Revit Structure your patterns can rotate with any object that uses a pattern. At this stage you are finished, as shown in Figure 17.6.

FIGURE 17.6
You've created the Styrofoam fill pattern.

Now that your pattern for Styrofoam is created, you can add it to a new 1:1 Legend view. Once within the view, use the Annotate tab and select the Filled Region button from the Detail panel. The Ribbon will change to the Create Filled Region Boundary tab. This Ribbon contains all sketch-related functions and controls. Zoom in a bit and use the Draw panel Rectangle tool to create a 1×1 box. Then click the Region Properties button on the Element panel, which displays the Instance Properties dialog box for filled regions. Since you still need to create your filled region style, click the Edit Type button; then in the Type Properties dialog box, click the Duplicate button and set the name to **Styrofoam**. Click OK. The dialog box closes and changes the active type appropriately. Next, change the fill pattern to match. You can either use the ellipsis ([...]) button to browse for the fill pattern, or, since you know the name, you can type **Styrofoam [Drafting]** and Revit Structure will assign it. Then decide whether you want your Styrofoam pattern to always hide other content by using an opaque background or let it overlay with other line work (choose Transparent). If you never want any line work to show through the region, leave this setting as Opaque (see Figure 17.7).

FIGURE 17.7
The Styrofoam Filled
Region Type properties

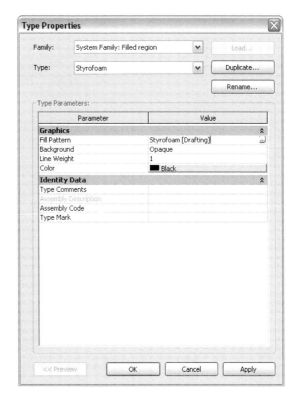

Once you have finished adjusting the Filled Region Type properties, click OK a few times to close all dialog boxes. Back in the drawing area, your rectangle is already done (see Figure 17.8). If warranted, you could change the rectangle line work by selecting the lines and then choosing another type from the Type Selector. In this case you may want the Thin Lines border. Simply click the Finish Region button on the Region panel. Then instantly your box is filled with the honeycomb pattern you defined earlier, and it is automatically a tighter pattern, matching your standards.

FIGURE 17.8
A Styrofoam hatch made
using a filled region

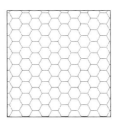

ADJUSTING CONTENT

After you have defined your line weights, line styles, and filled regions, you can then use them on your typical details or other types of families, such as annotation symbols. You have put all this work into your standards, and these features will be applied to any new content in your model. But unless you inject them into your various family files, those nonstandard elements will propagate into your model as you bring them in.

In some cases, depending on the file type, you can use Manage tab ➤ Transfer Project Standards button to bring your standards model into your family file. Another option is to copy/paste from one into another. Once your family file has the styles within it, you can select existing objects such as lines and use the Type Selector to switch them to your standard styles. When you have finished, click the Purge Unused button on the Manage tab to rid the file of the now-unused styles.

This can be a tedious task, but it is necessary if you are to create and use a truly seamless single set of standards. Keep records of the files you change, or use a separate file structure for your customized files, because new builds and new versions of Revit Structure families come out often and you don't want to overwrite your work accidentally.

Customizing Revit Structure to Save Time and Effort

Once your project models can create drawings that look good, then it is time to make Revit Structure easier to use! Although you're not making a visual that you can show off to your superiors, a few deft moves of your fingers on a couple of mission-critical Revit Structure support files can free up tons of time later on. Hopefully this free time then can be spent on more customization or learning a seldom-used feature of the program.

In this section we will explore enhancements that can be utilized to improve Revit Structure and your use of it. There is an `.INI` file where you can tweak Revit Structure to make it more user friendly. You can also empower Revit Structure by adding access to your own custom family files, but do it smart if you do. Also, you can customize tool shortcuts to speed your work with the software.

Editing the *Revit.INI* File

The `Revit.INI` file is where Revit presets library folders, obtained during installation or a network installation image. This file contains mostly code that you are better off adjusting via the Revit Structure application menu (the big R) button, via the Options button at the bottom of the screen. However, there are a few gems you can have only by manually editing the `Revit.INI` file.

First determine where your `Revit.INI` file is stored, which is no easy task in today's myriad of operating systems. The simplest method is to check out the properties of any Revit Structure 2010 shortcut link on your desktop or in your Start menu. The file will be in the same location as the `Revit.EXE` file. Please note that you should not make changes to the `Revit.INI` file while Revit is open.

Once you find the `Revit.INI` file, it is recommended that you make a backup copy. Once that is done, open `Revit.INI` for editing with Notepad. Now you are ready for the gems!

ENLARGING THE FONT IN TEMPORARY DIMENSION VALUES

No doubt you have noticed how Revit Structure will create many temporary albeit small dimensions as you draw or edit objects. The problem is that this text is somewhat small (8 point) and often can be placed poorly by the software. If you find yourself struggling to read these items, then take advantage of a tweak to make the text size bigger onscreen. Edit your `Revit.INI` file and look for a [Graphics] section. If it doesn't exist, then create it at the bottom of all the content. On the line following [Graphics], type **TempDimFontSizeInPoints=XX** where **XX** is a value normally larger than 8. A good start point is 14, 15, or 16. As you can see in Figure 17.9, the little helpful text is quite a bit bigger now.

FIGURE 17.9
New, easier-to-see temporary dimensions

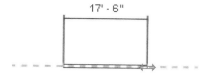

As for the font itself, it is very similar to Arial but isn't Arial. In fact, it isn't any normal font on your computer and does not ship with the operating system as Arial and others do. The font characters are defined by a font embedded in the software and cannot be changed.

RESETTING YOUR RECENT LIST

After using Revit for a day or so, hopefully your Recent Files area will be populated with your recent activities. Although this list may be handy, it may become bothersome to see all those entries every time you start Revit. What can you do? You can hack the `Revit.INI` file! Somewhere in your file, probably near the bottom, will be a running list of the last eight files you have accessed. This is helpful when working on one project, but imagine if you are working on several projects, but your file-naming convention isn't unique to each project!

This happens more often for families because they usually have similar names but can be customized per project. The problem is that you get only the filename in the list, which makes it easy to pick the wrong file since the folder could be different. Now it should be noted that if you hover over a recent file entry, Revit will provide a tooltip with the full folder path to the file. But that is a tedious method to use.

To fix this is simple; open the `Revit.INI` file and in the `[Recent File List]` area simply remove whatever filenames you don't want. You needn't bother with renumbering the ones you leave behind.

If you enjoy this tip, then put a shortcut on your desktop to your `Revit.INI` file. Then whenever you want to reset your list, open it up and make the change.

As you can see in Figure 17.10, you can find recently used files within the Application menu.

AVOIDING PRESS AND DRAG MISTAKES

One final helpful `Revit.INI` edit is a control to set the default status of the Press & Drag feature in Revit Structure. This selection method allows you to select a group of objects with no command active and then, by clicking a point in the drawing area, move them en masse to a new location.

If this seems like a non-issue, then you are not a new user to Revit Structure! More often than not, new users will inadvertently grab objects and move them and in some cases fail to notice. By turning this feature off at the right end of the status bar, as shown in Figure 17.11, you can protect your model from these sorts of mistakes.

FIGURE 17.10
The new Revit Structure 2010 Recent File list shown on the Application menu

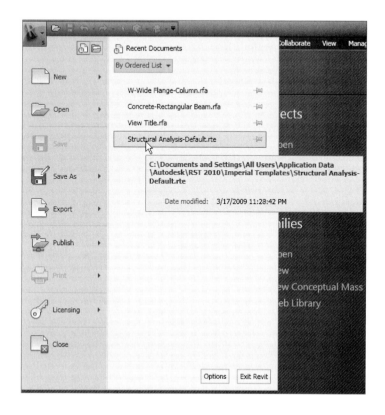

FIGURE 17.11
Turn off Press & Drag for new users.

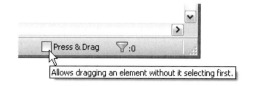

So why do the Revit.INI file edit? Revit Structure by default has the feature set to on, or (1). Do you think you can tell your new users and they will remember to shut this off? Probably not, so edit their Revit.INI file before they start and fix this code in their file:

```
[Selection]
AllowPressAndDrag=0
```

When Revit Structure fires up, the Press & Drag toggle will be off, thus protecting your user from making press and drag mistakes. Now if they turn the check box on, well, it is on then. Education is key.

Customizing Library Paths

You are probably aware of this already, but customizing library paths not only helps to implement standards but also, with proper organization, aids in your management activities. The key is understanding why it is important and then getting consensus on how to organize. Nothing is more frustrating than not being able to find a family you need in order to keep modeling. As you can see in Figure 17.12, the default installation will place all of your library and related family files on your local drive.

FIGURE 17.12
The default installation paths for library files found on the File Locations tab of the Options dialog box and the related Places dialog box

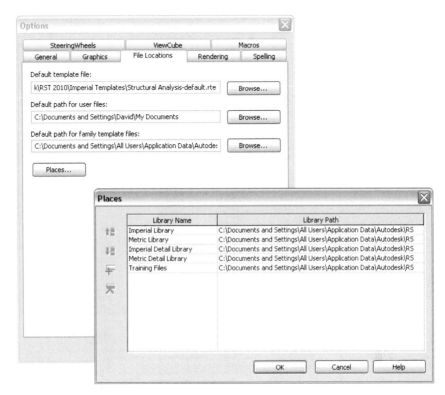

The first step is to develop a plan to share your library files across your network. Typically this involves assigning a directory location on your local server where every user has the same drive letters pointed to the same server share. For example, `\\server\software` could be mapped to each network user as the `S:` drive. Then on the server you would place the Revit Structure library files as they exist normally on the local C: drive.

So at this point you have `S:\Autodesk Revit Structure 2010\Imperial Library`; you then would have all your fellow Revit Structure users modify their Places dialog box to match the new server locations. Once this process is complete, you and your entire team will share the same set of templates and family files and have a new home in which to put custom files.

MAINTAINING YOUR LIBRARY

All is good in your world, running smoothly, and then after a little time passes you get word about a new build of Revit Structure. As a new and growing industry, Autodesk and the Revit Structure development team are always working on the next release of the program. But sometimes a bug is found, or a fix made, and Autodesk issues a patch to the software. At the same time, they may or may not include new and/or revised family files.

So you install the new build or version and then go to copy the new library files over your existing server located files. But you pause and wonder, what changed? Anything? Everything? What if the name of your own custom family file is now used by Autodesk for a similar family they created? If you copy it over, it will wipe out yours. Did you edit the wide flange catalog file to change the X to an x? That will be replaced as well.

Did you write a diary of all the changes you made 3–4 months ago when you rolled out the then-new release? Move with caution unless you like starting over. Okay then, what can be done to avert disaster in the future?

Creating Your Directories

The recommended method is to create your own library structure and from within each directory create a shortcut to the default files. We also recommend pointing all users to your library structure within their Places dialog box. If you take the time to customize the Steel Column family, then you probably want people using it before the out-of-the-box families.

For your family files, you assign a unique naming convention to all custom or revised family files. As shown earlier, we used a # prefix for all files created or changed.

If you are modeling and select a family-based object in the model without a # prefix, then you know you didn't modify it. If by chance you see the same family name with a # prefix, then you *know* you need to use that one instead. As an added benefit, family files prefixed with a # sign will be listed at the top of their section in the Project Browser and Type Selector.

When you name all family library directories with a # prefix, that tells all users that this directory is the company default structure. All family files and directories are stored on the server already, so it is easy to share.

Creating Shortcuts

The out-of-the-box content is not under the default directories users place in their Options File Search paths. Instead, placing shortcut links in your directories, such as `..\#Column\#Concrete`, would help isolate and organize any customized RFA files and a shortcut prefixed with a ! to the normal out-of-the-box location `..\Column\Concrete`. As a user, when you go to load a concrete column family, you would see #Family folders and a link to the default file location. You can then decide if you need the company standard or want the original files, in which case a single directory click will get you there.

WHY THE !?

Why place an exclamation point (!) in the shortcut names? The answer is so that users can distinguish between a true directory folder and a folder shortcut. In some cases a shortcut name will read the same as a real directory. You can use whatever character or naming convention you wish, but choose something unique. A symbol also conveys "default" or "out-of-the-box" to your users. When they click something with a ! in the folder name, they know where on the server they are going.

For example, say you need to load a detail component. You fire up the Load dialog box, where you are presented with all #-prefixed family files. More than likely, that is what you want, but on occasion you have not customized your own. So in that directory will be a shortcut link to the same family location under the out-of-the-box folder. The user can then click the link and will be sent into the stock location.

This probably seems confusing, so let's break it down. There are two directory structures, A and B. A has the same organization but contains only custom (#) family files. B, on the other hand, is right out of the box. Within the A structure are shortcut links to the same directory structure location in B. The user's options are all pointed to A directory structures. Take a look at Figure 17.13 for an example of this in use.

FIGURE 17.13
A custom # directory structure and default content locations

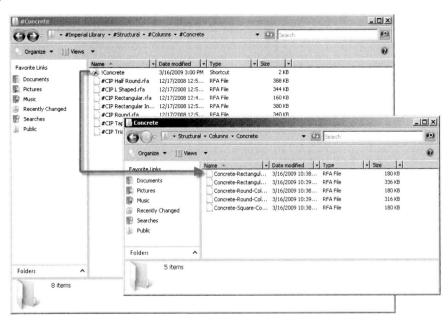

Defining Shortcut Keys

If you have used AutoCAD more than casually, you are probably aware of the ACAD.PGP file. You can use this file to define keystroke(s) to invoke a command. For example, you can use this file to specify that rather than using the menu or toolbar button, you simply press L and then Enter to get the Line command.

Revit Structure has similar customization features, albeit in the BIM world. You'll find the file KeyboardShortcuts.TXT alongside the Revit.EXE file. Once you find the file, simply edit it with Notepad. Here's an example entry:

```
"BM"    ribbon: "Home-Structure-Beam"
```

The "BM" indicates the series of keys to be pressed. That's followed by the exact Ribbon menu path to the command required (in this example, Home Ribbon ➤ Structure panel ➤ Beam tool). If you are not in an active command and you press the letter B, the Revit status bar will show *Shortcut B: ribbon Home|Structure|Beam* and the command will activate when you press Enter or the spacebar. If the command shown on the status bar is not what you want, you can press any arrow direction key (normally to the right of the Enter key) to skip through other B* shortcut key definitions.

Once you open your shortcut file, you will probably notice that most of the commands are not defined. But before you dive in and make a shortcut for every menu command, ask yourself what you need. For each menu item listed, many will be used seldom, if ever. Do you really need a shortcut to something you don't use and therefore won't remember when you actually do need it? You will probably just go up into the Ribbon menu and find it and then run from there. Commands you use every day are the ones you *should* customize.

To customize a shortcut item, find the command you want, remove the semicolon (;), and type in your one- or two-letter shortcut. For example,

```
;  ""    ribbon: "Home-Foundation-Isolated"
```

would become

```
"FI"    ribbon: "Home-Foundation-Isolated"
```

So then in Revit Structure, when you type FI, the Foundation Isolated command will start as if you had chosen it from the Ribbon. Nearly every key on the keyboard can be used for a shortcut, even function keys (although the process is little different). Since a function key has a letter and number, they are not quoted. For example, to press F7 and get the Options dialog box, the process would be

```
F7    ribbon: "Create-Annotate-Spelling"
```

Finally, you can use the same set of keystrokes (not including a double set of the same letter) for several commands. The first one listed in the KeyboardShortcuts.TXT file will be run first, but you then can use the arrow keys to step through any of the other commands with the same keyboard shortcut definition. If the order in the .TXT file doesn't fit your needs, you can reorder the command so that it does. But rather than moving items to the top, place a semicolon in front of the item being relocated (to shut it off). And then place a working version at the top. This will keep your shortcut file pristine, thus enabling you to make easy upgrades.

In previous Revit Structure versions, the KeyboardShortcuts.TXT file had one line per menu item. With Revit Structure 2010 this has been made more complicated by the introduction of the Ribbon. You may have noticed that many of the tabs contain very similar buttons but are tabbed with different names. Unfortunately this duplication is needed in the KeyboardShortcuts.TXT file as well. So that means if you want to customize a given command, it may need to be customized in several locations. You will need to be very studious in your edits to be sure to find all duplicated command entries.

 Real World Scenario

DEVELOPING SHORTCUTS

You should think about how you use the graphical user interface before assigning shortcuts. Normally, you will assign shortcuts to first-priority commands, such as Align and Copy, in either close proximity or using double letters. For example, Align could be AA, Copy could be CC, and Beam BB. Any Ribbon button used daily should get a shortcut that you can type easily with one hand. Next you assign shortcuts to second-priority menu item commands that you use often. Use an intelligent and consistent method so that you can remember the keystrokes — such as SY for Symbol. Those keys can be easy to reach with one hand and not so hard on the memory. Now feel free to change everything if you want. The out-of-the-box shortcut for Structural Wall is WA. But there is also a Wall (nonstructural) command. It makes more sense to me to make Structural Wall SW instead.

Want to take your customization to another level? Included with the Chapter 17 exercise files is a Microsoft Excel spreadsheet that is set up for easing the process of keyboard shortcut customization. As described earlier, many of the commands are duplicated in the .TXT file. By using the programming techniques in MS Excel, you have a means to edit a command once, and any duplicated entry will automatically be fixed as well.

Open up the RST2010 Keyboard Shortcuts Development.XLS file and review it prior to beginning to edit it. At the top of the file is the standard information regarding shortcut editing. Scrolling down you then see blue, orange, and green sections. The blue section is what when finished you copy/paste into a .TXT file to make your new KeyboardShortcuts.TXT file. The orange section is where you need to focus your attention; this area lists all the commands with duplicates removed. The green areas are the only areas where you need to do any editing.

As you customize a given command, your change will override the out-of-the-box (OOTB) entry. As you scroll down farther you will begin to notice ribbon lines on the left not being repeated on the right. This is because they are duplicates — you don't need to worry about them since you have already addressed them earlier in the .XLS file.

If, during your editing, a shortcut matches another shortcut but the menu item is different (meaning same shortcut for different commands), the Customize Here column will highlight the offending cells in red. If that happens, scroll down through the file and resolve or ignore the problem.

Once you finish customizing, copy the blue area onto the clipboard and paste it into a .TXT file and name it **KeyboardShortcuts.TXT**. Back up your original file and put the new one in its place. Launch Revit Structure and see if you get any errors. Any errors found will be saved into a KeyboardShortcuts.LOG file alongside the .TXT file.

As you can see, you can do a lot to speed up your work with simple and easy edits to your shortcuts. Although you cannot share a shortcut file on a network, your office should share the customization that you develop, if for no other reason than to let you sit at other stations from time to time to help users understand something and not become frustrated with different command shortcuts.

Modifying Your Model

Now that you have spent considerable time figuring out what your pen weights and line styles should be, you will want to apply them to a model file. You cannot just define these items; you must tell Revit Structure how to use them effectively for your benefit. You will make wholesale assignments and change everything in your model. Then, as needed, make changes at the view level.

Now you have the power to put Revit Structure work for you. You have modified your .INI file, and you have temporary dimension text you can actually read. You have your own custom files available to load before the OOTB files. And you have managed to speed up your user interface by assigning shortcuts to your frequently used commands. After all this, you are ready to see real results in your model by adjusting your object styles and applying visibility/graphic overrides when required. Then we'll check out the concept of color and see what it can do for you.

Fixing Object Styles

One of the first things people notice about Revit Structure is that it doesn't have layers. Almost every other CAD software package has layers (or levels) — how can Revit not have layers? Well, in a way it does, but not in the traditional sense. Everything in Revit Structure is an object of some sort. It could be a model object like a column, an annotation object like text, or even imported objects from an AutoCAD drawing file.

You use the Object Styles dialog box to control the model-wide look of everything in Revit Structure. To begin, use the Manage tab ➤ Settings drop-down ➤ Object Styles to open the Object Styles dialog box shown in Figure 17.14. This dialog box has three tabs. The first is Model Objects, where you define how all the various 3D model objects in Revit Structure look.

FIGURE 17.14
Object styles control how all objects in Revit Structure appear.

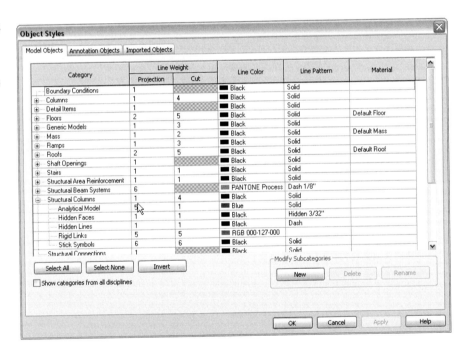

For each object type you have a control for projection lines and, if applicable, cut lines. You also have controls for color, pattern, and, if applicable, material. Each object category will expand into applicable conditions. For example, structural columns have a projection at the base level and then controls for analytical, hidden faces, hidden lines, rigid links, and stick symbols.

LEARNING OBJECT STYLES

It is beyond the scope of this book to explain every category. But there is a trick I used to learn and understand the controls. Take a model with all your various model types used, and change all object styles controls to some very obvious color of your choice. Now look at each object type individually, and one by one change each row in the Object Styles dialog box back to black (or another unique color). Look at each object type in plan, section, and elevation views and in each detail level (fine, medium, and coarse). As you change a given object style's row to another color, look at your views and note what is changing. You will soon learn that Floors – Slab Edges represents edge angles in plan views and that Floors – Common Edges applies to the line work between the metal deck and concrete slab in medium/fine section views when the deck is running parallel with the view. Before you deal with the next object type, set the one you just examined (and now understand) to black. This will help you avoid backtracking as you work your way through all the object types.

I also suggest that you leave rows in which you never see any change to an odd color, like hot pink. That way, you'll know in a glance that either you don't use that object type or you simply haven't been able to create a view to make that given property show itself. Do this in a real project and tell all team members to contact you if they ever see anything hot pink in color. You suddenly have expanded your investigation team beyond yourself, and before long those additional eyes will probably see the mysterious condition. Then you can deal with it, understand what it controls, and assign the proper line weight and pattern.

Referring back to Figure 17.14 for the Structural Columns category, if shown in a view (not cut), the primary control comes into play. Structural Columns – Projection defines the pen weight. The color on that row sets the visible color, just as the line pattern defines the line type to be used. In the case of columns, since there are many types of columns, you should not set material here as it will be used everywhere unless an instance material has been set.

The other Structural Columns category controls are fairly simple as well. Hidden faces come into play when a face of a column is hidden by itself. An example is a wide-flange column in an elevation turned with the flange facing the view. The line work for the hidden web is a hidden face. A concrete column that stops below a slab in a plan view is a hidden line. The Structural Columns Stick Symbols control applies to steel columns in coarse view detail level.

Each object category has its own set of controls, but many are similar and follow predicable rules. This consistency makes object styles the best way to control your graphic standards for a project model. Earlier in this chapter you learned about line weight and patterns. This is where you should apply those standards first. Whatever changes you make here apply to the entire model and all views that don't have overrides.

EXERCISE: SEEING THE DIFFERENCE

This exercise shows you the difference between an OOTB model appearance and an adjusted object styles model and how quickly it can be accomplished. Open the Chapter 17 exercise file Model Project.RVT (from the book's companion web page). This model has a basic structure laid out showing a number of object types. We have already created our preferred line patterns and line weights and set the concrete objects to have a solid hatching.

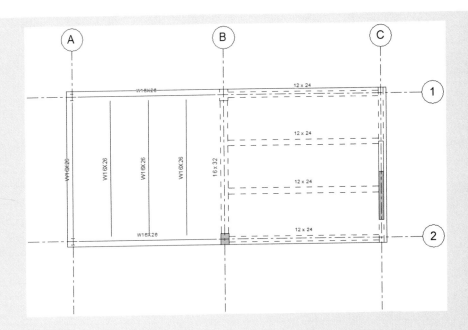

1. Under the Manage tab, choose the Settings drop-down and click the Object Styles command.

2. Change the Floors Primary Projection value from pen 2 to pen **7**.

3. Scroll down to Structural Columns and expand the category.

4. Change the Line Weight Cut value for the primary control from pen 4 to pen **8**.

5. Change the Hidden Lines Projection Line Weight from pen 1 to pen **6**. Also change the Line Pattern from Dash to **#Hidden** $\frac{1}{16}''$.

6. Scroll down more and expand the Structural Framing category.

7. Change the Structural Framing Girder Projection control from pen 6 to pen **10**.

8. Change the Hidden Lines Projection control from pen 1 to pen **5**, and change the Line Pattern from Dash to **#Hidden** $\frac{3}{32}''$.

9. Change the Structural Framing Joist Projection control from pen 4 to pen **10**.

10. Scroll down to Walls and expand the category.

11. Change the Walls Primary Projection from pen 2 to pen **7** and Cut from 5 to **8**. Change the Walls Hidden Lines Projection value from pen 2 to pen **6**. Change the Line Pattern from Dash to **#Hidden** $\frac{1}{8}''$.

12. Click OK to apply the changes and exit the dialog box.

Now as you can see in the following illustration, all visible model objects changed graphically (hopefully for the better).

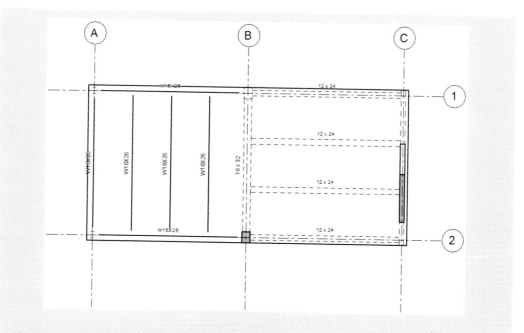

The key to making these adjustments is knowing your standards so that you can apply them. Print out a list of your pen weights along with sample sheet of line work so you can see what you are about to assign.

Adjusting the Visibility and Graphics

There will come a time when a given view needs a different set of object styles. It could be because the view scale is too large. In such cases you should utilize the differing view scale pen weights, as discussed earlier in this chapter. But what about for specific changes, such as making floors have a surface pattern, or hiding beams, or making some items halftone?

Enter Revit Structure's biggest dialog box, Visibility/Graphic Overrides. As you can see in Figure 17.15, this dialog box looks somewhat intimidating. Not only does it provide controls for the same object options shown in the Object Styles dialog box, but you can even set some object categories to halftone, transparent, and a different view detail level. In addition, using filters you can change only specific objects to look different, based on object type or just those selected objects.

When you go to use the Visibility/Graphic Overrides dialog box, your purpose will probably be to solve some specific problem. Simply make your change and go about your other work. In some cases, the changes will need to be repeated for other views, in which case you can use the View tab ➢ View Templates drop-down and then click Create Template from Current View command. This command will save your changes into a view template, and you will be able to recall and apply this template to other views, saving a lot of repetitive editing time.

FIGURE 17.15
Visibility/Graphic
Overrides
changes adjust
the current
view.

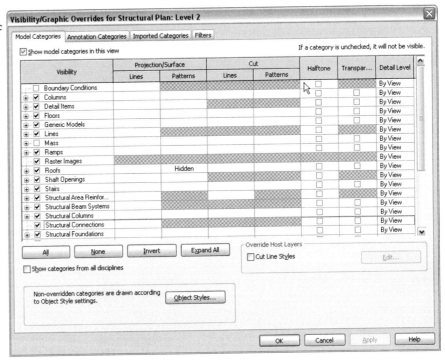

EXERCISE: CUSTOMIZING A VIEW

This exercise shows some view customization on the same model used for object styles. Open the Chapter 17 exercise file Visibility Graphics.RVT (from the book's companion web page). You will see that there are some objects added to a filter in order to control them.

1. Under the View tab click the Visibility/Graphics button to display the Visibility/Graphic Overrides dialog box.

2. Locate the Floors category, and click in the slot for Projection/Surface Patterns. You will see an Override button; click it.

3. In the Fill Pattern Graphics dialog box, change Pattern to Sand and click OK.

4. Locate the Structural Columns category and click in the slot for Cut Lines, and then click the Override button.

5. In the Line Graphics dialog box, change the Weight value to **8**.

6. Click the Patterns slot for Structural Columns and change the pattern to Solid Fill.

7. Click the Filters tab at the top of the Visibility/Graphic Overrides dialog box. Click the Add button.

8. In the Add Filters dialog box, select Demo from the list and click OK. This then displays the Demo filter with a visibility control like the one for model objects.

9. Click the Halftone toggle at the end of the line. Click OK to apply and close the Visibility/Graphic Overrides dialog box.

As shown in Figure 17.16, a number of things changed. The floor got a fill pattern applied to entire surface. The columns now have a thinner pen weight, and the concrete column got a solid black fill. In addition, a group of steel beams set for demolition is now halftone.

Overall, you've made quite dramatic differences with fewer than 30 seconds' worth of edits to the Visibility/Graphic Overrides dialog box. You only have to use your imagination to know the boundaries of this capability. In general, making changes this way should be limited to specific views for specific needs. This will ensure that your project standards are model wide, but you'll have a fallback solution when you need standards for specific views.

Modeling with Color

Many users of Revit Structure products have had previous experience with AutoCAD. Therefore, typically the first emotion when a new user fires up Revit Structure and starts modeling is "I miss color." Revit Structure by default is black and white; all objects are white or black depending on your background screen color. There are few instances of color; levels that have views referencing them have blue target symbols. And sections and elevation views are blue as well. Reference plane lines are green hidden lines.

So why is there no color in Revit? Is black and white so much better than color, and all those AutoCAD users have been doing it wrong for over 20 years? Revit Structure didn't start as an Autodesk-owned application. It was simply Revit and in many ways was competing with Autodesk products. The answer is, Revit Structure was made black and white so that it would *not* be like AutoCAD. Plain and simple, there was a marketing decision to be different, and the main way to be different was to go no-color.

FIGURE 17.16
The finished changes applied to the model

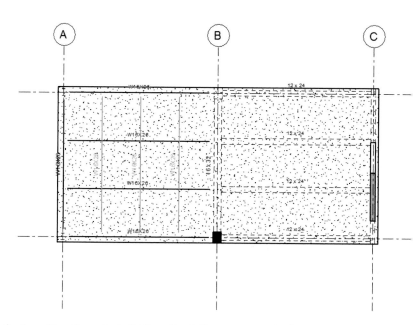

When you made the transition from AutoCAD to Revit Structure, no doubt you just accepted the black-and-white display. But perhaps you have poked around a little and discovered that color is there — it's just not used. Color is tedious to apply, but once you experiment with it in a model, applying differing color to columns, walls, beams, and the like, it will begin to feel familiar. You will then notice something simple and yet profound: it is easier to tell what you are looking when it is in color!

Interestingly Revit Structure doesn't use color to control pen weight as AutoCAD can, so color inherently won't affect your look unless you plot in color. But imagine you are zoomed into a tight area and you see a hidden line next to another hidden line. Which is a column and which is a beam? Well, you could hover your mouse above that line or select an object to know what it is, but wouldn't it be easier to simply know by its color? You would know visually whether a beam is aligned with the wall, or the wall is aligned with the beam, by the color of each and recognizing what is right and what is wrong.

The focus of this section isn't to propose a color scheme; that is up to you and your fellow modelers. What we suggest is to use color as an advantage in modeling with Revit Structure. It really can help. Just be aware when plotting to assign black and white and not color — unless you want color plots!

KNOWING WHAT TO LEAVE BLACK AND WHITE

Not everything in Revit Structure needs to be shown in color. For example, detail components you might draw in a drafting view have no 3D and gain no benefit. The same thing can be said for text in your model views; if you see text you obviously know what it is. A good rule to follow is that only model objects get color; all annotation and detail line work should be left black and white.

There's a side benefit to making line styles only black and white: if someone uses the Linework tool to paint something, such as a solid line of a model edge to be a hidden line style, you will then see black and white on a model object, telling you that some model fudging was going on. You can then investigate and correct any issues so that the model will automatically display a hidden line rather than faking it.

The Bottom Line

Ascertain what can and cannot be done easily.   Standards are there no matter what. What they are and how they are controlled are up to you. Before Revit Structure, users had various files provided with AutoCAD that determined what most of the standards were based on. A standard is many things, but a basic one specifies line weight, pattern, and style. In addition, you have filled patterns that can tone contained areas. You then bring all these definitions together and apply them to object styles, views, and objects to create your drawings.

> **Master It**   Develop line weights that meet your needs. Create line patterns and styles and then apply them to your model via the Object Styles dialog box. Address annotation and fill standards as well, all matching your required standards.

Enhance your model through customization.   Anyone using Revit Structure deserves to have their tool be as productive as possible. With a little bit of practice, you can take using Revit Structure to a new level.

> **Master It**   The temporary dimension values in Revit Structure are too small to read, so increase them! Follow that with organizing your firm's library files as well. Then improve usability by using command shortcuts, and take advantage of keyboard input speed.

Implement model standards and view overrides.   Once you have your standards in place, you then have to apply them to your model. There is no need to simply accept what Revit Structure can produce right out of the box.

> **Master It**   Take your standards and use them to control your model. Then when the need arises, tweak just about anything for a single view at a time. Can you break out of the black-and-white box and think in color again?

Chapter 18

Family Creation: Beyond the Provided Libraries

There are two ways you may have arrived at this chapter. One is you read through the book in its entirety and are now ready to start creating some families. The other way is you went out, bought the book, and flipped directly to this chapter with the sole purpose of learning this part of Revit Structure. Whatever path brought you to this point, you now know that Revit Structure is very much dependent on family objects to drive the model. For all of the advantages of Building Information Modeling (BIM) and the smooth workflow Revit Structure can provide, you will find that you are going virtually nowhere unless you have the content you need. Yes, Revit Structure does provide a rich library of content out of the box that will get you through most areas of a project, but what about the specialty content you need? It would be literally impossible for Revit Structure (or any CAD application for that matter) to provide a predefined custom family for every situation. Add to that the need to re-create that special family within your company's set standards, and the task becomes even more impossible.

Revit Structure acknowledges this and takes a different approach. Instead of attempting to provide a specific family for every situation, Revit Structure provides general templates (.rvt files) that allow you to choose the basic type of family object you want to create. Each family in Revit Structure is built with the flexibility to adapt to as many situations as possible. For example, say you need to add a lintel to your project. In AutoCAD, you might have a block that is inserted into your detail drawing. You can then edit the block scaling or explode and modify that block to suit your specific dimension requirements. Then you need another block or additional line work in plan to document the lintel. In Revit Structure, you make one lintel family starting with a Revit Structure family template, with parameters that allow you to change the size, shape, and anything else you need adjustable in the family. You can also create the family to display the line work in plan. Taking it a step further, you can even use the family to produce schedules and material takeoffs.

At its heart, Revit Structure is driven by families, and it depends on families to enable its parametric concept. Some families will be quite simple to create once you understand their basic structure and function. Families don't need to be complex to be well constructed. Others are going to be more difficult and will require more thoughtful consideration and good old-fashioned patience. Either way, learning the ins and outs of creating Revit Structure families is not something that will be accomplished overnight. Rome was not built in a day, but little parts of it sure were.

In this chapter you will learn to:

◆   Create a footing step family

◆   Create in-place families

◆   Create groups

Creating Families

In Revit Structure, a family is named *family* for a couple of reasons. One is the hierarchical concept that drives its organization and functionality. The second is the ability to deliver multiple types (or members) of the family to a project, all of which are contained in one package. It is similar to when a minivan pulls up to the picnic area of a local state park and eight people, all parents or siblings, start piling out of the vehicle. The same concept holds true for a Revit Structure family. The van represents the family and the eight members of the family on the picnic represent the different family types being delivered.

In Revit Structure, there are three kinds of families:

System family   Although you may not be aware, you have been using this family type throughout this book. A system family is defined within the project and is not an external file that needs to be loaded. It has a predefined purpose and capabilities that you cannot change, only use. You can edit a system family by modifying the parameters provided in the Element and Type Properties dialog boxes. You can also define the extents of many system families in Sketch mode. Some of the model elements contained within the project that are system families include

Walls

Wall footings (strip footings)

Floors (slabs)

Roofs

Stairs/ramps

Toposurfaces

Openings

Dimensions

There are also several system families that incorporate a component family, an external file, for a portion of their definition. These particular system families have additional flexibility to customize their look or the profile used to create them. Some of these include

Grids

Levels

Spot elevations

Spot coordinates

Railings

In-place family   This type of family resides completely within the model as well, but when you issue the Model In-Place tool and select the category of the in-place family, the Ribbon switches to the Family Editor. You can then create the family components in their required position without the need to insert and then position them correctly. Also, in many cases you will need to use the existing model elements to lay out the geometry of the in-place family. This functionality is very important in Revit Structure since there will always be areas of a model that need a custom touch.

Component family   This type of family is created and managed externally and then loaded into the Revit Structure model as needed. For instance, if you wanted to add a castellated beam to the model, you would have to load it from an external family file (file extension .rfa). By default, Revit Structure does not have this type of beam family loaded into the model. After you execute the Beam tool, you can load a new beam family by selecting Load Family in the Detail panel of the Ribbon. Then you can browse for the family you need, and it will be loaded into the project for future use. It is obviously preferable to have a library of families available for use, but in the interest of maintaining an organized model with a manageable file size, families shouldn't be loaded into the model until you actually need them.

Constructing a family in Revit Structure is a unique process, and you will probably find it unlike any of your experiences with other CAD applications. At first you may see the family-creation process as cumbersome and somewhat unwieldy. It may seem like more than it is worth to create a family for a model element that may be needed for only limited use, but then you realize how much potential your creation has. After some practice using the tools, you will see the overwhelming advantage of constructing these components. To get a feel for family creation, we will use a stepped footing example. It will be similar to the stepped footing you have already used in Chapter 8.

Creating a Family File

To begin creating a family file (.rfa), you should first decide on a template that is close to what you are trying to create. Revit Structure provides templates for most situations. For example, if you started a new truss family, you would begin with the Structural Trusses.rft file found in the Imperial Templates directory. Once this template is opened, the Ribbon reflects this with tools specific to the creation of trusses, as illustrated in Figure 18.1. Specific materials are preloaded into these templates as well, along with logical setting defaults related to the family category.

FIGURE 18.1
An example of the Structural Truss Family Editor Ribbon

The process for starting a new Revit Structure family is to choose New ➢ Family from the Revit Structure Application menu (the big R in the top-left corner). This will launch the New Family - Select Template File dialog box. You can now browse the Revit Structure Imperial (or Metric) Template library for your specific family category. For the example we will be creating, choose the Structural Foundation.rft template file, as shown in Figure 18.2.

Once you are in the desired template, you are basically on your own. As you can see, you are given very little graphical information to begin with. If you look at the Project Browser, you will see Revit Structure has provided several views of the family for you. These include a floor plan, four elevations, and a 3D view. The Project Browser allows you to navigate around the family just as you would navigate a Revit Structure project. You will most certainly use all of these views at some point, but for now let us concentrate on the Floor Plan: Ref. Level view.

FIGURE 18.2
The New Family dialog box, allowing you to choose from one of the predefined Revit Structure family templates

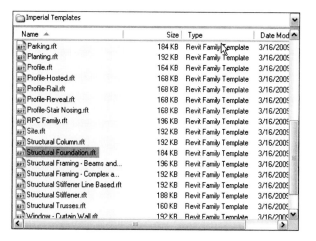

With the floor plan open, notice the two green dashed lines. These are reference planes. Depending on the template used, Revit Structure often will start you with at least two of these in plan view and usually a datum (a level) reference in elevation view, thus the floor plan name Ref. Level. When you are constructing a family, these reference planes are critical to your success. They are used to constrain the family, which allows the users input to determine the resulting geometry. To make a long story short, reference planes help define the family and control placement in the host model.

REFERENCE PLANES IN FAMILIES

In Figure 18.3, you will see two reference planes. These two reference planes are important, and you should always build from them when creating families. You should not modify or move these planes, as they define the origin and insertion point of the family. Follow these steps:

1. Select one of the reference planes. You will see the name of the reference plane, as shown in Figure 18.3. This particular name indicates it serves a specific purpose.

2. With the reference plane selected, choose Element Properties ➢ Instance Properties on the Ribbon.

   You will see this plane's specific reference is the center of the family in the front/back direction, which is reflected in the value of the Is Reference parameter. It has been named the same as its given reference for continuity (Name parameter).

3. You will also see a check box next to the Defines Origin parameter. Highlight and view the Instance properties of the vertical reference plane, and you will find it serves an identical function in the left/right direction.

   This further indicates that these two reference planes have special value, and each should be used as a datum when constructing families.

The family we are about to create is the footing step illustrated in Figure 18.4. The objective is to make the family dynamic enough to work with any stepped situation. This means the dimensions and geometry need to be flexible enough to allow the family to be placed manually and then adjusted to fit the needed condition.

FIGURE 18.3
These reference planes define the origin of the family and should be used as a starting point for family construction.

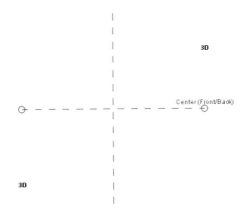

FIGURE 18.4
The finished footing step family

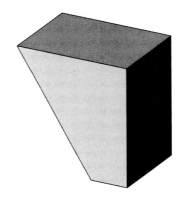

To create the required dimensional constraints, you will need to add additional reference planes offset from the existing reference planes shown in Figure 18.3.

To do so, focus your attention on the Ribbon. On the Create tab, you will see a Reference Plane button. When using this tool you have the choice of drawing reference planes from scratch or picking existing lines to create them.

1. Choose Reference Plane ➢ Pick Existing Line/Edge, as shown in Figure 18.5.

FIGURE 18.5
The Ribbon changes to Family Editor mode when creating or editing families.

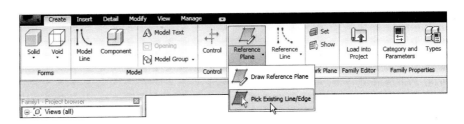

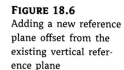

NOT ALL TEMPLATES ARE EQUAL

When you select an existing reference plane, you may find that a tool such as Copy is disabled. This means that the element has been "locked" by a software developer for some reason. Unfortunately, some families exhibit this condition and others do not; thus all templates have not been created equal, or consistent. Don't let this bother you; just sketch a new reference plane.

Once you have launched the Reference Plane tool with the Pick Existing Line/Edge option, you will notice the Options bar now contains an Offset edit box.

2. Assign an offset of **4'-0"** You can now create a reference plane 4'-0" from the existing vertical reference plane in the view window.

3. When you hover the cursor over the existing vertical reference plane, you will see a blue alignment line indicating the new reference plane to be created.

4. Move your cursor to either side of the vertical reference plane to assign your offset side. Click to place the new vertical reference plane. Your view should now look like Figure 18.6.

FIGURE 18.6

Adding a new reference plane offset from the existing vertical reference plane

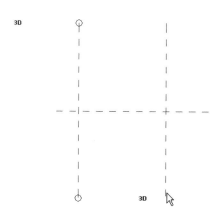

The strategy for this example has the insertion point at the right midpoint of the footing step when it is inserted into the model. The vertical origin plane will take care of this in the vertical plane. In the horizontal plane, however, you need to add two more reference planes to center the footing step on the horizontal origin plane. You need one above and one below.

1. To do this, start the Reference Plane tool with the Pick option as before.

2. Create an offset horizontal reference plane 1'-0" above and 1'-0" below the origin plane, leaving you with three horizontal reference planes, as shown in Figure 18.7.

At the bottom of the footing step it will be nice to have an extension, which will provide more bearing surface against the bulkhead of the wall step. Normally this is a 6" extension of the wall footing. We can build this feature right into the footing step family. Using the Reference Plane tool, offset a reference plane 6" to the left of the vertical origin plane. This will establish a plane to model any additional cover you may wish to add to the step. Later on, you will create an extrusion that will be locked to these planes. When the reference planes move, the extrusion will follow.

FIGURE 18.7
Adding two additional
reference planes to cen-
ter the footing step on
the horizontal origin
plane

FIGURE 18.7
Adding two additional
reference planes to cen-
ter the footing step on
the horizontal origin
plane

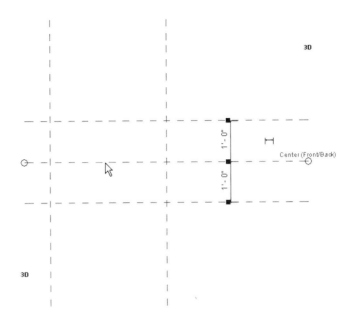

Center (Front/Back)

In plan view, the planes needed to create the footing step geometry have been accounted for. Now it is time to look at the third dimension.

In the Project Browser notice there are four elevation views predefined. Choose the front elevation. You can now see a Reference Level datum and three reference planes, including the two we added, in the plan view. You now need to add a reference plane that reflects the height of the footing step. To do this, follow the same procedure as you did in the plan view. You may notice there is a reference plane as well as the Reference Level datum at 0'-0". It is good practice to align the reference plane to the datum and lock these two elements together. The datum line is the strongest elevation reference in the family, and the reference plane is tackling the origin reference duties, so generally you will want them to be aligned. This will prevent the family from behaving erratically when placed in the model.

Using the Reference Plane tool, create a reference plane that is offset 4'-0" above 0'-0", as shown in Figure 18.8.

FIGURE 18.8
Establishing a reference
plane in an elevation
view is done exactly
as it is in plan view.
Remember to lock the
origin reference plane to
the datum elevation.

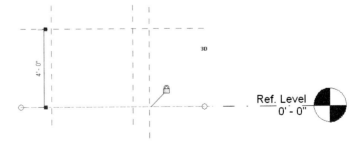

Ref. Level
0' - 0"

Since this is a relatively simple family, these are all the reference planes we will need. It is helpful to look at this procedure the same way you would look at the procedure for creating a steel-framed structure for a building. These reference planes are the structure of the family and serve as its backbone. Any additional elements we add are going to be locked to these planes and will be controlled by them. Once this family is loaded into the model, the reference planes we just added will not be visible, but the model elements such as the concrete step will be influenced and controlled by the planes.

Now that the reference planes are in place, it is time to add some parameters to your family. These parameters will serve as labels to control the dimensions of the reference planes. When you do this, the end user can go to the Element properties of the footing step and input new dimension values, creating different configurations of the same footing step family.

PARAMETERS AND LABELS

If you are thinking this is the fun part, then you are correct! Adding flexibility to families is at the heart of the functionality Revit Structure provides. Once you witness the potential of this concept, you will never want to go back to a traditional CAD platform again. Fundamentally this procedure is simple. Of course, when you begin creating more complicated families, it naturally gets more complex, but the base concept is grounded in simplicity. You need to dimension these reference planes so you can then add labels to those dimensions. Those labels reference parameters the user sees in the Element Properties dialog box. For instance, you added a reference plane 4′-0″ above 0′-0″ in the front elevation. The next step is to add a 4′-0″ dimension and label it Height. Now, the user can change the Height parameter to 5′-0″, and voilà! The footing step becomes 5′-0″ high. To start adding dimensions, do the following:

1. Return to the Ref. Level plan view. Again, one really nice thing about the Ribbon is that it makes it easy to get to the tools you need.

2. On the Detail tab of the Ribbon, in the Dimension panel, you will see an Aligned button. Click it, and place a 4′-0″ dimension, as shown in Figure 18.9. Be sure to dimension from the Center (Left/Right) reference plane.

   You should base your family dimensioning strategy from the origin reference planes whenever your family strategy allows. This will lead to much more stable families when it comes time to place the new component into your model. You should also note that a label can't be applied to a dimension string spanning more than two elements, so most dimensions in families will be placed individually. An often-used exception is when a string is used to define an equal-spacing constraint. You will be placing one such string a bit later.

3. Dimension the reference planes as shown in Figure 18.9. After the reference plane is dimensioned, you can then select the dimension.

FIGURE 18.9
Dimensioning the reference planes is the link between the physical geometry and the element parameters.

As is true for any Revit Structure element, once the item is selected, you will be presented with choices on the Options bar specific to the selection. In this case, we are interested in the Label option.

4. Select the <Add Parameter> item from the Label drop-down list, as shown in Figure 18.10.

Notice that there are two parameters already defined in the template and listed here too, Length and Width.

FIGURE 18.10
Once the dimension is selected, you can add a parameter from the Options bar.

The Parameter Properties dialog box, as illustrated in Figure 18.11, is very powerful despite its simplistic appearance. Some of the choices you make here are unchangeable, so be deliberate when you are creating these parameters. In the Parameter Properties dialog box, the first set of choices deals with the type of parameter you wish to use: Family Parameter or Shared Parameter. Each has a specific purpose.

FIGURE 18.11
The choices made in the Parameter Properties dialog box influence the behavior of the family.

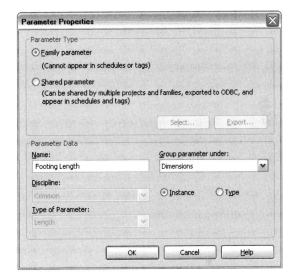

Shared Parameters

Shared parameters should be used when the parameter's value needs to be used by other families or projects. When shared parameters are created, information is stored in an external .txt file. This text file can be used while editing families and projects, and the parameters contained within can be added wherever they are needed. An example of a situation where you would want to use a shared parameter is if you were planning to nest the family within another that would then need access to its parameters, such as if you were creating a foundation family that included a nested pilaster. Shared parameters would allow you to change the pilaster's parameters within the foundation family.

Family Parameters

If you choose to create a family parameter (which is the default), it will be used by this family only and will not be accessible to other families. Given the specific nature of this type of parameter, it would be impractical to allow it to show up in schedules and tags because it is specific to only one family. You would wind up with a separate schedule or tag for each family. This is obviously not desirable, so Revit Structure does not allow it. A family parameter should be used when there is no need for the parameter's value to be used in another family.

For now, choose Family Parameter, as shown in Figure 18.11.

Parameter Data

The first item in the Parameter Data panel of the Parameter Properties dialog box is Name. Remember that you accessed this dialog box after selecting the 4'-0" dimension. For clarity, the parameter name should describe its purpose. This may be related to the item you are labeling or the dimension you are controlling. Do the following:

1. Name this parameter **Footing Length**.

   Notice the name Footing Length contains capital letters. This comes into play if the parameter is later used in a formula. Formulas are case sensitive and must include the exact parameter name. A popular convention is title case; that is, all the important words in the name are capitalized. However you choose to name your parameters, you should be consistent.

   Notice that the Discipline and Type of Parameter data fields have been automatically assigned and are unavailable for modification. They are not editable because Revit Structure knows you chose a dimension to apply this parameter to, so the Discipline value is automatically going to be Common, and the Type of Parameter value is going to be Length. Again, both of these values can make a huge difference if the parameters are used in a formula. This is the advantage of creating a parameter by selecting a dimension first. It isn't possible to assign the wrong type of parameter.

   The Group Parameter Under drop-down list allows you to categorize the parameter under a specific heading (Group) in the Instance Properties dialog box. This type of length parameter is almost always grouped under Dimensions. Some parameters may not lend themselves to one category over another, and that is why Revit Structure has provided a group called Other. Regardless, in these cases you will need to use good judgment.

2. Assign the Dimensions Group parameter.

   The next option is Instance or Type. This is arguably the most important choice of all. If you decide this will be an Instance parameter, you are saying, "I want this parameter to be independently editable, unique, for every instance of the family object." For example, if you select the footing step after you insert it into the model and open the Instance Properties dialog box, you will see a list of Instance parameters of the family. If you change any of these parameters without clicking the Edit Type button, only the footing step you selected will be modified with the changes you make. The rest of the footing steps in your project will remain unmodified. If you choose to create a Type parameter, you will need to first select the footing step in the model, then click the Element Properties drop-down list, and click the Type Properties tool. There you will find a list of Type parameters. If you edit these parameters, you will change all of the footing steps of the same family and type in the entire project. Then if you needed a different set of Type parameter values, you would need to duplicate the type to create a new one. For the footing step, you will be making all but one of the parameters Instance parameters.

3. For this parameter choose Instance.

4. Now click OK, and the dimension will contain the new label, as shown in Figure 18.12.

FIGURE 18.12
The Footing Length label has been added to the new dimension, which is now controlled by the Footing Length Instance parameter.

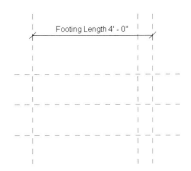

Now it is time to dimension and label the two 1'-0" offset reference planes you added earlier. The distance between these two reference planes represent the overall width. You will, however, need to tell Revit Structure that although the width will vary, it should always be equally spaced about the origin reference plane. To accomplish this, follow these steps:

1. Use the Aligned dimension tool and place a two-dimension string that includes all three horizontal reference planes.

2. Once the dimension has been placed and is still selected, click the blue EQ icon, but don't click the padlocks. This will create a relationship between the reference planes relative to the center reference.

3. Now add one more dimension to the overall 2'-0" width, select it, and create a parameter called **Footing Width**.

4. Make sure the parameter is grouped under Dimensions, as shown in Figure 18.13. This parameter should be created as a Type parameter.

   You also need to dimension the 6" offset reference plane and give it a parameter called **Footing Cover**, but let's do something a little different this time.

5. Dimension the 6" offset reference plane, but instead of selecting <Add Parameter> from the Label drop-down list, click the Types button located on the far right of the Ribbon in the Family Properties panel.

   This brings up the Family Types dialog box, as shown in Figure 18.13. While parameters that are used as labels for dimensions can be created through the Options bar drop-down, other kinds of parameters must be created here. You see the parameters you have already created here under Dimensions as well as the values that were automatically applied to them from the dimensions you labeled.

INSTANCE OR TYPE?

How can you tell if something is an instance or a type? When you see the parameter in the dialog box and also see (default), it is an Instance parameter. Otherwise it is a Type parameter. The default value is used when the family is placed in the project. Then you can change it as needed, but remember that you have to do this for each family when it is an Instance parameter.

---

6. In this dialog box on the right near the bottom you see the Parameters panel. Click the Add button and you will see a familiar dialog box.

FIGURE 18.13
To access the Family Types dialog box, click the Types button on the far right of the Ribbon in the Family Properties panel.

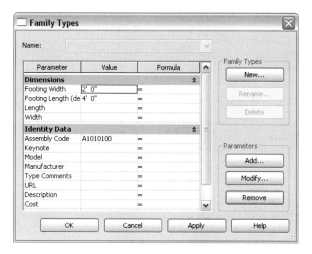

This is the same process as before, just a different way to go about it. Notice that the Discipline and Type of Parameter options are available here. That is because Revit Structure does not yet know this parameter is meant for a dimension label.

7. Create the Footing Cover parameter as you did the others before, taking care to select Common for Discipline and Length for the Type of Parameter option.

8. Set it to be an Instance parameter grouped under the Dimensions category. The parameter has been created but has not yet been applied to the dimension.

9. Click OK twice, and we will do something about that.

ZERO IS A NUMBER AFTER ALL

When you create a parameter using the Family Types dialog box, and it is intended to be used with a dimension, leave the default value set to 0'-0". Revit will change it to whatever value the dimension shows when you associate the parameter with the dimension. If you supply a value first and then associate it with the dimension, Revit will attempt to make the element move to reflect that value. This can cause some unintended changes to your family.

---

10. Back in the plan view, highlight the 6" dimension and look at the Label drop-down list. You will find the newly created Footing Cover parameter there.

11. Select it, and the label is applied and the parameter takes on the default value of the dimension. You can verify this by returning to the Family Types dialog box if you want.

These two methods achieved the same result but went about it a bit differently. Adding a label to a dimension is certainly more streamlined using the Label drop-down, but using the Family Types dialog box is required knowledge for anyone who creates families because there other types of parameters than those for dimensions. All of the necessary plan dimensions have now been added, as shown in Figure 18.14.

FIGURE 18.14

The reference planes now have the added dimensions and labels. Notice that the first two center reference planes are being used as the origin.

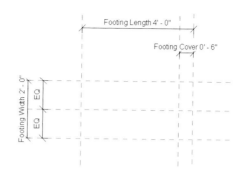

Are you starting to see the process? You build the geometry with reference planes, and then you dimension and apply parameters to them to make them parametric. To continue, follow these steps:

1. Display the front elevation where you added the reference plane 4'-0" offset of the datum elevation.

2. Add a dimension from the origin reference plane located at 0'-0" to the top reference plane you added previously. The procedure is the same as in plan view.

3. Select the dimension and use the Label drop-down menu to create a new parameter named **Footing Height**. Make it a Type parameter for now — we'll show you how you can change it later if needed

4. Apply it to the 4'-0" dimension, as illustrated in Figure 18.15.

FIGURE 18.15

The Footing Height dimension and parameter have been added.

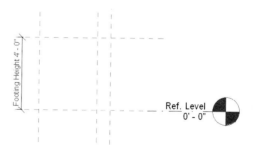

Now is a good time to test the family before you get too far along. If you were to wait until the family was finished to test it, the cause of any problems you may encounter would be much more difficult to determine. Once you have established the majority of the reference planes and have applied parameters to them, you can start to flex the family to shake out any unexpected results before adding the physical geometry:

1. To see how your family reacts to changes, click the Types button on the far right of the Ribbon to open the Family Types dialog box once again.

   Like most windows, this dialog box can be resized by dragging any edge or corner. The width of all columns will grow as you increase the width of the dialog box. In addition, if you hover the cursor over the line dividing the headers, you can adjust their widths individually.

2. Do this between the Parameter and Value headers, and drag slightly to the right so you can read the entire Parameter column.

   Notice that the parameters that have (default) next to their name. This indicates they are Instance parameters, and the value listed here is the value the parameter will have when it is initially inserted into a project.

   These parameters can be edited. If, for example, you forgot to make a parameter an Instance parameter, you can correct it by selecting the parameter in question and clicking the Modify button in the Parameters field in the lower right of the dialog box, as shown in Figure 18.16. This returns you to the Parameter Properties dialog box, where you can make needed changes.

3. For this footing step family, click Modify and make sure each of the parameters you added except Footing Width is an Instance parameter.

FIGURE 18.16
First select the parameter you wish to modify, and then choose Modify. Parameters can also be added or removed here.

To test the family, modify the value that was established to the right of the parameter name.

4. While still in the Front Elevation, drag the Family Types dialog box to the side so you can see the Footing Height dimension; then change the Footing Height value to **3′-0″** and click Apply.

   Notice that the reference plane representing the top of the footing step moved down to reflect the new value. The origin reference plane acts as an anchor in this situation, and you can now see why you should dimension from origin planes whenever possible.

5. Return the value to **4′-0″** and click OK. Now go to the Ref. Level plan view so you can test your other parameters.

6. After relaunching the Family Types dialog box, change the Footing Length value to **5′-0″**, click Apply, and then change it back to **4′-0″**.

7. Change the Footing Width value to **3′-0″** and click Apply.

   Notice that your reference planes move away from the origin reference planes even when an equal dimension string is involved. This procedure is called "flexing the family," and you should do this to test every parameter you create.

8. Return the Footing Width value to **2′-0″**.

   Now, suppose you wanted the Footing Cover value to be a function of the Footing Length value. You can achieve this by using a formula in the Family Types dialog box. To the right of the Value column, you will see a Formula column. Here Revit Structure will accept a formula and evaluate it, and the resulting value will be applied to the parameter. Again you can adjust the size of the dialog box or drag the column widths if you need to.

9. Open the Family Types dialog box, find the Footing Cover parameter, and under the Formula column type **Footing Length / 3**, as illustrated in Figure 18.17 (the formula is case sensitive).

When the Footing Length value changes, the Footing Cover value will equal the Footing Length value divided by 3. Formulas can contain mathematical functions, if/then statements, and much more. Consult the Revit Structure help file for the exact syntax and all supported expressions.

FIGURE 18.17
You can add a formula to the Formula column in the Family Types dialog box. Remember that the expressions are case sensitive.

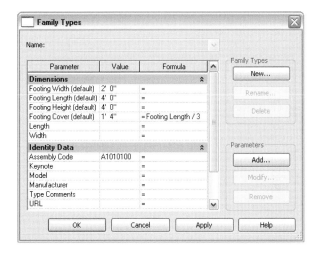

Now that the skeleton of the family is firmly in place, it is time to add the physical solid that you will see in the project. The extrusion that you will add will be locked to the reference planes that you have created and will be controlled by the values for each parameter.

Adding Extrusion Geometry

You have finally made it to the fun 3D part. Once the family is flexing correctly, the hard part is over, and you can usually wrap it up by adding a simple extrusion or two. There are, however, still a couple of tricky details to deal with. The first is establishing the plane you want the extrusion sketch to be drawn in. You will create this extrusion in the front elevation view, but if you start the Extrusion tool (Forms panel ➢ Create tab ➢ Solid ➢ Extrusion), Revit asks you to identify the work plane in which the sketch will be created. One thing to remember when adding an extrusion in Revit Structure is that the solid will always extrude based on how the reference plane was created; the start and end points influence the positive direction. In this case, you may want to sketch the extrusion on the back plane so the resulting geometry is effectively placed where it needs to be. You want to sketch in the back plane, but it does not show up as a choice in the work plane selection dialog box. Now is a good time to name the reference planes as needed.

In the Ref. Level plan view, the horizontal reference plane you added below the origin plane is at the front of the family, and the one you added above is at the back.

1. Select the front reference plane and choose Element Properties ➢ Instance Properties.

2. In the Instance Properties dialog box you will see a Name parameter. Name the reference plane **Front** and click OK.

3. Then repeat the procedure for the back plane and name it **Back**.

Notice that now when you select the back plane, you can see its name in the drawing area, as shown in Figure 18.18.

4. Switch to the Front Elevation view.

FIGURE 18.18
When the plane is selected, its name is visible. To name a plane, enter it in the Name parameter in the Instance Proper-ties dialog box.

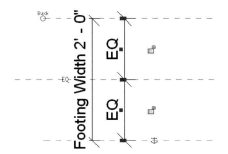

5. Choose Solid ➢ Extrusion from the Create tab on the Ribbon. The Work Plane dialog box will appear requesting that you specify the work plane you wish to use to sketch the extru-sion shape.

6. Now that it has a name, our preferred plane appears in the drop-down list. Select Reference Plane : Back, as shown in Figure 18.19. Click OK to close.

FIGURE 18.19
It is important to have a clear naming strat-egy for reference planes. New reference planes become available as a work plane selec-tion only after they have been named.

You will now find yourself in Sketch mode with a Create Extrusion tab to work from. The Options bar will also be of use to you. In the Draw panel of the Ribbon, you will find several options for sketching. One of the most useful is the Pick Lines option, especially when it is used in conjunction with the Lock option on the Options bar, as illustrated in Figure 18.20. While the lines can be sketched, aligned, and locked manually, this combination is usually more convenient.

Figure 18.21 shows the footing step shape. It is easiest to select the reference planes to create the sketch where possible.

7. Sketch the three lines that fall on reference planes using the Pick Lines and Lock options.

FIGURE 18.20

The Create Extrusion Ribbon tab with the Pick Lines and Lock options selected

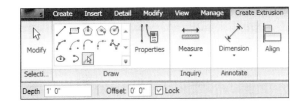

FIGURE 18.21

To draw the perimeter of the extrusion, select the reference planes with the Pick Lines tool and the Lock option. When sketching lines without the benefit of a reference plane, snap the ends to the reference plane intersections.

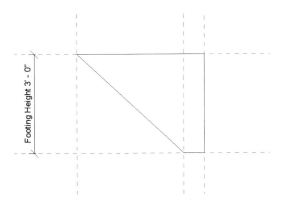

8. Select the Draw Lines option (top leftmost option in the Draw panel) and sketch in the diagonal line.

    Be sure to snap to the reference plane intersections when drawing the diagonal; use the keyboard shortcut for intersection (default is SI) to bring up only the intersection snap if needed.

9. Once you have the perimeter of the extrusion sketched in, use the Trim tool in the Edit panel of the Ribbon to clean up the corners.

Notice when you select a sketch line that you see the lock symbols for the three sides that are constrained to the reference planes. Next we will illustrate how you might accomplish this without the Pick Lines and Lock options:

1. Click the lock symbol for the right vertical sketch line to unlock it. Now select and drag the line a few inches to the right.

2. Choose the Align tool from the Edit panel of the Ribbon, and align the sketch line to the origin plane once again; pick the reference plane first.

3. Once this line is aligned, a lock symbol will appear but will remain unlocked. This is your opportunity to lock the sketch line to the reference plane, and you should do so now.

4. You can also align the end point of a sketch line if you need to. This align-and-lock combination is used often to constrain geometry when creating families.

Now that the perimeter is sketched and locked to the reference planes, you need to specify a material and an extrusion depth.

1. In the Element panel of the Ribbon, you will see the Extrusion Properties button. Click it and navigate down to the Material parameter.

2. The default material value is <By Category>. Since you know this footing step will be cast-in-place concrete, you can specify this as its material.

3. If you click within the Value field, a small browse button ([...]) will appear on the right side of the field. Once you click this button, the Materials dialog box will open.

4. Here you can select Concrete - Cast-in-Place Concrete and click OK.

   This returns you to the Instance Properties dialog box, where you will see this value added, as shown in Figure 18.22. If you do not assign a material, one will be automatically assigned using the default material for the category you specified for your family.

FIGURE 18.22
You can add a material by clicking the browse button in the Value field of the Material parameter.

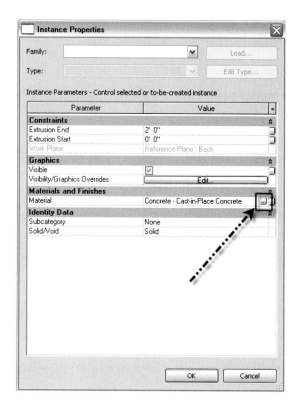

In the Instance Properties dialog box you will see three parameters, but only two that you can change here, Extrusion Start and Extrusion End, that deal with the extrusion's constraints, as shown in Figure 18.23. Since you know Extrusion Start refers to the plane the perimeter was sketched on (the back reference plane in this example, which you can see in Work Plane parameter), this value can remain 0. The Extrusion End parameter, however, needs to be the same as the Footing Width parameter. You could simply type the width in the Value field and the extrusion would adjust accordingly, but if you were to flex the model, the extrusion depth would remain at that fixed value you specified.

5. To apply the Footing Width value to this parameter, look to the right of the Value column. There is an = column. Within the = column you will see a small gray button, as pointed

out in Figure 18.23. Click this button (Associate Family Parameter), and you will get a list of length parameters to choose from.

FIGURE 18.23
Adding parameters to an extrusion is done through the small Associate Family Parameter button to the far right of the row.

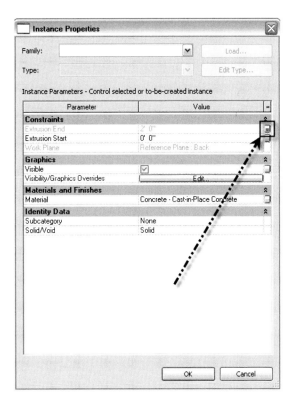

6. Select Footing Width, and now the Extrusion End parameter will match the value of the Footing Width parameter.

7. Click OK; now the small gray button shows an equal sign, and the field is grayed out.

As with many tasks in family creation and Revit Structural in general, there is usually more than one way to achieve an objective. For example, in this situation, instead of applying the Footing Width parameter to the extrusion width, you could choose to finish the extrusion and then align and lock it to the front and back reference planes in the Left or Right Elevation view.

8. Once the Extrusion End and the Material parameters have their values assigned, you are finished in this dialog box and can click OK.

9. On the far right of the Ribbon in the Extrusion panel, click Finish Extrusion.

10. Go to a 3D view to be sure the shape looks the way you expected it to.

At this point it is strongly recommended that you flex every parameter once again while viewing the family in 3D, as shown in Figure 18.24.

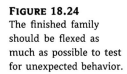

FIGURE 18.24
The finished family should be flexed as much as possible to test for unexpected behavior.

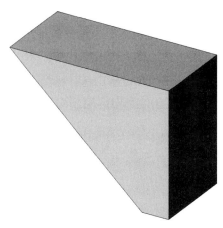

NAMING THE FAMILY AND SPECIFYING FAMILY TYPES

You name the family by saving the file with a specific name. If you have not already done so, click the Save button, browse to an appropriate location, and name the footing step family **Footing Step**. You can download the finished `Footing Step.rfa` file from this book's website at `www.sybex.com/go/masteringrevitstructure2010`.

You have one more thing to do before inserting this family into a project. You should always assign the family a category. In this case, it would be nice to be able to insert this family as an isolated foundation as opposed to a generic model. The ability to do this not only makes the process more organized but also allows this family to automatically join with adjacent foundations in most situations. To check or modify the family's assigned category, find the Family Properties panel on the right end of the Ribbon and click the Category and Parameters button. Notice in Figure 18.25 that this specific family is already categorized as Structural Foundations. This is because you used the Structural Foundation template when you created the family. If you had used a generic model, you would have had to modify the family category. Click OK once you have verified the family's category.

To add the family to a model, you need to either start a new project or open an existing one. The project file should be open but in the background, and the family file should be open and active.

1. Within the family file (`Footing Step.rfa`) click the Load Into Project button in the Family Editor panel of the Ribbon. The project will become active.

2. The Footing Step family now appears in the Type Selector as the current type. Click the Change Element Type drop-down, as shown in Figure 18.26.

You will see Footing Step as one of the choices in the Type Selector on the Options bar. Notice that this family is one of two isolated foundation families available (if you open a default template). The Footing Step family looks a little different from the Footing-Rectangular family. They both display a small preview of the family, but the Footing-Rectangular family has multiple types available, while your Footing Step family offers only the default type.

To create types of different sizes for your new family, switch back to the family file and click the Types button in the Family Properties panel. You will recognize the Family Types dialog box from when you added the parameters and flexed the family. In the upper right of the dialog box you will see a Family Types panel, as pointed out in Figure 18.27. Also notice that the Name drop-down at the top of your dialog box is currently not available. This is because only the default type exists.

FIGURE 18.25
To be sure this family is assigned the Structural Foundation category, click the Category and Parameters button on the Ribbon.

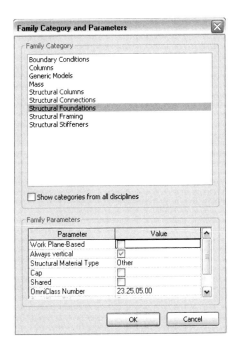

FIGURE 18.26
In a project, the Footing Step family is identified by its filename in the Type Selector.

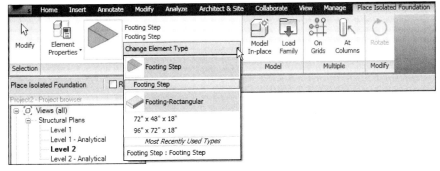

Imagine your project had two wall footing conditions you needed this family for. One was a wall footing step where the footing was always 3'-0" wide, and another was always 6'-0" wide. You can make a type for each of these conditions:

1. Under Family Types, click the New button, and you are immediately prompted for a name.

2. Name the new type **3'-0" Wide** and click OK. This will be a descriptive name for the width you are about to apply to the type. Notice that the Name drop-down now displays the name of your new type. This is an indication you are editing that particular type.

3. Change Footing Width to **3'-0"**.

4. Click New again, and add a type named **6'-0" Wide**. You guessed it, change the Footing Width value to **6'-0"** for this type. Notice that now you can switch between the types in your family, as illustrated in Figure 18.27.

FIGURE 18.27
By adding new types, you can switch between different-size configurations.

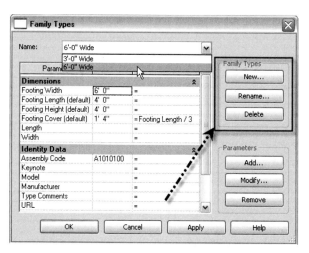

5. Simply select one from the Name drop-down and click Apply. The family updates in the drawing area, and its parameters are editable.

Once you have finished, you can load the updated family back into the project, and choose Overwrite to overwrite the existing version. Now when you execute the Isolated Footing tool within the project, you now have two variations of the same family: Footing Step: 3'-0" Wide and Footing Step: 6'-0" Wide. Because you created Footing Width as a type parameter, it can be different only in different types of the family. The Instance parameters are all freely editable in every instance regardless of type.

 **Real World Scenario**

WHEN TO STOP!

At my company we jumped right into using and customizing Revit Structure with little reservation. We took every AutoCAD block and rebuilt it as a Revit family file. In AutoCAD we had over 60 pile caps of various size and configurations. So we created a single family file with all forms in it. Seemed like a great idea at the time. Whenever we wanted to add something new, that proved to be a real hassle since we had to keep all the various types in the family in mind. The other major hassle was whenever a new type needed to be loaded, the single act of loading a single new type could take minutes, not seconds.

It is sometimes difficult to know where to draw the line as far as trying to capture every size configuration in individual family types. Typically you can create a family and provide the end user with two or three size configurations to use as templates. Once the user adds the family to a project, the provided types can be duplicated by selecting the family and choosing Element Properties ➢ Type Properties and clicking the Duplicate button. This will add a new type, just like within the family. In the case of the footing step family, once the user selects the step, blue shape handles will appear wherever an Instance parameter controls. Without even going to the Element properties, the user can simply stretch the footing step to the needed length and automatically join to adjacent foundations. You will notice that when you stretch the length, the cover automatically adjusts to a third of the length, thanks to the formula you added to control that particular parameter.

Some families you create are going to very simple. Some families you will attempt to create may require "Ninja" skills. Either way, it is quite obvious that the more you learn about creating stable, intelligent families, the more benefit you will reap by choosing to use Revit Structure. In many cases, success in Revit Structure and BIM in general depends on how proficient you are at creating families.

EXERCISE: CREATING A BRIDGING FAMILY

The following activity involves creating an uplift/joist bridging family. It includes family-creation concepts along with practical uses and applications. This family will be placed in a roof-framing plan by drawing a single line. The graphic representation will be a symbolic line in plan. In section view, there will be an angle seated on the bottom of the joist for detailing purposes. If at some point during the exercise you are prompted to save or you need to stop working on it for awhile, just save the file as **Joist Bridging.rfa**. The only steps you must complete first in order to save fully are those that require a sketch mode, like creating a solid sweep. Otherwise, you can save and return later.

1. To get started, open Revit Structure and in the Application menu (R in the upper-left corner) choose New ➢ Family. In the New Family dialog box, select `Generic Model line based.rft`. Notice that you are given three reference planes, a predrawn reference line, and a labeled dimension of Length. You will create a profile extrusion along this reference line. The Length parameter will be a variable that the user specifies graphically as the bridging is drawn in the plan view.

2. While in the plan view, on the Create tab in the Datum panel, select Reference Plane ➢ Pick Existing Line/Edge, and create two new reference planes by picking the two existing vertical reference planes. Each should be offset 1'-0" toward the center of the 4'-0" dimension.

3. Dimension the two new reference planes to the two existing references planes.

4. Select both new dimensions and add a label to each. Call the new label parameter **Symbolic Offsets**, group it under Graphics, and make it an Instance parameter.

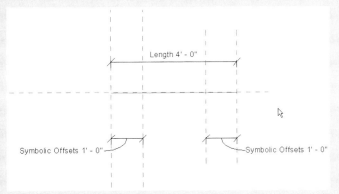

5. In the Family Properties panel of the Ribbon, click the Types button.

6. Change the Length value to **8'-0"**, and click Apply. If the right reference plane moved 4'-0" to the right and the Symbolic Offset reference plane went with it, you are good to go. Click OK.

Select the reference plane to the far left. Notice that it is already labeled. This is a good thing because some of the logistical work has been done for you in the template. This is the base origin of the entire family, so this is where you want to start your extrusion.

1. In the Project Browser, go to the Left elevation view.

2. Again, select Reference Plane ➤ Pick Existing Line/Edge, and create a new reference 1'-6" below the Ref. Level plane. This is the elevation where the angle shape will sit.

3. Align and lock the horizontal origin plane to the datum Ref. Level line, and add a dimension between the new reference plane and the horizontal Origin reference plane.

4. Add a label to this new dimension by selecting it and using the Label drop-down from the Options bar. Name it **Joist Depth**, choose Dimensions in the Group Parameter Under drop-down list, and make it an Instance parameter.

5. Click the Types button.

6. Near the bottom right of the dialog box in the Parameters frame, click the Add button.

7. Name the parameter **Joist Size**, under Type of Parameter choose Length, group it under Constraints, and make it an Instance parameter.

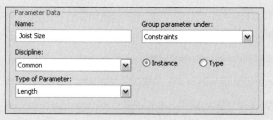

8. Click OK.

9. In the Family Types dialog box, give the new Joist Size parameter a value of **1'-6"**.

10. Create a Joist Depth formula, and type **Joist Size - 0' 1 1/4"**. Click Apply, and the Joist Depth value should change based on the formula result. You must provide "units" in the formula column; otherwise Revit will interpret the slash (/) as a divide symbol.

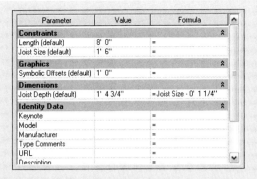

Parameter	Value	Formula	
Constraints			☆
Length (default)	8' 0''	=	
Joist Size (default)	1' 6''	=	
Graphics			☆
Symbolic Offsets (default)	1' 0''	=	
Dimensions			☆
Joist Depth (default)	1' 4 3/4''	=Joist Size - 0' 1 1/4''	
Identity Data			☆
Keynote		=	
Model		=	
Manufacturer		=	
Type Comments		=	
URL		=	
Description		=	

11. Click OK.

12. Select the bottom reference plane (the one $1'\text{-}4\frac{3}{4}''$ below the datum).

13. Select Element Properties ➢ Instance Properties from the Element panel of the Ribbon.

14. Name the plane **Bottom Reference** and click OK.

15. Open the Ref. Level floor plan.

16. On the Create tab, in the Work Plane panel, click the Set button, set the work plane to Bottom Reference, and click OK.

17. On the Create tab in the Datum panel, click the Reference Line button (not to be confused with Reference Plane). Draw a reference line from the leftmost reference plane to the rightmost reference plane in line with the Center (Front/Back) origin plane. However, you are not really drawing this one in the same place as the other reference line already in the view; it will be sketched on the bottom reference plane.

18. Choose a 3D view and verify that there are two reference lines visible.

19. Flex the family with the Family Types dialog box by changing the Length value to **9'-0''**. If both lines stretch, you are good to go. Reset the Length value back to **8'-0''**.

20. Navigate to the Left elevation view.

At this point you can draw some reference planes for the angle. This will only involve adding two additional reference planes, but this is a good time to think about your strategy in more depth. "Should I add more reference planes to provide additional functionality such as angle thickness?" There is no need to do so at this point, but when you are designing a family, always keep this option in mind. More effort will be required as the families become more complex, but the time spent contemplating your strategy will certainly pay off later.

1. From the Create tab, click the Reference Plane tool using the Pick Existing Line/Edge option, and offset one reference plane 0'-4'' above the bottom reference and the other one 0'-4'' to the right of the vertical origin plane.

2. Dimension the two new reference planes from the plane you used to create them.

3. Add a label to the dimension of the horizontal plane, and name it **Angle Height**. Group it under Dimensions, and make it a Type parameter.

4. Add a label to the dimension of the vertical plane called **Angle Depth**. Group it under Dimensions, and make it a Type parameter.

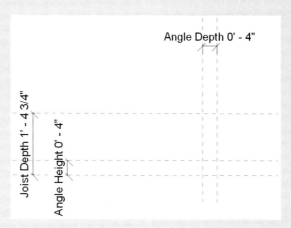

Now you can create the angle sweep. Since you have a reference line to use as the sweep path and two parameters controlling the size, all you need to do is sketch the angle profile.

1. Open the 3D view.

2. On the Create tab in the Forms panel choose Solid ➤ Sweep.

3. On the resulting Sweep tab in the Mode panel, select the Pick Path button. This will bring up a new Sweep ➤ Pick Path tab with Pick 3D Edges active by default in the Select panel.

4. Pick the reference line you just drew along the Center (Front/Back) origin plane. It will be the bottom one of the two. You can freely switch between views in this mode if you need to. In 3D you will see a node with a reference box at the midpoint. Click Finish Path.

5. This will result in a new Modify Profile tab. In the Edit panel, select the Edit Profile button.

6. In the Project Browser, open the Left Elevation view. This will allow you to sketch the angle in profile.

7. Draw the angle using the tools on the Sweep ➤ Edit Profile tab. You can make the angle $\frac{1}{4}''$ thick and use a $\frac{3}{8}''$ fillet for the interior radius. You can create the ends by drawing a $\frac{1}{4}''$ diameter circle with its center point on the outside edge of the angle, and then clean up the geometry using Trim.

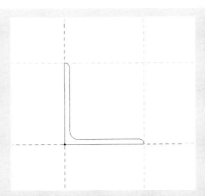

To ensure the angle will be controlled by the reference planes, you will need to align and lock the edges and endpoints to them. At first this may seem somewhat daunting, but once you get the hang of it, you can use this method for many purposes in Revit Structure.

1. Start by aligning and locking the end of the outside edge of the angle to the family reference plane it stops at. Click the Align button.

2. For the first alignment point, select the top horizontal reference plane that represents the top of the angle height.

3. For the second alignment point, select the endpoint of the magenta line representing the back of the angle. When a line's end point is highlighted, the line highlights as well. This allows you to choose the correct end point even though end points from both lines fall on the same point. You may have to use Tab key to cycle through to get the correct one. Once you align the end point to the reference plane, a blue lock icon will appear. Be sure to click this icon, locking the alignment in place.

4. Because the radial portion needs to be locked too, you need to repeat the process for the end-point of the arc. That means you basically have to align and lock two endpoints to the same reference plane.

5. Repeat the procedure for the horizontal leg lines of the angle where it intersects with the Angle Depth reference plane.

6. To the far right of the Sweep ➢ Edit Profile tab, click the Finish Profile button.

7. Again to the far right of the Ribbon, click the Finish Sweep button.

8. Flex the angle by clicking the Types button and changing the Angle Height and Angle Depth values.

9. Navigate to a 3D view and flex the Length and Joist Size parameters.

10. Save the file as `Joist Bridging.rfa`.

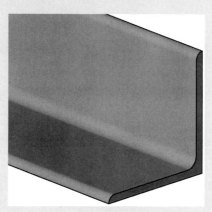

Now it is time to work on the graphical plan representation. In plan view, the symbolic line work will look like the following graphic:

Of course, this plan representation should also adjust to any scale change that may occur as well. To add the break marks at the end of the dashed lines, it would be prudent to make a separate annotation family (because this kind of family will adjust for scale as desired) and load it into this joist bridging family as a component.

1. From the Application menu, choose New ➢ Annotation Symbol.

2. Select `Generic Annotation.rft` as the template and click Open.

3. Read the red block of text and then delete it.

4. On the Create tab in the Detail panel, click the Line button, and draw the two arcs as illustrated here. You can use the Start-End-Radius arc tool and make them $\frac{1}{32}$″ x $\frac{1}{8}$″.

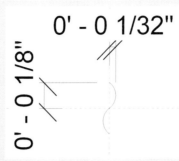

5. Save the file as **Tick Mark 1.rfa**.

6. Click the Load Into Projects button on the Create tab. Naturally, if you closed the file earlier, you'll need to open it again first.

7. If you have more than one file open, Revit will ask you which file you want to load the family in; select the Joist Bridging.rfa file. If your current view is a 3D view in the Joist Bridging family, when you use Load Family you will get the message that Revit "can't create this kind of element in the view in the current mode." The Tick Mark family is annotation, which cannot be used in 3D views. You can ignore the message and move to step 8.

8. In the Joist Bridging.rfa file, navigate to the Ref. Level plan view.

9. On the Create tab in the Work Plane panel, click the Set button.

10. Set the current work plane to Level: Ref. Level in the dialog box, and click OK.

11. On the Detail tab in the Detail panel, click the Symbol button.

12. Insert the Tick Mark 1 symbol at the intersections of the Center (Front/Back) reference plane and the symbolic offset planes.

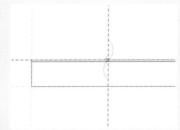

13. Align and lock the symbol both vertically and horizontally to the intersecting reference planes. Remember, select the reference planes first, and then click the symbol's embedded references. When you place your cursor over the symbol, a center line will appear, allowing you to select the symbol reference. You will probably need to use the Tab key to cycle through the possible references. Of course, remember to lock the symbol.

14. Repeat steps 11 through 13 for the other side.

15. Open the Family Types dialog box (Type button on the Family Properties panel on all of the Ribbon tabs), and flex the Symbolic Offsets parameter to test the constraints of the newly added symbols.

16. On the Detail tab, click the Symbolic Line button, and then in the Type Selector drop-down (Place Symbolic Lines tab ➤ Element panel), select Hidden Lines [Projection].

17. Draw a symbolic line between the intersections of the reference planes as shown in the graphic below, in which the line weight is exaggerated for clarity. Align and lock these symbolic lines to the reference planes they fall on. Although it is not always necessary to align and lock the endpoints of these lines to the perpendicular planes, it is a good practice to get in the habit of doing so. If you uncheck the Chain option before sketching the lines, you should get the option to lock the padlocks for the endpoints.

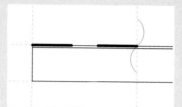

18. Repeat this procedure and draw another symbolic line at the other end. You may need to extend the Center (Front/Back) reference plane if you've increased the Length parameter. If you don't, you may not be able to snap to the intersection of the reference planes until you do. It is also "pinned," so you have to unpin it too.

One last thing to do before you load this family into a project for testing is to prevent the actual angle from being visible in plan view. This will enhance the functionality of the component and decrease the amount of RAM being gobbled up while viewing the plan.

1. Select the angle in any view.

2. On the Modify Sweep tab in the Form panel, click the Visibility Settings button.

3. In the Family Element Visibility Settings dialog box, in the View Specific Display frame, uncheck Plan/RCP. If you wanted to, you could even specify which display levels (Coarse, Medium, or Fine) the angle will be visible in.

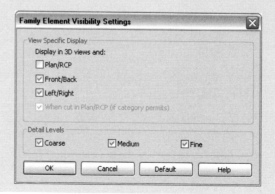

4. Click OK.

5. Click the Category and Parameters button in the Family Properties panel.

6. Change the Family category to Structural Framing. (After you do this, you may notice that Revit Structure changed the symbolic lines to a continuous line type. If so, you can highlight them and change them back to Hidden Lines [Projection]. We could have structured this exercise so that you wouldn't stumble into this issue, but then you wouldn't be aware that it mattered. You should define the category of your family as early as possible to avoid any rework like this.)

7. Click OK.

8. Start a new project, and place some 14K joists (or use your project with joists already established).

9. Load the Joist Bridging family into the new project.

10. On the Home tab, click the Beam button.

11. The Joist Bridging family should be the active type.

12. Click the Element Properties button.

13. Change the Joist Size value to the appropriate size. (Notice that the other values that were part of a formula in the family are grayed out.)

14. Place the bridging in plan view. When you first attempt to place the bridging, Revit Structure may default to Place on Face placement, and you'll see your cursor display the "you can't do this" sign, a circle with a slash through it. On the Place Beam tab ➤ Placement panel, verify that the Place on Work Plane button is active.

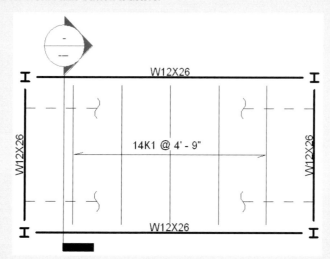

15. Cut a section along the joist where the bridging is. Vertically, it should fall at the base of the joist right where you want it. The nice thing is you can move the angle into the correct horizontal position in the section, and it will update the placement in plan view as well.

That completes this exercise. How did you do? In this exercise you created a joist bridging family. The family works by being drawn on a framing plan as a single line. As you have seen, the graphical result in the plan view is symbolic line work representation. In section view there is an angle seated on the bottom of the joist for detailing purposes.

The final version of this family and the tick mark symbol family are available for download from this book's website at www.sybex.com/go/masteringrevitstructure2010.

While creating an external family file is a very common practice, there will be times when you need to create a family that requires the surrounding model geometry to construct the family correctly. Or, if the family is so specific that you know it will never be used again, you can create what is called an *in-place* family.

In-Place Families

In-place families can be a very powerful tool to help you in the design process. They can also be restrictive if they are created beyond their usefulness. Normally an in-place family is designed to be just what its title implies. Although you can ultimately copy it around the model after it is created, an in-place family depends on specific placement within the model. That being said, if you are planning to create an in-place family, think about how many times it will need to be copied. If you find that you will need multiple instances of the family, creating an external family file (.rfa) may be the way to go. For example, Figure 18.28 shows two roofs and a special truss that was created between them using an in-place family. Because there will likely never be another project that would use these shapes, or any variation of them, it makes more sense to create an in-place family versus an external one.

FIGURE 18.28
This kind of geometry lends itself well to the use of in-place families.

An in-place family can be used in most situations where a 3D massing type element is required, but what the in-place mass tools produce are general shapes that help with conceptual design. That is the difference between a conceptual mass and an in-place family. When you create a 3D element as an in-place family, Revit Structure then knows that this is the final geometry and is a part of the actual model.

1. To start an in-place family, the first thing you need to do is go to the Model panel of the Home tab. Click the Component drop-down ➤ Model In-Place, as shown in Figure 18.29.

FIGURE 18.29
You will find the Model In-Place tool on the Home tab.

2. The Family Category and Parameters dialog box will open so you can define which category this family should belong to. In this example, you will add a truss to each side of the model.

   This is the same Family Category and Parameters dialog box you used earlier when creating the other families in this chapter.

3. Select Structural Framing as the family category. The next dialog box allows you to name the family.

   This is somewhat less important than specifying an accurate family category, but you should always adhere to good naming conventions because the name will be listed in the Project Browser.

4. For this example, type the name **Esthetic Trusses** and click OK. Once you have finished naming the new family, Revit Structure will provide a Model In-Place tab similar to what you saw while creating external families earlier in the chapter.

This is done to give you the full capability to create a family just as you would in the Family Editor mode, only this time you can use the existing geometry in the model as a guide — the best of both worlds! Also, you still have access to the Project Browser to navigate to the different project views.

Typically, creating an in-place family will be easier than creating an external family since this type of family usually does not need to be nearly as dynamic as an external family. The dimensions are usually fixed, and the nature of the placement is primarily static. There will be fewer, if any, variable dimensions. In the case of adding a specific item to the side of a building, the only reference planes you may need are the walls, floors, and roofs of the existing structure.

Since you are in the in-place Family Editor mode, you can now add as much 3D geometry as you wish. As we mentioned earlier, however, once you start adding 3D elements, Revit Structure will need you to define a work plane to reference. If the desired location of your in-place family is such that it can be sketched in plan, Revit will know to use the level as the work plane, but other views will require that the work plane be defined. For example, to create a truss profile in an elevation view, choose Solid ➢ Extrusion on the Model In-Place tab. Instead of simply letting you place the extrusion in the model, Revit Structure needs to know what you would like the work plane of the extrusion to be. It makes sense if you think about it. Revit Structure has no idea whether you want the geometry to sit on the wall or to be 100 miles back in the next county. When it prompts you for a work plane, Revit Structure allows you to pick something related to the building to establish the plane, as shown in Figure 18.30.

In this example, the face of a wall is being selected as the work plane in which to sketch the special truss, as illustrated in Figure 18.31. You can use most any item as a reference, including established gridlines.

Now you are essentially free to sketch anything you want. If you add reference planes, they will be invisible when you finish the family. If you choose to edit the family at a later date, the reference planes will reappear, as they are embedded in the family itself. Figure 18.32 illustrates an in-place family in production.

FIGURE 18.30

The Work Plane dialog box allows you to specify the location on the building where your sketch will reside. It is common to choose a wall or a framing member to establish a work plane.

FIGURE 18.31

Select the surface of the wall on which to sketch the new family.

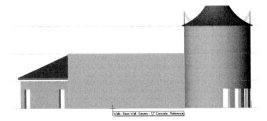

FIGURE 18.32

This is a sketch of an extrusion within an in-place family. Notice that you can easily draw any shape you need.

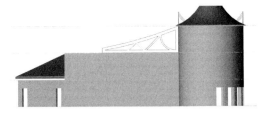

Once you have finished sketching the profile, choose Finish Extrusion on the far right of the Ribbon. Notice that when you do that, you are still in the Model In-Place mode. This means you can perform additional 3D functions. This is but one extrusion within the family. Any number of 3D shapes and elements can be included in a single in-place family. In addition, if you look at the Home and Annotate tabs, you will see that you can also insert components and detail components into the family.

To investigate the creation of an in-place family further, you can open the Revit Structure file called Gothic Structure.rvt and follow along with the next exercise.

EXERCISE: CREATING AN IN-PLACE FAMILY

This lesson walks you through the creation of a special truss family designed specifically for one building that will never be used again in another project.

1. Open the file, available at this book's website, called Gothic Structure.rvt.

2. The file should open by default in the section view called Truss Section - 1. If not, open the view called Truss Section - 1.

3. On the Home tab in the Model panel, choose Component ➤ Model In-Place.

4. For the Family Category value, select Structural Framing and click OK.

5. For the name, enter **Back Entry Truss**, and click OK.

6. On the Model In-Place tab, select Solid ➤ Extrusion.

7. You will encounter the Work Plane dialog box. Under Specify a New Work Plane, choose Pick a Plane, and click OK.

8. Select the back wall, place your cursor near the boundary edge of the arch opening in the wall, and watch for the tooltip: Walls: Basic Wall: Generic -12″ Concrete : Reference.

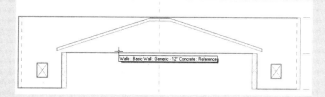

9. Now you are ready to start sketching. Remember, the 3D extrusion will extrude toward you depending on the direction in which the reference plane was created.

10. Sketch a truss shape, complex or simple — it doesn't matter. It must be a valid sketch, meaning no overlapping boundary lines or segments that fail to close/trim properly.

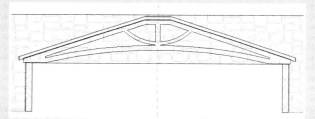

11. Click the Extrusion Properties button on the Create Extrusion tab ➤ Element panel.

12. In the Instance Properties dialog box, verify that the material selected is Wood - Birch.

13. Set the Extrusion Start value to 0′-0″ and the Extrusion End value to 0′-3″ and click OK.

14. On the far right of the Create Extrusion tab, click Finish Extrusion.

15. On the far right of the Ribbon, click Finish Model.

16. Go to the default 3D view, and rotate the view to check out your truss.

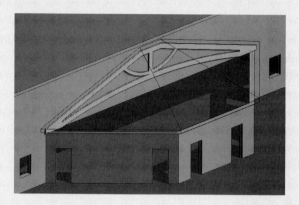

Now you will add a truss in the other direction. Just because you finished the Back Entry Truss family does not mean you cannot edit or continue working on the family at a later time.

1. Open the section view Truss Section - 2. This will bring you to the side view of the truss you just placed.

2. Select the truss you previously created, which is under the high point of the back roof against the building. It is only 0′-3″ wide/thick in this view from the side.

3. On the Modify Structural Framing tab in the Model panel, click the Edit In-Place button. This brings you back into the Model In-Place editing mode, as shown by the current Ribbon tab.

4. Select Solid ➢ Extrusion.

5. In the Work Plane dialog box, choose to specify a work plane by Name, and select Reference Plane : Center from the drop-down list. We prepared the file for you earlier by adding a reference plane in the plane view and naming it Center.

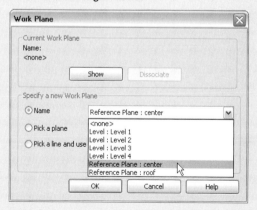

6. Sketch another truss profile.

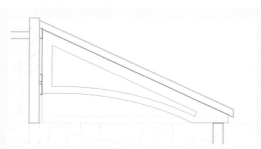

7. Click the Extrusion Properties button.

8. Set the End value to **0′-1 1/2″**.

9. Set the Start value to **- 0′-1 1/2″** (negative). These two settings place half the truss thickness on either side of the Center reference plane.

10. Click OK.

11. Click Finish Extrusion.

12. Click Finish Model.

13. Check out the truss in a 3D view.

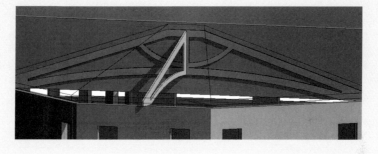

As you have just seen, you created the trusses while sketching in orthogonal views, which are equivalent to the task of sketching them in a 2D CAD elevation or section once. However, now that you have done this you can study and document the design in any other view that you need because they are 3D trusses, not just 2D line work in a single-view file. The ability to freely create any kind of required geometry in a 2D environment and achieve 3D results is crucial to BIM and the modeling process as a whole. As you can see from the previous exercise, you could easily elaborate on this truss system by adding two section view cuts along the hips and sketching the trusses in those views. Because the additions belong to the same family, you can enjoy greater organization and flexibility if you ever need to alter the trusses.

Another item in Revit Structure that allows for organization is the Group feature. The ability to take any typical geometric configuration and create a unified set of objects from it can be quite powerful.

Grouping

Families are useful and make Revit Structure effective. Groups extend this usefulness because families are associated with a single category, while a group is a collection of elements that can be associated with a variety of categories. Families also tend to be most effective if they are somewhat ambivalent about the project's specific use of them. Groups, on the other hand, can let you assemble a wide variety of otherwise innocuous families into a very useful, easily repeatable building condition that can be changed efficiently when or if required.

The concept of grouping has been around in Revit Structure for quite some time, and it is a simple procedure. You collect a bunch of components, group them together, and copy the entire group around the model. If you need to change anything within the group, you change one component, and the rest are updated automatically. It is as simple as that. Of course, not every situation will benefit from grouping, but when used correctly it can be very advantageous.

Before you create a group you need to first ask yourself, "Should this be a group?" Like anything in Revit Structure, if you try to use a specific feature beyond its usefulness, you are negating the benefit of that feature's functionality. You can wind up with a collection of groups that get confusing and, worse yet, will exponentially expand your file size. You also have two distinct types of groups: annotation and model. Revit Structure handles model components differently than annotation components, so there are two types of groups available. So with that in mind, let's start creating groups. In our example, a typical cross-bracing elevation will be grouped and then labeled accordingly.

The purpose of a group is to maintain consistency throughout the model by establishing typical conditions and configurations. The end goal, as is the overall end goal of BIM, is to ensure that a change made in one place will occur in every instance of that configuration. There will be times, however, when a copy of a specific group needs to have a stand-alone edit performed. Revit Structure takes this into consideration as well. But first, take a look at Figure 18.33. It is an elevation of two slightly different bracing schemes: Brace Frame A on the left and Brace Frame B on the right. It sure would be nice if these could be grouped and copied around the model. It would be even better if when the HSS sizes change, every instance of Brace Frame A and Brace Frame B would be updated.

FIGURE 18.33
These brace frames currently stand alone, but they will be grouped later.

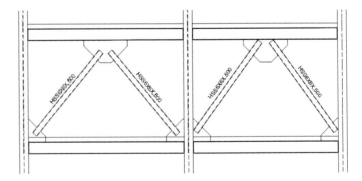

Creating a Group

To create the group containing the bracing, you must first select the items you want grouped, including any text and tags. Select the two HSS members, their tags, and the three gusset plates of the left brace frame. A Multi-Select tab is now available.

1. Click the Create Group button in the Create panel, as shown in Figure 18.34.

FIGURE 18.34
First select the items you want to group, and then click the Create Group button.

2. Once you click the Create Group button, a dialog box will appear, allowing you to name two separate items. One item is the model group, which contains all the model components you selected.

3. Name the model group **Brace Frame - A**. The second name is for any annotations that go with the components, tags in this case. If you have a group with no annotation, the detail group is omitted.

4. For this example, name the attached detail group **Brace Frame - A Tags**, as shown in Figure 18.35.

FIGURE 18.35
The Create Model Group dialog box allows you to name the model group as well as the attached detail (annotation) group.

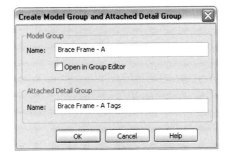

5. Once the group is created, you will see a blue grip at the bottom center of the group. This is the group origin, and it can be moved.

6. Place this origin where you want the group's insertion point to be. In this case, it would be a good idea to place it at the intersection of the grid line and the top of the lower framing member. See Figure 18.36.

Once the group has been established, it will appear in the Project Browser. Because the group contains model objects, it will appear under the Model heading under Groups. If you expand the model tree, it will expose the Brace Frame - A model group. Now if you expand the Brace Frame - A model group, you will see the attached detail group, indicated by the paperclip icon, as shown in Figure 18.37.

Now that you can see the group in the Project Browser, you can simply drag the group into the model and place it using the insertion point. When you are selecting the group item to drag into the model, be sure to drag the model group, not the attached detail group. Once the model group is placed, you will notice that the tags were not inserted along with it. This is because you may not want to include the annotation with every occurrence of the group. In many cases, you can annotate one typical group and assume the others are the same unless noted otherwise. In the event you do need to annotate each instance, you can annotate the entire group in one shot.

FIGURE 18.36
Drag the origin to the point that makes the most sense as an insertion point.

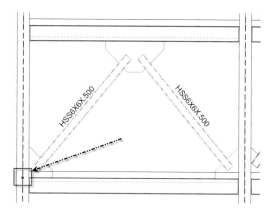

FIGURE 18.37
The group is displayed in the Project Browser. From here you can simply drag and drop the group into the model.

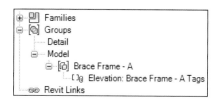

Once the group has been inserted, select it. You will see that the entire group is one entity with a blue dotted line indicating the perimeter of the group. You will be presented with the Modify Model Groups tab. In the Group panel there are four choices: Edit Group, Ungroup, Link, and Attached Detail Groups.

Editing a Group

The first choice, Edit Group, allows you to make changes to the group's configuration. Once you click the Edit Group button, you will be using the Group Edit mode. An Edit Group panel will appear on the Ribbon, as shown in Figure 18.38. You can click the plus sign to add elements to the group and the minus sign to remove elements from the group. The paperclip icon allows you to create and attach a new detail group to the model group, and the group properties button will display the group's Instance Properties dialog box. Any changes you make to the group are reflected in every instance of the group that exists in the model.

FIGURE 18.38
In Group Edit mode, you have access to the Edit Group panel on the Ribbon.

Ungrouping Elements

The Ungroup button removes the grouped elements from the group and returns the geometry to its original state, no longer part of the group. In a sense, using AutoCAD terminology, it "explodes" the group.

Linking Models

The Link option uses the group to create a separate Revit Structure model file, and then that file is linked back into your model. Once you execute this tool, Revit Structure will ask if you want to create a new project file or if you wish to find an existing model, as shown in Figure 18.39. Either way, the instance of the group will be replaced with a linked external file.

FIGURE 18.39
You can create a linked Revit Structure model by using the Link option. This can be advantageous in controlling file size.

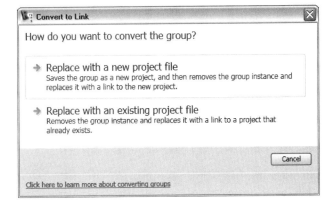

Normally you will create a new model, but there are some cases such as an architectural overlay where you may want to find an existing model. Once you choose between creating a new model and linking an existing one, Revit Structure will add the link to the Project Browser, as shown in Figure 18.40. You or another team member can now work on the link separately without having to start file sharing. This can become quite helpful in the waning days of a project.

FIGURE 18.40
The new link is added to the Project Browser.

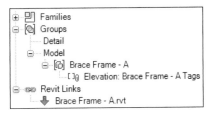

Another nice thing about the ability to turn a group into a linked Revit Structure model is that you can reverse the action. If you select the new link, you will notice a Bind button on the Options bar. You can bind any linked model (it does not have to start out as a group). Once the link is bound, it turns into a group. This can be helpful in many situations, but be aware of the file size of the linked file and what that will mean for the current model's file size once it is bound.

Once you click the Bind button, you will get a dialog box asking which items you want to bring into the current model. See Figure 18.41. If you choose to bring in levels and grids, you will create separate, uniquely named grids and levels. Be careful here, as this could overwhelm you with redundant information. In general, this is probably not a good idea.

FIGURE 18.41
Revit Structure gives
you the option of not
bringing in redundant
elements when you are
binding a link.

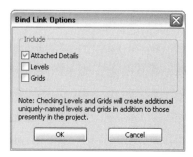

Inserting Annotations

The Attached Detail Groups button will insert the annotations that compose the attached detail group. This is a nice feature that allows you to annotate the model elements consistently. Once you click the Attached Detail Groups button, a dialog box will appear listing the attached details associated with that particular group, as shown in Figure 18.42. You can select a detail, and it will annotate the entire group.

FIGURE 18.42
This dialog box allows
you to select which
attached detail to attach.
Access this dialog box
by selecting the group
and then clicking the
Attached Detail Groups
button.

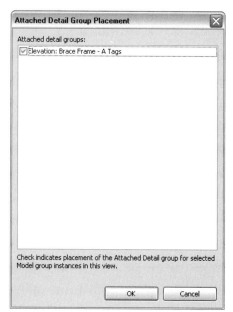

Editing Groups Independently

You will almost certainly run into a situation where you would like to make a slight modification to only one instance of a group without having to ungroup the set and create a brand-new grouping. This is allowed in Revit Structure. Once the group has been copied around, you can simply hover your cursor over the object you wish to modify within the group. Of course, the entire group will become highlighted, but once this occurs, press the Tab key on your keyboard to highlight the specific element. While the element is highlighted, right-click on it, and a small group icon will appear along with the shortcut menu, as shown in Figure 18.43. In the shortcut menu you will notice a Move to Project tool and an Exclude tool.

FIGURE 18.43
By selecting a single element in the group, you can either exclude it from the instance or move it back into the project.

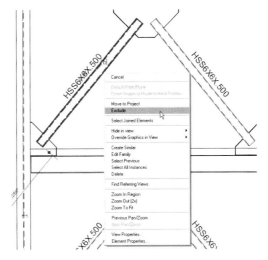

FIGURE 18.44
By hovering your cursor over a group with an excluded element, you can select the element and click the group icon on the member that was excluded to return it to its original place within the group.

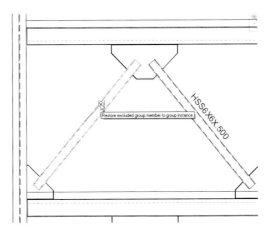

The Move to Project tool will create a copy of the selected element from the group and place it back into the project. The element that this tool is used on is still part of the group, but that same element is now hidden from view (excluded) for that instance of the group, and it won't be included in schedules. In contrast, the Exclude tool just hides the selected element in this instance of the group. You also have the option of clicking the group icon to exclude the element. If you choose to exclude the element from the group, Revit Structure hides it but remembers that instance of the element for later retrieval. After you select Exclude, you can hover your cursor back over the group to reveal hidden elements. After using Tab to select the desired element, you can click the group icon that appears to move the element back into the group, as shown in Figure 18.44. This icon works as a toggle to exclude and restore the selected element. You also have the option of using the shortcut menu and selecting Restore Excluded Member. In addition, if you want to restore all excluded elements, you can select the group as a whole and select Restore All Excluded from the shortcut menu. Keep in mind that should you use the Move to Project tool, the Restore All Excluded tool will make the hidden element visible again, and this will likely mean that there are two elements in exactly the same location. If this does happen, a message will appear warning you that there are now identical instances in the same place.

The following exercise allows you to create a group on your own using the provided Revit Structure model from this book's website.

EXERCISE: CREATING A BRACE FRAME GROUP

This exercise allows you to create a brace frame group and copy it throughout the model. As you make your way through this exercise, try to think about specific situations where you may want to use this feature.

1. Open the file titled Bracing Groups.rvt.

2. Select all the elements (seven) of the brace frame on the right. This includes the two HSS members, the three plates, and the tags. Be careful not to select the adjacent framing or the slab.

3. Click the Create Group button.

4. Name the model group **Brace Frame - B**.

5. Name the attached detail group **Brace Frame - B Tags**. (Note the option Open in Group Editor, which is useful if you need to make some changes right away.)

6. Click OK.

7. Find the grip dot that indicates the group's insert point of origin, and drag it to the left projected end of the HSS framing.

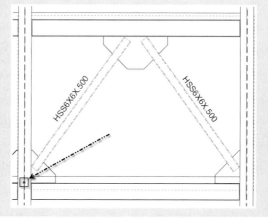

8. Expand the Project Browser under the Groups category, and find the new group.

9. Drag the new group into the bay above.

10. Select the new group.

11. Click the Attached Detail Groups button on the Ribbon.

12. Click the Elevation: Brace Frame - B Tags check box.

13. You can either repeat this procedure or simply copy the brace frame to each bay. Either way, fill in the rest of the bays above the original Brace Frame - B.

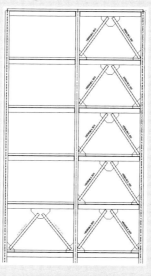

14. Select any one of the brace groups, and click Edit Group on the Ribbon.

15. Select the two HSS6X6X.500 brace members, and change them to W8x10s using the Type Selector.

16. Click Finish on the far right of the Ribbon.

17. All of the brace members are then updated.

As you can see, there are some real advantages to using groups within a Revit Structure model. Having a good grouping strategy and sharing it with everyone on the team, you will greatly increase your productivity in terms of organization and uniformity.

The Bottom Line

Create a footing step family.   Creating families is a vital skill. You create a family, such as a footing step family, by meticulously tying reference planes with dimensions and parameters. Then you add 3D solids to the references to achieve a flexible, useful family.

Master It When you start a new Revit Structure family from a template, there will be existing reference planes. How do these reference planes help in the creation of the family?

Create in-place families. You create specialized families, called in-place families, directly within the model, tying the family to the surrounding building. This allows you to more easily create custom geometry that will probably never be used in another model.

Master It What is the process for creating a custom family directly within the model?

Create groups. Adding groups to the model greatly reduces the time spent organizing and manipulating the configuration of certain items. Also, by linking a group, you can actually create a separate Revit Structure model and link it back into Revit Structure, similar to creating an x-ref in AutoCAD.

Master It You also learned that a linked Revit Structure file can be turned into an embedded group. Explain the procedure for this to occur.

Chapter 19

Advanced Structural Families

As you have been working through the chapters of this book, you have been learning how to use the basic libraries to obtain your model elements. You go to a library file and load in different types from a family for use in your project, such as a 3 × 6 from the lumber family. But as you gain experience and have to deal with the many objects that occur in a real-world scenario, you quickly find that the built-in libraries do not have everything you need. You'll get into more complex objects such as wood and steel trusses, tapered steel girders, and wood beam nailers, to name just a few. These objects will require more advanced modeling techniques.

This chapter looks at some of these objects that you will undoubtedly encounter and need to model and explores the more advanced methods required to construct them. Integral to this discussion is the notion of pure, solid modeling techniques that enable you to construct modeled objects. Using a combination of solid and void forms that can be extruded, revolved, swept, and blended, you will find that you can create almost any shape imaginable. These tools are located on Ribbon in the Home tab ➢ Model panel ➢ Model In-Place tool. In the examples presented in this chapter you will learn to use these tools to construct particular families for your project. When you have completed this chapter, you will have learned how to create more complex objects.

This is a tall order for one chapter, but you truly do want to move beyond simple techniques in order to unleash the real power of this program. We will break it all down into easy-to-follow steps that you can then apply to your own families when the need arises. The examples that you will learn in this chapter are not perfect, nor are they the final word on how these families might be done. Perhaps if you tinker a bit, you can improve them. The first object you will learn how to construct is a tapered girder family.

In this chapter you will learn to:

♦ Create a parametrically driven tapered steel girder family

♦ Construct an in-place bent beam family

♦ Adapt the steel wide-flange beam family by adding a nailer to its top

♦ Create an elevator pit family that can be dropped into your project

♦ Produce wood and steel truss families using the truss template

Creating Tapered Steel Girders

Tapered steel girders are a common element in many buildings but are not available in any Revit Structure family (see Figure 19.1). You will need to prepare your own at some point. Many long-span conditions, such as a gymnasium or a hotel lobby, use this type of girder. A tapered steel girder is one whose center depth is greater than the end depth, or it is flipped upward with the center higher than the endpoints. You could make a single nonparametric tapered girder specifically for your project by making an in-place family (it is nonparametric if it does not flex into different depths). But why not create a family that you can use over and over again and from which you can easily create different mid-span and end-span depths? That is the most efficient approach, though a little more thought provoking and challenging to create. When you are able to develop a truly flexible and reusable family from scratch, you begin to really unlock the power of Revit Structure.

FIGURE 19.1
Tapered steel girder types created from a parametric family

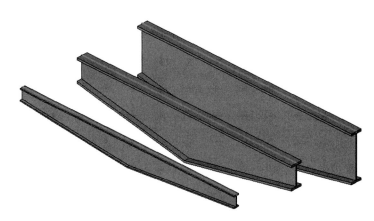

Defining the Basic Constraints

To get the process started, first you will create a new family, and then you will define the basic constraints of the shape. As you learned in the previous chapter on basic family creation, this is done by adding reference planes to which you will lock the girder sketch lines that define its shape. Those reference planes will be dimensioned, and then the dimensions will be enhanced so that they become labels (parameters) whose value may vary. Doing so will allow the shape to flex as you create different types.

Once you've defined the rules that your family will follow, you will create the shape by using the Swept Blend tool to create the tapered form, which will be attached to the reference planes. Finally you will adjust the visibility of the various family components so that they show correctly in coarse or 3D mode.

The first step in making a parametric tapered steel girder family is to open a new family template file and set up some reference planes, so do the following:

1. Start a new project so that we can use it to test the family as we progress.

2. Start a new family by choosing New ➢ Family on the Application menu.

3. Select Structural Framing - Beams and Braces for the template, and then click OK.

4. Once you're in the Family Editor, open the front elevation.

5. Select and delete the rectangular extrusion that you find there.

6. Set the Detail Level to Medium so the stick symbol will be hidden.

Now you will need to add five horizontal reference planes: one for the top flange of the girder, two for the end-span depth, and two that represent the mid-span girder depth (see Figure 19.2).

FIGURE 19.2

The front elevation with five added reference planes

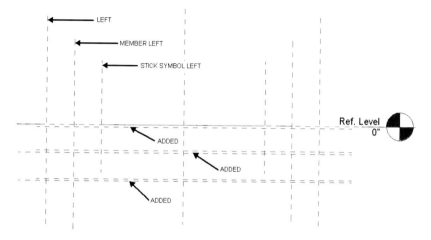

7. On the Datum panel of the Create tab click Reference Plane, then choose Draw Reference Plane from the drop-down list, and draw the five new horizontal reference planes:

    a. Draw one just below Ref. Level (about 1″ down).

    b. Then draw two (about 1″ apart) about 1′ below Ref. Level.

    c. Then draw another two about 2′ below Ref. Level.

Next go to the right view so that you can add four more vertical reference planes that will represent the flange width and the web thickness.

8. On the Create tab click Reference Plane, then choose Draw Reference Plane from the drop-down list, and draw four new vertical reference planes like those in Figure 19.3 (note that the girder profile has been ghosted in for the next few figures to make it easier for you to understand what we are doing). Draw two reference planes, at $\frac{1}{2}''$ and 3″, to the left of the center reference line and two to the right of it.

ADDING DIMENSIONS AND LABELS TO THE CONSTRAINTS

Now that the new reference planes have been added, you will dimension them and apply labels. Your values do not have to match the figure at this time. To dimension the reference planes do the following:

From the Dimension panel of the Detail tab of the Ribbon choose the Aligned Dimension tool. In the right view add seven defining dimensions to the reference lines (see Figure 19.4) for the following:

    ◆ Girder end depth

    ◆ Girder mid depth

FIGURE 19.3
Adding the reference planes to the right side view

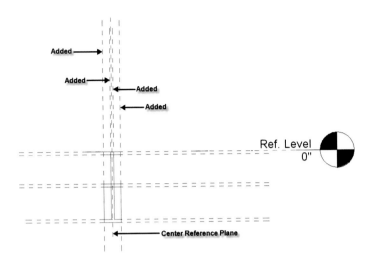

FIGURE 19.4
Adding dimensions to the right side view

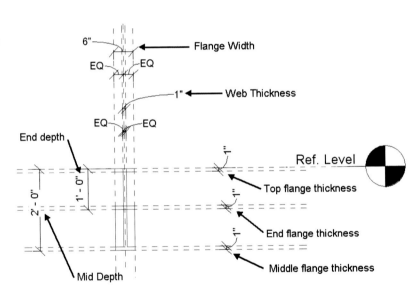

◆ Flange thickness in three locations: top, end, and middle

◆ Flange width (You must also use the EQ constraint to keep the flange symmetrical about the centerline.)

◆ Web thickness (You must also use the EQ constraint to keep the flange symmetrical about the centerline.)

Now that the reference planes are dimensioned, you will create the labels. You want to make the family parametric so that you can create different family types in your projects. To do this you will alter the dimensions you just added in order to create labels for end-span depth, mid-span depth, flange width, flange thickness, web width, and web thickness.

1. Select the End Span Depth dimension (1′-0″), right-click, and select Edit Label from the context menu.

2. Choose <Add Parameter>.

3. In the Parameter Properties dialog box, name the parameter **End Span Depth**.

AVOID MATH SYMBOLS IN PARAMETER NAMES

You should not include math symbols in parameter names, such as naming this one End-Span Depth. This will generate errors if the parameter is used in a formula. The hyphen in the name will be interpreted as a subtraction operation.

---

4. Choose Dimensions as the Group parameter.

5. Click the Type radio button to make it a Type parameter.

6. Click OK to complete the label (see Figure 19.5).

7. Repeat steps 1 through 6, and create the Mid Span Depth, Flange Width, Flange Thickness, and Web Thickness parameters. When completed, your reference planes should look like Figure 19.6.

FIGURE 19.5
Defining the End Span Depth label in the Parameter Properties dialog box

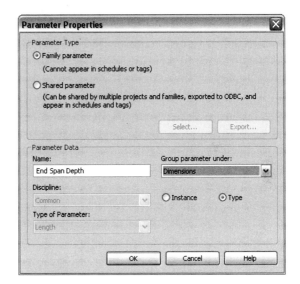

Now you need to start flexing the labels to test whether the reference lines you have created are working. Remember that you need to constantly test your family by flexing the different dimensions you have established.

1. On the Family Properties panel of the Create tab of the Ribbon, click Types.

2. Change the Mid Span Depth parameter to **5′-0″** and then click Apply.

3. Save the file.

FIGURE 19.6

Altering the dimensions to create the labels

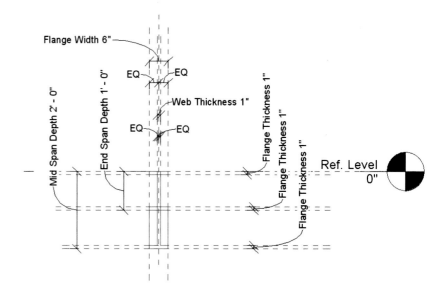

Did the bottom two reference lines stretch correctly to the new depth? If not, you need to cancel and check the problem areas. This process can get frustrating, but after awhile you will get the hang of it. Test the other labels in the same way until all are flexing correctly. Once you have the reference lines flexing correctly, open the Ref. Level plan view again.

CREATING THE TAPERED GIRDER GEOMETRY

You now will create the basic geometry of the tapered girder (look back at Figure 19.1). Once you have done that, you are almost finished creating this family. This part of the process will use a Solid Swept Blend to create half of the tapered girder.

1. Open the Ref. Level plan, if it is not already opened.

2. From the Forms panel on the Create tab click the Solid tool icon; then choose Swept Blend from the drop-down list.

3. From the Mode panel on the Swept Blend tab click Sketch Path.

4. Sketch a horizontal line along the Reference Plane : Center (Front/Back), from the left (leftmost) vertical reference line to the Center (Left/Right) reference line, and lock its ends to them.

CONSTRAINING THE ENDPOINT AND THE LINE TO THE REFERENCE PLANE

If you sketch the path above and just short of each reference plane, it is easy to use the Align tool to ensure that each endpoint and the line are properly constrained to each reference plane. It is easier to do this first than to figure out which one is wrong later.

---

5. Click Finish Path from the Path panel on the Swept Blend ➢ Sketch Path tab.

6. On the Edit panel of the Modify Profile 1 tab click Edit Profile, and then open the right elevation view.

7. On the Swept Blend ➢ Edit Profile tab, use the line tools to sketch lines that represent the end-span depth profile (see Figure 19.7).

FIGURE 19.7
Lock the sketch lines to the appropriate reference plane.

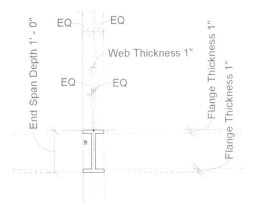

It is very important to make sure that the sketch lines are locked to the reference planes. To do so, follow these steps:

1. On the Modify tab select the Align feature.

2. Click a reference line and then the associated sketch line you want to match; then click the padlock icon to lock it.

3. Do this for all the sketch lines you have created for the end-span depth profile.

4. Click Finish Profile.

5. On the Mode panel of the Swept Blend tab, click Modify Profile 2.

6. On the Edit panel of the Modify Profile 2 tab, click Edit Profile.

7. On the Swept Blend ➢ Edit Profile tab, use the line tools to sketch lines that represent the mid-span depth profile, and lock them to the reference planes as you did with the end-span depth profile.

8. Click Finish Profile, and then click Finish Swept Blend.

Now go to a 3D view and flex the various values in the Family Types dialog box to test that the shape is stretching as you expect. When you are satisfied that the shape is flexing correctly, go to the front elevation view.

1. Highlight the swept blend, and mirror it about the vertical center line.

2. Lock the ends of both swept blends to the vertical center line (see Figure 19.8).

3. On the Modify tab click Join ➢ Join Geometry, and then join the two pieces together.

4. With the Align tool lock the ends of the tapered girder again to the left and right vertical reference planes.

FIGURE 19.8
Locking the two
segments of the
tapered girder to
the center line

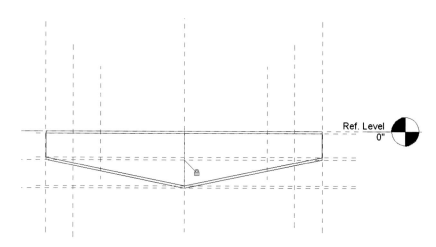

It is very important to make sure the sketch lines of the new mirrored solid are locked to the reference planes as well. To do so, use the Align tool. This can get a bit tedious, but pay close attention so that you get all of the lines. When you mirror the girder from one side, you may have to relock to the new reference planes on the other side.

You have now completed the tapered steel girder family (see Figure 19.9) and can make some family types.

FIGURE 19.9
The two profiles of
the solid swept blend
highlighted for half the
tapered girder

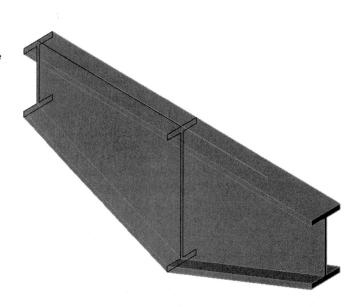

1. Select Types from the Family Properties panel on the Modify tab — or any other tab for that matter.

2. In the Family Types dialog box choose New.

3. Name the type **1′ x 2′**.

4. Change the End-Span Depth value to **1'-0″** and the Mid-Span Depth value to **2'-0″**.

5. Click Apply, and confirm that it is flexing okay.

6. Repeat steps 1 through 3, and create a 2' × 4' family type and a 3' × 5' family type.

7. Save the finished tapered girder.

WHAT SHOWS AS THE THUMBNAIL?

When you save the finished tapered girder, remember that the last view open when the file is saved/closed will determine what the thumbnail will be when users load the family into the project.

Now you are ready to test the finished tapered girder. It acts like any other beam object, and it also will work with a beam system.

1. Load the family into a new project.

2. On the Home tab click Beam.

3. Choose a tapered girder type, and draw it just as you would any other beam.

4. Go to a 3D view and check it out.

 **Real World Scenario**

OH-OH! WE HAVE A MAJOR PROBLEM HERE!

Did you notice one discrepancy in what we have done? Remember how you set the flange thickness dimension and label in the right side view? But in fact the lower flange is sloping. That means the dimension in the right side view is not really the thickness of the lower flange but is a little bigger, as illustrated in the following graphic.

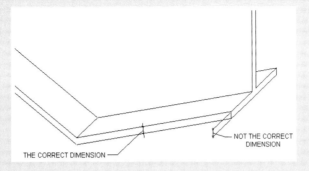

This turns out to be the most difficult and advanced part of creating this family. If you go to the front view and try to add a dimension and label for the sloping bottom flange, you will find that it becomes overconstrained. There is no way around it. So how can we overcome this dilemma? This problem even flummoxed the authors, who then had to contact Revit Structure headquarters for assistance. Coming to our aid was Jack Zhang Lee, one of the family-creation specialists.

To set the correct flange thickness for the sloped parts of the girder, we need to set the sloped angle beforehand (see the following illustration), so that we can then calculate the flange thickness with that angle. The angle for the tapered girder is a function of the overall length of the girder, so it can be computed only as a resultant value after placing the element. So you must test this family for accuracy in a project, not in the family file.

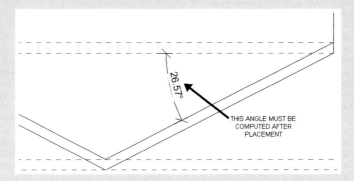

Yes, you can add formulas to your parameters for just this kind of purpose. Here is how it works.

In the family:

You create a new parameter, namely, **Length1**, and set Length1 equal to **Cut Length**.

In the Family Editor, Length1 may not represent the real physical length of the beam, but in the project it does refer to the real physical length of the component. The flange thickness could be calculated precisely in the project with the nested profile employed.

In the project:

The resultant angle is computed with the following formula (see the two illustrations):

$$\text{Bottom Flange Angle} = \text{atan}(2 *(\text{Mid Span Depth} - \text{End Span Depth}) / \text{Length1})$$

For the beam itself the cut length is computed with the following formula:

$$\text{Length1} = \text{Length} + 0'\ 1'' + \text{Start Extension} + \text{End Extension}$$

Then from that the Flange Vertical Thickness value is computed. Notice how the three parameters are grayed out in the dialog box. That is because they are resultant values that you cannot manually change.

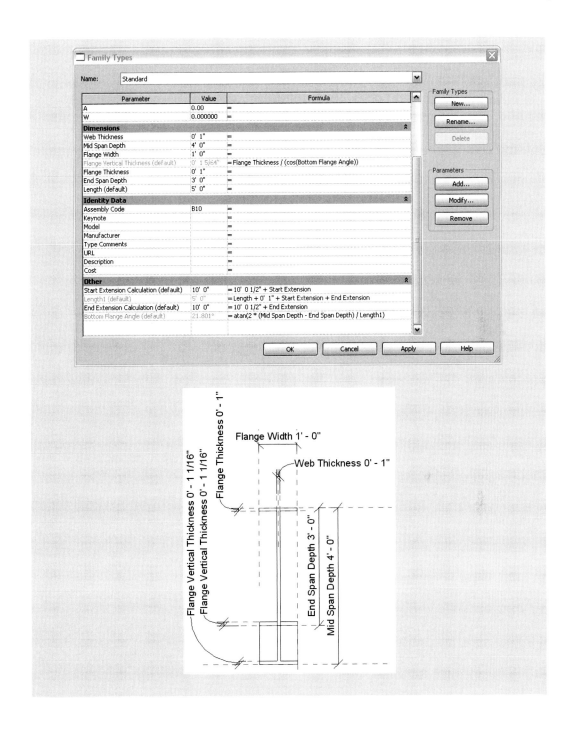

So there you have the answer to a very complex problem. I am sure we could go further in this discussion and keep tweaking the family, but we need to move on to our next advanced structural family. Maybe you can take a crack at it. You may find a better solution. When you get stuck with this sort of thing, it can be very taxing on your sanity! But stick with it, and look around on the Web for help in the AUGI Structural Forum or other such sites. Don't be afraid to ask for help. That's what we did.

 **Real World Scenario**

THE OLD 80-20 RULE

You may know the old saying usually referred to as the 80–20 rule. Known as the Pareto Principle, it points out that you probably wear 20 percent of the clothes in your closet 80 percent of the time. In the case of modeling, you will find that as you gain proficiency, 80 percent of the work will sail along. The client and your boss will be delighted that you have done the work and used only 20 percent of your drafting fee for the project. Life is wonderful at that point; high fives all around.

But then you find you have to model elements that cannot be done so easily and require huge workarounds or are so complex that it takes a monumental effort to complete them. Suddenly that 20 percent of the work takes 80 percent of your fee to accomplish. The boss is probably not so happy at this point.

That is one of the reasons why we are presenting these more complex families to you in this chapter. These are objects that can take a lot of time to do if you do not create families for them. Creating them anew each time you need them will considerably slow your progress and create needless work.

So do not get lulled asleep by your initial successes. When your project begins, try to scope out the elements that might cause you problems and prepare to deal with them. Let your boss know where you can expect difficulties and how much it will cost in time and effort to devise methods to deal with them. Don't get caught in the 80-20 trap.

We just worked through the process that you use to create a family from scratch. You got off to a good start because you used the template for beams and braces, which saved you a lot of work. You created the proper constraints for the tapered girder geometry. Then you overcame a big problem getting the sloping bottom flange to show the correct thickness. In the next section you will create a single in-place family within an existing project.

Creating Bent Steel Beams

Another common structural item you are bound to need while modeling your building is a bent beam (see Figure 19.10), whether in concrete or steel. You will probably be happy to learn that creating this one is not as involved as creating the tapered girder family. Earlier, in the chapter on framing, you saw that you can create many types of curved beams, but bent beams require a different approach. Since the bent beam is usually an isolated case, you may want to do only a quick model of it directly in your project. This will be accomplished by using the Model In-Place tool. Basically you create a solid sweep and apply a beam profile to it. Then you add a symbolic stick line for coarse detail mode display to finish out the family. But you do not go to the trouble of making the family parametric by creating labels for your dimensions so that it can stretch to many shapes. Let us break down the process and step through its creation.

FIGURE 19.10
Bent beams in a 3D view

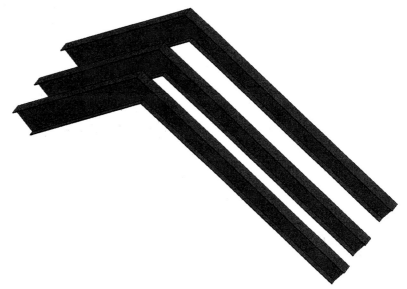

Here is how the procedure works. First you set up the file and start the in-place family:

1. Open a new Revit Structure project. It should start with Level 2 open. Change the scale to $\frac{1}{2}'' = 1'\text{-}0''$.

2. Draw a single horizontal grid line above the south elevation mark (a named reference plane also works).

3. On the Model panel of the Home tab, click the lower half of the split button for Component, and then choose Model In-Place from the pull-down list.

4. Select Structural Framing from the Family Category list, and click OK.

5. Name the in-place family **Bent Beam 1** (you may have others to construct).

6. Click OK, which puts you in the Family Editor environment but still within the context of your project, and you can now begin constructing the bent beam.

Next you will create a solid sweep. You will need to use a plan view and an elevation view as you construct it. First you will use the south elevation view to draw the path of the bent beam.

1. On the In-Place Modeling panel of the Model In-Place tab, click Solid ➢ Sweep. This will put you into Sketch mode.

2. Now double-click the South elevation in the Project Browser.

3. On the Home tab click Set on the Work Plane panel, and then choose Grid 1 as your active work plane (or select a named reference plane).

4. On the Sweep tab click the Sketch Path icon on the Mode panel.

5. Use the Line tool on the Draw panel to sketch the bent beam path, something like the one shown in Figure 19.11.

FIGURE 19.11
Sketching the 2D bent beam path in the elevation view

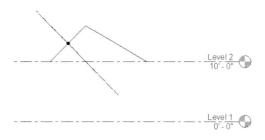

6. On the Path panel click Finish Path to complete the path.

7. Click Select Profile on the Mode panel of the Sweep tab.

8. On the Edit panel, use the drop-down list to select a W16X26 from the list of loaded profiles.

9. On the Options bar change the Angle value to **90** degrees in order to roll the profile into a web vertical position.

10. Click Finish Sweep, and the basic form is done.

11. Go to your 3D view and check out your progress.

Now you will apply a material to the bent beam.

1. Select the bent beam, and click the Element Properties tool on the Element panel on the Model In-Place tab.

2. Click the Materials parameter field, which then displays the Materials button, the small button with three dots. Click this button to open the Materials dialog box.

3. Select Metal - Steel - ASTM A36.

4. On the right side of the dialog box, click the Shading Swatch button. This displays the Color palette (see Figure 19.12).

5. Change the color to an RGB (red, green, blue) value of 128, 0, 0, a tone of dark red that makes the steel display more realistically.

6. Click OK until you exit all the dialog boxes.

You are still in the Model In-Place Family Editor, but now go to the 3D view and check out your results thus far. In the 3D view on the View Control bar, click Model Graphics Style. Select Shading with Edges to get a good display of the bent beam. It is always a good idea to check the 3D view as you work to make sure it looks right.

Now you will add a symbolic stick symbol line in plan view. Go to Level 2, and zoom in to the bent beam. You will probably see something like Figure 19.13. Notice that part of the bent beam is above the cut plane of the view and not visible. Adjust the Level 2 View Range until the entire bent beam is visible.

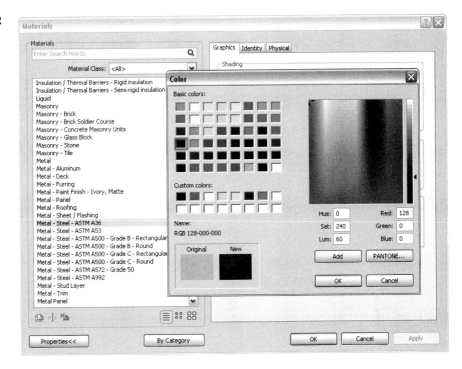

To add the stick symbol to the in-place family, do the following:

1. Click Symbolic Lines on the In-Place Modeling tab.

2. Select Stick Symbols [Projection] from the drop-down list on the Element panel.

3. Draw the line along the length of the bent beam, right on the center.

4. Press the Esc key, and then highlight the stick symbol.

5. Lock both ends of the stick symbol to the bent beam model (see Figure 19.14). You can use the Align tool for this.

Finally you will adjust the visibility of the family components so they show correctly in different detail modes:

1. With the stick symbol selected, click the Visibility Settings tool on the Visibility panel.

FIGURE 19.14
Locking the stick symbol
to the model endpoints

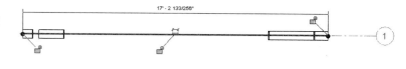

2. Uncheck Medium and Fine, as you do not want the stick symbol showing in those detail modes. Click OK to exit.

3. Select the bent beam sweep, and then click the Visibility Settings tool on the Form panel this time.

4. Uncheck Coarse, as you do not want the sweep showing in your coarse detail mode views. Click OK to exit.

5. Click Finish Family.

You have now completed the process of creating an in-place bent beam family. The bent beam can be copied and adapted for other instances as required. But it is important to remember that when in-place families are copied, each instance becomes its own new family. That is a real negative if you want to have many copies in your project, because each copy will have to be individually edited if you need to change the bent beam in any way. So if you think you will have many copies, best practice is to create the family externally and load it in. That type can then be copied, and both the original and the copies need be edited only once.

The next section walks you through creation of a wood nailer on a steel beam family.

Adding a Wood Nailer on a Steel Beam

So far in this chapter you have created a parametrically driven tapered girder family and an in-place bent beam family. In this section you will alter an existing family by adding a wood nailer. What is that? If you work with wood products much, you will know (see Figure 19.15). Many commercial structures are built using multiple materials such as wood and light steel framing. In order to attach wood members such as floor framing and plywood sheathing to a steel beam, wood members are bolted to the top, and sometimes to the bottom, flange of the beam. These are called *beam nailers*. Revit Structure does not ship with a family to accommodate this assembly, so you are going to learn how to do it yourself.

Now you could go about this by adding a wood member over a steel member independently of each other, but the process gets quite difficult to control that way. The best approach is to make your own family by adapting the basic wide-flange steel family in order to make your own integrated wood nailer family.

ADAPTING THE SHIPPED REVIT STRUCTURE FAMILIES

Adapting the basic families shipped with Revit Structure can be a very useful approach to creating your own families, and it is a great way to learn more advanced approaches to your work. Just be sure that you do not save the adapted family with the same name, or you will end up overwriting the original family. Each framing family has an associated text file, which serves as a database of information. Each line in the text file is a record that describes a certain type, or distinct shape, within the family. You will need to copy that file to the new family name as well.

FIGURE 19.15
Wood nailer on the top of a steel girder

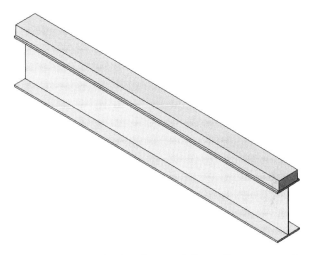

The procedure for creating the basic wood nailer family is as follows. First you need to set up the file:

1. Open a new default project.

2. On Level 2 draw a W16X26 beam.

3. Select the beam, and click Edit Family on the Family panel of the Modify Structural Framing tab.

4. Click Yes to open the W-Wide Flange beam family for editing.

5. Immediately save the family using the Save As option. Name it **W-Wide Flange with Top Nailer**.

Using Windows Explorer, you will next browse to your structural framing library in order to copy the text file associated with the family. Do you know where that is located? If you do not know, you can check under File Locations in the Options dialog box. The default location will be in your Documents and Settings folder. When you find the folder, do the following:

1. In the Steel Framing library copy the file W-Wide Flange.txt and save to a new file called: W-Wide Flange with Top Nailer.txt.

2. Go back to the Revit Structure file, and choose the right elevation view.

3. Zoom in on the top flange of the beam shape.

4. On the Graphics panel of the View tab, click Thin Lines to make it easier to see the beam lines.

5. Draw three reference planes above the top flange in order to anchor the three sides of the nailer (see Figure 19.16).

6. Select the existing vertical Center (Left/Right) reference plane, and click Pin on the Modify Reference Planes tab.

FIGURE 19.16
Draw three new reference planes above the top flange.

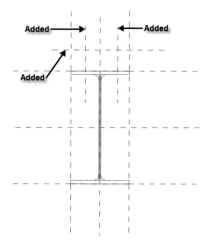

Now you will draw a solid extrusion over the top flange that represents the nailer:

1. From the Forms panel on the Create tab, click Solid ➢ Extrusion.

2. For the reference plane select Reference Plane : Center (Left/Right), as shown in Figure 19.17.

3. Sketch a rectangle to represent the nailer, and lock the four sides to the reference planes (see Figure 19.18).

4. Click Finish Extrusion.

FIGURE 19.17
Selecting the reference plane for the solid extrusion

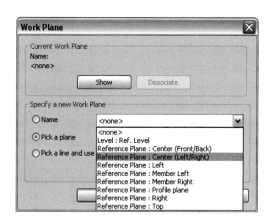

FIGURE 19.18
Lock the sketch lines to
the reference planes.

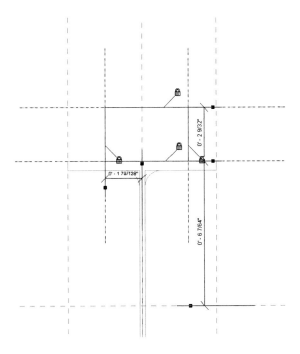

Next you will add dimensions to the reference planes and then create labels that will control
the nailer size:

1. Add dimensions to the added reference planes as shown in Figure 19.19.

2. Select the Nailer Depth dimension.

3. Right-click and select Edit Label.

FIGURE 19.19
Adding dimensions
to the nailer refer-
ence planes

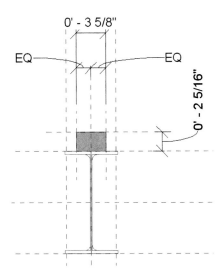

4. On the pull-down menu, select <Add Parameter>.

5. In the Parameter Properties dialog box, name the parameter **Nailer Depth**.

6. Group the parameter under Dimensions.

7. Click the Type radio button to make it a Type parameter.

8. Click OK to complete the label.

9. Repeat steps 2 through 8 to create the Nailer Width label.

Now it is time to flex the nailer to make sure it works correctly:

1. On the Detail tab click Types.

2. Under Dimensions change the Nailer Depth value to **2.5"** and the Nailer Width value to 5.5". Those values would be for a standard 3 × 6 profile of a piece of lumber.

3. Click Apply to demonstrate that the assembly can change to different shapes (see Figure 19.20). If you get a message that the shape is overconstrained, click Remove Constraints.

4. When you have finished testing, click OK to exit the dialog box.

FIGURE 19.20
The dimensions have been changed to labels.

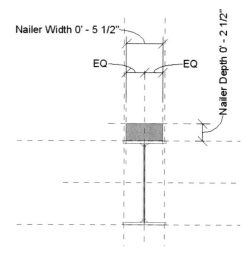

Now that the nailer profile is completed, the next step is to anchor the extents of it to the ends of the steel beam. Notice that we lock it to the reference plane and not to the actual steel member. That is always the best practice.

1. Go to the Ref. Level plan view.

2. On the Modify tab click Align.

3. Click the long reference plane at the beam end and then the one at the nailer end.

4. Close the lock, and then do the same for the other end.

Next you need to adjust the visibility of the nailer so that it does not show in coarse detail level:

1. Select the nailer, and then on the Modify Extrusion tab click the Visibility Settings tool.

2. Uncheck the Coarse check box, and then click OK to exit.

Finally, you will assign a material to the nailer. Most likely there is no wood material loaded, so you will need to create it:

1. With the nailer highlighted, click the Element Properties button on the Modify Extrusion tab.

2. In the Instance Properties dialog box, click into the Value box of the Material parameter, and then click the small button with three dots. This will display the Materials dialog box.

3. Click the blue icon at the bottom left of the dialog box to create a new material by duplicating the default material.

4. Call the new material **Wood - Dimensional Lumber**.

5. Click the Shading tab, and set the RGB values to **223, 192, 134**.

6. Click OK until you exit all the dialog boxes.

You have now-completed the family. Once again go to the right view, and then change the Model Graphics Style to Shaded with Edges. Does it resemble Figure 19.21? Go to the 3D view, and flex the family with various nailer sizes to make sure everything is working correctly. Now you are ready to load it into your project whenever needed. One nice aspect of this family is that the insertion will be from the top of the nailer, so setting its top in relation to your level can be done quite simply.

FIGURE 19.21
The finished nailer on a
steel beam, forming an
assembly

Modeling Wood Shear Walls

The next subject for you to explore is the creation of wood shear walls. Especially in seismic zones, the structural design and documentation of shear walls is essential to master. But what is the best practice in terms of modeling this type of element? It might be a retail store in a mixed-use project, or it might be a student housing project. Your structural model will need interior and exterior shear wall types as well as bearing wall types. Wood projects can be quite a challenge to model because they have many, many pieces, as opposed to a steel or concrete building. So modeling them takes a lot of planning and good modeling techniques.

Of particular importance to this type of wall family is to embed 2D detail components right into the family. You will take a generic wall type and create a 6″ wood shear wall with the required elements. The process you will use to accomplish this is to create a profile family first and embed the 2D components into it. Then you will add that profile to the wall family.

Using Detail Components in Wall Families

Using detail components in families is an important evolution in your practice, as we briefly discussed in Chapter 9. As you learn more about the family-creation process, you should look for ways to embed 2D components directly into the family.

The goal in doing so is to have the ability to cut a section through your model so that the result is as complete as possible. Having to add lots of 2D lines and detail components to your sections after they are placed in your project adds a lot of extra work, especially when the model starts flexing or you move the wall. The stand-alone 2D components you place in your sections tend not to follow the wall model and must be repositioned, oftentimes more than once. The wood shear wall is a good example of this. The shear wall will have plywood sheathing and top and bottom plates to which the studs are nailed. Why not have everything in one package?

To illustrate this idea look at Figure 19.22. There are four different wall types displayed in section view.

◆ On the left side is a generic 6″ wall that shows no detail of the wall. Lots of work to do there.

◆ Second from the left is a 6″ shear wall in which plywood sheathing has been added and cuts have been made to show the outline of the 3 × 6 nailers. That is a little better.

◆ Third from the left is a 6″ shear wall with plywood sheathing. It also has embedded detail components for the plates and the bolt at the bottom. Better still.

◆ On the far right side you see that a concrete curb has also been added as another option, so you need not draw it separately.

FIGURE 19.22
Wood shear wall creation using detail components

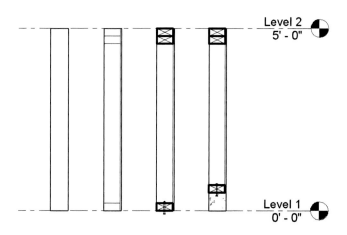

So which wall type would you like to use on your project? Of course, you might ask why we are not modeling all the wall studs and plates. The answer is that we could, but it would be very difficult to accurately place each stud. A worker building such a wall in the field would not find it all that useful to have such a model of framing plans. The important information for the design team is the overall wall length, the sheathing location, and the hold-down anchor locations at the end of the wall and at doorways.

First you will create the profile for the top and bottom plates similar to the way it was done in Chapter 9:

1. Browse to the Structural Library ➢ Profiles ➢ Structural ➢ Wood and open Dimension Lumber-Profile.

2. On the Family Properties panel of the Create tab click Types.

3. Click New, and name the new type **3x6**.

4. Set the b dimension to **5-$\frac{1}{2}$″** and the d dimension to **2-$\frac{1}{2}$″**; then click OK to exit.

5. On the Detail panel of the Create tab click Detail Component.

6. Click Yes to load a detail items family.

7. Choose Detail Components ➢ Div 06-Wood and Plastic ➢ 061100-Wood Framing, and then double-click Nominal Cut Lumber-Section.

8. Select a 3 × 6 component, and click OK to apply it and close the screen.

9. Rotate the component after placement, and then move it directly over the profile lines.

10. On the Applications menu choose Save As, and save the new profile with the name **Dimension Lumber-Profile with plate.rfa**.

11. Start a new default project, and go to Level 1. Save the project as **Wood Shear Wall Example**.

12. Go back to the new profile family, and load it into your new project file.

Now you are ready to begin the process of creating the wood shear wall. Do the following:

1. In the new project file on the Structure panel of the Home tab, select Structural Wall.

2. In the Type Selector choose Basic Wall: Generic - 6″.

3. Click the bottom half of the split button for the Element Properties tool on the Element panel of the Place Structural Wall tab, and then choose Type Properties from the drop-down list

4. Click Duplicate.

5. Name the new wall **6″ Wood Shear Wall**, and then click OK.

6. Click Edit in the Structure field, which will display the Edit Assembly dialog box.

7. Click the Preview button on the bottom left to expand the view.

8. Change the view to Section: Modify Type Attributes.

9. Click the Material for Structure [1] area, and select Wood - Stud Layer. Then click OK to close.

10. Change the thickness to **5$\frac{1}{2}$″** (the actual size of a 3 × 6).

11. Click Insert to add the sheathing layer. Highlight the new layer, and click Up to move it out of the Core Boundary area.

12. Change the Material value to Wood - Sheathing - Plywood, and then give it a thickness of $\frac{1}{2}''$.

13. Click Sweeps, and then in the Wall Sweeps dialog box click Add.

14. Set the following parameters for the sweep (see Figure 19.23):

    ◆ Profile: Dimension Lumber - Profile Plate: 3 × 6

    ◆ Material: Wood - Stud Layer

    ◆ Distance: $1\frac{1}{4}''$

    ◆ From: Base

    ◆ Side: Exterior

    ◆ Offset: $-3\frac{1}{4}''$ (note negative value)

15. Click OK to complete the addition of the sweep to the wall family.

FIGURE 19.23
Creating the bottom plate for the shear wall

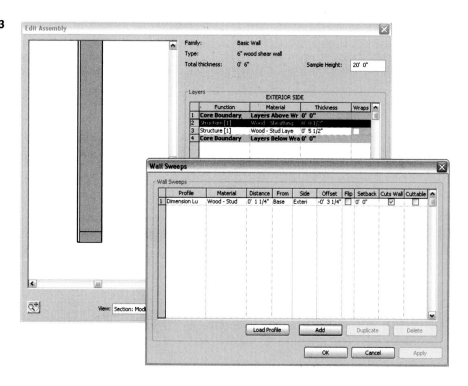

Next you will unlock the sheathing at the bottom of the wall so it can move independently in the vertical position after placement:

1. With the Sheathing layer still active click Modify, and then zoom in on the bottom of the wall in the preview. You can use the Steering Wheel tool in the bottom-left corner to navigate the preview window.

2. Click the bottom line of the sheathing layer until you see the lock; then unlock it (see Figure 19.24).

FIGURE 19.24
Unlocking the sheathing layer

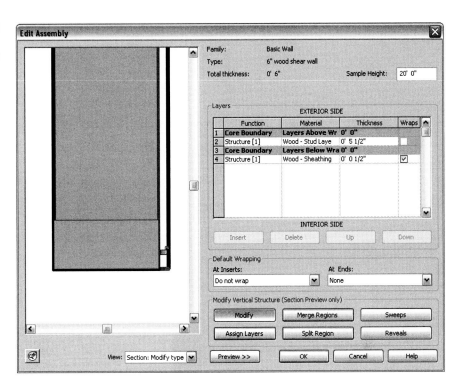

Next you will add two more profiles at the top of the wall to represent the top plates:

1. Click Sweeps and then Add.

2. Set the following parameters for the first top plate sweep:

- Profile: Dimension Lumber - Profile Plate: 3 × 6
- Material: Wood - Stud Layer
- Distance: $-1\frac{1}{4}''$ (note negative value)
- From: Top

◆ Side: Exterior

◆ Offset: -3$\frac{1}{4}$″ (note negative value)

3. Set the following parameters for the second top plate sweep:

◆ Profile: Dimension Lumber - Profile Plate: 3 × 6

◆ Material: Wood - Stud Layer

◆ Distance: -3$\frac{3}{4}$″ (note negative value)

◆ From: Top

◆ Side: Exterior

◆ Offset: -3$\frac{1}{4}$″ (note negative value)

4. Click OK to complete the addition of the two top plate sweeps to the wall family.

5. Click OK successively until you exit all dialog boxes.

Now draw a wall in plan view. Go to a section view, and change the detail mode to Medium. Your wall should look like that in Figure 19.25. Try pulling the sheathing layer up and down to make sure it is free to move. As a further example, you could create another profile family by adding a 2D detail component of a bolt in section to the file you created for the basic stud plate.

FIGURE 19.25
The completed shear wall with sheathing and top and bottom plates

There is a lot you can do there, and you will probably have to spend time getting used to this assembly. For now we will turn to creating an elevator pit family from scratch.

Developing Elevator Pits

Almost every multistory building is going to have an elevator pit and most likely a sump pit. You will have to show the pit opening and then the pit walls dashed to represent the pit on your floor plan. The pit can appear in different sections you might take for detailing purposes as well. In the 3D modeling world you need to model the pit as one important structural component of the project. If you do not model the pit, you risk losing the integrity of the model as a BIM solution.

The first and most obvious way to approach the pit construction is to simply add foundation walls and a slab at the bottom of the pit. But this will take some effort in getting all the pieces situated correctly, and display can be messy. The pit slab and walls also generally intersect and form a bearing surface that is a little harder to construct (see Figure 19.26). The inner pit footing line slopes up at an angle connecting to the pit slab. You will need to add a slab edge profile and then join all the geometry to get it looking right.

FIGURE 19.26
Elevator pit wall and
slab edge condition

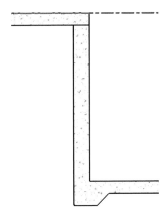

So instead of using that approach, what if you were to make a parametrically driven elevator pit family that could simply be loaded into your project and dropped onto the floor as a single unit? The 3D pit family would automatically attach to the underside of the floor slab and create the pit opening. The plan view would be exactly and cleanly displayed, and the whole thing could be pushed and pulled into place as one big assembly. For each project you could adapt the pit length, width, and depth dimensions to fit the particular installation in that building. Several types of pits could also be created on one floor.

Well, that elevator pit family is exactly what you are going to create in this section of the chapter (see Figure 19.27).

FIGURE 19.27
The elevator pit family
in cutaway view

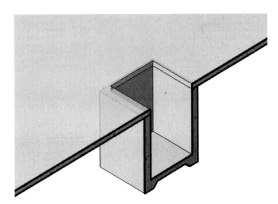

The procedure to create such a pit family can seem quite involved, so we will break it down into parts. You start a new family first and then add reference planes where the walls and pit slab will be located. You add dimensions to the reference planes that you later change to labels. Then you add solid extrusions for the walls and pit slab that are attached to the reference planes. Next you add void forms to make the floor opening and to sculpt the pit slab. Finally you add 2D symbolic lines and set the visibility for different detail levels.

To create an elevator pit family, follow these steps:

1. Open a new default project.

2. On the Application menu drop-down click New ➤ Family.

3. For the family template type select Generic Model Floor Based, and then click Open. You then will work on the floor that has already been created in the template. Using the floor-based template means that the pit will be hosted by a floor element.

Now you must establish reference planes to which you will attach the walls:

1. Make sure you are on the Ref. Level plan. Zoom extents (keyboard shortcut ZE) so that you can see the central reference plane axis.

2. On the Create tab click Reference Plane.

3. Draw eight reference planes around the central axis to represent the pit wall lines (see Figure 19.28). Do not worry about exact placement or dimension, but make it about 4'-0″ square.

4. Use Figure 19.28 as a guide to add dimensions to the reference planes. Lock only the four 8″ dimensions.

5. On the Create tab choose Solid ➤ Extrusion from the drop-down list.

FIGURE 19.28
Create eight reference planes around the center point of the slab.

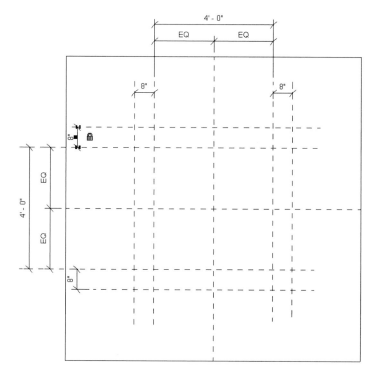

6. On the Create Extrusion tab select the Rectangle tool on the Draw panel.

7. Now draw two rectangles representing the inner and outer faces of the pit, and lock them to the reference plane (see Figure 19.29).

8. On the Element panel of the Create Extrusion tab choose Extrusion Properties, and make the Extrusion End value equal to **-5'-0"**. Click OK to close.

FIGURE 19.29
The wall lines are locked to the reference planes.

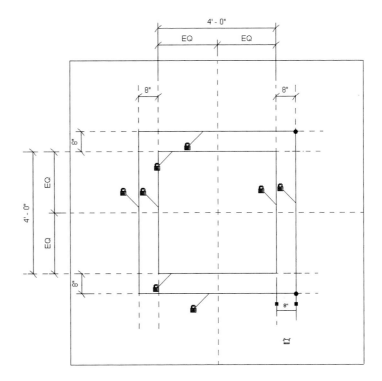

9. Click Finish Extrusion on the Extrusion panel to complete the walls.

Now you will create the pit slab:

1. On the Create tab click Solid ➤ Extrusion.

2. Draw a rectangle around the inner walls, and lock them to the inner reference planes (see Figure 19.30).

3. On the Element panel of the Create Extrusion tab, choose Extrusion Properties.

4. Make the Extrusion End value **-5'-0"** and the Extrusion Start value **-4'-0"**.

5. Click OK, and then click Finish Sketch to complete the pit slab.

Next you will create the opening in the host floor slab. You should still be in the Ref. Level view:

1. On the Model panel of the Create tab click Opening. This places you into Sketch mode.

2. Now Click the Rectangle tool on the Draw panel.

FIGURE 19.30
The pit slab lines are now locked to the reference planes.

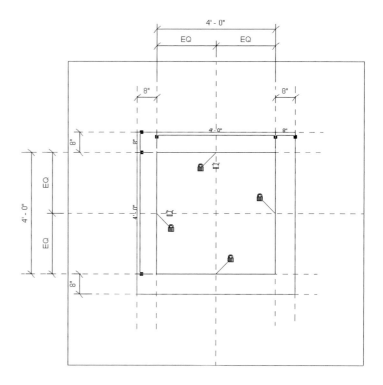

3. Create a rectangle around the inner walls of the pit and lock the lines.

4. Click Finish Sketch and there you have it; your basic pit is complete (see Figure 19.31). But it still is not parametric yet, is it? We still have a way to go.

The next step is to add a reference plane and dimensions to control the depth of the pit:

1. Go to the Front Elevation view.

2. Select Reference Plane on the Create tab and Pick Existing Line/Edge from the drop-down list.

3. Click the top of the pit slab line. Stretch the new reference plane line out to the left, and lock the geometry to it.

4. Repeat steps 2 and 3 for the bottom of the pit slab (see Figure 19.32).

   Note that the bottom of the slab and the bottom of wall solid forms must both be locked into the bottom reference plane. If you are having problems selecting either one, press the Tab key until you can select properly.

5. Add one dimension from the floor line to the top of the pit slab and one for the thickness of the pit slab.

6. On the Edit Geometry panel of the Modify tab, click Join ➤ Join Geometry from the drop-down list, and join the pit slab and walls together.

FIGURE 19.31
The slab opening is locked to the inner wall lines.

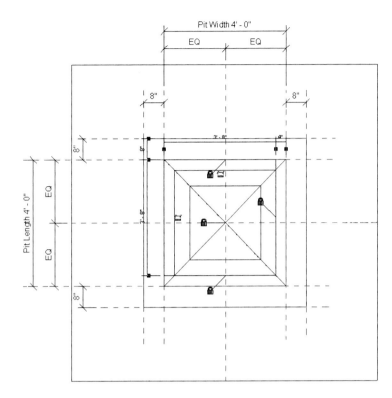

FIGURE 19.32
The pit slab lines are locked to the reference planes.

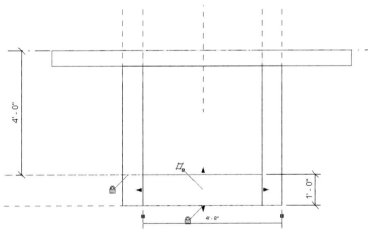

The next step adds a solid void blend to carve out the bottom of the slab so its edges look like Figure 19.34. The point is to make a bearing surface equal to 1'-0" around the pit. We already have the 8" pit wall and now must add another 4".

1. Go back to the Ref. Level plan view.

2. On the Forms panel of the Create tab, choose Void ➢ Blend.

3. On the Draw panel of the Create Void Blend Base Boundary tab, click the Rectangle tool.

4. On the Options bar set the Offset dimension equal to **-4″**. Click the upper left and lower right of the pit opening to create the base of the blend, as shown in Figure 19.33.

   Note: If the rectangle starts to appear on the outside of the slab, press the spacebar to make it go inside the walls.

FIGURE 19.33
Locking the void to the reference plane

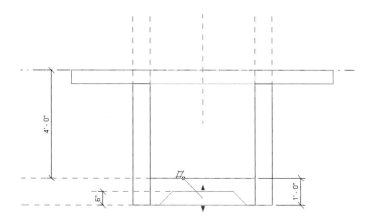

5. On the Mode panel click Edit Top.

6. On the Draw panel select the Rectangle tool, and set the offset dimensions to **-10″**. Click the upper left and lower right of the pit opening to create the top of the blend.

7. On the Element panel select Blend Properties, and set the First End value at **-5′-0″** and the Second End value at **-4′-6″**. Click OK to exit the dialog box.

8. Click Finish Blend to complete the void blend.

9. Go to the front elevation again. Select the void blend, and then align and lock the bottom to the bottom of pit slab reference plane (see Figure 19.34).

10. Add a reference plane for the top of the void, and lock the top of the blend to it. Make a 6″ dimension, and close the dimension lock.

You have now completed the basic geometry of your elevator pit family. The final step is to make it parametric by changing the dimensions you have created into labels. The labels will contain different values that will represent the various pit types that you will create:

1. In the front elevation select the Pit Depth dimension, right-click it, and select Edit Label.

2. Click Add Parameter.

3. In the Parameter Properties dialog box name the parameter **Pit Depth**.

4. Group the parameter under Dimensions.

5. Click the Type radio button to make it a Type parameter.

6. Click OK to complete the label (see Figure 19.35).

FIGURE 19.34
A solid void is added to sculpt the bottom of the pit slab.

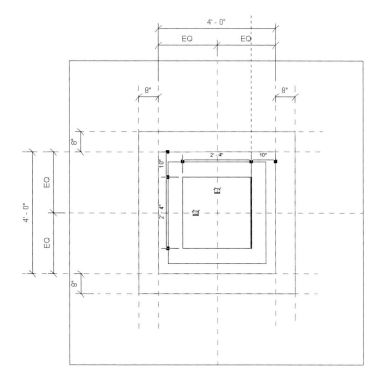

FIGURE 19.35
Defining the Pit Depth label in the Parameter Properties dialog box

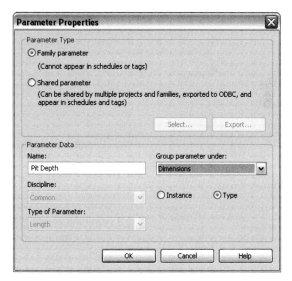

Now you need to start flexing the pit model to test whether the lines you have created are locked into the reference planes. Remember that you need to constantly test your family by flexing the different dimensions you have established.

1. Click Family Types on the Family tab.

2. Change the Pit Depth parameter to **6'-0"**, and then click Apply.

Did the model stretch correctly to the new depth? If not, you need to exit and check the problem areas. Most likely something is overconstrained or improperly locked to a reference plane. This can get frustrating, but after awhile you will get the hang of it. Once you have the model flexing correctly, choose the Ref. Level plan view again.

1. Go to the Ref. Plan view and repeat the process to create new labels for the Pit Length dimension and the Pit Width dimension.

2. Test them in the same way as you did the Pit Depth parameter to make sure the dimensions are flexing correctly to different sizes.

The final step to complete the elevator pit family is to add symbolic lines for your coarse mode display and to establish the visibility of the various parts of the family. If you use the family the way it is now, the plan view will not display appropriately (see Figure 19.36).

FIGURE 19.36
The final display must be configured using symbolic lines and visibility settings so it does not look like this.

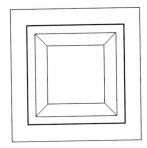

So do the following:

1. Open the front view.

2. Select the walls, and then click the Visibility Settings tool on the Form panel of the Modify Extrusion tab.

3. Uncheck the Coarse detail level, as shown in Figure 19.37. Click OK to exit.

4. Now do the same for the remaining solid and void forms.

5. Go back to the Ref. Level plan view.

6. On the Detail tab click Symbolic Line.

7. On the Place Symbolic Lines tab, click into the Type Selector and select Generic Models [Projection] from the pull-down list.

8. On the Visibility panel click the Visibility Settings tool.

9. Uncheck Medium and Fine so they do not show in those display modes; then click OK to exit the dialog box.

10. Draw a rectangle at the inner edges of the pit walls, and lock the lines to those reference planes.

11. From the Type Selector select Hidden Lines [Projection].

FIGURE 19.37
Use the Family
Element Visibility
Settings dialog box
to set view-specific
display charac-
teristics for your
family members.

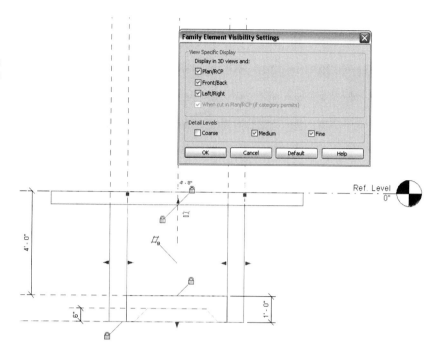

12. Draw a rectangle at the outer edges of the pit walls, and lock the lines to those reference planes.

13. On the Draw panel using the Generic Models [Projection] line type, click the Line tool, and then draw an *X* to represent the area of the pit opening.

Now the pit in coarse mode will look like Figure 19.38.

FIGURE 19.38
The pit plan view after
the Visibility settings are
completed, showing the
symbolic/model lines in
coarse mode

There you have it, a finished elevator pit family. It is time to take it for a test run. Start a new project, and on the first level add a 6″ concrete slab. Load the elevator pit family into the file. You will find the family under Generic Models. Drag it out, and drop it onto the floor (see Figure 19.39). Check out the plan view in coarse detail level to make it sure it is displaying correctly. Go to a 3D view, and notice how you can push and pull the pit around the slab. Take note as well how the walls automatically adjust to the floor depth and how the opening is automatically created in the floor slab.

You may now be getting a feel for the power of Revit Structure families and your ability to create your own families for the particular situations your project may demand. The next section focuses on another more advanced item, steel and wood trusses.

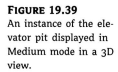

FIGURE 19.39
An instance of the elevator pit displayed in Medium mode in a 3D view.

Creating and Adding Steel and Wood Trusses

Trusses are one type of structural object that we did not cover in the chapter on structural framing. They tend to require more advanced thinking and planning. While there are many families available for loading into your model, you will come across many conditions that will require you to build your own families. Trusses in Revit Structure are treated as assemblies that are created with numerous pieces. The truss families consist of basic truss forms (see Figure 19.40) and individual elements that can be configured with different structural framing members and whose spacing can be adjusted. The basic forms have a top chord and a bottom chord, as well as vertical and diagonal members.

In this section you will look at two warehouse buildings that require the addition of truss framing (see Figure 19.41). For one you will see how to add and create a truss whose top and bottom chord elements are steel WT shapes and whose web members are double angles as a free span over the entire warehouse floor area. This is a very common truss configuration. For the other warehouse you will create a wooden truss whose vertical members must be specifically located over intermediate bearing walls. That will require editing of the truss form itself, and it is the more difficult of the two examples.

FIGURE 19.40
Various types of truss families available in the default libraries

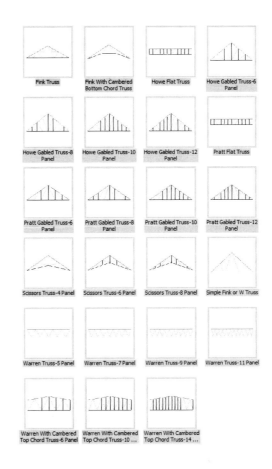

FIGURE 19.41
Two examples of warehouses requiring truss framing

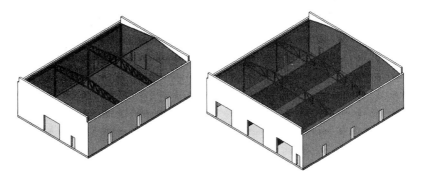

EXERCISE: ADDING A STEEL TRUSS TO YOUR PROJECT

In the following exercise you will add free-spanning steel truss to your project and then configure it for a particular condition.

1. Open Dataset_1901.rvt (from the book's companion web page at www.sybex.com/go/masteringrevitstructure2010).

2. In the Project Browser double-click Level 2.

3. Zoom closer to the section mark along grid line 2.

4. On Structure panel of the Home tab click Truss.

5. In the Type Selector choose Howe Flat Truss: Standard if it is not set already.

6. On the Element panel of the Place Truss tab, click the Element Properties icon; then choose Type Properties from the pull-down list.

7. Click Duplicate.

8. Name the new type **WT+DBL Angle**, and then click OK.

9. For Top Chord Structural Framing Type select WT-Structural Tee: WT9X25.

10. For Vertical and Diagonal Webs Structural Framing Types choose LL-Double Angle: 2L4X4X1/2.

11. For Bottom Chord Structural Framing Type select WT-Structural Tee: WT9X25 and change the Angle parameter to **180**.

12. Click OK until you exit the dialog boxes.

13. Draw the truss from grid A2 to grid B2.

14. Now go to section 1, which should look like the following illustration.

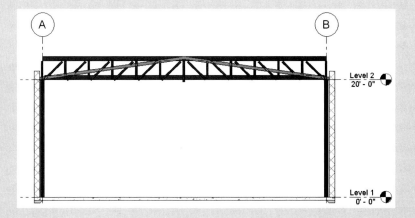

15. Select the truss form. (As you hover over the truss with your mouse, you will see a blue dashed-line representation. Pick that, not any of the individual pieces.)

16. On the Modify Structural Trusses tab, click the Element Properties button.

17. In the Instance Properties dialog box, change the Start Level and End Level offsets to **-2'-7$\frac{1}{2}$"**.

18. Click OK to exit the dialog box.

19. Select the truss form, and then on the Modify Truss panel click the Attach/Detach Top Chord tool. Select the sloping roof element. The truss form should realign with the roof.

20. Select one of the double-angle diagonals or verticals.

21. Click Element Properties ➢ Type Properties on the drop-down list. Change the Space parameter to the width of the WT, **91/256"**, so the double angle fits over the WT web.

22. Click OK until you exit the dialog boxes.

23. Finally, select all the vertical double-angle web members.

24. Open the Element Properties dialog box, and change their Start and End Extension values to **4$\frac{1}{2}$"** so they overlap the WTs.

25. Exit the dialog box, and you have completed the basic truss, which should look like the following illustration.

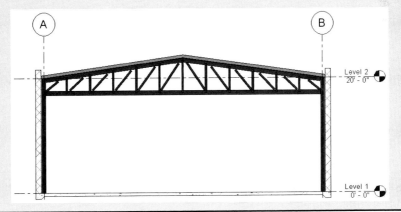

TINKERING WITH THE TRUSS MODEL

You can keep tinkering with the individual extensions and truss form to make it even more complete, as in the following illustration. Each member can be individually adjusted. For instance, each diagonal web member could be extended onto the WT web. Then you could cut the end so it is parallel to the chord member by using the Cut Geometry command. You can also add connection plates between the members. If you are working for a structural design firm and spending a lot of time on the plates, that might not make sense. You could document the connections with typical details and simply reference the elevation to those details. On the other hand, if you are working for a structural detailing firm or a contractor, you might want to develop each piece of the truss quite accurately.

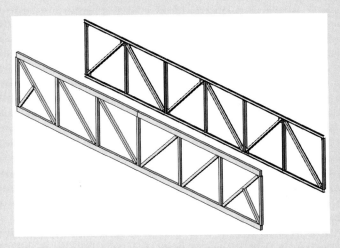

But be careful not to overwork the object, and keep in mind the view scale at which you will display the model as well as your final documentation needs. Do not make the model more detailed than necessary. If you do, you will just be burning your project fee with little return to show.

Working with the Truss Template to Create a Wood Truss

When the built-in libraries and the Truss Wizard cannot work for the condition required in your project, you can build your own truss family. On many projects you must specifically locate the vertical web members of the truss over intermediate supports, so you have to alter the basic spacing of the truss form. Using the truss family template makes the process much easier. The following explanation of this procedure will give you some first-hand experience in making your own truss.

In this second warehouse example, the vertical web members of the wood truss need to located at third points of the truss span because the truss is supported by wood shear walls below. The structural design calls for placing a vertical web member directly over each one. The overall span of the truss is 70′-0″, with the supporting shear walls at 23′-4″ center to center. Develop the truss in the following way:

1. Open Dataset_1902.rvt (from the book's companion web page at www.sybex.com/go/masteringrevitstructure2010).

2. On the Application menu select New ➤ Family.

3. For the family template type select Structural Trusses.

4. On the Family Properties panel of the Create tab click Types, and then in the Family Types dialog box change the Truss Length parameter to **70′-0″** and the Truss Height parameter to **4′-0″**. Click OK to close.

5. On the Detail panel of the Create tab, select Top Chord.

6. Sketch a line from the left reference plane to the right reference plane along the top reference plane. Lock the sketch line to the top reference plane.

7. On the Detail panel select Bottom Chord.

8. Sketch a line from the left reference plane to the right reference plane along the bottom reference plane. Lock the sketch line to the bottom chord reference plane only.

Now that the top and bottom chords are completed, the web will be constructed starting with the critical vertical web members that go over the walls.

1. Add a vertical reference plane between the left and center reference planes. These represent the main supports.

2. Add a dimension string between the three reference planes and make them EQ (see Figure 19.42).

3. Repeat step 2 for the right side of the truss center line.

FIGURE 19.42
Adding the intermediate reference planes

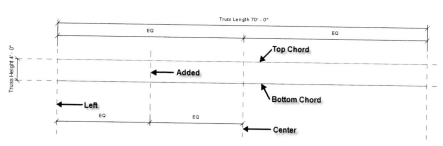

4. On the Detail panel of the Create tab click Web, and then sketch and lock vertical lines at the added reference planes between the top and bottom chords.

5. Using Figure 19.43 as a guide, add eight other vertical reference planes and then nine vertical lines (do not worry about exact placement). Do not add vertical members at the left and right reference planes.

6. Using Figure 19.43 as a guide, add dimension strings to the added web members.

7. Again using Figure 19.43 as a guide, add the diagonal double-angle truss web members between the vertical truss web members.

FIGURE 19.43
Adding the dimensions for the vertical web members in relation to the main supports

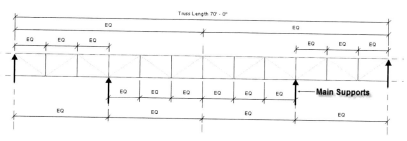

8. On the Insert tab on the Load From Library panel, click the Load Framing Family tool ➤ Structural ➤ Framing ➤ Wood ➤ Dimensional Lumber.

9. Click Open, and then select a 3 × 6 (which you will use for all the members of the truss), and click OK to load it into your project.

10. On the Truss Family tab choose Types, and then set the Structural Framing type for the Top, Bottom, Vertical, and Diagonal members to Dimensional Lumber : 3 × 6. Click OK to exit the dialog box.

The truss creation is completed. Now you will save and load the new truss family into your project and do the final configuration after adding it to the model:

1. Save your new truss family to your project directory with the name **Wood Truss Family**.

2. On the Truss Family tab, click Load into Project. (Since the family is already loaded into the project, you will get a warning message asking you if you want to overwrite it, which is what you want to do.)

3. Back in the building model, use the Project Browser to go to Level 2 if you are not there already.

4. In the Project Browser find the truss under Families ➤ Structural Trusses ➤ Wood Truss Family.

5. Draw the truss in plan view from grid A2 to grid B2.

6. Go to section 1.

7. Select the truss form, and click the Element Properties button on the Options bar.

8. In the Instance Properties dialog box, change the Start and End Level Offset value to -2'-0", and then click OK to exit the dialog box.

9. Highlight the truss form again.

10. On the Modify truss panel click the Attach/Detach tool.

11. Select the barrel roof element, and the truss top chord will reconfigure to its radius.

Now the truss is completed and placed into your project. It should look like the one in Figure 19.44. You can further refine the vertical and diagonal member ends as discussed earlier, depending on your requirements. Note that the truss's vertical web members are accurately placed in relation to the walls below it.

FIGURE 19.44
The final placed wood truss girder

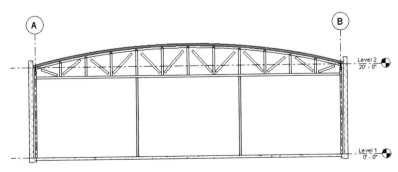

So that is the basic story on how to create, place, and configure structural trusses in a project. In the first case you inserted a truss form from the library and adjusted its spacing and members.

Then you created your own truss from scratch using the truss template for a very specific web placement.

That completes this chapter on advanced structural families. There is incredible modeling power awaiting you when you reach this skill level. So always keep working on your technique, and try to take it to the next level. You will find that you can save lots of time and effort by taking a more sophisticated approach to your projects, using such families as we have presented here. You surely have some good ideas that will apply to your own work that are not included here.

The Bottom Line

Create a parametrically driven tapered steel girder family. In the first section you learned how to develop a new family from scratch using the beam template. You used a blended sweep to create the taper on the lower flange of the girder. You had to introduce a number of new reference planes to which you could then attach the sketch lines of the girder. Adding dimensions between reference planes and making them labels gave you the ability to flex the shape and made the family truly parametric.

Master It What does "flexing the model" mean, and why is it important?

Construct an in-place bent beam family. The bent beam family was created inside the project as an example of an in-place family. You learned how to use a solid sweep form to sketch a path and a steel beam profile along a reference plane in order to create the desired shape.

Master It What elements are used to describe the bent beam family?

Adapt the steel wide-flange beam family by adding a nailer to its top. In this section you adapted the existing wide flange beam family by adding an extrusion onto its top. The extrusion represents the wood nailer and has the ability to flex into different shapes.

Master It What are the four main steps necessary to add an extrusion in the shape of a 3 × 6 to the wide-flange beam family?

Create an elevator pit family that can be dropped into your project. You learned to make an elevator pit family that could be easily inserted into your project. The pit form consists of solid extrusions and void extrusions working together. The whole family is floor based, so it can exist only when associated with a floor object in your model.

Master It What is the void blend used for in the elevator pit family?

Produce wood and steel truss families using the truss template. In the final section you first worked through an exercise in which you inserted a truss from the structural truss library and then reconfigured it to create a steel truss with WT top and bottom chords and double-angle web members.

Then you used the truss template to create a wood truss from scratch so that its vertical web members could be specifically located above supporting walls in a warehouse.

Master It After you inserted the wood truss into your building model, how did you make the top chord of the truss follow the barrel-shaped roof?

Appendices

In this Section you will find:

Appendix A

The Bottom Line

Each of The Bottom Line sections in the chapters suggest exercises to deepen skills and understanding. Sometimes there is only one possible solution, but often you are encouraged to use your skills and creativity to create something that builds on what you know and lets you explore one of many possible solutions.

Chapter 1: Inside Revit Structure

Use the graphical user interface. The Revit Structure GUI is an easy way to interact with your computer in order to efficiently create your project model and documents.

Master It There are several ways to launch a single command in Revit Structure. List the various ways in which the Beam command can be invoked. Which method is the quickest?

Solution You can invoke the Beam command by selecting the beam icon on the Home tab of the Ribbon or by typing BM on your keyboard.

One additional method that is often overlooked is the Create Similar command. If other beams already exist in the model, hovering your cursor over or selecting a beam and executing this command will launch the Beam command.

You can find the Create Similar command on the context menu or by typing CS on your keyboard.

The quickest method to invoke the Beam command is probably by typing the default shortcut: BM.

Understand the types of elements in the modeling environment. In the modeling environment, there are basic types of model and annotation elements that you use in the construction of the virtual model and construction documents that you derive from the model.

Master It Modeled elements have a defined hierarchy that consists of categories, families, types, and instances. Select a structural column and give examples of each of these four element properties.

Solution The category is Structural Columns.

An example of a column family is the W-Wide Flange-Column family.

An example of a type of column for this family is a W14X99.

An example of an instance of this type of column is the placement of a two-story W14X99 column at a grid intersection in a project. Each column placement is a singular instance with unique properties.

Create and manage project views.   Even though you are building a 3D model, most of the time you are working in views that present the model as if they are 2D views, such as plans and sections. Therefore, the view types become your working planes and must be sensibly arranged.

Master It   List all the major project view types discussed in this chapter.

Solution   The project view types discussed were plans, callouts, sections, elevations, drafting, legends, schedules, 3D, sheets, and plan regions.

Control the graphical display of elements in a project.   Creating the model is only half the story. You must also derive the 2D and 3D views you will need for your construction documents. Each of these views must be able to display the model, and those display controls are an essential subject to understand.

Master It   In your project you want to change the look of your masonry units on plans and elevations to match your company standards. Explain how to change the cut pattern for concrete masonry units to a diagonal pattern and the surface pattern to 8 × 8 block.

Solution   On the Manage tab of the Ribbon, click Materials to open the Materials dialog box. Highlight Masonry - Concrete Masonry Units. Click the Cut Pattern tab, and in the Fill Patterns dialog box change its setting to Diagonal Down. Click the Surface Pattern tab, and change its setting to Block 8 × 8. Then exit the Materials dialog box.

Chapter 2: Setting the Project Environment

Develop your own custom templates.   Knowing all of the items that you can store in a template file will help you avoid creating data that is the same over and over and make it easier to encourage following company standards.

Master It   What extension does a template file have? What types of things can be stored in a template file? What cannot be stored in a template?

Solution   A template file takes on the extension of .rte. Just about everything that is in a project can be stored in a template file. Some basic examples are materials, line weights, fill patterns, view templates, project settings, and text and dimension styles. More advanced examples include wall types, slab types, schedules, and sheet setup. Worksets cannot be placed in a template file.

Set project units and precision display.   Setting the units for your project and the precision of them is part of documenting your model for those who will be using it.

Master It   What are the three types of units in Revit Structure?

Solution   The three types of units in Revit Structure are Common, Structural, and Electrical.

Make adjustments to structure-specific settings.   Revit Structure has several areas of settings that are specific to how elements display for your documentation.

Master It   Where do you go to assign the global display of symbolic representations for different types of connections? What type of family template do you use to create a new symbol type?

Solution   To set the global display of symbols for different connection types, choose the Manage tab ➤ Project Settings panel ➤ Structural Settings tool. When creating a new symbol type for these connections, use the `Generic Annotation.rft` template with the appropriate category set to Brace in Plan View Symbols or Connection Symbols.

Organize the Project Browser.   Learning how to organize your browser depending on the workflow and requirements of the project will allow you to work more efficiently and keeps the browser free and clean of unused views.

Master It   For what two things can you create a browser view type in the Project Browser? When creating a new project parameter so that you can sort your sheets in the Project Browser, what category do you need to apply the new parameter to?

Solution   You can create a browser view type only for views and sheets in the Project Browser. When creating a new project parameter for sheets, you need to assign the parameter to the category Drawing Sheets.

Transfer standards into your project.   Being able to use settings and content from past or other current projects allows you to avoid duplicating your efforts over and over again and ensures that standards are kept.

Master It   What command is used to bring new line weight settings into a project that is using old line weight settings?

Solution   Use the Transfer Project Standards tool (Manage tab ➤ Project Settings panel ➤ Transfer Project Standards tool) to transfer standards from another template or project file into your current file.

Chapter 3: Starting To Model Your Project

Import and link CAD data.   Many of your projects are likely to start with bringing in an architect's CAD data. In this chapter you learned how to bring a DWG file into your Revit Structure model and manipulate it to conform to your company's standards.

Master It   Once you add a DWG to the model, you will find that the DWG does not look the way you would like it to. Name two methods of controlling how it looks.

Solution   By going to the Visibility/Graphic Overrides dialog box for that view, you can select the Imported Categories tab, where you can access all of the layers and change their display. You can also halftone the entire underlay.

Link and work with Revit files.   The power of Revit Structure shines when you can get a Revit model from the architect. You can link that model and perform a Copy/Monitor operation to add superior integration unseen in CAD applications.

Master It   Although the actual import of the Revit Architecture model is quite simple, you can copy specific objects from the Revit link and keep a live connection telling you if anything changes when the model reloads. How does Copy/Monitor work?

Solution   Once the link is inserted, click the Copy/Monitor tool located on the Collaborate tab of the Ribbon. You can then select the Revit link. The Ribbon will transform into the Copy/Monitor tab. You can select either Copy or Monitor, depending on the situation.

Create levels. One of the most compelling aspects of Revit Structure is its ability to contain the entire model in a single file. The ability to create levels and generate floor plan views that are associated with them is a huge part of this functionality.

> **Master It** As mentioned earlier, levels and plan views are connected. How does Revit Structure determine which level belongs to which plan view? What do you do if you need a new plan view based on an existing level?
>
> **Solution** If you change the name of a level, you will be prompted as to whether you want to rename the associated plan view. If you click Yes, the plan view will keep the identical name as the level. If you find yourself in a situation where you added levels but not plan views, choose the View tab ➢ Create panel➢ Plan Views drop-down ➢ Structural Plan tool. The resulting dialog box lists levels that do not have views associated with them. Removing the check from the Do Not Duplicate Existing Views check box will display all levels that are in your project.

Create grids. Revit Structure allows you to create grids "stick by stick." This freedom is crucial to being able to easily model any building shape needed.

> **Master It** In this chapter you learned how to create a grid. Once the gridlines are in place, you have to make further adjustments. Explain how to do so.
>
> **Solution** Once the grids are in place, select one of them. You will see a number of options once a single gridline is selected. You can turn the grid head on or off, add an elbow, and even create a new grid type to leave out the middle portion.

Chapter 4: Structural Columns

Work with the basic structural column family template. Understanding the differences between the various templates for a structural column will help you ensure that your structural columns behave properly when placed into your project.

> **Master It** What setting in a structural column family gives it the characteristics that help Revit Structure determine connection and attachment properties and whether the columns display in the Graphical Column Schedule?
>
> **Solution** The Structural Material setting in the structural column family specifies how other framing members behave when they frame to the column and how attachments behave when columns are attached to other elements. You can also use this setting to display only columns of certain material types in a GCS.

Place structural columns in your project. Knowing all the methods available for placing structural columns in your project and knowing when to use each one will help you place columns quickly and accurately into your project.

> **Master It** What are three options you can use to place structural columns in your project, and how can you quickly place them onto the upper levels?

Solution   You can put columns in your project by placing each column one at a time, or you can use the On Grids option, which will put a column at each grid intersection you select. If architectural columns are in the project, you can place columns by using the At Columns option. You can select and copy columns to the clipboard and then choose Paste Aligned to Levels.

Attach structural columns to other structural components.   To help maintain the top and bottom of a column's location and their relationship to other elements, they can be of different cut styles and justifications while being attached to various elements.

Master It   What types of elements can structural columns be attached to?

Solution   Structural columns can be attached to floors, roofs, foundations, structural framing members, reference planes, and reference levels.

Employ the methods of placing slanted columns.   Revit Structure allows you to place slanted columns into your project using similar methods used to place vertical columns. As you attach the top and base of a slanted columns to levels, you can set the slanted column's properties to determine how they behave when those levels are modified.

Master It   What view type does not allow a slanted column to be placed, and what are the two properties that can be specified in the Column Style setting to control how slanted columns behave when their top and base locations are modified?

Solution   A plan view does not permit placing a slanted column. In order for the Slanted Column tool to be available, you need to be in a 3D view or a section/elevation view. Setting the Column Style to Slanted - Angle Driven maintains the angle of the column (changing the endpoint locations), and setting it to Slanted - End Point Driven maintains the endpoint locations (changing the angle) when the top and base locations of the column are modified.

Document your model with the Graphical Column Schedule.   The Graphical Column Schedule can be generated automatically by Revit Structure and modified to exclude columns that you do not want displayed.

Master It   What methods are used to remove structural columns from the Graphical Column Schedule?

Solution   You can use several methods to remove structural columns from the GCS. You can choose to not schedule off-grid columns, to schedule by their material type, to use phasing, or to use filters to remove them.

Chapter 5: Floor Slabs and Roof Decks

Create a slab-on-grade with dropped slab edges.   Using the Slab command, you can create slabs-on-grade and apply dropped edges to them with the Slab Edge function. You can also edit the profile file for slab edges in order to create new types.

Master It   You have a new project and have to add a slab-on-grade and slab edge at the bottom level. How do you do it?

Solution   Using the Slab tool on the Foundation panel of the Home tab, you can create a new slab type that is appropriate for your project. You then add a slab edge. You may be required to make a new slab type depending on the actual one you are using. If the profile you need isn't already available in the library, you will need to create a new profile family whose Profile Usage value is assigned to Slab Edge.

Work with floor decks.   There are different methods for creating and editing roof diaphragms within Revit Structure. Composite roofs with metal deck can be created by sketching their profile in a plan view or extruding their sectional shapes.

Master It   Your project requires the metal deck to stop at the edge girder and the concrete to extend out one foot beyond to meet the inside face of the metal stud framing on the exterior. How do you accomplish this?

Solution   Create the floor deck type you need and create its geometry. While in Sketch mode, select the lines you wish to extend. On the Options bar under Cantilevers, enter the length you wish to cantilever the concrete portion of the deck beyond the support line.

Work with various kinds of roof decks.   Different methods exist for creating roofs that are other than planar. Those methods include using the slab subelement tools as well as creating more exotic roof shapes with solid modeling tools.

Creating warped roof decks requires more complicated techniques because the form has no flat planes. Revit Structure has tools that help you create and edit the ridge lines and elevation points that occur in most roof elements.

Master It   Your project has a main ridge line across the middle of the roof with two drains on two edges of the roof diaphragm at points that are at one-third of the edge distance. How would you create it?

Solution   In plan view, create the basic roof as a flat diaphragm. Highlight the deck; then add the lines and points from the subelement menu that will be used for the ridge line and drains. Adjust the values of the points and lines accordingly for your roof.

Create openings and depressions in your floors and roofs.   For nearly every project you will need to create shaft and incidental openings. The dimensions of openings such as elevator shafts that extend through several floors must be kept consistent. Revit Structure has the tools to help you accomplish that goal.

Master It   On a multistory building, you want to add shafts to the core areas for stairs and elevators. How would you do that?

Solution   On the Opening panel of the Modify tab of the Ribbon, click Shaft to create consistent openings that automatically penetrate all floors and roofs. Constrain the shaft opening to the top and bottom levels, and then extend it as necessary to go through the slabs and decks at each constraint point.

Chapter 6: Walls

Place walls in your model.   When you are adding walls to your Revit Structure model, you can rely on the fact that you will get both the width and height of the wall depending on that wall's type, as well as the height constraint you have set. Once the walls are placed in the model, you can easily adjust them to change when the building changes.

Master It   Walls are quite simple to place in the model, but they can also be inaccurate if they are not added to the model deliberately. What are three things to look out for when placing walls in the model?

Solution   The first thing to be sure of is the type of wall. Although you can change this later, it is good to at least be within the ballpark as to the overall width and structure. The second is the height offset, or the level to which the base and the top of the wall are set. Again, this can be changed later, but it is much easier to adjust these parameters as you are placing the wall. The third is the justification of the wall. This is probably the most crucial because if this is wrong, you may not notice it until you are dimensioning the walls. This could be at the end of the project, once you discover the overall dimensions are slightly incorrect.

Create new walls.   There is a good amount of functionality included in the process of building a new wall type. Furthermore, walls are a system family, which can be used as a basis for any additional wall type you may wish to create.

Master It   The walls in the default Revit Structure template are not going to be sufficient. Revit Structure provides the capability to modify a preconfigured wall type to suit your condition. Describe the procedures for:

◆   Creating a basic wall

◆   Creating a stacked wall

Solution   To create a new wall type, you first must find a wall close to the wall you wish to create. You can locate that wall either by using the Wall command or by finding that wall in the Project Browser. In the Instance Properties dialog box, click Edit Type, then click Duplicate (if you found the wall using the Wall command). Alternately, use the Project Brower and double-click on a wall type, then click Duplicate. Name as you wish. Open the Preview window and then click the Structure Edit button. If it is a compound wall, start adding layers and materials. If it is a stacked wall, set the Preview to Section; you can view the stack as you place wall types atop one another.

Modify walls in place.   When a wall has been placed, some additional functions are allowed in Revit Structure for modifying the wall.

Master It   Walls must conform to various conditions vertically, such as odd openings and a stepped base profile. Also, if you have a pitched roof, the tops of the walls need to be extended to meet the roof. Explain how these procedures can be performed.

Solution   Once the wall you want to edit is placed, set to an elevation view of that wall. Select the wall and look at the Modify Walls tab. If you would like to edit the profile (such as adding a footing step), click the Edit Profile button. Then, you can sketch the stepped profile as you please. If you need an opening, you can use the same edit profile method and sketch the opening, or you can go to the Modify tab, and from the Opening panel, click Wall. If you need to physically attach the wall to a pitched roof or a sloping floor, select the wall, and choose Attach from the Modify Walls tab. If you are choosing to attach the wall to a roof, click Top, and then select the roof. If it is a floor, select Bottom, then select the floor.

Chapter 7: Structural Framing

Understand structural framing families and properties.   Revit Structure modeling is a constraint-based system that allows the model to update as changes occur, keeping the overall relationships between elements the same.

Master It   Describe the two primary modeling constraints for attaching beams and braces, and explain why they are important.

Solution   Grids are the main horizontal constraints and levels are the main vertical constraints in your project. You can update them through the life of the project, and the model elements will stay attached and move with them. Framing members will be attached to their levels, and to grids if they are on them, in such a way that the model will be able to flex when design changes occur.

Add floor framing.   When you add floor framing to your project, you probably start with a fuzzy idea of the size and initially use a placeholder. As the design progresses and comes into sharper detail, you will update the size and spacing in many cases. The model must have a maximum of flexibility to make the editing practical.

Master It   You are in schematics and know the bay widths on your building will change considerably. You want your framing members in each bay to be about 10′ from center to center no matter how wide the bay becomes during the course of the design. What layout rule is the best to use in this case?

Solution   Using beam systems, the best layout rule to use in this case is the Maximum Spacing rule. This way, if the bay expands so that it would be necessary for the members to exceed the 10′ center-to-center setting, Revit will create additional framing members automatically and insert them into the beam system.

Add roof framing.   Roof framing must support roofs that slope from ridges to drains. That means all the support beams and girders must slope as well. During the design process the roof can change in shape and slope. Be aware that costly editing can eat away your at your design fee.

Master It   Calculating the end elevation for each sloping beam would be very time consuming and a nightmare to edit. What process do you use to most efficiently place the roof support system?

Solution   Use the Beam tool with the 3D Snapping enabled. You select all the columns that intersect the roof diaphragm and then attach them to its underside. Next, add girders by snapping from column top to column top until the entire column grid is connected. Now you can use the Beam System tool with the 3D parameter checked (in Beam System properties) so that the beams will intersect the sloping girders at top center.

Create moment and braced frames.   Moment and braced frames are an important element of many structural designs. Revit Structure has two methods of displaying the braces in a plan views: Parallel Line and Line with Angle. The symbols are placed automatically in plan view as you draw the braces in elevation view.

Master It   Which display type is the most informative of the braced frame layouts, and how do you set it to display correctly in plan view?

Solution   Line with Angle is the most informative brace symbol because it shows the location of end points and the direction of the diagonal braces in plan view. Using a solid line for brace up and a dashed line for brace down can alert the design team to conflicts with doors or windows adjacent to the diagonal brace.

Chapter 8: Forming the Foundations

Create and work with isolated foundations.   Knowing the various methods available for placing isolated foundations into your project allows you to quickly and accurately place them into your project.

Master It   What are some of the methods you can use to place isolated foundations into your project?

Solution   The default is the Single Pick option, which allows you to place a single isolated foundation by snapping to other elements in the model or by picking a random location. You can also choose the On Grids or At Columns tools from the Ribbon. The On Grids option for placement puts an isolated foundation at the intersection of the grids that are selected. The At Columns option for placement puts an isolated foundation at the base of the columns that are selected.

Create and work with wall foundations.   Unlike an isolated foundation, a wall foundation is a system family, which has most of its behavior predefined in Revit Structure. When working with the wall foundation, the value of the Structural Usage parameter determines how it behaves in your project.

Master It   What values can be assigned to the Structural Usage parameter, and what are their biggest differences?

Solution   There are two Structural Usage values to choose from, Bearing and Retaining. Bearing allows you to set an overall width for the footing with a foundation thickness, and it can be offset from the wall using the Instance parameter called Eccentricity. Retaining allows you to set a Toe Length and Heel Length for the footing. The overall width of the footing is determined by the Toe Length + Heel Length + Wall Width. The Toe and Heel Length Type parameters determine the footing offset instead of an Eccentricity parameter.

Create and work with foundation slabs.   Foundation slabs are created with the same methods you use to create a structural floor. Knowing how to work with structural floors means you already know how to work with foundation slabs.

Master It   What are the two biggest differences between a foundation slab and a structural floor?

Solution   The two biggest differences between a foundation slab and a structural floor are that a foundation slab is assigned to the Structural Foundation category, whereas a structural floor is assigned to the Floors category, and a foundation slab does not have the sloping capabilities that a structural floor has. You can slope it only by using a slope arrow to define a slope of an entire slab or a portion of a slab.

Chapter 9: Model Documentation

Add datum elements to your detail and section views.   Datum elements are necessary for your model because they are the anchors for your objects. Grids, dimensions, spot dimensions, and reference planes are basic constraints for elements within the model, and they give it the ability to flex as you are working through changes in the design of the structure.

Master It   Datum elements form the basic constraints for your project. If you want to manage the columns and framing members of your project, which kind of datum is best suited for this purpose? What datum element is intended to define the vertical information like floor-to-floor height in your project?

Solution   Grids are the basic horizontal constraints to which your structural elements will be attached. They are tied together and controlled with dimensions so that they flex when the dimensions change. Levels are the basic vertical constraints that you use to attach tops and bottoms of columns or beams to a particular level.

Add annotation elements such as text, tags, and symbols.   Once the model is moving forward in development, you need to efficiently add identifying tags, beam annotations, and text to your various views in order to document your design and prepare your sheets. Tagging elements is an essential task since it taps into the properties of the object. If the object changes type, the tag automatically updates. That then allows you to use the model as a physical database for building schedules of many kinds. Text and symbols also are used to further the documentation of your model.

Master It   Open Dataset_0901_Begin.rvt (from the book's companion web page at www.sybex.com/go/masteringrevitstructure2010), and then go to the second-floor plan. On the second floor, load and tag all steel members. Add a Beam System tag to at least one bay. Add a Span Direction tag to the floor. Go to the first floor and tag the columns. After placing the tags, highlight and use the grips to align them with one another for a better display. Add grid dimensions.

Solution   Load the tags by choosing Load Family on the Load from Library panel on the Insert tab, and then choose Imperial Library ➢ Annotations ➢ Structural. Hover the mouse cursor over the girders and click to add the beam tag. Make sure the Leader box is unchecked. For the bay in-fills, use the two types of Beam System tags. See `Dataset_0901_End.rvt` for the completed task.

Add detailing elements such as detailing lines and filled regions. Not everything should be modeled. It takes experience to find the correct level of modeling in your project. For instance, columns are modeled but base plates are not in a typical American design firm. But when taking sections and creating details, you have to add that information in 2D over the modeled objects. So you add detailing lines to show the column base plate and perhaps some earth hatching around it. These are detailing elements.

Master It Open `Dataset_0902_Begin.rvt` and then go to the callout of Section 6. Add detail lines to show piping 4′-0″ to the left of the column going through the slab, turning 90 degrees, and going through the slab. Use a hidden line style. Add earth hatching below the slab using a filled region. Add a repeating CMU component wall to the right of the column with its outside flush with the grade beam below.

Solution Use detail lines, filled regions, and repeating details to complete the task. See `Dataset_0902_End.rvt` for the completed task.

Create a typical details library. A critical task to accomplish if you want your project to be totally documented in Revit Structure is the management of typical detail libraries. Typical details can be imported from the 2D CAD library or created from scratch in Revit Structure. You import Revit Structure details individually as drafting views, which are then added to sheets. They can also be inserted as part of a whole sheet. In similar fashion, you can export individual drafting views or sheets of drafting views to use in another job or to add to your Revit Structure library of details.

Master It You have a new project to start and want to transfer your model and drafting views from an already completed project. How will you transfer the drafting views to the new project? What is the best way to transfer a section with model elements in it to another project as a typical drafting view?

Solution You will transfer the existing drafting views by using the Save to Library command and exporting the sheets, which will also export and keep organized the drafting views they contain. Then in the new project, you will use the Insert from File command to import the views and sheets for the section that contains model elements. The best practice is to use the Freeze Drawing command to transfer all mode elements to drafting view lines. Then you can export and re-import that drafting view easily.

Chapter 10: Modeling Rebar

Configure rebar settings. In Revit Structure you can place reinforcement as actual objects as opposed to simple drafting. To do this correctly, however, you need to extensively configure the rebar settings for graphics as well as performance.

Master It Walls, footings, and slabs have cover settings that allow you to place reinforcement in a more organized and accurate approach. How is this done?

Solution   On the Home tab find the Reinforcement panel and click the drop-down area to choose Rebar Cover Settings. In the resulting dialog box, you can add and change the cover settings needed for the project. Hopefully your company's template will have these settings preconfigured. To add these settings to objects in your model, simply select the object (such as a wall, slab, or footing) and click the Element Properties button on the Options bar. In the Instance Properties dialog box, you will see the Structural group. In this group you'll find the cover settings needed to control the not-to-exceed-rebar cover.

Model a 3D rebar.   Although Revit Structure uses a modeling approach, it is often necessary to be able to sketch reinforcement first and then add it to the 3D Shape Browser once it is completed.

Master It   Placing 3D reinforcement can be done in two different ways. Describe both.

Solution   To place preconfigured reinforcement, you can simply select the item you want to reinforce, such as a wall, slab, or footing. Then, click the associated icon on the Options bar that will allow you to place rebar perpendicular to the current work plane or parallel to the current work plane. Once you choose an option, Revit Structure will display the Shape Browser. You can then select a shape and add it to the model.

You can also click the Sketch button on the Options bar. This allows you to draft any rebar shape. Once you have finished sketching the reinforcement, Revit Structure will add it to the Shape Browser.

Add rebar shapes.   By default in Revit Structure, you have a multitude of reinforcements to choose from. These shapes are preloaded into the template file you are using. Revit Structure allows for the importing of additional shapes.

Master It   You may be working in a model that was created in an older Revit Structure version. The model will not have any rebar shapes. How do you import the shapes?

Solution   On the Insert Ribbon tab, find the Load from Library panel and click Load Family. In the resulting dialog box, browse to the `Rebar Shapes` folder. Click in the `Rebar Shapes` folder, and press Ctrl+A. This will select the entire contents of the folder. Click Open, and each rebar family will be brought into the model.

Chapter 11: Schedules and Quantities

Create schedules.   Revit Structure benefits from a strong link between schedules and data. Once a schedule is created, the elements and parameter values can be manipulated either in the model or in the schedule. Each will influence the other.

Master It   The Schedule Properties dialog box can be accessed in two ways. One way is to right-click on the schedule name in the Project Browser and select Properties. What is the second way of accessing the Schedule properties?

Solution   The Schedule Properties dialog box can also be accessed by right-clicking anywhere in the schedule view and selecting View Properties.

Create schedule keys.   Schedule keys can be used to control multiple parameter values by creating a key designation and applying it to model elements.

> **Master It**   How can you create additional parameters for use with schedule keys, and what are their restrictions?
>
> **Solution**   Additional parameters for use with schedule keys can be created by navigating to the Manage tab and selecting Project Parameters from the Project Settings panel. Then in the Project Parameters dialog box, click the Add button. Verify that the parameter type is set to Project Parameter, and in the Parameter Data area, verify that you are creating an Instance parameter. Set the other parameter data options as needed, and give the parameter a category from the list on the right side of the dialog box. This choice is derived from the element category you wish to use with the schedule key.

Create material takeoffs.   Material takeoffs are known as a fourth-dimension modeling use. Using Revit Structure to track cost and material can be a big advantage in any project. Once the tools are developed and the basic takeoffs are in place, the efficiency of these features will be greater than ever.

> **Master It**   A material takeoff is a bit different from a schedule; however, the two are similar in many ways. What is the primary difference between material takeoffs and schedules?
>
> **Solution**   In a material takeoff, the materials are listed as separate items named Material: <material property>. This type of data is not present in a normal schedule. Other than the additional properties of Material, regular schedules and material takeoffs are comparatively identical.

Export schedules to Microsoft Excel.   Keeping track of the quantities may not be in the designer's scope of work. Many times the task is assigned to an estimator who is not involved with the modeling process at all. This functionality allows the designer to output accurate model data to an estimator in a format that person can use.

> **Master It**   Once a schedule or material takeoff is created in Revit Structure, how is it exported to Excel?
>
> **Solution**   It is exported to a text file and then imported into Excel using the following process. With the schedule view active, navigate to the Application menu and select Export ➤ Reports ➤ Schedule. Set the desired options in the Export Schedule dialog box, and create the .txt file. To import the data, open Microsoft Excel and select Open using the Office button, which is similar to the Revit Application menu. For the files of type, select Text Files (*.prn; *.txt; *.csv). Walk through the three steps of the Text Import Wizard, open the file, and perform any additional formatting within Excel.

Create keynote legends.   Keynote legends are a great way to track items and materials in Revit. The keynote values and keynote text values are easily editable and create reliable keynotes for your drawings.

> **Master It**   A keynote is tied directly into the element type being scheduled. What is the procedure for giving an element a keynote value?

Solution   The keynote value can be selected at the time of tagging by browsing the keynote table tree, or it can be input directly into the keynote parameter in the Element Properties dialog box.

Chapter 12: Working with Sheets

Create a title block to display project information.   The basics of creating a title block include using line work, annotations, filled regions, labels, and images. Combining these basic elements to create parametric behavior will take you way beyond 2D drafting.

Master It   What are three ways you can make your title blocks parametric to autoadapt to changes that are made within your sheets?

Solution   At the very least you can add labels that display project information, add Yes/No parameters to control the display of Not for Construction, and add a Revision Schedule to track revisions made to sheets.

Create a Revision Schedule to your company standards.   Revision Schedules added to title blocks allow you to keep track of revisions on sheets. You can design these Revision Schedules to accommodate just about any company standard and title block configuration.

Master It   How do you rotate a Revision Schedule 90 degrees? How or where do you set a Revision Schedule to display its information from the bottom up?

Solution   To rotate a Revision Schedule in a title block, select one that is already placed on a sheet. With the Revision Schedule selected, set its rotation by choosing 90 degrees clockwise or 90 degrees counterclockwise from the Options bar.

To display a Revision Schedule from the bottom up, you will need to be in the title block family so you can select the properties of the schedule. Using the Element Properties dialog box for the schedule, click the Appearance button, and select the Bottom-Up option from the Graphics area.

Explore the behavior of the various view types when they are placed on a sheet.   When views are placed on sheets, new parameters become available that display information that is specific to how and where the views are placed. Each view can have a different behavior; knowing this behavior allows you to take advantage of it.

Master It   What are four parameters that become available in plan, elevation, detail, drafting, and 3D views when they are placed on a sheet? What types of views can be placed on a sheet more than once without being duplicated?

Solution   Several parameters become available for plan, elevation, detail, drafting, and 3D views when they are placed on a sheet. They are Rotation on Sheet, Title on Sheet, Detail Number, Sheet Number, Sheet Name, Referencing Sheet, and Referencing Detail.

Most views can be placed on only one sheet to allow Revit Structure to keep track of their location within the model. Some views do not require this behavior, so they can be placed on more than one sheet. They are schedules, Graphical Column Schedules, and legends.

Produce a drawing list/sheet index to keep track of your issued sheets.   Revit Structure lets you easily create a drawing list/sheet index to keep track of sheets.

Master It   How can you get additional information on your drawing list to manually account for issue names and descriptions as well as to show which sheets are being or have been issued?

Solution   Two methods can be used individually or together. First a special kind of schedule called a drawing list is used. You can add additional parameters to your drawing list when you create it initially or later by editing its properties. Once the list is created you can add information to denote which sheets are being issued and for what reason. The second method involves using a drafting view to create a schedule with just line work and annotation. You can place it alongside a drawing list to enhance the quality of the information you provide.

Control the behavior of revisions in your project.   You can control the tracking of revisions made to the model to reflect several standards that may be required as well as react to unknown project schedule changes.

Master It   How do you set a revision tag to display an alphabetic sequence "numbering" standard? How do you rearrange a revision to be put on hold so that it can be used after others instead?

Solution   Companies using alphabetic sequence "numbering" can set this behavior on a per-revision basis by choosing the Manage tab ➤ Project Settings ➤ Settings drop-down ➤ Sheet Issues/Revisions tool and setting the numbering method to Alphabetic in the Sheet Issues/Revisions dialog box. The same dialog box offers the Move Up, Move Down, Merge Up, and Merge Down buttons for rearranging revisions.

Chapter 13: Worksharing

Determine when to enable worksharing.   Looking past day 1 of your project to help determine the proper game plan for moving forward will make things go much smoother.

Master It   What can determine when you should enable worksharing?

Solution   If more than one person will be repeatedly working on a project, you should enable worksharing to avoid getting file read-only warnings. Large projects will need to be broken into worksets to increase performance. The ability to perform standards checking while other users are in the same model will increase productivity by allowing multiple users to be in the same project simultaneously.

Enable and set up the worksharing environment.   When working in Revit Structure, you'll almost always be in a multiuser environment. Knowing how to enable worksets and use the central and local files is important for communicating among team members.

Master It   How do you enable worksets, and where should the central and local files be saved?

Solution   Worksets can be enabled by choosing the Worksets tool from the Collaborate tab ➤ Worksets panel. After worksets are enabled, when you save the file Revit will create the central file, which should be saved on the network. Users should then create and work on local files that are saved onto their own workstation's hard drive.

Request and grant permission of elements. Working in a multiuser environment where you are sharing a project with ownership rights will eventually lead to team members tripping over one another. Understanding how borrowing elements works is important to work efficiently.

Master It What are the methods used so you can borrow an element(s)? What do you do if another team member has already borrowed an element(s) that you need?

Solution Borrowing individual elements is preferred over borrowing worksets. Elements are borrowed automatically as you edit objects, but it can be done manually by clicking the Make Element Editable icon (stacked cubes) or by right-clicking on the object and selecting Make Elements Editable. If another user has already borrowed an element that you need, you can request permission by making an Editing Request.

Stay in sync with other team members. Creating the central file and communicating with it using a local file is how to work effectively using Revit's worksharing features.

Master It What is the most flexible method to create a local file? What commands are used to get information back and forth between the central and local files?

Solution The most flexible method to create a local file is to use the Copy/Paste/Rename features through Windows Explorer. Once you're working in your local file, you use the Synchronize with Central tools and the Reload Latest tool to stay in sync with other users.

Properly maintain your project file. Keeping your central file as healthy as possible will decrease chances of file corruption and increase overall performance.

Master It When should you audit the central file? How should you go about upgrading your file to a new version?

Solution Performing an audit at least once a month on the central file will help keep it healthy and minimize file corruption. Prior to upgrading to a new version, create a backup file and do an audit on the central file. The audit of the central file should be done by using the Revit Structure version that it is currently saved in, but not at the same time an upgrade is taking place.

Chapter 14: Visualization

Determine what and when to model. Once you get going in Revit Structure, the ease of creating models is both a blessing and a curse. If you model too little, you don't achieve the desired result. If you model too much, then you will have so much more than you need, your renderings will take an excessive amount of time.

Master It Before modeling, develop a scope of what and when to model. Conduct team meetings with all project modelers so that everyone involved has rendering in mind as they do their work. Limit the complexity of your renderings by using appropriate detail levels.

Solution Create a project model document with instructions for what to and what not to model. This will include primary beam members as well as secondary and bracing elements. Using the View ribbon, choose the 3D View. Then rename your 3D view specifically for rendering purposes. Using the Detail level control at the bottom of the 3D View and set it to the Medium level for entire building views. For views that are connection specific, assign a Fine detail level so that complete member profiles can be seen.

Assign materials to your model.   Actually rendering in Revit Structure isn't hard — having something render worthy is the hard part. Materials make or break your renderings. You can make your model look real or *like* a real model.

> **Master It**   As you develop your families, assign materials so that you can render on demand later. Using the Materials dialog box, create materials for steel and concrete for when they are viewed at a distance. Adjust materials for rendering even if you won't be rendering now. This will reduce the time needed to prepare for when you are asked to produce images. For real photographic needs, use materials that have few repeating patterns so that no matter the point of view, the materials you use will maintain a level of smoothness.

> **Solution**   Using the Manage tab, choose Materials. Locate Concrete - Cast-in-Place Concrete and then select it. Then using the Render Appearance tab, click the Replace button. Then, in the Render Appearance Library dialog box, type Concrete as the search content. Then choose the single Concrete slide, and click OK to accept. Click OK again, and then you'll see that all basic concrete has a cleaner rendered look. For steel, once again use the Material dialog box, but this time look for Metal - Steel - ASTM A992: This is the typical material for major steel elements. Then, in the Render Appearance Library, select Paint Dark Red Matte. Once found, select it and click OK twice.

Define the quality and style of your renderings.   When you begin to render your model, you can be overwhelmed with all the settings at your disposal. You can define where the sun is, what time of day it is, what resolution to create, and how detailed your images should be.

> **Master It**   Take a look around in the real world. Get a sense of what structures look like when they are under construction. Things are often dark; you don't always have to light everything up. When you create renderings, save time and create high quality only at the very end. Use the Rendering system with Autodesk mental ray to define a sun, adjust exposure, control shadows, and create renderings. Then save your rendering to any number of image types.

> **Solution**   Using a 3D View, click the Teapot icon at the bottom of the view to open the Rendering dialog box. Use the Setting drop-down list, and select Medium. Under Lighting, change the direction of the Sun to Sunlight from Top Left. Change the Background Style to be Sky: No Clouds. Now click the Render button at the top of the Rendering dialog box. Once the process is complete, click the Adjust Exposure button and click Reset to Default at the top. Then change the Shadows value to 3 and click OK to close. Finally, click Export and save your rendered image to a JPEG format.

Export your models for other uses.   Exporting your model for outside use is a typical activity of the true professional. You don't use one kind of writing implement, so you should not use only one rendering application.

> **Master It**   Once you have a 3D view active, you can export it to a DWG or FBX file to use in an outside application. Use the FBX format if you have Revit Structure cameras you want to export as well. Use the DWG format with polymesh for direct import into 3ds Max Design.

But if you have very large models, you might want to use ACIS solids since that allows 3ds Max to control the meshing directly.

Solution   Using the Application menu choose Export ≻ CAD Formats ≻ DWG (or FBX if so desired). Then, on in the Export CAD Formats dialog box, click the DWG Properties tab, and change the Solids (3D Views only) control to Export as ACIS solids. Click Export to close and then save the file as needed.

Chapter 15: Revit Structural Analysis

Configure Revit Structure structural settings and create loads for your project.   The Structural Settings dialog box contains the tabs that will allow you to configure loads for your project. Load Cases, Load Natures, Load Combinations, and their usage form the basis for preparing your analytical model for export to analysis software.

Master It

1. True or False: Revit Structure has the ability to perform structural analysis.

2. True or False: Revit Structure cannot combine load cases.

3. True or False: A circular reference will occur when a system of beams frames back to the origin.

4. True or False: A good example of a typical boundary condition is the support of earth underneath a footing or a slab on grade.

5. Where are the settings located that allow you to turn on automatic checks for Member Supports and Analytical/Physical Model Consistency?

Solution

1. False. The analytical model must be exported to analysis software.

2. False. Revit can combine load cases.

3. True.

4. True.

5. The settings are located in Structural Settings dialog box, on the Analytical Model Settings tab.

Place analytical load patterns onto your model.   Loads are placed in the model in anticipation of using them for preliminary analysis. Several placement methods are possible within Revit Structure. Each of these methods can be applied in two ways.

Master It

1. Name the three different kinds of load placements.

2. The analytical properties of an element can depend on one of two things. What are they?

3. True or False: The Project Coordinate system directional guide is an icon that indicates the work plane for the load you are about to place.

4. What two ways can load placements be applied?

5. True or False: Adding a line load with host is a little less confusing than adding an area load since a line load has no z direction whatsoever.

Solution

1. The three kinds of load placement are line, point, and area loads.

2. The analytical model is dependent upon its host geometry, or it can be configured to extend to other members regardless of its host geometry.

3. True.

4. The load placements can be applied by clicking in the display area, or you can choose a host, resulting in six different ways to place a load.

5. True.

Import and export your virtual model from Revit Structure to structural analysis software. Once the loading is created and placed, the model is ready to be exported to an analysis application. Once the analysis is complete, it can then be imported back in to Revit Structure and will automatically update the model.

Master It

1. True or False: The integration links come prepackaged with Revit Structure.

2. When the application's dialog box is displayed, you will be given some choices. To what do they refer?

3. What type of file will Revit Structure export to the analysis application?

4. True or False: Importing and exporting to the analysis application exchanges the physical model back and forth between Revit Structure and the analysis application.

Solution

1. False. You have to go to the vendor's website and download the integration links and then install them.

2. They refer to the extent of elements that you are exporting and specific application questions you will need to answer for that particular analysis package.

3. Revit Structure will either export a file in that program's native extension or create a `.bim` file.

4. False. Only analysis data flows between the two applications.

Chapter 16: Project Phases and Design Options

Create project phases to manage element assignments. Creating and managing phases in a project is an important task that will help establish the sequence of construction of your structure. Phases apply existing and new statuses on elements so you can manage them. A good example of using phases is in distinguishing existing elements from new when you add a wing onto a hospital complex.

Master It   What steps do you take in developing phases for your building document set?

Solution   First you have to either use the existing phases or create new ones. Then you assign elements in your model to the different phases you have created. Finally you create views that display the phases the way the project requires. Be sure to pay close attention to your Element and View properties when you are working with phases.

Display project phases in your project views.   Views in Revit Structure are configured to display your various phases. Using the Phase and Phase Filter parameters, you set each view to display new, demo, or existing objects or any number of construction sequence views.

Master It   The current view's phase is set to New Construction, with only the Existing phase preceding it. Name the default phase filter that will show elements as they are described below:

1. All elements from the phase before New Construction

2. Demolished elements and all of the new elements that you add to your model

3. Only the new elements that you have added to your model

4. All elements, including existing, demolished, and temporary elements

5. All elements from the previous phase that were not demolished, as well as all added new elements

Solution

1. Show Previous Phase

2. Show Demo + New

3. Show New

4. Show All

5. Show Previous + New

Understand the relationship among phases, views, and elements.   It is critical to understand how these three relate to one another when using phasing. An element can display as existing in one view, demolished in another, and new in yet another. This is all governed with just four parameters, two for views and two for elements. Revit interprets the values stored in these parameters to determine how to display them in your views.

Master It   Match the following phase settings for elements with their corresponding phase status, assuming that they are visible in a view assigned to Phase: New.

1. Phase Created: Existing - Phase Demolished: None

2. Phase Created: Existing - Phase Demolished: New

3. Phase Created: New - Phase Demolished: None

4. Phase Created: New - Phase Demolished: New

Solution

1. Existing

2. Demolished

3. New

4. Temporary

Create design options to manage element assignments.   In a design situation, you have to create sets of design options in order to evaluate various issues and problem areas. All of these options are created and managed in one Revit Structure file. They are then displayed in various views that you create.

Master It   Answer the following questions:

1. How many options from an option set can be shown in one view?

2. What elements are not supported in design options?

3. What is a dedicated view?

4. How does the use of design options in your project save you time and resources?

Solution

1. No matter how many options are added to an option set, only one can be displayed in a view at a time, and it is called the primary option.

2. Levels, views, annotations, and 2D details are not supported in design options.

3. Dedicated views are developed to display one particular design option.

4. Using design options in your projects saves you considerable time and resources because you can display multiple design ideas easily without duplicating your project files.

Display design options in your project views.   Once design options are created in your project, you assign them to different views. Those views are then added to a sheet for comparison. In that way, you are able to evaluate and select primary options and discard ones you do not want as the design process progresses.

Master It   Some modeled elements in your project depend on other elements and so cannot be independently assigned to a design option. Name three of those types of elements.

Solution   Elements of this sort that are dependent on their host objects include the following:

◆ Inserts that cut their hosts

◆ Host sweeps and their hosts

◆ Curtain panels

◆ Window mullions

◆ Grids

◆ Topographical surfaces and building pads

◆ Attachments (walls to roofs/floors)

Also, elements that are added to a group must be in the same design option as the group.

Chapter 17: Standards: Increasing Revit Productivity

Ascertain what can and cannot be done easily. Standards are there no matter what. What they are and how they are controlled are up to you. Before Revit Structure, users had various files provided with AutoCAD that determined what most of the standards were based on. A standard is many things, but a basic one specifies line weight, pattern, and style. In addition, you have filled patterns that can tone contained areas. You then bring all these definitions together and apply them to object styles, views, and objects to create your drawings.

Master It Develop line weights that meet your needs. Create line patterns and styles and then apply them to your model via the Object Styles dialog box. Address annotation and fill standards as well, all matching your required standards.

Solution Research pen weights to learn which are most applicable to your firm's standards. Examine how your line patterns look, and adjust them to suit your needs. Do the same for fill patterns and the various annotation objects. You can then create your own line styles for use in your templates.

Enhance your model through customization. Anyone using Revit Structure deserves to have their tool be as productive as possible. With a little bit of practice, you can take using Revit Structure to a new level.

Master It The temporary dimension values in Revit Structure are too small to read, so increase them! Follow that with organizing your firm's library files as well. Then improve usability by using command shortcuts, and take advantage of keyboard input speed.

Solution Locate and open your `Revit.INI` file for editing in Notepad. Then add an entry for adjusting the `TempDimFontSizeInPoints` control. Once this entry is complete, modify your `KeyboardShortcuts.TXT` file to add one- or two-letter access to your favorite commands. From within Revit Structure, adjust your Options File Search paths to look to your custom family libraries first to enforce your standards automatically.

Implement model standards and view overrides. Once you have your standards in place, you then have to apply them to your model. There is no need to simply accept what Revit Structure can produce right out of the box.

Master It Take your standards and use them to control your model. Then when the need arises, tweak just about anything for a single view at a time. Can you break out of the black-and-white box and think in color again?

Solution After you have defined your standard containers, use object styles to define them for the entire model. You can use the Visibility/Graphic Overrides dialog box to refine a single view. Then take a complete model and adjust the object styles to use color and notice how much easier it is to understand the objects in it.

Chapter 18: Family Creation: Beyond the Provided Libraries

Create a footing step family.   Creating families is a vital skill. You create a family, such as a footing step family, by meticulously tying reference planes with dimensions and parameters. Then you add 3D solids to the references to achieve a flexible, useful family.

> **Master It**   When you start a new Revit Structure family from a template, there will be existing reference planes. How do these reference planes help in the creation of the family?

> **Solution**   By offsetting these lines and dimensioning to them, you can establish a strong origin while maintaining flexibility within the family. These reference planes will also serve as alignment lines when you are modifying them in the model.

Create in-place families.   You create specialized families, called in-place families, directly within the model, tying the family to the surrounding building. This allows you to more easily create custom geometry that will probably never be used in another model.

> **Master It**   What is the process for creating a custom family directly within the model?

> **Solution**   On the Home tab of the Ribbon, within the Model panel, click the lower half of the Component button and select Model In-Place. Then you can select the category from the Family Category and Parameters dialog box. You will then be prompted for a name. After this initial setup, you will be presented with the Model In-Place Ribbon, which contains the tools for creating model content in place. Once the desired model elements have been created, click Finish Model to return to the project environment.

Create groups.   Adding groups to the model greatly reduces the time spent organizing and manipulating the configuration of certain items. Also, by linking a group, you can actually create a separate Revit Structure model and link it back into Revit Structure, similar to creating an x-ref in AutoCAD.

> **Master It**   You also learned that a linked Revit Structure file can be turned into an embedded group. Explain the procedure for this to occur.

> **Solution**   By selecting the linked Revit model, you can click Bind Link from the Link panel on the Modify RVT Links tab of the Ribbon. From there you get a choice as to whether you want to include the attached details, levels, and grids from the linked file. Typically, you will not bind the levels and grids because this creates redundant instances, which Revit will rename as it imports them. The file that was a link is now a group in the project.

Chapter 19: Advanced Structural Families

Create a parametrically driven tapered steel girder family.   In the first section you learned how to develop a new family from scratch using the beam template. You used a blended sweep to create the taper on the lower flange of the girder. You had to introduce a number of new reference planes to which you could then attach the sketch lines of the girder. Adding dimensions between reference planes and making them labels gave you the ability to flex the shape and made the family truly parametric.

Master It   What does "flexing the model" mean, and why is it important?

Solution   Flexing the model tests the parametric constraints of the model. You create several family types and then apply them to see if the shape reacts properly to the new parameters. It is important to flex the model in order to prove that the sketch lines that have been built into the shape are working correctly.

Construct an in-place bent beam family.   The bent beam family was created inside the project as an example of an in-place family. You learned how to use a solid sweep form to sketch a path and a steel beam profile along a reference plane in order to create the desired shape.

Master It   What elements are used to describe the bent beam family?

Solution   The bent beam family consists of two elements: the solid sweep form and the symbolic stick symbol.

Adapt the steel wide-flange beam family by adding a nailer to its top.   In this section you adapted the existing wide flange beam family by adding an extrusion onto its top. The extrusion represents the wood nailer and has the ability to flex into different shapes.

Master It   What are the four main steps necessary to add an extrusion in the shape of a 3 × 6 to the wide-flange beam family?

Solution

1. First you copy the family file to a file with a new name.

2. Then you copy its associated text file as well to the same name.

3. Finally you create a solid extruded form with a beam profile.

4. You add labeled dimensions to your reference planes in order to make the solid form act parametrically.

Create an elevator pit family that can be dropped into your project.   You learned to make an elevator pit family that could be easily inserted into your project. The pit form consists of solid extrusions and void extrusions working together. The whole family is floor based, so it can exist only when associated with a floor object in your model.

Master It   What is the void blend used for in the elevator pit family?

Solution   The void blend is used to cut out the underside of the solid for the pit slab.

Produce wood and steel truss families using the truss template.   In the final section you first worked through an exercise in which you inserted a truss from the structural truss library and then reconfigured it to create a steel truss with WT top and bottom chords and double-angle web members.

Then you used the truss template to create a wood truss from scratch so that its vertical web members could be specifically located above supporting walls in a warehouse.

Master It After you inserted the wood truss into your building model, how did you make the top chord of the truss follow the barrel-shaped roof?

Solution To make the top chord of the truss follow the barrel-shaped roofline, you first highlight the truss that you have inserted, and then on the Options bar you click the Attach/Detach Top Chord button, and the top chord is then automatically reshaped. All web members are also extended. It was also of critical importance to drop the base elevation of the truss so that it could be attached without generating error messages.

The Gallery Up Close

Revit Structure is capable of modeling as well as creating documentation for a variety of building structures. To recognize what tools should be used and understand the various ways to create and document elements in a nonstandard structure, you need a good grasp of the techniques you've read about in this book.

As you'll see in this appendix, the tools provided in Revit Structure to aid in these efforts are not always used for the purpose for which they were intended. As we discuss the wide range of projects we've modeled and the strategies we employed when using Revit Structure in a real-world production environment, you should gain a good understanding of how to overcome structural issues.

In this appendix, we'll show you examples of real-world projects that we've worked on using Revit Structure. We'll explain what we've done to overcome challenges and roadblocks, and we'll discuss common situations that can be handled by stepping outside the box or taking a look from a different angle. We'll bring to light new workflow methods that you can experiment with to continue to push Revit Structure to new limits.

Mid-Rise with Multiple Structure Types

The hotel and residence shown in the following graphic is an 18-story structure with low-level ballroom and restaurant areas, as well as two levels of parking below grade. The main structure system is concrete, which supports the post-tension upper levels with concrete columns and shear walls. One level of supported parking below grade consists of a post-tension slab; the main street level is a two-way flat plate slab. Areas of the lower-level roofs are supported with a steel structural system consisting of columns, beams, and bar joists. The foundations used a mixture of conventional footings and pile caps, with piles and associated grade beams.

You can take several approaches when starting to model a project of this size as well as the various structural systems that it can use. Much depends on the schedule of the project and when the various portions need to be issued. For each project, regardless of its size, you must take into account its construction schedule, team member expectations, and limitations of the current software. Another factor is whether other design team disciplines are using BIM software or 2D CAD to produce their documentation.

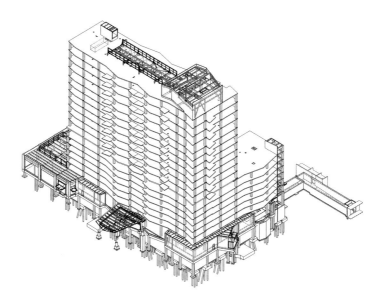

For this project, we issued an early foundation package, so much of the work up front involved designing the foundation. While doing this, we kept the upper portions of the model going, but only to exchange information back and forth with other disciplines to keep their design moving forward. For the upper portions of the structure, we focused on the modeling elements for design intent and not for documentation. The following images are examples of how we dispersed early design information to the team:

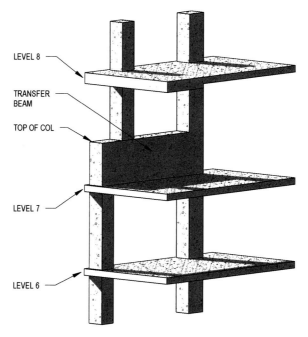

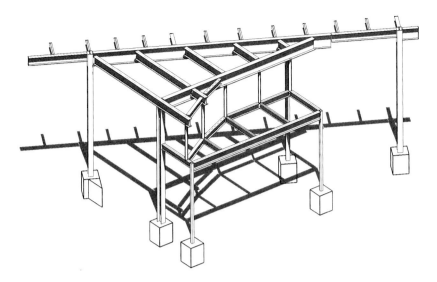

To help meet the quick construction schedules, we used strategies such as grouping floors for typical framing. For the foundation efforts, we were in full Documentation mode, at first creating many 3D views to portray the design to the contractor and other design team members. We tagged everything with labels and used spot dimensions to call off elevations. This allowed us to keep the documentation up to date as the design progressed and the model was coordinated.

Modeling Techniques

Since several systems were used on this project, we employed various modeling techniques while working on our construction documents. Also, with projects of this size you can wind up using several versions of software — which in most cases will make some modeling tasks that much easier. This project started out in Revit Structure 3, and we upgraded the project to Revit Structure 2009 for the last month or so of the construction phase. As we look back to day one, it would have been nice to start this project in Revit Structure 2009 or 2010 — we could have taken advantage of such improvements as warped slabs, more enhanced sloping beams, filters by criteria, dependent views, concrete joining, slab edge, foundation pads, enhanced spot dimensions, schedule columns offset from grids . . . . As new features are added, you have to be ready to adapt to them or make the decision to carry out your original modeling techniques. Many of the techniques used on this project were work-arounds for solutions that are now much easier to accomplish in the current version. Even though some of these work-around techniques have been replaced with added functionality, some are still methods that are preferred or at least another option that can be used for special situations in just about any project you come across.

PILE FOUNDATIONS

For the pile foundations, we used the Pile Cap families that shipped with Revit Structure. Not all shapes and pile cap types were available, so we created additional ones as needed, using the existing ones to start from. The structural design required that several of the piles had to be battered, which meant we had to create separate families for the various locations to accurately show the location of the battered piles. Since the cap families nest in a shared pile family, we were able to schedule the individual piles, which allowed us to keep an up-to-date count of the total number of piles at the various design stages of the project. We assigned additional parameters to the families to include more information to be scheduled, such as bearing capacity and whether the piles were battered. As you can see in the following view, showing the foundations providing support enhanced the visual aspect and put the design in perspective for those viewing it.

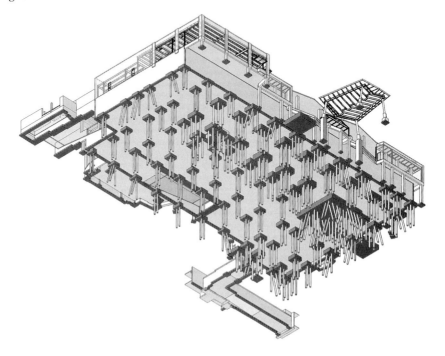

COLUMNS

Concrete columns were modeled with the "model as you build it" approach. They were modeled individually floor to floor, with their tops attached to the underside of the slab or column capitals. We created additional text parameters in the properties of the concrete column families for reinforcing so column reinforcing could be scheduled. Because the columns were modeled floor to floor, we were able to put all column-reinforcing information into each object in text form. Aside from creating construction documents, this information was also displayed in views via tags for checking the integrity of the model as well as more efficient checking of shop drawings.

SLABS

We used the slab tools to model the slabs as well as any dropped slabs or column capitals. Using the slab tools for these elements gave us more flexibility in modeling the various shapes and sizes that were needed throughout the project. For instance, if an 8″ slab required an 8″ dropped slab, we'd create a new slab type called Dropped Slab − 8″. This slab would be placed with the same reference as the 8″ slab with an offset of −8″. With the slabs named to reflect their use, we created schedules for calling out reinforcing and for calculating concrete volumes.

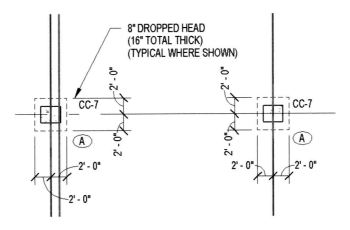

We decided to make the slab thickness the depth of the dropped slab and not the overall thickness so that we did not have to rely on the concrete joining behavior. With this method, the dropped slab displays as a hidden line regardless of its join behavior. This is only one strategy that can be used for modeling dropped slabs. Another method is to create a slab type that is the overall thickness of the slab at the capital. The two slabs would automatically join together, cutting out the areas of overlapped concrete. Using this method would eliminate having to maintain an offset for the dropped slab but in return will not accurately reflect the total volume of concrete in the slabs.

Several of the upper levels had recessed balconies (shown in the following graphic) that were at the exterior of the building. With the Revit Structure version at the time we modeled these recesses, and we used an in-place family that existed for each level. Each family contained individual void blends to form the recess. We used a void blend sketched in a section view because the balcony was sloping and each corner of the recess was at a different elevation. We placed reference planes inside the family over the top of the recessed lines to give us the ability to dimension to the recessed edges. Without adding these reference planes, we would not have been able to select the recess edge as a dimension reference point.

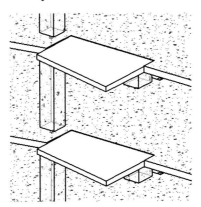

With the current version of Revit Structure, modeling recessed slabs like this is much easier. One method involves using the slab tools in Revit Structure. You model the core slab around the recessed slabs and then come back with individual slabs at each recess. With this method, you can treat each recess as its own slab, thus giving you the ability to control the various elevations of the recess slab by using the elevation tools located on the Options bar when you select the slab. When complete, all of the slab types will be automatically joined to show one monolithic slab. You will also need to use the Variable option in the Edit Assembly dialog box for the slab. Setting the Variable option will keep the bottom of the slab flat rather than sloping with the top surface.

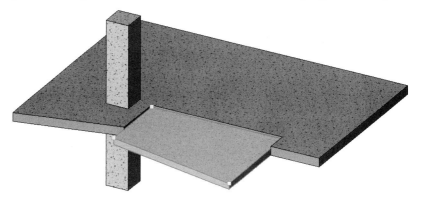

Screen Wall Framing

Screen walls (shown here) are often required on structures to mainly conceal mechanical equipment. These types of structures can typically be modeled by using structural columns and beams.

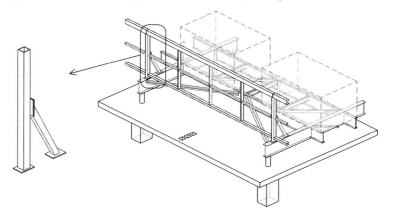

The vertical supports and its kickers were all typical at the perimeter, so for this project we created a column family that we used specifically for the screen wall. We used Revit Structure's HSS Tube Steel Column family as the template. In our new family, we reassigned the base constraints of the column as well as added new geometry for the plates and kicker brace by using extrusions. Once the family was loaded back into the project, all locations where this framing was required instantly updated. We assigned the new geometry visibility settings to allow the proper display depending on the type of view. Modeling to this detail helped us to detect conflicts with the mechanical units as well as ensure that any required clear space was not being encroached on. As the location and slope of the kickers were revised to accommodate the ever-changing mechanical units, this method helped us make those changes quickly.

Sloped Canopy

This project also had a unique canopy structure. Without Revit Structure, we would probably *still* be trying to figure out how it was all going to come together with regard to its connection requirements and relationship with the architectural skin. For this project, we chose to model the canopy as its own model. This allowed us to have several design option models to choose from. Each design was easier to modify and maintain as a separate model. This approach also enabled us to link the entire structure into each canopy model to show images of the various design concepts and how they related to the structure. In the end, the chosen canopy design concept was linked back into the master Revit Structure model, where we added it to the documentation set. At this point, we were able to create plans and sections to facilitate documenting the model.

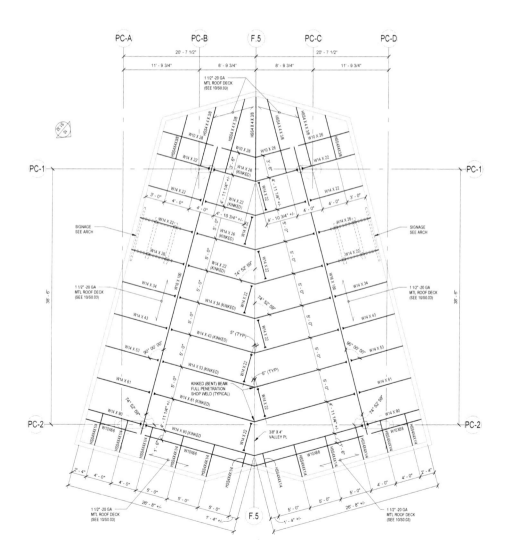

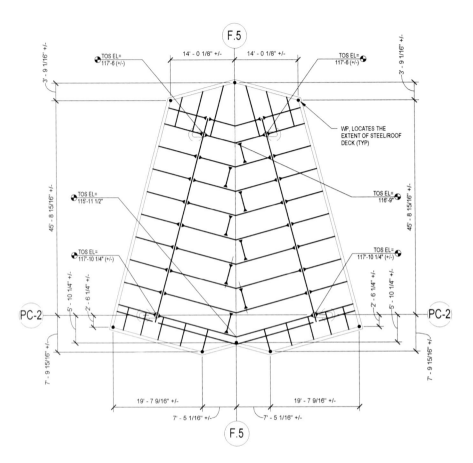

With Revit Structure's ability to create multiple views of the model at different scales, we were able to create separate plans to dimension the location of the steel and for denoting top-of-steel elevations. This resulted in plans that were clear and to the point.

Concrete Pan and Joist Structures

Concrete pan and joist structures (like the ones shown here as well as on the color insert pages) may require more expertise — or at least a few pointers — in using Revit Structure to achieve a good set of documentation while still keeping as much information in the model as you can. The last few versions of Revit Structure improved the program's capabilities with regard to concrete framing and how it joins. Starting with the 2009 version of Revit Structure, not only do the concrete framing members automatically join to other members of the same material, but you can also control the types of beam-to-beam join types, similar to how you can with a wall corner or intersection. This works with rectangular shapes, but in a pan and joist system the members are tapered on their sides, thus making the Edit Beam Joins tool unusable. For a pan and joist system, you will have to develop other methods to overcome some of the limitations of the software for the tapered shapes that this system requires.

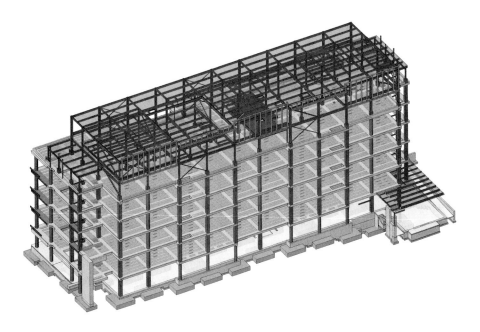

Before you start to model this type of system, make a list of everything you want to get out of your model. How will the model be used? Do you want the ability to cut and annotate sections from the model, like the one shown here, or will sections be created by using a drafting view?

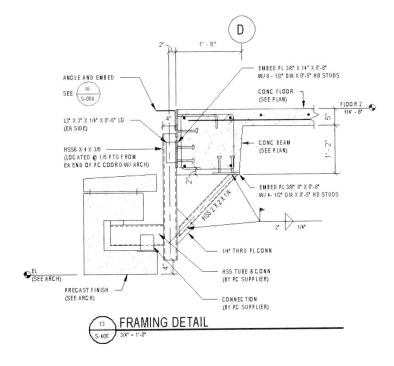

Are you using the model only for geometry display, or will you be building in additional information that can be scheduled by using the properties of each individual element? If you are using the model only for geometry display, then you could probably just model each floor with a slab and cut extrusion. Or you could model each floor as one big in-place family, with several extrusions to form the pan and joist system. (Of course, with this method you will have zero intelligence in the model. All information denoting these members will be 2D text, and it will be difficult to have Revit Structure automatically create a schedule.) Will the model be used for collaboration by another discipline? Do you want to calculate concrete volumes? Questions like these will help you determine the best approach to take before you start modeling a project with this structural system. We prefer to discuss the method that allows you to put as much information into the model as you can, accurately model the system, and easily extract accurate information out of the model to be displayed for your documentation.

What's in the Family

When Revit Structure was first released, it did not feature families that we could accurately use for a pan and joist system. We had to start from the basic rectangular beam family and develop our own families for the typical shapes that we required. At first, we had created shapes for a concrete tapered beam, a tapered beam with a shallow pan, a tapered joist, and a tapered bridging member. These all were just two basic shapes used in the pan and joist system. We created separate families for each to give us more flexibility in scheduling as well as assign color for the surface material so we could visually display the various structural components of the system. Families for these two basic shapes are located in Revit Structure's `Imperial Library\Structural\Framing\Concrete` folder. Even though some of these families are available to you after installing Revit Structure, it is important for you to realize that you will still have to develop certain families of your own and even project-specific families as you get further along into your modeling adventure. Just because everything is not available out of the box doesn't mean that modeling a pan and joist system cannot be done successfully.

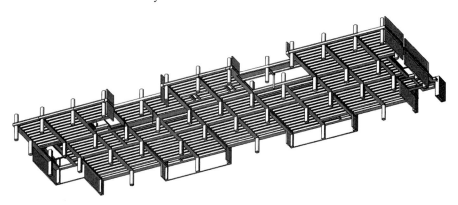

As you get further along in a concrete pan and joist structure, you will begin to see that you must create new family shapes to help model the structure accurately. You will also want to keep in mind that if every framing member needs to be scheduled as well as annotated based on the member's properties, you must choose a modeling method that will allow you to do that. This is where you will want to get your in-house family creator expert involved. Many families can be created quickly by starting from a current family, or similar ones can be used by adding more advanced functionality to them. You will have to create many families specifically for a project. The more projects you do, the more families you may break out from being project-specific and add them to your standard family library.

The basic tapered beam family shown next has parameters that help control the geometry that are different for controlling the geometry of a rectangular beam. The first are the parameters for the Taper Left Dim and Taper Right Dim. These parameters are driven by a Yes/No setting as properties of the tapered beam and have formulas assigned to them. When the user chooses, Revit Structure will display the edges of the beam tapered (yes) or show them straight (no), as in a rectangular beam. This allows you to use the tapered beam as an interior beam, with the beam tapered on both sides, or at an edge condition, where only one side is tapered. You must coordinate the Slab Thickness parameter with the slab thickness that the tapered beam is being placed under. This keeps the taper dimension accurately shown, automatically displays the bottom edge of the beams as hidden lines when the beam is not joined to the slab, and ensures accurate totals of volume counts for the slab and beams.

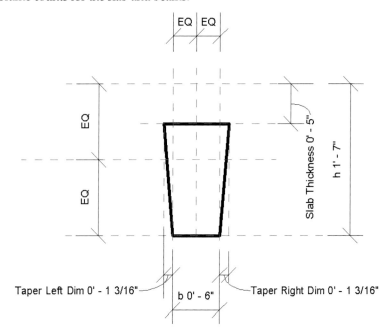

The next basic family shown is for the condition where a beam is deeper than the beam or joist adjacent to it. This type of beam is tapered only for the depth of the adjacent beams and has vertical faces for the deeper portions of the beam.

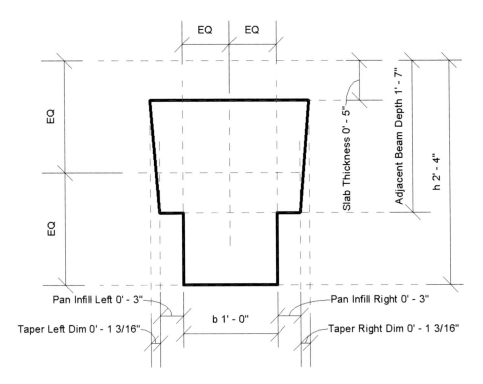

The same parameters exist for this family as the one described earlier. Additional parameters have been added to this family to control the Pan Infill Left and Pan Infill Right, as well as the Adjacent Beam Depth. To achieve the proper display of line work on plan, you need to always have these options set correctly. In order for an adjacent beam to join and display properly, the Adjacent Beam Depth parameter must be set to the proper depth. Setting any of the Pan Infill parameters to 0 along with turning of the taper will create an edge beam condition. This family could be taken one step further to add another level of functionality by expanding the Adjacent Beam Depth parameter so you set it differently for a Left or a Right condition.

There is also a parameter setting in the family called Display in Hidden Views that defines how the hidden lines of concrete behave in the project. This parameter will become available only when the family is set to a Concrete material. For the families mentioned earlier, this option is set to Edges Hidden by Beam Itself. This setting allows the bottom of the tapered concrete beam line to display as a hidden line rather than where the taper meets the slab.

Along with creating the geometry of the family, you will want to add in text parameters to give you the ability to put all of the reinforcing information into each element you create. Make a list of required parameters that matches your methods of scheduling. Once you have this list, add the parameters to your shared parameter text file. Each family that you create — as well as those families that are created in place — should have these shared parameters incorporated into them. For families that are created in place, the shared parameters can be added as project parameters. Developing your families to hold text such as reinforcing information will allow you set up Revit Structure to automatically create and maintain your schedules, as shown here:

BEAM MARK NUMBER	PLAN SIZE	BEAM SIZE		TOP BARS (LEFT)	BOTTOM BARS (CENTER)	TOP BARS (RIGHT)	STIRRUPS			REMARKS
		WIDTH	DEPTH				LEFT	RIGHT	TYPE	
B2-001	35 X 36	35"	36"	10-#9	5-#9	10-#9	12	12	S	TOP BARS CONTINUOUS
B2-002	35/43 X 19	35"	19"		5-#7	5-#8	8	8	S	TOP BARS CONTINUOUS (REF DETAIL 12/S004)
B2-003	43 x 19	43"	19"		5-#6	5-#6	8	8	S	
B2-004	26/37 X 19	26"	19"	5-#7	5-#7		8	8	S	TOP BARS CONTINUOUS (REF DETAIL 12/S004)
B2-005	30 X 24	30"	24"	5-#9	5-#9	5-#8	10	10	S	
B2-006	30 X 19	30"	19"		5-#7	6-#9	8	8	S	

Table title: CONCRETE BEAM SCHEDULE - LEVEL 2

Workaround Solutions

So, what do you do when a beam does not join as well as you hoped it would, or the line work shown on plan is not displaying correctly? You can take advantage of solutions such as using the Line Work tool, opening by face, or placing a slab as an in-fill slab to either finish what you couldn't accomplish with the Revit Structure tapered beam capabilities or to just put the finishing touches on your documentation. Again, try using the version of Revit Structure you have and the families that come with it — then decide whether you need to invest in creating custom families or workarounds.

In the following image, the plan view displays line work correctly for the condition at a beam-to-beam join at a sharp corner. However, the accuracy of the model is not correct. Also note that the form work for a pan and joist system comes with 90-degree ends. The form work pans will stop short of the beam, leaving a triangular area filled with concrete. You can address problem areas such as the corner beam intersection and the triangular in-fills by using the Slab tool.

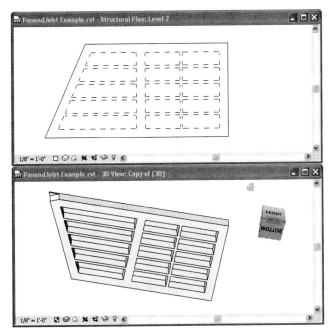

Create a slab type and call it something like **Slab Infill – 24″**. It should reflect the depth of the beam for the pan and joist system or the depth of the beam minus the slab thickness. Use this slab type to add the additional geometry that we mentioned earlier. If you are using the Slab Thickness parameter in the beam families, consider making this slab type the thickness of the overall beam depth minus the slab thickness. You would then offset the in-fill slab by the thickness of the slab. Use the same method for setting up your tapered beam families to help maintain consistency in your model.

In the following image, on the left is a slab in Sketch mode with multiple closed-loop sketch lines to model the in-fill areas. These in-fill slabs can be modeled as separate slabs or several individual slabs all in one slab sketch. You will need to decide which method is best for you. These in-fill slabs should automatically join to the slab and beam members as long as the materials are the same. On the right is both a plan view and a below view, indicating that the model is now shown accurately for both model coordination as well as documentation.

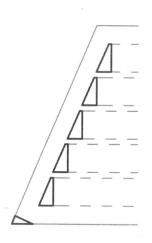
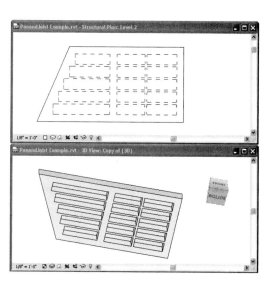

Other techniques, such as an opening By Face, can be used to cope or carve out tapered portions of the beam at openings or oddball shapes of beams. Using this approach may be a bit handier than creating a whole new family for a specific condition. You first select the plane of the element through which you will be placing an opening. Then you place sketch lines to form a closed loop in the shape needed to create the look you want. This method not only should create the desired look in plan but also should be reflected in the 3D content of the model.

Tools such as the Linework and Cut Profile tools (which are located on the Ribbon in the Modify tab ➤ Edit Linework panel) can help you fix unsatisfying areas of your documentation where it is not necessary to reflect the 3D intent throughout the model. Both of these tools are considered 2D or view-specific tools. This means that you may get the look you desire in a particular view, but it will not be reflected in all views of the model. The Linework tool can be used to change the line type of lines that are not displaying correctly or to selectively remove lines that should not be displayed. The Cut Profile tool is useful in sections where you need to change the configuration of an element. You select the object you wish to change the shape of and add sketch lines to remove or add to the shape in a 2D manner. The new sketch boundary automatically takes on the selected object's material.

As you can see, a lot can go into a pan and joist structural system when you are modeling it in Revit Structure. Taking the time to discuss what you want, or what others hope to get out of the model, will certainly help you determine the best modeling techniques.

Projects with Miscellaneous Framing

Sometimes taking a step back to see what you want to get out of your model in the end might just help you get to that finish line faster. Some methods may not work for every project — which is why you need to spend the time up front with fellow in-house team members and other design team associates who will be working on the project to discuss what you want to put into the model.

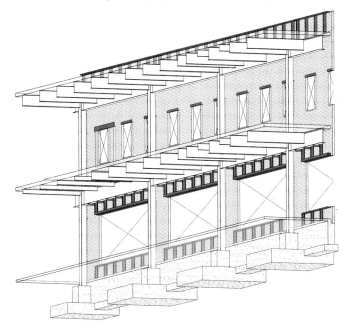

For this two-story medical building, we tried a few things that we would never think of attempting on some of our larger projects. We created all-in-one Opening/Lintel families and Brick Support Frame families. Why wouldn't we attempt that on larger projects? Well, if we tried to model to this degree and then expected to maintain the accuracy as things changed, or had to deal with possible performance issues, we might still be working weekends to make up for lost time. During our assessment of this project, we felt that enough of the design was decided, which meant things were not going to change (or at least *shouldn't* change). The schedule was pretty well set, and the model was small enough that we felt we could easily maintain it. What did we hope to get out of the project? Our goals were to develop schedules that linked to the modeled geometry, maintain accuracy, be able to share the accuracy with the clients to help coordinate with their sections, and make an attempt at scheduling quantities.

Loose Lintel Opening Family

We started the Loose Lintel Opening family from the Generic Model wall-based family template. We used a cut extrusion to cut the opening in the wall. We used model lines to display the X through the opening cut. We added reference planes and parameters to control the left and right bearing lengths. In addition, we created shared parameters that allowed the lintel properties to be linked into schedules. For the loose lintel, we used a solid sweep with an angle profile assigned to it so we could swap out the angle sizes that we needed for the various opening widths. We set the visibility parameters of the model lines and geometry so they would display in a specific way depending on the detail level of the view and whether it was a 3D, plan, or section view.

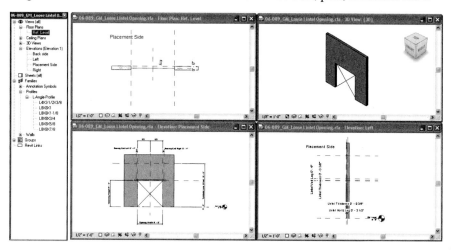

Once the family was working correctly with all of the desired functionality, we loaded it into the project and everything worked as expected. When we started looking at the plan, we said to ourselves, "Wouldn't it be nice to be able to tag and schedule all of these lintels we just placed?" Well, that was our next step. We figured that taking another hour or so building in this functionality might save us some time down the road. If it didn't save us time on this project, it would certainly save us time on the next one.

We added a symbolic line with its ends locked to the reference planes that controlled the bearing lengths. This allowed the symbolic line to accurately display the correct bearing length. Since openings can be placed at various heights, we added a parameter for floor-to-floor height so each opening we placed could control the vertical elevation of the symbolic line and thus would be properly placed in the view range that it needed to be shown in. Because the symbolic line was part of the family, we could tag it just like any other element in Revit Structure. At this point we had a lintel family that modeled the geometry accurately, its behavior was automated depending on the settings it was being viewed in, and its properties could be scheduled. Creating this family for this project has opened our minds (and hopefully yours) to other ideas with similar workflow methods. Taking this approach for this type of project proved to be an enhancement to our workflow.

Brick Support Frame Families

We also created families that consisted of channel frames with light-gauge stud in-fill. These frames were required at the top of some of the larger openings in addition to being used for their sills. These families consisted of vertical and horizontal channel families created from solid sweeps that were nested into the master family. We then placed these nested channel families in an array parameter that allowed us to adjust the channel spacing to the length of the span. The basic setup was the same for both family types. Nesting the individual families into one another gave us more control over the behavior of the arrays that we used, and it also enabled us to create family Type parameters to swap out channel shapes with HSS tube steel shapes.

The Brick Support Frame family shown here had a horizontal kicker angle that we were able to attach to the bottom of beams in the project by aligning and locking a reference plane set to an Instance parameter. When beam sizes changed, the kicker brace changed with it. This not only put additional information into our model for a more accurate set of details, but it also helped the architect visualize and coordinate the extra structure required for the design.

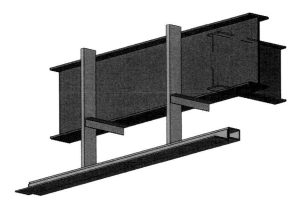

The support frame shown next also nested in an embed plate family. This did not add much benefit to the project, but the plate was automatically displayed in our section views and also made our 3D views a bit more attractive. We were having fun and things were going good — which made it hard to know when to stop.

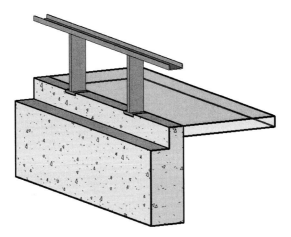

Once you gain a better understanding of how families work, you will find that you can build more functionality into your projects. Seeing all of these frames while viewing the project can be a bit overwhelming, but when you take a closer look, all of the information exists in one spot: the family. If changes need to be made, you make those changes in the family or by using the parameter functionality built into it. All those locations will update to your changes. As you learn to work with families and parameter types, you will be able to allow your model to maintain itself.

A Campus Design

Consider how you might approach the modeling setup for a campus with seven structures: two multistory classrooms, a library, a food services building, a gymnasium, an administration building, and a parking structure. Will you model all seven buildings in one Revit Structure file? Probably not. If you could, you might use worksets to divvy up all the buildings into discrete parts. For a project of this size, though, you will have several people handling the modeling and the documentation who will need constant access to the file. The engineers will also be involved in studying the model and possibly taking advantage of the analytical model. That could make for a lot of performance issues. Even though Revit Structure files tend to be smaller than their architectural counterparts, which range from 17MB to 32MB each, putting all seven in one file would make the file nearly 200MB.

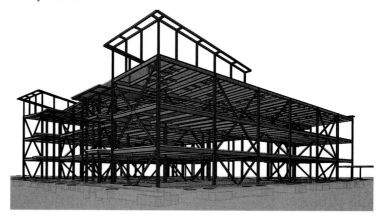

A better approach is to model each building separately; make each structure its own central file. By setting up the project this way, you ensure that several people can work easily in each file. Each file can have its own set of worksets. That is the approach taken by the team who worked on the LAUSD Central High School campus project. This approach can work for any campus-style design project.

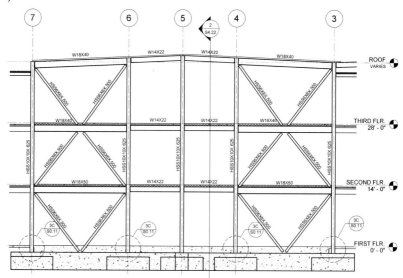

The toughest decision was how to work on two classroom buildings that were basically the same, except for a few areas. It was that "except" that swayed the decision to make two separate models in separate files. So many times in real practice when you are told that buildings are identical, they really are not — and the frustration level can really build.

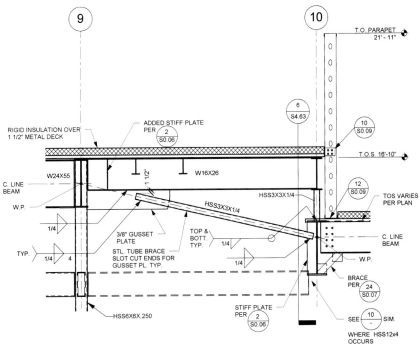

We decided to create an overall site file. When we created the individual files, we first inserted the architectural 2D site plan, and each new building was located at its correct position within the campus. We then linked each building model into the overall site plan file using the Origin-to-Origin setting so that they all appeared in their correct position.

Each of the seven files contained sheet files for plan, elevation, and section work for that particular structure. So one downside is that plotting required opening all of the Revit files and involved many organizational duties.

The other major concern was where to locate the Typical Detail sheets. Those ended up in the overall site file. The overall site plan also became a central file so a number of people could be working at the same time on the typical details. One nice benefit of placing the typical details in the overall site file involved the creation of a drawing list for the project. The drawing list schedule was able to extract all the sheet information from the seven linked files and compile them into one list. That was a great help in coordinating the set.

Besides the typical details, the site file contains several sheets of overall model views. You get a great feel for the whole campus when you take some perspective snapshots from the ground level looking across the campus. With products like Autodesk NavisWorks, you can easily cruise building to building through the whole site. For client presentations, this was the file we used.

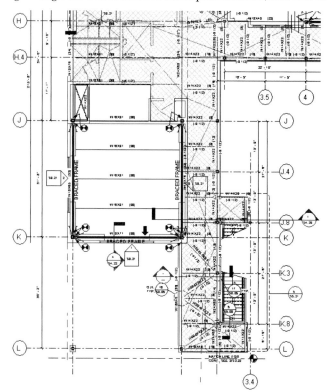

A Hollywood Studio Project at NBC Universal

The NBC Live Show at Universal is to be the new home of the famous "Tonight Show." This was a high-profile project indeed. It had a demanding design and construction schedule since it had to be ready for the changing of the guard in 2009, as Jay Leno exited and Conan O'Brien took over the show. The project had two main parts: retrofitting and remodeling the existing Stage 1, and adding a new support building.

The existing stage in itself is quite famous. It was the first TV production stage built on the Universal lot back in the 1950s for the great comedian Jack Benny and his TV show. There is a lot of history at the Universal lot, and it was satisfying to work on a structure with such a storied past.

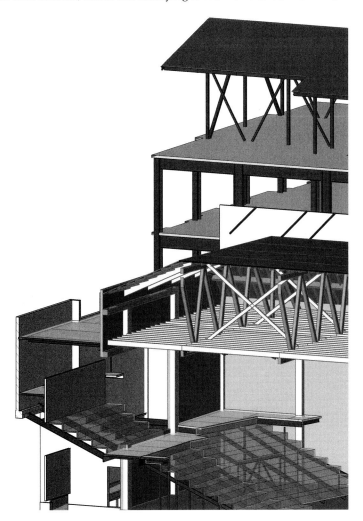

The stage was made of 6″ tilt-up concrete walls. Wood trusses carried the roof with lumber rafters and ceiling joists attached across the truss bottom chord. Wood cross bracing finished the existing roof design.

The new support building is a four-story steel and concrete structure with moment frames as the main seismic restraint system. There is also a full basement. The building has heavy Spanish roof tiles, so the roof needed to be strong to carry the weight as well as being braced diagonally on four sides.

We added a new front entry and a back fly house (which holds all the sets). All new work in the stage area was done in the new Revit Structure file. We went back to the original stage file to demolish portions, such as the many new openings in the exterior tilt-up walls.

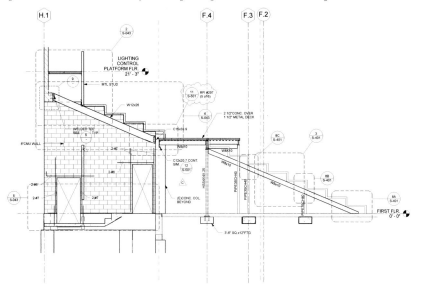

Our approach to modeling the project in Revit Structure involved the creation of two files: one for the existing stage, which was then linked to the second file containing the new support building. We set the Phase Created parameter for all elements in the stage area to Existing. The linked file was half-toned in each view to distinguish it from the new work.

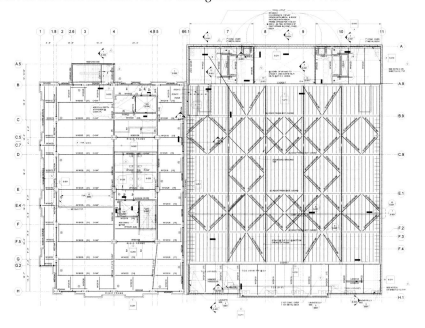

Our approach to typical details in this project was different than for most other Revit Structure projects. Rather than insert stock typical details and adjust them, we derived most of those details in this project from the model. A good example is the foundation details. We created one cross section through the foundation area showing a wall footing, tie beam, and column isolated footing from the model. The detail displays the exterior wall detailing as well and shows how it locks into the first-floor slab.

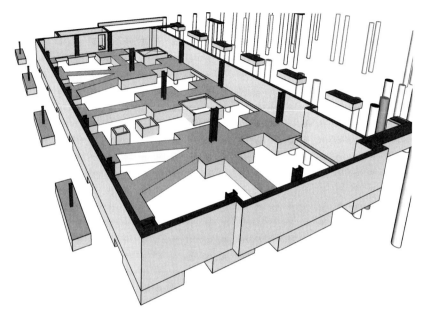

That detail represented most of the foundation area detailing. So rather than having to adapt a stock detail, we deemed this approach more efficient and direct.

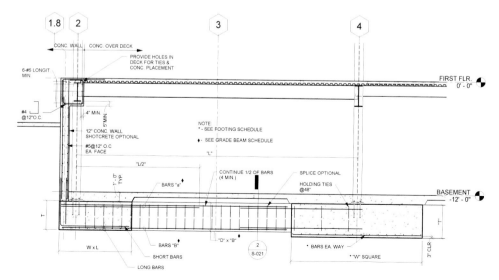

Another interesting problem was a change that occurred during construction. Two mechanical equipment platforms on the roof were found to be too tall after they were erected. On one platform we decided to remove the posts and diagonal braces and bring the platform framing down onto the roof.

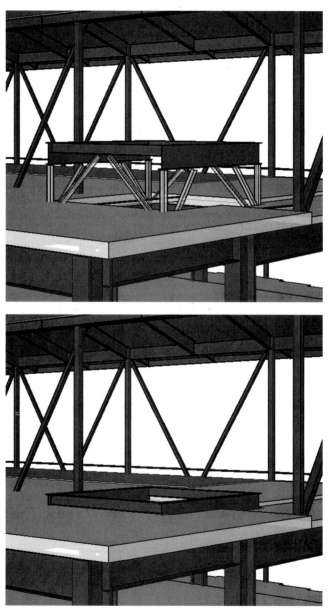

We made the effort much simpler by creating two design options and using phasing. One option represented the existing condition. The members to be removed were designated to be demolished and could be shown as hidden lines in the elevations. The other design option represented the new finished condition. We could then enable the two options as needed in the various views and document them to show the existing and new conditions.

This was not a huge project in terms of square feet, but as you see it had many conditions that had to be modeled in order to achieve a model that had sufficient integrity. Not every project is an 80-story high rise or an airport terminal. For the average structural firm, Revit Structure will do just fine in modeling structures. The mix of new and existing portions as well as the mix of steel, concrete, and wood can be just as demanding to design and model as that new fancy high rise.

If the boss asks if it wouldn't be easier to just do it in AutoCAD, your answer should be, ''No way! Let me do it in Revit Structure!'' Don't look back.

The Historic Rose Bowl Locker Room and Media Center Project

This is another high-profile project with a demanding schedule. The historic Rose Bowl was built in the early 1920s in the city of Pasadena, California. The UCLA football team is now one of the main tenants. A bigger and better locker room was required along with a new media center. The team was anxious to move into their new facility.

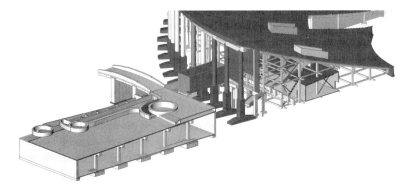

The Rose Bowl consists of a set of structures added over the years. As originally built, the Rose Bowl was a horseshoe shape, open at the south end. The south end was closed in the late 1920s and is the only part that is not sitting on grade. It is supported by concrete columns, braces, and beams.

In the initial design, the locker room was going to be under the south end of the bowl. But after development, that design was abandoned because it was too difficult to accomplish due to the nature of the existing structure. The south end of the Rose Bowl is so full of concrete columns, beams, and braces that it looks more like a spaghetti bowl!

Then began the next design effort: to locate the locker rooms just outside the stadium under the parking lot, with connecting tunnels onto the playing field. The media center remained tucked under the south end as a one-story structure.

The structural engineer on this project was contracted to provide all the engineering services required for the Rose Bowl. We decided that the entire existing historic bowl would be modeled. That sounds like a huge undertaking, and it was complex but doable. By centralizing the work into one ongoing model, we could divide the cost between successive contracts. The more complete the model, the better resource it became for facility management uses. This then was a real BIM solution.

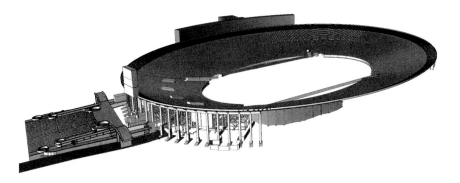

The bowl shape could be created in a straightforward way by using a solid sweep to create the basic shape. We drew the profile and then swept 360 degrees to create the basic bowl shape. Most of the Rose Bowl structure is sitting on the ground. Fascinating old photographs are available showing mule-drawn wagons in the 1920s as they removed dirt from the site.

The new locker room scheme uses precast columns and girders. The roof is made of precast concrete double-T planks. Walls are cast-in-place concrete.

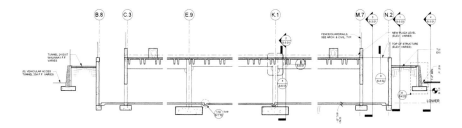

The Wall of Champions was another important design consideration in that we had to maintain accessibility. It showcases Rose Bowl history and is located on the south end. The precast concrete roof planks over the locker rooms are covered with about a foot of soil, with paving above that.

We added elaborate concrete landscaping walls, with new stairs and a second slab-on-Styrofoam leading up to the Wall of Champions. All this was accomplished in Revit Structure with very little 2D work required.

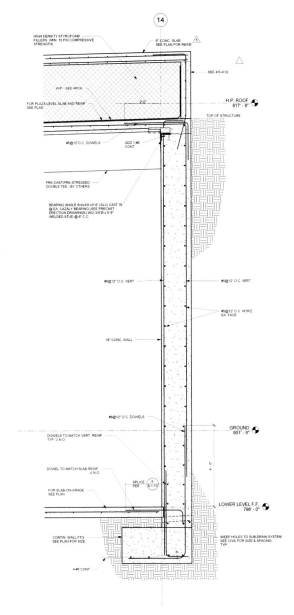

One of the main design problems with the new scheme involved constructing the tunnel while avoiding the many large foundations supporting the existing bowl and the large stadium sign. Ensuring the integrity and accuracy of the model became a crucial task that required successive site surveys. We created walkthroughs through the tunnels, and it became quite simple to spot any intrusion by the existing foundations. The tunnel construction also used design options. Options were required because the contractor wanted to explore the possibility of using masonry walls instead of concrete.

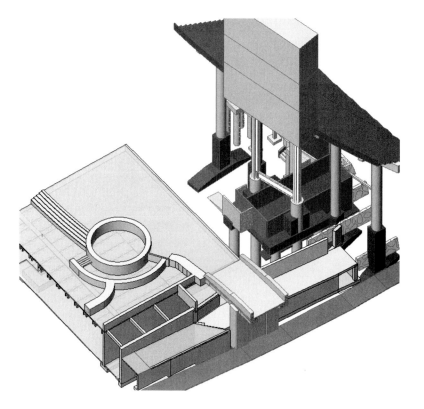

In the end, the second design scheme in the parking lot was adopted. We completed the design and construction work in record time with few RFIs, and now the team has moved in.

A Church Project

Religious structures come in many forms. In this case the project is a Roman Catholic church whose design is inspired by historic churches of California as well as Catholic tradition. As such, it has a nave, a large sanctuary, and a transept forming a traditional cross with a large dome over its altar. The Lady of the Most Blessed Trinity Chapel at St. Thomas Aquinas College is situated on a prominent site so that it is visible to all those passing through this beautiful Southern California valley north of Los Angeles.

Because the church is in a valley, though, the site had a steep slope. One of the toughest design questions we faced was whether to in-fill the site and construct the church floor on grade or construct a partially supported floor. Which way was the most economical? Modeling the structure helped in that determination. Using the topography features in Revit Structure, we were able to import the 2D CAD site survey and construct a 3D site plan. It took a few hours to add contour points over the 2D contour lines and create the 3D topography. With that in place, we could cut sections through the model and see exactly where the existing hillside was located, which was a great aid while we were figuring how to step the foundation down the slope. In the end, the design decision was to use a partially supported floor.

We also decided early in the design process that the church steeple would not be designed by the structural engineer but instead would be separately designed and built by others. As you see, it does not appear in the model views.

The church walls are made of masonry with a concrete foundation. The circular walls in the back proved difficult to create, especially since they were modeled in an earlier version of Revit Structure. Placing openings in the curved walls and adding the rounded roof framing was a real chore. New versions of Revit Structure make it easier to accomplish these tasks.

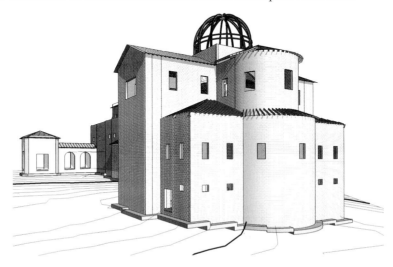

The altar area was the most demanding to model and engineer, because of the confluence of elements there. The dome had to be supported with arched walls below. The altar area was stepped, and several wood roof areas converged. We abstracted a partial model of that area, which became very useful in assessing the integrity of our design. We modeled the dome structural elements using an in-place family using a solid sweep to create the curved vertical steel members, then arrayed them about the circle.

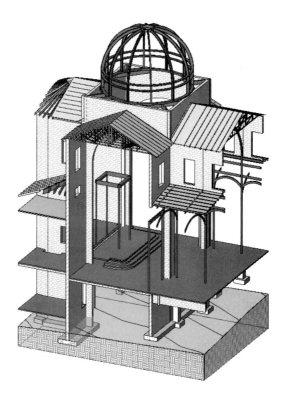

Most of the roofs in the sanctuary and transept areas were made from wood trusses. We created the trusses in Revit Structure using a simple solid extrusion, grouped and then arrayed as necessary. We did this step before the Truss Wizard was available. The lower roof portions were constructed of lumber members framing into light steel framing members with nailers on top. Curved steel tube framing was required throughout the sanctuary area in order to support the architectural finishes.

A Student Housing Project

Wood materials are used extensively in many parts of the United States and Canada. With the high price of concrete and steel because of worldwide demand, we can expect to see more structures built of lumber products in the future, a renewable resource in this green era. But modeling in wood has its own challenges. There are so many pieces of wood to contend with that you must be very careful in how you approach the virtual model.

This student housing project uses wood and light steel framing. Wood shear walls form the main seismic resisting system. There are two four-story structures for housing and a one-story support building.

Shear Walls

The walls of the structures did not contain individual studs. For the purpose of composing construction documents, that was not necessary. As you saw in Chapter 19, in the shear wall definitions the plywood sheathing was added as a vertical layer. The top and bottom plates were inserted as sweeps with embedded detail components. That way when a section was cut the wood sheathing and plates would automatically display. We created interior and exterior shear wall and bearing wall family types to give us greater control over the display and addition of curbs at the ground level. A 6″ curb could be added directly into the family. In plan view we created separate plans for the shear walls and the floor framing. This way, the view was much less cluttered. We used annotated symbols to indicate hold-down anchor locations as well as shear wall types and extents.

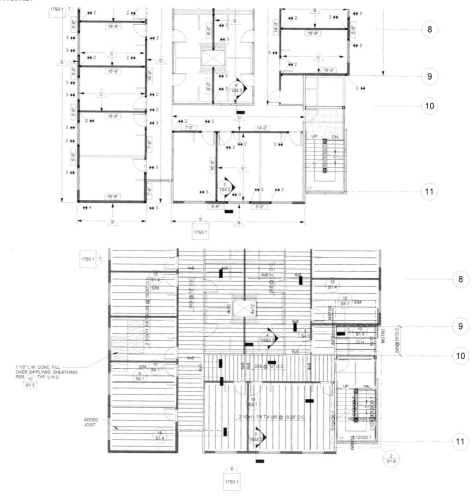

Floor Framing

Floor framing consisted of wood I-joists in the room areas and lumber in the shorter corridor areas. As opposed to the walls, all floor framing members were modeled. Most floor framing was created using the Beam System with a Maximum Spacing setting of 16″ center to center.

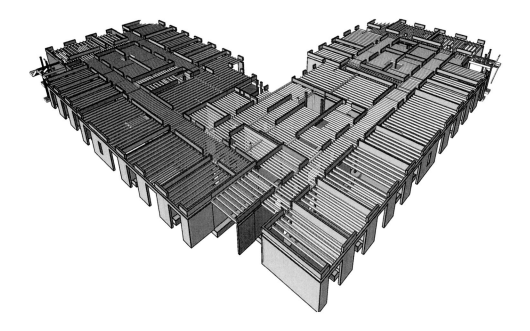

Roof Trusses

The roof trusses on this project were very demanding. The trusses spanned the building and were supported on the shear walls in the corridors below. The centers of the truss were all along the same ridge line. But the extents of the trusses varied depending on the roof footprint at any one location. For a shorter truss, the ends were simply clipped and a vertical member inserted.

The truss spacing was at 2′ center to center, so there were a tremendous number of different types, each with its own length. So how could we model those? And could they be edited easily if necessary during the design process?

The answer to the problem was to construct a truss family. We created the truss family in elevation as a solid extrusion. On each end we added a solid void with an instance label. That way, we could insert a truss into the roof and then adjust the voids on each end to shorten the length as needed. Then that could be arrayed over the area the truss length represented.

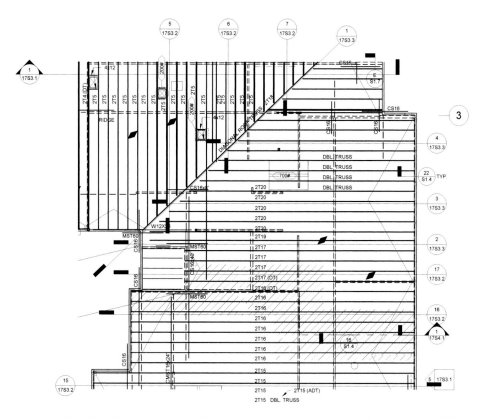

As was said earlier, having to deal with so many pieces of timber can be frustrating. Editing can be difficult, so plan well.

Final Thoughts

Hopefully we have shown you that all types of projects and structural systems can be accomplished by using Revit Structure. It may not always be crystal clear how these project types or structural systems should be modeled, but honestly, two projects that use the same structural system may be handled two completely different ways. Or the size or unique framing requirements may have to be modeled or documented in a certain way that the out-of-the-box program can't address. It is important for you to think about how you will approach each project before you start. Consider the downstream effects. Think about what you and the design team want to get out of the model, and model within those expectations. A lot of situations will pop up midway through a project, but as you overcome the small roadblocks and figure out ways to move through them, you will be able to carry your solutions into future projects.

Index